T0264322

Introduction to Statistical Pattern Recognition

Second Edition

This is a volume in
COMPUTER SCIENCE AND SCIENTIFIC COMPUTING

Editor: WERNER RHEINBOLDT

Introduction to Statistical Pattern Recognition

Second Edition

Keinosuke Fukunaga

School of Electrical Engineering
Purdue University
West Lafayette, Indiana

An Imprint of Elsevier

San Diego San Francisco New York Boston
London Sydney Tokyo

This book is printed on acid-free paper. ♾

Copyright © 1990 by Academic Press
All rights reserved.
No part of this publication may be reproduced or transmitted in any form or by any means, electronic or mechanical, including photocopy, recording, or any information storage and retrieval system, without permission in writing from the publisher.

Permissions may be sought directly from Elsevier's Science and Technology Rights Department in Oxford, UK. Phone: (44) 1865 843830, Fax: (44) 1865 853333, e-mail: permissions@elsevier.co.uk. You may also complete your request on-line via the Elsevier homepage: http://www.elsevier.com by selecting "Customer Support" and then "Obtaining Permissions".

ACADEMIC PRESS
An Imprint of Elsevier
525 B Street, Suite 1900, San Diego, CA 92101-4495 USA
http://www.academicpress.com

Academic Press
24-28 Oval Road, London NW1 7DX United Kingdom
http://www.hbuk/ap/

Morgan Kaufmann
340 Pine Street, Sixth Floor, San Francisco, CA 94104-3205
http://mkp.com

Library of Congress Cataloging-in-Publication Data
Fukunaga, Keinosuke.
Introduction to statistical pattern recognition / Keinosuke Fukunaga. — 2nd ed.
p. cm.
Includes bibliographical references.

ISBN-13: 978-0-12-269851-4 ISBN-10: 0-12-269851-7
1. Pattern perception — Statistical methods. 2. Decision-making — — Mathematical models. 3. Mathematical statistics. I. Title.
0327.F85 1990
006.4 — dc20 89-18195
CIP

ISBN-13: 978-0-12-269851-4
ISBN-10: 0-12-269851-7

Printed and bound in the United Kingdom
Transferred to Digital Printing, 2011

To Reiko, Gen, and Nina

Contents

Preface

This book presents an introduction to statistical pattern recognition. Pattern recognition in general covers a wide range of problems, and it is hard to find a unified view or approach. It is applied to engineering problems, such as character readers and waveform analysis, as well as to brain modeling in biology and psychology. However, statistical decision and estimation, which are the subjects of this book, are regarded as fundamental to the study of pattern recognition. Statistical decision and estimation are covered in various texts on mathematical statistics, statistical communication, control theory, and so on. But obviously each field has a different need and view. So that workers in pattern recognition need not look from one book to another, this book is organized to provide the basics of these statistical concepts from the viewpoint of pattern recognition.

The material of this book has been taught in a graduate course at Purdue University and also in short courses offered in a number of locations. Therefore, it is the author's hope that this book will serve as a text for introductory courses of pattern recognition as well as a reference book for the workers in the field.

Acknowledgments

The author would like to express his gratitude for the support of the National Science Foundation for research in pattern recognition. Much of the material in this book was contributed by the author's past co-workers, T. F. Krile, D. R. Olsen, W. L. G. Koontz, D. L. Kessell, L. D. Hostetler, P. M. Narendra, R. D. Short, J. M. Mantock, T. E. Flick, D. M. Hummels, and R. R. Hayes. Working with these outstanding individuals has been the author's honor, pleasure, and delight. Also, the continuous discussion with W. H. Schoendorf, B. J. Burdick, A. C. Williams, and L. M. Novak has been stimulating. In addition, the author wishes to thank his wife Reiko for continuous support and encouragement.

The author acknowledges those at the Institute of Electrical and Electronics Engineers, Inc., for their authorization to use material from its journals.

Chapter 1

INTRODUCTION

This book presents and discusses the fundamental mathematical tools for statistical decision-making processes in pattern recognition. It is felt that the decision-making processes of a human being are somewhat related to the recognition of patterns; for example, the next move in a chess game is based upon the present pattern on the board, and buying or selling stocks is decided by a complex pattern of information. The goal of pattern recognition is to clarify these complicated mechanisms of decision-making processes and to automate these functions using computers. However, because of the complex nature of the problem, most pattern recognition research has been concentrated on more realistic problems, such as the recognition of Latin characters and the classification of waveforms. The purpose of this book is to cover the mathematical models of these practical problems and to provide the fundamental mathematical tools necessary for solving them. Although many approaches have been proposed to formulate more complex decision-making processes, these are outside the scope of this book.

1.1 Formulation of Pattern Recognition Problems

Many important applications of pattern recognition can be characterized as either waveform classification or classification of geometric figures. For example, consider the problem of testing a machine for normal or abnormal operation by observing the output voltage of a microphone over a period of time. This problem reduces to discrimination of waveforms from good and bad machines. On the other hand, recognition of printed English characters corresponds to classification of geometric figures. In order to perform this type of classification, we must first measure the observable characteristics of the sample. The most primitive but assured way to extract all information contained in the sample is to measure the time-sampled values for a waveform, $x(t_1), \ldots, x(t_n)$, and the grey levels of pixels for a figure, $x(1), \ldots, x(n)$, as shown in Fig. 1-1. These n measurements form a vector X. Even under the normal machine condition, the observed waveforms are different each time the observation is made. Therefore, $x(t_i)$ is a *random variable* and will be expressed, using boldface, as $\mathbf{x}(t_i)$. Likewise, X is called a *random vector* if its components are random variables and is expressed as $\mathbf{X}$. Similar arguments hold for characters: the observation, $x(i)$, varies from one A to another and therefore $\mathbf{x}(i)$ is a random variable, and $\mathbf{X}$ is a random vector.

Thus, each waveform or character is expressed by a vector (or a *sample*) in an n-dimensional space, and many waveforms or characters form a distribution of $\mathbf{X}$ in the n-dimensional space. Figure 1-2 shows a simple two-dimensional example of two distributions corresponding to normal and abnormal machine conditions, where points depict the locations of samples and solid lines are the contour lines of the probability density functions. If we know these two distributions of $\mathbf{X}$ from past experience, we can set up a boundary between these two distributions, $g(x_1, x_2) = 0$, which divides the two-dimensional space into two regions. Once the boundary is selected, we can classify a sample without a class label to a normal or abnormal machine, depending on $g(x_1, x_2) < 0$ or $g(x_1, x_2) > 0$. We call $g(x_1, x_2)$ a *discriminant function*, and a network which detects the sign of $g(x_1, x_2)$ is called a *pattern recognition network*, a *categorizer*, or a *classifier*. Figure 1-3 shows a block diagram of a classifier in a general n-dimensional space. Thus, in order to design a classifier, we must study the characteristics of the distribution of $\mathbf{X}$ for each category and find a proper discriminant function. This process is called *learning* or *training*, and samples used to design a classifier are called *learning* or *training samples*. The discussion can be easily extended to multi-category cases.

Thus, pattern recognition, or decision-making in a broader sense, may be considered as a problem of estimating density functions in a high-dimensional space and dividing the space into the regions of categories or classes. Because

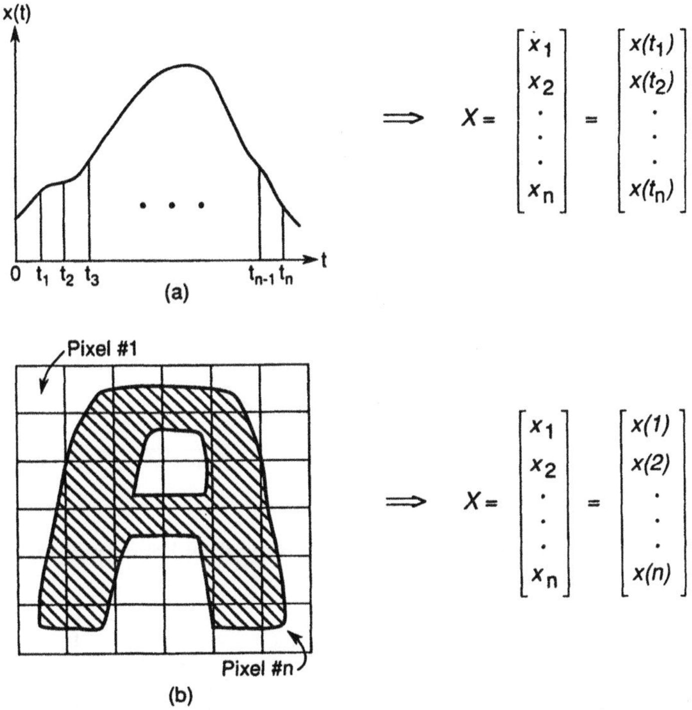

Fig. 1-1 Two measurements of patterns: (a) waveform; (b) character.

of this view, *mathematical statistics* forms the foundation of the subject. Also, since vectors and matrices are used to represent samples and linear operators, respectively, a basic knowledge of *linear algebra* is required to read this book. Chapter 2 presents a brief review of these two subjects.

The first question we ask is what is the theoretically best classifier, assuming that the distributions of the random vectors are given. This problem is *statistical hypothesis testing*, and the *Bayes classifier* is the best classifier which minimizes the probability of classification error. Various hypothesis tests are discussed in Chapter 3.

The probability of error is the key parameter in pattern recognition. The error due to the Bayes classifier (the *Bayes error*) gives the smallest error we can achieve from given distributions. In Chapter 3, we discuss how to calculate the Bayes error. We also consider a simpler problem of finding an upper bound of the Bayes error.

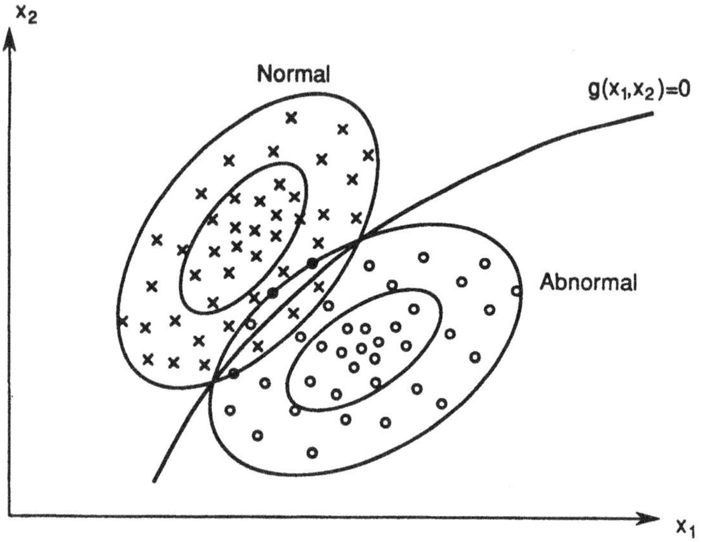

Fig. 1-2 Distributions of samples from normal and abnormal machines.

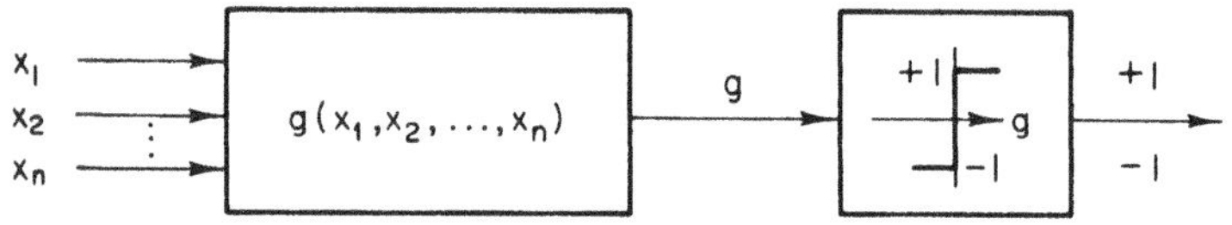

Fig. 1-3 Block diagram of a classifier.

Although the Bayes classifier is optimal, its implementation is often difficult in practice because of its complexity, particularly when the dimensionality is high. Therefore, we are often led to consider a simpler, *parametric classifier*. Parametric classifiers are based on assumed mathematical forms for either the density functions or the discriminant functions. *Linear, quadratic*, or *piecewise classifiers* are the simplest and most common choices. Various design procedures for these classifiers are discussed in Chapter 4.

Even when the mathematical forms can be assumed, the values of the parameters are not given in practice and must be estimated from available samples. With *a finite number of samples*, the estimates of the parameters and subsequently of the classifiers based on these estimates become random variables. The resulting classification error also becomes a random variable and is biased with a variance. Therefore, it is important to understand how the number of samples affects classifier design and its performance. Chapter 5 discusses this subject.

When no parametric structure can be assumed for the density functions, we must use *nonparametric techniques* such as the *Parzen* and *k-nearest neighbor* approaches for estimating density functions. In Chapter 6, we develop the basic statistical properties of these estimates.

Then, in Chapter 7, the nonparametric density estimates are applied to classification problems. The main topic in Chapter 7 is the estimation of the Bayes error without assuming any mathematical form for the density functions. In general, nonparametric techniques are very sensitive to the number of control parameters, and tend to give heavily biased results unless the values of these parameters are carefully chosen. Chapter 7 presents an extensive discussion of how to select these parameter values.

In Fig. 1-2, we presented decision-making as dividing a high-dimensional space. An alternative view is to consider decision-making as a *dictionary search*. That is, all past experiences (learning samples) are stored in a memory (a dictionary), and a test sample is classified to the class of the closest sample in the dictionary. This process is called the *nearest neighbor classification rule*. This process is widely considered as a decision-making process close to the one of a human being. Figure 1-4 shows an example of the decision boundary due to this classifier. Again, the classifier divides the space into two regions, but in a somewhat more complex and sample-dependent way than the boundary of Fig. 1-2. This is a nonparametric classifier discussed in Chapter 7.

From the very beginning of the computer age, researchers have been interested in how a human being learns, for example, to read English characters. The study of *neurons* suggested that a single neuron operates like a linear classifier, and that a combination of many neurons may produce a complex, piecewise linear boundary. So, researchers came up with the idea of a *learning machine* as shown in Fig. 1-5. The structure of the classifier is given along with a number of unknown parameters $w_0, \ldots, w_\tau$. The input vector, for example an English character, is fed, one sample at a time, in sequence. A teacher stands beside the machine, observing both the input and output. When a discrepancy is observed between the input and output, the teacher notifies the machine, and the machine changes the parameters according to a predesigned algorithm. Chapter 8 discusses how to change these parameters and how the parameters converge to the desired values. However, changing a large number of parameters by observing one sample at a time turns out to be a very inefficient way of designing a classifier.

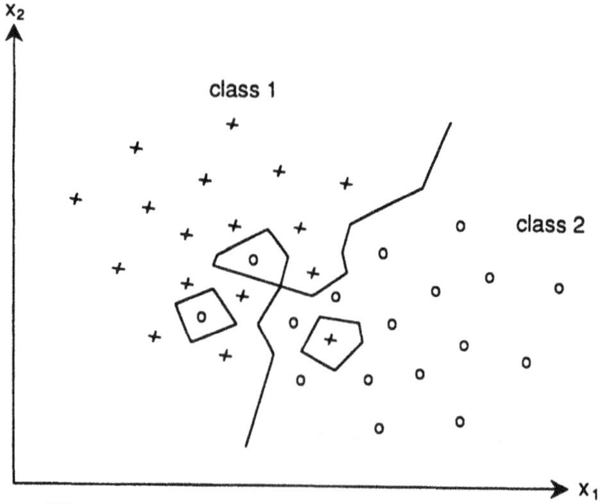

Fig. 1-4 Nearest neighbor decision boundary.

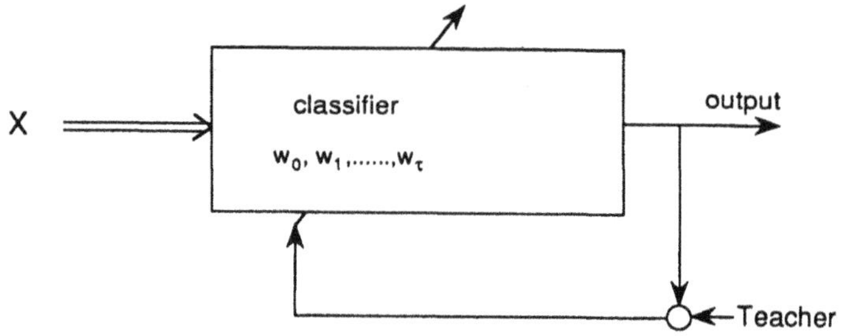

Fig. 1-5 A learning machine.

We started our discussion by choosing time-sampled values of waveforms or pixel values of geometric figures. Usually, the number of measurements n becomes high in order to ensure that the measurements carry all of the information contained in the original data. This high-dimensionality makes many pattern recognition problems difficult. On the other hand, classification by a human being is usually based on a small number of features such as the peak value, fundamental frequency, etc. Each of these measurements carries significant information for classification and is selected according to the physical meaning of the problem. Obviously, as the number of inputs to a classifier becomes smaller, the design of the classifier becomes simpler. In order to enjoy this advantage, we have to find some way to select or extract important features from the observed samples. This problem is called *feature selection* or *extraction* and is another important subject of pattern recognition. However, it should be noted that, as long as features are computed from the measurements, the set of features cannot carry more classification information than the measurements. As a result, the Bayes error in the feature space is always larger than that in the measurement space.

Feature selection can be considered as a mapping from the n-dimensional space to a lower-dimensional feature space. The mapping should be carried out without severely reducing the class separability. Although most features that a human being selects are nonlinear functions of the measurements, finding the optimum nonlinear mapping functions is beyond our capability. So, the discussion in this book is limited to linear mappings.

In Chapter 9, *feature extraction for signal representation* is discussed in which the mapping is limited to orthonormal transformations and the mean-square error is minimized. On the other hand, in *feature extraction for classification*, mapping is not limited to any specific form and the class separability is used as the criterion to be optimized. Feature extraction for classification is discussed in Chapter 10.

It is sometimes important to decompose a given distribution into several clusters. This operation is called *clustering* or *unsupervised classification* (or *learning*). The subject is discussed in Chapter 11.

1.2 Process of Classifier Design

Figure 1-6 shows a flow chart of how a classifier is designed. After data is gathered, samples are normalized and registered. Normalization and registration are very important processes for a successful classifier design. However, different data requires different normalization and registration, and it is difficult to discuss these subjects in a generalized way. Therefore, these subjects are not included in this book.

After normalization and registration, the class separability of the data is measured. This is done by estimating the Bayes error in the measurement space. Since it is not appropriate at this stage to assume a mathematical form for the data structure, the estimation procedure must be nonparametric. If the Bayes error is larger than the final classifier error we wish to achieve (denoted by ε_0), the data does not carry enough classification information to meet the specification. Selecting features and designing a classifier in the later stages

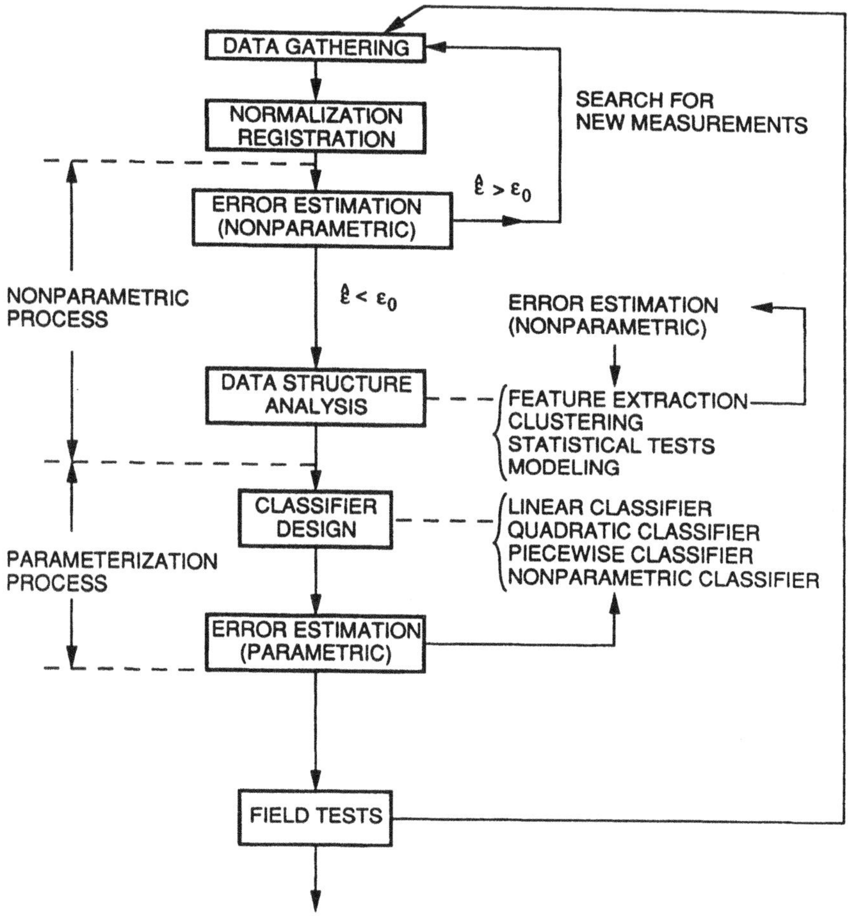

Fig. 1-6 A flow chart of the process of classifier design.

merely increase the classification error. Therefore, we must go back to data gathering and seek better measurements.

Only when the estimate of the Bayes error is less than ε_0, may we proceed to the next stage of data structure analysis in which we study the characteristics of the data. All kinds of data analysis techniques are used here which include feature extraction, clustering, statistical tests, modeling, and so on. Note that, each time a feature set is chosen, the Bayes error in the feature space is estimated and compared with the one in the measurement space. The difference between them indicates how much classification information is lost in the feature selection process.

Once the structure of the data is thoroughly understood, the data dictates which classifier must be adopted. Our choice is normally either a linear, quadratic, or piecewise classifier, and rarely a nonparametric classifier. Nonparametric techniques are necessary in off-line analyses to carry out many important operations such as the estimation of the Bayes error and data structure analysis. However, they are not so popular for any on-line operation, because of their complexity.

After a classifier is designed, the classifier must be evaluated by the procedures discussed in Chapter 5. The resulting error is compared with the Bayes error in the feature space. The difference between these two errors indicates how much the error is increased by adopting the classifier. If the difference is unacceptably high, we must reevaluate the design of the classifier.

At last, the classifier is tested in the field. If the classifier does not perform as was expected, the data base used for designing the classifier is different from the test data in the field. Therefore, we must expand the data base and design a new classifier.

Notation

n	Dimensionality
L	Number of classes
N	Number of total samples
N_i	Number of class i samples
ω_i	Class i
P_i	*A priori* probability of ω_i
$X = [x_1 \, x_2 \, \ldots \, x_n]^T$	Vector
$\mathbf{X} = [\mathbf{x}_1 \, \mathbf{x}_2 \, \ldots \, \mathbf{x}_n]^T$	Random vector
$p_i(X) = p_i(x_1, x_2, \ldots, x_n)$	Conditional density function of ω_i
$p(X) = \sum_{i=1}^{L} P_i p_i(X)$	Mixture density function
$q_i(X) = P_i p_i(X)/p(X)$	*A posteriori* probability of ω_i given X
$M_i = E\{\mathbf{X} \mid \omega_i\}$	Expected vector of ω_i

$M = E\{\mathbf{X}\} = \sum_{i=1}^{L} P_i M_i$	Expected vector of the mixture density
$\Sigma_i = E\{(\mathbf{X}-M_i)(\mathbf{X}-M_i)^T \mid \omega_i\}$	Covariance matrix of ω_i
$\Sigma = E\{(\mathbf{X}-M)(\mathbf{X}-M)^T\}$	
$= \sum_{i=1}^{L} \{P_i \Sigma_i + P_i (M_i - M)(M_i - M)^T\}$	Covariance matrix of the mixture density

References

1. K. Fukunaga, "Introduction to Statistical Pattern Recognition," Academic Press, New York, 1972.
2. R. O. Duda and P. E. Hart, "Pattern Classification and Scene Analysis," Wiley, New York, 1973.
3. P. R. Devijver and J. Kittler, "Pattern Recognition: A Statistical Approach," Prentice-Hall, Englewood Cliffs, New Jersey, 1982.
4. A. K. Agrawala (ed.), "Machine Recognition of Patterns," IEEE Press, New York, 1977.
5. L. N. Kanal, Patterns in pattern recognition: 1968-1972, *Trans. IEEE Inform. Theory*, IT-20, pp. 697-722, 1974.
6. P. R. Krishnaiah and L. N. Kanal (eds.), "Handbook of Statistics 2: Classification, Pattern Recognition and Reduction of Dimensionality," North-Holland, Amsterdam, 1982.
7. T. Y. Young and K. S. Fu (eds.), "Handbook of Pattern Recognition and Image Processing," Academic Press, New York, 1986.

Chapter 2

RANDOM VECTORS AND THEIR PROPERTIES

In succeeding chapters, we often make use of the properties of random vectors. We also freely employ standard results from linear algebra. This chapter is a review of the basic properties of a random vector [1,2] and the related techniques of linear algebra [3-5]. The reader who is familiar with these topics may omit this chapter, except for a quick reading to become familiar with the notation.

2.1 Random Vectors and their Distributions

Distribution and Density Functions

As we discussed in Chapter 1, the input to a pattern recognition network is a *random vector* with n variables as

$$\mathbf{X} = [\mathbf{x}_1 \mathbf{x}_2 \ \ldots \ \mathbf{x}_n]^T , \tag{2.1}$$

where T denotes the transpose of the vector.

Distribution function: A random vector may be characterized by a *probability distribution function*, which is defined by

$$P(x_1, \ldots, x_n) = Pr\{\mathbf{x}_1 \le x_1, \ldots, \mathbf{x}_n \le x_n\} , \tag{2.2}$$

where $Pr\{A\}$ is the probability of an event A. For convenience, we often write (2.2) as

$$P(X) = Pr\{\mathbf{X} \le X\} . \tag{2.3}$$

Density function: Another expression for characterizing a random vector is the *density function*, which is defined as

$$p(X) = \lim_{\substack{\Delta x_1 \to 0 \\ \vdots \\ \Delta x_n \to 0}} \frac{Pr\{x_1 < \mathbf{x}_1 \le x_1 + \Delta x_1, \ldots, x_n < \mathbf{x}_n \le x_n + \Delta x_n\}}{\Delta x_1 \ldots \Delta x_n}$$

$$= \partial^n P(X)/\partial x_1 \ldots \partial x_n . \tag{2.4}$$

Inversely, the distribution function can be expressed in terms of the density function as follows:

$$P(X) = \int_{-\infty}^{X} p(Y)\, dY = \int_{-\infty}^{x_1} \ldots \int_{-\infty}^{x_n} p(y_1, \ldots, y_n)\, dy_1 \ldots dy_n , \tag{2.5}$$

where $\int_{-\infty}^{X} \{\cdot\}\, dY$ is a shorthand notation for an n-dimensional integral, as shown. The density function $p(X)$ is not a probability but must be multiplied by a certain region $\Delta x_1 \ldots \Delta x_n$ (or ΔX) to obtain a probability.

In pattern recognition, we deal with random vectors drawn from different classes (or categories), each of which is characterized by its own density function. This density function is called the *class i density* or *conditional density of class i*, and is expressed as

$$p(X \mid \omega_i) \text{ or } p_i(X) \qquad (i=1, \ldots, L) , \tag{2.6}$$

where ω_i indicates class i and L is the number of classes. The unconditional density function of $\mathbf{X}$, which is sometimes called the *mixture density function*, is given by

$$p(X) = \sum_{i=1}^{L} P_i p_i(X) , \tag{2.7}$$

where P_i is *a priori probability* of class i.

***A posteriori* probability:** The *a posteriori probability* of ω_i given X, $P(\omega_i \mid X)$ or $q_i(X)$, can be computed by using the *Bayes theorem*, as follows:

$$q_i(X) = \frac{P_i p_i(X)}{p(X)} . \tag{2.8}$$

This relation between $q_i(X)$ and $p_i(X)$ provides a basic tool in hypothesis testing which will be discussed in Chapter 3.

Parameters of Distributions

A random vector **X** is fully characterized by its distribution or density function. Often, however, these functions cannot be easily determined or they are mathematically too complex to be of practical use. Therefore, it is sometimes preferable to adopt a less complete, but more computable, characterization.

Expected vector: One of the most important parameters is the *expected vector* or *mean* of a random vector **X**. The expected vector of a random vector **X** is defined by

$$M = E\{\mathbf{X}\} = \int X p(X)\, dX , \tag{2.9}$$

where the integration is taken over the entire X-space unless otherwise specified.

The ith component of M, m_i, can be calculated by

$$m_i = \int x_i p(X)\, dX = \int_{-\infty}^{+\infty} x_i p(x_i)\, dx_i , \tag{2.10}$$

where $p(x_i)$ is the *marginal density* of the ith component of X, given by

$$p(x_i) = \underbrace{\int_{-\infty}^{+\infty} \cdots \int_{-\infty}^{+\infty}}_{n-1} p(X)\, dx_1 \ldots dx_{i-1}\, dx_{i+1} \ldots dx_n . \tag{2.11}$$

Thus, each component of M is actually calculated as the expected value of an individual variable with the marginal one-dimensional density.

The *conditional expected vector* of a random vector **X** for ω_i is the integral

$$M_i = E\{\mathbf{X} \mid \omega_i\} = \int X p_i(X)\, dX , \tag{2.12}$$

where $p_i(X)$ is used instead of $p(X)$ in (2.9).

Covariance matrix: Another important set of parameters is that which indicates the dispersion of the distribution. The *covariance matrix* of **X** is defined by

$$\Sigma = E\{(\mathbf{X}-M)(\mathbf{X}-M)^T\} = E\left\{ \begin{bmatrix} \mathbf{x}_1 - m_1 \\ \vdots \\ \mathbf{x}_n - m_n \end{bmatrix} [\mathbf{x}_1 - m_1 \dots \mathbf{x}_n - m_n] \right\}$$

$$= E\left\{ \begin{bmatrix} (\mathbf{x}_1 - m_1)(\mathbf{x}_1 - m_1) & \dots & (\mathbf{x}_1 - m_1)(\mathbf{x}_n - m_n) \\ \vdots & & \vdots \\ (\mathbf{x}_n - m_n)(\mathbf{x}_1 - m_1) & \dots & (\mathbf{x}_n - m_n)(\mathbf{x}_n - m_n) \end{bmatrix} \right\}$$

$$= \begin{bmatrix} E\{(\mathbf{x}_1 - m_1)(\mathbf{x}_1 - m_1)\} & \dots & E\{(\mathbf{x}_1 - m_1)(\mathbf{x}_n - m_n)\} \\ \vdots & & \vdots \\ E\{(\mathbf{x}_n - m_n)(\mathbf{x}_1 - m_1)\} & \dots & E\{(\mathbf{x}_n - m_n)(\mathbf{x}_n - m_n)\} \end{bmatrix}$$

$$= \begin{bmatrix} c_{11} & \dots & c_{1n} \\ & \vdots & \\ c_{n1} & \dots & c_{nn} \end{bmatrix} . \tag{2.13}$$

The components c_{ij} of this matrix are

$$c_{ij} = E\{(\mathbf{x}_i - m_i)(\mathbf{x}_j - m_j)\} \quad (i,j = 1,\dots,n) . \tag{2.14}$$

Thus, the diagonal components of the covariance matrix are the *variances* of individual random variables, and the off-diagonal components are the *covariances* of two random variables, $\mathbf{x}_i$ and $\mathbf{x}_j$. Also, it should be noted that all covariance matrices are symmetric. This property allows us to employ results from the theory of symmetric matrices as an important analytical tool.

Equation (2.13) is often converted into the following form:

$$\Sigma = E\{\mathbf{X}\mathbf{X}^T\} - E\{\mathbf{X}\}M^T - ME\{\mathbf{X}^T\} + MM^T = S - MM^T \;, \tag{2.15}$$

where

$$S = E\{\mathbf{X}\mathbf{X}^T\} = \begin{bmatrix} E\{\mathbf{x}_1\mathbf{x}_1\} & \dots & E\{\mathbf{x}_1\mathbf{x}_n\} \\ \vdots & & \vdots \\ E\{\mathbf{x}_n\mathbf{x}_1\} & \dots & E\{\mathbf{x}_n\mathbf{x}_n\} \end{bmatrix} . \tag{2.16}$$

Derivation of (2.15) is straightforward since $M = E\{\mathbf{X}\}$. The matrix S of (2.16) is called the *autocorrelation matrix* of $\mathbf{X}$. Equation (2.15) gives the relation between the covariance and autocorrelation matrices, and shows that both essentially contain the same amount of information.

Sometimes it is convenient to express c_{ij} by

$$c_{ii} = \sigma_i^2 \quad \text{and} \quad c_{ij} = \rho_{ij}\sigma_i\sigma_j \;, \tag{2.17}$$

where σ_i^2 is the *variance* of $\mathbf{x}_i$, $\text{Var}\{\mathbf{x}_i\}$, or σ_i is the *standard deviation* of $\mathbf{x}_i$, $\text{SD}\{\mathbf{x}_i\}$, and ρ_{ij} is the *correlation coefficient* between $\mathbf{x}_i$ and $\mathbf{x}_j$. Then

$$\Sigma = \Gamma R \Gamma \tag{2.18}$$

where

$$\Gamma = \begin{bmatrix} \sigma_1 & 0 & \dots & 0 \\ 0 & \sigma_2 & & \cdot \\ \cdot & & \cdot & \cdot \\ \cdot & & & \cdot \\ \cdot & & & \\ 0 & \dots & & \sigma_n \end{bmatrix} \tag{2.19}$$

and

$$R = \begin{bmatrix} 1 & \rho_{12} & \dots & \rho_{1n} \\ \rho_{12} & 1 & & \cdot \\ \cdot & & \cdot & \cdot \\ \cdot & & & \cdot \\ \cdot & & & \\ \rho_{1n} & & \dots & 1 \end{bmatrix} \qquad (|\rho_{ij}| \le 1) \,. \tag{2.20}$$

Thus, Σ can be expressed as the combination of two types of matrices: one is the diagonal matrix of standard deviations and the other is the matrix of the correlation coefficients. We will call R a *correlation matrix*. Since standard deviations depend on the scales of the coordinate system, the correlation matrix retains the essential information of the relation between random variables.

Normal Distributions

An explicit expression of $p(X)$ for a *normal distribution* is

$$N_X(M, \Sigma) = \frac{1}{(2\pi)^{n/2} |\Sigma|^{1/2}} \exp\{-\frac{1}{2} d^2(X)\} , \tag{2.21}$$

where $N_X(M, \Sigma)$ is a shorthand notation for a normal distribution with the expected vector M and covariance matrix Σ, and

$$d^2(X) = (X - M)^T \Sigma^{-1} (X - M) = \text{tr}\{\Sigma^{-1}(X - M)(X - M)^T\}$$

$$= \sum_{i=1}^{n} \sum_{j=1}^{n} h_{ij}(x_i - m_i)(x_j - m_j) , \tag{2.22}$$

where h_{ij} is the i, j component of Σ^{-1}. The term $\text{tr}A$ is the trace of a matrix A and is equal to the summation of the diagonal components of A. As shown in (2.21), a normal distribution is a simple exponential function of a distance function (2.22) that is a positive definite quadratic function of the x's. The coefficient $(2\pi)^{-n/2} |\Sigma|^{-1/2}$ is selected to satisfy the probability condition

$$\int p(X)\, dX = 1 . \tag{2.23}$$

Normal distributions are widely used because of their many important properties. Some of these are listed below.

(1) *Parameters that specify the distribution:* The expected vector M and covariance matrix Σ are sufficient to characterize a normal distribution uniquely. All moments of a normal distribution can be calculated as functions of these parameters.

(2) *Uncorrelated-independent:* If the $\mathbf{x}_i$'s are mutually uncorrelated, then they are also independent.

(3) *Normal marginal densities and normal conditional densities:* The marginal densities and the conditional densities of a normal distribution are all normal.

(4) *Normal characteristic functions:* The characteristic function of a normal distribution, $N_X(M, \Sigma)$, has a normal form as

$$\psi(\Omega) = E\{\exp[j\Omega^T \mathbf{X}]\} = \exp\{-\frac{1}{2}\Omega^T \Sigma \Omega + j\Omega^T M\} , \qquad (2.24)$$

where $\Omega = [\omega_1 \ \dots \ \omega_n]^T$ and ω_i is the ith frequency component.

(5) *Linear transformations:* Under any nonsingular linear transformation, the distance function of (2.22) keeps its quadratic form and also does not lose its positive definiteness. Therefore, after a nonsingular linear transformation, a normal distribution becomes another normal distribution with different parameters.

Also, it is always possible to find a nonsingular linear transformation which makes the new covariance matrix diagonal. Since a diagonal covariance matrix means uncorrelated variables (independent variables for a normal distribution), we can always find for a normal distribution a set of axes such that random variables are independent in the new coordinate system. These subjects will be discussed in detail in a later section.

(6) *Physical justification:* The assumption of normality is a reasonable approximation for many real data sets. This is, in particular, true for processes where random variables are sums of many variables and the *central limit theorem* can be applied. However, normality should not be assumed without good justification. More often than not this leads to meaningless conclusions.

2.2 Estimation of Parameters

Sample Estimates

Although the expected vector and autocorrelation matrix are important parameters for characterizing a distribution, they are unknown in practice and should be estimated from a set of available samples. This is normally done by using the *sample estimation* technique [6,7]. In this section, we will discuss the technique in a generalized form first, and later treat the estimations of the expected vector and autocorrelation matrix as the special cases.

Sample estimates: Let $\mathbf{y}$ be a function of $\mathbf{x}_1, \dots, \mathbf{x}_n$ as

$$\mathbf{y} = f(\mathbf{x}_1, \dots, \mathbf{x}_n) \qquad (2.25)$$

with the expected value m_y and variance σ_y^2:

$$m_y = E\{\mathbf{y}\} \quad \text{and} \quad \sigma_y^2 = \text{Var}\{\mathbf{y}\} . \tag{2.26}$$

Note that all components of M and S of $\mathbf{X}$ are special cases of m_y. More specifically, when $\mathbf{y} = \mathbf{x}_1^{i_1} \ldots \mathbf{x}_n^{i_n}$ with positive integer i_k's, the corresponding m_y is called the $(i_1 + \ldots + i_n)$*th order moment*. The components of M are the first order moments, and the components of S are the second order moments.

In practice, the density function of $\mathbf{y}$ is unknown, or too complex for computing these expectations. Therefore, it is common practice to replace the expectation of (2.26) by the average over available samples as

$$\hat{\mathbf{m}}_y = \frac{1}{N}\sum_{k=1}^{N}\mathbf{y}_k , \tag{2.27}$$

where $\mathbf{y}_k$ is computed by (2.25) from the kth sample $\mathbf{X}_k$. This estimate is called the *sample estimate*. Since all N samples $\mathbf{X}_1, \ldots, \mathbf{X}_N$ are randomly drawn from a distribution, it is reasonable to assume that the $\mathbf{X}_k$'s are mutually independent and identically distributed (iid). Therefore, $\mathbf{y}_1, \ldots, \mathbf{y}_N$ are also iid.

Moments of the estimates: Since the estimate $\hat{\mathbf{m}}_y$ is the summation of N random variables, it is also a random variable and characterized by an expected value and variance. The expected value of $\hat{\mathbf{m}}_y$ is

$$E\{\hat{\mathbf{m}}_y\} = \frac{1}{N}\sum_{k=1}^{N} E\{\mathbf{y}_k\}$$

$$= \frac{1}{N}\sum_{k=1}^{N} m_y = m_y . \tag{2.28}$$

That is, the expected value of the estimate is the same as the expected value of $\mathbf{y}$. An estimate that satisfies this condition is called an *unbiased estimate*. Similarly, the variance of the estimate can be calculated as

$$\text{Var}\{\hat{\mathbf{m}}_y\} = E\{(\hat{\mathbf{m}}_y - m_y)^2\} = \frac{1}{N^2}\sum_{k=1}^{N}\sum_{\ell=1}^{N} E\{(\mathbf{y}_k - m_y)(\mathbf{y}_\ell - m_y)\}$$

$$= \frac{1}{N^2}\sum_{k=1}^{N} E\{(\mathbf{y}_k - m_y)^2\}$$

$$= \frac{1}{N}\sigma_y^2 . \tag{2.29}$$

Since $\mathbf{y}_1, \ldots, \mathbf{y}_N$ are mutually independent, $E\{(\mathbf{y}_k - m_y)(\mathbf{y}_\ell - m_y)\} = E\{\mathbf{y}_k - m_y\}E\{\mathbf{y}_\ell - m_y\} = 0$ for $k \neq \ell$. The variance of the estimate is seen to be $1/N$ times the variance of $\mathbf{y}$. Thus, $\mathrm{Var}\{\hat{\mathbf{m}}_y\}$ can be reduced to zero by letting N go to ∞. An estimate that satisfies this condition is called a *consistent estimate*. All sample estimates are unbiased and consistent regardless of the functional form of f.

The above discussion can be extended to the covariance between two different estimates. Let us introduce another random variable $\mathbf{z} = g(\mathbf{x}_1, \ldots, \mathbf{x}_n)$. Subsequently, m_z and $\hat{\mathbf{m}}_z$ are obtained by (2.26) and (2.27) respectively. The covariance of $\hat{\mathbf{m}}_y$ and $\hat{\mathbf{m}}_z$ is

$$\begin{aligned}
\mathrm{Cov}\{\hat{\mathbf{m}}_y, \hat{\mathbf{m}}_z\} &= E\{(\hat{\mathbf{m}}_y - m_y)(\hat{\mathbf{m}}_z - m_z)\} \\
&= \frac{1}{N^2}\sum_{k=1}^{N}\sum_{\ell=1}^{N} E\{(\mathbf{y}_k - m_y)(\mathbf{z}_\ell - m_z)\} \\
&= \frac{1}{N^2}\sum_{k=1}^{N} E\{(\mathbf{y}_k - m_y)(\mathbf{z}_k - m_z)\} \\
&= \frac{1}{N}\,\mathrm{Cov}\{\mathbf{y},\mathbf{z}\} .
\end{aligned} \tag{2.30}$$

Again, $E\{(\mathbf{y}_k - m_y)(\mathbf{z}_\ell - m_z)\} = E\{\mathbf{y}_k - m_y\}E\{\mathbf{z}_\ell - m_z\} = 0$ for $k \neq \ell$, because $\mathbf{y}_k$ and $\mathbf{z}_\ell$ are independent due to the independence between $\mathbf{X}_k$ and $\mathbf{X}_\ell$.

In most applications, our attention is focused on the first and second order moments, the *sample mean* and *sample autocorrelation matrix*, respectively. These are defined by

$$\hat{\mathbf{M}} = \frac{1}{N}\sum_{k=1}^{N}\mathbf{X}_k \tag{2.31}$$

and

$$\hat{\mathbf{S}} = \frac{1}{N}\sum_{k=1}^{N}\mathbf{X}_k\,\mathbf{X}_k^T . \tag{2.32}$$

Note that all components of (2.31) and (2.32) are special cases of (2.25). Therefore, $\hat{\mathbf{M}}$ and $\hat{\mathbf{S}}$ are unbiased and consistent estimates of M and S respectively.

Example 1: For $\hat{\mathbf{m}}_i$, the ith component of $\hat{\mathbf{M}}$, the corresponding $\mathbf{y}$ is $\mathbf{x}_i$. If the moments of $\mathbf{x}_i$ are given as $E\{\mathbf{x}_i\} = m_i$, $\text{Var}\{\mathbf{x}_i\} = \sigma_i^2$, and $\text{Cov}\{\mathbf{x}_i,\mathbf{x}_j\} = \rho_{ij}\sigma_i\sigma_j$, then the moments of $\hat{\mathbf{m}}_i$ are computed by (2.28), (2.29), and (2.30), resulting in $E\{\hat{\mathbf{m}}_i\} = m_i$, $\text{Var}\{\hat{\mathbf{m}}_i\} = \sigma_i^2/N$, and $\text{Cov}\{\hat{\mathbf{m}}_i,\hat{\mathbf{m}}_j\} = \rho_{ij}\sigma_i\sigma_j/N$. They may be rewritten in vector and matrix forms as

$$E\{\hat{\mathbf{M}}\} = M \ , \tag{2.33}$$

$$\text{Cov}\{\hat{\mathbf{M}}\} = E\{(\hat{\mathbf{M}} - M)(\hat{\mathbf{M}} - M)^T\} = \frac{1}{N}\Sigma \ , \tag{2.34}$$

where $\text{Cov}\{\hat{\mathbf{M}}\}$ is the covariance matrix of $\hat{\mathbf{M}}$.

Example 2: For $\hat{\mathbf{s}}_{ij}$, the i, j component of $\hat{\mathbf{S}}$, the corresponding $\mathbf{y}$ is $\mathbf{x}_i\mathbf{x}_j$. Therefore,

$$E\{\hat{\mathbf{s}}_{ij}\} = s_{ij} \ , \tag{2.35}$$

$$\text{Var}\{\hat{\mathbf{s}}_{ij}\} = \frac{1}{N}\text{Var}\{\mathbf{x}_i\mathbf{x}_j\} = \frac{1}{N}[E\{\mathbf{x}_i^2\mathbf{x}_j^2\} - E^2\{\mathbf{x}_i\mathbf{x}_j\}] \ , \tag{2.36}$$

$$\begin{aligned} \text{Cov}\{\hat{\mathbf{s}}_{ij},\hat{\mathbf{s}}_{k\ell}\} &= \frac{1}{N}\text{Cov}\{\mathbf{x}_i\mathbf{x}_j,\mathbf{x}_k\mathbf{x}_\ell\} \\ &= \frac{1}{N}[E\{\mathbf{x}_i\mathbf{x}_j\mathbf{x}_k\mathbf{x}_\ell\} - E\{\mathbf{x}_i\mathbf{x}_j\}E\{\mathbf{x}_k\mathbf{x}_\ell\}] \ . \end{aligned} \tag{2.37}$$

Central Moments

The situation is somewhat different when we discuss *central moments* such as variances and covariance matrices. If we could define $\mathbf{y}$ for the i, j component of Σ as

$$\mathbf{y} = (\mathbf{x}_i - m_i)(\mathbf{x}_j - m_j) \tag{2.38}$$

with the given expected values m_i and m_j, then

$$E\{\hat{\mathbf{m}}_y\} = E\{\mathbf{y}\} = \rho_{ij}\sigma_i\sigma_j \ . \tag{2.39}$$

The sample estimate is unbiased. In practice, however, m_i and m_j are unknown, and they should be estimated from available samples. When the sample means are used, (2.38) must be changed to

$$\mathbf{y} = (\mathbf{x}_i - \hat{\mathbf{m}}_i)(\mathbf{x}_j - \hat{\mathbf{m}}_j) . \tag{2.40}$$

Then

$$E\{\hat{\mathbf{m}}_y\} = E\{\mathbf{y}\} \neq \rho_{ij}\sigma_i\sigma_j . \tag{2.41}$$

That is, the expectation of the sample estimate is still the same as the expected value of $\mathbf{y}$ given by (2.40). However, the expectation of (2.40) is not equal to that of (2.38) which we want to estimate.

Sample covariance matrix: In order to study the expectation of (2.40) in a matrix form, let us define the sample estimate of a covariance matrix as

$$\hat{\Sigma} = \frac{1}{N}\sum_{k=1}^{N}(\mathbf{X}_k - \hat{\mathbf{M}})(\mathbf{X}_k - \hat{\mathbf{M}})^T . \tag{2.42}$$

Then

$$\begin{aligned}\hat{\Sigma} &= \frac{1}{N}\sum_{k=1}^{N}\{(\mathbf{X}_k - M) - (\hat{\mathbf{M}} - M)\}\{(\mathbf{X}_k - M) - (\hat{\mathbf{M}} - M)\}^T \\ &= \frac{1}{N}\sum_{k=1}^{N}(\mathbf{X}_k - M)(\mathbf{X}_k - M)^T - (\hat{\mathbf{M}} - M)(\hat{\mathbf{M}} - M)^T .\end{aligned} \tag{2.43}$$

Thus, taking the expectation of $\hat{\Sigma}$

$$\begin{aligned}E\{\hat{\Sigma}\} &= \Sigma - E\{(\hat{\mathbf{M}} - M)(\hat{\mathbf{M}} - M)^T\} \\ &= \Sigma - \frac{1}{N}\Sigma = \frac{N-1}{N}\Sigma .\end{aligned} \tag{2.44}$$

That is, (2.44) shows that $\hat{\Sigma}$ is a *biased estimate* of Σ. This bias can be eliminated by using a modified estimate for the covariance matrix as

$$\hat{\Sigma} = \frac{1}{N-1}\sum_{k=1}^{N}(\mathbf{X}_k - \hat{\mathbf{M}})(\mathbf{X}_k - \hat{\mathbf{M}})^T . \tag{2.45}$$

Both (2.42) and (2.45) are termed a *sample covariance matrix*. In this book, we use (2.45) as the estimate of a covariance matrix unless otherwise stated, because of its unbiasedness. When N is large, both are practically the same.

Variances and covariances of $\hat{\mathbf{c}}_{ij}$: The variances and covariances of $\hat{\mathbf{c}}_{ij}$ (the i, j component of $\hat{\Sigma}$) are hard to compute exactly. However, approximations may be obtained easily by using $\hat{\Sigma}_a = (1/N)\sum_{k=1}^{N}(\mathbf{X}_k - M)(\mathbf{X}_k - M)^T$ in place of $\hat{\Sigma}$ of (2.42). The i, j component of $\hat{\Sigma}_a$ as an approximation of $\hat{\mathbf{c}}_{ij}$ is then given by

$$\hat{\mathbf{c}}_{ij} \cong \frac{1}{N}\sum_{k=1}^{N}(\mathbf{x}_{ik} - m_i)(\mathbf{x}_{jk} - m_j) , \tag{2.46}$$

where $\mathbf{x}_{ik}$ is the ith component of the kth sample $\mathbf{X}_k$. The right hand side of (2.46) is the sample estimate of $E\{(\mathbf{x}_i - m_i)(\mathbf{x}_j - m_j)\}$. Therefore, the arguments used to derive (2.28), (2.29), and (2.30) can be applied without modification, resulting in

$$E\{\hat{\mathbf{c}}_{ij}\} \cong c_{ij} , \tag{2.47}$$

$$\text{Var}\{\hat{\mathbf{c}}_{ij}\} \cong \frac{1}{N}\text{Var}\{(\mathbf{x}_i - m_i)(\mathbf{x}_j - m_j)\} , \tag{2.48}$$

and

$$\text{Cov}\{\hat{\mathbf{c}}_{ij},\hat{\mathbf{c}}_{k\ell}\} \cong \frac{1}{N}\text{Cov}\{(\mathbf{x}_i - m_i)(\mathbf{x}_j - m_j), (\mathbf{x}_k - m_k)(\mathbf{x}_\ell - m_\ell)\} . \tag{2.49}$$

Note that the approximations are due to the use of $\hat{\mathbf{m}}_i$ on the left side and m_i on the right side. Both sides are practically the same for a large N.

Normal case with approximation: Let us assume that samples are drawn from a normal distribution, $N_X(0,\Lambda)$, where Λ is a diagonal matrix with components $\lambda_1, \ldots, \lambda_n$. Since the covariance matrix is diagonal, $\mathbf{x}_i$ and $\mathbf{x}_j$ for $i \neq j$ are mutually independent. Therefore, (2.48) and (2.49) are further simplified to

$$\text{Var}\{\hat{\mathbf{c}}_{ij}\} \cong \frac{1}{N}\text{Var}\{\mathbf{x}_i\}\text{Var}\{\mathbf{x}_j\} = \frac{\lambda_i\lambda_j}{N} , \tag{2.50}$$

$$\text{Var}\{\hat{\mathbf{c}}_{ii}\} \cong \frac{1}{N}\text{Var}\{\mathbf{x}_i^2\} = \frac{1}{N}[E\{\mathbf{x}_i^4\} - E^2\{\mathbf{x}_i^2\}]$$

$$= \frac{1}{N}[3\lambda_i^2 - \lambda_i^2] = \frac{2\lambda_i^2}{N} , \tag{2.51}$$

and

$$\text{Cov}\{\hat{\mathbf{c}}_{ij}\ \hat{\mathbf{c}}_{k\ell}\} \cong \frac{1}{N}[E\{\mathbf{x}_i\mathbf{x}_j\mathbf{x}_k\mathbf{x}_\ell\} - E\{\mathbf{x}_i\mathbf{x}_j\}E\{\mathbf{x}_k\mathbf{x}_\ell\}]$$

$$= 0 \quad \text{except } \{i{=}k \text{ and } j{=}\ell\}\ . \tag{2.52}$$

The reader may confirm (2.52) for all possible combinations of i, j, k, and ℓ. When $i=k$ and $j=\ell$, $\text{Cov}\{\hat{\mathbf{c}}_{ij}, \hat{\mathbf{c}}_{k\ell}\}$ becomes $\text{Var}\{\hat{\mathbf{c}}_{ij}\}$, which is given in (2.50).

Also, the covariance between $\hat{\mathbf{m}}_i$ and $\hat{\mathbf{c}}_{k\ell}$ may be computed in approximation as follows:

$$\text{Cov}\{\hat{\mathbf{m}}_i,\hat{\mathbf{c}}_{k\ell}\} \cong \frac{1}{N}\ \text{Cov}\{\mathbf{x}_i,\ \mathbf{x}_k\mathbf{x}_\ell\}$$

$$= \frac{1}{N}[E\{\mathbf{x}_i\mathbf{x}_k\mathbf{x}_\ell\} - E\{\mathbf{x}_i\}E\{\mathbf{x}_k\mathbf{x}_\ell\}]$$

$$= 0\ , \tag{2.53}$$

because $E\{\mathbf{x}_i\mathbf{x}_k\mathbf{x}_\ell\} = 0$ and $E\{\mathbf{x}_i\} = 0$ for a zero-mean normal distribution.

Normal case without approximation: When samples are drawn from a normal distribution, the variances and covariances for $\hat{\mathbf{c}}_{ij}$ of (2.45) are known without approximation. In order to see the effects of the approximation on (2.50)-(2.52), let us study the exact solutions here. Again, for simplicity, let us assume a zero expected vector and a diagonal covariance matrix Λ.

It is known that the sample variance $\hat{\mathbf{c}}_{ii} = 1/(N-1)\sum_{k=1}^{N}(\mathbf{x}_{ik} - \hat{\mathbf{m}}_i)^2$ for a normal $\mathbf{x}_i$ has a *gamma distribution* as [2]

$$p_{\hat{c}_{ii}}(z) = \frac{\alpha_i^{\beta+1}}{\Gamma(\beta+1)} z^{\beta} e^{-\alpha_i z} u(z)\ , \tag{2.54}$$

where

$$\beta+1 = \frac{N-1}{2} \quad \text{and} \quad \alpha_i = \frac{N-1}{2\lambda_i}\ , \tag{2.55}$$

and $\Gamma(\cdot)$ is the gamma function and $u(\cdot)$ is a step function. The expected value and variance of (2.54) are also known as

$$E\{\hat{\mathbf{c}}_{ii}\} = \frac{\beta+1}{\alpha_i} = \lambda_i \ , \tag{2.56}$$

$$\mathrm{Var}\{\hat{\mathbf{c}}_{ii}\} = \frac{\beta+1}{\alpha_i^2} = \frac{2\lambda_i^2}{N-1} \ . \tag{2.57}$$

On the other hand, the moments of $\hat{\mathbf{c}}_{ij} = 1/(N-1)\sum_{k=1}^{N} (\mathbf{x}_{ik}-\hat{\mathbf{m}}_i)(\mathbf{x}_{jk}-\hat{\mathbf{m}}_j)$ for $i \neq j$ can be computed as follows:

$$E\{\hat{\mathbf{c}}_{ij}\} = \frac{1}{N-1}\sum_{k=1}^{N} E\{\mathbf{x}_{ik} - \hat{\mathbf{m}}_i\}E\{\mathbf{x}_{jk} - \hat{\mathbf{m}}_j\} = 0 \ , \tag{2.58}$$

$$\mathrm{Var}\{\hat{\mathbf{c}}_{ij}\} = \frac{1}{(N-1)^2}\sum_{k=1}^{N}\sum_{\ell=1}^{N} E\{(\mathbf{x}_{ik}-\hat{\mathbf{m}}_i)(\mathbf{x}_{i\ell}-\hat{\mathbf{m}}_i)\}E\{(\mathbf{x}_{jk}-\hat{\mathbf{m}}_j)(\mathbf{x}_{j\ell}-\hat{\mathbf{m}}_j)\}$$

$$= \frac{1}{(N-1)^2}\sum_{k=1}^{N}\left(\frac{N-1}{N}\right)^2\lambda_i\lambda_j = \frac{\lambda_i\lambda_j}{N} \ . \tag{2.59}$$

The expectations can be broken into the product of two expectations because $\mathbf{x}_i$ and $\mathbf{x}_j$ are mutually independent. $E\{(\mathbf{x}_{ik}-\hat{m}_i)(\mathbf{x}_{i\ell}-\hat{m}_i)\} = \lambda_i\,\delta_{k\ell}\,(N-1)/N$, because $\mathbf{X}_k$ and $\mathbf{X}_\ell$ are independent. Similarly, the covariances are

$$\mathrm{Cov}\{\hat{\mathbf{c}}_{ij},\hat{\mathbf{c}}_{k\ell}\} = 0 \quad \text{except } \{i=k \text{ and } j=\ell\} \ , \tag{2.60}$$

because some of the $(\mathbf{x}_{..} - \hat{\mathbf{m}}_.)$ terms are independent from the others and $E\{\mathbf{x}_{..} - \hat{\mathbf{m}}_.\} = 0$.

Note that (2.59) and (2.60) are the same as (2.50) and (2.52) respectively. Equation (2.51) may be obtained from (2.57) by using the approximation of $N-1 \cong N$. This confirms that the approximations are good for a large N.

2.3 Linear Transformation

Linear Transformation

When an n-dimensional vector $\mathbf{X}$ is transformed linearly to another n-dimensional vector $\mathbf{Y}$, $\mathbf{Y}$ is expressed as a function of $\mathbf{X}$ as

$$\mathbf{Y} = A^T \mathbf{X} , \tag{2.61}$$

where A is an $n \times n$ matrix. Then, the expected vector and covariance matrix of $\mathbf{Y}$ are

$$M_Y = E\{\mathbf{Y}\} = A^T E\{\mathbf{X}\} = A^T M_X , \tag{2.62}$$

$$\begin{aligned} \Sigma_Y &= E\{(\mathbf{Y} - M_Y)(\mathbf{Y} - M_Y)^T\} \\ &= A^T E\{(\mathbf{X} - M_X)(\mathbf{X} - M_X)^T\} A \\ &= A^T \Sigma_X A , \end{aligned} \tag{2.63}$$

where the following rule of matrices (matrices need not be square) is used

$$(AB)^T = B^T A^T . \tag{2.64}$$

A similar rule, which holds for the inversion of matrices, is

$$(AB)^{-1} = B^{-1} A^{-1} . \tag{2.65}$$

This time, the existence of $(AB)^{-1}$, A^{-1}, and B^{-1} is required.

Example 3: The distance function of (2.22) for Y can be calculated as

$$\begin{aligned} d_Y^2(Y) &= (Y - M_Y)^T \Sigma_Y^{-1} (Y - M_Y) \\ &= (X - M_X)^T A A^{-1} \Sigma_X^{-1} (A^T)^{-1} A^T (X - M_X) \\ &= (X - M_X)^T \Sigma_X^{-1} (X - M_X) \\ &= d_X^2(X) . \end{aligned} \tag{2.66}$$

That is, the distance of (2.22) is invariant under any nonsingular ($|A| \neq 0$) linear transformation.

Example 4: If $\mathbf{X}$ is normal with M_X and Σ_X, $\mathbf{Y}$ is also normal with M_Y and Σ_Y. Since the quadratic form in the exponential function is invariant, the density function of $\mathbf{Y}$ is

$$p(Y) = \frac{1}{|A|(2\pi)^{n/2}|\Sigma_X|^{1/2}} \exp\{-\frac{1}{2} d_Y^2(Y)\} , \tag{2.67}$$

where $|A|$ is the Jacobian of this linear transformation. Recalling (2.63) and a determinant rule

$$\Sigma_Y = A^T \Sigma_X A \rightarrow |\Sigma_Y| = |A^T||\Sigma_X||A| = |\Sigma_X||A|^2 , \tag{2.68}$$

$p(Y)$ becomes

$$p(Y) = \frac{1}{(2\pi)^{n/2}|\Sigma_Y|^{1/2}} \exp\{-\frac{1}{2} d_Y^2(Y)\} . \tag{2.69}$$

Thus, **Y** is a normal distribution with the expected vector M_Y and covariance matrix Σ_Y.

Orthonormal Transformation

Let us shift our coordinate system to bring the expected vector M to the origin. We use Z for the new coordinate system.

$$Z = X - M . \tag{2.70}$$

Then the quadratic form of (2.22) becomes

$$d_Z^2(Z) = Z^T \Sigma^{-1} Z . \tag{2.71}$$

Let us find a vector Z which maximizes $d_Z^2(Z)$ subject to the condition $Z^T Z = 1$ (constant). This is obtained by

$$\frac{\partial}{\partial Z}\{Z^T \Sigma^{-1} Z - \mu(Z^T Z - 1)\} = 2\Sigma^{-1} Z - 2\mu Z = 0 , \tag{2.72}$$

where μ is a Lagrange multiplier. The term $\partial/\partial Z$ consists of n partial derivatives $[\partial/\partial z_1 \; \partial/\partial z_2 \; \ldots \; \partial/\partial z_n]^T$. The result is

$$\Sigma^{-1} Z = \mu Z \quad or \quad \Sigma Z = \lambda Z \quad (\lambda = 1/\mu) , \tag{2.73}$$

$$Z^T Z = 1 . \tag{2.74}$$

In order that a nonnull Z may exist, λ must be chosen to satisfy the determinant equation

$$|\Sigma - \lambda I| = 0 . \tag{2.75}$$

This is called the *characteristic equation* of the matrix Σ. Any value of λ that satisfies this equation is called an *eigenvalue*, and the Z corresponding to a given λ

is called an *eigenvector*. When Σ is a symmetric $n \times n$ matrix, we have n real eigenvalues $\lambda_1, \ldots, \lambda_n$ and n real eigenvectors $\phi_1, \ldots, \phi_n$. The eigenvectors corresponding to two different eigenvalues are orthogonal. This can be proved as follows: For λ_i, ϕ_i and λ_j, $\phi_j (\lambda_i \neq \lambda_j)$,

$$\Sigma\phi_i = \lambda_i\phi_i \quad \text{and} \quad \Sigma\phi_j = \lambda_j\phi_j \ . \tag{2.76}$$

Multiplying the first equation by ϕ_j^T, the second by ϕ_i^T, and subtracting the second from the first gives

$$(\lambda_i - \lambda_j)\phi_j^T\phi_i = \phi_j^T\Sigma\phi_i - \phi_i^T\Sigma\phi_j = 0 \ , \tag{2.77}$$

since Σ is a symmetric matrix. Since $\lambda_i \neq \lambda_j$,

$$\phi_j^T\phi_i = 0 \ . \tag{2.78}$$

Thus, (2.73), (2.74), and (2.78) can be rewritten as

$$\Sigma\Phi = \Phi\Lambda \ , \tag{2.79}$$

$$\Phi^T\Phi = I \ , \tag{2.80}$$

where Φ is an $n \times n$ matrix, consisting of n eigenvectors as

$$\Phi = [\phi_1 \ \ldots \ \phi_n] \tag{2.81}$$

and Λ is a diagonal matrix of eigenvalues as

$$\Lambda = \begin{bmatrix} \lambda_1 & & & 0 \\ & \cdot & & \\ & & \cdot & \\ & & & \cdot \\ 0 & & & \lambda_n \end{bmatrix} , \tag{2.82}$$

and I is the identity matrix. The matrices Φ and Λ will be called the *eigenvector matrix* and the *eigenvalue matrix*, respectively.

Let us use Φ as the transformation matrix A of (2.61) as

$$\mathbf{Y} = \Phi^T\mathbf{X} \ . \tag{2.83}$$

Then, from (2.63),

$$\Sigma_Y = \Phi^T \Sigma_X \Phi = \Lambda \ , \tag{2.84}$$

where the following relationships are used:

$$(\Phi^T)^T = \Phi \ , \tag{2.85}$$

$$\Phi^{-1} = \Phi^T \quad \text{[from (2.80)]} \tag{2.86}$$

Equation (2.84) leads to the following important conclusions:

(1) The transformation of (2.83) may be broken down to n separate equations $\mathbf{y}_i = \phi_i^T \mathbf{X}$ $(i=1,\ldots,n)$. Since $\phi_i^T X$ is $\|\phi_i\| \|X\| \cos\theta = \|X\| \cos\theta$ where θ is the angle between the two vectors ϕ_i and X, y_i is the projected value of X on ϕ_i. Thus, Y represents X in the new coordinate system spanned by $\phi_1, \ldots, \phi_n$, and (2.83) may be interpreted as a coordinate transformation.

(2) We can find a linear transformation to *diagonalize* a covariance matrix in the new coordinate system. This means that we can obtain uncorrelated random variables in general and independent random variables for normal distributions.

(3) The transformation matrix is the eigenvector matrix of Σ_X. Since the eigenvectors are the ones that maximize $d_Z^2(Z)$, we are actually selecting the principal components of the distribution as the new coordinate axes. A two-dimensional example is given in Fig. 2-1.

(4) The eigenvalues are the variances of the transformed variables, $\mathbf{y}_i$'s.

(5) This transformation is called an *orthonormal transformation*, because (2.80) is satisfied. In orthonormal transformations, Euclidean distances are preserved since

$$\|Y\|^2 = Y^T Y = X^T \Phi \Phi^T X = X^T X = \|X\|^2 \ . \tag{2.87}$$

Whitening Transformation

After applying the orthonormal transformation of (2.83), we can add another transformation $\Lambda^{-1/2}$ that will make the covariance matrix equal to I.

$$\mathbf{Y} = \Lambda^{-1/2} \Phi^T \mathbf{X} = (\Phi \Lambda^{-1/2})^T \mathbf{X} \ , \tag{2.88}$$

$$\Sigma_Y = \Lambda^{-1/2} \Phi^T \Sigma_X \Phi \Lambda^{-1/2} = \Lambda^{-1/2} \Lambda \Lambda^{-1/2} = I \ . \tag{2.89}$$

This transformation $\Phi \Lambda^{-1/2}$ is called the *whitening transformation* or the

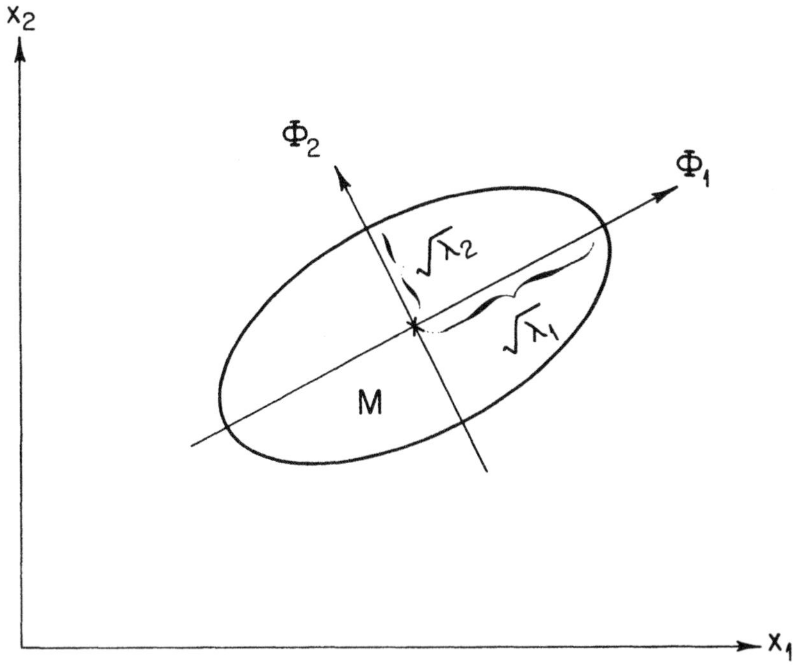

Fig. 2-1 Eigenvalues and eigenvectors of a distribution.

whitening process. The purpose of the second transformation $\Lambda^{-1/2}$ is to change the scales of the principal components in proportion to $1/\sqrt{\lambda_i}$. Figure 2-2 shows a two-dimensional example.

A few properties of the whitening transformation are pointed out here as follows.

(1) Whitening transformations are not orthonormal transformations because

$$(\Phi\Lambda^{-1/2})^T(\Phi\Lambda^{-1/2}) = \Lambda^{-1/2}\Phi^T\Phi\Lambda^{-1/2} = \Lambda^{-1} \neq I \; . \tag{2.90}$$

Therefore, Euclidean distances are not preserved:

$$\|Y\|^2 = Y^TY = X^T\Phi\Lambda^{-1}\Phi^TX = X^T\Sigma_X^{-1}X \neq \|X\|^2 \; . \tag{2.91}$$

(2) After a whitening transformation, the covariance matrix is invariant under any orthonormal transformation, because

$$\Psi^T I \Psi = \Psi^T\Psi = I \; . \tag{2.92}$$

This property will be used for simultaneous diagonalization of two matrices.

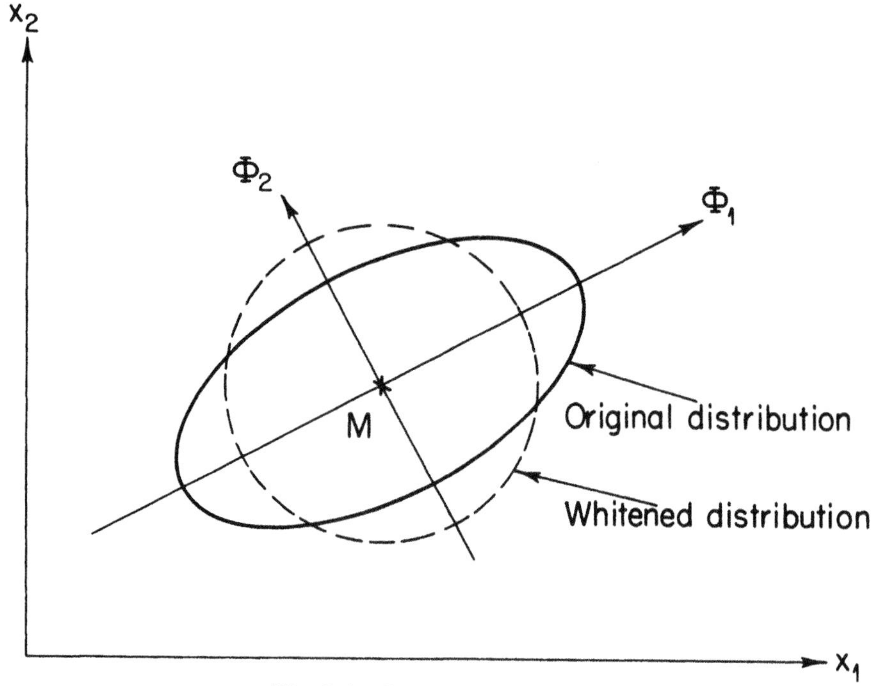

Fig. 2-2 Whitening process.

Sample generation: In pattern recognition experiments, it is often necessary to generate samples which are to be normally distributed according to a given expected vector M and covariance matrix Σ. In general, the variables are correlated and this makes the generation of samples complex. However, the generation of normal samples with the expected vector 0 and covariance matrix I is easy. Therefore, samples may be generated as follows:

(1) From the given Σ, find the whitening transformation of $Y = \Lambda^{-1/2}\Phi^T X$. In the transformed space, $\Sigma_Y = I$.

(2) Generate N independent, normally distributed numbers for each y_i $(i=1, \ldots, n)$ with zero expected value and unit variance. Then, form N vectors $\mathbf{Y}_1, \ldots, \mathbf{Y}_N$.

(3) Transform back the generated samples to the X-space by $\mathbf{X}_k = \Phi\Lambda^{1/2}\mathbf{Y}_k$ $(k=1, \ldots, N)$.

(4) Add M to the samples in the X-space as $\mathbf{X}_k + M$ $(k = 1, \ldots, N)$.

Simultaneous Diagonalization

We can diagonalize two symmetric matrices Σ_1 and Σ_2 simultaneously by a linear transformation. The process is as follows:

(1) First, we whiten Σ_1 by

$$\mathbf{Y} = \Theta^{-1/2}\Phi^T\mathbf{X} , \tag{2.93}$$

where Θ and Φ are the eigenvalue and eigenvector matrices of Σ_1 as

$$\Sigma_1\Phi = \Phi\Theta \quad \text{and} \quad \Phi^T\Phi = I . \tag{2.94}$$

Then, Σ_1 and Σ_2 are transformed to

$$\Theta^{-1/2}\Phi^T\Sigma_1\Phi\Theta^{-1/2} = I , \tag{2.95}$$

$$\Theta^{-1/2}\Phi^T\Sigma_2\Phi\Theta^{-1/2} = K . \tag{2.96}$$

In general, K is not a diagonal matrix.

(2) Second, we apply the orthonormal transformation to diagonalize K. That is,

$$\mathbf{Z} = \Psi^T\mathbf{Y} , \tag{2.97}$$

where Ψ and Λ are the eigenvector and eigenvalue matrices of K as

$$K\Psi = \Psi\Lambda \quad \text{and} \quad \Psi^T\Psi = I . \tag{2.98}$$

As shown in (2.92), the first matrix I of (2.95) is invariant under this transformation. Thus,

$$\Psi^T I \Psi = \Psi^T\Psi = I , \tag{2.99}$$

$$\Psi^T K \Psi = \Lambda . \tag{2.100}$$

Thus, both matrices are diagonalized. Figure 2-3 shows a two-dimensional example of this process. The combination of steps (1) and (2) gives the overall transformation matrix $\Phi\Theta^{-1/2}\Psi$.

Alternative approach: The matrices $\Phi\Theta^{-1/2}\Psi$ and Λ can be calculated directly from Σ_1 and Σ_2 without going through the two steps above. This is done as follows:

Theorem We can diagonalize two symmetric matrices as

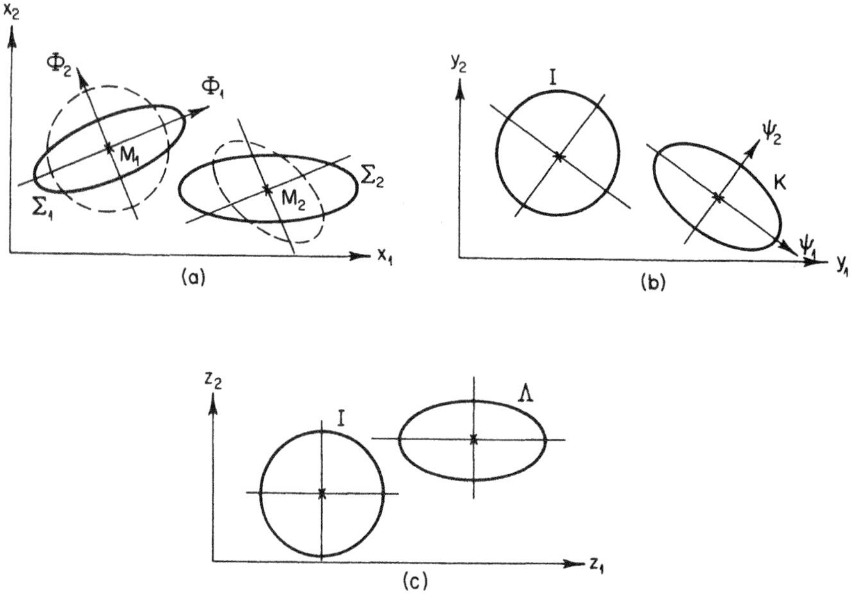

Fig. 2-3 Simultaneous diagonalization.

$$A^T \Sigma_1 A = I \quad \text{and} \quad A^T \Sigma_2 A = \Lambda , \tag{2.101}$$

where Λ and A are the eigenvalue and eigenvector matrices of $\Sigma_1^{-1}\Sigma_2$.

$$\Sigma_1^{-1}\Sigma_2 A = A\Lambda . \tag{2.102}$$

Proof Since λ's are the eigenvalues of K from (2.98),

$$|K - \lambda I| = 0 . \tag{2.103}$$

Replacing K and I by (2.95) and (2.96),

$$|\Theta^{-1/2}\Phi^T| \, |\Sigma_2 - \lambda\Sigma_1| \, |\Phi\Theta^{-1/2}| = 0 . \tag{2.104}$$

Since the transformation matrix $\Phi\Theta^{-1/2}$ is nonsingular, $|\Theta^{-1/2}\Phi^T| \neq 0$ and $|\Phi\Theta^{-1/2}| \neq 0$. Therefore,

$$|\Sigma_2 - \lambda\Sigma_1| = 0 \quad \textit{or} \quad |\Sigma_1^{-1}\Sigma_2 - \lambda I| = 0 . \tag{2.105}$$

Thus, λ's are the eigenvalues of $\Sigma_1^{-1}\Sigma_2$.

For the eigenvectors, inserting (2.96) into (2.98) yields

$$\Theta^{-1/2}\Phi^T\Sigma_2\Phi\Theta^{-1/2}\Psi = \Psi\Lambda \ , \tag{2.106}$$

or

$$\Sigma_2\Phi\Theta^{-1/2}\Psi = (\Theta^{-1/2}\Phi^T)^{-1}\Psi\Lambda \ . \tag{2.107}$$

By (2.95), $(\Theta^{-1/2}\Phi^T)^{-1}$ can be replaced by $\Sigma_1\Phi\Theta^{-1/2}$.

$$\Sigma_2(\Phi\Theta^{-1/2}\Psi) = \Sigma_1(\Phi\Theta^{-1/2}\Psi)\Lambda \ , \tag{2.108}$$

or

$$\Sigma_1^{-1}\Sigma_2(\Phi\Theta^{-1/2}\Psi) = (\Phi\Theta^{-1/2}\Psi)\Lambda \ . \tag{2.109}$$

Thus, the transformation matrix $A = \Phi\Theta^{-1/2}\Psi$ is calculated as the eigenvector matrix of $\Sigma_1^{-1}\Sigma_2$.

One fact should be mentioned here. The eigenvectors ϕ_i of a symmetric matrix are orthogonal and satisfy $\phi_i^T\phi_j = 0$ for $i \neq j$. However, $\Sigma_1^{-1}\Sigma_2$ is not symmetric in general, and subsequently the eigenvectors ζ_i are not mutually orthogonal. Instead, the ζ_i's are orthogonal with respect to Σ_1: that is, $\zeta_i^T\Sigma_1\zeta_j = 0$ for $i \neq j$. Furthermore, in order to make the ζ_i's *orthonormal* with respect to Σ_1 to satisfy the first equation of (2.101), the scale of ζ_i must be adjusted by $\sqrt{\zeta_i^T\Sigma_1\zeta_i}$ such that

$$\frac{\zeta_i^T}{\sqrt{\zeta_i^T\Sigma_1\zeta_i}}\Sigma_1\frac{\zeta_i}{\sqrt{\zeta_i^T\Sigma_1\zeta_i}} = 1 \ . \tag{2.110}$$

Simultaneous diagonalization of two matrices is a very powerful tool in pattern recognition, because many problems of pattern recognition consider two distributions for classification purposes. Also, there are many possible modifications of the above discussion. These depend on what kind of properties we are interested in, what kind of matrices are used, etc. In this section we will show one of the modifications that will be used in later chapters.

Modification:

Theorem Let a matrix Q be given by a linear combination of two symmetric matrices Q_1 and Q_2 as

$$Q = a_1Q_1 + a_2Q_2 \ , \tag{2.111}$$

where a_1 and a_2 are positive constants. If we normalize the eigenvectors with respect to Q as the first equation of (2.101), Q_1 and Q_2 will share the same eigenvectors, and their eigenvalues will be reversely ordered as

$$\lambda_1^{(1)} > \lambda_2^{(1)} > \ldots > \lambda_n^{(1)} \quad \text{for } Q_1 , \tag{2.112}$$

$$\lambda_1^{(2)} < \lambda_2^{(2)} < \ldots < \lambda_n^{(2)} \quad \text{for } Q_2 . \tag{2.113}$$

Proof Let Q and Q_1 be diagonalized simultaneously such that

$$A^T Q A = I \quad \text{and} \quad A^T Q_1 A = \Lambda^{(1)} , \tag{2.114}$$

where

$$Q^{-1} Q_1 A = A \, \Lambda^{(1)} . \tag{2.115}$$

Then Q_2 is also diagonalized because, from (2.111) and (2.114),

$$A^T Q_2 A = \frac{I - a_1 \Lambda^{(1)}}{a_2} = \Lambda^{(2)} , \tag{2.116}$$

or

$$\lambda_i^{(2)} = \frac{1 - a_1 \lambda_i^{(1)}}{a_2} . \tag{2.117}$$

Therefore, Q_1 and Q_2 share the same eigenvectors that are normalized with respect to Q because of the first equation of (2.114) and, if $\lambda_i^{(1)} > \lambda_j^{(1)}$, then $\lambda_i^{(2)} < \lambda_j^{(2)}$ from (2.117).

Example 5: Let S be the mixture autocorrelation matrix of two distributions whose autocorrelation matrices are S_1 and S_2. Then

$$\begin{aligned} S &= E\{\mathbf{X}\mathbf{X}^T\} \\ &= P_1 E\{\mathbf{X}\mathbf{X}^T \mid \omega_1\} + P_2 E\{\mathbf{X}\mathbf{X}^T \mid \omega_2\} = P_1 S_1 + P_2 S_2 . \end{aligned} \tag{2.118}$$

Thus, by the above theorem, we can diagonalize S_1 and S_2 with the same set of eigenvectors. Since the eigenvalues are ordered in reverse, the eigenvector with the largest eigenvalue for the first distribution has the least eigenvalue for the second, and vice versa. This property can be used to extract features important to distinguish two distributions [8].

2.4 Various Properties of Eigenvalues and Eigenvectors

As we saw in the diagonalization processes, the eigenvalues and eigenvectors of symmetric matrices play an important role. In this section, we review various properties of eigenvalues and eigenvectors, which will simplify discussions in later chapters. Most of the matrices we will be dealing with are covariance and autocorrelation matrices, which are symmetric. Therefore, unless specifically stated, we assume that matrices are symmetric, with real eigenvalues and eigenvectors.

Orthonormal Transformations

Theorem An eigenvalue matrix Λ is invariant under any orthonormal linear transformation.

Proof Let A be an orthonormal transformation matrix and let it satisfy

$$A^T A = I \quad or \quad A^T = A^{-1} . \tag{2.119}$$

By this transformation, Q is converted to $A^T Q A$ [see (2.63)]. If the eigenvalue and eigenvector matrices of $A^T Q A$ are Λ and Φ,

$$\Phi^T (A^T Q A) \Phi = \Lambda , \tag{2.120}$$

$$(A\Phi)^T Q (A\Phi) = \Lambda . \tag{2.121}$$

Thus, Λ and $A\Phi$ should be the eigenvalue and eigenvector matrices of Q. This transformation matrix $A\Phi$ satisfies the orthonormal condition as

$$(A\Phi)^T (A\Phi) = \Phi^T A^T A \Phi = \Phi^T \Phi = I . \tag{2.122}$$

Positive Definiteness

Theorem If all eigenvalues are positive, Q is a positive definite matrix.

Proof Consider a quadratic form

$$d^2 = X^T Q X . \tag{2.123}$$

We can rewrite X as ΦY, where Φ is the eigenvector matrix of Q. Then

$$d^2 = (\Phi Y)^T Q (\Phi Y) = Y^T \Phi^T Q \Phi Y = Y^T \Lambda Y = \sum_{i=1}^{n} \lambda_i y_i^2 , \tag{2.124}$$

where the λ_i's are the eigenvalues of Q. If these eigenvalues are all positive, then d^2 is positive, unless Y is a zero vector. From the relation between Y and X, we see that d^2 must be positive for all nonzero X as well. Therefore, Q is positive definite.

When Q is a covariance or autocorrelation matrix, the λ_i's are the variances or second order moments after the orthonormal transformation to diagonalize Q. Therefore, all λ_i's should be positive for both cases, and both covariance and autocorrelation matrices are positive definite.

Trace

Theorem The trace of Q is the summation of all eigenvalues and is invariant under any orthonormal transformation. That is,

$$\operatorname{tr} Q = \sum_{i=1}^{n} \lambda_i . \tag{2.125}$$

Proof First for general rectangular matrices $A_{n \times m}$ and $B_{m \times n}$,

$$\operatorname{tr}[A_{n \times m} B_{m \times n}] = \operatorname{tr}[B_{m \times n} A_{n \times m}] , \tag{2.126}$$

because

$$\sum_{i=1}^{n} \sum_{j=1}^{m} a_{ij} b_{ji} = \sum_{j=1}^{m} \sum_{i=1}^{n} b_{ji} a_{ij} , \tag{2.127}$$

where a_{ij} and b_{ji} are the components of $A_{n \times m}$ and $B_{m \times n}$. Using (2.126),

$$\sum_{i=1}^{n} \lambda_i = \operatorname{tr} \Lambda = \operatorname{tr}(\Phi^T Q \Phi) = \operatorname{tr}(Q \Phi \Phi^T) = \operatorname{tr} Q . \tag{2.128}$$

As we proved before, the eigenvalues are invariant under any orthonormal transformation. Therefore, any function of eigenvalues is also invariant.

When Q is a covariance or autocorrelation matrix, the above theorem states that the summation of the variances or second order moments of individual variables is invariant under any orthonormal transformation.

Theorem If Λ and Φ are the eigenvalue and eigenvector matrices of Q, the eigenvalue and eigenvector matrices of Q^m for any integer m are Λ^m and Φ respectively. That is,

$$Q\Phi = \Phi\Lambda \quad \rightarrow \quad Q^m\Phi = \Phi\Lambda^m \ . \tag{2.129}$$

Proof Using $Q\Phi = \Phi\Lambda$,

$$Q^m\Phi = Q^{m-1}\Phi\Lambda = Q^{m-2}\Phi\Lambda^2 = \ldots = \Phi\Lambda^m \ . \tag{2.130}$$

Theorem The trace of Q^m is the summation of λ_i^m's, and invariant under any orthonormal transformation. That is,

$$\text{tr}\, Q^m = \text{tr}\, \Lambda^m = \sum_{i=1}^{n} \lambda_i^m \ . \tag{2.131}$$

Example 6: Let us consider n eigenvalues, $\lambda_1, \ldots, \lambda_n$, as the samples drawn from the distribution of a random variable $\boldsymbol{\lambda}$. Then we can calculate all sample moments of the distribution of $\boldsymbol{\lambda}$ by

$$\hat{E}\{\boldsymbol{\lambda}^m\} = \frac{1}{n}\sum_{i=1}^{n}\lambda_i^m = \frac{1}{n}\text{tr}\, Q^m \ , \tag{2.132}$$

where $\hat{E}\{\cdot\}$ indicates the sample estimate of $E\{\cdot\}$. Particularly, we may use

$$\hat{E}\{\boldsymbol{\lambda}\} = \frac{1}{n}\text{tr}\, Q = \frac{1}{n}\sum_{i=1}^{n} q_{ii} \ , \tag{2.133}$$

$$\begin{aligned} \hat{\text{V}}\text{ar}\{\boldsymbol{\lambda}\} &= \frac{1}{n}\text{tr}\, Q^2 - \{\frac{1}{n}\text{tr}\, Q\}^2 \\ &= \frac{1}{n}\sum_{i=1}^{n}\sum_{j=1}^{n} q_{ij}^2 - \frac{1}{n^2}\left(\sum_{i=1}^{n} q_{ii}\right)^2 \ . \end{aligned} \tag{2.134}$$

Example 7: Equation (2.131) is used to find the largest eigenvalue because

$$\lambda_1^m + \ldots + \lambda_n^m \cong \lambda_1^m \quad \text{for } m >> 1 \ , \tag{2.135}$$

where λ_1 is assumed to be the largest eigenvalue. For example, if we select

$m = 16$, we need to multiply matrices four times as $Q \to Q^2 \to Q^4 \to Q^8 \to Q^{16}$, and take the trace of Q^{16} to estimate the largest eigenvalue.

Determinant and Rank

Theorem The determinant of Q is equal to the product of all eigenvalues and is invariant under any orthonormal transformation. That is,

$$|Q| = |\Lambda| = \prod_{i=1}^{n} \lambda_i \ . \tag{2.136}$$

Proof Since the determinant of the product of matrices is the product of the determinants of the matrices,

$$|\Lambda| = |\Phi^T||Q||\Phi| = |Q||\Phi^T||\Phi| = |Q| \ . \tag{2.137}$$

Theorem The rank of Q is equal to the number of nonzero eigenvalues.

Proof Q can be expressed by

$$Q = \Phi\Lambda\Phi^T = \sum_{i=1}^{n} \lambda_i \phi_i \phi_i^T \ , \tag{2.138}$$

where the ϕ_i's are linearly independent vectors with mutually orthonormal relations. Therefore, if we have $(n-r)$ zero λ_i's, we can express Q by r linearly independent vectors, which is the definition of rank r.

Three applications of the above theorems are given as follows:

Relation between $|S|$ and $|\Sigma|$: We show the relation between the determinants of the covariance and autocorrelation matrices [from (2.15)]:

$$|S| = |\Sigma + MM^T| \ . \tag{2.139}$$

Applying the simultaneous diagonalization of (2.101) for $\Sigma_1 = \Sigma$ and $\Sigma_2 = MM^T$, we have $A^T(\Sigma + MM^T)A = I + \Lambda$. Therefore,

$$|\Sigma + MM^T| = \frac{\prod_{i=1}^{n}(1+\lambda_i)}{|A|^2} = \{\prod_{i=1}^{n}(1+\lambda_i)\}|\Sigma| \ , \tag{2.140}$$

where $1/|A|^2 = |\Sigma|$ is obtained from (2.101). On the other hand, since the rank of MM^T is one, the λ_i's should satisfy the following conditions

$$\lambda_1 \neq 0, \quad \lambda_2 = \ldots = \lambda_n = 0 , \tag{2.141}$$

$$\sum_{i=1}^{n} \lambda_i = \lambda_1 = \mathrm{tr}(A^T M M^T A) = \mathrm{tr}(M^T A A^T M) = M^T \Sigma^{-1} M , \tag{2.142}$$

where $AA^T = \Sigma^{-1}$ is obtained from (2.101), and $\mathrm{tr}(M^T\Sigma^{-1}M) = M^T\Sigma^{-1}M$ because $M^T\Sigma^{-1}M$ is a scalar. Thus,

$$|S| = |\Sigma|(1 + M^T\Sigma^{-1}M) . \tag{2.143}$$

Small sample size problem: When only m samples are available in an n-dimensional vector space with $m < n$, the sample autocorrelation matrix $\hat{S}$ is calculated from the samples as

$$\hat{S} = \frac{1}{m}\sum_{i=1}^{m} X_i X_i^T . \tag{2.144}$$

That is, $\hat{S}$ is a function of m or less linearly independent vectors. Therefore, the rank of $\hat{S}$ should be m or less. The same conclusion can be obtained for a sample covariance matrix. However, the $(X_i - \hat{M})$'s are not linearly independent, because they are related by $\sum_{i=1}^{m}(X_i - \hat{M}) = 0$. Therefore, the rank of a sample covariance matrix is $(m-1)$ or less. This problem, which is called a small sample size problem, is often encountered in pattern recognition, particularly when n is very large. For this type of problem, instead of calculating eigenvalues and eigenvectors from an $n \times n$ matrix, the following procedure is more efficient [9].

Let $X_1, \ldots, X_m$ $(m < n)$ be samples. The sample autocorrelation matrix of these samples is

$$\hat{S}_{n\times n} = \frac{1}{m}\sum_{i=1}^{m} X_i X_i^T = \frac{1}{m}(UU^T)_{n\times n} , \tag{2.145}$$

where $U_{n\times m}$ is called a *sample matrix* and defined by

$$U = [X_1 \ \ldots \ X_m]_{n\times m} . \tag{2.146}$$

Instead of using the $n \times n$ matrix $\hat{S}_{n\times n}$ of (2.145), let us calculate the eigenvalues and eigenvectors of an $m \times m$ matrix $(U^T U)_{m\times m}$ as

$$\frac{1}{m}(U^T U)_{m\times m}\Phi_{m\times m} = \Phi_{m\times m}\Lambda_{m\times m} . \tag{2.147}$$

Multiplying U into (2.147) from the left side, we obtain

$$\frac{1}{m}(UU^T)_{n\times n}(U\Phi)_{n\times m} = (U\Phi)_{n\times m}\Lambda_{m\times m} \ . \tag{2.148}$$

Thus, $(U\Phi)_{n\times m}$ and $\Lambda_{m\times m}$ are the m eigenvectors and eigenvalues of $\hat{S} = (UU^T)_{n\times n}/m$. The other $(n-m)$ eigenvalues are all zero and their eigenvectors are indefinite. The advantage of this calculation is that only an $m \times m$ matrix is used for calculating m eigenvalues and eigenvectors. The matrix $(U\Phi)_{n\times m}$ represents orthogonal vectors but not orthonormal ones. In order to obtain orthonormal vectors V_i, we have to divide each column vector of $(U\Phi)_{n\times m}$ by $(m\lambda_i)^{1/2}$ as

$$V_i = \frac{1}{(m\lambda_i)^{1/2}}U\phi_i \quad or \quad V_{n\times m} = \frac{1}{m^{1/2}}(U\Phi\Lambda^{-1/2})_{n\times m} \ , \tag{2.149}$$

because, from (2.147),

$$V^TV = \frac{1}{m}\Lambda^{-1/2}\Phi^TU^TU\Phi\Lambda^{-1/2}$$

$$= \Lambda^{-1/2}\Phi^T\Phi\Lambda\Phi^T\Phi\Lambda^{-1/2} = \Lambda^{-1/2}\Lambda\Lambda^{-1/2} = I \ . \tag{2.150}$$

Near-singular matrix: In many pattern recognition problems, n may be very large, for example 100. However, only a few eigenvalues, such as 10, are dominant, so that

$$\lambda_1 + \ldots + \lambda_n \cong \lambda_1 + \ldots + \lambda_k \quad (k \ll n) \ . \tag{2.151}$$

This means that in a practical sense we are handling Σ (or S) with rank k, even though the mathematical rank of Σ is still n. Therefore, it is very inefficient to use an $n \times n$ matrix to find k eigenvalues and eigenvectors, even when we have a sample size greater than n. In addition to this inefficiency, we face some computational difficulty in handling a large, near-singular matrix. For example, let us consider the calculation of Σ^{-1} or $|\Sigma|$. The determinant $|\Sigma|$ is $\prod_{i=1}^{n}\lambda_i$ and $(n-k)$ λ_i's are very close to zero. If we have $n = 100$, $k = 10$, and $\lambda_1 + \ldots + \lambda_{10} = 0.9$ out of $\lambda_1 + \ldots + \lambda_{100} = 1$, $|\Sigma|$ becomes

$$\prod_{i=1}^{10}\lambda_i \times \prod_{j=11}^{100}\lambda_j = \prod_{i=1}^{10}\lambda_i \times (0.1/90)^{90} \cong \prod_{i=1}^{10}\lambda_i \times 10^{-270}$$

for the assumption of $\lambda_{11} = \lambda_{12} = \ldots = \lambda_{100}$.

Fortunately, in pattern recognition problems, $|\Sigma|$ is rarely computed directly. Instead, $\ln|\Sigma|$ is commonly used, which can be computed from the eigenvalues as

$$\ln|\Sigma| = \sum_{i=1}^{n} \ln\lambda_i \ . \tag{2.152}$$

For the above example, $\ln|\Sigma| = \Sigma_{i=1}^{10} \ln\lambda_i + 90 \ln(0.1/90) = \Sigma_{i=1}^{10} \ln\lambda_i - 612.2$.

As far as the inverse is concerned, each element of Σ^{-1} is given by the ratio of a cofactor (the determinant of an $(n-1)\times(n-1)$ matrix B) and $|\Sigma|$. The cofactor is the product of $(n-1)$ eigenvalues of B, while $|\Sigma|$ is the product of n eigenvalues of Σ. Assuming that $(n-1)$ eigenvalues of the denominator are, roughly speaking, cancelled out with $(n-1)$ eigenvalues of the numerator, $|B|/|\Sigma|$ is proportional to $1/\lambda_k$ where λ_k is one of the eigenvalues of Σ. Therefore, although $|\Sigma|$ becomes extremely small as the above example indicates, each element of Σ^{-1} does not go up to an extremely large number. In order to avoid $|B|/|\Sigma| = 0/0$ in computation, it is suggested to use the following formula to compute the inverse matrix.

$$\Sigma^{-1} = \sum_{i=1}^{n} \frac{1}{\lambda_i} \phi_i \phi_i^T \ . \tag{2.153}$$

Again, the eigenvalues and eigenvectors of Σ are computed first, and then Σ^{-1} is obtained by (2.153). Recall from (2.129) that, if Λ and Φ are the eigenvalue and eigenvector matrices of Σ, Λ^{-1} and Φ are the eigenvalue and eigenvector matrices of Σ^{-1}. Also, any matrix Q can be expressed by (2.138), using the eigenvalues and eigenvectors.

Matrix Inversion

Diagonalization of matrices is particularly useful when we need the inverse of matrices.

From (2.66), a distance function is expressed by

$$d_X^2(X) = (X - M)^T \Sigma^{-1} (X - M) = (Y - D)^T \Lambda^{-1} (Y - D)$$

$$= \sum_{i=1}^{n} \frac{(y_i - d_i)^2}{\lambda_i} , \tag{2.154}$$

where $D = [d_1 \ldots d_n]^T$ and Λ are the expected vector and diagonal covariance matrix of **Y** after the diagonizing transformation. For two distributions, the distance functions are, by simultaneous diagonalization,

$$d_1^2(X) = (X - M_1)^T \Sigma_1^{-1} (X - M_1) = (Y - D_1)^T I^{-1} (Y - D_1)$$
$$= \sum_{i=1}^{n} (y_i - d_{1i})^2 , \tag{2.155}$$

$$d_2^2(X) = (X - M_2)^T \Sigma_2^{-1} (X - M_2) = (Y - D_2)^T \Lambda^{-1} (Y - D_2)$$
$$= \sum_{i=1}^{n} \frac{(y_i - d_{2i})^2}{\lambda_i} . \tag{2.156}$$

When distance computations are heavily involved in practice, it is suggested to transform the original data samples $\mathbf{X}_i$ to $\mathbf{Y}_i$ before processing the data. This saves a significant amount of computation time.

Relation between $\mathbf{S}^{-1}$ and Σ^{-1}: We show the inverse matrix of an autocorrelation matrix in terms of the covariance matrix and expected vector. From (2.15),

$$S^{-1} = (\Sigma + MM^T)^{-1} . \tag{2.157}$$

Applying the simultaneous diagonalization of (2.101) for $\Sigma_1 = \Sigma$ and $\Sigma_2 = MM^T$, we have $A^T(\Sigma + MM^T)A = I + \Lambda$, or $\Sigma + MM^T = (A^T)^{-1} (I + \Lambda)A^{-1}$. Taking the inverse,

$$(\Sigma + MM^T)^{-1} = A(I + \Lambda)^{-1} A^T , \tag{2.158}$$

where Λ is given in (2.141) and (2.142). Therefore,

$$(I + \Lambda)^{-1} = \begin{bmatrix} 1+\lambda_1 & & & & 0 \\ & 1 & & & \\ & & \cdot & & \\ & & & \cdot & \\ 0 & & & & 1 \end{bmatrix}^{-1} = \begin{bmatrix} \frac{1}{1+\lambda_1} & & & & 0 \\ & 1 & & & \\ & & \cdot & & \\ & & & \cdot & \\ 0 & & & & 1 \end{bmatrix}$$

$$= \begin{bmatrix} 1-\frac{\lambda_1}{1+\lambda_1} & & & & 0 \\ & 1 & & & \\ & & \cdot & & \\ & & & \cdot & \\ & & & & \cdot \\ 0 & & & & 1 \end{bmatrix} = I - \frac{1}{1+\lambda_1}\Lambda \,. \tag{2.159}$$

Inserting (2.159) into (2.158),

$$S^{-1} = AA^T - \frac{1}{1+\lambda_1} A\Lambda A^T = \Sigma^{-1} - \frac{\Sigma^{-1}MM^T\Sigma^{-1}}{1+\lambda_1}$$

$$= \Sigma^{-1} - \frac{\Sigma^{-1}MM^T\Sigma^{-1}}{1+M^T\Sigma^{-1}M} \,, \tag{2.160}$$

where $AA^T = \Sigma^{-1}$ and $A\Lambda A^T = \Sigma^{-1}MM^T\Sigma^{-1}$ are obtained from (2.101). If we would like to calculate $M^TS^{-1}M$ in terms of $M^T\Sigma^{-1}M$,

$$M^TS^{-1}M = M^T\Sigma^{-1}M - \frac{(M^T\Sigma^{-1}M)^2}{1+M^T\Sigma^{-1}M} = \frac{M^T\Sigma^{-1}M}{1+M^T\Sigma^{-1}M} \,. \tag{2.161}$$

Or,

$$M^T\Sigma^{-1}M = \frac{M^TS^{-1}M}{1-M^TS^{-1}M} \,. \tag{2.162}$$

Pseudoinverse: One way of calculating the *pseudoinverse* of a singular square matrix is as follows. Let Q be a singular matrix with rank r, then Q can be expressed by the eigenvalues and eigenvectors as

$$Q = \Phi\Lambda\Phi^T = \sum_{i=1}^{r} \lambda_i \phi_i \phi_i^T \,. \tag{2.163}$$

If we express Q^* by

$$Q^* = \sum_{i=1}^{r} \frac{1}{\lambda_i} \phi_i \phi_i^T \,, \tag{2.164}$$

then

$$QQ^* = \sum_{i=1}^{r}\sum_{j=1}^{r} \frac{\lambda_i}{\lambda_j} \phi_i \phi_i^T \phi_j \phi_j^T = \sum_{i=1}^{r} \phi_i \phi_i^T$$

$$= \Phi \left[\begin{array}{cccc|cccc} 1 & 0 & & & & & & \\ & 1 & & & & 0 & & \\ & & \cdot & & & & & \\ & & & \cdot & & & & \\ 0 & & & 1 & & & & \\ \hline & & & & 0 & & & \\ & 0 & & & & \cdot & & \\ & & & & & & \cdot & \\ & & & & & & & 0 \end{array} \right] \Phi^T . \tag{2.165}$$

$$\qquad\qquad r \qquad\qquad\qquad n-r$$

Therefore, Q^* is the inverse matrix of Q in the subspace spanned by r eigenvectors, and satisfies

$$QQ^*Q = Q . \tag{2.166}$$

Generalized inverse: Equation (2.166) suggests a general way to define the "inverse" of a rectangular (not square) singular matrix [10]. The *generalized inverse* of an $m \times n$ matrix R of rank r is an $n \times m$ matrix $R^\#$ *satisfying*

$$RR^\# R = R , \tag{2.167}$$

$$O^\# = O^T . \tag{2.168}$$

The column vectors of R are seen to be eigenvectors of the $m \times m$ matrix $(RR^\#)$, among which the r's are linearly independent with eigenvalues equal to 1. Also, $(m-r)$ eigenvalues of $(RR^\#)$ must be zero. The matrix $(RR^\#)$ has the properties of a projection matrix and is useful in linear regression analysis [6].

A particular form of $R^\#$ *is* most often used. Let B be an $m \times r$ matrix whose columns are the linearly independent columns of R. Then R can be expressed by

$$R_{m\times n} = B_{m\times r}C_{r\times n} \ . \tag{2.169}$$

Since B^TB is an $r \times r$ nonsingular matrix, C can be obtained by

$$C = (B^TB)^{-1}B^TR \ . \tag{2.170}$$

From (2.170), C has rank r so that CC^T is also an $r \times r$ nonsingular matrix. The *pseudoinverse* R^* of R is defined by

$$R^* = C^T(CC^T)^{-1}(B^TB)^{-1}B^T \ . \tag{2.171}$$

It can be shown that R^* satisfies (2.167) and is therefore a generalized inverse. Further, R^* is unique. The pseudoinverse is the most often used generalized inverse.

Standard Data and Experimental Procedure

Throughout this book the following data will be used:

Type of distribution: normal,
Dimension: $n = 8$ unless specified otherwise,
Number of classes: $L = 2$,
Distribution parameters:

$$M_1 = 0 = [0 \ldots 0]^T \ , \quad M_2 = M = [m_1 \ldots m_8]^T \ ,$$

$$\Sigma_1 = I = \begin{bmatrix} 1 & & 0 \\ & \ddots & \\ 0 & & 1 \end{bmatrix} , \quad \Sigma_2 = \Lambda = \begin{bmatrix} \lambda_1 & & 0 \\ & \ddots & \\ 0 & & \lambda_8 \end{bmatrix} .$$

Data I-I:

$$m_1 = m, \quad m_2 = \ldots = m_8 = 0 \ ,$$

$$\lambda_1 = \ldots = \lambda_8 = 1 \ .$$

In this data, both Σ_1 and Σ_2 are I. The value of m controls the overlap between the two distributions. Unless m (or $\sqrt{M^TM}$ or $\|M_2 - M_1\|$) is specified otherwise, we use $m = 2.56$, which gives the Bayes error of 10%. Also, unless specified otherwise, we assume $n = 8$. Even when n changes, the Bayes error stays the same for a fixed m.

Data I-4I:

$$m_1 = \ldots = m_8 = 0 ,$$

$$\lambda_1 = \ldots = \lambda_8 = 4 .$$

In this data, the two expected vectors are the same, but the covariance matrices are different. The Bayes error varies depending on the value of the λ_i's as well as n, and becomes about 9% for $\lambda_1 = \ldots = \lambda_8 = 4$. Again, unless specified otherwise, we use $n = 8$ for this data.

Data I-Λ:

i	1	2	3	4	5	6	7	8
m_i	3.86	3.10	0.84	0.84	1.64	1.08	0.26	0.01
λ_i	8.41	12.06	0.12	0.22	1.49	1.77	0.35	2.73

In this data [11], both the expected vectors and the covariance matrices differ, and the Bayes error is 1.9% as will be shown in Chapter 3. The dimensionality of this data is fixed and cannot be changed.

Generally, parametric algorithms which work well for Data *I-I* will not work for Data *I-4I*, and vice versa. So, it is important to understand which algorithms fit which data. Any reasonable nonparametric algorithm must work for all types of data, since the algorithm should not depend on the structure of a particular data set.

Even though the covariance matrices for these three data sets are diagonal, they still represent the general case, since any two non-diagonal covariances can be simultaneously diagonalized by a linear transformation. Also, a coordinate shift can bring M_1 to the origin of the coordinate system without any loss of generality.

The dimensionality of 8 was selected for the following reasons. When the dimensionality is low (e.g., 1 or 2), all experimental results can be explained easily using an engineer's intuition. Unfortunately, this is no longer true when the dimensionality becomes high (for example, 32 or 64). Often, experimental conclusions obtained using low-dimensional data cannot be extended to high-dimensional cases. However, running experiments with high-dimensional data requires a large amount of memory and frequently consumes a lot of computer time. The dimensionality of 8 is a compromise; high-dimensional phenomena can be observed with relatively inexpensive data-handling costs.

Experimental procedure: When an experiment is called for, a number of samples, N_i $(i = 1,2)$, are generated according to the specified parameters. Normally $N_i = 100$ is selected for $n=8$, unless specified otherwise. Using these N_i samples per class, the planned experiment is conducted. This process is repeated τ times. For each trial, N_i samples per class must be generated *independently*. Normally $\tau=10$ is used in this book, unless specified otherwise. Then, the τ experimental results are averaged and the standard deviation is computed.

Data RADAR: In addition to the three standard data sets mentioned above, a set of millimeter-wave radar data is used in this book in order to test algorithms on high-dimensional real data. Each sample is a range profile of a target observed using a high resolution millimeter-wave radar. The samples were collected by rotating a Chevrolet Camaro and a Dodge Van on a turntable, taking approximately 8,800 readings over a complete revolution. The magnitude of each range profile was time-sampled at 66 positions (range bins), and the resulting 66-dimensional vector was normalized by energy. Furthermore, each normalized time-sampled value, x_i, was transformed to y_i by $y_i = x_i^{0.4}$ $(i = 1, \ldots, 66)$. The justification of this transformation will be discussed in Chapter 3. The vectors were then selected at each half-degree of revolution to form 720 sample sets. These sets (720 samples from each class) are referred to in this book as Data RADAR. When a large number of samples is needed, 8,800 samples per class will be used.

Computer Projects

1. Generate samples from a normal distribution specified by

$$n = 2, \quad N = 100, \quad M = \begin{bmatrix} 1 \\ 2 \end{bmatrix}, \quad \text{and} \quad \Sigma = \begin{bmatrix} 4 & 4 \\ 4 & 9 \end{bmatrix} .$$

2. Plot the generated samples.

3. Compute the sample mean, $\hat{\mathbf{M}}$, and sample covariance matrix, $\hat{\Sigma}$

4. Repeat 1 and 3, 10 times. Compute the sample mean and sample variance for each component of $\hat{\mathbf{M}}$ and $\hat{\Sigma}$ *over 10 trials*.

5. Repeat 4 for $N=10$, 20, and 40, and examine the effect of the sample size.

6. Simultaneously diagonalize Σ and $\hat{\Sigma}$ *and form a vector* $\mathbf{V}=[\boldsymbol{\lambda}_1 \boldsymbol{\lambda}_2]^T$. *Compute the sample mean and sample covariance of* $\mathbf{V}$ *over 10 trials.*

Problems

1. Compute and plot $q_1(x)$ and $q_2(x)$ for $p_1(x)=N_x(0,1)$ and $p_2(x)=N_x(1,2)$.

2. Let $p(X)$ be $N_X(M,\Sigma)$ with

$$X=\begin{bmatrix} x_1 \\ x_2 \end{bmatrix}, \quad M=\begin{bmatrix} m_1 \\ m_2 \end{bmatrix}, \quad \text{and} \quad \Sigma=\begin{bmatrix} \sigma_1^2 & \rho\sigma_1\sigma_2 \\ \rho\sigma_1\sigma_2 & \sigma_2^2 \end{bmatrix}.$$

Show that

$$p(x_1)=N_{x_1}(m_1,\ \sigma_1^2) \quad (\textit{a marginal density}),$$

$$p(x_1|x_2)=N_{x_1}(m_1+\rho\sigma_1(x_2-m_2)/\sigma_2\ ,\ \sigma_1^2(1-\rho^2))$$

$$(\textit{a conditional density}).$$

3. For the distribution of Problem 2, plot the contour lines for

$$d^2(X)=1,\ 4,\ \text{and } 9\ ,$$

where the parameters are selected as

$$m_1=1,\ m_2=2,\ \sigma_1^2=1,\ \sigma_2^2=2,$$

$$\rho=-1,\ -0.5,\ 0,\ 0.5,\ 1\ .$$

4. A two-dimensional random vector becomes $[a\ b]^T$, $[-a\ -b]^T$, $[-c\ d]^T$ or $[c\ -d]^T$ with probability of 1/4 for each.

(a) Compute the expected vector and covariance matrix.

(b) Find the condition for a, b, c, and d to satisfy in order to obtain $\rho = 0$.

(c) Find the conditions for a, b, c and d to satisfy in order to obtain $\rho = +1$ and $\rho = -1$.

5. Let $\hat{\mathbf{m}}$ be the sample mean of N samples, $\mathbf{x}_1, \ldots, \mathbf{x}_N$, drawn from $N_x(m, \sigma^2)$. Find the expected value and variance of $(\hat{\mathbf{m}}-m)^2$, and confirm that $\text{Var}\{(\hat{\mathbf{m}}-m)^2\} \sim 1/N^2$.

6. Let

$$\Sigma_1 = \begin{bmatrix} 1 & 0.5 \\ 0.5 & 1 \end{bmatrix} \quad \text{and} \quad \Sigma_2 = \begin{bmatrix} 1+\sqrt{3}/4 & 0.5 \\ 0.5 & 1-\sqrt{3}/4 \end{bmatrix} .$$

Diagonalize these two matrices simultaneously.

7. Prove that $S^{-1}M$ and $\Sigma^{-1}M$ are the same vector with different lengths.

8. Express a non-zero eigenvalue and the corresponding eigenvector of $\Sigma^{-1}MM^T$ in terms of Σ and M. (Hint: The rank of $\Sigma^{-1}MM^T$ is one.)

9. Let S be an $n \times n$ matrix, composed of two vectors M_1 and M_2 as $S = M_1M_1^T + M_2M_2^T$. The lengths of M_1 and M_2 are 1 and 2 respectively, and their mutual angle is 60°. Compute the eigenvalues of S.

10. After the mixture of two distributions is normalized by a shift and a linear transformation, the expected vectors and covariance matrices satisfy the following equations.

$$P_1(\Sigma_1 + M_1M_1^T) + P_2(\Sigma_2 + M_2M_2^T) = I ,$$

$$P_1M_1 + P_2M_2 = 0 .$$

Calculate the followings in terms of P_1, P_2, and M_1

(a) $(P_1\Sigma_1 + P_2\Sigma_2)^{-1}$,

(b) $(M_2 - M_1)^T (P_1\Sigma_1 + P_2\Sigma_2)^{-1} (M_2 - M_1)$,

(c) $|P_1\Sigma_1 + P_2\Sigma_2|$.

References

1. R. V. Hogg and A. T. Craig, "Introduction to Mathematical Statistics (Second Edition)," Macmillan, New York, 1965.
2. A. Papoulis, "Probability, Random Variables, and Stochastic Processes," McGraw-Hill, New York, 1965.
3. B. Noble and J. W. Daniel, "Applied Linear Algebra (Second Edition)," Prentice-Hall, Englewood Cliffs, New Jersey, 1977.
4. S. R. Searle, "Matrix Algebra Useful for Statistics," Wiley, New York, 1982.
5. J. H. Wilkinson, "Algebraic Eigenvalue Problem," Oxford Univ. Press, London and New York, 1965.
6. R. Deutsch, "Estimation Theory," Prentice-Hall, Englewood Cliffs, New Jersey, 1965.
7. A. Gelb (ed.), "Applied Optimal Estimation," MIT Press, Cambridge, 1974.
8. K. Fukunaga and W. L. G. Koontz, Application of the Karhunen-Loéve expansion to feature selection and ordering, *Trans. IEEE Computers*, C-19, pp. 311-318, 1970.
9. J. A. McLaughlin and J. Raviv, *N*th order autocorrelations in pattern recognition, *Inform. and Contr.*, 12, pp. 121-142, 1968.
10. R. Penrose, On the generalized inverse of a matrix, *Proc. Cambridge Philos. Soc.*, 51, pp. 406-413, 1955.
11. T. Marill and D. M. Green, On the effectiveness of receptors in recognition systems, *Trans. IEEE Inform. Theory*, IT-9, pp. 11-27, 1963.

Chapter 3

HYPOTHESIS TESTING

The purpose of pattern recognition is to determine to which category or class a given sample belongs. Through an observation or measurement process, we obtain a set of numbers which make up the observation vector. The observation vector serves as the input to a decision rule by which we assign the sample to one of the given classes. Let us assume that the observation vector is a random vector whose conditional density function depends on its class. If the conditional density function for each class is known, then the pattern recognition problem becomes a problem in statistical hypothesis testing.

3.1 Hypothesis Tests for Two Classes

In this section, we discuss two-class problems, which arise because each sample belongs to one of two classes, ω_1 or ω_2. The conditional density functions and the *a priori* probabilities are assumed to be known.

The Bayes Decision Rule for Minimum Error

Bayes test: Let X be an observation vector, and let it be our purpose to determine whether X belongs to ω_1 or ω_2. A decision rule based simply on probabilities may be written as follows:

$$q_1(X) \underset{\omega_2}{\overset{\omega_1}{\gtrless}} q_2(X) , \tag{3.1}$$

where $q_i(X)$ is *a posteriori probability* of ω_i given X. Equation (3.1) indicates that, if the probability of ω_1 given X is larger than the probability of ω_2, X is classified to ω_1, and vice versa. The *a posteriori* probability $q_i(X)$ may be calculated from the *a priori* probability P_i and the conditional density function $p_i(X)$, using *Bayes theorem*, as

$$q_i(X) = \frac{P_i p_i(X)}{p(X)} \tag{3.2}$$

where $p(X)$ is the mixture density function. Since $p(X)$ is positive and common to both sides of the inequality, the decision rule of (3.1) can be expressed as

$$P_1 p_1(X) \underset{\omega_2}{\overset{\omega_1}{\gtrless}} P_2 p_2(X) \tag{3.3}$$

or

$$\ell(X) = \frac{p_1(X)}{p_2(X)} \underset{\omega_2}{\overset{\omega_1}{\gtrless}} \frac{P_2}{P_1} . \tag{3.4}$$

The term $\ell(X)$ is called the *likelihood ratio* and is the basic quantity in hypothesis testing. We call P_2/P_1 the *threshold value* of the likelihood ratio for the decision. Sometimes it is more convenient to write the *minus-log likelihood ratio* rather than writing the likelihood ratio itself. In that case, the decision rule of (3.4) becomes

$$h(X) = -\ln \ell(X) = -\ln p_1(X) + \ln p_2(X) \underset{\omega_2}{\overset{\omega_1}{\gtrless}} \ln \frac{P_1}{P_2} . \tag{3.5}$$

The direction of the inequality is reversed because we have used the negative logarithm. The term $h(X)$ is called *the discriminant function.* Throughout this book, we assume $P_1 = P_2$, and set the threshold $\ln P_1/P_2 = 0$ for simplicity, unless otherwise stated.

Equation (3.1), (3.4), or (3.5) is called the *Bayes test for minimum error.*

Bayes error: In general, the decision rule of (3.5), or any other decision rule, does not lead to perfect classification. In order to evaluate the performance of a decision rule, we must calculate the *probability of error*, that is, the probability that a sample is assigned to the wrong class.

The *conditional error* given X, $r(X)$, due to the decision rule of (3.1) is either $q_1(X)$ or $q_2(X)$ whichever smaller. That is,

$$r(X) = \min[q_1(X), q_2(X)] \ . \tag{3.6}$$

The total error, which is called the *Bayes error*, is computed by $E\{r(\mathbf{X})\}$.

$$\begin{aligned} \varepsilon = E\{r(\mathbf{X})\} &= \int r(X)p(X)dX \\ &= \int \min[P_1p_1(X), P_2p_2(X)]dX \\ &= P_1\int_{L_2} p_1(X)dX + P_2\int_{L_1} p_2(X)dX \\ &= P_1\varepsilon_1 + P_2\varepsilon_2 \ , \end{aligned} \tag{3.7}$$

where

$$\varepsilon_1 = \int_{L_2} p_1(X)\, dX \quad \text{and} \quad \varepsilon_2 = \int_{L_1} p_2(X)\, dX \ . \tag{3.8}$$

Equation (3.7) shows several ways to express the Bayes error, ε. The first line is the definition of ε. The second line is obtained by inserting (3.6) into the first line and applying the Bayes theorem of (3.2). The integral regions L_1 and L_2 of the third line are the regions where X is classified to ω_1 and ω_2 by this decision rule, and they are called the ω_1- and ω_2*–regions*. In L_1, $P_1p_1(X) > P_2p_2(X)$, and therefore $r(X) = P_2p_2(X)/p(X)$. Likewise, $r(X) = P_1p_1(X)/p(X)$ in L_2 because $P_1p_1(X) < P_2p_2(X)$ in L_2. In (3.8), we distinguish two types of errors: one results from misclassifying samples from ω_1 and the other results from misclassifying samples from ω_2. The total error is a weighted sum of these errors.

Figure 3-1 shows an example of this decision rule for a simple one-dimensional case. The decision boundary is set at $x=t$ where $P_1p_1(x) = P_2p_2(x)$, and $x < t$ and $x > t$ are designated to L_1 and L_2 respectively. The resulting errors are $P_1\varepsilon_1 = B + C$, $P_2\varepsilon_2 = A$, and $\varepsilon = A + B + C$, where A, B, and C indicate the areas, for example, $B = \int_t^{t'} P_1p_1(x)\,dx$.

This decision rule gives the smallest probability of error. This may be demonstrated easily from the one-dimensional example of Fig. 3-1. Suppose that the boundary is moved from t to t', setting up the new ω_1- and ω_2–regions as L_1' and L_2'. Then, the resulting errors are $P_1\varepsilon_1' = C$, $P_2\varepsilon_2' = A + B + D$, and $\varepsilon' = A + B + C + D$, which is larger than ε by D. The same is true when the

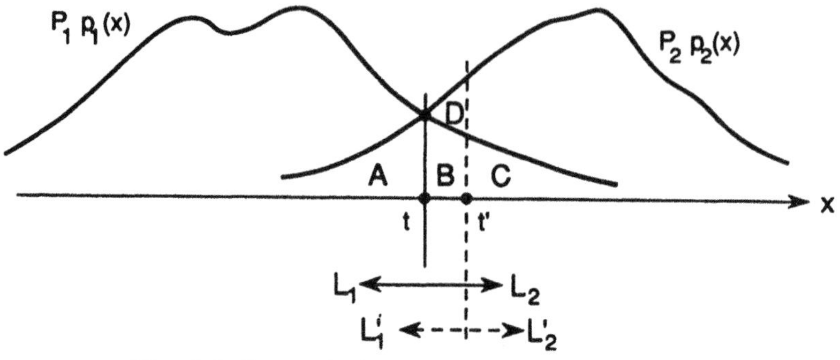

Fig. 3-1 Bayes decision rule for minimum error.

boundary is shifted to the left. This argument can be extended to a general n-dimensional case.

The computation of the Bayes error is a very complex problem except in some special cases. This is due to the fact that ε is obtained by integrating high-dimensional density functions in complex regions as seen in (3.8). Therefore, it is sometimes more convenient to integrate the density function of $\mathbf{h} = h(\mathbf{X})$ of (3.5), which is one-dimensional:

$$\varepsilon_1 = \int_{\ln(P_1/P_2)}^{+\infty} p_h(h \mid \omega_1)dh \ , \tag{3.9}$$

$$\varepsilon_2 = \int_{-\infty}^{\ln(P_1/P_2)} p_h(h \mid \omega_2)dh \ , \tag{3.10}$$

where $p_h(h \mid \omega_i)$ is the conditional density of $\mathbf{h}$ for ω_i. However, in general, the density function of $\mathbf{h}$ is not available, and very difficult to compute.

Example 1: When the $p_i(X)$'s are normal with expected vectors M_i and covariance matrices Σ_i, the decision rule of (3.5) becomes

$$\begin{aligned} h(X) &= -\ln \ell(X) \\ &= \frac{1}{2}(X-M_1)^T\Sigma_1^{-1}(X-M_1) - \frac{1}{2}(X-M_2)^T\Sigma_2^{-1}(X-M_2) + \frac{1}{2}\ln\frac{|\Sigma_1|}{|\Sigma_2|} \\ &\underset{\omega_2}{\overset{\omega_1}{\gtrless}} \ln\frac{P_1}{P_2} \ . \end{aligned} \tag{3.11}$$

Equation (3.11) shows that the decision boundary is given by a quadratic form in X. When $\Sigma_1 = \Sigma_2 = \Sigma$, the boundary becomes a linear function of X as

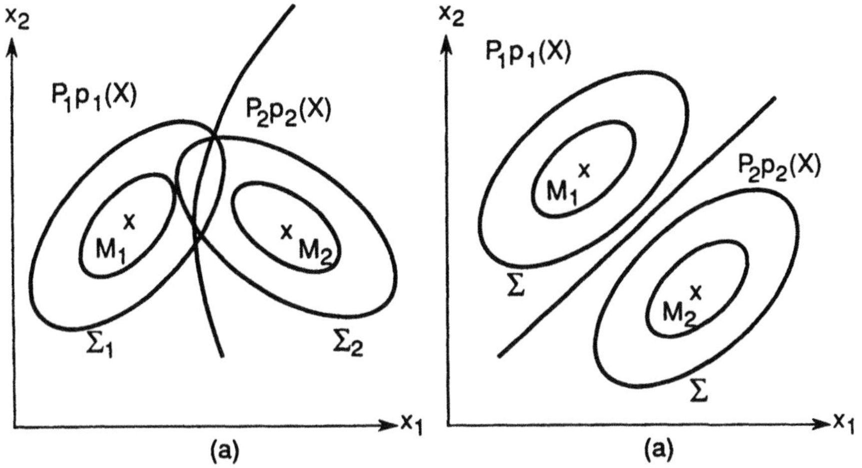

Fig. 3-2 Decision boundaries for normal distributions: (a) $\Sigma_1 \neq \Sigma_2$; (b) $\Sigma_1 = \Sigma_2$.

$$h(X) = (M_2 - M_1)^T \Sigma^{-1} X + \frac{1}{2}(M_1^T \Sigma^{-1} M_1 - M_2^T \Sigma^{-1} M_2) \underset{\omega_2}{\overset{\omega_1}{\gtrless}} \ln \frac{P_1}{P_2} . \tag{3.12}$$

Figure 3-2 shows two-dimensional examples for $\Sigma_1 \neq \Sigma_2$ and $\Sigma_1 = \Sigma_2$.

Example 2: Let us study a special case of (3.11) where

$$M_i = 0 \quad \text{and} \quad \Sigma_i = \begin{bmatrix} 1 & \rho_i & \cdots & \rho_i^{n-1} \\ \rho_i & 1 & & \vdots \\ \vdots & & \ddots & \rho_i \\ \rho_i^{n-1} & \cdots & \rho_i & 1 \end{bmatrix} . \tag{3.13}$$

This type of covariance matrix is often seen, for example, when *stationary random processes* are time-sampled to form random vectors. The explicit expressions for Σ_i^{-1} and $|\Sigma_i|$ are known for this covariance matrix as

$$\Sigma_i^{-1} = \frac{1}{1-\rho_i^2} \begin{bmatrix} 1 & -\rho_i & 0 & \cdots & 0 \\ -\rho_i & 1+\rho_i^2 & -\rho_i & \ddots & \vdots \\ 0 & \ddots & \ddots & \ddots & 0 \\ \vdots & \ddots & & 1+\rho_i^2 & -\rho_i \\ 0 & \cdots & 0 & -\rho_i & 1 \end{bmatrix} , \tag{3.14}$$

$$|\Sigma_i| = (1-\rho_i^2)^{n-1} . \tag{3.15}$$

Therefore, the quadratic equation of (3.11) becomes

$$\left[\frac{1+\rho_1^2}{1-\rho_1^2} - \frac{1+\rho_2^2}{1-\rho_2^2} \right] \sum_{i=1}^{n} x_i^2 - \left[\frac{\rho_1^2}{1-\rho_1^2} - \frac{\rho_2^2}{1-\rho_2^2} \right] (x_1^2 + x_n^2)$$

$$- \left[\frac{2\rho_1}{1-\rho_1^2} - \frac{2\rho_2}{1-\rho_2^2} \right] \sum_{i=1}^{n-1} x_i x_{i+1} + (n-1) \ln \frac{1-\rho_1^2}{1-\rho_2^2} \underset{\omega_2}{\overset{\omega_1}{\gtrless}} \ln \frac{P_1}{P_2} , \tag{3.16}$$

where the second term shows the edge effect of terminating the observation of random processes within a finite length, and this effect diminishes as n gets large. If we could ignore the second and fourth terms and make $\ln(P_1/P_2) = 0$ $(P_1 = P_2)$, the decision rule becomes $(\Sigma x_i x_{i+1})/(\Sigma x_i^2) \gtrless t$; that is, the decision is made by estimating the correlation coefficient and thresholding the estimate. Since $\rho_1 \neq \rho_2$ is the only difference between ω_1 and ω_2 in this case, this decision rule is reasonable.

Example 3: When $\mathbf{x}_k$'s are mutually independent and exponentially distributed,

$$p_i(X) = \prod_{k=1}^{n} \frac{1}{\alpha_{ik}} \exp\left[-\frac{1}{\alpha_{ik}} x_k \right] u(x_k) \quad (i=1,2) , \tag{3.17}$$

where α_{ik} is the parameter of the exponential distribution for $\mathbf{x}_k$ and ω_i, and $u(\cdot)$ is the step function. Then, $h(X)$ of (3.5) becomes

$$h(X) = \sum_{k=1}^{n} \left[\frac{1}{\alpha_{1k}} - \frac{1}{\alpha_{2k}} \right] x_k + \sum_{k=1}^{n} \ln \frac{\alpha_{1k}}{\alpha_{2k}} . \tag{3.18}$$

The Bayes decision rule becomes a linear function of x_k's.

The Bayes Decision Rule for Minimum Cost

Often in practice, minimizing the probability of error is not the best criterion to design a decision rule because the misclassifications of ω_1- and ω_2-samples may have different consequences. For example, the misclassification of a cancer patient to normal may have a more damaging effect than the misclassification of a normal patient to cancer. Therefore, it is appropriate to assign a cost to each situation as

$$c_{ij} = \text{cost of deciding } X \in \omega_i \text{ when } X \in \omega_j . \tag{3.19}$$

Then, the *conditional cost of deciding* $X \in \omega_i$ given X, $r_i(X)$, is

$$r_i(X) = c_{i1}q_1(X) + c_{i2}q_2(X) . \tag{3.20}$$

The decision rule and the resulting *conditional cost* given X, $r(X)$, are

$$r_1(X) \underset{\omega_2}{\overset{\omega_1}{\gtrless}} r_2(X) \tag{3.21}$$

and

$$r(X) = \min[r_1(X), r_2(X)] . \tag{3.22}$$

The total *cost* of this decision is

$$\begin{aligned} r = E\{r(\mathbf{X})\} &= \int \min[r_1(X), r_2(X)]p(X)\,dX \\ &= \int \min[c_{11}q_1(X) + c_{12}q_2(X), c_{21}q_1(X) + c_{22}q_2(X)]p(X)\,dX \\ &= \int \min[c_{11}P_1p_1(X) + c_{12}P_2p_2(X), c_{21}P_1p_1(X) + c_{22}P_2p_2(X)]\,dX \\ &= \int_{L_1} [c_{11}P_1p_1(X) + c_{12}P_2p_2(X)]\,dX \\ &\quad + \int_{L_2} [c_{21}P_1p_1(X) + c_{22}P_2p_2(X)]\,dX , \end{aligned} \tag{3.23}$$

where L_1 and L_2 are determined by the decision rule of (3.21).

The boundary which minimizes r of (3.23) can be found as follows. First, rewrite (3.23) as a function of L_1 alone. This is done by replacing $\int_{L_2} p_i(X)dX$ with $1 - \int_{L_1} p_i(X)dX$, since L_1 and L_2 do not overlap and cover the entire domain. Thus,

$$r = (c_{21}P_1 + c_{22}P_2) + \int_{L_1} [(c_{11}-c_{21})P_1p_1(X) + (c_{12}-c_{22})P_2p_2(X)]dX \ . \tag{3.24}$$

Now our problem becomes one of choosing L_1 such that r is minimized. Suppose, for a given value of X, that the integrand of (3.24) is negative. Then we can decrease r by assigning X to L_1. If the integrand is positive, we can decrease r by assigning X to L_2. Thus the *minimum cost decision rule* is to assign to L_1 those X's and only those X's, for which the integrand of (3.24) is negative. This decision rule can be stated by the following inequality:

$$(c_{12}-c_{22})P_2p_2(X) \underset{\omega_2}{\overset{\omega_1}{\gtrless}} (c_{21}-c_{11})P_1p_1(X) \tag{3.25}$$

or

$$\frac{p_1(X)}{p_2(X)} \underset{\omega_2}{\overset{\omega_1}{\lessgtr}} \frac{(c_{12}-c_{22})P_2}{(c_{21}-c_{11})P_1} \ . \tag{3.26}$$

This decision rule is called the *Bayes test for minimum cost.*

Comparing (3.26) with (3.4), we notice that the Bayes test for minimum cost is a likelihood ratio test with a different threshold from (3.4), and that the selection of the cost functions is equivalent to changing the *a priori* probabilities P_i. Equation (3.26) is equal to (3.4) for the special selection of the cost functions

$$c_{21} - c_{11} = c_{12} - c_{22} \ . \tag{3.27}$$

This is called a *symmetrical cost function.* For a symmetrical cost function, the cost becomes the probability of error, and the test of (3.26) minimizes the probability of error.

Different cost functions are used when a wrong decision for one class is more critical than one for the other class.

The Neyman — Pearson Test

The Neyman-Pearson test follows from a third formulation of the hypothesis test problem. Recall that we can commit two types of errors in a two-class decision problem. Let the probabilities of these two errors again be ε_1 and ε_2. The *Neyman-Pearson decision rule* is the one which minimizes ε_1, subject to ε_2 being equal to a constant, say ε_0. To determine this decision rule, we must find the minimum of

$$r = \varepsilon_1 + \mu(\varepsilon_2 - \varepsilon_0) , \tag{3.28}$$

where μ is a Lagrange multiplier. Inserting ε_1 and ε_2 of (3.8) into (3.28),

$$\begin{aligned} r &= \int_{L_2} p_1(X)dX + \mu\left\{\int_{L_1} p_2(X)dX - \varepsilon_0\right\} \\ &= (1 - \mu\varepsilon_0) + \int_{L_1} \{\mu p_2(X) - p_1(X)\}\, dX . \end{aligned} \tag{3.29}$$

Using the same argument as in the derivation of (3.25) from (3.24), r can be minimized by selecting L_1 and L_2 as

$$\mu p_2(X) \underset{\omega_2}{\overset{\omega_1}{\gtrless}} p_1(X) \tag{3.30}$$

or

$$\frac{p_1(X)}{p_2(X)} \underset{\omega_2}{\overset{\omega_1}{\lessgtr}} \mu . \tag{3.31}$$

Comparing (3.31) with (3.26), we can conclude that the Neyman-Pearson test does not offer any new decision rule but relies on the likelihood ratio test, as did the Bayes test. However, the preceding discussion shows that the likelihood ratio test is the test which minimizes the error for one class, while maintaining the error for the other class constant.

The threshold μ is the solution, for a given ε_0, of the following equation:

$$\varepsilon_2 = \int_{L_1} p_2(X)dX = \varepsilon_0 . \tag{3.32}$$

Or, using the density function of $h(\mathbf{X})$ of (3.10),

$$\varepsilon_2 = \int_{-\infty}^{\mu} p_h(h \mid \omega_2)dh = \varepsilon_0 \ . \tag{3.33}$$

However, an analytical solution is not possible in general. So, we must find μ experimentally or numerically. Since $p_h(h \mid \omega_2) \geq 0$, ε_2 of (3.33) is a monotonic function of μ, and increases as μ increases. Therefore, after calculating ε_2's for several μ's, we can find the μ which gives a specified ε_0 as ε_2.

Example 4: Let us consider two-dimensional normal distributions with $M_1 = [-1,0]^T$, $M_2 = [+1,0]^T$, $\Sigma_1 = \Sigma_2 = I$, and $P_1 = P_2 = 0.5$. Then, from (3.12) and (3.31), the decision boundary can be expressed by

$$h(X) = \{[+1\ 0] - [-1\ 0]\} \begin{bmatrix} x_1 \\ x_2 \end{bmatrix} + \frac{1}{2}\left\{[-1\ 0]\begin{bmatrix} -1 \\ 0 \end{bmatrix} - [+1\ 0]\begin{bmatrix} +1 \\ 0 \end{bmatrix}\right\} = 2x_1 \underset{\omega_2}{\overset{\omega_1}{\gtrless}} -\ln \mu \ . \tag{3.34}$$

The decision boundaries for various μ's are lines parallel to the x_2-axis, as shown in Fig. 3-3, and the corresponding errors ε_2's are given in Table 3-1. For example, if we would like to maintain $\varepsilon_2 = 0.09$, then μ becomes 2 from Table 3-1, and the decision boundary passes (-0.34) of x_1.

TABLE 3-1

RELATION BETWEEN μ AND ε_2

μ:	4	2	1	$\frac{1}{2}$	$\frac{1}{4}$
ε_2:	0.04	0.09	0.16	0.25	0.38

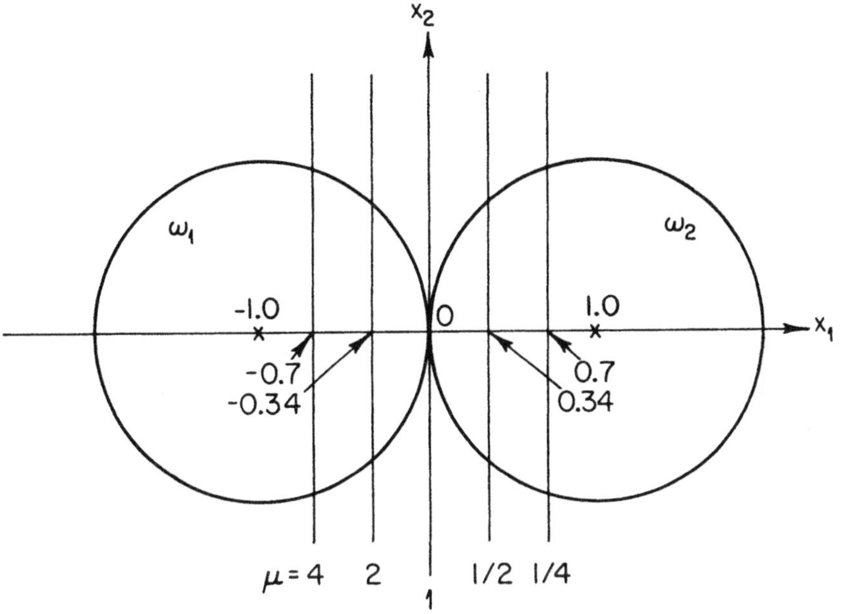

Fig. 3-3 Neyman — Pearson boundaries.

The Minimax Test

In the Bayes test for minimum cost, we notice that the likelihood ratio is compared with a threshold value which is a function of P_i. Therefore, in order to design a decision rule which minimizes the cost, we need to know the values of P_i beforehand. After the design is completed, the decision rule stays optimum only if the P_i's stay the same. Unfortunately in practice, the P_i's vary after the decision rule is fixed. The *minimax* test is designed to protect the performance of the decision rule, even if the P_i's vary unexpectedly.

First, let us express the cost of (3.24) in terms of P_1. Since $P_1 + P_2 = 1$, P_2 is uniquely determined by P_1. Inserting $P_2 = 1 - P_1$ into (3.24), and replacing $\int_{L_1} p_1(X)dX$ by $1 - \int_{L_2} p_1(X)dX$,

$$r = c_{22} + (c_{12} - c_{22})\int_{L_1} p_2(X)\, dX + P_1[(c_{11} - c_{22})$$

$$+ (c_{21}-c_{11})\int_{L_2} p_1(X)dX - (c_{12}-c_{22})\int_{L_1} p_2(X)\,dX] \,. \tag{3.35}$$

Equation (3.35) shows that, once L_1 and L_2 are determined, r is a linear function of P_1. In Fig. 3-4, the curved line represents an example of the Bayes

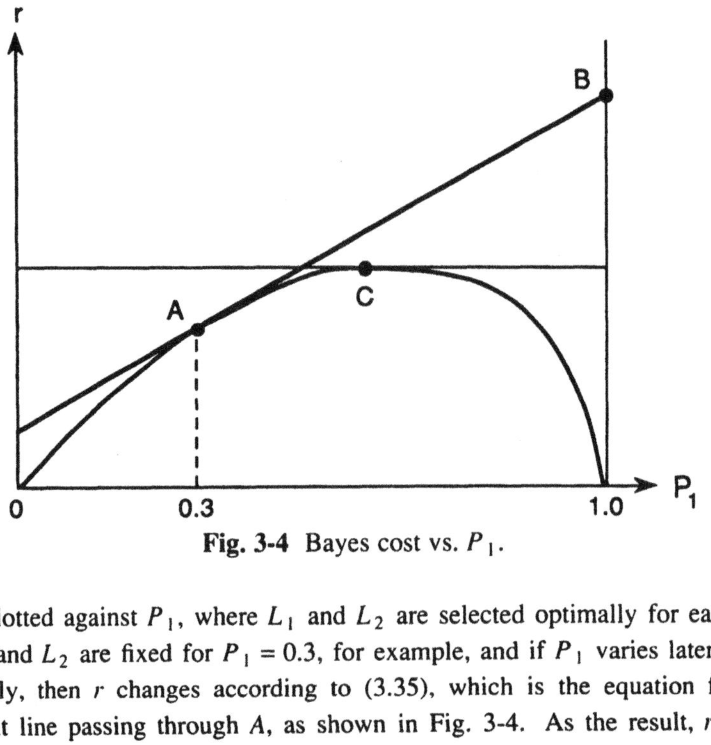

Fig. 3-4 Bayes cost vs. P_1.

cost plotted against P_1, where L_1 and L_2 are selected optimally for each P_1. If L_1 and L_2 are fixed for $P_1 = 0.3$, for example, and if P_1 varies later unexpectedly, then r changes according to (3.35), which is the equation for the straight line passing through A, as shown in Fig. 3-4. As the result, r could become much larger than we expected when we design the decision rule (for example, r can go up to B when P_1 becomes 1). In order to prevent this deterioration of performance, we choose L_1 and L_2 to make the coefficient of P_1 zero in (3.35) regardless of the predicted value for P_1. Then, the straight line becomes the tangent at the point C where the Bayes cost curve is maximum. This selection of L_1 and L_2 guarantees that the maximum Bayes cost is minimized after the threshold value is fixed, regardless of the change of P_1. This decision rule is called the *minimax test*.

Thus, in the minimax test, the boundary is designed to satisfy

$$(c_{11}-c_{22}) + (c_{21}-c_{11})\int_{L_2} p_1(X)dX - (c_{12}-c_{22})\int_{L_1} p_2(X)dX = 0 \,. \tag{3.36}$$

If we select the special set of cost functions

$$c_{11} = c_{22} \quad \text{and} \quad c_{12} = c_{21} , \tag{3.37}$$

(3.36) becomes

$$\int_{L_2} p_1(X)\,dX = \int_{L_1} p_2(X)\,dX . \tag{3.38}$$

That is, the decision boundary is still determined by the likelihood ratio, but the threshold is selected to satisfy $\varepsilon_1 = \varepsilon_2$.

Operating Characteristics

So far, we have found that the likelihood ratio test is commonly used for various tests, and only the selection of the threshold varies depending on the test. Extending this, it is a common practice to plot the relation between ε_1 and ε_2 by changing the value of the threshold continuously. This curve is called the *operating characteristic* [5]. Figure 5 shows an example of the operating characteristics where ε_1 and $1-\varepsilon_2$ are used for the x- and y-axes in log scale. Three curves in Fig. 3-5 show the performance of the likelihood ratio test for 30, 20, and 9 features which are selected from the same data set. They indicate that 30 and 20 features give almost identical performance for a wide range of operating points, while 9 features give much poor performance. From such curves, the designer of the decision rule can select a proper operating point and the corresponding threshold, depending on one's need.

Burdick's chart: Various combinations of log and linear scales are used for operating characteristics. However, the following scale gives a straight line when $h(\mathbf{X})$ of (3.5) is normally distributed for both ω_1 and ω_2 [6].

Let $\Phi(\alpha)$ be a *normal error function* defined by

$$\Phi(\alpha) = \int_{-\infty}^{\alpha} \frac{1}{\sqrt{2\pi}} e^{-x^2/2}\,dx . \tag{3.39}$$

If $\mathbf{h}$ is distributed as $N_h(m_1,\sigma_1^2)$ for ω_1 and $N_h(m_2,\sigma_2^2)$ for ω_2, and t is the value of the threshold as shown in Fig. 3-6, then

$$\varepsilon_1 = \Phi\left(\frac{m_1-t}{\sigma_1}\right) \quad \text{and} \quad \varepsilon_2 = \Phi\left(\frac{t-m_2}{\sigma_2}\right) . \tag{3.40}$$

Or, taking the inverse operation,

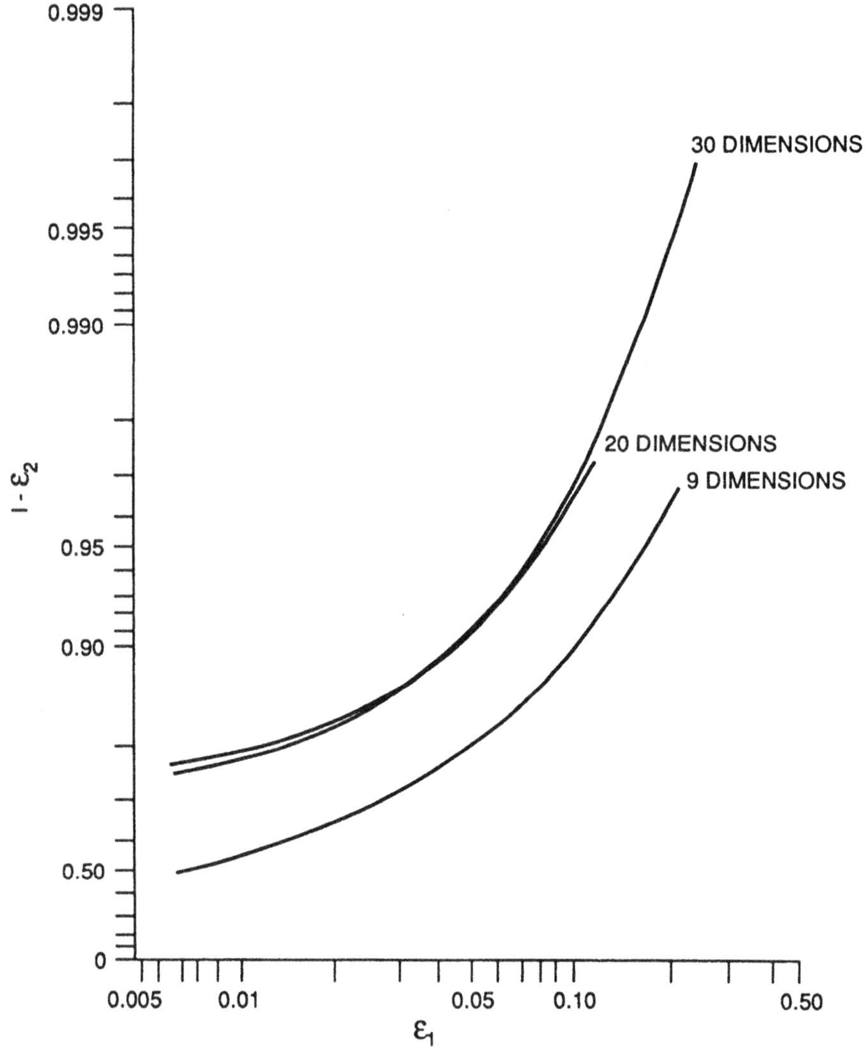

Fig. 3-5 An example of operating characteristics.

$$\frac{m_1 - t}{\sigma_1} = \Phi^{-1}(\varepsilon_1) \quad \text{and} \quad \frac{t - m_2}{\sigma_2} = \Phi^{-1}(\varepsilon_2) \,. \tag{3.41}$$

Eliminating t from these two equations, we can obtain the relation between $\Phi^{-1}(\varepsilon_1)$ and $\Phi^{-1}(\varepsilon_2)$ as

$$\Phi^{-1}(\varepsilon_2) = -\frac{\sigma_1}{\sigma_2}\Phi^{-1}(\varepsilon_1) + \frac{m_1-m_2}{\sigma_2} . \tag{3.42}$$

That is, if $\Phi^{-1}(\varepsilon_1)$ and $\Phi^{-1}(\varepsilon_2)$ are used as the x- and y-axes, we have a

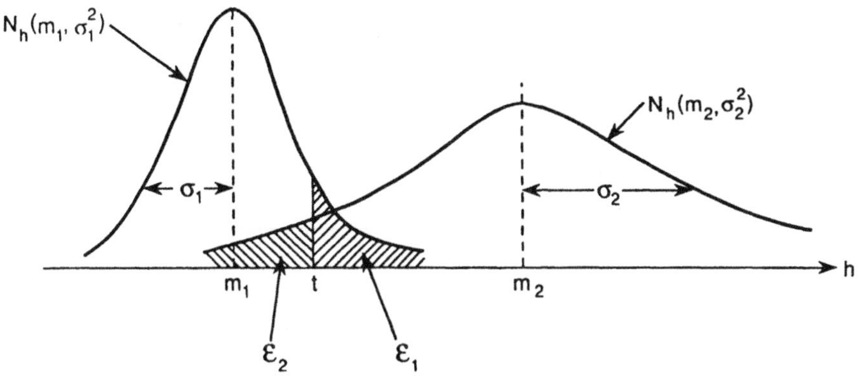

Fig. 3-6 Normal distributions of **h**.

straight line with $-\sigma_1/\sigma_2$ as the slope and $(m_1-m_2)/\sigma_2$ as the y-cross point. Figure 3-7 shows the chart, where both $\Phi^{-1}(\varepsilon)$ and ε scales are shown. Note that $\Phi^{-1}(\varepsilon) = -2, -1, 0, 1, 2$ correspond to $\varepsilon = 2.3, 15.9, 50.0, 84.1, 97.7$ (%).

For Data *I-I*, $h(X)$ becomes a linear function of X as shown in (3.12), and therefore $h(\mathbf{X})$ becomes normal if $\mathbf{X}$ is normal. The straight line operating characteristic is shown in Fig. 3-7 with the corresponding threshold values.

The advantage of using this scale is that we may see whether the distributions of $h(\mathbf{X})$ for ω_1 and ω_2 are close to normal or not. Also, we can measure some of the parameters, $-\sigma_1/\sigma_2$ and $(m_1-m_2)/\sigma_2$, from the line.

3.2 Other Hypothesis Tests

In this section, other hypothesis tests will be discussed. They are multihypothesis tests, single hypothesis tests, reject option, and composite hypothesis tests.

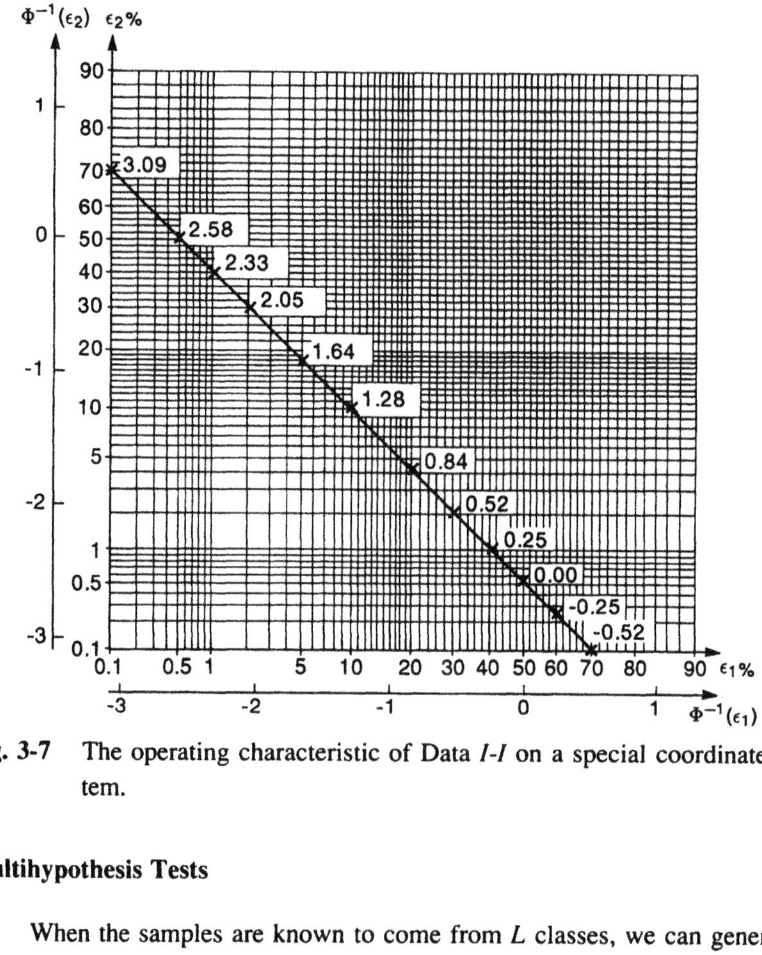

Fig. 3-7 The operating characteristic of Data *I-I* on a special coordinate system.

Multihypothesis Tests

When the samples are known to come from L classes, we can generalize the binary hypothesis testing problem.

First, if our decision is simply based on probabilities, the decision rule is

$$q_k(X) = \max_i q_i(X) \quad \rightarrow \quad X \in \omega_k \, . \tag{3.43}$$

Or, by the Bayes theorem,

$$P_k p_k(X) = \max_i P_i p_i(X) \quad \rightarrow \quad X \in \omega_k \, . \tag{3.44}$$

Since X belongs to ω_j with the probability of $q_j(X)$, the decision rule of (3.43) misclassifys X from ω_j $(j \neq k)$ to ω_k with the same probability. Summing up these, the conditional probability of error given X, due to (3.43), becomes

$r(X) = q_1(X) + \ldots + q_{k-1}(X) + q_{k+1}(X) + \ldots + q_L(X) = 1 - q_k(X)$, and the Bayes error is the expected value of $r(\mathbf{X})$ over $\mathbf{X}$. That is,

$$r(X) = 1 - \max_i q_i(X) \quad \text{and} \quad \varepsilon = E\{r(\mathbf{X})\} . \tag{3.45}$$

When cost functions are involved, the decision rule becomes

$$r_k(X) = \min_i r_i(X) \quad \rightarrow \quad X \in \omega_k \tag{3.46}$$

where $r_i(X)$ is a simple extension of (3.20) to L classes as

$$r_i(X) = \sum_{j=1}^{L} c_{ij} q_j(X) \tag{3.47}$$

and c_{ij} is the cost of deciding $X \in \omega_i$ when $X \in \omega_j$. Substituting (3.47) into (3.46) and using the Bayes theorem,

$$\sum_{j=1}^{L} c_{kj} P_j p_j(X) = \min_i \sum_{j=1}^{L} c_{ij} P_j p_j(X) \quad \rightarrow \quad X \in \omega_k . \tag{3.48}$$

The resulting conditional cost given X and the total cost are

$$r(X) = \min_i r_i(X) \quad \text{and} \quad r = E\{r(\mathbf{X})\} . \tag{3.49}$$

Example 5: When $c_{ii} = 0$ and $c_{ij} = 1$ for $i \neq j$, $r_i(X)$ of (3.47) becomes

$$r_i(X) = \sum_{j=1}^{L} q_j(X) - q_i(X) = 1 - q_i(X) . \tag{3.50}$$

Therefore, the decision rule of (3.46) and the resulting conditional cost of (3.49) become (3.43) and (3.45), respectively.

Single Hypothesis Tests

So far, we have assumed that our task is to classify an unknown sample to one of L classes. However, in practice, we often face the problem in which one class is well defined while the others are not. For example, when we want to distinguish targets from all other possible nontargets, the nontargets may include trucks, automobiles, and all kinds of other vehicles as well as trees and clutter discretes. Because of the wide variety, it is almost impossible to study the distributions of all possible nontargets before a decision rule is designed.

Single hypothesis schemes have been proposed to solve this problem. Typically, they involve measuring the distance of the object from the target mean (normalized by the target covariance matrix), and applying a threshold to determine if it is or is not a target. This technique works well when the dimensionality of the data, n, is very low (such as 1 or 2). However, as n increases, the error of this technique increases significantly. The mapping from the original n-dimensional feature space to a one-dimensional distance space destroys valuable classification information which existed in the original feature space. In order to understand this phenomena, let us study here the statistics of the distance.

Distribution of the distance: Let us consider a distribution of $\mathbf{X}$ with the expected vector M and the covariance matrix Σ. Then, the normalized distance of $\mathbf{X}$ from M is

$$\mathbf{d}^2 = (\mathbf{X}-M)^T\Sigma^{-1}(\mathbf{X}-M) = \mathbf{Z}^T\mathbf{Z} = \sum_{i=1}^{n}\mathbf{z}_i^2 \ , \tag{3.51}$$

where $\mathbf{Z} = A^T(\mathbf{X}-M)$ and A is the whitening transformation. Since the expected vector and covariance matrix of $\mathbf{Z}$ are 0 and I respectively, the $\mathbf{z}_i$'s are uncorrelated, and $E\{\mathbf{z}_i\} = 0$ and $\mathrm{Var}\{\mathbf{z}_i\} = 1$. Thus, the expected value and variance of $\mathbf{d}^2$ are

$$E\{\mathbf{d}^2\} = n\ E\{\mathbf{z}_i^2\} = n \tag{3.52}$$

$$\mathrm{Var}\{\mathbf{d}^2\} = E\{(\mathbf{d}^2)^2\} - E^2\{\mathbf{d}^2\}$$

$$= \sum_{i=1}^{n}E\{\mathbf{z}_i^4\} + \sum_{i=1}^{n}\sum_{\substack{j=1\\ i\neq j}}^{n}E\{\mathbf{z}_i^2\mathbf{z}_j^2\} - n^2E^2\{\mathbf{z}_i^2\} \ . \tag{3.53}$$

When the $\mathbf{z}_i^2$'s are uncorrelated (this is satisfied when the $\mathbf{z}_i$'s are independent), and $E\{\mathbf{z}_i^4\}$ is independent of i, the variance of $\mathbf{d}^2$ can be further simplified to

$$\mathrm{Var}\{\mathbf{d}^2\} = n\ \gamma\ , \tag{3.54}$$

where

$$\gamma = E\{\mathbf{z}_i^4\} - E^2\{\mathbf{z}_i^2\} = E\{\mathbf{z}_i^4\} - 1 . \tag{3.55}$$

For normal distributions, when the $\mathbf{z}_i$'s are uncorrelated, they are also independent. Therefore, (3.55) can be used to compute $\text{Var}\{\mathbf{d}^2\}$, and $\gamma = 2$. Figure 3-8 shows the distribution of $\mathbf{d}^2$ with the mean n and the standard deviation $\sqrt{n\gamma}$.

Example 6: Let the $\mathbf{x}_i$'s be mutually independent and identically distributed with a *gamma density function*, which is characterized by two parameters α and β as in (2.54). Using $m = E\{\mathbf{x}_i\}$ and $\sigma^2 = \text{Var}\{\mathbf{x}_i\}$, (3.51) becomes

$$\mathbf{d}^2 = \frac{1}{\sigma^2}\sum_{i=1}^{n}(\mathbf{x}_i - m)^2 . \tag{3.56}$$

Then, γ is

$$\gamma = \frac{E\{(\mathbf{x}_i - m)^4\} - \sigma^4}{\sigma^4}$$

$$= 2 + \frac{6}{\beta + 1} , \tag{3.57}$$

where the second line is obtained by using the mth order moments of a gamma density as

$$E\{\mathbf{x}^m\} = \frac{(\beta+m)\ldots(\beta+1)}{\alpha^m} . \tag{3.58}$$

An *exponential distribution* is a special case of a gamma distribution with $\beta = 0$, for which γ becomes 8. On the other hand, $\gamma = 2$ is obtained by letting β be ∞. Recall from (3.55) that γ for a normal distribution is 2.

Example 7: In (3.52) and (3.54), only the first and second order moments of $\mathbf{d}^2$ are given. However, if the $\mathbf{z}_i$'s are normal, the density function of $\mathbf{d}^2$ is known as [7].

$$p_{d^2}(\zeta) = \frac{1}{2^{n/2}\Gamma(n/2)}\zeta^{\frac{n-2}{2}} e^{-\zeta/2} u(\zeta) , \tag{3.59}$$

which is the gamma density with $\beta = n/2 - 1$ and $\alpha = 1/2$.

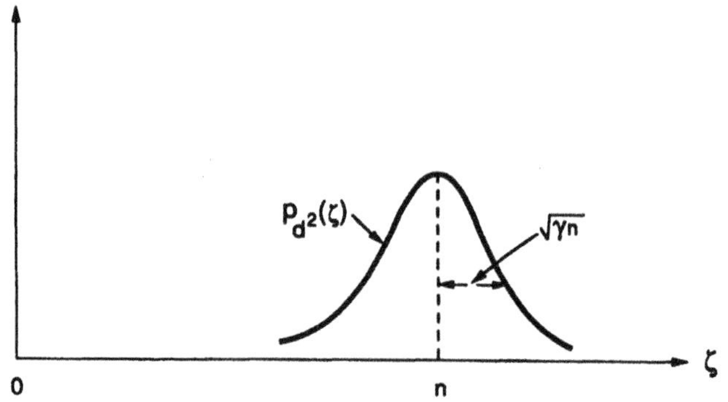

Fig. 3-8 The distribution of $\mathbf{d}^2$.

The expected value and variance of the gamma distribution are computed from α and β as

$$E\{\mathbf{d}^2\} = \frac{\beta+1}{\alpha} = n \, , \tag{3.60}$$

$$\text{Var}\{\mathbf{d}^2\} = \frac{\beta+1}{\alpha^2} = 2n \, , \tag{3.61}$$

which are identical to (3.52) and (3.54). Since the $\mathbf{z}_i$'s are obtained by a linear transformation from $\mathbf{X}$, the $\mathbf{z}_i$'s are normal if $\mathbf{X}$ is normal.

Also, note that (3.59) becomes an exponential distribution for $n=2$. It is known that coherent (complex) radar signatures have real and imaginary parts that tend to be independent. Therefore, if both parts are normally distributed, the magnitude-square of these two parts, $(real)^2 + (imaginary)^2$, will exhibit an exponential distribution.

It is important to realize from Fig. 3-8 that, if samples are drawn from a normal distribution in a high-dimensional space, most samples fall in a doughnut-type ring and no samples fall in the center region where the value of the density function is largest. Because of this phenomena, two distributions could be classified with little error, even when they share the same expected vectors, as long as the covariance matrices are different. In order to understand why this happens, let us look at the example of Fig. 3-9. This figure shows the contour lines of a normal distribution with covariance matrix I. The probability mass of region A, an n-dimensional hypersphere with radius a, is $Pr\{A\} = c\, a^n p(X_A)$ where c is a constant and X_A is located somewhere in A.

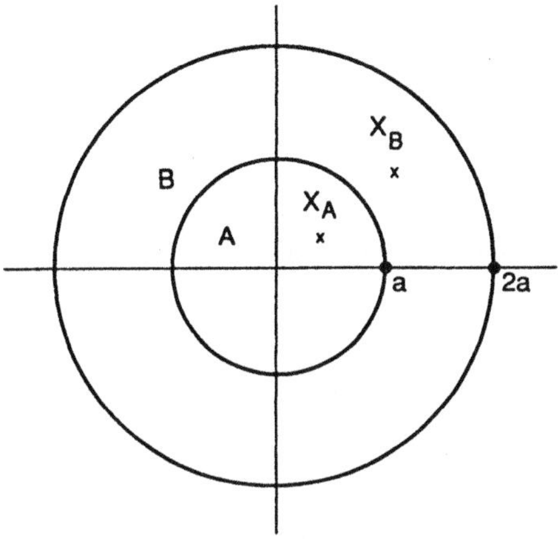

Fig. 3-9 Probability coverage.

On the other hand, for the outer ring, region B, with radius between a and $2a$, $Pr\{B\} = c[(2a)^n - a^n]\ p(X_B) = c(2^n-1)a^n p(X_B)$, where X_B is located somewhere in B. Therefore, $Pr\{B\}/Pr\{A\} = (2^n-1)p(X_B)/p(X_A)$. This becomes, for example, 2×10^{18} for n=64 and $p(X_A)/p(X_B) = 10$. That is, the probability of having a sample in region A is so much smaller than the probability for region B, that we would never see samples in A by drawing a resonable number (say 10^4) of samples.

Performance of a single hypothesis test: Suppose that two classes are distributed with expected vectors $M_1 = 0$ and $M_2 = M$, and covariance matrices $\Sigma_1 = I$ and $\Sigma_2 = \Lambda$ (a diagonal matrix with λ_i's as the components), respectively. Without loss of generality, any two covariance matrices can be simultaneously diagonalized to I and Λ, and a coordinate shift can bring the expected vector of ω_1 to zero. As shown in (3.52) and (3.54), $E\{\mathbf{d}^2 | \omega_1\} = n$ and $\text{Var}\{\mathbf{d}^2 | \omega_1\} = \gamma n$, and $\gamma = 2$ if the ω_1-distribution is normal. On the other hand, the distance of an ω_2-sample from the ω_1-expected vector, 0, is

$$\begin{aligned}\mathbf{d}^2 &= \mathbf{X}^T\mathbf{X} = (\mathbf{X} - M + M)^T(\mathbf{X} - M + M) \\ &= (\mathbf{X} - M)^T(\mathbf{X} - M) + 2M^T(\mathbf{X} - M) + M^TM \\ &= \text{tr}\,[(\mathbf{X} - M)(\mathbf{X} - M)^T] + 2M^T(\mathbf{X} - M) + M^TM\ . \end{aligned} \tag{3.62}$$

Taking the expectation with respect to ω_2,

$$E\{\mathbf{d}^2 | \omega_2\} = \text{tr}\,[E\{(\mathbf{X}-M)(\mathbf{X}-M)^T | \omega_2\}] + M^T M$$

$$= \text{tr}\,\Lambda + M^T M = \sum_{i=1}^{n} \lambda_i + M^T M \,. \tag{3.63}$$

Likewise, the variance can be computed as

$$\text{Var}\{\mathbf{d}^2 | \omega_2\} = E\{(\mathbf{d}^2)^2 | \omega_2\} - E^2\{\mathbf{d}^2 | \omega_2\} \,. \tag{3.64}$$

When the ω_2-distribution is normal,

$$E\{(\mathbf{d}^2)^2 | \omega_2\} = E\{(\mathbf{X}-M)^T(\mathbf{X}-M)(\mathbf{X}-M)^T(\mathbf{X}-M) | \omega_2\}$$

$$+ 4\, M^T E\{(\mathbf{X}-M)(\mathbf{X}-M)^T | \omega_2\} M$$

$$+ (M^T M)^2 + 2\, E\{(\mathbf{X}-M)^T(\mathbf{X}-M) | \omega_2\} M^T M$$

$$= 3\sum_{i=1}^{n} \lambda_i^2 + \sum_{i \neq j}\sum \lambda_i \lambda_j + 4\sum_{i=1}^{n} \lambda_i m_i^2$$

$$+ (\sum_{i=1}^{n} m_i^2)^2 + 2(\sum_{i=1}^{n} \lambda_i)(\sum_{i=1}^{n} m_i^2) \,, \tag{3.65}$$

where m_i is the ith component of M. Subtracting $E^2\{\mathbf{d}^2 | \omega_2\}$ of (3.63), we obtain

$$\text{Var}\{\mathbf{d}^2 | \omega_2\} = 2\sum_{i=1}^{n} \lambda_i^2 + 4\sum_{i=1}^{n} \lambda_i m_i^2 \,. \tag{3.66}$$

Example 8: For Data *I-I* with n variables, $\lambda_i = 1$. Therefore,

$$E\{\mathbf{d}^2 | \omega_1\} = n \quad \text{and} \quad \text{Var}\{\mathbf{d}^2 | \omega_1\} = 2n \,, \tag{3.67}$$

$$E\{\mathbf{d}^2 | \omega_2\} = n + M^T M \quad \text{and} \quad \text{Var}\{\mathbf{d}^2 | \omega_2\} = 2n + 4M^T M \,. \tag{3.68}$$

If we assume normal distributions for $\mathbf{d}^2$, we can design the Bayes classifier and compute the Bayes error in the d-space, ε_d. The normality assumption for $\mathbf{d}^2$ is reasonable for high-dimensional data because $\mathbf{d}^2$ is the summation of n terms as seen in (3.51), and the central limit theorem can be applied. The ε_d is determined by n and $M^T M$, while $M^T M$ specifies the Bayes error in the X-space, ε_X. In order to show how much classification information is lost by mapping the n-dimensional X into the one-dimensional $\mathbf{d}^2$, the relation between

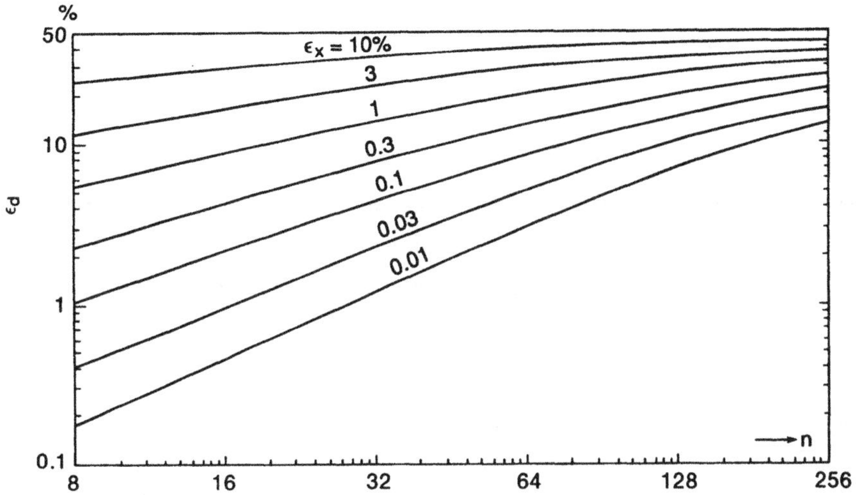

Fig. 3-10 Performance of a single hypothesis test for Data *I-I*.

ε_X and ε_d for various values of n is plotted in Fig. 3-10. For example, when $n = 64$, $\varepsilon_X = 0.1\%$ is increased to $\varepsilon_d = 8.4\%$. This is the price we must pay when we do not know where the second distribution is located relative to the first distribution for a fixed $\|M\|$.

Ranking procedure: So far, we have pointed out that mapping the n-dimensional $\mathbf{X}$ into the one-dimensional $\mathbf{d}^2$ and classifying samples by thresholding $\mathbf{d}^2$ produce a large increase in error. However, the error may be reduced significantly by using different approaches for different applications. For example, let our problem be to select one object for targeting out of many objects detected in a field. Then, we may rank the objects according to their distances from the selected target mean, and choose the closest one as the one to target. This *ranking*, instead of thresholding, reduces the classification error of the selected object. However, it must be noted that this problem is different from the conventional one, in which all objects are classified and the number of misclassified objects are counted as the error.

Assuming that k_1 ω_1-samples and k_2 ω_2-samples are available for ranking, the probability of acquiring one of the k_1 ω_1-samples by this procedure (the probability of correct classification) can be expressed as [8-9]

$$P_a = \int_0^1 k_1 (1-u_1)^{k_1-1} (1-u_2)^{k_2} du_1 \ , \tag{3.69}$$

where

$$u_i(t) = \int_0^t p_{d^2}(\zeta \mid \omega_i) d\zeta \tag{3.70}$$

and $p_{d^2}(\zeta \mid \omega_i)$ is the density function of $\zeta = \mathbf{d}^2$ for ω_i. As seen in (3.70), $u_i(t)$ is the probability of a sample from ω_i falling in $0 \le \zeta < t$. Thus, $u_1(t) = 1-\varepsilon_1$ and $u_2(t) = \varepsilon_2$ in the d-space when the threshold is chosen at $d^2 = t$. In (3.69), du_1, $(1-u_1)^{k_1-1}$, and $(1-u_2)^{k_2}$ represent the probability of one of k_1 ω_1-samples falling in $t \le \zeta < t + \Delta t$, k_1-1 of ω_1-samples falling in $t + \Delta t \le \zeta < \infty$, and all k_2 ω_2-samples falling in $t + \Delta t \le \zeta < \infty$ respectively. The product of these three gives the probability of the combined event. Since the acquisition of any one of the k_1 ω_1-samples is a correct classification, the probability is multiplied by k_1. The integration is taken with respect to t from 0 to ∞, that is, with respect to u_1 from 0 to 1.

TABLE 3-2

EFFECT OF THE RANKING PROCEDURE

ε_X (%)	ε_d (%)	$1 - P_a$ (%)	
		$k_1 = k_2 = 5$	$k_1 = k_2 = 20$
1.0	10.0	0.9	0.6
5.0	24.0	8.9	4.4
10.0	32.0	17.6	14.9
20.0	42.0	34.2	32.0

Table 3-2 shows $(1-P_a)$'s for Data *I-I* and $n = 20$. Specifying ε_X as 1, 5, 10, and 20 %, we computed the corresponding $\|M\|$'s, from which ε_d's were obtained assuming that both $p_{d^2}(\zeta \mid \omega_1)$ and $p_{d^2}(\zeta \mid \omega_2)$ in (3.70) are normal. Then, the integrations of (3.69) and (3.70) were carried out numerically for normal $p_{d^2}(\zeta \mid \omega_i)$'s. Table 3-2 indicates that the ranking procedure is effective, particularly for small ε_X's. Also, the errors are smaller for larger k_1 and k_2's.

Test of normality: Despite its importance, it has been difficult to test whether a given data set is normal or not. If the dimensionality of the data is low, we could use a conventional chi-square test [10]. But obviously the number of cells increases exponentially with the dimensionality and the test is impractical for high-dimensional data sets. Measuring the variance of $\mathbf{d}^2$ provides an estimate of γ in (3.54) which may be used to test for normality of a high-dimensional distribution. Also, the parameter β could be determined for a gamma density function according to (3.57). However, it must be cautioned that this procedure tests only one marginal aspect of the distribution, however important that aspect, and does not guarantee the overall normality of the distribution even if the samples pass the test.

When $\mathbf{X}$ is normal and M and Σ are given, the density function of $\mathbf{d}^2 = (\mathbf{X}-M)^T\Sigma^{-1}(\mathbf{X}-M)$ is given in (3.59), which is a gamma distribution. This may be extended to the case where the sample mean and sample covariance matrix are used in place of M and Σ as

$$\zeta = \frac{1}{N-1}(\mathbf{X}-\hat{\mathbf{M}})^T\hat{\mathbf{\Sigma}}^{-1}(\mathbf{X}-\hat{\mathbf{M}}) , \tag{3.71}$$

where

$$\hat{\mathbf{M}} = \frac{1}{N}\sum_{i=1}^{N}\mathbf{X}_i \quad \text{and} \quad \hat{\mathbf{\Sigma}} = \frac{1}{N}\sum_{i=1}^{N}(\mathbf{X}_i-\hat{\mathbf{M}})(\mathbf{X}_i-\hat{\mathbf{M}})^T . \tag{3.72}$$

When $\mathbf{X}$ is normal, ζ has the *beta-distribution* given by [11]

$$p_\zeta(\zeta) = \frac{\Gamma\left(\frac{N-1}{2}\right)}{\Gamma\left(\frac{n}{2}\right)\Gamma\left(\frac{N-n-1}{2}\right)}\zeta^{\frac{n}{2}-1}(1-\zeta)^{\frac{N-n-1}{2}-1} \qquad 0 \le \zeta \le 1 . \tag{3.73}$$

The expected value and variance of ζ may be computed by using

$$\int_0^1 x^b(1-x)^c dx = \frac{\Gamma(b+1)\Gamma(c+1)}{\Gamma(b+c+2)} . \tag{3.74}$$

The results are

$$E\{\zeta\} = \frac{n}{N-1} , \tag{3.75}$$

$$\text{Var}\{\zeta\} = \frac{2n}{(N-1)^2} \frac{1-(n+1)/N}{1+1/N} \cong \frac{2n}{(N-1)^2} . \tag{3.76}$$

Because ζ of (3.71) is $1/(N-1)$ times the distance, (3.75) and the right-most term of (3.76) correspond to (3.60) and (3.61) respectively.

Thus, the test of normality may be performed in the following two levels.

(1) Compute the sample variance of ζ of (3.71), and check whether it is close to (3.76) or not. When $N >> n$, $2n/(N-1)^2$ may be used to approximate (3.76).

(2) Plot the empirical distribution function of ζ by using $\zeta(\mathbf{X}_1), \ldots, \zeta(\mathbf{X}_N)$ and the theoretical distribution function from (3.73), and apply the *Kolmogorov-Smirnov* test [10].

Variable transformation: When variables are causal (i.e. positive), the distribution of each variable may be approximated by a gamma density. In this case, it is advantageous to convert the distribution to a normal-like one by applying a transformation such as

$$y = x^{\nu} \qquad (0 < \nu < 1) , \tag{3.77}$$

which is called the *power transformation*. The normal-like is achieved by making γ of (3.54), $E\{(\mathbf{y}-\bar{\mathbf{y}})^4\} - E^2\{(\mathbf{y}-\bar{\mathbf{y}})^2\}$, close to 2 under the condition that $E\{(\mathbf{y}-\bar{\mathbf{y}})^2\} = 1$, where $\bar{\mathbf{y}} = E\{\mathbf{y}\}$.

Assuming a gamma density function of (2.54) for $\mathbf{x}$, let us compute the moments of $\mathbf{y}$ as

$$E\{\mathbf{y}^m\} = \frac{\alpha^{\beta+1}}{\Gamma(\beta+1)} \int_0^{\infty} x^{\nu m} x^{\beta} e^{-\alpha x} dx$$

$$= \frac{1}{\alpha^{m\nu}} \frac{\Gamma(\beta+1+m\nu)}{\Gamma(\beta+1)} . \tag{3.78}$$

Therefore,

$$\gamma = \frac{E\{(y-\bar{y})^4\} - E^2\{(y-\bar{y})^2\}}{E^2\{(y-\bar{y})^2\}}$$

$$= \frac{E\{y^4\} - 4E\{y^3\}E\{y\} + 6E\{y^2\}E^2\{y\} - 3E^4\{y\}}{[E\{y^2\} - E^2\{y\}]^2} . \tag{3.79}$$

Note in (3.79) that the α's of the numerator are cancelled out with the α's of the denominator, and γ is a function of β and ν only. Figure 3-11 shows plots of γ as a function of ν for various values of β. Figure 3-11 indicates that we

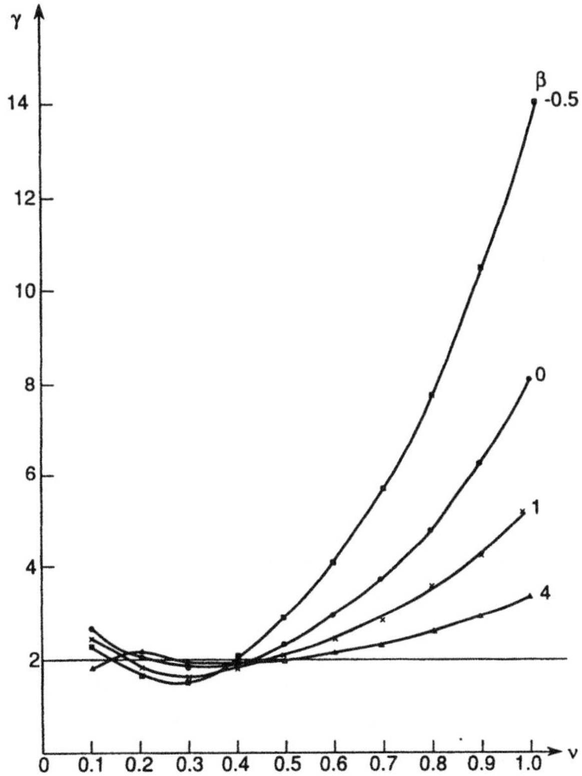

Fig. 3-11 Relation between γ and α for various β.

can make γ close to 2 for a wide range of β by selecting $\nu = 0.4$. This transformation with $\nu = 0.4$ was applied to obtain Data RADAR of Chapter 2.

Reject Option

When $r(X)$ of (3.6) is close to 0.5, the conditional error of making the decision given X is high. So, we could postpone decision-making and call for a further test. This option is called *reject*. Setting a threshold for $r(X)$, we may define the *reject region*, $L_R(t)$, and *reject probability*, $R(t)$, as

$$L_R(t) = \{X: r(X) \geq t\} , \tag{3.80}$$

$$R(t) = Pr\{r(\mathbf{X}) \geq t\} = \int_{L_R(t)} p(X)\, dX . \tag{3.81}$$

Then, the resulting error, $\varepsilon(t)$, is

$$\varepsilon(t) = \int_{\bar{L}_R(t)} \min[P_1 p_1(X), P_2 p_2(X)]\, dX , \tag{3.82}$$

where $\bar{L}_R$ is the complementary region of L_R. When the minus-log likelihood test is used, (3.80) can be converted to

$$-\ln\left[\frac{1-t}{t}\right] + \ln\frac{P_1}{P_2} \leq h(X) = -\ln\frac{p_1(X)}{p_2(X)}$$
$$\leq \ln\left[\frac{1-t}{t}\right] + \ln\frac{P_1}{P_2} . \tag{3.83}$$

The left and right side inequalities are obtained from $r(X) = P_2 p_2(X)/[P_1 p_1(X) + P_2 p_2(X)] \geq t$ when $P_1 p_1(X) > P_2 p_2(X)$, and $r(X) = P_1 p_1(X)/[P_1 p_1(X) + P_2 p_2(X)] \geq t$ when $P_1 p_1(X) < P_2 p_2(X)$, respectively. Thus, any sample X which satisfies (3.83) is rejected. On the other hand, the ω_1-sample satisfying $h(X) > \ln(1-t)/t + \ln P_1/P_2$ and the ω_2-sample satisfying $h(X) < -\ln(1-t)/t + \ln P_1/P_2$ are misclassified.

Figure 3-12 shows the relationship between $\varepsilon(t)$ and $R(t)$ for a simple one-dimensional example. As seen in Fig. 3-12, as t increases from 0 to 0.5, $\varepsilon(t)$ increases from 0 to the Bayes error, and $R(t)$ decreases from 1 to 0.

Error-reject curve: The relation between $R(t)$ and $\varepsilon(t)$ resembles the operating characteristics in which ε_1 and ε_2 are related with decision threshold as the parameter. Therefore, the *error-reject curve*, which plots $\varepsilon(t)$ as the

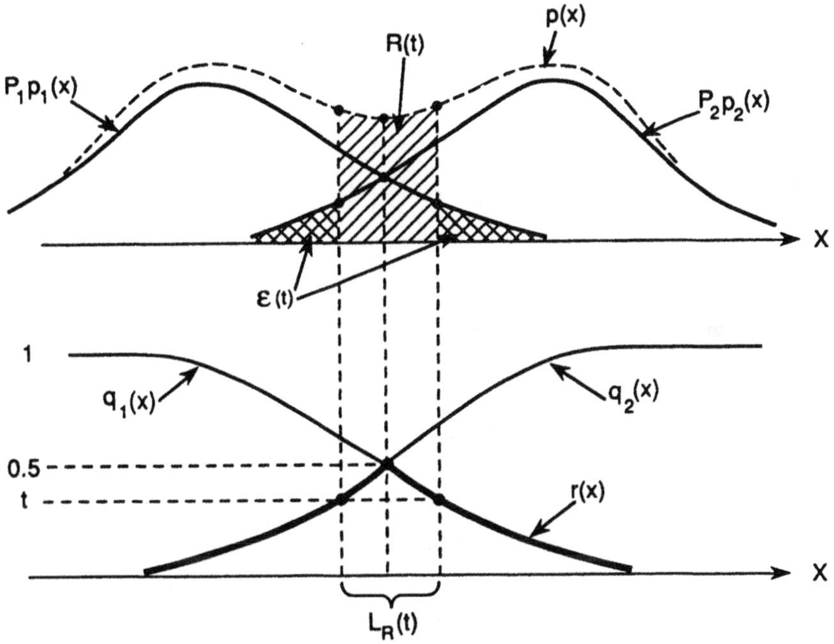

Fig. 3-12 Reject region and probability.

function of $R(t)$, could be used as another indicator of the system behavior [12-13].

For example, we can study, by using the error-reject curve, the effect of the sample size used to design a decision rule as follows:

Experiment 1: The error-reject curve for Data *I-I*

Data: *I-I* (Normal, $M^TM = 3^2, 4^2$)

Dimensionality: $n = 5$, 20, 100

Classifier: Linear classifier of (3.84)

Sample size: $N_1 = N_2 = kn$, $k = 2, 10, 50$ (Design)

$N_1 = N_2 = 100n$ (Test)

No. of trials: $\tau = 10$

Results: Fig. 3-13 [13]

In this experiment, the two covariance matrices are the same, and the Bayes classifier becomes linear as in (3.12). In addition, since the effect of design sample size on the error-reject curve is our concern in this experiment, the M_i and Σ in (3.12) are replaced by their respective estimates $\hat{M}_i$ and $\hat{\Sigma}$ as

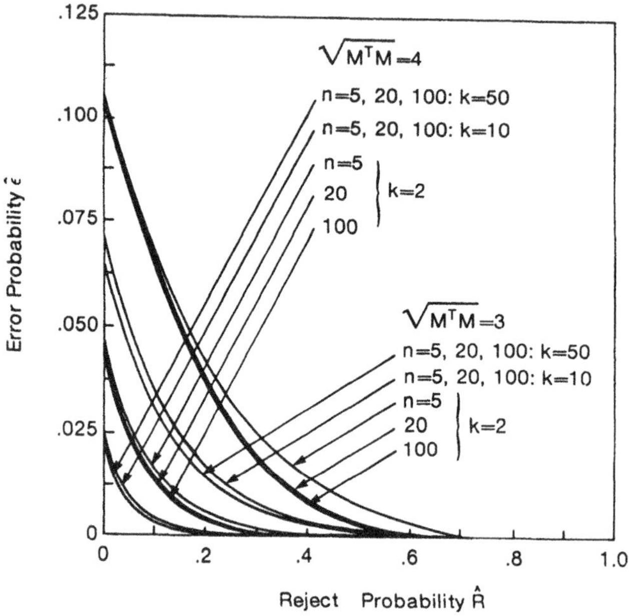

Fig. 3-13 Error-reject curves for Data *I-I*.

$$\hat{h}(X) = (\hat{M}_2 - \hat{M}_1)^T \hat{\Sigma}^{-1} X + \frac{1}{2}(\hat{M}_1^T \hat{\Sigma}^{-1} \hat{M}_1 - \hat{M}_2^T \hat{\Sigma}^{-1} \hat{M}_2) , \tag{3.84}$$

where $\hat{M}_i$ is the sample mean and $\hat{\Sigma}$ is the sample covariance matrix estimated from (N_1+N_2) samples. The test sample, which was generated independently of the design samples, was classified by using (3.83) and (3.84), and labeled according to either "correct", "error", or "reject". The numbers of error and reject samples were counted and divided by (N_1+N_2) to give $\hat{\varepsilon}(t)$ and $\hat{R}(t)$, respectively. A large number of test samples was used to minimize the variation of the result due to the finite number of test samples. Figure 3-13 shows the error-reject curves, which are the averages of the 10-trial results. The mean performance depends almost entirely on the ratio $k = N/n$. As a rule of thumb, it appears that k must be 10 or greater for the mean performance reasonably to approximate the asymptotic one. This conclusion for the whole of the error-reject curves is an extension of the same conclusion for the error without rejection.

Experiment 2: The error-reject curve for Data *I*-Λ

Data: Case I - *I*-Λ (Normal, $n = 8$)

Case II - *I*-Λ except $M_1 = M_2$

Classifier: Quadratic classifier of (3.11) with $\hat{M}_i$, $\hat{\Sigma}_i$

Sample size: $N_1 = N_2 = kn$, $k =$ 2,4,8,50 (Design)

$N_1 = N_2 = 100n = 800$ (Test)

No. of trials: $\tau = 10$

Results: Fig. 3-14 [13]

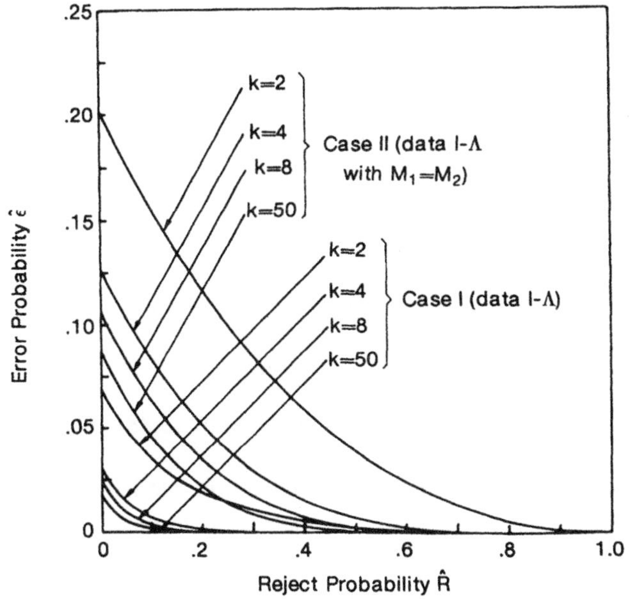

Fig. 3-14 Error-reject curves for Data *I*-Λ.

In this experiment, the two covariance matrices are different, and the Bayes classifier becomes quadratic as in (3.11). Again, M_i and Σ_i in (3.11) are replaced by their estimates $\hat{M}_i$ and $\hat{\Sigma}_i$. The resulting error-reject curves are shown in Fig. 3-14. The general dependency on the ratio $k = N/n$ is present, but now a somewhat larger number of design samples is needed for good results. The effect of the design sample size on the classification error will be readdressed in Chapter 5 in more detail.

As the error-reject curve suggests, $\varepsilon(t)$ may be expressed explicitly in terms of $R(t)$. When t is increased by Δt, the reject region is reduced by

$\Delta L_R(t)$, resulting in a reduction of $R(t)$ and an increase of $\varepsilon(t)$. However, as Fig. 3-12 suggests, the change of $\varepsilon(t)$ occurs in two different ways, depending on the right and left sides of $L_R(t)$. That is, on the right side the ω_1-error increases, while on the left side the ω_2-error increases. Therefore, defining ΔL_1 and ΔL_2 as the change of the reject region in the right and left sides,

$$\Delta\varepsilon = \varepsilon(t+\Delta t) - \varepsilon(t) = \int_{\Delta L_1} P_1 p_1(X) dX + \int_{\Delta L_2} P_2 p_2(X)\, dX \,. \tag{3.85}$$

On the other hand,

$$-\Delta R = R(t) - R(t+\Delta t) = \int_{\Delta L_1} p(X)\, dX + \int_{\Delta L_2} p(X)\, dX \,. \tag{3.86}$$

Since $t \cong P_1 p_1(X)/p(X)$ in ΔL_1 and $t \cong P_2 p_2(X)/p(X)$ in ΔL_2, (3.86) can be modified to

$$-t\,\Delta R \cong \int_{\Delta L_1} \frac{P_1 p_1(X)}{p(X)} p(X) dX + \int_{\Delta L_2} \frac{P_2 p_2(X)}{p(X)} p(X) dX$$

$$= \int_{\Delta L_1} P_1 p_1(X)\, dX + \int_{\Delta L_2} P_2 p_2(X)\, dX = \Delta\varepsilon \,. \tag{3.87}$$

Therefore, integrating (3.87) from 0 to t,

$$\varepsilon(t) = -\int_0^t \zeta dR(\zeta) \,. \tag{3.88}$$

Thus, once we know $R(t)$, $\varepsilon(t)$ can be computed by (3.88) [12].

Model validity tests: In pattern recognition, we have a set of data, and often assume a system model (the mathematical form of distributions) from which the data were drawn. A typical example is the normality assumption. Then, we need a procedure to test the model validity in order to assure a reasonable fit of the model with the data. Since the description of the model is a specification of probability distributions in n dimensions, it at first appears that we face the difficult problem of multivariate goodness of fit tests. We avoid this problem by using a transformation of the data to univariate statistics and apply goodness of fit tests in one dimension. The reject probability is one of the transformations.

The reject probability of (3.81) reveals that $1-R(t)$ is the distribution function of a random variable $r(\mathbf{X})$, $P_r(t)$.

$$P_r(t) = Pr\{r(\mathbf{X}) < t\} = 1 - R(t) \,. \tag{3.89}$$

Also, we know that $\varepsilon(t)$ is determined from $R(t)$ by (3.88). These facts suggest that appropriate statistics of $r(\mathbf{X})$ can be used for model validity tests, and that the error-reject curve is one option among many possible choices. Three other possibilities are listed as follows [13].

(1) *A test based on the mean of* $r(\mathbf{X})$*:* Since the Bayes error is $E\{r(\mathbf{X})\}$, the sample mean of $r(\mathbf{X})$ from the data can be compared with the Bayes error obtained from the model. This tests only one moment of the distribution of $r(\mathbf{X})$. Therefore, although simple, this does not provide sufficient information to compare two models.

(2) *Chi-square goodness-of-fit test:* The empirical distribution function, $\hat{\mathbf{P}}_r(t)$, is obtained from $r(\mathbf{X}_1), \ldots, r(\mathbf{X}_N)$, and compared with $1-R(t)$ of the model by the chi-square test. This procedure divides the space into a finite number of bins according to the reject threshold values. The test is conducted to compare the empirical probability in each bin with the predicted one.

(3) *Kolmogorov-Smirnov test for R(t):* The empirical distribution function of $r(\mathbf{X})$ is compared with $1-R(t)$ by measuring the maximum difference between them.

For details regarding the use, definition, and critical values of these tests, the reader is refered to [10].

Composite Hypothesis Tests

Sometimes $p_i(X)$ is not given directly, but is given by the combination of $p(X|\Theta_i)$ and $p(\Theta_i|\omega_i)$, where $p(X|\Theta_i)$ is the conditional density function of $\mathbf{X}$ assuming a set of parameters or a parameter vector Θ_i, and $p(\Theta_i|\omega_i)$ is the conditional density function of $\boldsymbol{\Theta}_i$ assuming class ω_i. In this case, we can calculate $p_i(X)$ by

$$p_i(X) = \int p(X|\Theta_i)p(\Theta_i|\omega_i)\,d\Theta_i \;. \tag{3.90}$$

Once $p_i(X)$ is obtained, the likelihood ratio test can be carried out for $p_1(X)$ and $p_2(X)$, as described in the previous sections. That is,

$$\ell(X) = \frac{p_1(X)}{p_2(X)} = \frac{\int p(X|\Theta_1)p(\Theta_1|\omega_1)d\Theta_1}{\int p(X|\Theta_2)p(\Theta_2|\omega_2)d\Theta_2} \;. \tag{3.91}$$

This is the *composite hypothesis test.*

Example 9: Two distributions are known to be normal, with fixed covariance matrices Σ_1 and Σ_2 for given expected vectors M_1 and M_2. The expected vectors $\mathbf{M}_1$ and $\mathbf{M}_2$ are also known to be normally distributed, with the expected vectors M_{10} and M_{20} and covariance matrices K_1 and K_2. Then according to (3.90),

$$p_i(X) = \int \frac{1}{(2\pi)^n |\Sigma_i|^{1/2} |K_i|^{1/2}} \exp[-\frac{1}{2}(X - M_i)^T \Sigma_i^{-1} (X - M_i)$$

$$- \frac{1}{2}(M_i - M_{i0})^T K_i^{-1} (M_i - M_{i0})] dM_i \ . \tag{3.92}$$

This can be calculated by diagonalizing Σ_i and K_i simultaneously. The result is

$$p_i(X) = \frac{1}{(2\pi)^{n/2} |\Sigma_i + K_i|^{1/2}}$$

$$\times \exp[-\frac{1}{2}(X - M_{io})^T (\Sigma_i + K_i)^{-1} (X - M_{io})] \ . \tag{3.93}$$

Knowing that $p_i(X)$ is normal when $p(X | M_i)$ and $p(M_i | \omega_i)$ are normal, we can simply calculate the expected vector and covariance matrix of X assuming ω_i:

$$\begin{aligned} E\{\mathbf{X} | \omega_i\} &= \int X p_i(X) dX = \iint X p(X | M_i) p(M_i | \omega_i) dX \, dM_i \\ &= \int [\int X p(X | M_i) dX] p(M_i | \omega_i) dM_i \\ &= \int M_i p(M_i | \omega_i) dM_i \\ &= M_{i0} \ , \end{aligned} \tag{3.94}$$

$$\begin{aligned} &E\{(\mathbf{X} - M_{i0})(\mathbf{X} - M_{i0})^T | \omega_i\} \\ &= \int [\int (X - M_{i0})(X - M_{i0})^T p(X | M_i) dX] p(M_i | \omega_i) \, dM_i \\ &= \int [\Sigma_i + (M_i - M_{i0})(M_i - M_{i0})^T] p(M_i | \omega_i) \, dM_i \\ &= \Sigma_i + K_i \ . \end{aligned} \tag{3.95}$$

The result is the same as (3.93).

3.3 Error Probability in Hypothesis Testing

Associated with any decision rule is a *probability of error*. The probability of error is the most effective measure of a decision rule's usefulness. In general, the calculation of error probability is very difficult, although the concept is quite simple. In order to evaluate (3.8), we must perform an n-dimensional integration in a complicated region. A more promising procedure is to determine the density function of the likelihood ratio, and integrate it in the one-dimensional h-space, as in (3.9) and (3.10). This is possible for normal distributions, and will be discussed in this section. However, if the distributions are not normal, finding the density function of $\mathbf{h}$ is very difficult. Thus, in many practical problems, we either employ experimental techniques such as Monte Carlo simulation, or we seek bounds on the error probabilities. We will discuss error bounds in the next section.

Linear Boundaries

When the distributions are normal with equal covariance matrices, $\Sigma_1 = \Sigma_2 = \Sigma$, the minus-log likelihood ratio becomes a linear function of X as shown in (3.12). Since (3.12) is a linear transformation from an n-dimensional space to one-dimension, $h(\mathbf{X})$ is a normal random variable when $\mathbf{X}$ is a normally distributed random vector. The expected value and variance of $h(\mathbf{X})$ can be calculated as follows:

$$\eta_i = E\{h(\mathbf{X}) \mid \omega_i\}$$

$$= (M_2 - M_1)^T \Sigma^{-1} E\{\mathbf{X} \mid \omega_i\} + \frac{1}{2}(M_1^T \Sigma^{-1} M_1 - M_2^T \Sigma^{-1} M_2) . \tag{3.96}$$

Since $E\{\mathbf{X} \mid \omega_i\} = M_i$, (3.96) becomes

$$\eta_1 = -\frac{1}{2}(M_2 - M_1)^T \Sigma^{-1} (M_2 - M_1) = -\eta , \tag{3.97}$$

$$\eta_2 = +\frac{1}{2}(M_2 - M_1)^T \Sigma^{-1} (M_2 - M_1) = +\eta . \tag{3.98}$$

Also,

$$\sigma_i^2 = E[\{h(\mathbf{X}) - \eta_i\}^2 \mid \omega_i]$$

$$= E[\{(M_2 - M_1)^T \Sigma^{-1} (\mathbf{X} - M_i)\}^2 \mid \omega_i]$$

$$= (M_2 - M_1)^T \Sigma^{-1} E\{(\mathbf{X} - M_i)(\mathbf{X} - M_i)^T \mid \omega_i\} \Sigma^{-1} (M_2 - M_1)$$

$$= (M_2 - M_1)^T \Sigma^{-1} (M_2 - M_1) = 2\eta \ . \tag{3.99}$$

The above holds because $E\{(\mathbf{X} - M_i)(\mathbf{X} - M_i)^T \mid \omega_i\}$ is Σ_i $(=\Sigma)$, as was shown in (2.13).

Figure 3-15 shows the density functions of $h(\mathbf{X})$ for ω_1 and ω_2, and the

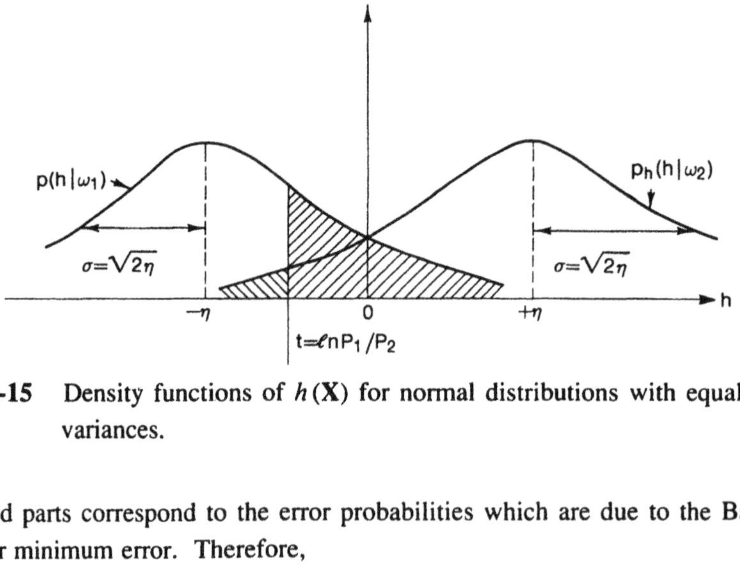

Fig. 3-15 Density functions of $h(\mathbf{X})$ for normal distributions with equal covariances.

hatched parts correspond to the error probabilities which are due to the Bayes test for minimum error. Therefore,

$$\varepsilon_1 = \int_t^{\infty} p_h(h \mid \omega_1)dh = \int_{(t+\eta)/\sigma}^{+\infty} \frac{1}{\sqrt{2\pi}} e^{-\zeta^2/2} d\zeta = 1 - \Phi(\frac{t+\eta}{\sigma}) \ , \tag{3.100}$$

$$\varepsilon_2 = \int_{-\infty}^{t} p_h(h \mid \omega_2)dh = \int_{-\infty}^{(t-\eta)/\sigma} \frac{1}{\sqrt{2\pi}} e^{-\zeta^2/2} d\zeta = \Phi(\frac{t-\eta}{\sigma}) \ , \tag{3.101}$$

where $\Phi(\cdot)$ is the normal error function of (3.39), and

$$t = \ln \frac{P_1}{P_2} , \tag{3.102}$$

$$\sigma^2 = \sigma_1^2 = \sigma_2^2 = 2\eta . \tag{3.103}$$

Thus, when the density function of the likelihood ratio is normal, the probabilities of error can be obtained from the table of $\Phi(\cdot)$.

General Error Expression

Error expression: Before computing the error of the quadratic classifier for normal distributions, let us express the error of a classifier in a general form. Let a classifier be

$$h(X) \underset{\omega_2}{\overset{\omega_1}{\gtrless}} 0 . \tag{3.104}$$

Then, the ω_1-error is

$$\begin{aligned} \varepsilon_1 &= \int_{h(X)>0} p_1(X)\, dX = \int u(h(X)) p_1(X)\, dX \\ &= \frac{1}{2\pi} \iint [\pi\delta(\omega) + \frac{1}{j\omega}] e^{j\omega h(X)} p_1(X)\, d\omega\, dX \\ &= \frac{1}{2} + \frac{1}{2\pi} \iint \frac{e^{j\omega h(X)}}{j\omega} p_1(X)\, d\omega\, dX , \end{aligned} \tag{3.105}$$

where $u(\cdot)$ is the step function. The second line is obtained by using the fact that the Fourier transform of a step function, $u(h)$, is $[\pi\delta(\omega) + 1/j\omega]$. Likewise, the ω_2-error is

$$\begin{aligned} \varepsilon_2 &= \int_{h(X)<0} p_2(X)\, dX = \int u(-h(X)) p_2(X)\, dX \\ &= \frac{1}{2\pi} \iint [\pi\delta(\omega) - \frac{1}{j\omega}] e^{j\omega h(X)} p_2(X)\, d\omega\, dX \\ &= \frac{1}{2} - \frac{1}{2\pi} \iint \frac{e^{j\omega h(X)}}{j\omega} p_2(X)\, d\omega\, dX . \end{aligned} \tag{3.106}$$

Then, the total error becomes

$$\varepsilon = P_1\varepsilon_1 + P_2\varepsilon_2$$
$$= \frac{1}{2} + \frac{1}{2\pi}\iint \frac{e^{j\omega h(X)}}{j\omega}\tilde{p}(X)\,d\omega\,dX , \tag{3.107}$$

where

$$\tilde{p}(X) = P_1 p_1(X) - P_2 p_2(X) . \tag{3.108}$$

That is, the error is a function of $h(X)$ and $\tilde{p}(X)$, which specify the classifier and the test distributions, respectively.

Another interpretation of (3.105) is given as follows. Let us define the *characteristic function* of $h(\mathbf{X})$ for ω_1, $F_1(\omega)$, as

$$F_1(\omega) = E\{e^{j\omega h(\mathbf{X})} \mid \omega_1\} = \int e^{j\omega h(X)} p_1(X)\,dX$$
$$= \int e^{j\omega h} p_h(h \mid \omega_1)\,dh . \tag{3.109}$$

That is, $F_1(\omega)$ may be obtained through an n-dimensional integration using $p_1(X)$ or through a one-dimensional integration using $p_h(h \mid \omega_1)$. Since $F_1(\omega)$ is the Fourier transform of $p_h(h \mid \omega_1)$, except for the sign of $j\omega$, the inverse Fourier transform from $F_1(\omega)$ to $p_h(h \mid \omega_1)$ is given by

$$p_h(h \mid \omega_1) = \frac{1}{2\pi}\int F_1(\omega)e^{-j\omega h}d\omega \tag{3.110}$$

or

$$p_h(-h \mid \omega_1) = \frac{1}{2\pi}\int F_1(\omega)e^{j\omega h}d\omega . \tag{3.111}$$

Equation (3.111) indicates that $F_1(\omega)$ is the Fourier transform of $p_h(-h \mid \omega_1)$. The multiplication by $[\pi\delta(\omega) + 1/j\omega]$ in the Fourier domain corresponds to an integration in the time domain from $-\infty$ to t. Therefore, from the second line of (3.105) and the first line of (3.109)

$$\begin{aligned}
\varepsilon_1 &= \frac{1}{2\pi}\int[\pi\delta(\omega) + \frac{1}{j\omega}]F_1(\omega)d\omega \\
&= \frac{1}{2\pi}\int[\pi\delta(\omega) + \frac{1}{j\omega}]F_1(\omega)e^{j\omega h}d\omega \,|_{h=0} \\
&= \int_{-\infty}^{0} p_h(-h \,|\, \omega_1)\, dh \\
&= \int_{0}^{\infty} p_h(h \,|\, \omega_1)\, dh \; . \qquad (3.112)
\end{aligned}$$

Likewise, for ω_2, multiplying by $[\pi\delta(\omega) - 1/j\omega]$ in the Fourier domain corresponds to an integration in the time domain from t to $+\infty$. Therefore,

$$\varepsilon_2 = \int_{0}^{\infty} p_h(-h \,|\, \omega_2)\, dh = \int_{-\infty}^{0} p_h(h \,|\, \omega_2)\, dh \; . \qquad (3.113)$$

Procedure to compute the error: Thus, when a classifier and test distributions are given, the error of the classifier can be computed as follows [14]:

(1) Compute the characteristic function, $F_i(\omega)$, by carrying out the n-dimensional integration of (3.109). For quadratic classifiers with normal test distributions, the explicit expression for $F_i(\omega)$ can be obtained, as will be discussed later.

(2) Carry out the inverse operations of (3.105) and (3.106) as

$$\begin{aligned}
\varepsilon_i &= \frac{1}{2} \pm \frac{1}{2\pi}\int_{-\infty}^{+\infty} \frac{F_i(\omega)}{j\omega}\, d\omega \\
&= \frac{1}{2} \pm \frac{1}{\pi}\int_{0}^{\infty} \frac{\text{Im}[F_i(\omega)]}{\omega}\, d\omega \\
&= \frac{1}{2} \pm \frac{1}{\pi}\int_{0}^{\infty} \frac{|F_i(\omega)|}{\omega}\sin\{\angle F_i(\omega)\}\, d\omega \; , \qquad (3.114)
\end{aligned}$$

where + and − are used for $i = 1$ and 2, respectively. The real and imaginary parts of $F_i(\omega)$ are even and odd. Therefore, the real and imaginary parts of $F_i(\omega)/\omega$ are odd and even, which lead us to the second line of (3.114). Note that this integration is one-dimensional. Therefore, we can carry out the integration numerically, even if $F_i(\omega)$ is a complicated function and not integrable explicitly.

Example 10: In order to confirm the above discussion, let us study a simple case with two normal distributions: $N_X(0,I)$ and $N_X(M,I)$. From (3.12), the Bayes classifier becomes

$$h(X) = M^T X - \frac{1}{2} M^T M \, , \tag{3.115}$$

and the ω_1-density function $N_X(0,I)$ is expressed by

$$p_1(X) = \frac{1}{(2\pi)^{n/2}} \exp[-\frac{1}{2} X^T X] \, . \tag{3.116}$$

Therefore,

$$F_1(\omega) = \int e^{j\omega h(X)} p_1(X) \, dX$$

$$= \int \frac{1}{(2\pi)^{n/2}} \exp\left[-\frac{1}{2}(X^T X - 2j\omega M^T X + j\omega M^T M)\right] dX$$

$$= \int N_X(j\omega M, I) \exp\left[-\frac{\omega^2}{2} M^T M - \frac{1}{2} j\omega M^T M\right] dX$$

$$= \exp\left[-\frac{\omega^2}{2} M^T M - \frac{1}{2} j\omega M^T M\right] . \tag{3.117}$$

Equation (2.24) shows the characteristic function of a multivariate normal distribution, and (3.117) is a special case for one-dimension. Therefore, taking the inversion,

$$p_h(h \mid \omega_1) = \frac{1}{\sqrt{2\pi}\sqrt{M^T M}} \exp\left[-\frac{(h + M^T M/2)^2}{2M^T M}\right] . \tag{3.118}$$

That is, the ω_1-distribution of $\mathbf{h}$ has $E\{\mathbf{h} \mid \omega_1\} = -M^T M/2$ and $\mathrm{Var}\{\mathbf{h} \mid \omega_1\} = M^T M$, which are identical to (3.97) and (3.99) for $M_1=0$, $M_2=M$, and $\Sigma_1=\Sigma_2=I$.

Quadratic Classifiers

For a normal test distribution: When the quadratic classifier of (3.11) is designed and tested on a normal distribution $p_T(X)$, $h(X)$ and $p_T(X)$ can be given as

$$h(X) = \frac{1}{2}(X-M_1)^T\Sigma_1^{-1}(X-M_1) - \frac{1}{2}(X-M_2)^T\Sigma_2^{-1}(X-M_2) + \frac{1}{2}\ln\frac{|\Sigma_1|}{|\Sigma_2|} - t \tag{3.119}$$

and

$$p_T(X) = \frac{1}{(2\pi)^{n/2}|\Sigma_T|^{1/2}}\exp\left[-\frac{1}{2}(X-M_T)^T\Sigma_T^{-1}(X-M_T)\right] . \tag{3.120}$$

where t of (3.119) is a threshold. Applying simultaneous diagonalization and a coordinate shift, $Y = A^T(X-M_T)$,

$$A^T\Sigma_T A = I \quad \text{and} \quad A^T(\Sigma_1^{-1}-\Sigma_2^{-1})^{-1}A = \Lambda . \tag{3.121}$$

Then, M_i and Σ_i are converted to

$$A^T(M_i - M_T) = D_i \quad \text{and} \quad A^T\Sigma_i A = K_i \quad (i=1,2) . \tag{3.122}$$

Thus, in the Y-space

$$h(Y) = \frac{1}{2}Y^T\Lambda^{-1}Y - V^TY + c , \tag{3.123}$$

$$p_T(Y) = \frac{1}{(2\pi)^{n/2}}\exp\left[-\frac{1}{2}Y^TY\right] , \tag{3.124}$$

where

$$V = K_1^{-1}D_1 - K_2^{-1}D_2 , \tag{3.125}$$

$$c = \frac{1}{2}(D_1^TK_1^{-1}D_1 - D_2^TK_2^{-1}D_2) + \frac{1}{2}\ln\frac{|K_1|}{|K_2|} - t . \tag{3.126}$$

The characteristic function $F_T(\omega)$ can be computed now as

$$F_T(\omega) = \int e^{j\omega h(Y)} p_T(Y) dY$$

$$= \int \frac{1}{(2\pi)^{n/2}} \exp\left[-\frac{1}{2} Y^T (I - j\omega\Lambda^{-1}) Y - j\omega V^T Y\right] \exp[j\omega c] dY$$

$$= \int \frac{1}{(2\pi)^{n/2}} \prod_{i=1}^{n} \exp\left[-\frac{1}{2}(1-j\omega/\lambda_i)\left\{y_i + \frac{j\omega v_i}{1-j\omega/\lambda_i}\right\}^2\right]$$

$$\exp\left[-\frac{1}{2}\frac{\omega^2 v_i^2}{1-j\omega/\lambda_i}\right] \exp[j\omega c] dY$$

$$= \left\{\prod_{i=1}^{n} \frac{1}{\sqrt{1-j\omega/\lambda_i}} \exp\left[-\frac{1}{2}\frac{\omega^2 v_i^2}{1-j\omega/\lambda_i}\right]\right\} \exp[j\omega c] , \qquad (3.127)$$

where y_i, v_i, and λ_i are the components of Y, V, and Λ respectively. Depending on whether the error is generated by $h(X) > 0$ or $h(X) < 0$, the error must be computed as

$$\varepsilon_T = \begin{cases} \int_0^{\infty} p_h(h \mid \omega_T) dh = \dfrac{1}{2} + \dfrac{1}{2\pi} \int \dfrac{F_T(\omega)}{j\omega} d\omega , \\[2ex] \int_{-\infty}^{0} p_h(h \mid \omega_T) dh = \dfrac{1}{2} - \dfrac{1}{2\pi} \int \dfrac{F_T(\omega)}{j\omega} d\omega . \end{cases} \qquad (3.128)$$

The integration of (3.128) must be carried out numerically. This integration is not simple but is possible, because it is one-dimensional.

The result of (3.128) is quite general, because we may select the test distribution independently of the parameters used for design [15]. However, the cases most frequently encountered in practice are $M_T = M_i$ and $\Sigma_T = \Sigma_i$ (i=1,2). Therefore, let us find v_i, λ_i, and c for these cases.

$\mathbf{M_T = M_1}$ and $\mathbf{\Sigma_T = \Sigma_1}$: In this case, we apply simultaneous diagonalization and a coordinate shift such that

$$A^T\Sigma_1 A = I, \quad A^T\Sigma_2 A = \mu, \quad \text{and} \quad A^T(M_2-M_1) = L\ . \tag{3.129}$$

Then, $(\Sigma_1^{-1}-\Sigma_2^{-1})^{-1}$ is also transformed to a diagonal matrix Λ by A as

$$\Lambda = A^T(\Sigma_1^{-1}-\Sigma_2^{-1})^{-1}A = A^T[A(I-\mu^{-1})A^T]^{-1}A$$
$$= (I-\mu^{-1})^{-1}\ . \tag{3.130}$$

Since $M_T = M_1$, $D_1 = 0$ and $D_2 = A^T(M_2-M_1) = L$ from (3.122). Also, $K_1 = I$ and $K_2 = \mu$ from (3.122) and (3.129). Therefore, inserting these into (3.125) and (3.126), V and c are

$$V = -\mu^{-1}L\ , \tag{3.131}$$

$$c = -\frac{1}{2}L^T\mu^{-1}L - \frac{1}{2}\ln|\mu| - t\ . \tag{3.132}$$

That is, after computing μ and L by (3.129), we replace λ_i and v_i of (3.127) by

$$\frac{1}{\lambda_i} = 1 - \frac{1}{\mu_i} \quad \text{and} \quad v_i = -\frac{\ell_i}{\mu_i}\ , \tag{3.133}$$

where μ_i and ℓ_i are the components of μ and L. Then ε_1 is computed by the first equation of (3.128).

$M_T = M_2$ and $\Sigma_T = \Sigma_2$: After applying the transformation of $Y = A^T(X-M_2)$ where A is determined by (3.129), a further transformation of $Z = \mu^{-1/2}Y$ is applied. Then, (3.129) is modified to

$$\mu^{-1/2}I\mu^{-1/2} = \mu^{-1}\ ,\ \mu^{-1/2}\mu\mu^{-1/2} = I\ , \quad \text{and}$$

$$\mu^{-1/2}A^T(M_1-M_2) = -\mu^{-1/2}L\ . \tag{3.134}$$

Also, $(\Sigma_1^{-1}-\Sigma_2^{-1})^{-1}$ is diagonalized as

$$\Lambda = \mu^{-1/2}(I-\mu^{-1})^{-1}\mu^{-1/2} = (\mu-I)^{-1}\ . \tag{3.135}$$

Since $M_T = M_2$ this time, $D_1 = -\mu^{-1/2}L$, $D_2 = 0$, $K_1 = \mu^{-1}$, and $K_2 = I$ from (3.122) and (3.134). Therefore, inserting them into (3.125) and (3.126), V and

c are computed as

$$V = -\mu\mu^{-1/2}L = -\mu^{1/2}L \,, \tag{3.136}$$

$$c = \frac{1}{2}L^T\mu^{-1/2}\mu\mu^{-1/2}L - \frac{1}{2}\ln|\mu| - t$$

$$= \frac{1}{2}L^TL - \frac{1}{2}\ln|\mu| - t \,. \tag{3.137}$$

That is, after computing μ and L by (3.129), we calculate λ_i, v_i, and c of (3.127) by using (3.135), (3.136), and (3.137). Then ε_2 is computed by the second equation of (3.128).

Example 11: The technique was applied to Data I-Λ ($n = 8$) in which two normal distributions have significantly different covariance matrices. First, the density functions of **h** for ω_1 and ω_2 are numerically computed by using (3.110) and plotted in Fig. 3-16 [14]. Note that these density functions are skewed from a normal distribution. The Bayes error was computed using (3.128), resulting in

$$\varepsilon_1 = 1.6\%, \quad \varepsilon_2 = 2.2\%, \quad \text{and} \quad \varepsilon = 1.9\% \,, \tag{3.138}$$

where $P_1 = P_2 = 0.5$ and $t = 0$ are used.

Approximations

Since the quadratic equation of (3.11) represents the summation of many terms, the central limit theorem suggests that the distribution of $h(\mathbf{X})$ could be close to normal. If that is true, we only need to compute $E\{h(\mathbf{X})|\omega_i\}$ and $\mathrm{Var}\{h(\mathbf{X})|\omega_i\}$. Then, the error can be calculated from a normal error table.

Expected value of h(X): The expected values can be calculated easily regardless of the distributions of **X** as follows:

$$E\{h(\mathbf{X})|\omega_1\} = \frac{1}{2}\,\mathrm{tr}\,[\Sigma_1^{-1}E\{(\mathbf{X}-M_1)(\mathbf{X}-M_1)^T|\omega_1\}]$$

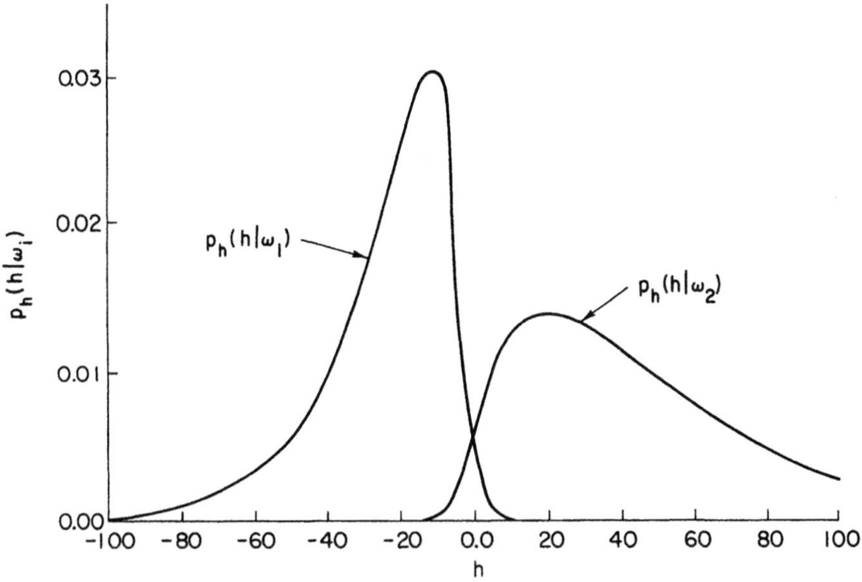

Fig. 3-16 Density functions of $h(\mathbf{X})$ for Data I-Λ.

$$
\begin{aligned}
&- \frac{1}{2} \operatorname{tr} [\Sigma_2^{-1} E\{(\mathbf{X}-M_1)(\mathbf{X}-M_1)^T \\
&- (M_2-M_1)(\mathbf{X}-M_1)^T - (\mathbf{X}-M_1)(M_2-M_1)^T \\
&+ (M_2-M_1)(M_2-M_1)^T | \omega_1 \}] + \frac{1}{2} \ln \frac{|\Sigma_1|}{|\Sigma_2|} - t \\
&= \frac{1}{2} \operatorname{tr} \{I - \Sigma_2^{-1}\Sigma_1\} - \frac{1}{2}(M_2-M_1)^T \Sigma_2^{-1} (M_2-M_1) \\
&+ \frac{1}{2} \ln \frac{|\Sigma_1|}{|\Sigma_2|} - t \, .
\end{aligned}
\tag{3.139}
$$

Likewise, for ω_2

$$E\{h(\mathbf{X})|\omega_2\} = \frac{1}{2}\,\mathrm{tr}\,\{\Sigma_1^{-1}\Sigma_2 - I\} + \frac{1}{2}(M_1-M_2)\Sigma_1^{-1}(M_1-M_2)$$

$$+\frac{1}{2}\ln\frac{|\Sigma_1|}{|\Sigma_2|} - t\,. \qquad (3.140)$$

Or, after simultaneous diagonalization from Σ_1 and Σ_2 to I and Λ by $Y = A^T X$,

$$E\{h(\mathbf{Y})|\omega_1\} = \frac{1}{2}\sum_{i=1}^{n}[(1-\frac{1}{\lambda_i}) - \frac{(d_{2i}-d_{1i})^2}{\lambda_i} + \ln\frac{1}{\lambda_i}] - t\,, \qquad (3.141)$$

$$E\{h(\mathbf{Y})|\omega_2\} = \frac{1}{2}\sum_{i=1}^{n}[(\lambda_i-1) + (d_{2i}-d_{1i})^2 + \ln\frac{1}{\lambda_i}] - t\,, \qquad (3.142)$$

where d_{ki} is the ith component of $D_k = A^T M_k$.

An interesting property emerges from (3.141) and (3.142). That is, if $t = 0$,

$$E\{h(\mathbf{Y})|\omega_1\} \le 0 \quad \text{and} \quad E\{h(\mathbf{Y})|\omega_2\} \ge 0 \qquad (3.143)$$

regardless of the distributions of **X**. These inequalities may be proved by using $\ln x \le x-1$. From (3.141), $(1-1/\lambda_i) + \ln(1/\lambda_i) \le 0$ and $-(d_{2i}-d_{ii})^2/\lambda_i \le 0$ yield $E\{h(\mathbf{Y})|\omega_1\} \le 0$ for $t = 0$. Also, from (3.142), $(\lambda_i-1) - \ln\lambda_i \ge 0$ and $(d_{2i}-d_{1i})^2 \ge 0$ yield $E\{h(\mathbf{Y})|\omega_2\} \ge 0$ for $t = 0$.

Variance of h(X): The computation of the variance is more involved. Therefore, only the results for normal distributions are presented here. The reader is encouraged to confirm these results. It is suggested to work in the Y-space where the two covariances are diagonalized to I and Λ.

$$\text{Var}\{h(\mathbf{X})|\omega_1\} = \frac{1}{2}\sum_{i=1}^{n}\left[\left(1-\frac{1}{\lambda_i}\right)^2 + 2\frac{(d_{2i}-d_{1i})^2}{\lambda_i^2}\right]$$

$$= \frac{1}{2}\text{ tr }\{(I-\Sigma_2^{-1}\Sigma_1)^2\}$$

$$+ (M_2-M_1)^T\Sigma_2^{-1}\Sigma_1\Sigma_2^{-1}(M_2-M_1)\,, \qquad (3.144)$$

$$\text{Var}\{h(\mathbf{X})|\omega_2\} = \frac{1}{2}\sum_{i=1}^{n}[(\lambda_i-1)^2 + 2\lambda_i(d_{2i}-d_{1i})^2]$$

$$= \frac{1}{2}\text{tr }\{(\Sigma_1^{-1}\Sigma_2-I)^2\}$$

$$+ (M_1-M_2)^T\Sigma_1^{-1}\Sigma_2\Sigma_1^{-1}(M_1-M_2)\,. \qquad (3.145)$$

3.4 Upper Bounds on the Bayes Error

It is evident from the preceding discussion that the calculation of the error probability is, in general, a difficult task. Even when observation vectors have a normal distribution, we must resort to numerical techniques. However, a closed-form expression for the error probability is the most desirable solution for a number of reasons. Not only is the computational effort greatly reduced, since we need only to evaluate a formula, but more importantly, the use of the closed-form solution provides insight into the mechanisms causing the errors. This information is useful later when we consider the problem of feature selection.

When we cannot obtain a closed-form expression for the error probability, we may take some other approach. We may seek either an approximate expression for the error probability, or an upper bound on the error probability. In this section, we will discuss some *upper bounds of error probability*.

The Chernoff and Bhattacharyya Bounds

Chernoff bound: The Bayes error is given in (3.7) as

$$\varepsilon = \int \min[P_1 p_1(X), P_2 p_2(X)]\, dX \,. \tag{3.146}$$

An upper bound of the integrand may be obtained by making use of the fact that

$$\min[a, b] \le a^s b^{1-s} \qquad 0 \le s \le 1 \tag{3.147}$$

for $a, b \ge 0$. Equation (3.147) simply states that the geometric mean of two positive numbers is larger than the smaller one. The statement can be proved as follows. If $a<b$, the left side of (3.147) is a, and the right side can be rewritten as $a \times (b/a)^{1-s}$. Since $(b/a) > 1$ and $1-s \ge 0$ for $0 \le s \le 1$, the right side becomes larger than the left side. Likewise, if $a>b$, the left side of (3.147) is b, and the right side is rewritten as $b \times (a/b)^s$, which is larger than b because $(a/b) > 1$ and $s \ge 0$. Using the inequality of (3.147), ε can be bounded by

$$\varepsilon_u = P_1^s P_2^{1-s} \int p_1^s(X) p_2^{1-s}(X)\, dX \quad \text{for} \quad 0 \le s \le 1 \,, \tag{3.148}$$

where ε_u indicates an upper bound of ε. This ε_u is called the *Chernoff bound* [16]. The optimum s can be found by minimizing ε_u.

When two density functions are normal as $N_X(M_1,\Sigma_1)$ and $N_X(M_2,\Sigma_2)$, the integration of (3.148) can be carried out to obtain a closed-form expression for ε_u. That is,

$$\int p_1^s(X) p_2^{1-s}(X) dX = e^{-\mu(s)} \tag{3.149}$$

where

$$\mu(s) = \frac{s(1-s)}{2}(M_2-M_1)^T[s\Sigma_1 + (1-s)\Sigma_2]^{-1}(M_2-M_1)$$

$$+ \frac{1}{2} \ln \frac{|s\Sigma_1 + (1-s)\Sigma_2|}{|\Sigma_1|^s |\Sigma_2|^{1-s}} \,. \tag{3.150}$$

This expression of $\mu(s)$ is called the *Chernoff distance*. For this case, the optimum s can be easily obtained by plotting $\mu(s)$ for various s with given M_i and Σ_i. The optimum s is the one which gives the maximum value for $\mu(s)$.

Bhattacharyya bound: If we do not insist on the optimum selection of s, we may obtain a less complicated upper bound. One of the possibilities is to select $s = 1/2$. Then, the upper bound is

$$\varepsilon_u = \sqrt{P_1 P_2} \int \sqrt{p_1(X) p_2(X)}\, dX = \sqrt{P_1 P_2}\, e^{-\mu(1/2)} \tag{3.151}$$

in general, and for normal distributions

$$\mu(1/2) = \frac{1}{8}(M_2 - M_1)^T \left[\frac{\Sigma_1 + \Sigma_2}{2} \right]^{-1} (M_2 - M_1) + \frac{1}{2} \ln \frac{\left| \frac{\Sigma_1 + \Sigma_2}{2} \right|}{\sqrt{|\Sigma_1||\Sigma_2|}} . \tag{3.152}$$

The term $\mu(1/2)$ is called the *Bhattacharyya distance*, and will be used as an important measure of the separability of two distributions [17].

When $\Sigma_1 = \Sigma_2 = \Sigma$, the Chernoff distance, (3.150), becomes

$$\mu(s) = \frac{s(1-s)}{2}(M_2 - M_1)^T \Sigma^{-1} (M_2 - M_1) . \tag{3.153}$$

In this case, the optimum s can be obtained by solving

$$\frac{d\mu(s)}{ds} = \frac{1-2s}{2}(M_2 - M_1)^T \Sigma^{-1} (M_2 - M_1) = 0 . \tag{3.154}$$

The solution is $s = 0.5$. That is, the Bhattacharyya distance is the optimum Chernoff distance when $\Sigma_1 = \Sigma_2$.

As seen in (3.151), $\varepsilon_u = \sqrt{P_1 P_2} \exp[-\mu(1/2)]$ or $\ln \varepsilon_u = -\mu(1/2) - \ln \sqrt{P_1 P_2}$. Figure 3-17 shows the relation between $\mu(1/2)$ and ε_u for $P_1 = P_2 = 0.5$.

Throughout this book, we use the Bhattacharyya distance rather than the Chernoff because of its simplicity. However, all discussions about the Bhattacharyya distance in this book could be extended to the Chernoff.

As seen in (3.152), the Bhattacharyya distance consists of two terms. The first or second term disappears when $M_1 = M_2$ or $\Sigma_1 = \Sigma_2$, respectively. Therefore, the first term gives the class separability due to the mean-difference, while the second term gives the class separability due to the covariance-

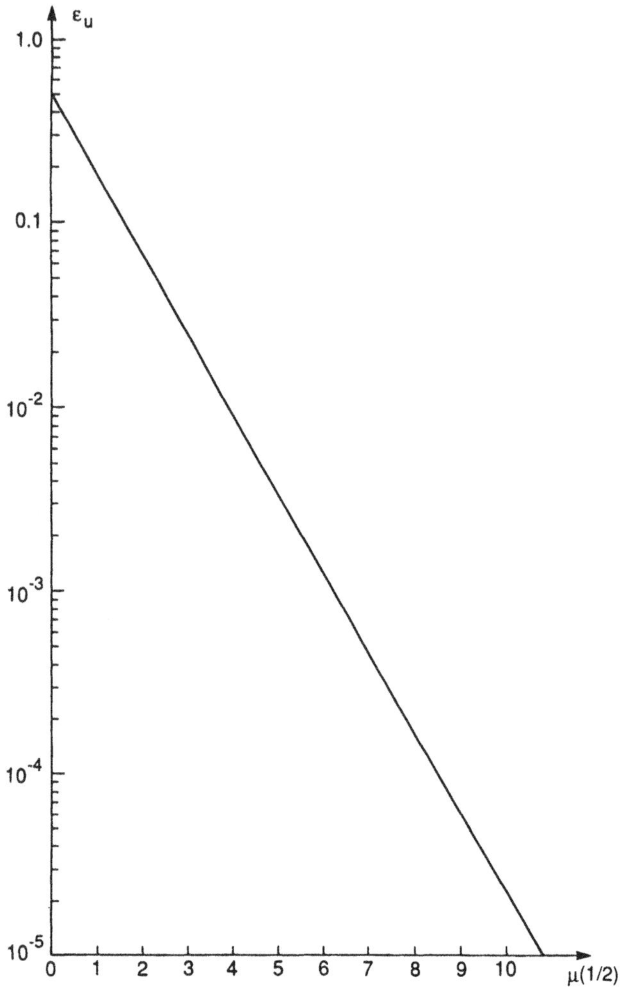

Fig. 3-17 Relation between $\mu(1/2)$ and ε_u.

difference. It is important to know which term is dominant, because it determines what type of a classifier must be designed for given distributions.

Example 12: Figure 3-18 shows the Chernoff distance $\mu(s)$ for DATA I-Λ. Although the two covariance matrices are significantly different in this case, the optimum s is $s_0 = 0.58$, which is close to 0.5. Also, the resulting bound of $\varepsilon_u = 0.5e^{-\mu(s_0)} = 0.046$ (assuming $P_1 = P_2 = 0.5$) is very close to the

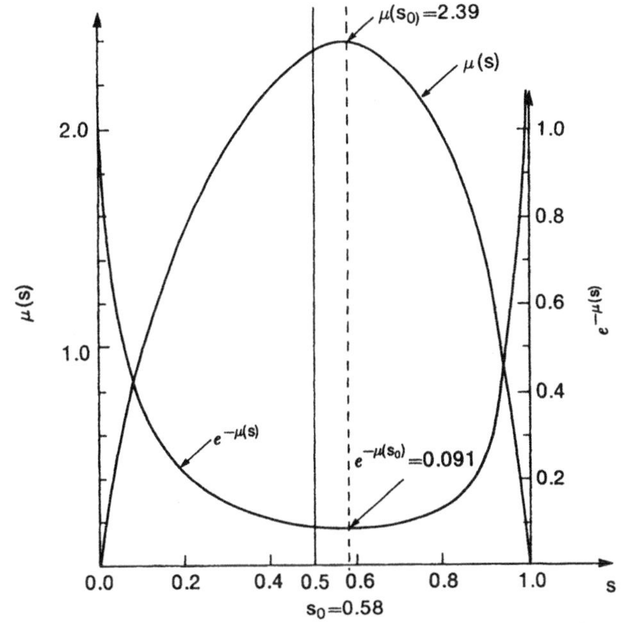

Fig. 3-18 Error bound vs. *s*.

Bhattacharyya bound of $\varepsilon_u = 0.5\ e^{-\mu(1/2)} = 0.048$. The Bayes error for this data is $\varepsilon = 0.019$.

Example 13: Let us compute the Bhattacharyya distance between two normal distributions, $N_X(0,I)$ and $N_X(0,\Lambda)$, which share the same mean. Since the first term of μ disappears in this case,

$$\mu(1/2) = \frac{1}{2}\sum_{i=1}^{n} \ln \frac{1+\lambda_i}{2\sqrt{\lambda_i}} . \tag{3.155}$$

Since $(1+\lambda_i)/2\sqrt{\lambda_i} \geq 1$ regardless of the value of λ_i (λ_i is the variance and positive), $\ln (1+\lambda_i)/2\sqrt{\lambda_i} \geq 0$, where the equality holds only when $\lambda_i = 1$. Therefore, as n goes to ∞ with $\lambda_i \neq 1$, $\mu(1/2)$ can go to ∞. This example shows that, even if $M_1 = M_2$, the Bayes error in a high-dimensional space could become very small with different covariance matrices.

Example 14: Let $\mathbf{x}_i$ $(i=1, \ldots, n)$ be independent and identically distributed random variables. The density functions of $\mathbf{x}_i$ for ω_1 and ω_2 are uniform in [0.4, 0.6] for ω_1 and [0, 1] for ω_2. The Bhattacharyya bound for these two distributions is

$$\begin{aligned}\varepsilon_u &= \sqrt{P_1 P_2} \int \sqrt{p_1(X) p_2(X)}\, dX \\ &= \sqrt{P_1 P_2} \prod_{i=1}^{n} \int_{-\infty}^{+\infty} \sqrt{p_1(x_i) p_2(x_i)}\, dx_i \\ &= \sqrt{P_1 P_2} \prod_{i=1}^{n} \int_{0.4}^{0.6} \sqrt{5}\, dx_i \\ &= \sqrt{P_1 P_2}\, 0.447^n \,. \end{aligned} \tag{3.156}$$

Thus, ε_u becomes small as n increases. When $n=1$ and $P_1=P_2=0.5$, ε_u is 0.224 while the Bayes error is 0.1.

Other bounds: Many other bounds can be derived similarly. One of them is the *asymptotic nearest neighbor error*, which is a tighter upper bound of the Bayes error than the Bhattacharyya bound, as given by

$$\varepsilon \le 2 \int \frac{P_1 p_1(X) P_2 p_2(X)}{p(X)}\, dX \le \int \sqrt{P_1 p_1(X) P_2 p_2(X)}\, dX \,. \tag{3.157}$$

The inequalities are verified by proving $\min[a,b] \le 2ab/(a+b) \le \sqrt{ab}$ for any positive a and b. If $a>b$, the left inequality becomes $b < 2b/(1+b/a)$. Since $b/a < 1$, the inequality holds. The case for $a<b$ can be proved similarly. The right inequality holds, because $a+b-2\sqrt{ab} = (\sqrt{a} + \sqrt{b})^2 \ge 0$.

These measures of class separability have a common structure. In the Bayes error, $P_1 p_1(X)$ and $P_2 p_2(X)$ are integrated in L_2 and L_1 respectively, thus measuring the overlap of two distributions exactly. In both the nearest neighbor error and the Bhattacharyya bound, this overlap was approximated by integrating the product of $P_1 p_1(X)$ and $P_2 p_2(X)$. However, in order to ensure that the dimension of the integrand is one of a density function, $P_1 p_1(X) P_2 p_2(X)$ is divided by the mixture density $p(X)$ in the nearest neighbor error while the product is square-rooted in the Bhattacharyya bound. The properties of the nearest neighbor error will be discussed extensively in Chapter 7.

Validity of the Bhattacharyya Distance

The Bhattacharyya distance for normal distributions, (3.152), is a very convenient equation to evaluate class separability. Even for non-normal cases, (3.152) seems to be a reasonable equation, measuring in the first term the distance between M_1 and M_2 normalized by the average covariance matrix, and in the second term the distance due to the covariance-difference. The question here is how widely (3.152) can be used. Since we cannot examine all possible non-normal distributions, we limit our discussion to a family of gamma distributions. Also, in order to avoid complexity, we present only one-dimensional cases. Note that, if two diagonalized covariance matrices are used, $\mu(1/2)$ of (3.152) is the summation of the Bhattacharyya distances of individual variables.

μ for gamma densities: When two one-dimensional distributions are gamma as shown in (2.54), $\int\sqrt{p_1(x)p_2(x)}\,dx$ can be computed as

$$\int_{-\infty}^{+\infty}\sqrt{p_1(x)p_2(x)}\,dx = \frac{\alpha_1^{\frac{\beta_1+1}{2}}\alpha_2^{\frac{\beta_2+1}{2}}}{\sqrt{\Gamma(\beta_1+1)\Gamma(\beta_2+1)}}\int_0^{\infty} x^{\frac{\beta_1+\beta_2}{2}} e^{-\frac{\alpha_1+\alpha_2}{2}x}\,dx$$

$$= \frac{\Gamma\left(\frac{\beta_1+\beta_2+2}{2}\right)}{\sqrt{\Gamma(\beta_1+1)\Gamma(\beta_2+1)}}\,\frac{\alpha_1^{\frac{\beta_1+1}{2}}\alpha_2^{\frac{\beta_2+1}{2}}}{\left(\frac{\alpha_1+\alpha_2}{2}\right)^{\frac{\beta_1+\beta_2+2}{2}}}\,, \tag{3.158}$$

where α_i and β_i are the parameters of the gamma distribution for ω_i. Or, taking the minus-log of (3.158),

$$\mu_0 = \frac{\beta_1+\beta_2+2}{2}\left[\ln\left\{\left(\frac{\alpha_1}{\alpha_2}\right)^{\frac{\beta_2+1}{\beta_1+\beta_2+2}} + \left(\frac{\alpha_2}{\alpha_1}\right)^{\frac{\beta_1+1}{\beta_1+\beta_2+2}}\right\} - \ln 2\right]$$

$$- \ln \frac{\Gamma\left(\frac{\beta_1+\beta_2+2}{2}\right)}{\sqrt{\Gamma(\beta_1+1)\Gamma(\beta_2+1)}} . \tag{3.159}$$

On the other hand, when (3.152) is used to compute μ,

$$\mu_g = \frac{1}{8} \frac{\left(\frac{\beta_1+1}{\alpha_1} - \frac{\beta_2+1}{\alpha_2}\right)^2}{\frac{1}{2}\left(\frac{\beta_1+1}{\alpha_1^2} + \frac{\beta_2+1}{\alpha_2^2}\right)} + \frac{1}{2} \ln \frac{\frac{1}{2}\left(\frac{\beta_1+1}{\alpha_1^2} + \frac{\beta_2+1}{\alpha_2^2}\right)}{\sqrt{\frac{\beta_1+1}{\alpha_1^2}\frac{\beta_2+1}{\alpha_2^2}}} . \tag{3.160}$$

This is based on $E\{\mathbf{x}|\omega_i\} = (\beta_i+1)/\alpha_i$ and $\mathrm{Var}\{\mathbf{x}|\omega_i\} = (\beta_i+1)/\alpha_i^2$ as in (2.56) and (2.57).

In many applications, β_1 and β_2 are equal or close to each other. Therefore, in order to simplify the discussion of comparing (3.159) and (3.160), let us assume $\beta_1 = \beta_2 = \beta$. Then,

$$\mu_0 = \frac{\beta+1}{2} \ln \frac{1}{4}\left(\frac{\alpha_1}{\alpha_2} + \frac{\alpha_2}{\alpha_1} + 2\right) \tag{3.161}$$

and

$$\mu_g = \frac{\beta+1}{4}\left[1 - \frac{2}{\alpha_1/\alpha_2 + \alpha_2/\alpha_1}\right] + \frac{1}{2} \ln \frac{1}{2}\left(\frac{\alpha_1}{\alpha_2} + \frac{\alpha_2}{\alpha_1}\right) . \tag{3.162}$$

Figure 3-19 shows the relation between μ_0 and μ_g for various values of β. For a given β and μ_0, (3.161) is solved to find the corresponding α_1/α_2, which is inserted to (3.162) to compute μ_g. The values for μ_0 are selected between 0 and 2 which corresponds to ε_u between 0.5 and 0.068 from Fig. 3-17. Figure 3-19 indicates that μ_g could be significantly different from μ_0, particularly for smaller β's.

Variable transformation: The power transformation of (3.77) tends to convert a gamma distribution to a normal-like one. Therefore, it must make μ_g

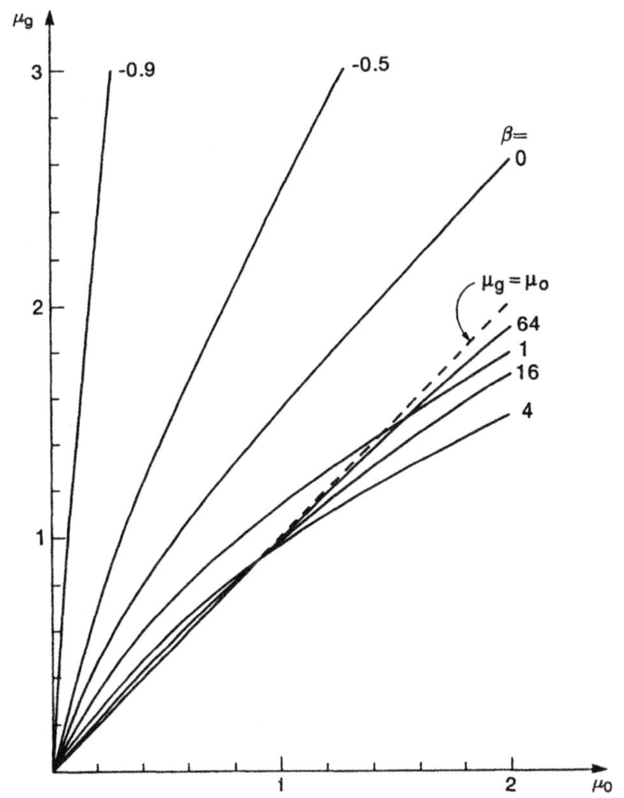

Fig. 3-19 Relation between μ_0 and μ_g for gamma densities.

closer to μ_0 so that μ_g could be used for a wider range of distributions. The mth order moments of the transformed variable, $\mathbf{y}$, are given in (3.78). Thus,

$$E\{\mathbf{y} \mid \omega_i\} = \frac{1}{\alpha_i^{\nu}} \frac{\Gamma(\beta_i+1+\nu)}{\Gamma(\beta_i+1)} = \frac{A}{\alpha_i^{\nu}} , \tag{3.163}$$

$$\mathrm{Var}\{\mathbf{y} \mid \omega_i\} = \frac{1}{\alpha_i^{2\nu}} \frac{\Gamma(\beta_i+1)\Gamma(\beta_i+1+2\nu)-\Gamma^2(\beta_i+1+\nu)}{\Gamma^2(\beta_i+1)} = \frac{B}{\alpha_i^{2\nu}} . \tag{3.164}$$

Then, using $\beta_1 = \beta_2 = \beta$ for simplicity, μ_g in the y-space is

$$\mu_g = \frac{1}{8} \frac{A^2 \left[\frac{1}{\alpha_1^{\nu}} - \frac{1}{\alpha_2^{\nu}} \right]^2}{\frac{B}{2} \left[\frac{1}{\alpha_1^{2\nu}} + \frac{1}{\alpha_2^{2\nu}} \right]} + \frac{1}{2} \ln \frac{\frac{B}{2} \left[\frac{1}{\alpha_1^{2\nu}} + \frac{1}{\alpha_2^{2\nu}} \right]}{\sqrt{\frac{B}{\alpha_1^{2\nu}} \frac{B}{\alpha_2^{2\nu}}}}$$

$$= \frac{A^2}{4B} \left[1 - \frac{2}{(\alpha_1/\alpha_2)^{\nu} + (\alpha_2/\alpha_1)^{\nu}} \right] + \frac{1}{2} \ln \frac{1}{2} \left[\left[\frac{\alpha_1}{\alpha_2} \right]^{\nu} + \left[\frac{\alpha_2}{\alpha_1} \right]^{\nu} \right] . \tag{3.165}$$

Figure 3-20 shows the relation between μ_0 of (3.161) and μ_g of (3.165) for $\nu = 1/2$, $1/4$ and $\beta = 0, -0.5$. For larger β's, the curves become very close to the $\mu_g = \mu_0$ line. These curves indicate that μ_0 and μ_g are now much closer than the ones of Fig. 3-19. Thus, μ_g of (3.165) may be used for a wider range of β.

Once variables are transformed to normal-like distributions, we can evaluate the class separability more easily. Also, the design of a classifier becomes easier, because a standard quadratic classifier could be adopted, rather than designing a complicated classifier depending on the underlying distributions.

Before leaving this subject, we would like to point out two important properties of this variable transformation.

The first point is that the correlation coefficients are relatively unaffected by the transformation of (3.77). In order to see this, let us expand $\mathbf{y}_i = \mathbf{x}_i^{\nu}$ around $\bar{\mathbf{x}}_i = E\{\mathbf{x}_i\}$ by a Taylor series up to the first order term.

$$\mathbf{y}_i = \mathbf{x}_i^{\nu} \cong \bar{\mathbf{x}}_i^{\nu} + \nu\, \bar{\mathbf{x}}_i^{\nu-1} (\mathbf{x}_i - \bar{\mathbf{x}}_i) . \tag{3.166}$$

Then,

$$E\{\mathbf{y}_i\} \cong \bar{\mathbf{x}}_i^{\nu} , \tag{3.167}$$

$$\mathrm{Var}\{\mathbf{y}_i\} \cong E\{(\mathbf{y}_i - \bar{\mathbf{x}}_i^{\nu})^2\} \cong (\nu \bar{\mathbf{x}}_i^{\nu-1})^2 \mathrm{Var}\{\mathbf{x}_i\} , \tag{3.168}$$

and

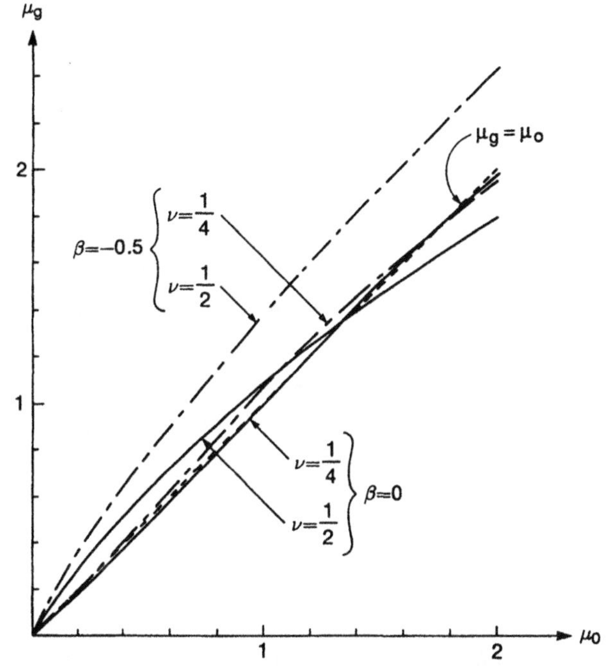

Fig. 3-20 Relation between μ_0 and μ_g after transformation.

$$\rho_{y_iy_j} \cong \frac{E\{(\mathbf{y}_i-\bar{\mathbf{x}}_i^{\nu})(\mathbf{y}_j-\bar{\mathbf{x}}_j^{\nu})\}}{\sqrt{\mathrm{Var}\{\mathbf{y}_i\}\mathrm{Var}\{\mathbf{y}_j\}}}$$

$$\cong \frac{(\nu\bar{\mathbf{x}}_i^{\nu-1})(\nu\bar{\mathbf{x}}_j^{\nu-1})E\{(\mathbf{x}_i-\bar{\mathbf{x}}_i)(\mathbf{x}_j-\bar{\mathbf{x}}_j)\}}{\sqrt{(\nu\bar{\mathbf{x}}_i^{\nu-1})^2\mathrm{Var}\{\mathbf{x}_i\}(\nu\bar{\mathbf{x}}_j^{\nu-1})^2\,\mathrm{Var}\{\mathbf{x}_j\}}}$$

$$= \rho_{x_ix_j} \,. \tag{3.169}$$

That is, by the first order approximation, $\rho_{y_iy_j} = \rho_{x_ix_j}$. Whether the first order approximation is good enough or not depends on the distribution.

Example 15: Let us study an exponential distribution and $\nu = 1/4$. In the exponential distribution, $\beta=0$ and $E^2\{\mathbf{x}\} = \mathrm{Var}\{\mathbf{x}\}$. Therefore, the second order approximation of (3.167) becomes

$$
\begin{aligned}
E\{\mathbf{y}\} &\cong \bar{\mathbf{x}}^{\nu} + \frac{\nu(1-\nu)}{2}\bar{\mathbf{x}}^{\nu-2}E\{(\mathbf{x}-\bar{\mathbf{x}})^2\} \\
&= [1 + \frac{\nu(1-\nu)}{2}]\bar{\mathbf{x}}^{\nu} \\
&\cong (1 - 0.094)\bar{\mathbf{x}}^{1/4} \ .
\end{aligned}
\tag{3.170}
$$

This is reasonably close to $\bar{\mathbf{x}}^{1/4}$ which is the first order approximation. Probably, the first order approximation in this case would be acceptable for qualitative discussions.

The second point is that, by changing ν of the transformation, the weights of the first and second terms of the Bhattacharyya distance vary. The smaller ν is, the more the first term tends to dominate. That is, the class separability comes more from the mean-difference than the covariance-difference. This means that we may have a better chance to design a linear classifier after the transformation with a small ν.

Furthermore, when two gamma density functions of $\mathbf{x}$ share the same β, we can achieve $\text{Var}\{\mathbf{y}|\omega_1\} = \text{Var}\{\mathbf{y}|\omega_2\}$ by using another popular *log-transformation* $\mathbf{y} = \ln \mathbf{x}$ [18]. Suppose that $\mathbf{x}$ has a gamma density of (2.54) and we apply $\mathbf{y} = \ln \mathbf{x}$, then

$$
E\{\mathbf{y}\} = \frac{\alpha^{\beta+1}}{\Gamma(\beta+1)}\int_0^{\infty}(\ln x)x^{\beta}e^{-\alpha x}dx = -\ln \alpha + \frac{\Gamma'(\beta+1)}{\Gamma(\beta+1)} \ , \tag{3.171}
$$

$$
E\{\mathbf{y}^2\} = \frac{\alpha^{\beta+1}}{\Gamma(\beta+1)}\int_0^{\infty}(\ln x)^2x^{\beta}e^{-\alpha x}\,dx = E^2\{\mathbf{y}\} + \sum_{i=1}^{\infty}\frac{1}{(\beta+1+i)^2} \ , \tag{3.172}
$$

where $\Gamma'(\beta+1) = d\Gamma(x)/dx\,|_{\beta+1}$. Therefore,

$$
\text{Var}\{\mathbf{y}\} = \sum_{i=0}^{\infty}\frac{1}{(\beta+1+i)^2} \ . \tag{3.173}
$$

The integrations of (3.171) and (3.172) are obtained from an integral table [19]. Note from (3.173) that $\text{Var}\{\mathbf{y}\}$ is independent of α. Therefore, if two classes have different α's but the same β, the variance-difference between the two classes disappears, and the class separability comes from the mean-difference only. Thus, after the transformation, the Bhattacharyya distance in the y-space becomes

$$\mu_g = \frac{1}{8} \frac{(\ln \alpha_1 - \ln \alpha_2)^2}{\sum_{i=1}^{\infty} \frac{1}{(\beta+1+i)^2}} . \tag{3.174}$$

The relation between μ_0 of (3.161) and μ_g of (3.174) is plotted in Fig. 3-21. Figure 3-21 shows that μ_g tends to be smaller than μ_0. This could be acceptable, because $\sqrt{P_1 P_2} \exp[-\mu_g]$ still gives an upper bound of the Bayes error although the bound is not as good as μ_0.

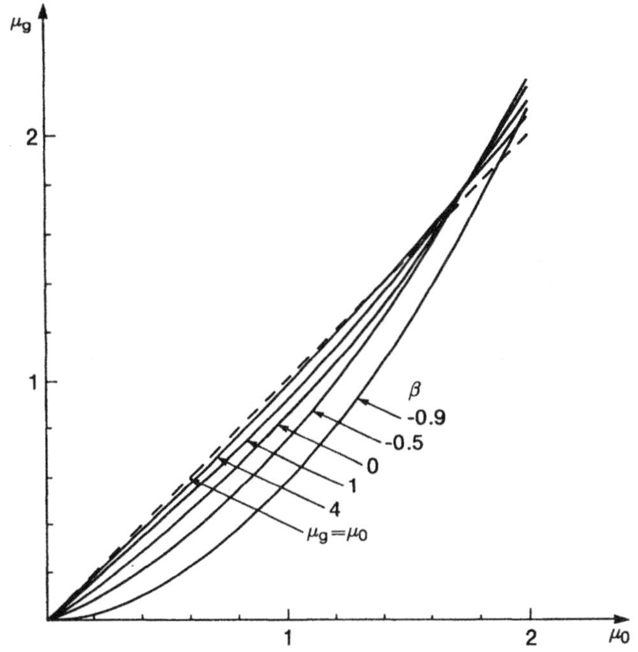

Fig. 3-21 Relation between μ_0 and μ_g after log transformation.

The above advantage of the log-transformation is often cancelled by the disadvantage that the distribution of **y** tends to have a long negative tail when **x** is distributed in [0, 1]. The tail generates more error when a standard quadratic or linear classifier is used.

Thus, when the application of a transformation is considered, a careful study must be conducted, and a proper transformation suitable to the given distributions must be selected.

3.5 Sequential Hypothesis Testing

In the problems considered so far, all of the information about the sample to be classified is presented at one instant. The classifier uses the single observation vector to make a decision via Bayes rule since no further observations will be made, and, as a result, we essentially have no control over the error, unless we can modify the observation process.

In many practical problems, however, the observations are sequential in nature, and more and more information becomes available as time procedes. For example, the vibration of a machine is observed to determine whether the machine is in good or bad condition. In this case, a sequence of observed waveforms should belong to the same category: either "good" or "bad" condition. Another popular example is a radar detection problem. Again the sequence of return pulses over a certain period of time should be from the same class: either existence or nonexistence of a target. A basic approach to problems of this type is the averaging of the sequence of observation vectors. This has the effect of filtering the noise and reducing the observed vectors down to the expected vector. Thus, it is possible, at least theoretically, to achieve zero error, provided that the expected vectors of the two classes are not the same. However, since obtaining an infinite number of observation vectors is obviously not feasible, it is necessary to have a condition, or rule, which helps us decide when to terminate the observations. The *sequential hypothesis test*, the subject of this section, is a mathematical tool for this type of problem.

The Sequential Test

Let $\mathbf{X}_1, \ldots, \mathbf{X}_m$ be the random vectors observed in sequence. These are assumed to be drawn from the same distribution and thus to be independent and identically distributed. Using the joint density functions of these m vectors, $p_i(X_i, \ldots, X_m)$ ($i = 1,2$), the minus-log likelihood ratio becomes

$$s = -\ln \frac{p_1(X_1, \ldots, X_m)}{p_2(X_1, \ldots, X_m)} = \sum_{i=1}^{m} \left[-\ln \frac{p_1(X_i)}{p_2(X_i)} \right]$$

$$= \sum_{i=1}^{m} h(X_i) , \tag{3.175}$$

where $h(X) = -\ln p_1(X)/p_2(X)$ is the likelihood ratio for an individual observation vector. The s of (3.175) is compared with a threshold such as $\ln P_1/P_2$ for the Bayes classifier, and the group of the samples $\{X_1, \ldots, X_m\}$ is classified to ω_1 or ω_2, depending on $s < 0$ or $s > 0$ (assuming $\ln P_1/P_2 = 0$). The expected values and variances of **s** for ω_1 and ω_2 are

$$E\{\mathbf{s} | \omega_i\} = \sum_{j=1}^{m} E\{h(\mathbf{X}_j) | \omega_i\} = m\, \eta_i , \tag{3.176}$$

$$\text{Var}\{\mathbf{s} | \omega_i\} = \sum_{j=1}^{m} \text{Var}\{h(\mathbf{X}_j) | \omega_i\} = m\, \sigma_i^2 , \tag{3.177}$$

since the $h(\mathbf{X}_j)$'s are also independent and identically distributed with mean η_i and variance σ_i.

When the Bayes classifier is used for $h(X)$, it can be proved that $\eta_1 \le 0$ and $\eta_2 \ge 0$ as follows:

$$\eta_1 = E\left\{ -\ln \frac{p_1(\mathbf{X})}{p_2(\mathbf{X})} | \omega_1 \right\} = \int \left\{ \ln \frac{p_2(X)}{p_1(X)} \right\} p_1(X)\, dX$$

$$\le \int \left\{ \frac{p_2(X)}{p_1(X)} - 1 \right\} p_1(X)\, dX = \int p_2(X) dX - \int p_1(X)\, dX = 0 , \tag{3.178}$$

$$\eta_2 = E\left\{ -\ln \frac{p_1(\mathbf{X})}{p_2(\mathbf{X})} | \omega_2 \right\} = -\int \left\{ \ln \frac{p_1(X)}{p_2(X)} \right\} p_2(X)\, dX$$

$$\geq -\int \left\{ \frac{p_1(X)}{p_2(X)} - 1 \right\} p_2(X)\, dX = 0 \,, \tag{3.179}$$

where the inequalities are derived from $\ln x \leq x - 1$. The equalities in (3.178) and (3.179) hold only when $p_1(X) = p_2(X)$.

Thus, as m increases, $E\{\mathbf{s} | \omega_1\}$ decreases and $E\{\mathbf{s} | \omega_2\}$ increases in proportion to m, while the standard deviations increase in proportion to $\sqrt{m}$. This is true regardless of $p_1(X)$ and $p_2(X)$ as long as $p_1(X) \neq p_2(X)$. Therefore, the density functions of $\mathbf{s}$ for ω_1 and ω_2 become more separable as m increases. Also, by the central limit theorem, the density function of $\mathbf{s}$ tends toward a normal distribution for large m.

Example 16: In order to see the effect of m easily, let us study a simple example in which $h(\mathbf{X})$ is distributed as $N_h(-\eta, 1)$ for ω_1 and $N_h(+\eta, 1)$ for ω_2. Then, $\mathbf{s}$ is distributed as $N_s(-m\eta, m)$ for ω_1 and $N_s(+m\eta, m)$ for ω_2. Therefore, the Bayes error of the sequential classifier for $P_1 = P_2 = 0.5$ is

$$\varepsilon = \int_{\eta\sqrt{m}}^{+\infty} \frac{1}{\sqrt{2\pi}} e^{-x^2/2} dx = 1 - \Phi(\eta\sqrt{m}) \,, \tag{3.180}$$

where $\Phi(\cdot)$ is the normal error function. Figure 3-22 shows the relation between ε and m for various η.

In practice, the $p_i(X)$'s are not known, and the Bayes classifier is hard to design. Therefore, in place of the Bayes classifier, some classifiers such as the quadratic classifier of (3.11) and the linear classifier of (3.12) are often used. These two classifiers satisfy

$$E\{h(\mathbf{X}) | \omega_1\} \leq 0 \quad \text{and} \quad E\{h(\mathbf{X}) | \omega_2\} \geq 0 \tag{3.181}$$

regardless of the distributions of $\mathbf{X}$ as shown in (3.143), (3.97), and (3.98) respectively. Note here that (3.97) and (3.98) can be derived from (3.96) regardless of the selection of Σ. Therefore, by increasing m, we can make the errors of these classifiers as small as we like. However, note from (3.97) and (3.98) that $E\{h(\mathbf{X}) | \omega_1\} = E\{h(\mathbf{X}) | \omega_2\} = 0$ for $M_1 = M_2$. Therefore, when $M_1 = M_2$, we cannot use the linear classifier of (3.12) for sequential operation.

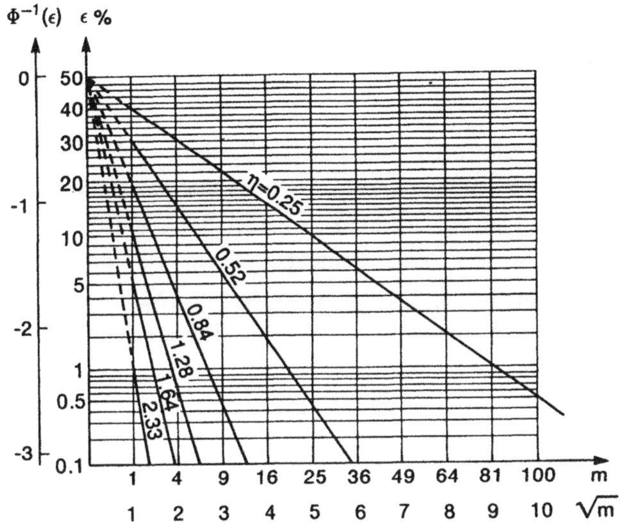

Fig. 3-22 Effect of the number of observations.

On the other hand, the $E\{h(\mathbf{X})|\omega_i\}$'s for the quadratic classifier do not become zero unless both means and covariance matrices are the same for ω_1 and ω_2, as seen in (3.139) and (3.140).

The effectiveness of m for reducing the error is significantly diminished when samples and subsequently $h(\mathbf{X}_j)$'s are correlated. This can be observed by computing the variance of $\mathbf{s}$ for correlated $\mathbf{h}$'s as

$$\mathrm{Var}\{\mathbf{s}|\omega_i\} = \sum_{j=1}^{m} \mathrm{Var}\{h(\mathbf{X}_j)|\omega_i\} + \sum_{j=1}^{m}\sum_{\substack{k=1 \\ j\neq k}}^{m} E\{(h(\mathbf{X}_j)-\eta_i)(h(\mathbf{X}_k)-\eta_i)|\omega_i\} . \tag{3.182}$$

That is, the second term does not disappear and contributes to increase $\mathrm{Var}\{\mathbf{s}|\omega_i\}$.

Example 17: Suppose that $\mathrm{Var}\{h(\mathbf{X}_j)|\omega_i\} = \sigma_i^2$, and $E\{(h(\mathbf{X}_j)-\eta_i)(h(\mathbf{X}_k)-\eta_i)|\omega_i\} = \rho_i^{|j-k|}\sigma_i^2$. Then, the second term of (3.182) becomes $2\sigma_i^2[\rho_i(m-1) + \rho_i^2(m-2) + \ldots + \rho_i^{m-1}]$. When $\rho_i = 0.5$ and m=10 are used, it becomes $16\sigma_i^2$. Therefore, $\mathrm{Var}\{\mathbf{s}|\omega_i\} = 26\sigma_i^2$ instead of $10\sigma_i^2$ for $\rho_i = 0$.

When $\rho_i = 1$, $\text{Var}\{s \mid \omega_i\} = m\sigma_i^2 + 2\sigma_i^2[(m-1)+\ldots+1] = m^2\sigma_i^2$. Therefore, the error of the sequential classifier is the same as the one of a classifier with a single observation, regardless of the value of m.

Multi-sensor fusion: The multi-sensor fusion problem may be handled in a similar way as the sequential test. Suppose that m different sensors (such as radar, infrared, and so on) are used to gather data, and the *ith* sensor generates a vector $\mathbf{X}_i$ with k_i measurements. Then, we form a vector with $(k_1 + \ldots + k_m)$ components, concatinating $\mathbf{X}_1, \ldots, \mathbf{X}_m$. However, often in practice, $\mathbf{X}_1, \ldots, \mathbf{X}_m$ are mutually independent. Therefore, the Bayes classifier becomes

$$h(X_1, \ldots, X_m) = -\ln \frac{p_1(X_1, \ldots, X_m)}{p_2(X_1, \ldots, X_m)}$$

$$= \sum_{i=1}^{m} \left[-\ln \frac{p_{X_i}(X_i \mid \omega_1)}{p_{X_i}(X_i \mid \omega_2)} \right] \underset{\omega_2}{\overset{\omega_1}{\gtrless}} \ln \frac{P_1}{P_2} , \tag{3.183}$$

where $-\ln p_{X_i}(X_i \mid \omega_1)/p_{X_i}(X_i \mid \omega_2)$ is the minus-log likelihood ratio for the *ith* sensor outputs. The Bayes classifier for the multi-sensor system can be designed by computing the minus-log likelihood ratio for each individual sensor outputs, adding these ratios, and thresholding the summation. Note that (3.183) is similar to (3.175). However, there is a difference between the multi-sensor and sequential classifiers in that each likelihood function is different for the multi-sensor classifier, while it is the same for the sequential classifier. When the outputs of different sensors are correlated, we need to treat the problem in the $(k_1+\ldots+k_m)$-dimensional space.

The Wald Sequential Test

Wald sequential test: Instead of fixing m, we may terminate the observations when s of (3.175) reaches a certain threshold value. That is

$$\begin{aligned} s_m \le a \quad &\rightarrow X's \in \omega_1 , \\ a < s_m < b \quad &\rightarrow \text{take the } (m+1)\text{th sample} , \\ b \le s_m \quad &\rightarrow X's \in \omega_2 , \end{aligned} \tag{3.184}$$

where s_m is used instead of s to indicate the number of observations, and a and b are thresholds to determine ω_1 and ω_2, respectively. This decision rule is called the *Wald sequential test* [20].

The error of the Wald sequential test is controlled by a and b; that is, as the absolute values of a and b increase, the error decreases, while the number of observations required to reach the decision increases. The relation between the threshold values and the error can be expressed by

$$\varepsilon_1 = \sum_{j=1}^{\infty} \int_b^{+\infty} p_{s_j}(s_j \mid \omega_1)\, ds_j \,, \tag{3.185}$$

$$\varepsilon_2 = \sum_{j=1}^{\infty} \int_{-\infty}^{a} p_{s_j}(s_j \mid \omega_2)\, ds_j \,. \tag{3.186}$$

Theoretically, we should be able to find a and b from (3.185) and (3.186) for any given ε_1 and ε_2.

A simpler way to find the threshold values was developed by Wald. The procedure is as follows: At the mth observation, the likelihood ratio is tested as

$$\ell_m = \frac{p_1(X_1, \ldots, X_m)}{p_2(X_1, \ldots, X_m)} \geq A \rightarrow X's \in \omega_1$$

$$\leq B \rightarrow X's \in \omega_2 \,. \tag{3.187}$$

Therefore,

$$\sum_{m=1}^{\infty} \int_{\ell_m \geq A} p_1(X_1, \ldots, X_m)\, dX_1 \ldots dX_m$$

$$\geq A \sum_{m=1}^{\infty} \int_{\ell_m \geq A} p_2(X_1, \ldots, X_m)\, dX_1 \ldots dX_m \,, \tag{3.188}$$

$$\sum_{m=1}^{\infty}\int_{\ell_m \le B} p_1(X_1,\ldots,X_m)\,dX_1\ldots dX_m$$
$$\le B\sum_{m=1}^{\infty}\int_{\ell_m \le B} p_2(X_1,\ldots,X_m)\,dX_1\ldots dX_m\,. \tag{3.189}$$

The left side of (3.188) includes all X's which belong to ω_1 and are classified correctly; hence, it should be $1-\varepsilon_1$. On the other hand, the right side of (3.188) includes all X's which belong to ω_2 and are misclassified as ω_1; hence, it should be ε_2. By the same argument, the left and right sides of (3.189) become ε_1 and $1-\varepsilon_2$, respectively. Therefore, (3.188) and (3.189) are rewritten as

$$1-\varepsilon_1 \ge A\varepsilon_2\,, \tag{3.190}$$

$$\varepsilon_1 \le B(1-\varepsilon_2)\,, \tag{3.191}$$

or

$$\frac{1-\varepsilon_1}{\varepsilon_2} \ge A\,, \tag{3.192}$$

$$\frac{\varepsilon_1}{1-\varepsilon_2} \le B\,. \tag{3.193}$$

Thus, for any given ε_1 and ε_2, A and B are obtained by (3.192) and (3.193). When the minus-log likelihood ratio is used, A and B should be converted to

$$a = -\ln A \ge -\ln\frac{1-\varepsilon_1}{\varepsilon_2}\,, \tag{3.194}$$

$$b = -\ln B \le -\ln\frac{\varepsilon_1}{1-\varepsilon_2}\,. \tag{3.195}$$

When the increments $h(X_j)$ are small, the likelihood ratio will exceed the threshold values A and B by only a small amount at the stage where ω_i is chosen.

Thus, the inequalities of the above equations can be replaced by equalities, and A and B are approximately determined by $(1-\varepsilon_1)/\varepsilon_2$ and $\varepsilon_1/(1-\varepsilon_2)$. Or, ε_1 and ε_2 can be expressed in terms of A and B as

$$\varepsilon_1 \cong \frac{B(A-1)}{A-B} , \tag{3.196}$$

$$\varepsilon_2 \cong \frac{1-B}{A-B} . \tag{3.197}$$

A few remarks concerning the properties of the Wald sequential test are in order.

(1) For the derivation of (3.192) and (3.193), $\mathbf{X}_1, \mathbf{X}_2, \ldots$ do not need to be independent and identically distributed.

(2) It can be proved that the Wald test terminates with probability 1 [20].

(3) The Wald test minimizes the average number of observations to achieve a given set of errors, ε_1 and ε_2 [21].

Expected number of observations: In the Wald sequential test, the average number of observations varies, depending on the distributions and the error we would like to achieve. In order to discuss this subject, let $\mathbf{m}$ be the number of observations needed to reach the upper or lower threshold value. The term $\mathbf{m}$ is a random variable. Equation (3.175) is rewritten as

$$\mathbf{s} = \sum_{j=1}^{\mathbf{m}} h(\mathbf{X}_j) \tag{3.198}$$

Then $\mathbf{s}$ should be either a or b of (3.184), with

$$\begin{aligned}
&\mathbf{s} = a \ \ (\textit{accept } \omega_1) \textit{ with probability } 1-\varepsilon_1 \ \ \textit{when } \ \mathbf{X}'s \in \omega_1 , \\
&\mathbf{s} = a \ \ (\textit{accept } \omega_1) \textit{ with probability } \varepsilon_2 \ \ \textit{when } \ \mathbf{X}'s \in \omega_2 , \\
&\mathbf{s} = b \ \ (\textit{accept } \omega_2) \textit{ with probability } \varepsilon_1 \ \ \textit{when } \ \mathbf{X}'s \in \omega_1 , \\
&\mathbf{s} = b \ \ (\textit{accept } \omega_2) \textit{ with probability } 1-\varepsilon_2 \ \ \textit{when } \ \mathbf{X}'s \in \omega_2 .
\end{aligned} \tag{3.199}$$

Therefore,

$$E\{\mathbf{s} \mid \omega_1\} = a(1-\varepsilon_1) + b\varepsilon_1 , \tag{3.200}$$

$$E\{\mathbf{s}|\omega_2\} = a\varepsilon_2 + b(1-\varepsilon_2) . \tag{3.201}$$

On the other hand, since (3.198) is a random sum, it is known that

$$E\{\mathbf{s}|\omega_i\} = E\{E\{\mathbf{s}|\mathbf{m},\omega_i\}\} = E\{\mathbf{m}\eta_i|\omega_i\} = E\{\mathbf{m}|\omega_i\}\eta_i , \tag{3.202}$$

where $E\{h(\mathbf{X}_j)|\omega_i\}$ is equal to η_i, regardless of j. Thus, the *average number of observations* needed to reach the decisions is

$$E\{\mathbf{m}|\omega_1\} = \frac{a(1-\varepsilon_1)+b\varepsilon_1}{\eta_1} , \tag{3.203}$$

$$E\{\mathbf{m}|\omega_2\} = \frac{a\varepsilon_2+b(1-\varepsilon_2)}{\eta_2} . \tag{3.204}$$

Example 18: Let us consider an example with normal distributions. Then, $h(X_j)$ becomes the quadratic equation of (3.11), and $\eta_i = E\{h(\mathbf{X}_j)|\omega_i\}$ is given by (3.139) or (3.140). On the other hand, we can select ε_1 and ε_2 as we like, and a, b, $a(1-\varepsilon_1)+b\varepsilon_1$, and $a\varepsilon_2+b(1-\varepsilon_2)$ are subsequently determined, as shown in Table 3-3.

TABLE 3-3

AVERAGE NUMBER OF OBSERVATIONS

$\varepsilon_1 = \varepsilon_2$:	10^{-2}	10^{-3}	10^{-4}	10^{-5}	10^{-6}
$-a = b$:	4.6	6.9	9.2	11.5	13.8
$a(1-\varepsilon_1)+b\varepsilon_1$:	-4.6	-6.9	-9.2	-11.5	-13.8
$a\varepsilon_2+b(1-\varepsilon_2)$:	4.6	6.9	9.2	11.5	13.8

In order to get an idea how many observations are needed, let us consider one-dimensional distributions with equal variances. In this case, (3.97) and (3.98) become

$$\eta_1 = -\frac{(m_2-m_1)^2}{2\sigma^2} \quad \text{and} \quad \eta_2 = +\frac{(m_2-m_1)^2}{2\sigma^2} . \tag{3.205}$$

If we assume $(m_2-m_1)/\sigma = 1$, then we have heavy overlap with $\varepsilon_1 = \varepsilon_2 = 0.31$ by the observation of one sample. However, we can achieve

10^{-6} as ε_1 and ε_2 by observing an average of 27.6 samples. This indicates how errors can be significantly reduced by using a relatively small number of observations.

Computer Projects

Two normal distributions are specified by the following parameters.

$$M_1 = M_2 = \begin{bmatrix} 0 \\ 0 \end{bmatrix}, \quad \Sigma_1 = \begin{bmatrix} 1 & 0.5 \\ 0.5 & 1 \end{bmatrix}, \quad \Sigma_2 = \begin{bmatrix} 1 & -0.5 \\ -0.5 & 1 \end{bmatrix},$$

$$P_1 = P_2 = 0.5 .$$

1. Generate 100 samples from each class.
2. Design the Bayes classifier for minimum error by using given M_i, Σ_i and P_i (the theoretical classifier). Classify the generated samples by the classifier, and count the number of misclassified samples.
3. Plot the theoretical distribution function derived from (3.73) and the empirical distribution functions of (3.71), and test the normality of the generated samples.
4. Plot the operating characteristics by classifying the generated samples with the theoretical classifier.
5. Plot the error-reject curve by classifying the generated samples with the theoretical classifier.
6. Compute the theoretical Bayes error for the given normal distributions.
7. Changing the threshold value t in Project 6, plot the theoretical operating characteristics and error-reject curve, and compare them with the results of Projects 4 and 5.
8. Plot the Chernoff bound as a function of s, and find the optimum s and the minimum Chernoff bound.
9. Perform the sequential classification for $m = 9$ and 25. Generate 100 m-sample-groups-from each class and count the number of misclassified m-sample-groups.

Problems

1. Two one-dimensional distributions are uniform in [0, 2] for ω_1 and [1, 4] for ω_2, and $P_1 = P_2 = 0.5$.

   (a) Find the Bayes boundary for minimum error, and compute the Bayes error.

   (b) Plot the operating characteristics.

   (c) Find the Neyman-Pearson boundary with $\varepsilon_2 = 0.25$.

   (d) Find the minimax boundary.

   (e) Compute the Chernoff bound, and find the optimal s.

   (f) Compute the Bhattacharyya bound.

2. Two normal distributions are characterized by

$$P_1 = P_2 = 0.5 ,$$

$$M_1 = \begin{bmatrix} +1 \\ 0 \end{bmatrix}, \quad M_2 = \begin{bmatrix} -1 \\ 0 \end{bmatrix}, \quad \Sigma_1 = \Sigma_2 = \begin{bmatrix} 1 & 0.5 \\ 0.5 & 1 \end{bmatrix}.$$

   (a) Draw the Bayes decision boundary to minimize the probability of error.

   (b) Draw the Bayes decision boundary to minimize the cost with $c_{11} = c_{22} = 0$ and $c_{12} = 2c_{21}$.

3. Repeat Problem 2 for

$$\Sigma_1 = \begin{bmatrix} 1 & 0.5 \\ 0.5 & 1 \end{bmatrix} \quad \text{and} \quad \Sigma_2 = \begin{bmatrix} 1 & -0.5 \\ -0.5 & 1 \end{bmatrix}.$$

4. Assuming that $c_{11} = c_{22} = 0$ and $c_{12} = c_{21}$ in Problem 2, plot the relationship between the threshold values of the likelihood ratio and the probabilities of errors.

   (a) Plot the operating characteristics.

   (b) Find the total error when the Neyman-Pearson test is performed with $\varepsilon_1 = 0.05$.

   (c) Find the threshold value and the total error for the minimax test.

(d) Plot the error-reject curve.

5. Two normal distributions are characterized by

$$P_1 = 0.6, \quad P_2 = 0.4 ,$$

$$M_1 = \begin{bmatrix} 2 \\ 4 \end{bmatrix}, \quad M_2 = \begin{bmatrix} 6 \\ 8 \end{bmatrix}, \quad \Sigma_1 = \Sigma_2 = \begin{bmatrix} 4 & 3 \\ 3 & 9 \end{bmatrix} .$$

Compute the Bayes error for $c_{11} = c_{22} = 0$ and $c_{12} = c_{21}$.

6. Show how to derive the variances of (3.144) and (3.145) for normal distributions.

7. Let $\mathbf{x}_i$ $(i=1, \ldots, n)$ be independent and identically distributed random variables, whose distributions are exponential with the parameters α_1 for ω_1 and α_2 for ω_2. Find $E\{h(\mathbf{X}) | \omega_i\}$ where $h(\mathbf{X})$ is the quadratic equation of (3.11).

8. The equivocation is given by

$$\frac{-1}{2\ln 2} \int \sum_{i=1}^{2} P_i p_i(X) \ln \frac{P_i p_i(X)}{p(X)} \, dX .$$

Prove that the equivocation is larger than the asymptotic nearest neighbor error but smaller than the Bhattacharyya error bound.

9. When two distributions are normal with an equal covariance matrix, Σ, both the Bayes error, ε, and the Bhattacharyya bound, ε_u, are expressed as functions of $\ell = (M_2 - M_1)^T \Sigma^{-1} (M_2 - M)$. Plot ε and ε_u vs. ℓ.

10. Three distributions are normal with

$$M_1 = M_2 = M_3 = \begin{bmatrix} 0 \\ 0 \end{bmatrix}, \quad \Sigma_1 = \begin{bmatrix} \sigma_n^2 & 0 \\ 0 & \sigma_n^2 \end{bmatrix},$$

$$\Sigma_2 = \begin{bmatrix} \sigma_n^2 + \sigma_s^2 & 0 \\ 0 & \sigma_n^2 \end{bmatrix}, \quad \Sigma_3 = \begin{bmatrix} \sigma_n^2 & 0 \\ 0 & \sigma_n^2 + \sigma_s^2 \end{bmatrix} .$$

The cost matrix is

$$\begin{bmatrix} 0 & 1 & 1 \\ 1 & 0 & a \\ 1 & a & 0 \end{bmatrix}$$

where $0 \le a < 1$ and $P_2 = P_3 = p$.

(a) Find the Bayes boundary and plot it in the X-coordinate system.

(b) Write an expression for the probabilities of errors. (Do not evaluate the integrals.)

11. Two distributions are normal with

$$P_1 = P_2 = 0.5, \qquad M_1 = \begin{bmatrix} 0 \\ 0 \end{bmatrix}, \qquad M_2 = \begin{bmatrix} 1 \\ 0 \end{bmatrix},$$

$$\Sigma_1 = \Sigma_2 = \begin{bmatrix} 1 & 0.5 \\ 0.5 & 1 \end{bmatrix}.$$

(a) Calculate the threshold values for the Wald sequential test for $\varepsilon_1 = \varepsilon_2 = 10^{-3}$, 10^{-5}, and 10^{-7}.

(b) Find the average number of observations required.

(c) Fixing the number of observations as obtained in (b), compute the error of the sequential classifier with fixed m.

References

1. C. K. Chow, An optimum character recognition system using decision functions, *Trans. IRE Electronic Computers*, EC-6, pp. 247-254, 1957.

2. A. Wald, "Statistical Decision Functions," Wiley, New York, 1950.

3. D. Blackwell and M. A. Girshick, "Theory of Games and Statistical Decisions," Wiley, New York, 1954.

4. T. S. Furguson, "Mathematical Statistics: A Decision Theoretic Approach," Academic Press, New York, 1967.

5. H. L. Van Trees, "Detection, Estimation, and Modulation Theory: Part I," Wiley, New York, 1968.

6. B. J. Burdick, Private communication, 1984.

7. A. Papoulis, "Probability, Random Variables, and Stochastic Processes," p. 250, McGraw-Hill, New York, 1965.

8. K. Fukunaga, R. R. Hayes, and L. M. Novak, The acquisition probability for a minimum distance one-class classifier, *Trans. IEEE Aerospace and Electronic Systems*, AES-23, pp. 493-499, 1987.

9. R. R. Parenti and E. W. Tung, A statistical analysis of the multiple-target, multiple-shot target acquisition problem, Project Report TT-43, Lincoln Laboratory, M.I.T., 1981.

10. G. E. Noether, "Elements of Non-Parametric Statistics," Wiley, New York, 1967.

11. K. Fukunaga and D. L. Kessell, Error evaluation and model validation in statistical pattern recognition, Purdue University, Technical report TR-EE-72-73, Chapter 6, 1972.

12. C. K. Chow, On optimum recognition error and reject tradeoff, *Trans. IEEE Inform. Theory*, IT-16, pp. 41-46, 1970.

13. K. Fukunaga and D. L. Kessell, Application of optimum error-reject functions, *Trans. IEEE Inform. Theory*, IT-18, pp. 814-817, 1972.

14. K. Fukunaga and T. F. Krile, Calculation of Bayes recognition error for two multivariate Gaussian distributions, *Trans. IEEE Computers*, C-18, pp. 220-229, 1969.

15. L. M. Novak, On the sensitivity of Bayes and Fisher classifiers in radar target detection, *Proc. 18th Asilomar Conference on Circuit, Systems, and Computers*, Pacific Grove, CA, 1984.

16. H. Chernoff, A measure of asymptotic efficiency for tests of a hypothesis based on the sum of observations, *Ann. Math. Stat.*, 23, pp. 493-507, 1952.

17. A. Bhattacharyya, On a measure of divergence between two statistical populations defined by their probability distributions, *Bull. Calcutta Math. Soc.*, 35, pp. 99-110, 1943.

18. S. D. Martinez, Private communication, 1988.

19. I. S. Gradshteyn and I. M. Ryzhik, "Tables of Integrals, Series, and Products," Academic Press, New York, 1980.

20. A. Wald, "Sequential Analysis," Wiley, New York, 1947.

21. A. Wald and J. Wolfowitz, Optimum character of the sequential probability ratio test, *Ann. Math. Stat.*, 19, pp. 326-339, 1948.

Chapter 4

PARAMETRIC CLASSIFIERS

The Bayes likelihood ratio test has been shown to be optimal in the sense that it minimizes the cost or the probability of error. However, in order to construct the likelihood ratio, we must have the conditional probability density function for each class. In most applications, we must estimate these density functions using a finite number of sample observation vectors. Estimation procedures are available, and will be discussed in Chapters 6 and 7. However, they may be very complex or require a large number of samples to give accurate results.

Even if we can obtain the densities, the likelihood ratio test may be difficult to implement; time and storage requirements for the classification process may be excessive. Therefore, we are often led to consider a simpler procedure for designing a pattern classifier. In particular, we may specify the mathematical form of the classifier, leaving a finite set of parameters to be determined. The most common choices are linear, quadratic, or piecewise classifiers which we will discuss in this chapter.

First, we will consider under what conditions the Bayes classifier becomes quadratic, linear, or piecewise. We will then develop alternative methods for deriving "good" parametric classifiers even when these conditions are not met.

The reader should be reminded, however, that the Bayes classifier is the best classifier in all cases. No parametric classifier will exceed the performance of the likelihood ratio test.

4.1 The Bayes Linear Classifier

For two normal distributions, the Bayes decision rule can be expressed as a quadratic function of the observation vector X as

$$\frac{1}{2}(X - M_1)^T \Sigma_1^{-1} (X - M_1) - \frac{1}{2}(X - M_2)^T \Sigma_2^{-1} (X - M_2) + \frac{1}{2} \ln \frac{|\Sigma_1|}{|\Sigma_2|} \underset{\omega_2}{\overset{\omega_1}{\gtrless}} \ln \frac{P_1}{P_2} . \tag{4.1}$$

When both covariance matrices are equal, that is when $\Sigma_1 = \Sigma_2 = \Sigma$, (4.1) reduces to a linear function of X as

$$(M_2 - M_1)^T \Sigma^{-1} X + \frac{1}{2}(M_1^T \Sigma^{-1} M_1 - M_2^T \Sigma^{-1} M_2) \underset{\omega_2}{\overset{\omega_1}{\gtrless}} \ln \frac{P_1}{P_2} . \tag{4.2}$$

Furthermore, if the covariance matrix is the identity matrix, I, then we can view $\mathbf{X}$ as an observation corrupted by *white noise*. The components of $\mathbf{X}$ are uncorrelated and have unit variance. The Bayes decision rule reduces to

$$(M_2 - M_1)^T X + \frac{1}{2}(M_1^T M_1 - M_2^T M_2) \underset{\omega_2}{\overset{\omega_1}{\gtrless}} \ln \frac{P_1}{P_2} . \tag{4.3}$$

There have been a number of classifiers, such as the correlation classifier and the matched filter, developed in the communication field for signal detection problems [1]. We will discuss here how these classifiers are related to the Bayes classifier.

Correlation Classifier

The product $M_i^T \mathbf{X}$ is called the *correlation* between M_i and $\mathbf{X}$. When $\mathbf{X}$ consists of time-sampled values taken from a continuous random process, $\mathbf{x}(t)$, we can write the correlation as

$$M_i^T \mathbf{X} = \sum_{j=1}^{n} m_i(t_j) \mathbf{x}(t_j) . \tag{4.4}$$

In the continuous case, the correlation becomes an integral, that is

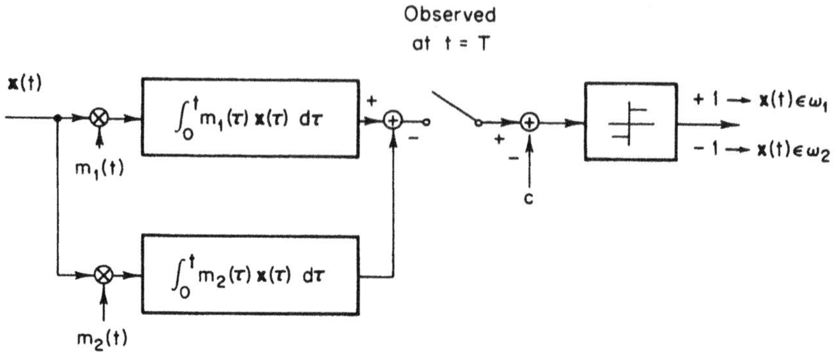

Fig. 4-1 Block diagram of a correlation classifier.

$$\sum_{j=1}^{n} m_i(t_j)\mathbf{x}(t_j) \quad \rightarrow \quad \int_0^T m_i(t)\mathbf{x}(t)\,dt \ . \tag{4.5}$$

We can see that the classifier (4.3) compares the difference in the correlations of $\mathbf{X}$ with M_1 and M_2 with a threshold to make a decision. Thus, we may call it a *correlation classifier*. The structure of the correlation classifier is shown in Fig. 4-1, and is written as

$$M_1^T X - M_2^T X \underset{\omega_2}{\overset{\omega_1}{\lessgtr}} c \ . \tag{4.6}$$

If c is selected as $(M_1^T M_1 - M_2^T M_2)/2 - \ln P_1/P_2$, (4.6) becomes identical to (4.3). Thus, in order for the correlation classifier to be the Bayes classifier, the distributions must be normal with the equal covariance matrix I for both ω_1 and ω_2.

Matched Filter

The correlation between M_i and $\mathbf{X}$ can also be considered as the output of a linear filter. Suppose we construct functions $g_i(t)$ such that

$$g_i(T-t) = m_i(t) \ . \tag{4.7}$$

The relation between $g_i(t)$ and $m_i(t)$ is illustrated in Fig. 4-2. Then, clearly,

$$\int_0^T m_i(t)\mathbf{x}(t)\,dt = \int_0^T g_i(T-t)\mathbf{x}(t)\,dt \ . \tag{4.8}$$

Thus, the correlation is the output of a linear filter whose impulse response is $g_i(t)$. This filter is called a *matched filter*. The matched filter classifier, which

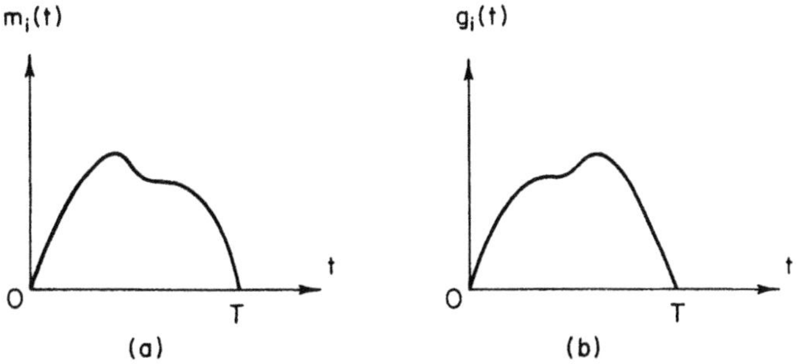

Fig. 4-2 Relation between $m_i(t)$ and $g_i(t)$.

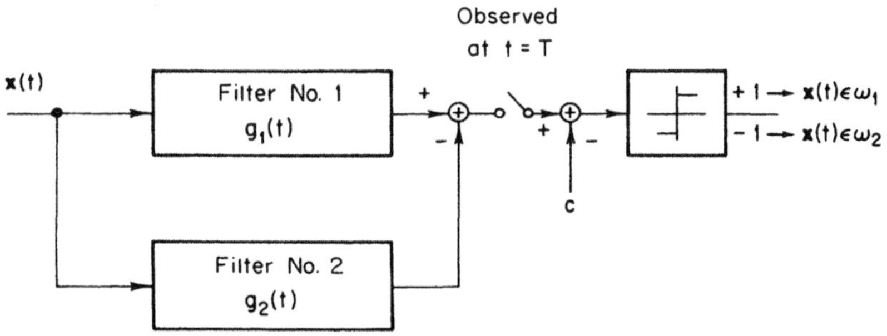

Fig. 4-3 Block diagram of a matched filter classifier.

performs the same function as the correlation classifier, is shown in Fig. 4-3. Again, the matched filter becomes the Bayes classifier with a proper threshold, when the distributions are normal with the equal covariance I.

Distance Classifier

The correlation and matched filter classifiers are directly related to another popular classifier called a *distance classifier* as follows.

Suppose we multiply (4.3) by 2, and then add and subtract $X^T X$ from the left-hand side. The resulting decision rule is

$$(X^T X - 2M_1^T X + M_1^T M_1) - (X^T X - 2M_2^T X + M_2^T M_2) \underset{\omega_2}{\overset{\omega_1}{\lessgtr}} 2 \ln \frac{P_1}{P_2} , \tag{4.9}$$

or

$$\|X - M_1\|^2 - \|X - M_2\|^2 \underset{\omega_2}{\overset{\omega_1}{\gtrless}} 2 \ln \frac{P_1}{P_2} . \tag{4.10}$$

Now the decision rule has the geometrical interpretation of comparing the Euclidean distances from X to M_1 and M_2 according to a threshold. When $P_1 = P_2 = 0.5$, the decision boundary is the perpendicular *bisector* of the line joining M_1 and M_2, as shown in Fig. 4-4.

Nonwhite Observation Noise

In the more general case when $\Sigma_1 = \Sigma_2 \neq I$, the observation noise is correlated and is often called *colored noise*. The Bayes classifier of (4.2) should be used in this case instead of (4.3). However, it is still useful to view the decision rule of (4.2) as a correlation classifier or a distance classifier. To see this, we introduce the "whitening" transformation, $\mathbf{Y} = A^T\mathbf{X}$, where

$$A^T \Sigma A = I . \tag{4.11}$$

It is important to note that as long as Σ is positive definite, A exists and is nonsingular. Thus, the whitening transformation is reversible, and the observation $\mathbf{Y}$ can be classified as effectively as $\mathbf{X}$.

The expected vector of $\mathbf{Y}$ is

$$D_i = E\{\mathbf{Y} | \omega_i\} = A^T M_i \qquad (i = 1,2) \tag{4.12}$$

for class ω_i, and the covariance of $\mathbf{Y}$ is I for both classes. Hence, all of the discussion of the preceding section applies to $\mathbf{Y}$ if we replace M_i [or $m_i(t)$] with D_i [or $d_i(t)$].

In the continuous time case, the transformation becomes an integral as

$$\mathbf{Y} = A^T\mathbf{X} \quad \rightarrow \quad \mathbf{y}(t) = \int_0^T a(t,\tau)\mathbf{x}(\tau)\, d\tau . \tag{4.13}$$

The kernel, $a(t,\tau)$, can be viewed as the impulse response of a *whitening filter*. A possible structure for this classifier is shown in Fig. 4-5. We see that we have the correlation classifier of Fig. 4-1 modified by the addition of whitening filters.

Example 1: Figure 4-6 shows a two-dimensional example in which a whitening transformation is effective. Although the two distributions of Fig.

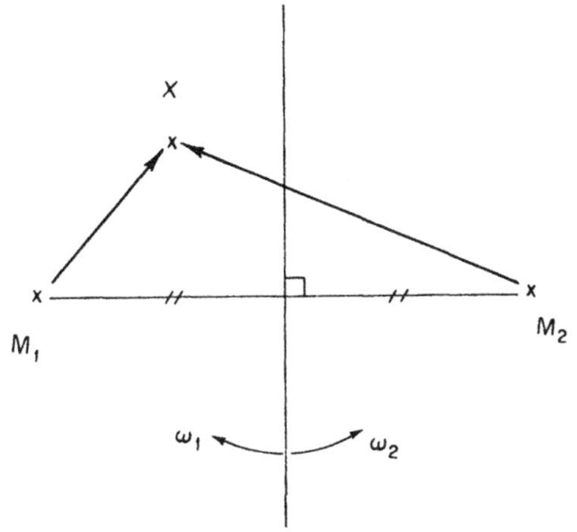

Fig. 4-4 A classifier by Euclidean distances.

4-6(a) are very much separable by the Bayes classifier of (4.2), the bisector classifier or simple correlation gives a poor classification. The narrow distributions of Fig. 4-6(a) occur when $\mathbf{x}_1$ and $\mathbf{x}_2$ are highly correlated. Particularly, when $\mathbf{x}_1, \mathbf{x}_2, \ldots$ are the time-sampled values of waveforms, adjacent $\mathbf{x}_i$'s are usually highly correlated and show this type of distribution. The whitening transformation changes these two distributions to the circular ones of Fig. 4-6(b) such that the Bayes classifier becomes the bisector.

Other Bayes Linear Classifiers

The Bayes classifier becomes linear for some other distributions such as independent exponential distributions and the distributions of independent binary variables. We will discuss these cases in this section.

Independent exponential distributions: When the $\mathbf{x}_i$'s are mutually independent and exponentially distributed for both ω_1 and ω_2, the Bayes classifier becomes linear as shown in (3.18).

Independent binary variables: When the $\mathbf{x}_j$'s are binary, either +1 or −1, the density function of $\mathbf{x}_j$ for ω_i is expressed by

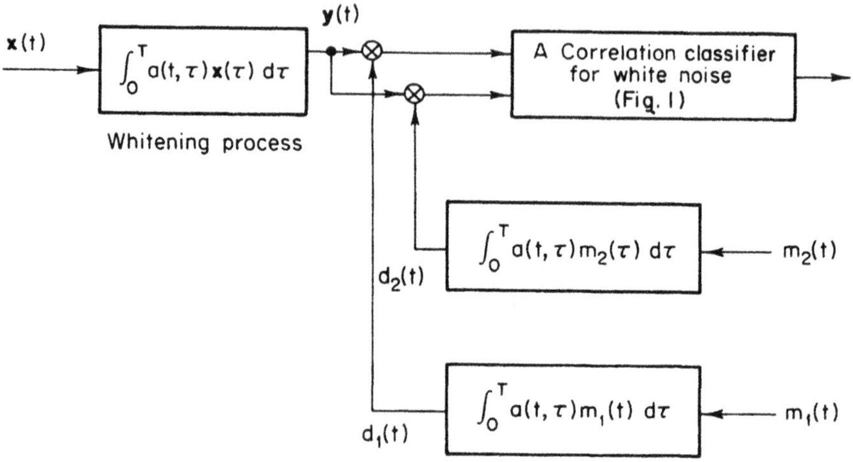

Fig. 4-5 A correlation classifier for colored noise.

$$P_r\{\mathbf{x}_j = x_j \mid \omega_i\} = P_{ij}^{(1+x_j)/2}(1-P_{ij})^{(1-x_j)/2} , \tag{4.14}$$

where

$$P_{ij} = P_r\{\mathbf{x}_j = 1 \mid \omega_i\} . \tag{4.15}$$

Note that (4.14) becomes P_{ij} for $x_j = +1$, and $(1-P_{ij})$ for $x_j = -1$. For

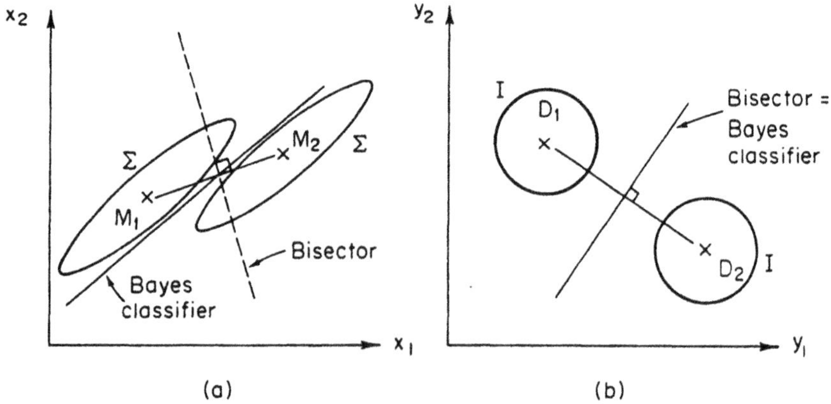

Fig. 4-6 Effect of a whitening process.

independent $\mathbf{x}_j$'s, the density function of the binary random vector $\mathbf{X}$ is

$$P_r\{\mathbf{X} = X \mid \omega_i\} = \prod_{j=1}^{n} P_r\{\mathbf{x}_j = x_j \mid \omega_i\} . \tag{4.16}$$

Thus, the minus-log likelihood ratio of (4.16) becomes

$$h(X) = -\ln \frac{P_r\{\mathbf{X} = X \mid \omega_1\}}{P_r\{\mathbf{X} = X \mid \omega_2\}}$$

$$= -\sum_{j=1}^{n} \left[\frac{1+x_j}{2} \ln \frac{P_{1j}}{P_{2j}} + \frac{1-x_j}{2} \ln \frac{1-P_{1j}}{1-P_{2j}} \right]$$

$$= -\frac{1}{2} \left\{ \sum_{j=1}^{n} \left[\ln \frac{P_{1j}(1-P_{2j})}{P_{2j}(1-P_{1j})} \right] x_j + \sum_{j=1}^{n} \ln \frac{P_{1j}(1-P_{1j})}{P_{2j}(1-P_{2j})} \right\} . \tag{4.17}$$

This is a linear function of x_j.

4.2 Linear Classifier Design

Linear classifiers are the simplest ones as far as implementation is concerned, and are directly related to many known techniques such as correlations and Euclidean distances. However, in the Bayes sense, linear classifiers are optimum only for normal distributions with equal covariance matrices. In some applications such as signal detection in communication systems, the assumption of equal covariance is reasonable because the properties of the noise do not change very much from one signal to another. However, in many other applications of pattern recognition, the assumption of equal covariance is not appropriate.

Many attempts have been made to design the best linear classifiers for normal distributions with unequal covariance matrices and non-normal distributions. Of course, these are not optimum, but in many cases the simplicity and robustness of the linear classifier more than compensate for the loss in performance. In this section, we will discuss how linear classifiers are designed for these more complicated cases.

Since it is predetermined that we use a linear classifier regardless of the given distributions, our decision rule should be

$$h(X) = V^T X + v_o \underset{\omega_2}{\overset{\omega_1}{\gtrless}} 0 . \tag{4.18}$$

The term $h(X)$ is a linear function of X and is called a *linear discriminant function.* Our design work is to find the optimum coefficients $V = [v_1 \ldots v_n]^T$ and the threshold value v_o for given distributions under various criteria. The linear discriminant function becomes the minus-log likelihood ratio when the given distributions are normal with equal covariance matrices.

However, the reader should be cautioned that no linear classifiers work well for the distributions which are not separated by the mean-difference but separated by the covariance-difference. In this case, we have no choice but to adopt a more complex classifier such as a quadratic one. The first and second terms of the Bhattacharyya distance, (3.152), will indicate where the class separability comes from, namely mean- or covariance-difference.

Optimum Design Procedure

Equation (4.18) indicates that an n-dimensional vector X is projected onto a vector V, and that the variable, $y = V^T X$, in the projected one-dimensional h-space is classified to either ω_1 or ω_2, depending on whether $y < -v_o$ or $y > -v_o$. Figure 4-7 shows an example in which distributions are projected onto two vectors, V and V'. On each mapped space, the threshold, v_0, is chosen to separate the ω_1- and ω_2-regions, resulting in the hatched error probability. As seen in Fig. 4-7, the error on V is smaller than that on V'. Therefore, the optimum design procedure for a linear classifier is to select V and v_o which give the smallest error in the projected h-space.

When $\mathbf{X}$ is normally distributed, $h(\mathbf{X})$ of (4.18) is also normal. Therefore, the error in the h-space is determined by $\eta_i = E\{h(\mathbf{X}) | \omega_i\}$ and $\sigma_i^2 = \text{Var}\{h(\mathbf{X}) | \omega_i\}$, which are functions of V and v_o. Thus, as will be discussed later, the error may be minimized with respect to V and v_o. Even if $\mathbf{X}$ is not normally distributed, $h(\mathbf{X})$ could be close to normal for large n, because $h(\mathbf{X})$ is the summation of n terms and the central limit theorem may come into effect. In this case, a function of η_i and σ_i^2 could be a reasonable criterion to measure the class separability in the h-space.

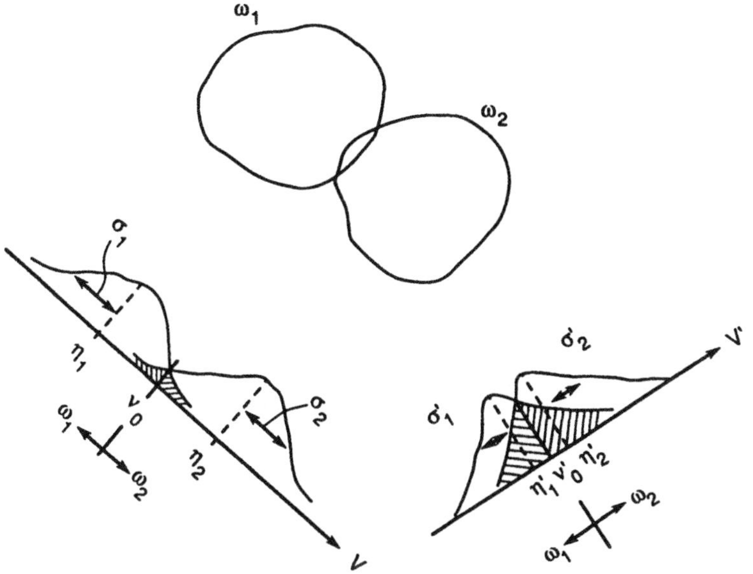

Fig. 4-7 An example of linear mapping.

The expected values and variances of $h(\mathbf{X})$ are

$$\eta_i = E\{h(\mathbf{X})|\omega_i\} = V^T E\{\mathbf{X}|\omega_i\} + v_o = V^T M_i + v_o \,, \tag{4.19}$$

$$\sigma_i^2 = \text{Var}\{h(\mathbf{X})|\omega_i\} = V^T E\{(\mathbf{X}-M_i)(\mathbf{X}-M_i)^T|\omega_i\}V$$
$$= V^T \Sigma_i V \,. \tag{4.20}$$

Let $f(\eta_1,\eta_2,\sigma_1^2,\sigma_2^2)$ be any criterion to be minimized or maximized for determining the optimum V and v_o. Then, the derivatives of f with respect to V and v_o are

$$\frac{\partial f}{\partial V} = \frac{\partial f}{\partial \sigma_1^2}\frac{\partial \sigma_1^2}{\partial V} + \frac{\partial f}{\partial \sigma_2^2}\frac{\partial \sigma_2^2}{\partial V} + \frac{\partial f}{\partial \eta_1}\frac{\partial \eta_1}{\partial V} + \frac{\partial f}{\partial \eta_2}\frac{\partial \eta_2}{\partial V} \,, \tag{4.21}$$

$$\frac{\partial f}{\partial v_o} = \frac{\partial f}{\partial \sigma_1^2}\frac{\partial \sigma_1^2}{\partial v_o} + \frac{\partial f}{\partial \sigma_2^2}\frac{\partial \sigma_2^2}{\partial v_o} + \frac{\partial f}{\partial \eta_1}\frac{\partial \eta_1}{\partial v_o} + \frac{\partial f}{\partial \eta_2}\frac{\partial \eta_2}{\partial v_o} \,. \tag{4.22}$$

On the other hand, from (4.19) and (4.20)

$$\frac{\partial \sigma_i^2}{\partial V} = 2\Sigma_i V \, , \quad \frac{\partial \eta_i}{\partial V} = M_i \, , \tag{4.23}$$

$$\frac{\partial \sigma_i^2}{\partial v_o} = 0 \, , \quad \frac{\partial \eta_i}{\partial v_o} = 1 \, . \tag{4.24}$$

Substituting (4.23) and (4.24) into (4.21) and (4.22), and equating (4.21) and (4.22) to zero,

$$2\left[\frac{\partial f}{\partial \sigma_1^2}\Sigma_1 + \frac{\partial f}{\partial \sigma_2^2}\Sigma_2\right]V = -\left[\frac{\partial f}{\partial \eta_1}M_1 + \frac{\partial f}{\partial \eta_2}M_2\right], \tag{4.25}$$

$$\frac{\partial f}{\partial \eta_1} + \frac{\partial f}{\partial \eta_2} = 0 \, . \tag{4.26}$$

Substituting (4.26) into (4.25), and solving (4.25) for V, the optimum V can be computed. However, it should be noted that the error in the h-space depends only on the direction of V, and not on the size of V. Therefore, for simplicity, we eliminate any constant term (not a function of M_i and Σ_i) multiplying to V, resulting in

$$V = [s\Sigma_1 + (1-s)\Sigma_2]^{-1}(M_2 - M_1) \, , \tag{4.27}$$

where

$$s = \frac{\partial f/\partial \sigma_1^2}{\partial f/\partial \sigma_1^2 + \partial f/\partial \sigma_2^2} \, . \tag{4.28}$$

Note that the optimum V has the form of (4.27) regardless of the selection of f. The effect of f appears only in s of (4.28). In (4.2), the Bayes classifier for normal distributions with the equal covariance matrix Σ has $V = \Sigma^{-1}(M_2 - M_1)$. Replacing this Σ by the averaged covariance matrix $[s\Sigma_1 + (1-s)\Sigma_2]$, we can obtain the optimum V of (4.27).

Once the functional form of f is selected, the optimum v_o is obtained as the solution of (4.26).

Example 2: Let us consider the *Fisher criterion* which is given by

$$f = \frac{(\eta_1 - \eta_2)^2}{\sigma_1^2 + \sigma_2^2} . \tag{4.29}$$

This criterion measures the difference of two means normalized by the averaged variance. The derivatives of f with respect to σ_1^2 and σ_2^2 are

$$\frac{\partial f}{\partial \sigma_1^2} = \frac{\partial f}{\partial \sigma_2^2} = \frac{-(\eta_1 - \eta_2)^2}{(\sigma_1^2 + \sigma_2^2)^2} . \tag{4.30}$$

Therefore, $s = 0.5$ and the optimum V is

$$V = [\frac{1}{2}\Sigma_1 + \frac{1}{2}\Sigma_2]^{-1}(M_2 - M_1) . \tag{4.31}$$

The $h(\mathbf{X})$ with V of (4.31) and the resulting linear classifier are called the *Fisher discriminant function* and *Fisher linear classifier*, respectively [2]. The Fisher criterion does not depend on v_o, because the subtraction of η_2 from η_1 eliminates v_o from (4.19). Therefore, we cannot determine the optimum v_o by maximizing this criterion.

Example 3: Another possible criterion is

$$f = \frac{P_1\eta_1^2 + P_2\eta_2^2}{P_1\sigma_1^2 + P_2\sigma_2^2} . \tag{4.32}$$

This criterion measures the *between-class scatter* (around zero) normalized by the *within-class scatter*, and will be discussed in Chapter 10. For this criterion,

$$\frac{\partial f}{\partial \sigma_i^2} = \frac{-P_i(P_1\eta_1^2 + P_2\eta_2^2)}{(P_1\sigma_1^2 + P_2\sigma_2^2)^2} . \tag{4.33}$$

Thus, $s = P_1$ and the optimum V is

$$V = [P_1\Sigma_1 + P_2\Sigma_2]^{-1}(M_2 - M_1) . \tag{4.34}$$

On the other hand,

$$\frac{\partial f}{\partial \eta_i} = \frac{2P_i\eta_i}{P_1\sigma_1^2 + P_2\sigma_2^2} . \tag{4.35}$$

Substituting (4.35) into (4.26), and rewriting (4.26) by using (4.19)

$$V^T[P_1M_1 + P_2M_2] + v_o = 0 , \tag{4.36}$$

or

$$v_o = -V^T[P_1M_1 + P_2M_2] . \tag{4.37}$$

Equation (4.37) indicates that, if V is multiplied by a constant α, v_o is also changed by a factor of α. The decision made by $V^TX + v_o \gtrless 0$ is equivalent to the decision of $\alpha V^TX + \alpha v_o \gtrless 0$ for any positive α. This confirms that the scale of V is irrelevant in our discussion.

Optimum Design for Normal Distributions

Theoretical approach: When the distributions of $h(\mathbf{X})$ are normal, we can find the V and v_0 which minimize the Bayes error in the h-space. The Bayes error in the h-space is expressed as a function of η_i and σ_i^2 as

$$\varepsilon = P_1\int_{-\eta_1/\sigma_1}^{+\infty} \frac{1}{\sqrt{2\pi}} e^{-\zeta^2/2} d\zeta + P_2\int_{-\infty}^{-\eta_2/\sigma_2} \frac{1}{\sqrt{2\pi}} e^{-\zeta^2/2}\, d\zeta . \tag{4.38}$$

For this criterion, the derivatives of ε are

$$\frac{\partial\varepsilon}{\partial\sigma_1^2} = \frac{-P_1}{\sqrt{2\pi}} e^{-(\eta_1/\sigma_1)^2/2} \frac{\eta_1}{\sigma_1^3} = \frac{P_1}{\sqrt{2\pi}\,\sigma_1} e^{-(\eta_1/\sigma_1)^2/2} \left[\frac{-\eta_1}{\sigma_1^2}\right] , \tag{4.39}$$

$$\frac{\partial\varepsilon}{\partial\sigma_2^2} = \frac{P_2}{\sqrt{2\pi}} e^{-(\eta_2/\sigma_2)^2/2} \frac{\eta_2}{\sigma_2^3} = \frac{P_2}{\sqrt{2\pi}\,\sigma_2} e^{-(\eta_2/\sigma_2)^2/2} \left[\frac{\eta_2}{\sigma_2^2}\right] , \tag{4.40}$$

$$\frac{\partial\varepsilon}{\partial\eta_1} = \frac{P_1}{\sqrt{2\pi}\,\sigma_1} e^{-(\eta_1/\sigma_1)^2/2} , \tag{4.41}$$

$$\frac{\partial\varepsilon}{\partial\eta_2} = \frac{-P_2}{\sqrt{2\pi}\,\sigma_2} e^{-(\eta_2/\sigma_2)^2/2} . \tag{4.42}$$

Therefore, from (4.26)

$$\frac{P_1}{\sqrt{2\pi}\,\sigma_1} e^{-(\eta_1/\sigma_1)^2/2} = \frac{P_2}{\sqrt{2\pi}\,\sigma_2} e^{-(\eta_2/\sigma_2)^2/2} . \tag{4.43}$$

That is, v_o must be selected to make the two density functions of $h(\mathbf{X})$ equal at $h(\mathbf{X}) = 0$. Substituting (4.43) into (4.39) and (4.40), and using (4.28)

$$s = \frac{-\eta_1/\sigma_1^2}{-\eta_1/\sigma_1^2 + \eta_2/\sigma_2^2} , \tag{4.44}$$

and

$$[s\Sigma_1 + (1-s)\Sigma_2] \, V = (M_2 - M_1) , \tag{4.45}$$

where s stays between 0 and 1 because $\eta_1 < 0$ and $\eta_2 > 0$. Thus, if we can find V and v_o which satisfy (4.43) and (4.45), these V and v_o minimize the error of (4.38) [3]. Unfortunately, since η_i and σ_i^2 are functions of V and v_o, the explicit solution of these equations has not been found. Thus, we must use an iterative procedure to find the solution.

Before discussing the iterative process, we need to develop one more equation to compute v_o from s and V. This is done by substituting η_1 and η_2 of (4.19) into (4.44), and by solving (4.44) for v_o. The result is

$$v_o = -\frac{s\sigma_1^2 V^T M_2 + (1-s)\sigma_2^2 V^T M_1}{s\sigma_1^2 + (1-s)\sigma_2^2} . \tag{4.46}$$

The iterative operation is carried out by changing the parameter s with an increment of Δs as follows [4]:

Procedure I to find s (the theoretical method):

(1) Calculate V for a given s by
$V = [s\Sigma_1 + (1-s)\Sigma_2]^{-1}(M_2 - M_1)$.

(2) Using the V obtained, compute σ_i^2 by (4.20), v_o by (4.46), and η_i by (4.19) in that sequence.

(3) Calculate ε by (4.38).

(4) Change s from 0 to 1.

The s which minimizes ε can be found from the ε vs. s plot.

The advantage of this process is that we have only one parameter s to adjust. This makes the process very much simpler than solving (4.43) and (4.45) with $n + 1$ variables.

Example 4: Data *I*-Λ is used, and ε vs. s is plotted in Fig. 4-8. As seen in Fig. 4-8, ε is not particularly sensitive to s around the optimum point.

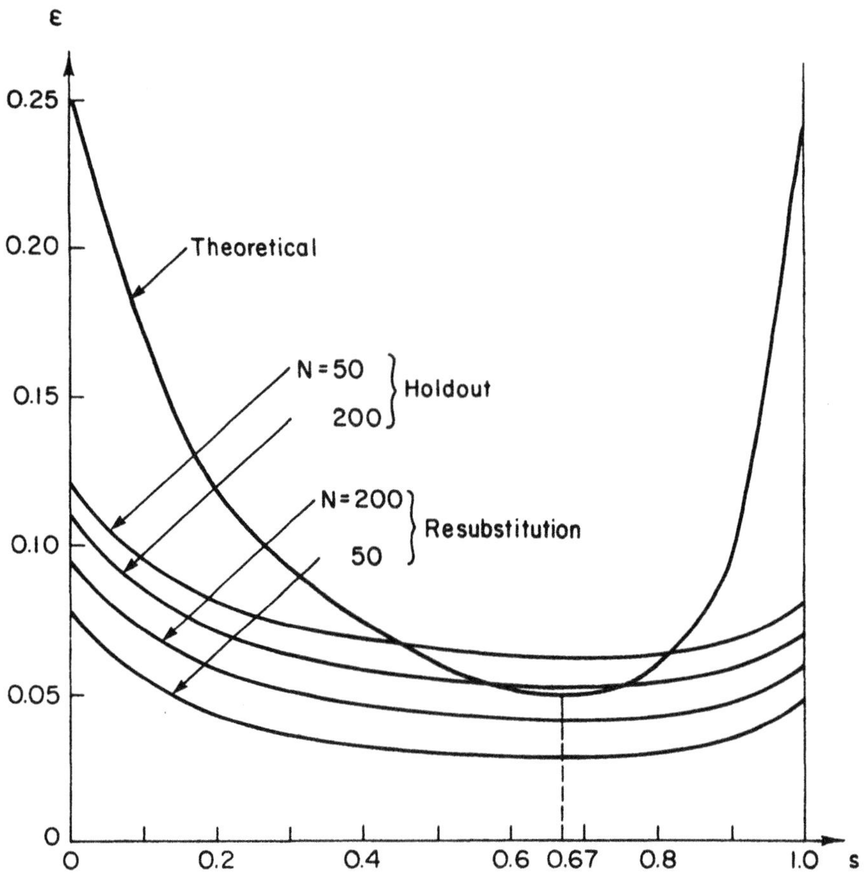

Fig. 4-8 Error vs. s.

The optimized error is 5% by the best linear discriminant function, while the Bayes classifier with a quadratic form gives 1.9%, as shown in Example 3-11.

Sample-based approach: The iterative process mentioned above is based on the closed-form expression of the error. Also, M_i and Σ_i are assumed to be given. However, if only a set of samples is available without any prior knowledge, M_i and Σ_i must be estimated. Furthermore, we could replace the error calculation by an empirical error-counting based on available samples. Assuming that N samples are available from each class, the procedure to find the optimum linear classifier is as follows.

Procedure II to find s (the resubstitution method):

(1) Compute the sample mean, $\hat{M}_i$, and sample covariance matrix, $\hat{\Sigma}_i$.

(2) Calculate V for a given s by $V = [s\hat{\Sigma}_1 + (1-s)\hat{\Sigma}_2]^{-1}(\hat{M}_2-\hat{M}_1)$.

(3) Using the V obtained, compute $y_j^{(i)} = V^T X_j^{(i)}$ $(i = 1,2;$ $j = 1, \ldots, N)$, where $X_j^{(i)}$ is the jth ω_i-sample.

(4) The $y_j^{(1)}$ and $y_j^{(2)}$'s, which do not satisfy $y_j^{(1)} < -v_o$ and $y_j^{(2)} > -v_o$, are counted as errors. Changing v_o from $-\infty$ to $+\infty$, find the v_o which gives the smallest error.

(5) Change s from 0 to 1, and plot the error vs. s.

Note that in this process no assumption is made on the distributions of **X**. Also, the criterion function, f, is never set up. Instead of using an equation for f, the empirical error-count is used. The procedure is based solely on our knowledge that the optimum V must have the form of $[s\Sigma_1 + (1-s)\Sigma_2]^{-1}(M_2-M_1)$.

In order to confirm the validity of the procedure, the following experiment was conducted.

Experiment 1: Finding the optimum s (Procedure II)
Data: I-Λ (Normal, $n = 8$, $\varepsilon = 1.9\%$)
Sample size: $N_1 = N_2 = 50, 200$
No. of trials: $\tau = 10$
Results: Fig. 4-8

Samples were generated and the error was counted according to Procedure II. The averaged error over 10 trials vs. s is plotted in Fig. 4-8. Note that the error of Procedure II is smaller than the error of Procedure I. This is due to the fact that the same samples are used for both designing and testing the classifier. This method of using available samples is called the *resubstitution method*, and produces an optimistic bias. The bias is reduced by increasing the sample size as seen in Fig. 4-8. In order to avoid this bias, we need to assure independence between design and test samples, as follows:

Procedure III to find s (the holdout method):

(1) Divide the available samples into two groups: one is called the *design sample* set, and the other is called the *test sample* set.

(2) Using the design samples, follow steps (1)-(4) of Procedure II to find the V and v_o for a given s.

(3) Using V and v_o found in step (2), classify the test samples by (4.18), and count the number of misclassified samples.

(4) Change s from 0 to 1, and plot the error vs. s.

In order to confirm the validity of Procedure III, the following experiment was conducted.

Experiment 2: Calculation of the error (Procedure III)
Data: I-Λ (Normal, $n = 8$, $\varepsilon = 1.9\%$)
Sample size: $N_1 = N_2 = 50, 200$ (Design)
$N_1 = N_2 = 50, 200$ (Test)

No. of trials: $\tau = 10$
Results: Fig. 4-8

Again, samples were generated and the error was counted according to Procedure III. The averaged error over 10 trials vs. s is plotted in Fig. 4-8. The error of this procedure is larger than the error of Procedure I at the optimum s. This method of using available samples is called the *holdout method*, and produces a pessimistic bias. As N goes to ∞, both the optimistic and pessimistic biases are reduced to zero, and the errors of Procedures II and III converge to the error of Procedure I at the optimum s. Also, Fig. 4-8 shows that Procedure I does not give as good a performance as Procedures II and III when s is not optimum. This is due to the use of (4.46) to determine v_0 for the entire region of s. Equation (4.46) is the condition for v_0 to satisfy at the optimum point. When s is not optimum, (4.46) may not be an appropriate equation to obtain the best v_0. In Data I-Λ, the two covariance matrices are significantly different. Thus, the averaged covariance $[s\Sigma_1+(1-s)\Sigma_2]$ varies wildly with s. Despite this variation, both Procedures II and III keep the error curves flat for a wide range of s by adjusting the threshold v_0. This indicates that the proper selection of v_0 is critical in classifier design.

Since Procedures II and III produce different s's, V's, v_o's, and ε's, we need to know which s, V, v_o, and ε to use. Once a classifier has been designed by using N samples and implemented, the classifier is supposed to classify samples which were never used in design. Therefore, the error of Procedure III is the one to indicate the performance of the classifier in operation. However, the error of Procedure III alone does not tell how much the error can be reduced if we use a larger number of design samples. The error of the ideal classifier, which is designed with an infinite number of design samples, lies somewhere between the errors of Procedures II and III. Therefore, in order to predict the asymptotic error experimentally, it is common practice to run both Procedures II and III. As far as the parameter selection of the classifier is concerned, we can get better estimates of these parameters by using a larger number of design samples. Therefore, if the available sample size is fixed, we had better use all samples to design the classifier. Thus, the s, V, and v_o obtained by Procedure II are the ones which must be used in classifier design.

Before leaving this subject, the reader should be reminded that the criteria discussed in this section can be used to evaluate the performance of a linear classifier regardless of whether the classifier is optimum or not. For a given linear classifier and given test distributions, η_i and σ_i^2 are computed from (4.19) and (4.20), and they are inserted into a chosen criterion to evaluate its performance. When the distributions of $\mathbf{X}$ are normal for both ω_1 and ω_2, $h(\mathbf{X})$ becomes normal. Thus, we can use the error of (4.38).

Optimum Design of a Nonlinear Classifier

So far, we have limited our discussion to a linear classifier. However, we can extend the previous discussion to a more general nonlinear classifier.

General nonlinear classifier: Let $y(X)$ be a general discriminant function with X classified according to

$$y(X) \underset{\omega_2}{\overset{\omega_1}{\gtrless}} 0 . \tag{4.47}$$

Also, let $f(\eta_1,\eta_2,s_1^2,s_2^2)$ be the criterion to be optimized with respect to $y(X)$, where

$$\eta_i = E\{y(\mathbf{X}) \mid \omega_i\} = \int y(X) p_i(X)\, dX \ , \tag{4.48}$$

$$s_i^2 = E\{y^2(\mathbf{X}) \mid \omega_i\} = \int y^2(X) p_i(X)\, dX \ . \tag{4.49}$$

Since $s_i^2 = \eta_i^2 + \sigma_i^2$, $f(\eta_1, \eta_2, s_1^2, s_2^2)$ is a function of η_1, η_2, σ_1^2, and σ_2^2 also. The reason why s_i^2 is used instead of σ_i^2 is that the second order moments are easier to handle than the central second order moments in which the means must be subtracted. The variation of f, δf, due to the variation of $y(X)$, $\delta y(X)$, is expressed by

$$\delta f = \frac{\partial f}{\partial s_1^2} \delta s_1^2 + \frac{\partial f}{\partial s_2^2} \delta s_2^2 + \frac{\partial f}{\partial \eta_1} \delta \eta_1 + \frac{\partial f}{\partial \eta_2} \delta \eta_2 \ , \tag{4.50}$$

where $\delta\eta_i$ and δs_i^2 are computed from (4.48) and (4.49) as

$$\delta \eta_i = \int \delta y(X) p_i(X)\, dX \ , \tag{4.51}$$

$$\delta s_i^2 = \int 2y(X) \delta y(X) p_i(X)\, dX \ . \tag{4.52}$$

Substituting (4.51) and (4.52) into (4.50), δf becomes

$$\delta f = \int \left[2 \left\{ \frac{\partial f}{\partial s_1^2} p_1(X) + \frac{\partial f}{\partial s_2^2} p_2(X) \right\} y(X) \right.$$

$$\left. + \left\{ \frac{\partial f}{\partial \eta_1} p_1(X) + \frac{\partial f}{\partial \eta_2} p_2(X) \right\} \right] \delta y(X)\, dX \ . \tag{4.53}$$

In order to make $\delta f = 0$ regardless of $\delta y(X)$, the $[\cdot]$ term in the integrand must be zero. Thus

$$y(X) = -\frac{1}{2}\left[\frac{\partial f}{\partial \eta_1}\frac{p_1(X)}{\frac{\partial f}{\partial s_1^2}p_1(X)+\frac{\partial f}{\partial s_2^2}p_2(X)} + \frac{\partial f}{\partial \eta_2}\frac{p_2(X)}{\frac{\partial f}{\partial s_1^2}p_1(X)+\frac{\partial f}{\partial s_2^2}p_2(X)}\right]$$

$$= a_1\frac{sp_1(X)}{sp_1(X)+(1-s)p_2(X)} + a_2\frac{(1-s)p_2(X)}{sp_1(X)+(1-s)p_2(X)} , \tag{4.54}$$

where

$$s = \frac{\partial f/\partial s_1^2}{\partial f/\partial s_1^2 + \partial f/\partial s_2^2} = \frac{\partial f/\partial \sigma_1^2}{\partial f/\partial \sigma_1^2 + \partial f/\partial \sigma_2^2} , \tag{4.55}$$

$$a_i = -\frac{\partial f/\partial \eta_i}{2\partial f/\partial s_i^2} = -\frac{\partial f/\partial \eta_i}{2\partial f/\partial \sigma_i^2} . \tag{4.56}$$

Note that $\partial f/\partial \sigma_i^2 = (\partial f/\partial s_i^2)(\partial s_i^2/\partial \sigma_i^2) = \partial f/\partial s_i^2$ since $s_i^2 = \sigma_i^2 + \eta_i^2$. The optimum solution, (4.54), may be interpreted as $y(X) = a_1 q_1(X) + a_2 q_2(X) = a_2 + (a_1 - a_2) q_1(X)$, where $q_1(X)$ is a posteriori probability function of ω_1 with a priori probability of s. On the other hand, the Bayes classifier is $q_1(X) \lessgtr q_2(X)$, and subsequently the Bayes discriminant function is $h(X) = q_2(X) - q_1(X) = 1 - 2q_1(X) \gtrless 0$. Therefore, if we seek the discriminant function by optimizing a criterion $f(\eta_1, \eta_2, s_1^2, s_2^2)$, we obtain the Bayes discriminant function as the solution, except that different constants are multiplied and added to $q_1(X)$. The difference in the added constants can be eliminated by adjusting the threshold, and the difference in the multiplied constants does not affect the decision rule, as was discussed previously.

The above result further justifies the use of the criterion $f(\eta_1, \eta_2, \sigma_1^2, \sigma_2^2)$. The criterion not only provides a simple solution for linear classifier design, but also guarantees the best solution in the Bayes sense for general nonlinear classifier design. This guarantee enhances the validity of the criterion, although the above analysis does not directly reveal the procedure for obtaining the optimum nonlinear solution.

Linear classifier: When we limit the mathematical form of $y(X)$ to $y = V^T X$, the variation of $y(X)$ comes from the variation of V. Therefore,

$$\delta y(X) = \delta V^T X \ . \tag{4.57}$$

Inserting (4.57) into (4.53), and using $y(X) = V^T X = X^T V$,

$$\delta f = \delta V^T \int \left[2XX^T V \left\{ \frac{\partial f}{\partial s_1^2} p_1(X) + \frac{\partial f}{\partial s_2^2} p_2(X) \right\} \right.$$

$$\left. + X \left\{ \frac{\partial f}{\partial \eta_1} p_1(X) + \frac{\partial f}{\partial \eta_2} p_2(X) \right\} \right] dX$$

$$= \delta V^T \left[2 \left\{ \frac{\partial f}{\partial s_1^2} S_1 + \frac{\partial f}{\partial s_2^2} S_2 \right\} V + \left\{ \frac{\partial f}{\partial \eta_1} M_1 + \frac{\partial f}{\partial \eta_2} M_2 \right\} \right] , \tag{4.58}$$

where $S_i = E\{\mathbf{X}\mathbf{X}^T | \omega_i\}$ is the autocorrelation matrix of ω_i. Since $\delta f = 0$ regardless of δV^T, $[\cdot]$ must be zero. Thus,

$$2 \left[\frac{\partial f}{\partial \sigma_1^2} S_1 + \frac{\partial f}{\partial \sigma_2^2} S_2 \right] V = - \left[\frac{\partial f}{\partial \eta_1} M_1 + \frac{\partial f}{\partial \eta_2} M_2 \right] , \tag{4.59}$$

where $\partial f / \partial s_i^2$ is replaced by $\partial f / \partial \sigma_i^2$ in order to maintain the uniformity of expressions. Note that (4.59) is the same as (4.25), except that S_i is used in (4.59) while Σ_i is used in (4.25). This is due to the difference in criteria we used; $f(\eta_1, \eta_2, s_1^2, s_2^2)$ for (4.59) and $f(\eta_1, \eta_2, \sigma_1^2, \sigma_2^2)$ for (4.25). Since $s_i^2 = \eta_i^2 + \sigma_i^2$, $f(\eta_1, \eta_2, s_1^2, s_2^2)$ is also a function of η_1, η_2, σ_1^2, and σ_2^2. Therefore, both (4.59) and (4.25) must give the same optimum V.

In order to confirm the above argument, let us prove that $V = [sS_1 + (1-s)S_2]^{-1} \ [(\partial f / \partial \eta_1) M_1 + (\partial f / \partial \eta_2) M_2]$ is the same vector as $V = [s\Sigma_1 + (1-s)\Sigma_2]^{-1} \ [(\partial f / \partial \eta_1) M_1 + (\partial f / \partial \eta_2) M_2]$ except for its length. Since the result must be independent of where the coordinate origin is, let us choose M_1 as the coordinate origin for simplicity. Then, M_1 and M_2 are replaced by 0 and $M = M_2 - M_1$. Ignoring the constant $(\partial f / \partial \eta_2)$, we start from

$$V = [sS_1 + (1-s)S_2]^{-1} M \ . \tag{4.60}$$

Since $S_1 = \Sigma_1$ and $S_2 = \Sigma_2 + MM^T$,

$$sS_1 + (1-s)S_2 = [s\Sigma_1 + (1-s)\Sigma_2] + (1-s)MM^T . \tag{4.61}$$

Using (2.160),

$$\bar{S}^{-1} = \bar{\Sigma}^{-1} - \frac{(1-s)\bar{\Sigma}^{-1}MM^T\bar{\Sigma}^{-1}}{1 + (1-s)M^T\bar{\Sigma}^{-1}M} , \tag{4.62}$$

where $\bar{S} = [sS_1+(1-s)S_2]$ and $\bar{\Sigma} = [s\Sigma_1+(1-s)\Sigma_2]$. Multiplying M from the right side,

$$\bar{S}^{-1}M = \bar{\Sigma}^{-1}M - \frac{(1-s)M^T\bar{\Sigma}^{-1}M}{1 + (1-s)M^T\bar{\Sigma}^{-1}M}\bar{\Sigma}^{-1}M$$

$$= \frac{1}{1 + (1-s)M^T\bar{\Sigma}^{-1}M}\bar{\Sigma}^{-1}M . \tag{4.63}$$

That is, $\bar{S}^{-1}M$ and $\bar{\Sigma}^{-1}M$ are the same vector except for their lengths.

Minimum Mean-Square Error

The mean-square error is a popular criterion in optimization problems. Therefore, in this section, we will study how the concept of the mean-square error may be applied to linear classifier design.

Let $\gamma(X)$ be the *desired output* of the classifier which we would like to design. The possible functional forms for $\gamma(X)$ will be presented later. Then, the mean-square error between the actual and desired outputs is

$$\bar{\varepsilon}^2 = E\{(h(\mathbf{X}) - \gamma(\mathbf{X}))^2\}$$

$$= E\{h^2(\mathbf{X})\} - 2E\{h(\mathbf{X})\gamma(\mathbf{X})\} + E\{\gamma^2(\mathbf{X})\} . \tag{4.64}$$

We minimize this criterion with respect to V and v_o. Since the third term of (4.64) is not a function of V and v_o, the minimization is carried out for the summation of the first and second terms only.

Two different functional forms of $\gamma(X)$ are presented here as follows:

(1) *$\gamma(X) = -1$ for $X \in \omega_1$ and $+1$ for $X \in \omega_2$*: Since $h(X)$ is supposed to be either negative or positive, depending on $X \in \omega_1$ or $X \in \omega_2$, -1 and $+1$ for $\gamma(X)$ are a reasonable choice. Then

$$E\{h(\mathbf{X})\gamma(\mathbf{X})\} = P_1\, E\{h(\mathbf{X})(-1)\,|\,\omega_1\} + P_2\, E\{h(\mathbf{X})(+1)\,|\,\omega_2\}$$

$$= -P_1\eta_1 + P_2\eta_2 \,. \tag{4.65}$$

On the other hand, the first term of (4.64), $E\{h^2(\mathbf{X})\}$, is the second order moment of $h(\mathbf{X})$, and is expressed by

$$E\{h^2(\mathbf{X})\} = P_1(\sigma_1^2 + \eta_1^2) + P_2(\sigma_2^2 + \eta_2^2) \,. \tag{4.66}$$

Therefore, $\overline{\varepsilon}^2$ is a function of η_1, η_2, σ_1^2, and σ_2^2. Since $\partial\overline{\varepsilon}^2/\partial\sigma_i^2 = P_i$, the optimum V according to (4.27) is

$$V = [P_1\Sigma_1 + P_2\Sigma_2]^{-1}(M_2 - M_1) \,. \tag{4.67}$$

(2) $\gamma(X) = q_2(X) - q_1(X)$: This is the Bayes discriminant function (recalling $q_1(X) \lessgtr q_2(X)$ or $h(X) = q_2(X) - q_1(X) \gtrless 0$). Therefore, if we can match the designed discriminant function with the Bayes one, the result must be desirable. For this $\gamma(X)$,

$$E\{h(\mathbf{X})\gamma(\mathbf{X})\} = \int h(X)\frac{P_2 p_2(X) - P_1 p_1(X)}{p(X)}\, p(X)\, dX$$

$$= P_2\int h(X)p_2(X)\, dX - P_1\int h(X)p_1(X)\, dX$$

$$= P_2\eta_2 - P_1\eta_1 \,, \tag{4.68}$$

which is identical to (4.65). Also, note that $E\{h^2(\mathbf{X})\}$ is not affected by $\gamma(\mathbf{X})$, and is equal to (4.66).

Thus, for both cases, the mean-square error expressions become the same except for the constant term $E\{\gamma^2(\mathbf{X})\}$, and the resulting optimum classifiers are the same. Also, note that the mean-square errors for these $\gamma(X)$'s are a special case of a general criterion function $f(\eta_1,\eta_2,\sigma_1^2,\sigma_2^2)$. This is not surprising, since the mean-square error consists of the first and second order moments of $h(\mathbf{X})$. However, it is possible to make the mean-square error a different type of criterion than $f(\eta_1,\eta_2,\sigma_1^2,\sigma_2^2)$ by selecting $\gamma(X)$ in a different way. This is the subject of the next section.

Other Desired Outputs and Search Techniques

In pattern recognition, the classifier should be designed by using samples near the decision boundary; samples far from the decision boundary are less important to the design. However, if we fix the desired output $\gamma(\mathbf{X})$ and try to minimize the mean-square error between $h(\mathbf{X})$ and $\gamma(\mathbf{X})$, larger $h(\mathbf{X})$'s contribute more to the mean-square error. This has long been recognized as a disadvantage of a mean-square error approach in pattern recognition. In this section, we discuss a modification which reduces this effect.

New notation for the discriminant function: Before proceeding, let us introduce new notations which will simplify the discussion later. Instead of (4.18), we will write the linear discriminant function as

$$h(X) = -V^T X - v_o > 0 \quad \text{for} \quad X \in \omega_1 \,, \tag{4.69}$$

$$h(X) = V^T X + v_o > 0 \quad \text{for} \quad X \in \omega_2 \,. \tag{4.70}$$

Furthermore, if we introduce a new vector to express a sample as

$$Z = [-1 \; -x_1 \; \ldots \; -x_n]^T \quad \text{for} \quad X \in \omega_1 \,, \tag{4.71}$$

$$Z = [+1 \; x_1 \; \ldots \; x_n]^T \quad \text{for} \quad X \in \omega_2 \,, \tag{4.72}$$

then, the discriminant function becomes simply

$$h(Z) = W^T Z = \sum_{i=0}^{n} w_i z_i > 0 \,, \tag{4.73}$$

where z_0 is either +1 or −1, and $w_i = v_i$ $(i = 0, 1, \ldots, n)$.

Thus, our design procedure is

(1) to generate a new set of vectors Z's from X's, and

(2) to find W^T so as to satisfy (4.73) for as many Z's as possible.

Desired outputs: Using the notation of (4.73), new desired outputs will be introduced. Also, the expectation in (4.64) is replaced by the sample mean to obtain the following mean-square errors:

(1)
$$\bar{\varepsilon}^2 = \frac{1}{N}\sum_{j=1}^{N}\{W^T Z_j - |W^T Z_j|\}^2 , \tag{4.74}$$

(2)
$$\bar{\varepsilon}^2 = \frac{1}{N}\sum_{j=1}^{N}\{sign(W^T Z_j) - 1\}^2 , \tag{4.75}$$

(3)
$$\bar{\varepsilon}^2 = \frac{1}{N}\sum_{j=1}^{N}\{W^T Z_j - \gamma(Z_j)\}^2 , \tag{4.76}$$

$\gamma(Z_j)$: *a variable with constraint* $\gamma(Z_j) > 0$,

where N is the total number of samples, and $sign(\cdot)$ is either +1 or −1 depending on the sign of its argument. In (4.74), $\gamma(Z_j)$ is selected as $|W^T Z_j|$ so that, only when $W^T Z_j < 0$, the contribution to $\bar{\varepsilon}^2$ is made with $(W^T Z_j)^2$ weighting. On the other hand, (4.75) counts the number of samples which give $W^T Z_j < 0$. In the third criterion, we adjust $\gamma(Z_j)$ as variables along with W. However, the $\gamma(Z_j)$'s are constrained to be positive.

These criteria perform well, but, because of the nonlinear functions such as $|\cdot|$, $sign(\cdot)$, and $\gamma(Z_j) > 0$, the explicit solutions of W which minimize these criteria are hard to obtain. Therefore, a search technique, such as the gradient method, must be used to find the optimum W.

The gradient method for minimizing a criterion is given by

$$W(\ell + 1) = W(\ell) - \rho \frac{\partial \bar{\varepsilon}^2}{\partial W} \Big|_{W(\ell)} , \tag{4.77}$$

where ℓ indicates the ℓth iterative step, and ρ is a positive constant.

Again, we cannot calculate $\partial \bar{\varepsilon}^2 / \partial W$ because of the nonlinear functions involved in $\bar{\varepsilon}^2$. However, in the linear case of (4.64), $\partial \bar{\varepsilon}^2 / \partial W$ can be obtained as follows. Replacing the expectation of (4.64) by the sample mean,

$$\overline{\varepsilon}^2 = \frac{1}{N}\sum_{j=1}^{N}\{W^T Z_j - \gamma(Z_j)\}^2$$

$$= \frac{1}{N}(U^T W - \Gamma)^T (U^T W - \Gamma) , \tag{4.78}$$

where

$$U = [Z_1 \ldots Z_N]_{(n+1)\times N} , \tag{4.79}$$

$$\Gamma = [\gamma(Z_1) \ldots \gamma(Z_N)]^T . \tag{4.80}$$

The U and Γ are called the *sample matrix* and the *desired output vector*, respectively. Taking the derivative of (4.78) with respect to W,

$$\frac{\partial \overline{\varepsilon}^2}{\partial W} = \frac{2}{N} U (U^T W - \Gamma) . \tag{4.81}$$

By analogy to (4.81), the following correction terms have been suggested for the criteria [5]:

(1) $$W(\ell + 1) = W(\ell) - \frac{2\rho}{N} U [U^T W(\ell) - | U^T W(\ell) |] , \tag{4.82}$$

(2) $$W(\ell + 1) = W(\ell) - \frac{2\rho}{N} U [sign\{U^T W(\ell)\} - \Gamma_0 \}] , \tag{4.83}$$

(3) $$W(\ell + 1) = W(\ell) - \frac{2\rho}{N} U [U^T W(\ell) - \Gamma(\ell)] , \tag{4.84}$$

$$\Gamma(\ell + 1) = \Gamma(\ell) + \frac{2\rho}{N} [U^T W(\ell) - \Gamma(\ell)] + L(\ell) , \tag{4.85}$$

where

(a) $|U^T W|$ is a vector whose components are the absolute values of the corresponding components of $U^T W$;

(b) $sign(U^T W)$ is a vector whose components are +1 or −1 depending on the signs of the corresponding components of $U^T W$;

(c) $\Gamma_0 = [1 \ 1 \ \ldots \ 1]^T$;

(d) $L(\ell)$ is a penalty vector whose components are functions of the corresponding components of $\Gamma(\ell)$.

A different approach is to treat the problem of finding a feasible solution of (4.73) as a linear programming problem with an artificially created cost vector. For this approach, it is suggested that the reader refers to a text in linear programming.

A word of caution is in order here. In addition to its complexity, all of the above approaches have a more fundamental disadvantage. For examples of (4.82) and (4.83), the classifier is designed, based only on the misclassified samples in the boundary region. For a good classifier the number of the misclassified samples tends to be small, and sometimes it is questionable whether these samples represent the true statistics of the boundary structure. As the result, the resubstitution error, using the same sample set for both design and test, tends to be severely biased toward the optimistic side. Therefore, it is advisable that independent samples always be used to test the performance of the classifier.

An iterative process and its convergence: In order to see how the iterative process works, let us consider the third criterion of (4.76), in which $\gamma(Z_j)$ are adjusted along with W under the constraint $\gamma(Z_j) > 0$. Also, let us assume that our coordinate system has already been transformed to whiten the sample covariance matrix, such that

$$UU^T = NI \,. \tag{4.86}$$

Since the result of the procedure should not depend on the coordinate system, this transformation simplifies the discussion without loss of generality. Then the mean-square error becomes

$$\overline{\varepsilon}^2 = \frac{1}{N}(W^TU-\Gamma^T)(U^TW-\Gamma) = W^TW-\frac{2}{N}W^TU\Gamma+\frac{1}{N}\Gamma^T\Gamma \,. \tag{4.87}$$

The gradients of $\overline{\varepsilon}^2$ with respect to W and Γ are

$$\frac{\partial\overline{\varepsilon}^2}{\partial W} = 2(W - \frac{1}{N}U\Gamma) \,, \tag{4.88}$$

$$\frac{\partial\overline{\varepsilon}^2}{\partial \Gamma} = \frac{2}{N}(\Gamma - U^TW) \,. \tag{4.89}$$

In order to satisfy the constraint $\gamma(Z_j) > 0$, a modification is made as follows:

(1) Positiveness of the γ's can be guaranteed if we start with positive numbers and never decrease their values.

This can be done by modifying Γ in proportion to

$$\Delta\Gamma = C + |C| \tag{4.90}$$

instead of C, where

$$C = U^T W - \Gamma . \tag{4.91}$$

Thus, the components of the vector $\Delta\Gamma$ are positive or zero, depending on whether the corresponding components of C are positive or negative. Thus, $\Gamma(\ell + 1)$ is

$$\Gamma(\ell + 1) = \Gamma(\ell) + \rho\,\Delta\Gamma = \Gamma(\ell) + \rho(C + |C|) , \tag{4.92}$$

where ρ is a properly selected positive constant. In this process, the γ's are always increased at each iterative step, and W is adjusted to reduce the error between $\gamma(Z_j)$ and $W^T Z_j$. However, one should be reminded that the scale of γ's and, subsequently, the scale of W does not change the essential structure of the classifier. That is, $W^T Z_j$ is the same classifier as $\alpha W^T Z_j$ where α is a positive constant.

(2) On the other hand, there are no restrictions on W. Therefore, for a given Γ, we can select W to satisfy $\partial \overline{\varepsilon^2} / \partial W = 0$ in (4.88).

$$W = \frac{1}{N} U \Gamma \tag{4.93}$$

or,

$$W(\ell + 1) = \frac{1}{N} U \Gamma(\ell + 1) = \frac{1}{N} \{ U\Gamma(\ell) + \rho U\, \Delta\Gamma(\ell) \}$$

$$= W(\ell) + \frac{\rho}{N} U\, \Delta\Gamma(\ell) . \tag{4.94}$$

$W(\ell + 1)$ minimizes $\overline{\varepsilon^2}$ for a given $\Gamma(\ell + 1)$ at each iterative step.

In order to see how W converges by this optimization process, let us study the norm of C. The vector C makes the correction for both Γ and W. Also, from (4.91) and (4.87),

$$\|C\|^2 = 0 \quad \to \quad U^T W = \Gamma \quad \to \quad \bar{\varepsilon}^2 = 0 \,. \tag{4.95}$$

As ℓ increases, the change of $\|C(\ell)\|^2$ can be calculated by substituting (4.92) and (4.94) into (4.91). The result is

$$\|C(\ell+1)\|^2 - \|C(\ell)\|^2$$

$$= -2\rho C^T(\ell)[I - \frac{U^T U}{N}]\Delta\Gamma(\ell) + \rho^2 \Delta\Gamma^T(\ell)[I - \frac{U^T U}{N}]\Delta\Gamma(\ell) \,. \tag{4.96}$$

On the other hand, from (4.91), (4.93), and (4.86),

$$C^T U^T U = (W^T U - \Gamma^T) U^T U = (N W^T - \Gamma^T U^T) U = 0 \tag{4.97}$$

and

$$2C^T \Delta\Gamma = \{(C + |C|)^T + (C - |C|)^T\}(C + |C|)$$

$$= (C + |C|)^T (C + |C|) = \Delta\Gamma^T \Delta\Gamma \,. \tag{4.98}$$

Therefore, (4.96) can be simplified as

$$\|C(\ell+1)\|^2 - \|C(\ell)\|^2 = -\Delta\Gamma^T(\ell)[\rho^2 \frac{U^T U}{N} + (\rho - \rho^2) I]\, \Delta\Gamma(\ell)$$

$$= -[\rho^2 \frac{\|U\, \Delta\Gamma(\ell)\|^2}{N} + (\rho - \rho^2)\|\Delta\Gamma(\ell)\|^2] \leq 0$$

$$\text{for } 0 < \rho < 1 \,. \tag{4.99}$$

The equality holds only when $\|\Delta\Gamma\|^2 = 0$. Thus, as ℓ increases, $\|C(\ell)\|^2$ decreases monotonically, until $\|\Delta\Gamma\|^2$ equals zero. It means either $\|C\|^2 = 0$ or $C = -|C|$ from (4.90). When $\|C\|^2 = 0$, we can achieve $\bar{\varepsilon}^2 = 0$ [see (4.95)]. On the other hand, when $C = -|C|$, all components of C become negative or zero and the iteration stops with $U^T W \leq \Gamma$ satisfied from (4.91).

Linearly separable cases: When there exists a linear classifier to separate two distributions without error, we call this *linearly separable*. We will prove here that $C = -|C|$ never happens in linearly separable cases. This is done by establishing a contradiction as follows.

For a linearly separable case, there exists a W^* for a given U which satisfies

$$U^T W^* > 0 . \tag{4.100}$$

Therefore, if $C = -|C|$ (or $C \le 0$) occurs at the ℓth iterative step,

$$C^T(U^T W^*) = (UC)^T W^* < 0 . \tag{4.101}$$

On the other hand, using (4.91), (4.86), and (4.93), UC can be obtained as

$$\begin{aligned} UC &= U(U^T W(\ell) - \Gamma(\ell)) \\ &= NW(\ell) - U\Gamma(\ell) \\ &= 0 . \end{aligned} \tag{4.102}$$

This contradict (4.101), and $C = -|C|$ cannot happen.

Thus, the inequality of (4.99) holds only when $\|C\|^2 = 0$. That is, $\|C(\ell)\|^2$ continues to decrease monatonically with ℓ until $\|C\|^2$ equals zero.

4.3 Quadratic Classifier Design

When the distributions of **X** are normal for both ω_1 and ω_2, the Bayes discriminant function becomes the quadratic equation of (4.1). Even for non-normal **X**, the quadratic classifier is a popular one: it works well for many applications. Conceptually, it is easy to accept that the classification be made by comparing the normalized distances $(X - M_i)^T \Sigma_i^{-1} (X - M_i)$ with a proper threshold.

However, very little is known about how to design a quadratic classifier, except for estimating M_i and Σ_i and inserting these estimates into (4.1). Also, quadratic classifiers may have a severe disadvantage in that they tend to have significantly larger biases than linear classifiers particularly when the number of design samples are relatively small. This problem will be addressed in Chapter 5.

Design Procedure of a Quadratic Classifier

The general quadratic classifier may be expressed as

$$h(X) = X^T Q X + V^T X + v_o \underset{\omega_2}{\overset{\omega_1}{\gtrless}} 0 , \tag{4.103}$$

where Q, V, and v_o are a matrix, vector, and scalar, respectively. Therefore, we can optimize $f(\eta_1,\eta_2,\sigma_1^2,\sigma_2^2)$ ($\eta_i = E\{h(\mathbf{X})|\omega_i\}$ and $\sigma_i^2 = \text{Var}\{h(\mathbf{X})|\omega_i\}$) with respect to Q, V, and v_o as was done in linear classifier design. Unfortunately, the number of parameters, $[n(n+1)/2]+n+1$, is too large, and σ_i^2 is the function of the third and fourth order moments of $\mathbf{X}$. Therefore, it is not practical to optimize $f(\eta_1,\eta_2,\sigma_1^2,\sigma_2^2)$.

Linearization: Another possibility is to interpret (4.103) as a linear equation as

$$h(X) = \sum_{i=1}^{n}\sum_{j=1}^{n} q_{ij} x_i x_j + \sum_{i=1}^{n} v_i x_i + v_o$$

$$= \sum_{i=1}^{\frac{n(n+1)}{2}} \alpha_i y_i + \sum_{i=1}^{n} v_i x_i + v_o , \tag{4.104}$$

where q_{ij} and v_i are the components of Q and V. Each of the new variables, y_i, represents the product of two x's, and α is the corresponding q. Since (4.104) is a linear discriminant function, we can apply the optimum design procedure for a linear classifier, resulting in

$$[\alpha_1 \ldots \alpha_{n(n+1)/2} v_1 \ldots v_n]^T = [s K_1 + (1-s)K_2]^{-1}(D_2 - D_1) , \tag{4.105}$$

where D_i and K_i are the expected vector and covariance matrix of $Z = [Y^T X^T]^T$ with $[n(n+1)/2]+n$ variables. Since the y's are the product of two x's, K_i includes the third and fourth order moments of $\mathbf{X}$. Again, the number of variables is too large to compute (4.105) in practice.

Data display: A practical solution to improve the quadratic classifier of (4.1) is to plot samples in a coordinate system, where $d_1^2(X) =$

$(X-M_1)^T\Sigma_1^{-1}(X-M_1)$ and $d_2^2(X) = (X-M_2)^T\Sigma_2^{-1}(X-M_2)$ are used as the x- and y-axes respectively, and to draw the classifier boundary by using human judgement. Figure 4-9 shows an example where the data used for this plot was a 40-dimensional radar signature. If the density functions of $\mathbf{X}$ are normal for both ω_1 and ω_2, the Bayes classifier is a 45° line with the y-cross point determined by $\ln |\Sigma_1|/|\Sigma_2|$ ($P_1 = P_2 = 0.5$ in this data), as seen in (4.1). In Fig. 4-9, it is seen that the Bayes classifier for normal distributions is not the best

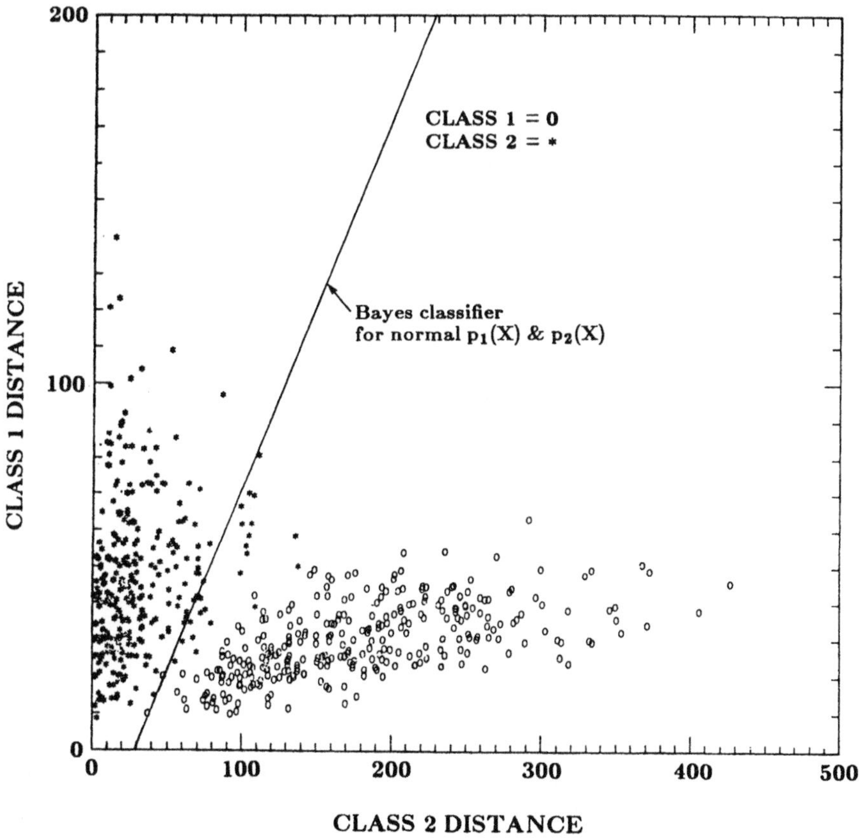

Fig. 4-9 d^2-display of a radar data.

classifier for this data. Changing both the slope and y-cross point, we can set up a better boundary. Or, we could even adopt a curve (not a straight line) for the classifier. That is,

$$d_2^2 = \alpha\, d_1^2 + \beta \tag{4.106}$$

or

$$d_2^2 = g\,(d_1^2)\ . \tag{4.107}$$

In a high-dimensional space, we cannot plot samples to see the distribution. Therefore, we must rely on mathematical tools to guide us in finding a reasonable boundary. Once samples are mapped down to a two-dimensional space as in Fig. 4-9, we can see the distribution and use our own judgement to set up the boundary. However, the structure of the boundary should not be too complex, because the boundary must work not only for the current, existing samples but also for samples which will come in the future. We can always draw a very complex boundary to classify the existing samples without error, but the boundary may misclassify many of the future samples.

Stationary Processes

The quadratic classifier for stationary processes: When $\mathbf{x}_i$ is the ith time-sampled value of a *stationary random process*, $\mathbf{x}(t)$, the contribution of $\mathbf{x}_i$ in the discriminant function must be independent of i. The same is true for $\mathbf{x}_i^2$ and $\mathbf{x}_i\mathbf{x}_{i+j}$ for fixed j's. Therefore, (4.104) may be simplified to

$$h(X) = q_o(\sum_{i=1}^{n} x_i^2) + 2q_1(\sum_{i=1}^{n-1} x_i x_{i+1}) + \ldots + 2q_{n-1}(x_1 x_n)$$

$$+\, v(\sum_{i=1}^{n} x_i) + v_o\ . \tag{4.108}$$

This is a linear discriminant function of new variables, $y_o = \Sigma x_i^2$, $y_1 = \Sigma x_i x_{i+1}, \ldots, y_{n-1} = x_1 x_n$, $y_n = \Sigma x_i$. However, now the number of variables is reduced to $n+1$, and we need to find only $n+2$ coefficients, $q_0, \ldots, q_{n-1}$, v, and v_0.

Orthonormality of the Fourier transform: Stationary processes have another desirable property, namely that the elements of the *(discrete) Fourier transform*, $\mathbf{F}(k)$ and $\mathbf{F}(\ell)$, of the process are uncorrelated. In order to show this, let us define the discrete Fourier transform of the time-sampled values of a random process, $\mathbf{x}(0), \ldots, \mathbf{x}(n-1)$, as

$$F(k) = \sum_{\ell=0}^{n-1} x(\ell) W^{k\ell} \qquad (k = 0, \ldots, n-1) , \tag{4.109}$$

where W is

$$W = e^{-j\frac{2\pi}{n}} \tag{4.110}$$

and W satisfies

$$\sum_{k=0}^{n-1} W^{k\ell} = \begin{cases} n & \text{for } \ell = 0 \\ 0 & \text{for } \ell \neq 0 . \end{cases} \tag{4.111}$$

Then, the inverse Fourier transform becomes

$$x(\ell) = \frac{1}{n} \sum_{k=0}^{n-1} F(k) W^{-k\ell} \qquad (\ell = 0, \ldots, n-1) . \tag{4.112}$$

In a stationary process, the first and second order moments of $\mathbf{x}(k)$ must satisfy

$$m = E\{\mathbf{x}(k)\} , \tag{4.113}$$

$$R(k-\ell) = E\{\mathbf{x}(k)\mathbf{x}(\ell)\} , \tag{4.114}$$

where m and $R(\cdot)$ are called the *mean* and *autocorrelation function* of the process. We assume that the process is real. Note that m is independent of k, and $R(\cdot)$ depends only on the difference between k and ℓ and is independent of k itself.

Using (4.113) and (4.114), the expected values and second order moments of the $\mathbf{F}(k)$'s can be computed as follows.

$$E\{\mathbf{F}(k)\} = m\sum_{\ell=0}^{n-1} W^{k\ell} = \begin{cases} nm & \text{for } k = 0 \\ 0 & \text{for } k \neq 0 , \end{cases} \tag{4.115}$$

$$E\{\mathbf{F}(k)\mathbf{F}^*(\ell)\} = \sum_{r=0}^{n-1}\sum_{s=0}^{n-1} E\{\mathbf{x}(r)\mathbf{x}(s)\} W^{kr} W^{-\ell s}$$

$$= \sum_{r=1}^{n-1}\sum_{s=0}^{n-1} R(r-s) W^{k(r-s)} W^{(k-\ell)s}$$

$$= \sum_{u=0}^{n-1}\sum_{s=0}^{n-1} R(u) W^{ku} W^{(k-\ell)s}$$

$$= \left(\sum_{u=0}^{n-1} R(u) W^{ku}\right)\left(\sum_{s=0}^{n-1} W^{(k-\ell)s}\right)$$

$$= \begin{cases} n\sum_{u=0}^{n-1} R(u) W^{ku} & \text{for } k = \ell \\ 0 & \text{for } k \neq \ell , \end{cases} \tag{4.116}$$

where $R(r-s) = R(s-r)$ for a real $\mathbf{x}(t)$ is used to derive the third line from the second, and $F^*(\ell)$ is the complex conjugate of $F(\ell)$. The variances and covariances of the $\mathbf{F}(k)$'s are

$$\text{Var}\{\mathbf{F}(k)\} = E\{\mathbf{F}(k)\mathbf{F}^*(k)\} - E\{\mathbf{F}(k)\}E\{\mathbf{F}^*(k)\}$$

$$= \begin{cases} n\sum_{u=0}^{n-1} R(u) - n^2 m^2 & \text{for } k = 0 \\ n\sum_{u=1}^{n-1} R(u) W^{ku} & \text{for } k \neq 0 , \end{cases} \tag{4.117}$$

and

$$\mathrm{Cov}\{\mathbf{F}(k),\mathbf{F}(\ell)\} = E\{\mathbf{F}(k)\mathbf{F}^*(\ell)\} - E\{\mathbf{F}(k)\}E\{\mathbf{F}^*(\ell)\}$$

$$= 0 \quad \text{for} \quad k \neq \ell \, . \tag{4.118}$$

That is, $\mathbf{F}(k)$ and $\mathbf{F}(\ell)$ are uncorrelated. It means that the covariance matrices of $\mathbf{X}$ for all classes are simultaneously diagonalized by the Fourier transform, if the random processes are stationary.

The quadratic classifier in the Fourier domain: Thus, if the $\mathbf{F}(k)$'s are normally distributed, we can design a quadratic classifier in the Fourier domain as

$$h = \frac{1}{2}\sum_{j=0}^{n-1} v_{1j}\,|F(j) - E\{\mathbf{F}(j)|\omega_1\}|^2 - \frac{1}{2}\sum_{j=0}^{n-1} v_{2j}\,|F(j) - E\{\mathbf{F}(j)|\omega_2\}|^2$$

$$+ v_o \, , \tag{4.119}$$

where

$$v_{ij} = \frac{1}{\mathrm{Var}\{\mathbf{F}(j)|\omega_i\}} \, , \tag{4.120}$$

$$v_o = \frac{1}{2}\sum_{j=0}^{n-1} \ln \frac{\mathrm{Var}\{\mathbf{F}(j)|\omega_1\}}{\mathrm{Var}\{\mathbf{F}(j)|\omega_2\}} \, . \tag{4.121}$$

Note in (4.119) that, since the covariance matrices of the $\mathbf{F}(j)$'s for both ω_1 and ω_2 are diagonal, all cross terms between $\mathbf{F}(j)$ and $\mathbf{F}(k)$ disappear.

A modification of the quadratic classifier can be made by treating (4.119) as a linear classifier and finding the optimum v_{1j}, v_{2j}, and v_o instead of using (4.120) and (4.121). In this approach, we need to optimize only $2n+1$ parameters, v_{ij} ($i = 1,2;\ j = 0,\ldots,n-1$) and v_0.

Approximation of Covariance Matrices

Most of the difficulty in designing quadratic classifiers comes from the covariance matrices. If we could impose some structure on the covariance matrix, it would become much easier to design a quadratic classifier. Also, the required design sample size would be reduced, and the classifier would become more insensitive to variations in the test distributions. One possible structure is the *toeplitz form*, based on the stationarity assumption. An example is seen in (3.13). However, the stationarity assumption is too restrictive and is not well suited to most applications in pattern recognition.

Toeplitz approximation of a correlation matrix: Another possibility is to assume the *toeplitz form only for the correlation matrices*, allowing each individual variable to have its own mean and variance. That is, departing from (4.113) and (4.114)

$$m_k = E\{\mathbf{x}(k)\} , \tag{4.122}$$

$$R(k-\ell) = E\{\mathbf{x}(k)\mathbf{x}(\ell)\} = \sigma_k \sigma_\ell \rho_{|k-\ell|} + m_k m_\ell , \tag{4.123}$$

where $\sigma_k^2 = \text{Var}\{\mathbf{x}(k)\}$, and $\rho_{|k-\ell|}$ is the correlation coefficient between $\mathbf{x}(k)$ and $\mathbf{x}(\ell)$ which depends only on $|k-\ell|$. Expressing the covariance matrix as $\Sigma = \Gamma R \Gamma$ from (2.18), the inverse matrix and the determinant are

$$\Sigma^{-1} = \Gamma^{-1} R^{-1} \Gamma^{-1}$$

$$= \begin{bmatrix} 1/\sigma_1 & & 0 \\ & \ddots & \\ 0 & & 1/\sigma_n \end{bmatrix} \begin{bmatrix} 1 & \rho_1 & \cdots & \rho_{n-1} \\ \rho_1 & 1 & & \vdots \\ \vdots & & \ddots & \rho_1 \\ \rho_{n-1} & \cdots & \rho_1 & 1 \end{bmatrix}^{-1} \begin{bmatrix} 1/\sigma_1 & & 0 \\ & \ddots & \\ 0 & & 1/\sigma_n \end{bmatrix} , \tag{4.124}$$

$$\ln |\Sigma| = \ln |\Gamma||R||\Gamma|$$

$$= \sum_{i=1}^{n} \ln \sigma_i^2 + \ln |R| . \tag{4.125}$$

Thus, we can focus our attention on R^{-1} and $\ln|R|$. A particular form of the toeplitz matrix, (3.13), has the closed forms for the inverse and determinant as seen in (3.14) and (3.15). Rewritting these.

$$R = \begin{bmatrix} 1 & \rho & \cdots & \rho^{n-1} \\ \rho & 1 & & \vdots \\ \vdots & & \ddots & \rho \\ \rho^{n-1} & \cdots & \rho & 1 \end{bmatrix} , \tag{4.126}$$

$$R^{-1} = \frac{1}{1-\rho^2} \begin{bmatrix} 1 & -\rho & 0 & \cdots & 0 \\ -\rho & 1+\rho^2 & \ddots & \ddots & \vdots \\ 0 & \ddots & \ddots & & 0 \\ \vdots & \ddots & & 1+\rho^2 & -\rho \\ 0 & \cdots & 0 & -\rho & 1 \end{bmatrix} , \tag{4.127}$$

$$|R| = (1-\rho^2)^{n-1} . \tag{4.128}$$

Thus, using (4.126) as the form to approximate the correlation matrix, the estimation process of an approximated covariance matrix is given as follows:

(1) Estimate σ_i^2 by the sample variance, $\hat{\sigma}_i^2$.

(2) Estimate $c_{i,i+1} = \rho_{i,i+1}\sigma_i\sigma_{i+1}$ by the sample covariance, $\hat{c}_{i,i+1}$, and divide $\hat{c}_{i,i+1}$ by $\hat{\sigma}_i\hat{\sigma}_{i+1}$ to obtain the estimate of $\hat{\rho}_{i,i+1}$.

(3) Average $\hat{\rho}_{i,i+1}$ over $i = 1, \ldots, n-1$, to get $\hat{\rho}$.

(4) Insert $\hat{\rho}$ into (4.126) to form $\hat{R}$.

Note that only $(n+1)$ parameters, σ_i $(i = 1, \ldots, n)$ and ρ, are used to approximate a covariance matrix.

Example 5: Figure 4-10 shows the correlation matrix for Camaro of Data RADAR. The radar transmitted a left circular electro-magnetic wave, and received left and right circular waves, depending on whether the wave bounced an even or odd number of times off the target surface. With 33 time-sampled values from each return, we form a vector with 66 variables. The first 33 are from the left-left and the latter 33 are from the left-right. The two triangular parts of Fig. 4-10 show the correlation matrices of the left-left and left-right. In both matrices, adjacent time-sampled variables are seen to be highly correlated, but the correlation disappears quickly as the intervals between two sampling points increase. The ith sampling point of the left-left and the ith sampling point of the left-right are the returns from the same target area. Therefore, they are somewhat correlated, which is seen in the rectangular part of Fig. 4-10.

The toeplitz form of (4.126) cannot approximate the rectangular part of Fig. 4-10 properly. Therefore, we need to modify the form of the approximation. The structure of Fig. 4-10 is often seen in practice, whenever several signals are observed from the same source. In the radar system of Example 5, we have two returns. In infrared sensors, it is common to observe several wavelength components. Furthermore, if we extend our discussion to two-dimensional images, the need for the form of Fig. 4-10 becomes more evident as follows.

Block toeplitz: Let $\mathbf{x}(i,j)$ be a variable sampled at the i,j position in a two-dimensional random field as illustrated in Fig. 4-11. Also, let us assume toeplitz forms for correlation coefficients as

```
+51111111110abb001111211111122112 211110a1121bcbb01111111111111112
 +621111110a0bb01110111111111112 121110a1111bccba1112111111111111
  +521111110abb0111a112111111122 12111000111bbcba1111111211111111
   +5111011abbaa1110111111111111 11111000111abbb01111111112212211
    +411111aaab01111111101111111 11111001111bbbb01111111112111111
     +52100abbb000111111101111121 1111112221accccba011111211112111
      +741bcdddbbb01111221111111 1211234431beeeddcba12112210111111
       +73aceeeccc012212211111111 0111224442beffeddcb1222211010a011
        +72beeedcb12222211110011 10a1112332befffedca12221111110010
         +61deecba22222101111001 1a01aa12220defedca0111210111100 11
          +6accb022222110111110a1 2011abba022bdddb0221111101111111
           +5ab01121000000000110a0 1010bcccb021abb01220000100100 1111
            +63110abbbaabbbaaaabb 0aabcddddca23332210bcbbbbbaaba0a0
             +721abcccbcbbbbcbbbb bbbbccdedcb2334321bcccccbbbbbabbb
              +620bcccbccbbbbbba0 bbbbccceec03334331abccbbbbbbb0abb
               +520bbaaabb010a001 aa000bbcb0210023310abaaa00baa1100
                +62aaa0a000000011 11100abba111ba12321a0110111001101
                 +61011010000111 1 21111abb011abba133200121111111101
                  +521111111111111 21110bb0110bccba132212211222112 11
                   +6221111121111 11111aa1110ccccba012222122221112 11
                    +521011122111 11121011210ccdccba012221121111121
                     +52211122211 11122111220ccdcba012112111111221
                      +6211112222 10111001220ccccb01111121111112111
                       +521221112 10111002221ccccba11122222111111 1
                        +62221112 11111002221ccccb0122222222111111 1
                         +6221112 111110a1111bbbba01112211111111111
                          +631111 1111110111 1bbbba01111221111111122
                           +72211 11121001111bcbb00111111111111122
                            +4222 11221001111bcbba01122211111112222
                             +732 11110011110bbbba00121212211111222
                              +62 1111111111abbbba001111221111 11221
                               +5 11111001210cbbb011111111122212211
                                + 11110b01111bbbb011122222222112211
                                  +3111001121bbcba12111112112111122
                                   +621111110bcbba11111101122101112
                                    +51011110bcbb01111110022110 1112
                                     +4111110cccba01122111221111122
                                      +632210cdccbaaa11111111110022
                                       +7421bcdcccbbba00000aaa0a011
                                        +731beedddccba000010a00aa11
                                         +72beeeedcca11111110110011
                                          +60eeeedcb01222222 1121112
                                           +5beedb1101222222 1121122
                                            +5acb121ab0110110011111
                                             +633310bccbcbbbbbbbaab
                                              +7521bbbcccbbcbccbbcc
                                               +731abbcccbbcbbbbbcc
                                                +620bccccbbbbbabbb
                                                 +62accbbaa0aa01011
                                                  +61bbaaa011111112
                                                   +610110111111111
                                                    +62111111111111
                                                     +6321112111111
                                                      +732212211111
                                                       +63222211111
                                                        +6212111111
                                                         +522210111
                                                          +63211111
                                                           +6201111
                                                            +522112
                                                             +72111
                                                              +4111
                                                               +711
                                                                +31
                                                                 +5
                                                                  +
```

```
 0.00 <  a  < -0.05
-0.05 <  b  < -0.15
-0.15 <  c  < -0.25
-0.25 <  d  < -0.35
-0.35 <  e  < -0.45
-0.45 <  f  < -0.55
-0.55 <  g  < -0.65
-0.65 <  h  < -0.75
-0.75 <  i  < -0.85
-0.85 <  j  < -0.95
-0.95 <  k  < -1.00
 0.00 <  0  <  0.05
 0.05 <  1  <  0.15
 0.15 <  2  <  0.25
 0.25 <  3  <  0.35
 0.35 <  4  <  0.45
 0.45 <  5  <  0.55
 0.55 <  6  <  0.65
 0.65 <  7  <  0.75
 0.75 <  8  <  0.85
 0.85 <  9  <  0.95
 0.95 <  +  <  1.00
```

Fig. 4-10 Correlation coefficients of Data RADAR.

$$\rho[\mathbf{x}(i,j),\mathbf{x}(i+k,j)] = \rho_k^{(c)} , \tag{4.129}$$

$$\rho[\mathbf{x}(i,j),\mathbf{x}(i,j+\ell)] = \rho_\ell^{(r)} , \tag{4.130}$$

$$\rho[\mathbf{x}(i,j),\mathbf{x}(i+k,j+\ell)] = \rho_k^{(c)}\rho_\ell^{(r)} . \tag{4.131}$$

That is, the correlation coefficient between $\mathbf{x}(i,j)$ and $\mathbf{x}(i+k,j)$, which is called the *column correlation coefficient*, $\rho_k^{(c)}$, depends only on k. The same is true for the *row correlation coefficient*, $\rho_\ell^{(r)}$. The correlation coefficient between

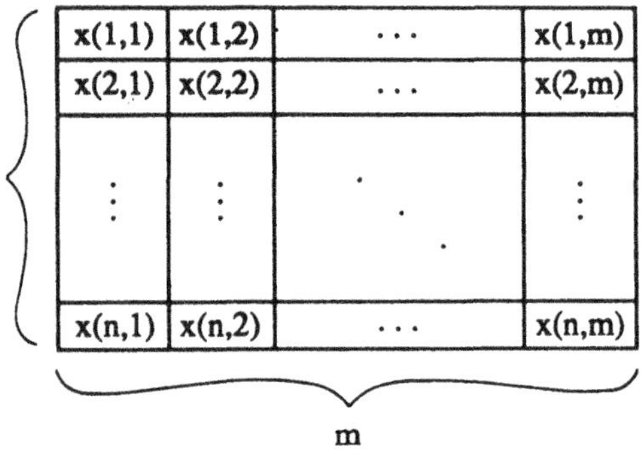

Fig. 4-11 Two-dimensional pixel array.

$\mathbf{x}(i,j)$ and $\mathbf{x}(i+k,j+\ell)$ is assumed to be the product of $\rho_k^{(c)}$ and $\rho_\ell^{(r)}$.

If we form a vector with nm variables by stacking columns of the received image as

$$X = [x(1,1)\ldots x(n,1)\ldots x(1,m)\ldots x(n,m)]^T \tag{4.132}$$

the correlation matrix has the *block toeplitz* form

$$R_c \otimes R_r = \begin{bmatrix} R_c & \rho_1^{(r)}R_c & \cdots & \rho_{m-1}^{(r)}R_c \\ \rho_1^{(r)}R_c & R_c & \cdots & \rho_{m-2}^{(r)}R_c \\ \vdots & \vdots & \ddots & \vdots \\ \rho_{m-1}^{(r)}R_c & \rho_{m-2}^{(r)}R_c & \cdots & R_c \end{bmatrix} , \tag{4.133}$$

where

$$R_r = \begin{bmatrix} 1 & \rho_1^{(r)} & \cdots & \rho_{m-1}^{(r)} \\ \rho_1^{(r)} & 1 & & \vdots \\ \vdots & & \ddots & \rho_1^{(r)} \\ \rho_{m-1}^{(r)} & \cdots & \rho_1^{(r)} & 1 \end{bmatrix}, \tag{4.134}$$

$$R_c = \begin{bmatrix} 1 & \rho_1^{(c)} & \cdots & \rho_{n-1}^{(c)} \\ \rho_1^{(c)} & 1 & & \vdots \\ \vdots & & \ddots & \rho_1^{(c)} \\ \rho_{n-1}^{(c)} & \cdots & \rho_1^{(c)} & 1 \end{bmatrix}. \tag{4.135}$$

Many properties of the block toeplitz matrix are known, and listed as follows without proof [6].

(1) $A \otimes B \neq A \otimes B$, (4.136)

(2) $(A \otimes B)(C \otimes D) = AC \otimes BD$, (4.137)

(3) $(A \otimes B)^T = A^T \otimes B^T$, (4.138)

(4) $(A \otimes B)^{-1} = A^{-1} \otimes B^{-1}$, (4.139)

(5) $\mathrm{tr}(A \otimes B) = (\mathrm{tr}\, A)(\mathrm{tr}\, B)$, (4.140)

(6) $(A \otimes B)(\Phi \otimes \Psi) = (\Phi \otimes \Psi)(\Lambda \otimes \mu)$ (4.141)

where $A\Phi = \Phi\Lambda$ and $B\Psi = \Psi\mu$

Φ, Ψ: eigenvector matrices of A and B

Λ, μ: eigenvalue matrices of A and B,

(7) $|A \otimes B| = |\Lambda|^m |\mu|^n = |A|^m |B|^n$ (4.142)

where A and B are $n \times n$ and $m \times m$ matrices.

When a quadratic classifier is designed, Properties (4) and (7) are particularly useful.

Example 6: For Data RADAR, $n = 33$ and $m = 2$. Both R_c and R_r matrices of (4.134) and (4.135) are formed based on the assumption that the toeplitz form of (4.126) holds. Then, the correlation matrix for ω_i is

$$R_i = \begin{bmatrix} R_{ci} & \rho_i^{(r)} R_{ci} \\ \rho_i^{(r)} R_{ci} & R_{ci} \end{bmatrix} \quad \text{and} \quad R_{ci} = \begin{bmatrix} 1 & \rho_i^{(c)} & \cdots & \rho_i^{(c)n-1} \\ \rho_i^{(c)} & 1 & & \vdots \\ \vdots & & \ddots & \rho_i^{(c)} \\ \rho_i^{(c)n-1} & \cdots & \rho_i^{(c)} & 1 \end{bmatrix} . \tag{4.143}$$

The inverse matrix and determinant of R_i are

$$R_i^{-1} = \frac{1}{1-\rho_i^{(r)2}} \begin{bmatrix} R_{ci}^{-1} & -\rho_i^{(r)} R_{ci}^{-1} \\ -\rho_i^{(r)} R_{ci}^{-1} & R_{ci}^{-1} \end{bmatrix} , \tag{4.144}$$

$$R_{ci}^{-1} = \frac{1}{1-\rho_i^{(c)2}} \begin{bmatrix} 1 & -\rho_i^{(c)} & 0 & \cdots & 0 \\ -\rho_i^{(c)} & 1+\rho_i^{(c)2} & & \ddots & \vdots \\ 0 & \ddots & \ddots & \ddots & 0 \\ \vdots & \ddots & & 1+\rho_i^{(c)2} & -\rho_i^{(c)} \\ 0 & \cdots & 0 & -\rho_i^{(c)} & 1 \end{bmatrix} , \tag{4.145}$$

and

$$|R_i| = (1-\rho_i^{(c)2})^{2(n-1)} (1-\rho_i^{(r)2})^n . \tag{4.146}$$

In order to verify the effectiveness of the above approximation, the following two experiments were conducted.

Experiment 3: Computation of the Bhattacharyya distance

Data: RADAR

Dimension: $n = 66$

Sample size: $N_1 = N_2 = 8800, 720, 360$

Approximation: Toeplitz approximation for $\hat{\Sigma}_i$

No. of trials: $\tau = 1$

Results: Table 4-1

TABLE 4-1

EFFECT OF TOEPLITZ APPROXIMATION

	$N_1 = N_2$	Without Approx.	Toeplitz Approx.
$\mu(1/2)$	8,800	0.64	0.73
	720	1.57	0.77
	360	2.52	0.81
ε_Q (%)	4,400 (Design) 4,400 (Test)	20.2	26.3
	720 (Design) 4,400 (Test)	25.9	26.6
	360 (Design) 4,400 (Test)	30.1	26.8

In this experiment, the sample mean $\hat{M}_i$ and sample covariance matrix $\hat{\Sigma}_i$ were estimated from N_i samples, and the correlation matrix of $\hat{\Sigma}_i$ was approximated by the toeplitz form of (4.143). Using $\hat{M}_i$ and the approximated $\hat{\Sigma}_i$, the Bhattacharyya distance was computed and was compared with the one computed from $\hat{M}_i$ and $\hat{\Sigma}_i$ (without the approximation). Both are fairly close for $N_i = 8800$, indicating the validity of the approximation. Furthermore, since the approximated covariance matrices depend on a smaller number of parameters, its estimates are less sensitive to the sample size. Without approximation, the effect of the sample size is evident. That is, $\mu(1/2)$ increases as N_i decreases.

However, with approximation, the effect of the sample size is significantly reduced.

Experiment 4: Error of the quadratic classifier

Data: RADAR

Dimension: $n = 66$

Sample size: $N_1 = N_2 = 4400, 720, 360$ (Design)

$N_1 = N_2 = 4400$ (Test)

Approximation: Toeplitz approximation for $\hat{\Sigma}_i$ (Design only)

No. of trials: $\tau = 1$

Results: Table 4-1

In this experiment, $\hat{M}_i$ and the approximated $\hat{\Sigma}_i$ were used to design the quadratic classifier of (4.1), and independent 4400 samples per class were tested. The results were compared with the error of the quadratic classifier designed without the approximation. The error of the approximated case is somewhat larger than the error without approximation. However, with approximation, the effect of the sample size is virtually eliminated.

The performance evaluation of the toeplitz approximation can be carried out experimentally as seen in Experiments 3 and 4. That is, the means and the parameters of the covariance matrices are estimated from design samples, and the quadratic classifier based on these estimated parameters is tested by independent test samples.

However, when the distributions of **X** are normal with given M_i and Σ_i, the performance of the quadratic classifier with the toeplitz approximation can be evaluated theoretically as follows.

(1) Average the first off-diagonal terms of R_i from the given Σ_i and form the toeplitz approximation as in (4.143).

(2) Using the given M_i and approximated Σ_i, design the quadratic classifier of (4.1).

(3) Compute the error by testing the original distributions of $N_X(M_i,\Sigma_i)$'s. Since Σ_i's used for design (the toeplitz approximations) are dif-

ferent from the ones used for test (given Σ_i's), the algorithm of (3.119)-(3.128) must be used to calculate the theoretical error.

4.4 Other Classifiers

In this section, we will discuss subjects which were left out in the previous discussions. They are the piecewise classifiers and some of the properties in binary inputs.

Piecewise Classifiers

If we limit our discussion to two-class problems, quadratic or linear classifiers have wide applications. However, when we have to handle three or more classes, a single quadratic or linear classifier cannot be adopted effectively. Even in two-class problems, the same is true when each class consists of several clusters. For these cases, a set of classifiers, which is called a *piecewise classifier*, gives increased flexibility.

Piecewise quadratic for multiclass problems: For multiclass problems, the multihypothesis test in the Bayes sense gives the best classifier with regard to minimizing the error. That is, from (3.44)

$$P_k p_k(X) = \max_i P_i p_i(X) \quad \rightarrow \quad X \in \omega_k \, . \tag{4.147}$$

If the distributions of $\mathbf{X}$ for L classes are normal, (4.147) is replaced by

$$\min_i [\frac{1}{2}(X - M_i)^T \Sigma_i^{-1} (X - M_i) + \frac{1}{2} \ln |\Sigma_i| - \ln P_i] \, , \tag{4.148}$$

where max is changed to min because of the minus-log operation. Note that the normalized distance of X from each class mean, M_i, must be adjusted by two constant terms, $(1/2)\ln|\Sigma_i|$ and $\ln P_i$. Equation (4.148) forms a *piecewise quadratic* boundary.

Piecewise quadratic for multicluster problems: For multicluster problems, the boundary is somewhat more complex. Assuming that $L = 2$, and that each distribution consists of m_i normal clusters with the cluster probability of P_{ij} for the jth cluster, the Bayes classifier becomes

$$P_1 \sum_{j=1}^{m_1} \frac{P_{1j}}{(2\pi)^{n/2} |\Sigma_{1j}|^{1/2}} \exp[-\frac{1}{2}(X-M_{1j})^T \Sigma_{1j}^{-1} (X-M_{1j})]$$

$$\underset{\omega_2}{\overset{\omega_1}{\lessgtr}} P_2 \sum_{j=1}^{m_2} \frac{P_{2j}}{(2\pi)^{n/2} |\Sigma_{2j}|^{1/2}} \exp[-\frac{1}{2}(X-M_{2j})^T \Sigma_{2j}^{-1} (X-M_{2j})] \qquad (4.149)$$

where M_{ij} and Σ_{ij} are the expected vector and covariance matrix of the jth cluster in ω_i. Or, defining the distances as

$$d_{ij}^2(X) = \frac{1}{2}(X-M_{ij})^T \Sigma_{ij}^{-1} (X-M_{ij}) + \frac{1}{2} \ln |\Sigma_{ij}| - \ln P_i - \ln P_{ij} \,, \qquad (4.150)$$

the classifier becomes

$$\sum_{j=1}^{m_1} e^{-d_{1j}^2(X)} \underset{\omega_2}{\overset{\omega_1}{\lessgtr}} \sum_{j=1}^{m_2} e^{-d_{2j}^2(X)} \,. \qquad (4.151)$$

Note that the decision of (4.151) is different from min $d_{ij}^2(X)$, which is the Bayes decision if we treat this problem as an (m_1+m_2)-class problem. Also, it should be realized that the distances are adjusted by $\ln P_{ij}$ as well as $\ln P_i$.

Piecewise linear classifiers: When all covariance matrices are the same in multiclass problems, $X^T \Sigma_i^{-1} X$ and $\ln |\Sigma_i|$ of (4.148) are common among all classes, and (4.148) is reduced to

$$\max_i [M_i^T \Sigma^{-1} X - \frac{1}{2} M_i^T \Sigma^{-1} M_i + \ln P_i] \,, \qquad (4.152)$$

where Σ is the common covariance matrix, and min of (4.148) is changed to max in (4.152) because of the change of sign. That is, X is classified to the class with the highest correlation between X and $\Sigma^{-1} M_i$. Again, the correlation must be adjusted by constant terms.

When covariance matrices are different among classes but close to each other, we may replace Σ of (4.152) by the averaged covariance.

Another alternative, particularly when covariance matrices are not close to each other, is to set a linear discriminant function for each pair of classes, and to optimize the coefficients. Let each discriminant function be

$$h_{ij}(X) = V_{ij}^T X + v_{ij0} \qquad (i,j = 1,\ldots,L:\ i \neq j)\ . \tag{4.153}$$

The signs of V_{ij} are selected such that the distribution of ω_i is located on the positive side of $h_{ij}(X)$ and ω_j on the negative side. Therefore,

$$h_{ij}(X) = -h_{ji}(X)\ . \tag{4.154}$$

Let us assume that the region for each class is convex, as shown in Fig. 4-12.

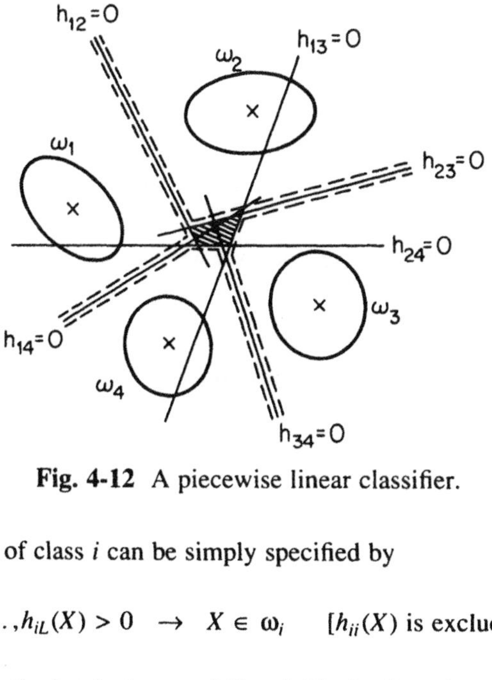

Fig. 4-12 A piecewise linear classifier.

Then, the region of class i can be simply specified by

$$h_{i1}(X) > 0, \ldots, h_{iL}(X) > 0 \ \rightarrow\ X \in \omega_i \qquad [h_{ii}(X) \text{ is excluded}]\ . \tag{4.155}$$

As evidenced by the hatched part of Fig. 4-12, the L regions given by (4.155) do not necessarily cover the entire space. When a sample falls in this region, the piecewise linear classifier cannot decide the class of this sample; we call this a *reject region*. Implementation of (4.155) consists of $(L-1)$ linear discriminant functions and a logical AND circuit with $(L-1)$ inputs of $sign\{h_{ij}(X)\}$, as shown in Fig. 4-13. Since the network has two cascaded circuits, the piecewise linear classifier is sometimes called a *layered machine*. When the assumption of convexity does not hold, we have to replace the AND gate by a more complex logic circuit. Consequently, the classifier becomes too

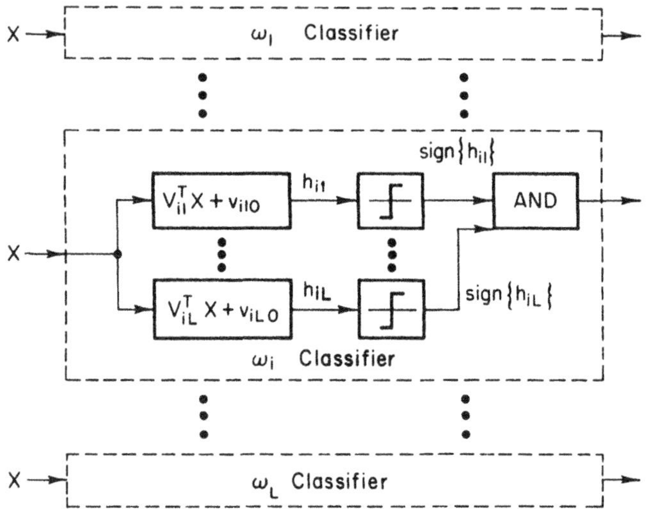

Fig. 4-13 Implementation of a piecewise linear classifier.

complicated to be practical. Therefore, we will limit our discussion to convex regions here.

The probability of error for each class, ε_i, can be expressed in terms of the $(L-1)$-dimensional distribution function as

$$\varepsilon_i = 1 - Pr\{h_{i1}(\mathbf{X}) > 0, \ldots, h_{iL}(\mathbf{X}) > 0 \mid \mathbf{X} \in \omega_i\}$$

$$= 1 - \int_0^\infty \ldots \int_0^\infty p(h_{i1}, \ldots, h_{iL} \mid \omega_i) dh_{i1} \ldots dh_{iL} \tag{4.156}$$

$$[h_{ii}(\mathbf{X}) \text{ is excluded}] .$$

The total error is

$$\varepsilon = \sum_{i=1}^{L} P_i \varepsilon_i . \tag{4.157}$$

Knowing the structure of piecewise linear classifiers, our problem is how to design the V's and v_0's for a given set of L distributions. Because of the complexity involved, solutions for this problem are not as clear-cut as in a linear classifier.

Three approaches are mentioned briefly:

(1) We can adjust the V's and v_0's so as to minimize ε of (4.157). Since it is difficult to get an explicit mathematical expression for ε, the error should be calculated numerically each time when we adjust the V's and v_0's. When $\mathbf{X}$ is distributed normally for all classes, some simplification can be achieved, since the $\mathbf{h}$'s are also normally distributed and $p(h_{i1}, \ldots, h_{iL} \mid \omega_i)$ is given by an explicit mathematical expression. Even for this case, the integration of an $(L-1)$-dimensional normal distribution in the first quadrant must be carried out in a numerical way, using techniques such as the Monte Carlo method.

(2) Design a linear discriminant function between a pair of classes according to one of the methods discussed previously for two-class problems. $\binom{L}{2}$ discriminant functions are calculated. Then, use them as a piecewise linear discriminant function without further modification. When each class distribution is quite different from the others, further modification can result in less error. However, in many applications, the decrease in error is found to be relatively minor by the further adjustment of V's and v_0's.

(3) We can assign the desired output $\gamma(\mathbf{X})$ for a piecewise linear discriminant function and minimize the mean-square error between the desired and actual outputs in order to find the optimum V's and v_0's. The desired outputs could be fixed or could be adjusted as variables with constraints. Unfortunately, even for piecewise linearly separable data, there is no proof of convergence.

Binary Inputs

In Section 4.1, we showed that for independent binary inputs the Bayes classifier becomes linear. In this section, we will discuss other properties of binary inputs.

When we have n binary inputs forming an input vector X, the number of all possible inputs is 2^n, $\{X_0, \ldots, X_{2^n-1}\}$ [see Table 4-2 for example]. Then the components of X_j, $x_{kj} (k = 1, \ldots, n)$, satisfy

$$\frac{1}{2^n}\sum_{j=0}^{2^n-1} x_{kj} = 0 , \tag{4.158}$$

$$\frac{1}{2^n}\sum_{j=0}^{2^n-1} x_{kj}^2 = 1 , \tag{4.159}$$

$$\frac{1}{2^n}\sum_{j=0}^{2^n-1} x_{kj}x_{\ell j} = 0 \qquad (k \neq \ell) , \tag{4.160}$$

where x_{kj} is either +1 or −1. Thus, if we define the sample matrix as

$$U = \underbrace{\begin{bmatrix} 1 & 1 & \dots & 1 \\ X_0 & X_1 & \dots & X_{2^n-1} \end{bmatrix}}_{2^n} \Bigg\} \; n+1 , \tag{4.161}$$

then the row vectors of U are mutually orthonormal, that is

$$UU^T = 2^n I . \tag{4.162}$$

Example 7: Table 4-2 shows an example of three binary inputs. We can easily see that (4.158)-(4.162) are all satisfied.

Let $\gamma(X)$ be the desired output of a pattern recognition network for the input X. The $\gamma(X)$ is not necessarily a binary number. One of the design procedures which may be used to realize this network by a linear discriminant function is to minimize the mean-square error between $\gamma(X)$ and $V^TX + v_0$. The mean-square error can be expressed by

$$\overline{\varepsilon^2} = \frac{1}{2^n}\sum_{j=0}^{2^n-1}\{(V^TX_j + v_o) - \gamma(X_j)\}^2 = \frac{1}{2^n}(W^TU - \Gamma^T)(U^TW - \Gamma) \tag{4.163}$$

where W and Γ are the same as the ones used in (4.78). Therefore, the W which minimizes $\overline{\varepsilon^2}$ is

TABLE 4-2
ALL POSSIBLE BINARY INPUTS

	X_0	X_1	X_2	X_3	X_4	X_5	X_6	X_7
x_0	1	1	1	1	1	1	1	1
x_1	−1	1	−1	1	−1	1	−1	1
x_2	−1	−1	1	1	−1	−1	1	1
x_3	−1	−1	−1	−1	1	1	1	1
x_1x_2	1	−1	−1	1	1	−1	−1	1
x_1x_3	1	−1	1	−1	−1	1	−1	1
x_2x_3	1	1	−1	−1	−1	−1	1	1
$x_1x_2x_3$	−1	1	1	−1	1	−1	−1	1

$$\frac{\partial \bar{\varepsilon}^2}{\partial W} = \frac{2}{2^n} U(U^T W - \Gamma) = 2(W - \frac{1}{2^n} U\Gamma) = 0 \,, \tag{4.164}$$

$$W = \frac{1}{2^n} U\Gamma \,. \tag{4.165}$$

Thus, the coefficients of the linear discriminant function are given by the correlation between the desired output and the input X. The above discussion is identical to that of the general linear discriminant function. However, it should be noted that for binary inputs $UU^T = NI$ is automatically satisfied without transformation.

As an example of $\gamma(X)$, let us use

$$\gamma(X) = p(X)\{q_2(X) - q_1(X)\} = P_2 p_2(X) - P_1 p_1(X) \,. \tag{4.166}$$

The term $\gamma(X)$ would be positive for $P_1 p_1(X) < P_2 p_2(X)$ or $q_1(X) < q_2(X)$, and be negative otherwise. Also, the absolute value of $\gamma(X)$ depends on $p_1(X)$ and $p_2(X)$. When n is large but the number of observed samples N is far less than 2^n, the correlation of (4.165) can be computed only by N multiplications and additions, instead of 2^n [7].

Table 4-2 suggests that we can extend our vector $X = [x_1 \ldots x_n]^T$ to

$$Y = \underbrace{[1 \;\; x_1 \; \ldots \; x_n \; (x_1 x_2) \; \ldots \; (x_1 x_2 \ldots x_n)]^T}_{2^n} \, . \tag{4.167}$$

Then, the sample matrix for this extended vector becomes a square matrix as

$$U_Y = \underbrace{[Y_0 \;\; Y_1 \ldots Y_{2^n-1}]}_{2^n} \}\, 2^n \, . \tag{4.168}$$

The row vectors of U_Y are also orthonormal, such that

$$U_Y U_Y^T = 2^n I \, . \tag{4.169}$$

A linear discriminant function for Y is

$$\sum_{j=0}^{2^n-1} w_j y_j = w_0 + \sum_{j=1}^{n} w_j x_j + \sum_i \sum_j w_{\ell} x_i x_j + \ldots + w_{2^n-1} x_1 \ldots x_n \, . \tag{4.170}$$

In accordance with the reasoning applied to derive (4.165), we can determine W of (4.170) by

$$W = \frac{1}{2^n} U_Y \Gamma \, . \tag{4.171}$$

The following should be noted here:

(1) Any desired output is expressed by $W^T Y$ without error.

(2) Since y_ℓ's are mutually orthonormal, $\overline{\varepsilon}^2$ due to the elimination of $w_\ell y_\ell$ from $W^T Y$ is w_ℓ^2.

(3) The $\overline{\varepsilon}^2$ determined by the linear discriminant function of $V^T X + v_0$ is

$$\overline{\varepsilon}^2 = \sum_{j=n+1}^{2^n-1} w_j^2 \, . \tag{4.172}$$

Computer Projects

1. Repeat Example 4, and obtain Fig. 4-8.

2. Repeat Experiment 1 for $N_i = 50, 100, 200, 400$ and plot the error vs. s.

3. Repeat Experiment 2 for $N_i = 50, 100, 200, 400$ and plot the error vs. s.

4. Design the optimum linear classifier by minimizing the mean-square error of (4.76). Use 100 generated samples per class from Data I-Λ for design, and test independently generated 100 samples per class. Observe the difference between this error (the error of the holdout method) and the one of the resubstitution method.

5. Two 8-dimensional normal distributions are characterized by $P_1 = P_2 = 0.5$, $M_1 = M_2 = 0$, $\Sigma_i = \sigma_i^2 R_i$ where R_i is given in (4.126) with $\sigma_1^2 = \sigma_2^2 = 1$, $\rho_1 = 0.5$, and $\rho_2 = -0.5$.
   (a) Compute the Bayes error theoretically.
   (b) Generate N_i design samples per class, and compute the sample mean $\hat{M}_i$ and sample covariance $\hat{\Sigma}_i$.
   (c) Approximate the correlation matrix of $\hat{\Sigma}_i$ by the toeplitz form of (4.126).
   (d) Design the quadratic classifier with $\hat{M}_i$ and the approximated $\hat{\Sigma}_i$.
   (e) Generate 1000 test samples, and classify them by the quadratic classifier designed in (d).
   (f) Repeat (b)-(e) 10 times, and compute the average and standard deviation of the error.
   (g) Compare the error of (f) with the error of (a) for various N_i. Suggested N_i's are 10, 20, and 40.

Problems

1. Let $\mathbf{x}_j$ $(j = 1, \ldots, n)$ be independent and identically distributed with an exponential density function

$$p_i(x_j) = \frac{1}{\lambda_i} \exp[-\frac{x_j}{\lambda_i}]\, u(x_j) \qquad (i = 1,2)$$

where $u(\cdot)$ is the step function.

   (a) Find the density function of the Bayes discriminant function $h(X)$.

(b) Assuming that the density functions of $h(\mathbf{X})$ for ω_1 and ω_2 can be approximated by normal densities, compute the approximated value of the Bayes error for $n = 8$, $\lambda_2/\lambda_1 = 2.5$, and $P_1 = P_2 = 0.5$.

2. Two normal distributions are characterized by

$$P_1 = P_2 = 0.5, \quad M_1 = \begin{bmatrix} -1 \\ 0 \end{bmatrix}, \quad M_2 = \begin{bmatrix} +1 \\ 0 \end{bmatrix},$$

$$\Sigma_1 = \Sigma_2 = \begin{bmatrix} 4 & 3 \\ 3 & 4 \end{bmatrix}.$$

Calculate the errors due to the Bayes classifier and the bisector.

3. Using the same data as in Problem 2 except

$$\Sigma_1 = \begin{bmatrix} 4 & 3 \\ 3 & 4 \end{bmatrix} \quad \text{and} \quad \Sigma_2 = \begin{bmatrix} 4 & -3 \\ -3 & 4 \end{bmatrix},$$

find the linear discriminant function which maximizes the Fisher criterion, and minimize the error by adjusting the threshold.

4. Using the same data as in Problem 3, find the optimum linear discriminant function which minimizes the probability of error. Show that the error is smaller than the one of Problem 3. (Check the errors for $s = 0$, 0.02 and 0.25.)

5. Design the optimum linear classifier by minimizing the mean-square error of

$$\overline{\varepsilon^2} = E\{(V^T\mathbf{X} + v_0 - \gamma(\mathbf{X}))^2\}$$

where $\gamma(X) = +1$ for $X \in \omega_2$ and -1 for $X \in \omega_1$. Without using the procedure discussed in this chapter, take the derivative of $\overline{\varepsilon^2}$ with respect to V and v_0, equate the derivative to zero, and solve the equation for V. Setting the mixture mean, $M_0 = P_1M_1 + P_2M_2$, as the coordinate origin, confirm that the resulting optimum V is

$$V = [P_1\Sigma_1 + P_2\Sigma_2]^{-1}(M_2 - M_1) .$$

6. Prove that $E\{\mathbf{F}(j\omega_1)\mathbf{F}^*(j\omega_2)\} = 0$ for $\omega_1 \neq \omega_2$ where $\mathbf{F}(j\omega)$ is the Fourier transform of a stationary random process, $\mathbf{x}(t)$, as

$$F(j\omega) = \int_{-\infty}^{+\infty} x(t)\, e^{-j\omega t}\, dt .$$

7. Two stationary normal distributions are characterized by $P_1 = P_2 = 0.5$, $M_1 = 0$, $M_2 = \Delta[1 \ldots 1]^T$, and $\Sigma = \Sigma_1 = \Sigma_2 = \sigma^2 R$ where R is given in (4.126).

(a) Compute the Bayes error for $n = 10$, $\Delta = 2$, $\sigma^2 = 1$, and $\rho = 0.5$.

(b) Using the same numbers as in (a), compute the error when $N_X(M_1,\sigma^2 I)$ and $N_X(M_2,\sigma^2 I)$ are used to design the classifier and $N_X(M_1,\Sigma)$ and $N_X(M_2,\Sigma)$ are used to test the classifier.

8. Repeat Problem 7 for a two-dimensional random field of $n \times n$. The vertical and horizontal correlation matrices are the same and specified by (4.126).

9. Design a linear classifier by minimizing the mean-square error for the data given in the following Table, assuming $P_1 = P_2 = 0.5$.

x_1	x_2	x_3	$p_1(X)$	$p_2(X)$
−1	−1	−1	1/3	0
+1	−1	−1	1/24	1/8
−1	+1	−1	1/24	1/8
+1	+1	−1	0	1/3
−1	−1	+1	1/3	0
+1	−1	+1	1/24	1/8
−1	+1	+1	1/24	1/8
+1	+1	+1	0	1/3

10. In the design of a piecewise linear classifier, propose a way to assign the desired output so that we can apply the technique of minimizing the mean-square error.

References

1. H. L. VanTrees, "Detection, Estimation, and Modulation Theory: Part I," Wiley, New York, 1968.
2. A. Fisher, "The Mathematical Theory of Probabilities," Vol. 1, Macmillan, New York, 1923.
3. T. W. Anderson and R. R. Buhadur, Classification into two multivariate normal distributions with different covariance matrices, *Ann. Math. Stat.*, 33, pp. 422-431, 1962.
4. D. W. Peterson and R. L. Mattson, A method of finding linear discriminant functions for a class of performance criteria, *Trans. IEEE Inform. Theory*, IT-12, pp. 380-387, 1966.
5. Y. C. Ho and R. L. Kashyap, An algorithm for linear inequalities and its applications, *Trans. IEEE Electronic Computers*, EC-14, pp. 683-688, 1965.
6. C. W. Therrien and K. Fukunaga, Properties of separable covariance matrices and their associated Gaussian random processes, *Trans. IEEE Pattern Anal. and Machine Intell.*, PAMI-6, pp. 652-656, 1984.
7. K. Fukunaga and T. Ito, A design theory of recognition functions in self-organizing systems, *Trans. IEEE Electronic Computers*, EC-14, pp. 44-52, 1965.

Chapter 5

PARAMETER ESTIMATION

As discussed in the previous chapters, once we express the density functions in terms of parameters such as expected vectors and covariance matrices, we can design the likelihood ratio classifier to partition the space. Another alternative is to express the discriminant function in terms of a number of parameters, assuming a mathematical form such as a linear or quadratic function. Even in this case, the discriminant function often becomes a function of expected vectors and covariance matrices, as seen in Chapter 4. In either case, we call it the *parametric approach*. The parametric approach is generally considered less complicated than its counterpart, the *nonparametric approach*, in which mathematical structures are not imposed on either the density functions or the discriminant function.

In the previous chapters, we have assumed that the values of the parameters are given and fixed. Unfortunately, in practice their true values are never known, and must be estimated from a finite number of available samples. This is done by using the *sample estimation* technique presented in Section 2.2. However, the estimates are random variables and vary around the expected values.

The statistical properties of sample estimates may be obtained easily as discussed in Section 2.2. However, in pattern recognition, we deal with functions of these estimates such as the discriminant function, the density function, the classification error, and so on. Therefore, we need to know how the outputs of these functions are affected by the random variations of parameters. More specifically, we are interested in the *biases* and *variances* of these functions. They depend on the functional form as well as the number of samples used to estimate the parameters. We will discuss this subject in this chapter. First, the problem will be addressed in a *general form*, and then the *Bhattacharyya distance* will be studied.

A more important quantity in pattern recognition is the *probability of error*, which is expressed as a complicated function of two sets of parameters: one is the set of parameters which specify a classifier, and the other is the set of parameters which specify the distributions to be tested. Because these two sets are involved, the estimation of the error is complex and difficult to discuss. In this chapter, we will show how the estimated error is affected by the design and test samples. Also, the discussion is extended to include several error estimation techniques such as the *holdout*, *leave-one-out*, and *resubstitution* methods as well as the *bootstrap* method.

5.1. Effect of Sample Size in Estimation

General Formulation

Expected value and variance: Let us consider the problem of estimating $f(y_1,\ldots,y_q)$ by $f(\hat{\mathbf{y}}_1,\ldots,\hat{\mathbf{y}}_q)$, where f is a given function, the y_i's are the true parameter values, and the $\hat{\mathbf{y}}_i$'s are their *estimates*. In this section, we will derive expressions for the expected value and variance of $f(\hat{\mathbf{y}}_1,\ldots,\hat{\mathbf{y}}_q)$, and discuss a method to estimate $f(y_1,\ldots,y_q)$.

Assuming that the deviation of $\hat{\mathbf{y}}_i$ from y_i is small, $f(\hat{\mathbf{Y}})$ can be expanded by a Taylor series up to the second order terms as

$$\hat{\mathbf{f}} \triangleq f(\hat{\mathbf{Y}}) \cong f(Y) + \sum_{i=1}^{q} \frac{\partial f}{\partial y_i} \Delta \mathbf{y}_i + \frac{1}{2} \sum_{i=1}^{q} \sum_{j=1}^{q} \frac{\partial^2 f}{\partial y_i \partial y_j} \Delta \mathbf{y}_i \Delta \mathbf{y}_j$$

$$= f(Y) + \frac{\partial f^T}{\partial Y} \Delta \mathbf{Y} + \frac{1}{2} \operatorname{tr} \left[\frac{\partial^2 f}{\partial Y^2} \Delta \mathbf{Y} \Delta \mathbf{Y}^T \right] , \tag{5.1}$$

where $Y = [y_1 \ldots y_q]^T$, $\hat{\mathbf{Y}} = [\hat{\mathbf{y}}_1 \ldots \hat{\mathbf{y}}_q]^T$, and $\Delta \mathbf{Y} = \hat{\mathbf{Y}} - Y$.

If the estimates are *unbiased*,

$$E\{\Delta \mathbf{Y}\} = 0 \tag{5.2}$$

and subsequently the *expected value* of $\hat{\mathbf{f}}$ is

$$E\{\hat{\mathbf{f}}\} \cong f + \frac{1}{2} \operatorname{tr} \left[\frac{\partial^2 f}{\partial Y^2} E\{\Delta \mathbf{Y} \Delta \mathbf{Y}^T\} \right] . \tag{5.3}$$

Similarly, the *variance* of $\hat{\mathbf{f}}$ can be derived as

$$\mathrm{Var}\{\hat{\mathbf{f}}\} \cong E\left\{ \left[\frac{\partial f^T}{\partial Y} \Delta \mathbf{Y} + \frac{1}{2} \operatorname{tr} \left[\frac{\partial^2 f}{\partial Y^2} \Delta \mathbf{Y} \Delta \mathbf{Y}^T \right] - \frac{1}{2} \operatorname{tr} \left[\frac{\partial^2 f}{\partial Y^2} E\{\Delta \mathbf{Y} \Delta \mathbf{Y}^T\} \right] \right]^2 \right\}$$

$$\cong E\left\{ \left[\frac{\partial f^T}{\partial Y} \Delta \mathbf{Y} \right]^2 \right\} = \frac{\partial f^T}{\partial Y} E\{\Delta \mathbf{Y} \Delta \mathbf{Y}^T\} \frac{\partial f}{\partial Y} , \tag{5.4}$$

where the approximation from the first line to the second line is made by discarding terms higher than second order.

Equation (5.3) shows that $\hat{\mathbf{f}}$ is a *biased estimate* in general and that the *bias* depends on $\partial^2 f / \partial Y^2$ and $E\{\Delta \mathbf{Y} \Delta \mathbf{Y}^T\}$, where $\partial^2 f / \partial Y^2$ is determined by the functional form of f and $E\{\Delta \mathbf{Y} \Delta \mathbf{Y}^T\}$ is determined by the distribution of $\hat{\mathbf{Y}}$, $p(\hat{Y})$, and the number of samples, N, used to compute $\hat{\mathbf{Y}}$. Likewise, the variance depends on $\partial f / \partial Y$ and $E\{\Delta \mathbf{Y} \Delta \mathbf{Y}^T\}$.

Estimation of f: For many estimates, the effects of $p(\hat{Y})$ and N on $E\{\Delta \mathbf{Y} \Delta \mathbf{Y}^T\}$ can be separated as

$$E\{\Delta \mathbf{Y} \Delta \mathbf{Y}^T\} = g(N)\, K(p(\hat{Y})) , \tag{5.5}$$

where the scalar g and the matrix K are functions determined by how $\hat{\mathbf{Y}}$ is computed. Substituting (5.5) into (5.3),

$$E\{\hat{\mathbf{f}}\} \cong f + \nu\, g(N)\,, \tag{5.6}$$

where $\nu = \text{tr}\,\{\partial^2 f/\partial Y^2\; K(p(\hat{Y}))\}/2$ is independent of N and treated as a constant determined by the underlying problem. This leads to the following procedure to estimate f.

(1) Change the sample size N as $N_1, N_2, \ldots, N_\ell$. For each N_i, compute $\hat{\mathbf{Y}}$ and subsequently $\hat{\mathbf{f}}$ empirically. Repeat the experiment τ times, and approximate $E\{\hat{\mathbf{f}}\}$ by the sample mean of the τ experimental results.

(2) Plot these empirical points $E\{\hat{\mathbf{f}}\}$ vs. $g(N)$. Then, find the line best fitted to these points. The slope of this line is ν and the y-cross point is the improved estimate of f. There are many possible ways of selecting a line. The standard procedure would be the minimum mean-square error approach.

Parametric Formulation

Moments of parameters: In the parametric approach, most of the expressions we would like to estimate are functions of expected vectors and covariance matrices. In this section, we will show how the general discussion of the previous section can be applied to this particular family of parameters.

Assume that N samples are drawn from each of two n-dimensional normal distributions with expected vectors and covariance matrices given by

$$\begin{aligned} M_1 &= 0\;, \quad \Sigma_1 = I \quad (= \Lambda_1)\,, \\ M_2 &= M\;, \quad \Sigma_2 = \Lambda \quad (= \Lambda_2)\,. \end{aligned} \tag{5.7}$$

Without loss of generality, any two covariance matrices can be *simultaneously diagonalized* to I and Λ, and a *coordinate shift* can bring the expected vector of one class to zero. Normality is assumed here for simplicity. However, the discussion can be extended to non-normal cases easily. The extension will be presented at the end of this section. Also, $N_1 = N_2 = N$ is assumed here. For $N_1 \neq N_2$, a similar discussion could be developed, although the results are a little more complex. In order to simplify the notation, Λ_r $(r = 1,2)$ are used to indicate the diagonalized class covariances, where $\Lambda_1 = I$ and $\Lambda_2 = \Lambda$.

The parameters M_i and Σ_i can be estimated without bias by the *sample mean* and *sample covariance matrix*

$$\hat{\mathbf{M}}_r = \frac{1}{N}\sum_{j=1}^{N}\mathbf{X}_j^{(r)} , \tag{5.8}$$

$$\hat{\boldsymbol{\Sigma}}_r = \frac{1}{N-1}\sum_{j=1}^{N}(\mathbf{X}_j^{(r)}-\hat{\mathbf{M}}_r)(\mathbf{X}_j^{(r)}-\hat{\mathbf{M}}_r)^T , \tag{5.9}$$

where $\mathbf{X}_j^{(r)}$ is the jth sample vector from class r. Thus, the parameter vector $\hat{\mathbf{Y}}$ of (1) consists of $2[n+n(n+1)/2]$ components

$$\hat{\mathbf{Y}} = \left[\hat{\mathbf{m}}_1^{(1)} \ldots \hat{\mathbf{m}}_n^{(1)}\ \hat{\mathbf{m}}_1^{(2)} \ldots \hat{\mathbf{m}}_n^{(2)}\ \hat{\mathbf{c}}_{11}^{(1)} \ldots \hat{\mathbf{c}}_{nn}^{(1)}\ \hat{\mathbf{c}}_{11}^{(2)} \ldots \hat{\mathbf{c}}_{nn}^{(2)}\right]^T , \tag{5.10}$$

where $\hat{\mathbf{m}}_i^{(r)}$ is the ith component of $\hat{\mathbf{M}}_r$, and $\hat{\mathbf{c}}_{ij}^{(r)}$ $(i \geq j)$ is the ith row and jth column component of $\hat{\boldsymbol{\Sigma}}_r$.

The random variables of (5.10) satisfy the following statistical properties, where $\Delta\mathbf{m}_i^{(r)} = \hat{\mathbf{m}}_i^{(r)} - m_i^{(r)}$ and $\Delta\mathbf{c}_{ij}^{(r)} = \hat{\mathbf{c}}_{ij}^{(r)} - c_{ij}^{(r)}$:

(1) The sample mean and covariance matrix are unbiased:

$$E\{\Delta\mathbf{m}_i^{(r)}\} = 0 \quad \text{and} \quad E\{\Delta\mathbf{c}_{ij}^{(r)}\} = 0 . \tag{5.11}$$

(2) Samples from different classes are independent:

$$E\{\Delta\mathbf{m}_i^{(1)}\Delta\mathbf{m}_j^{(2)}\} = E\{\Delta\mathbf{m}_i^{(1)}\}\ E\{\Delta\mathbf{m}_j^{(2)}\} = 0 ,$$

$$E\{\Delta\mathbf{c}_{ij}^{(1)}\Delta\mathbf{c}_{k\ell}^{(2)}\} = E\{\Delta\mathbf{c}_{ij}^{(1)}\}\ E\{\Delta\mathbf{c}_{k\ell}^{(2)}\} = 0 ,$$

$$E\{\Delta\mathbf{m}_i^{(r)}\Delta\mathbf{c}_{k\ell}^{(s)}\} = E\{\Delta\mathbf{m}_i^{(r)}\}\ E\{\Delta\mathbf{c}_{k\ell}^{(s)}\} = 0 \quad \text{for } r \neq s . \tag{5.12}$$

(3) The covariance matrices of the sample means are diagonal [see (2.34)]:

$$E\{(\hat{\mathbf{M}}_r - M_r)(\hat{\mathbf{M}}_r - M_r)^T\} = \frac{1}{N}\Lambda_r$$

or

$$E\{\Delta\mathbf{m}_i^{(r)}\Delta\mathbf{m}_j^{(r)}\} = \frac{\lambda_i^{(r)}}{N}\delta_{ij} \tag{5.13}$$

where $\lambda_i^{(r)}$ is the ith diagonal component of Λ_r.

(4) The third order central moments of a normal distribution are zero:

$$E\{\Delta\mathbf{m}_i^{(r)}\Delta\mathbf{c}_{k\ell}^{(r)}\} = 0 . \tag{5.14}$$

(5) The fourth order central moments of a normal distribution are [see (2.57), (2.59), and (2.60)]:

$$E\left\{\Delta\mathbf{c}_{ij}^{(r)}\Delta\mathbf{c}_{k\ell}^{(r)}\right\} = \begin{cases} \dfrac{\lambda_i^{(r)}\lambda_j^{(r)}}{N} & \text{for } i \neq j,\ i = k,\ j = \ell \\ \dfrac{2\lambda_i^{(r)2}}{N-1} \cong \dfrac{2\lambda_i^{(r)2}}{N} & \text{for } i = j = k = \ell \\ 0 & \text{otherwise .} \end{cases} \tag{5.15}$$

Note that, in the equal index case of (5.15), $N-1$ is replaced by N for simplicity.

Moments of $\hat{\mathbf{f}}$: Although we have not shown the higher order moments of $\mathbf{y}_i$'s other than the second, it is not so difficult to generalize the discussion to obtain

$$\hat{\mathbf{f}} = f + \sum_{i=1}^{\infty}\mathbf{0}^{(i)} \tag{5.16}$$

and

$$E\{\mathbf{0}^{(1)}\} = E\{\mathbf{0}^{(3)}\} = \ldots = 0 ,$$

$$E\{\mathbf{0}^{(2)}\} \sim 1/N,\quad E\{\mathbf{0}^{(4)}\} \sim 1/N^2, \ldots \tag{5.17}$$

where $\mathbf{0}^{(i)}$ is the ith order term of the Taylor expansion in (5.1) [see Problem

2-5]. Since N is large in general, we terminate the expansion at the second order throughout this book.

Substituting (5.10) through (5.15) into (5.3), the bias term of the estimate, $E\{\Delta\mathbf{f}\} = E\{\hat{\mathbf{f}}\} - f$, becomes

$$E\{\Delta\mathbf{f}\} \cong \frac{1}{2}\,\mathrm{tr}\left[\frac{\partial^2 f}{\partial Y^2}E\{\Delta\mathbf{Y}\Delta\mathbf{Y}^T\}\right] = \frac{1}{2}\sum_{i=1}^{q}\sum_{j=1}^{q}\frac{\partial^2 f}{\partial y_i \partial y_j}E\{\Delta\mathbf{y}_i\Delta\mathbf{y}_j\}$$

$$= \frac{1}{2}\sum_{r=1}^{2}\left[\sum_{i=1}^{n}\frac{\partial^2 f}{\partial m_i^{(r)2}}E\{\Delta\mathbf{m}_i^{(r)2}\} + \sum_{i=1}^{n}\frac{\partial^2 f}{\partial c_{ii}^{(r)2}}E\{\Delta\mathbf{c}_{ii}^{(r)2}\}\right.$$

$$\left. + \sum_{i=1}^{n}\sum_{j=1}^{i-1}\frac{\partial^2 f}{\partial c_{ij}^{(r)2}}E\{\Delta\mathbf{c}_{ij}^{(r)2}\}\right]$$

$$\cong \frac{1}{2N}\sum_{r=1}^{2}\left[\sum_{i=1}^{n}\frac{\partial^2 f}{\partial m_i^{(r)2}}\lambda_i^{(r)} + \sum_{i=1}^{n}\frac{\partial^2 f}{\partial c_{ii}^{(r)2}}2\lambda_i^{(r)2}\right.$$

$$\left. + \sum_{i=1}^{n}\sum_{j=1}^{i-1}\frac{\partial^2 f}{\partial c_{ij}^{(r)2}}\lambda_i^{(r)}\lambda_j^{(r)}\right]. \tag{5.18}$$

Note that the effect of N is successfully separated, and that $g(N)$ of (5.5) becomes $1/N$. This is true for any functional form of f, provided f is a function of the expected vectors and covariance matrices of two normal distributions.

Similarly, the variance can be computed from (5.4), resulting in

$$\mathrm{Var}\{\hat{\mathbf{f}}\} \cong \frac{1}{N}\sum_{r=1}^{2}\left[\sum_{i=1}^{n}\left(\frac{\partial f}{\partial m_i^{(r)}}\right)^2\lambda_i^{(r)} + \sum_{i=1}^{n}\left(\frac{\partial f}{\partial c_{ii}^{(r)}}\right)^2 2\lambda_i^{(r)2}\right.$$

$$\left. + \sum_{i=1}^{n}\sum_{j=1}^{i-1}\left(\frac{\partial f}{\partial c_{ij}^{(r)}}\right)^2\lambda_i^{(r)}\lambda_j^{(r)}\right]. \tag{5.19}$$

Note that, in order to calculate the bias and variance, we only need to compute $\partial f/\partial m_i^{(r)}$, $\partial f/\partial c_{ij}^{(r)}$, $\partial^2 f/\partial m_i^{(r)2}$, and $\partial^2 f/\partial c_{ij}^{(r)2}$ for $r = 1,2$.

Non-normal cases: Even when the distributions of $\mathbf{X}$ are not normal, (5.11), (5.12), and (5.13) are valid as the first and second order moments.

However, the third and fourth order moments, (5.14) and (5.15), must be modified according to (2.53), (2.48), and (2.49), resulting in

$$E\{\Delta \mathbf{m}_i^{(r)} \Delta \mathbf{c}_{k\ell}^{(r)}\} \cong \frac{1}{N} \operatorname{Cov}\{\Delta \mathbf{x}_i^{(r)}, \Delta \mathbf{x}_k^{(r)} \Delta \mathbf{x}_\ell^{(r)}\} , \tag{5.20}$$

$$E\{\Delta \mathbf{c}_{ij}^{(r)} \Delta \mathbf{c}_{k\ell}^{(r)}\} \cong \begin{cases} \dfrac{1}{N} \operatorname{Var}\{\Delta \mathbf{x}_i^{(r)} \Delta \mathbf{x}_j^{(r)}\} & \text{for } i \neq j,\ i = k,\ j = \ell \\ \dfrac{1}{N} \operatorname{Var}\{\Delta \mathbf{x}_i^{(r)2}\} & \text{for } i = j = k = \ell \\ \dfrac{1}{N} \operatorname{Cov}\{\Delta \mathbf{x}_i^{(r)} \Delta \mathbf{x}_j^{(r)},\ \Delta \mathbf{x}_k^{(r)} \Delta \mathbf{x}_\ell^{(r)}\} & \text{otherwise}. \end{cases} \tag{5.21}$$

Subsequently, $E\{\Delta \mathbf{f}\}$ of (5.18) and $\operatorname{Var}\{\Delta \mathbf{f}\}$ of (5.19) must be modified. However, it must be noted that both (5.20) and (5.21) are proportional to $1/N$. Thus, even for non-normal cases, we can isolate the effect of the sample size, and $g(N)$ of (5.5) becomes $1/N$. This means that we can adopt the estimation procedure of f of (5.6).

Bhattacharyya Distance

A popular measure of similarity between two distributions is the *Bhattacharyya distance*

$$\mu = \frac{1}{8}(M_2 - M_1)^T \left[\frac{\Sigma_1 + \Sigma_2}{2} \right]^{-1} (M_2 - M_1)$$

$$+ \frac{1}{2} \ln \frac{\left| \dfrac{\Sigma_1 + \Sigma_2}{2} \right|}{\sqrt{|\Sigma_1|}\sqrt{|\Sigma_2|}} . \tag{5.22}$$

Since μ is a function of M_1, M_2, Σ_1, and Σ_2, it is a member of the family of functions discussed previously.

If two distributions are normal, the Bhattacharyya distance gives an upper bound of the Bayes error, ε, as discussed in Chapter 3. The first and second terms of (5.22), μ_1 and μ_2, measure the difference between the two distributions due to the mean and covariance shifts respectively.

When $\hat{\mathbf{M}}_i$ and $\hat{\mathbf{\Sigma}}_i$ of (5.8) and (5.9) are used to compute μ, the resulting $\hat{\mu}$ differs from its true value. The bias and variance of $\hat{\mu}$ can be obtained using (5.18) and (5.19).

First term μ_1: From (5.22), the derivatives of μ_1 with respect to M_r are

$$\frac{\partial \mu_1}{\partial M_r} = (-1)^r \frac{1}{4} \bar{\Sigma}^{-1} (M_2 - M_1) , \tag{5.23}$$

$$\frac{\partial^2 \mu_1}{\partial M_r^2} = \frac{1}{4} \bar{\Sigma}^{-1} , \tag{5.24}$$

where $\bar{\Sigma} = (\Sigma_1 + \Sigma_2)/2$. The derivatives of μ_1 with respect to $c_{ij}^{(r)}$ can be obtained from (A.31) and (A.32). That is,

$$\frac{\partial \mu_1}{\partial c_{ij}^{(r)}} = \frac{\partial \mu_1}{\partial \bar{c}_{ij}} \frac{\partial \bar{c}_{ij}}{\partial c_{ij}^{(r)}} = -\frac{2-\delta_{ij}}{16} \frac{m_i m_j}{\bar{\lambda}_i \bar{\lambda}_j} , \tag{5.25}$$

$$\frac{\partial^2 \mu_1}{\partial c_{ij}^{(r)2}} = \frac{\partial^2 \mu_1}{\partial \bar{c}_{ij}^2} \left[\frac{\partial \bar{c}_{ij}}{\partial c_{ij}^{(r)}} \right]^2 = \frac{2-\delta_{ij}}{32 \bar{\lambda}_i \bar{\lambda}_j} \left[\frac{m_i^2}{\bar{\lambda}_i} + \frac{m_j^2}{\bar{\lambda}_j} \right] , \tag{5.26}$$

where $\bar{c}_{ij} = (c_{ij}^{(1)} + c_{ij}^{(2)})/2$, $\bar{\lambda}_i = (\lambda_i^{(1)} + \lambda_i^{(2)})/2$, and $m_i = m_i^{(2)} - m_i^{(1)}$.

Substituting (5.23) through (5.26) into (5.18) and (5.19), and noting that $\lambda_i^{(1)} = 1$ and $\lambda_i^{(2)} = \lambda_i$,

$$E\{\Delta \mu_1\} \cong \frac{1}{4N} \left[n + \sum_{i=1}^{n} \sum_{j=1}^{n} \frac{m_j^2 (1+\lambda_i \lambda_j)}{(1+\lambda_j)^2 (1+\lambda_i)} + \sum_{i=1}^{n} \frac{m_i^2 (1+\lambda_i^2)}{(1+\lambda_i)^3} \right] , \tag{5.27}$$

$$\text{Var}\{\hat{\mu}_1\} \cong \frac{1}{4N} \left[\sum_{i=1}^{n} \frac{m_i^2}{1+\lambda_i} + \sum_{i=1}^{n} \sum_{j=1}^{n} \frac{m_i^2 m_j^2 (1+\lambda_i \lambda_j)}{2(1+\lambda_i)^2 (1+\lambda_j)^2} \right] . \tag{5.28}$$

Second term μ_2: Similarly, the derivatives of μ_2 can be obtained from (A.37) and (A.38). The results are

$$\frac{\partial \mu_2}{\partial M_r} = 0 \quad \text{and} \quad \frac{\partial^2 \mu_2}{\partial M_r^2} = 0 \,, \tag{5.29}$$

$$\frac{\partial \mu_2}{\partial c_{ij}^{(r)}} = \frac{\delta_{ij}}{4} \left[\frac{1}{\bar{\lambda}_i} - \frac{1}{\lambda_i^{(r)}} \right] , \tag{5.30}$$

$$\frac{\partial^2 \mu_2}{\partial c_{ij}^{(r)2}} = \frac{2-\delta_{ij}}{4} \left[\frac{1}{\lambda_i^{(r)}\lambda_j^{(r)}} - \frac{1}{2\bar{\lambda}_i\bar{\lambda}_j} \right] . \tag{5.31}$$

Substituting (5.29) through (5.31) into (5.18) and (5.19), and noting that $\lambda_i^{(1)} = 1$ and $\lambda_i^{(2)} = \lambda_i$,

$$E\{\Delta\mu_2\} \cong \frac{1}{4N} \left[n(n+1) - \sum_{i=1}^{n}\sum_{j=1}^{n} \frac{1+\lambda_i\lambda_j}{(1+\lambda_i)(1+\lambda_j)} - \sum_{i=1}^{n} \frac{1+\lambda_i^2}{(1+\lambda_i)^2} \right] , \tag{5.32}$$

$$\mathrm{Var}\{\hat{\mu}_2\} \cong \frac{1}{2N} \sum_{i=1}^{n} \left[\left(\frac{1}{1+\lambda_i} - \frac{1}{2} \right)^2 + \left(\frac{1}{1+\lambda_i} - \frac{1}{2\lambda_i} \right)^2 \lambda_i^2 \right] . \tag{5.33}$$

Discussions and experimental verification: Table 5-1 shows the dependence of $E\{\Delta\mu_1\}$ and $E\{\Delta\mu_2\}$ on n and k $(=N/n)$ for three different cases [4]. In the first case, two sets of samples are drawn from the same source $N_X(O,I)$, a normal distribution with zero mean and identity covariance matrix. The second and third cases are Data *I-I* and Data *I-4I* (with variable n), respectively. As Table 5-1 indicates, for all three cases, $E\{\Delta\mu_1\}$ is proportional to $1/k$ while $E\{\Delta\mu_2\}$ is proportional to $(n+1)/k$. Also, note that $E\{\Delta\mu_1\}$ is the same for the first and third cases because the sources have the same mean. Similarly, $E\{\Delta\mu_2\}$ is the same for the first and second cases because the sources share a covariance matrix.

Since the trend is the same for all three cases, let us study the first case closely. Table 5-1 demonstrates that, in high-dimensional spaces ($n >> 1$), $E\{\Delta\mu_2\} = 0.125(n+1)/k$ dominates $E\{\Delta\mu_1\} = 0.25/k$. Also, $E\{\Delta\mu_2\} = 0.125(n+1)/k$ indicates that an increasingly large value of k is required to maintain a constant value of $E\{\hat{\mu}\}$ $(= E\{\hat{\mu}_1\} + E\{\hat{\mu}_2\})$ as the dimensionality increases. For example, Table 5-2 shows the value of k required to obtain

TABLE 5-1

SAMPLE BIAS EXPRESSIONS FOR THE BHATTACHARYYA DISTANCE

	Same Source $N_X(0,I)\ N_X(0,I)$	Data *I-I* $N_X(0,I)\ N_X(M,I)$	Data *I-4I* $N_X(0,I)\ N_X(0,4I)$
m_i	$m_i = 0$	$m_1 = 2.56$ $m_i = 0\ (i \neq 1)$	$m_i = 0$
λ_i	$\lambda_i = 1$	$\lambda_i = 1$	$\lambda_i = 4$
μ_1	0	0.82	0
μ_2	0	0	0.11 n
ε	50%	10%	Depends on n
$E\{\Delta\mu_1\}$	$\frac{0.25}{k}$	$\frac{0.35}{k}$	$\frac{0.25}{k}$
$E\{\Delta\mu_2\}$	$0.125\frac{n+1}{k}$	$0.125\frac{n+1}{k}$	$0.08\frac{n+1}{k}$

TABLE 5-2

VALUES OF k AND N REQUIRED TO MAINTAIN $E\{\hat{\mu}\} \leq 0.223$

n	4	8	16	32	64	128
k	3.9	6.2	10.7	19.6	39.6	73.4
$N = nk$	16	50	172	628	2407	9396

$E\{\hat{\mu}\} = 0.223$ [4]. In this example, two sets of samples are drawn from the same source. Therefore, if an infinite number of samples is generated, the distributions of two sets are identical (the Bayes error of 50% or $\mu = 0$). However, with a finite number of samples, $E\{\mu\}$ is no longer equal to zero, indicating that there exists a difference between two generated distributions. According to (3.151), $E\{\mu\} = 0.223$ means that the overlap between them (the Bayes error) is less than 40%. The larger $E\{\mu\}$ is, the smaller the overlap becomes.

Only 16 samples (3.9 times the dimensionality) are needed to achieve $E\{\hat{\mu}\} = 0.223$ in a 4 dimensional space, while 9396 samples (73.4 times the dimensionality) are needed in a 128 dimensional space. This result is sharply contrasted with the common belief that a fixed multiple of the dimensionality, such as 10, could be used to determine the sample size.

Since the theoretical results of (5.27) and (5.32) for biases and (5.28) and (5.33) for variances are approximations, we conducted three sets of experiments to verify the closeness of the approximations.

Experiment 1: Computation of μ_1 and μ_2

Data: *I-I*, *I-4I*, *I*-Λ (Normal)

Dimensionality: $n = 4, 8, 16, 32, 64$ (for *I-I*, *I-4I*)

$n = 8$ (for *I*-Λ)

Sample size: $N_1 = N_2 = kn$, $k = 3, 5, 10, 20, 40$

No. of trials: $\tau = 10$

Results: Tables 5-3, 5-4, 5-5 [4]

Tables 5-3 and 5-4 present a comparison of the theoretical predictions (first lines) and the means of the 10 trials (second lines) for Data *I-I* and Data *I-4I* respectively. These tables show that the theoretical predictions of the biases match the experimental results very closely. The third lines of Tables 5-3 and 5-4 shows the theoretical predictions of the standard deviations from (5.28) and (5.33). The fourth lines present the experimental standard derivations from the 10 trials. Again the theoretical predictions match the experimental results closely. It should be noted that the variances for $\hat{\mu}_2$ of Data *I-I* and $\hat{\mu}_1$ of Data *I-4I* are zero theoretically. This suggests that the variances for these cases come from the Taylor expansion terms higher than second order, and therefore are expected to be smaller than the variances for the other cases. This is confirmed by comparing the variances between $\hat{\mu}_1$ and $\hat{\mu}_2$ in each Table. Also, note that the variances of $\hat{\mu}_2$ for Data *I-4I* are independent of n. The similar results for Data *I*-Λ are presented in Table 5-5. The experimental results are well predicted by the theoretical equations for a wide range of k.

Verification of the estimation procedure: The estimation procedure of (5.6) was tested on Data RADAR as follows.

TABLE 5-3

$\hat{\mu}$ FOR DATA *I-I*

k	n = 4	8	16	32	64
3	1.1101	1.0758	1.0587	1.0502	1.0459
	1.0730	0.9933	1.0502	1.0754	1.0825
	0.3531	0.2497	0.1765	0.1248	0.0883
	0.4688	0.3791	0.2221	0.1551	0.0955
5	0.9946	0.9740	0.9638	0.9586	0.9561
	1.0941	1.0702	1.0396	0.9659	0.9764
	0.2735	0.1934	0.1368	0.0967	0.0684
	0.3867	0.2745	0.1542	0.1091	0.0733
10	0.9080	0.8977	0.8926	0.8900	0.8887
	0.9593	0.9277	0.8421	0.9128	0.8911
	0.1934	0.1368	0.0967	0.0684	0.0483
	0.2240	0.1424	0.1045	0.0720	0.0709
20	0.8647	0.8595	0.8570	0.8557	0.8551
	0.8778	0.8891	0.8261	0.8685	0.8361
	0.1368	0.0967	0.0684	0.0483	0.0342
	0.1356	0.1060	0.0929	0.0455	0.0387
40	0.8430	0.8405	0.8392	0.8385	0.8382
	0.7917	0.8251	0.8578	0.8343	0.8444
	0.0967	0.0684	0.0483	0.0342	0.0242
	0.0786	0.1118	0.0522	0.0283	0.0271

(a) $E\{\hat{\mu}_1\}$ $(\mu_1 = 0.82)$

k	n = 4	8	16	32	64
3	0.2083	0.3750	0.7083	1.3750	2.7083
	0.2546	0.4106	0.8930	1.7150	3.2875
	0.0000	0.0000	0.0000	0.0000	0.0000
	0.0787	0.0653	0.0588	0.0776	0.1083
5	0.1250	0.2250	0.4250	0.8250	1.6250
	0.1133	0.2791	0.5244	0.9252	1.8035
	0.0000	0.0000	0.0000	0.0000	0.0000
	0.0266	0.0785	0.0581	0.0302	0.0775
10	0.0625	0.1125	0.2125	0.4125	0.8125
	0.0803	0.1179	0.2280	0.4365	0.8578
	0.0000	0.0000	0.0000	0.0000	0.0000
	0.0339	0.0191	0.0218	0.0279	0.0234
20	0.0313	0.0563	0.1063	0.2063	0.4063
	0.0389	0.0566	0.1079	0.2099	0.4129
	0.0000	0.0000	0.0000	0.0000	0.0000
	0.0101	0.0140	0.0132	0.0154	0.0058
40	0.0156	0.0281	0.0531	0.1031	0.2031
	0.0170	0.0282	0.0561	0.1034	0.2061
	0.0000	0.0000	0.0000	0.0000	0.0000
	0.0072	0.0084	0.0086	0.0046	0.0063

(b) $E\{\hat{\mu}_2\}$ $(\mu_2 = 0)$

TABLE 5-4

$\hat{\mu}$ FOR DATA *I*-4*I*

k	n = 4	8	16	32	64
3	0.0833	0.0833	0.0833	0.0833	0.0833
	0.1435	0.1212	0.1051	0.1118	0.1061
	0.0000	0.0000	0.0000	0.0000	0.0000
	0.0971	0.0633	0.0415	0.0385	0.0160
5	0.0500	0.0500	0.0500	0.0500	0.0500
	0.0489	0.0709	0.0579	0.0545	0.0605
	0.0000	0.0000	0.0000	0.0000	0.0000
	0.0284	0.0314	0.0141	0.0209	0.0071
10	0.0250	0.0250	0.0250	0.0250	0.0250
	0.0192	0.0267	0.0266	0.0276	0.0262
	0.0000	0.0000	0.0000	0.0000	0.0000
	0.0151	0.0124	0.0066	0.0079	0.0035
20	0.0125	0.0125	0.0125	0.0125	0.0125
	0.0135	0.0156	0.0139	0.0120	0.0141
	0.0000	0.0000	0.0000	0.0000	0.0000
	0.0055	0.0071	0.0036	0.0038	0.0025
40	0.0063	0.0063	0.0063	0.0063	0.0063
	0.0066	0.0082	0.0056	0.0062	0.0065
	0.0000	0.0000	0.0000	0.0000	0.0000
	0.0045	0.0050	0.0021	0.0014	0.0010

(a) $E\{\hat{\mu}_1\}$ $(\mu_1 = 0)$

k	n = 4	8	16	32	64
3	0.5796	1.1326	2.2385	4.4503	8.8739
	0.7129	1.0732	2.4527	4.7841	9.3263
	0.1732	0.1732	0.1732	0.1732	0.1732
	0.1447	0.1653	0.2332	0.1893	0.1642
5	0.5263	1.0366	2.0572	4.0983	8.1806
	0.5081	1.0063	2.1341	4.1041	8.4000
	0.1342	0.1342	0.1342	0.1342	0.1342
	0.1119	0.1546	0.1129	0.0868	0.1209
10	0.4863	0.9646	1.9212	3.8343	7.6606
	0.4901	0.9463	1.9345	3.8014	7.6630
	0.0949	0.0949	0.0949	0.0949	0.0949
	0.1016	0.0722	0.0759	0.0702	0.1206
20	0.4663	0.9286	1.8532	3.7023	7.4006
	0.4708	0.9331	1.8277	3.7019	7.4049
	0.0671	0.0671	0.0671	0.0671	0.0671
	0.0658	0.0686	0.0966	0.0394	0.0672
40	0.4473	0.9106	1.7886	3.5769	7.1536
	0.4713	0.8937	1.8058	3.6374	7.2596
	0.0474	0.0474	0.0474	0.0474	0.0474
	0.0444	0.0328	0.0353	0.0563	0.0392

(b) $E\{\hat{\mu}_2\}$ $(\mu_2 = 0.11\,n)$

TABLE 5-5

$\hat{\mu}$ FOR DATA *I*-Λ

	Mean		Standard deviation	
k	Theor.	Expt.	Theor.	Expt.
3	1.6453	1.5056	0.3529	0.4995
5	1.4951	1.5104	0.2734	0.1650
10	1.3824	1.3864	0.1933	0.1997
20	1.3261	1.3266	0.1367	0.1712
40	1.2970	1.3104	0.0967	0.0658

(a) $E\{\hat{\mu}_1\}$ $(\mu_1 = 1.27)$

	Mean		Standard deviation	
k	Theor.	Expt.	Theor.	Expt.
3	1.4431	1.5695	0.1746	0.2081
5	1.3002	1.2287	0.1352	0.1446
10	1.1929	1.1638	0.0956	0.0766
20	1.1393	1.1255	0.0676	0.0539
40	1.1125	1.1093	0.0478	0.0405

(b) $E\{\hat{\mu}_2\}$ $(\mu_2 = 1.09)$

Experiment 2: Estimation of μ

Data: RADAR (Real data, $n = 66$, $\varepsilon =$ unknown)

$\hat{\mu}_N$: μ estimated by using $N_1 = N_2 = N$ samples

N	No. of sets per class	$\hat{\mu}_N$
8800	1	0.64
720	1	1.57
360	2	2.52*

Estimation procedure:

$$\left. \begin{aligned} 1.57 &= \mu + v/720 \\ 2.52 &= \mu + v/360 \end{aligned} \right\} \rightarrow \mu = 0.62$$

(*A set of 720 samples per class is divided to two sets of 360 samples. With two sets from each class, there are 4 possible combinations of selecting one set from each class and forming a two-class problem. $\hat{\mu}_{360}$ here is the average of the 4 cases.)

Although the radar data is not guaranteed to be normal, the above results indicate that the prediction of the true μ from a relatively small number of samples (720 per class for the 66 dimensional space) seems possible. Also, note that $\hat{\mu}_{360}$, $\hat{\mu}_{720}$, and $\hat{\mu}_{8800}$ are significantly different. Without the compensation, $\hat{\mu}_{360}$ and $\hat{\mu}_{720}$ could not provide a useful upper bound of the Bayes error.

5.2 Estimation of Classification Errors

An even more important measurement in pattern recognition is the expected performance of a classifier. The discriminant functions for some popular classifiers, including the linear and quadratic classifiers, are functions of M_1, M_2, Σ_1, and Σ_2. Thus, they are the members of the family of functions presented in the previous section. However, unlike the Bhattacharyya distance, the degradation of the expected classifier performance due to a finite sample size comes from two sources: the finite sample set used for design and the finite number of test samples. Thus, we need to study both their effects.

For the two-class problem, a classifier can be expressed by

$$h(X) \underset{\omega_2}{\overset{\omega_1}{\gtrless}} 0 , \tag{5.34}$$

where $h(X)$ is the discriminant function of an n-dimensional vector X. The *probabilities of error* for this classifier from ω_1 and ω_2 are from (3.105) and (3.106)

$$\varepsilon_1 = \int_{h(X)>0} p_1(X)\,dX = \frac{1}{2} + \frac{1}{2\pi}\iint \frac{e^{j\omega h(X)}}{j\omega} p_1(X) d\omega dX , \tag{5.35}$$

$$\varepsilon_2 = \int_{h(X)<0} p_2(X)\,dX = \frac{1}{2} - \frac{1}{2\pi}\iint \frac{e^{j\omega h(X)}}{j\omega} p_2(X) d\omega dX , \tag{5.36}$$

where $p_i(X)$ represents the class i distribution to be tested. The *total probability of error* is

$$\begin{aligned} \varepsilon &= P_1\varepsilon_1 + P_2\varepsilon_2 \\ &= \frac{1}{2} + \frac{1}{2\pi}\iint \frac{e^{j\omega h(X)}}{j\omega} \tilde{p}(X) d\omega dX , \end{aligned} \tag{5.37}$$

where

$$\tilde{p}(X) = P_1 p_1(X) - P_2 p_2(X) . \tag{5.38}$$

Effect of Test Samples

Error expression: When a finite number of samples is available for testing a given classifier, an *error-counting procedure* is the only feasible possibility in practice. That is, the samples are tested by the classifier, and the number of misclassified samples is counted. The other alternative is to estimate the test densities from the samples, and to integrate them in complicated regions. This procedure is, as seen in Chapter 3, complex and difficult even for normal distributions with known expected vectors and covariance matrices.

In the error-counting procedure, $p_i(X)$ of (5.38) may be replaced by

$$\hat{\mathbf{p}}_i(X) = \frac{1}{N_i}\sum_{j=1}^{N_i}\delta(X - \mathbf{X}_j^{(i)}) , \tag{5.39}$$

where $\mathbf{X}_1^{(i)}, \ldots, \mathbf{X}_{N_i}^{(i)}$ are N_i test samples drawn from $p_i(X)$, and $\delta(\cdot)$ is a unit impulse function.

Thus, the estimate of the error probability is

$$\hat{\varepsilon} = \frac{1}{2} + \frac{1}{2\pi}\iint\frac{e^{j\omega h(X)}}{j\omega}[\frac{P_1}{N_1}\sum_{j=1}^{N_1}\delta(X - \mathbf{X}_j^{(1)}) - \frac{P_2}{N_2}\sum_{j=1}^{N_2}\delta(X - \mathbf{X}_j^{(2)})]d\omega dX$$

$$= \frac{1}{2} + \frac{P_1}{N_1}\sum_{j=1}^{N_1}\boldsymbol{\alpha}_j^{(1)} - \frac{P_2}{N_2}\sum_{j=1}^{N_2}\boldsymbol{\alpha}_j^{(2)} , \tag{5.40}$$

where

$$\boldsymbol{\alpha}_j^{(i)} = \frac{1}{2\pi}\int\frac{e^{j\omega h(\mathbf{X}_j^{(i)})}}{j\omega}d\omega . \tag{5.41}$$

Since $\boldsymbol{\alpha}_j^{(i)}$ is the inverse Fourier transform of $1/j\omega$, it becomes $sign(h(\mathbf{X}_j^{(i)}))/2$. That is, $\boldsymbol{\alpha}_j^{(i)}$ is either $+1/2$ or $-1/2$, depending on $h(\mathbf{X}_j^{(i)}) > 0$ or $h(\mathbf{X}_j^{(i)}) < 0$. For $i = 1$, the $\boldsymbol{\alpha}_j^{(1)}$'s are $+1/2$ for misclassified $\mathbf{X}_j^{(1)}$'s and $-1/2$ for correctly classified $\mathbf{X}_j^{(1)}$'s. Thus, summing up these $\boldsymbol{\alpha}_j^{(1)}$'s

$$\frac{1}{N_1}\sum_{j=1}^{N_1}\boldsymbol{\alpha}_j^{(1)} = \frac{1}{2N_1}[(\#\text{ of }\omega_1\text{-errors}) - (\#\text{ of }\omega_1\text{-corrects})]$$

$$= \frac{1}{N_1}(\#\text{ of }\omega_1\text{-errors}) - \frac{1}{2} , \tag{5.42}$$

where (# of ω_1-corrects) = N_1 - (# of ω_1-errors) is used to obtain the second line from the first. Likewise, for $i = 2$,

$$\frac{1}{N_2}\sum_{j=1}^{N_2}\boldsymbol{\alpha}_j^{(2)} = -\frac{1}{N_2}(\#\text{ of }\omega_2\text{-errors}) + \frac{1}{2} . \tag{5.43}$$

Substituting (5.42) and (5.43) into (5.40),

$$\hat{\varepsilon} = P_1 \frac{(\#\text{ of } \omega_1\text{-errors})}{N_1} + P_2 \frac{(\#\text{ of } \omega_2\text{-errors})}{N_2} . \tag{5.44}$$

That is, $\hat{\varepsilon}$ of (5.40) is the error obtained by counting the number of misclassified samples with a given classifier.

Moments of $\hat{\varepsilon}$: The expected value of $\boldsymbol{\alpha}_j^{(i)}$ with respect to $\mathbf{X}_j^{(i)}$ (w.r.t. the test sample) is

$$\bar{\alpha}_i = E_t\{\boldsymbol{\alpha}_j^{(i)}\} = \frac{1}{2\pi}\iint \frac{e^{j\omega h(X)}}{j\omega} p_i(X) d\omega dX$$

$$= \begin{cases} \varepsilon_1 - \dfrac{1}{2} & \text{for } i=1 \\ \dfrac{1}{2} - \varepsilon_2 & \text{for } i=2 . \end{cases} \tag{5.45}$$

The second line of (5.45) can be obtained from (5.35) and (5.36) respectively. The second order moments are also computed as

$$E_t\{\boldsymbol{\alpha}_j^{(i)2}\} = E_t\{[\frac{1}{2\pi}\int \frac{e^{j\omega h(\mathbf{X})}}{j\omega} d\omega]^2\} = E_t\{[\frac{1}{2} sign(h(\mathbf{X}))]^2\}$$

$$= \frac{1}{4} , \tag{5.46}$$

$$E_t\{\boldsymbol{\alpha}_j^{(i)} \boldsymbol{\alpha}_\ell^{(k)}\} = \bar{\alpha}_i \bar{\alpha}_k \qquad \text{for } i \neq k \text{ or } j \neq \ell . \tag{5.47}$$

Equation (5.47) is obtained because $\boldsymbol{\alpha}_j^{(i)}$ and $\boldsymbol{\alpha}_\ell^{(k)}$ are independent due to the independence between $\mathbf{X}_j^{(i)}$ and $\mathbf{X}_\ell^{(k)}$.

From (5.40) and (5.45)-(5.47),

$$E_t\{\hat{\varepsilon}\} = \frac{1}{2} + P_1\bar{\alpha}_1 - P_2\bar{\alpha}_2$$

$$= \frac{1}{2} + P_1(\varepsilon_1 - \frac{1}{2}) - P_2(\frac{1}{2} - \varepsilon_2) = \varepsilon \,, \tag{5.48}$$

$$\text{Var}_t\{\hat{\varepsilon}\} = \frac{P_1^2}{N_1}\text{Var}_t\{\boldsymbol{\alpha}_j^{(1)}\} + \frac{P_2^2}{N_2}\text{Var}_t\{\boldsymbol{\alpha}_j^{(2)}\}$$

$$= \frac{P_1^2}{N_1}[\frac{1}{4} - (\varepsilon_1 - \frac{1}{2})^2] + \frac{P_2^2}{N_2}[\frac{1}{4} - (\frac{1}{2} - \varepsilon_2)^2]$$

$$= P_1^2\frac{\varepsilon_1(1-\varepsilon_1)}{N_1} + P_2^2\frac{\varepsilon_2(1-\varepsilon_2)}{N_2} \,. \tag{5.49}$$

That is, $\hat{\varepsilon}$ is an unbiased and consistent estimate, no matter what $h(X)$ is used.

Error counting approach: When the *error counting procedure* is used, the effect of test samples can be analyzed in a more direct way. In order to estimate ε_i, N_i samples are drawn from ω_i and tested by a given classifier. Let $\hat{\boldsymbol{\tau}}_i$ be the number of misclassified samples. Then, the random variables $\hat{\boldsymbol{\tau}}_1$ and $\hat{\boldsymbol{\tau}}_2$ are independent, and each is *binomially distributed* as

$$Pr\{\hat{\boldsymbol{\tau}}_1 = \tau_1, \hat{\boldsymbol{\tau}}_2 = \tau_2\} = \prod_{i=1}^{2} Pr\{\hat{\boldsymbol{\tau}}_i = \tau_i\}$$

$$= \prod_{i=1}^{2} \begin{bmatrix} N_i \\ \tau_i \end{bmatrix} \varepsilon_i^{\tau_i}(1 - \varepsilon_i)^{N_i - \tau_i} \,. \tag{5.50}$$

The ω_i-error, ε_i, is estimated by $\hat{\boldsymbol{\tau}}_i/N_i$ and, subsequently, the total probability of error is estimated by

$$\hat{\varepsilon} = \sum_{i=1}^{2} P_i \frac{\hat{\boldsymbol{\tau}}_i}{N_i} \,. \tag{5.51}$$

The expected value and variance of the binomial distribution are known, and thus

$$E\{\hat{\varepsilon}\} = P_1\varepsilon_1 + P_2\varepsilon_2 = \varepsilon \,, \tag{5.52}$$

$$\mathrm{Var}\{\hat{\varepsilon}\} = \sum_{i=1}^{2} P_i^2 \frac{\varepsilon_i(1-\varepsilon_i)}{N_i} \,. \tag{5.53}$$

These are the same as (5.48) and (5.49).

Effect of Design Samples

It is more difficult to discuss the effect of using a *finite number of design samples*. Although we would like to keep the formula as general as possible, in this section a specific family of discriminant functions is investigated to help determine which approximations should be used.

Error expression: Assume that the discriminant function is a function of two expected vectors, M_1 and M_2, and two covariance matrices, Σ_1 and Σ_2. Typical examples are the *quadratic* and *linear classifiers* as

$$h(X) = \frac{1}{2}(X-M_1)^T\Sigma_1^{-1}(X-M_1) - \frac{1}{2}(X-M_2)^T\Sigma_2^{-1}(X-M_2) + \frac{1}{2}\ln\frac{|\Sigma_1|}{|\Sigma_2|} \,, \tag{5.54}$$

$$h(X) = (M_2-M_1)^T\overline{\Sigma}^{-1}X + \frac{1}{2}(M_1^T\overline{\Sigma}^{-1}M_1 - M_2^T\overline{\Sigma}^{-1}M_2) \,, \tag{5.55}$$

where $\overline{\Sigma} = (\Sigma_1+\Sigma_2)/2$. When only a finite number of design samples is available and M_i and Σ_i are estimated from them, h becomes a random variable and

$$\Delta\mathbf{h}(X) = \hat{\mathbf{h}}(X) - h(X) = \sum_{k=1}^{\infty}\mathbf{0}^{(k)} \,, \tag{5.56}$$

where $\hat{\mathbf{h}}(X) = h(X, \hat{\mathbf{M}}_1, \hat{\mathbf{M}}_2, \hat{\Sigma}_1, \hat{\Sigma}_2)$, $h(X) = h(X, M_1, M_2, \Sigma_1, \Sigma_2)$, and $\mathbf{0}^{(k)}$ is the kth order term of the Taylor series expansion in terms of the variations of $\hat{\mathbf{M}}_i$ and $\hat{\Sigma}_i$. If the design samples are drawn from normal distributions, and $\hat{\mathbf{M}}_i$ and $\hat{\Sigma}_i$ are unbiased estimates (e.g., the sample mean and sample covariance),

(5.16) and (5.17) show

$$E_d\{\mathbf{0}^{(1)}\} = 0,\ \ E_d\{\mathbf{0}^{(2)}\} \sim 1/\mathcal{n},$$
$$E_d\{\mathbf{0}^{(3)}\} = 0,\ \ E_d\{\mathbf{0}^{(4)}\} \sim 1/\mathcal{n}^2, \ldots \tag{5.57}$$

where E_d indicates the expectation with respect to the design samples, and $\mathcal{n}$ is the number of design samples (while N indicates the number of test samples). Therefore, from (5.56) and (5.57),

$$E_d\{\Delta\mathbf{h}(X)\} \sim 1/\mathcal{n},\ \ E_d\{\Delta\mathbf{h}^2(X)\} \sim 1/\mathcal{n},$$
$$E_d\{\Delta\mathbf{h}^3(X)\} \sim 1/\mathcal{n}^2,\ \ E_d\{\Delta\mathbf{h}^4(X)\} \sim 1/\mathcal{n}^2, \ldots . \tag{5.58}$$

Assuming that $\mathcal{n}$ is reasonably large, we can eliminate $E\{\Delta\mathbf{h}^m(X)\}$ for m larger than 2.

From (5.37), the error of a random classifier for given test distributions is expressed by

$$\hat{\boldsymbol{\varepsilon}} = \frac{1}{2} + \frac{1}{2\pi}\iint \frac{e^{j\omega\hat{\mathbf{h}}(X)}}{j\omega}\tilde{p}(X)d\omega dX . \tag{5.59}$$

When $\Delta\mathbf{h}$ is small, we may use the following approximation

$$e^{j\omega\hat{\mathbf{h}}(X)} = e^{j\omega h(X)}e^{j\omega\Delta\mathbf{h}(X)} \cong e^{j\omega h(X)}[1 + j\omega\Delta\mathbf{h}(X) + \frac{(j\omega)^2}{2}\Delta\mathbf{h}^2(X)] . \tag{5.60}$$

Then, $\Delta\boldsymbol{\varepsilon} = \hat{\boldsymbol{\varepsilon}} - \varepsilon$ can be approximated by

$$\Delta\boldsymbol{\varepsilon} \cong \frac{1}{2\pi}\iint\{\Delta\mathbf{h}(X) + \frac{j\omega}{2}\Delta\mathbf{h}^2(X)\}e^{j\omega h(X)}\tilde{p}(X)d\omega dX . \tag{5.61}$$

Bayes classifier: When $h(X)$ is the Bayes classifier for the given test distributions, $\tilde{p}(X) = 0$ at $h(X) = 0$. In this case, the Bayes error, ε, is the minimum error and $\Delta\boldsymbol{\varepsilon}$ of (5.61) must be always positive. In order to confirm the validity of the error expression (5.59), let us prove $\Delta\boldsymbol{\varepsilon} \geq 0$ as an exercise.

The first step to prove $\Delta\boldsymbol{\varepsilon} \geq 0$ is to show that the first order variation of (5.61) is zero regardless of $\Delta\mathbf{h}(X)$, as follows.

$$\frac{1}{2\pi}\iint \Delta\mathbf{h}(\mathbf{X})e^{j\omega h(X)}\tilde{p}(X)d\omega dX = \int \Delta\mathbf{h}(X)\delta(h(X))\tilde{p}(X)dX$$

$$= \int_{h(X)=0} \Delta\mathbf{h}(X)\tilde{p}(X)dX = 0\ , \tag{5.62}$$

where we used the fact that the inverse Fourier transform of 1 is $\delta(\cdot)$. Equation (5.62) becomes zero because $\tilde{p}(X) = 0$ at $h(X) = 0$.

The second step involves showing that the second order variation of (5.61) is positive regardless of $\Delta\mathbf{h}(X)$.

$$\frac{1}{2\pi}\iint \frac{j\omega}{2}\Delta\mathbf{h}^2(X)e^{j\omega h(X)}\tilde{p}(X)d\omega\, dX = \frac{1}{2}\int \Delta\mathbf{h}^2(X)\frac{d\delta(h)}{dh}\tilde{p}(X)\, dX\ . \tag{5.63}$$

The derivative of the unit impulse, $d\delta(h)/dh$, is zero except in the region very close to $h(X) = 0$, where $d\delta(h)/dh > 0$ for $h < 0$ and $d\delta(h)/dh < 0$ for $h > 0$. On the other hand, $\tilde{p}(X) > 0$ for $h < 0$ and $\tilde{p}(X) < 0$ for $h > 0$. Since $\Delta\mathbf{h}^2(X) > 0$ regardless of $\Delta\mathbf{h}(X)$, (5.63) is always positive.

Bias: The expected value of $\hat{\boldsymbol{\varepsilon}}$, $\bar{\varepsilon}$, with respect to the design samples is

$$\bar{\varepsilon} = E_d\{\hat{\boldsymbol{\varepsilon}}\} = \frac{1}{2} + \frac{1}{2\pi}\iint \frac{E_d\{e^{j\omega\hat{\mathbf{h}}(X)}\}}{j\omega}\tilde{p}(X)d\omega dX$$

$$= \varepsilon + \overline{\Delta\varepsilon}\ . \tag{5.64}$$

Then, the *bias*, $\overline{\Delta\varepsilon}$, may be approximated by

$$\overline{\Delta\varepsilon} \cong \frac{1}{2\pi}\iint E_d\{\Delta\mathbf{h}(X) + \frac{j\omega}{2}\Delta\mathbf{h}^2(X)\}e^{j\omega h(X)}\tilde{p}(X)d\omega dX\ . \tag{5.65}$$

When h is a function of q parameters, $y_1, \ldots, y_q$, $\Delta\mathbf{h}$ is, from (5.1)

$$\Delta\mathbf{h} \cong \sum_{i=1}^{q}\frac{\partial h}{\partial y_i}\Delta\mathbf{y}_i + \frac{1}{2}\sum_{i=1}^{q}\sum_{j=1}^{q}\frac{\partial^2 h}{\partial y_i \partial y_j}\Delta\mathbf{y}_i\Delta\mathbf{y}_j\ . \tag{5.66}$$

Thus, discarding terms of higher order than 2,

$$E_d\{\Delta\mathbf{h}\} \cong \frac{1}{2}\sum_{i=1}^{q}\sum_{j=1}^{q}\frac{\partial^2 h}{\partial y_i \partial y_j}E_d\{\Delta\mathbf{y}_i\Delta\mathbf{y}_j\} , \tag{5.67}$$

$$E_d\{\Delta\mathbf{h}^2\} \cong \sum_{i=1}^{q}\sum_{j=1}^{q}\frac{\partial h}{\partial y_i}\frac{\partial h}{\partial y_j}E_d\{\Delta\mathbf{y}_i\Delta\mathbf{y}_j\} . \tag{5.68}$$

Note that $E_d\{\Delta\mathbf{y}_i\} = 0$, assuming that unbiased estimates are used. Substituting (5.67) and (5.68) into (5.65),

$$\overline{\Delta\varepsilon} \cong \frac{1}{2\pi}\iint \frac{1}{2}\sum_{i=1}^{q}\sum_{j=1}^{q}\left[\frac{\partial^2 h}{\partial y_i \partial y_j} + j\omega\frac{\partial h}{\partial y_i}\frac{\partial h}{\partial y_j}\right] \times E_d\{\Delta\mathbf{y}_i\Delta\mathbf{y}_j\}e^{j\omega h(X)}\tilde{p}(X)d\omega dX . \tag{5.69}$$

Furthermore, if the parameters come from M_1, M_2, Σ_1, and Σ_2 of two normal distributions, as in (5.10), $\overline{\Delta\varepsilon}$ becomes

$$\overline{\Delta\varepsilon} \cong \frac{1}{2\mathcal{N}}\frac{1}{2\pi}\iint\sum_{r=1}^{2}\left[\sum_{i=1}^{n}\left\{\frac{\partial^2 h}{\partial m_i^{(r)2}} + j\omega\left[\frac{\partial h}{\partial m_i^{(r)}}\right]^2\right\}\lambda_i^{(r)} + \sum_{i=1}^{n}\left\{\frac{\partial^2 h}{\partial c_{ii}^{(r)2}} + j\omega\left[\frac{\partial h}{\partial c_{ii}^{(r)}}\right]^2\right\}2\lambda_i^{(r)2} + \sum_{i=1}^{n}\sum_{j=1}^{i-1}\left\{\frac{\partial^2 h}{\partial c_{ij}^{(r)2}} + j\omega\left[\frac{\partial h}{\partial c_{ij}^{(r)}}\right]^2\right\}\lambda_i^{(r)}\lambda_j^{(r)}\right]e^{j\omega h(X)}\tilde{p}(X)d\omega dX . \tag{5.70}$$

Equation (5.69) is a very general expression for the bias of the error, which is valid regardless of the selection of $h(X)$, P_i, and $p_i(X)$. The term $E\{\Delta\mathbf{y}_i\Delta\mathbf{y}_j\}$ gives the effect of the sample size, $\mathcal{N}$. Therefore, if (5.5) is satisfied, $\overline{\Delta\varepsilon}$ can be expressed by $\nu g(\mathcal{N})$ where ν is determined by $h(X)$, P_i, and $p_i(X)$, and the estimation procedure of (5.6) can be applied. Furthermore, if $h(X)$ is a function of M_1, M_2, Σ_1, and Σ_2, $g(\mathcal{n})$ becomes $1/\mathcal{n}$ as is seen in (5.70). The quadratic and linear classifiers of (5.54) and (5.55) belong to this case. Therefore, for these classifiers,

$$\bar{\varepsilon} \cong \varepsilon + \frac{v}{\mathcal{n}} . \tag{5.71}$$

The v of (5.71) is determined by the underlying problem, and stays constant for experiments with various sample sizes. Thus, we may choose various values of $\mathcal{n}$ as $\mathcal{n}_1, \ldots, \mathcal{n}_\ell$, and measure $\hat{\varepsilon}$. Computing $\bar{\varepsilon}$ as the average of several independent trials, we may solve (5.71) for ε and v by a line fit technique.

Experiment 3: Estimation of the error for the quadratic classifier

Data: RADAR (Real data, $n = 66$, $\varepsilon =$ unknown)

Classifier: Quadratic classifier of (5.54)

Test samples: $N_1 = N_2 = 4400$ (one set)

Design samples: $\mathcal{n}_1 = \mathcal{n}_2 = 4400, 720, 360$

$\hat{\varepsilon}_{\mathcal{n}}$: The error of the quadratic classifier when $\mathcal{n}$ design samples per class are used.

$\mathcal{n}$	No. of sets per class	$\hat{\varepsilon}_{\mathcal{n}}$ (%)
4400	1	20.2
720	1	25.9
360	2	30.1*

(*average of 4 possible combinations of 2 sets from each class - see Experiment 2.)

Estimation procedure:

$$\left.\begin{array}{l} 25.9 = \varepsilon + v/720 \\ 30.1 = \varepsilon + v/360 \end{array}\right\} \rightarrow \varepsilon = 21.7\%$$

The estimated error by line fitting, 21.7%, is reasonably close to $\hat{\varepsilon}_{4400} = 20.2\%$. This confirms that we can predict the potential performance of the quadratic classifier even if the available sample size is relatively small for a high-dimensional space ($\mathcal{n}_1 = \mathcal{n}_2 = 720$ for $n = 66$.) Also, note that $\hat{\varepsilon}_{720} = 25.9\%$ and $\hat{\varepsilon}_{360} = 30.1\%$ are much higher than $\hat{\varepsilon}_{4400} = 20.2\%$. This suggests that neither $\hat{\varepsilon}_{720}$ nor $\hat{\varepsilon}_{360}$ can be used as reasonable estimates of the true performance of this quadratic classifier.

Quadratic classifier: Although we do not need to know the value of ν to conduct Experiment 3 to estimate ε, ν can be computed by obtaining the partial derivatives of h and carrying through the integration of (5.69) for a specific classifier. When the quadratic classifier of (5.54) with the parameters of (5.8) and (5.9) is adopted, the partial derivatives of h are, from (A.29)-(A.32) and (A.36)-(A.38),

$$\frac{\partial h}{\partial M_r} = (-1)^r \Lambda_r^{-1}(X-M_r) , \tag{5.72}$$

$$\frac{\partial^2 h}{\partial M_r^2} = (-1)^{r+1}\Lambda_r^{-1} , \tag{5.73}$$

$$\frac{\partial h}{\partial c_{ij}^{(r)}} = (-1)^r \frac{1}{2}\left[(2-\delta_{ij})\frac{(x_i-m_i^{(r)})(x_j-m_j^{(r)})}{\lambda_i^{(r)}\lambda_j^{(r)}} - \frac{\delta_{ij}}{\lambda_i^{(r)}}\right] , \tag{5.74}$$

$$\frac{\partial^2 h}{\partial c_{ij}^{(r)2}} = (-1)^{r+1}\frac{2-\delta_{ij}}{2}\left\{\left[\frac{(x_i-m_i^{(r)})^2}{\lambda_i^{(r)2}\lambda_j^{(r)}} + \frac{(x_j-m_j^{(r)})^2}{\lambda_i^{(r)}\lambda_j^{(r)2}}\right] - \frac{1}{\lambda_i^{(r)}\lambda_j^{(r)}}\right\} . \tag{5.75}$$

Substituting (5.72)-(5.75) into (5.70), and noting that $\lambda_i^{(1)} = 1$, $\lambda_i^{(2)} = \lambda_i$, $m_i^{(1)} = 0$ and $m_i^{(2)} = m_i$, ν of (5.71) becomes

$$\nu_q = \frac{1}{2\pi}\iint f_q(X,\omega)e^{j\omega h(X)}\tilde{p}(X)d\omega dX , \tag{5.76}$$

where

$$f_q(X,\omega) = \frac{1}{2}\left[(n+1)\sum_{i=1}^{n}\left\{x_i^2 - \frac{(x_i-m_i)^2}{\lambda_i}\right\}\right.$$

$$\left. + j\omega\left[n+\frac{1}{2}\sum_{i=1}^{n}\sum_{j=1}^{n}\left\{x_i^2x_j^2 + \frac{(x_i-m_i)^2(x_j-m_j)^2}{\lambda_i\lambda_j}\right\}\right]\right] . \tag{5.77}$$

The integration of (5.76) can be carried out by using the procedure discussed in

Section 3.3. First, we get the closed-form solution for the integration with respect to X, and then take the one-dimensional integration with respect to ω numerically.

For the simplest case of Data *I-I*, we can obtain the explicit expression for the integration of (5.76). In Data *I-I*, $p_1(X)$ and $p_2(X)$ are normal $N_X(0,I)$ and $N_X(M,I)$ respectively. Then, $e^{j\omega h(X)}p_i(X)$ may be rewritten as

$$e^{j\omega h(X)}p_1(X) = \frac{\sqrt{2\pi}}{\sqrt{M^TM}} e^{-M^TM/8} N_\omega(-\frac{j}{2}, \frac{1}{M^TM}) N_X(j\omega M, I) , \tag{5.78}$$

$$e^{j\omega h(X)}p_2(X) = \frac{\sqrt{2\pi}}{\sqrt{M^TM}} e^{-M^TM/8} N_\omega(\frac{j}{2}, \frac{1}{M^TM}) N_X((1+j\omega)M, I) , \tag{5.79}$$

where $N_\omega(a,b)$ and $N_X(D,K)$ are normal density functions of ω and X with the expected value a and variance b for N_ω, and the expected vector D and covariance matrix K for N_X.

Since $f_q(X,\omega)$ is a linear combination of $x_i^k x_j^\ell$ $(k,\ell \le 4)$ as seen in (5.77), $\int f_q(X,\omega)N_X(\cdot,\cdot)dX$ is the linear combination of the moments of $N_X(\cdot,\cdot)$. The result of the integration becomes a polynomial in ω

$$\begin{aligned}\gamma_i(\omega) = {} & \frac{(M^TM)^2}{2}(j\omega)^5 \mp (M^TM)^2(j\omega)^4 + \frac{M^TM}{2}(n+5+3M^TM)(j\omega)^3 \\ & \mp \frac{M^TM}{2}(n+5+2M^TM)(j\omega)^2 \\ & + \frac{1}{4}\left[n(n+7)+(5n+9)M^TM+(M^TM)^2\right](j\omega) \mp \frac{(n+1)M^TM}{2} ,\end{aligned} \tag{5.80}$$

where $-$ and $+$ of $\mp$ are for $i = 1$ and 2 respectively. Again, the $\int \gamma_i(\omega)N_\omega(\cdot,\cdot)d\omega$ is a linear combination of the moments of $N_\omega(\cdot,\cdot)$. Thus, v_q for $P_1 = P_2 = 0.5$ is

$$v_q = \frac{1}{4\sqrt{2\pi M^T M}} e^{-M^T M/8}$$

$$\times \left[n^2 + (1+\frac{M^T M}{2})n + \{\frac{(M^T M)^2}{16} - \frac{M^T M}{2} - 1\} \right] . \tag{5.81}$$

In order to verify (5.81), the following experiment was conducted.

Experiment 4: Error of the quadratic classifier

Data: *I-I* (Normal, $M^T M = 2.56^2$, $\varepsilon = 10\%$)
Dimensionality: $n = 4, 8, 16, 32, 64$
Classifier: Quadratic classifier of (5.54)
Design samples: $\mathcal{N}_1 = \mathcal{N}_2 = kn$, $k = 3, 5, 10, 20, 40$
Test: Theoretical using (3.119)-(3.128)
No. of trials: $\tau = 10$
Results: Table 5-6 [4]

In this experiment, kn samples are generated from each class, M_i and Σ_i are estimated by (5.8) and (5.9), and the quadratic classifier of (5.54) is designed. Testing was conducted by integrating the true normal distributions, $p_1(X) = N_X(O,I)$ and $p_2(X) = N_X(M,I)$, in the class 2 and 1 regions determined by this quadratic classifier, respectively [see (3.119)-(3.128)]. The first line of Table 5-6 shows the theoretical bias computed from (5.71) and (5.81), and the second and third lines are the average and standard deviation of the bias from the 10 trials of experiment. The theoretical prediction accurately reflects the experimental trends. Notice that v is proportional to n^2 for $n >> 1$. Also, note that the standard deviations are very small.

In theory, the Bayes error decreases monotonously, as the number of measurements, n, increases. However, in practice, when a fixed number of samples is used to design a classifier, the error of the classifier tends to increase as n gets large as shown in Fig. 5-1. This trend is called the *Hughes phenomena* [5]. The difference between these two curves is the bias due to finite design samples, which is roughly proportional to $n^2/\mathcal{N}$ for a quadratic classifier.

Linear classifier: The analysis of the linear classifier, (5.55), proceeds in a similar fashion. The partial derivatives of h may be obtained by using (A.30) and (A.33)-(A.35) as follows.

TABLE 5-6

QUADRATIC CLASSIFIER DEGRADATION FOR DATA *I-I* (%)

		n = 4	8	16	32	64
		14.50	16.89	21.15	30.67	48.94
	3	16.68	20.41	22.04	26.73	31.31
		3.51	2.35	2.89	1.95	1.33
		12.70	14.14	16.91	22.40	33.36
	5	14.03	16.40	17.34	20.81	25.54
		2.11	1.86	0.91	0.57	0.74
		11.35	12.07	13.45	16.20	21.68
k	10	11.52	12.40	13.66	15.73	19.34
		0.81	0.61	0.70	0.54	0.85
		10.67	11.03	11.73	13.10	15.84
	20	10.77	11.05	11.90	13.93	15.13
		0.21	0.23	0.51	0.22	0.32
		10.34	10.52	10.86	11.55	12.92
	40	10.37	10.57	10.87	11.50	12.75
		0.24	0.13	0.13	0.13	0.18

$$\frac{\partial h}{\partial M_r} = (-1)^r \bar{\Sigma}^{-1} (X - M_r) , \tag{5.82}$$

$$\frac{\partial^2 h}{\partial M_r^2} = (-1)^{r+1} \bar{\Sigma}^{-1} , \tag{5.83}$$

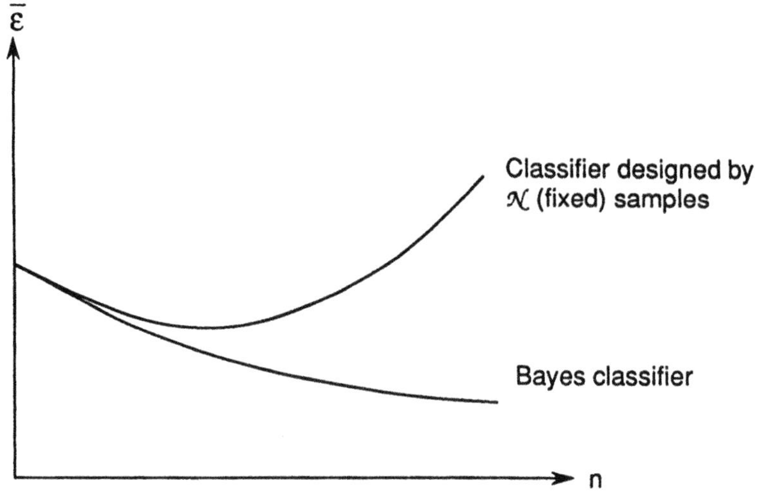

Fig. 5-1 An example of Hughes phenomena.

$$\frac{\partial h}{\partial c_{ij}^{(r)}} = \frac{\partial h}{\partial \bar{c}_{ij}} \frac{\partial \bar{c}_{ij}}{\partial c_{ij}^{(r)}} = -\frac{1}{2\bar{\lambda}_i \bar{\lambda}_j}(\alpha_{ij} + \alpha_{ji} - \delta_{ij}\alpha_{ij}) , \tag{5.84}$$

$$\frac{\partial^2 h}{\partial c_{ij}^{(r)2}} = \frac{\partial^2 h}{\partial \bar{c}_{ij}^2} \left[\frac{\partial \bar{c}_{ij}}{\partial c_{ij}^{(r)}} \right]^2 = \frac{2}{4\bar{\lambda}_i \bar{\lambda}_j} \left[\frac{\alpha_{ii}}{\bar{\lambda}_i} + \frac{\alpha_{jj}}{\bar{\lambda}_j} - \delta_{ij} \frac{\alpha_{ii}}{\bar{\lambda}_i} \right] , \tag{5.85}$$

where

$$\alpha_{ij} = (m_i^{(2)} - m_i^{(1)})x_j + \frac{1}{2}(m_i^{(1)} m_j^{(1)} - m_i^{(2)} m_j^{(2)}) , \tag{5.86}$$

and $\bar{c}_{ij} = (c_{ij}^{(1)} + c_{ij}^{(2)})/2$ and $\bar{\lambda}_i = (\lambda_i^{(1)} + \lambda_i^{(2)})/2$.

In particular, when $\lambda_i^{(1)} = 1$, $\lambda_i^{(2)} = \lambda_i$, $m_i^{(1)} = 0$, and $m_i^{(2)} = m$, (5.84)-(5.86) become

$$\frac{\partial h}{\partial c_{ij}^{(r)}} = -\frac{2}{(1+\lambda_i)(1+\lambda_j)}(\alpha_{ij} + \alpha_{ji} - \delta_{ij}\alpha_{ij}) , \tag{5.87}$$

$$\frac{\partial^2 h}{\partial c_{ij}^{(r)2}} = \frac{4}{(1+\lambda_i)(1+\lambda_j)} \left[\frac{\alpha_{ii}}{1+\lambda_i} + \frac{\alpha_{jj}}{1+\lambda_j} - \delta_{ij} \frac{\alpha_{ii}}{1+\lambda_i} \right] , \tag{5.88}$$

where

$$\alpha_{ij} = m_i x_j - \frac{1}{2} m_i m_j = \frac{m_i}{2}(2x_j - m_j) \ . \tag{5.89}$$

Substituting (5.82)-(5.89) into (5.70), ν of (5.71) becomes

$$\nu_\ell = \frac{1}{2\pi} \iint f_\ell(X,\omega) e^{j\omega h(X)} \tilde{p}(X) d\omega dX \ , \tag{5.90}$$

where

$$f_\ell(X,\omega) = \sum_{i=1}^{n} \left[\frac{1-\lambda_i}{1+\lambda_i} + (2x_i - m_i) \left\{ \frac{(1+\lambda_i^2) m_i}{(1+\lambda_i)^3} + \frac{m_i}{(1+\lambda_i)^2} \sum_{j=1}^{n} \frac{1+\lambda_i\lambda_j}{1+\lambda_j} \right\} \right]$$

$$+ \frac{j\omega}{2} \left[4 \sum_{i=1}^{n} \left\{ \frac{x_i^2}{(1+\lambda_i)^2} + \frac{(x_i - m_i)^2 \lambda_i}{(1+\lambda_i)^2} \right\} \right.$$

$$\left. + \sum_{i=1}^{n} \sum_{j=1}^{n} \frac{m_i(2x_j - m_j)(1+\lambda_i\lambda_j)}{(1+\lambda_i)^2(1+\lambda_j)^2} \left\{ m_i(2x_j - m_j) + m_j(2x_i - m_i) \right\} \right] . \tag{5.91}$$

Since $f_\ell(X,\omega)$ is a linear combination of x_i^k $(k \le 2)$, ν_ℓ can be theoretically computed for Data *I-I*, resulting in

$$\nu_\ell = \frac{1}{2\sqrt{2\pi M^T M}} e^{-M^T M/8} [(1 + \frac{M^T M}{4})n - 1] \ . \tag{5.92}$$

Equation (5.92) was experimentally verified in the same manner as (5.81). The results are shown in Table 5-7.

Experiment 5: Error of the linear classifier

Data: *I-I* (Normal, $M^T M = 2.56^2$, $\varepsilon = 10\%$)
Dimensionality: $n = 4, 8, 16, 32, 64$
Classifier: Linear classifier of (5.55)
Design samples: $\mathcal{N}_1 = \mathcal{N}_2 = kn$, $k = 3, 5, 10, 20, 40$
Test: Theoretical using the normal error table
No. of trials: $\tau = 10$
Results: Table 5-7 [4]

TABLE 5-7

LINEAR CLASSIFIER DEGRADATION FOR DATA *I-I* (%)

		n				
		4	8	16	32	64
		12.73	12.87	12.94	12.98	13.00
	3	14.37	14.36	13.36	13.02	13.19
		3.65	1.74	1.35	.81	.40
		11.64	11.72	11.77	11.79	11.80
	5	11.65	12.23	12.07	11.99	12.07
		1.28	1.53	.71	.48	.41
		10.82	10.86	10.88	10.89	10.90
k	10	10.50	10.89	10.93	10.86	10.92
		.30	.41	.24	.21	.19
		10.41	10.43	10.44	10.45	10.45
	20	10.39	10.39	10.58	10.40	10.45
		.21	.18	.26	.11	.08
		10.20	10.22	10.22	10.22	10.22
	40	10.22	10.27	10.21	10.23	10.22
		.21	.14	.09	.05	.04

Comparison of (5.81) and (5.92) reveals an important distinction between quadratic and linear classifiers. For Data *I-I*, the two covariances are the same. Thus, if the true underlying parameters are used, the quadratic classifier of (5.54) becomes identical to the linear classifier of (5.55). However, when the estimated covariances, $\hat{\Sigma}_1 \neq \hat{\Sigma}_2$, are used, the classifier of (5.54) differs from that of (5.55). As a result, $E\{\Delta\varepsilon\}$ for the quadratic classifier is proportional to $n^2/\mathcal{N}$ $(= n/k)$ while $E\{\Delta\varepsilon\}$ for the linear classifier is proportional to $n/\mathcal{N}(= 1/k)$ as in (5.81) and (5.92) when $n >> 1$. Although it depends on the values of n and $M^T M$, we may generally conclude that ν_q is larger than ν_ℓ for $n >> 1$. This implies that many more samples are needed to properly design a quadratic classifier than a linear classifier. It is believed in general that the linear classifier is more robust (less sensitive to parameter estimation errors) than the quadratic classifier, particularly in high-dimensional spaces. The above results support this belief both theoretically and experimentally.

Also note that for large n, ν_ℓ / n is proportional to $1/k$. This indicates that, as far as the design of a linear classifier is concerned, a fixed multiple could be used to determine the sample size from the dimensionality. However, (5.92) indicates that the value of the multiple depends on $M^T M$, which measures the separability between two distributions with a common covariance matrix I. In particular, the less the separability between the two distributions, the greater k must be for a fixed bias.

Variance: The variance of $\hat{\boldsymbol{\varepsilon}}$ may be computed from (5.59) and (5.64) as

$$\mathrm{Var}_d\{\hat{\boldsymbol{\varepsilon}}\} = \frac{1}{4\pi^2} \iiiint \frac{E_d\{e^{j\omega_1 \hat{\mathbf{h}}(X)} e^{j\omega_2 \hat{\mathbf{h}}(Y)}\}}{j\omega_1 j\omega_2} \tilde{p}(X)\tilde{p}(Y) d\omega_1 d\omega_2 dX dY$$
$$- (\bar{\varepsilon} - \frac{1}{2})^2 . \tag{5.93}$$

Applying the same approximation as (5.60) and keeping up to the second order terms of $\Delta\mathbf{h}$,

$$e^{j\omega_1 \hat{\mathbf{h}}(X)} e^{j\omega_2 \hat{\mathbf{h}}(Y)} = e^{j\omega_1 h(X)} e^{j\omega_2 h(Y)} e^{j\omega_1 \Delta\mathbf{h}(X)} e^{j\omega_2 \Delta\mathbf{h}(Y)}$$
$$\cong e^{j\omega_1 h(X)} e^{j\omega_2 h(Y)} [1 + j\omega_1 \Delta\zeta_1(X)$$
$$+ j\omega_2 \Delta\zeta_2(Y) - \omega_1 \omega_2 \Delta\mathbf{h}(X) \Delta\mathbf{h}(Y)] , \tag{5.94}$$

where

$$\Delta\zeta_i(X) = \Delta\mathbf{h}(X) + \frac{j\omega_i}{2} \Delta\mathbf{h}^2(X) . \tag{5.95}$$

Thus, (5.93) can be expanded to

$$\mathrm{Var}_d\{\hat{\varepsilon}\} \cong \frac{1}{2\pi}\iint \frac{e^{j\omega_1 h(X)}}{j\omega_1}\tilde{p}(X)d\omega_1 dX \cdot \frac{1}{2\pi}\iint \frac{e^{j\omega_2 h(Y)}}{j\omega_2}\tilde{p}(Y)d\omega_2 dY$$

$$+\frac{1}{2\pi}\iint E_d\{\Delta\zeta_1(X)\}e^{j\omega_1 h(X)}\tilde{p}(X)d\omega_1 dX \cdot \frac{1}{2\pi}\iint \frac{e^{j\omega_2 h(Y)}}{j\omega_2}\tilde{p}(Y)d\omega_2 dY$$

$$+\frac{1}{2\pi}\iint \frac{e^{j\omega_1 h(X)}}{j\omega_1}\tilde{p}(X)d\omega_1 dX \cdot \frac{1}{2\pi}\iint E_d\{\Delta\zeta_2(Y)\}e^{j\omega_2 h(Y)}\tilde{p}(Y)d\omega_2 dY$$

$$+\frac{1}{4\pi^2}\iiiint E_d\{\Delta\mathbf{h}(X)\Delta\mathbf{h}(Y)\}e^{j\omega_1 h(X)}e^{j\omega_2 h(Y)}\tilde{p}(X)\tilde{p}(Y)d\omega_1 d\omega_2 dX dY$$

$$-(\bar{\varepsilon}-\frac{1}{2})^2 . \tag{5.96}$$

The first line of (5.96) is $(\varepsilon-1/2)^2$ from (5.37), and the second and third lines are each $(\varepsilon-1/2)\overline{\Delta\varepsilon}$ from (5.65). Furthermore, the summation of the first, second, third, and fifth lines is $(\varepsilon-1/2)^2 + 2(\varepsilon-1/2)\overline{\Delta\varepsilon} - (\bar{\varepsilon}-1/2)^2 = -\overline{\Delta\varepsilon}^2$ where $\bar{\varepsilon} = \varepsilon + \overline{\Delta\varepsilon}$. Since $\overline{\Delta\varepsilon}$ is proportional to $E_d\{\Delta\mathbf{h}(X) + j\omega\Delta\mathbf{h}^2(X)/2\}$ $(\sim 1/\mathcal{N})$ from (5.65) and (5.58), $\overline{\Delta\varepsilon}^2$ is proportional to $1/\mathcal{N}^2$ and can be neglected for a large $\mathcal{N}$. Thus, only the fourth line remains uncancelled. Thus,

$$\mathrm{Var}_d\{\hat{\varepsilon}\} \cong \frac{1}{4\pi^2}\iiiint E_d\{\Delta\mathbf{h}(X)\Delta\mathbf{h}(Y)\}$$

$$\times e^{j\omega_1 h(X)}e^{j\omega_2 h(Y)}\tilde{p}(X)\tilde{p}(Y)d\omega_1 d\omega_2 dX dY$$

$$= \iint E_d\{\Delta\mathbf{h}(X)\Delta\mathbf{h}(Y)\}\delta(h(X))\delta(h(Y))\tilde{p}(X)\tilde{p}(Y)dXdY \tag{5.97}$$

$$= \int_{h(X)=0}\int_{h(Y)=0} E_d\{\Delta\mathbf{h}(X)\Delta\mathbf{h}(Y)\}\tilde{p}(X)\tilde{p}(Y)dXdY .$$

Equation (5.97) indicates that the integration is carried out along the classification boundary where $h(X) = 0$. When $h(X)$ is the Bayes classifier, $\tilde{p}(X)$ of (5.38) must be zero at the boundary. Thus, (5.97) becomes 0. Since we neglected the higher order terms of $\Delta\mathbf{h}(X)$ in the derivation of (5.97), the actual $\mathrm{Var}_d\{\hat{\varepsilon}\}$ is not zero, but proportional to $1/\mathcal{N}^2$ according to (5.58). When $h(X)$ is not the Bayes classifier, $\tilde{p}(X)$ is no longer equal to zero at $h(X) = 0$. Thus, we may observe a variance dominated by a term proportional to $E_d\{\Delta\mathbf{h}(X)\Delta\mathbf{h}(Y)\}$. Since $E_d\{\Delta\mathbf{h}(X)\Delta\mathbf{h}(Y)\}$ is a second order term, it is proportional to $1/\mathcal{N}$.

In order to confirm the above theoretical conclusion, we can look at the third line of Table 5-6, which is the standard deviation of 10 trials in Experiment 4. Also, Fig. 5-2 shows the relationship between $1/k (= n/\mathcal{N})$ and the

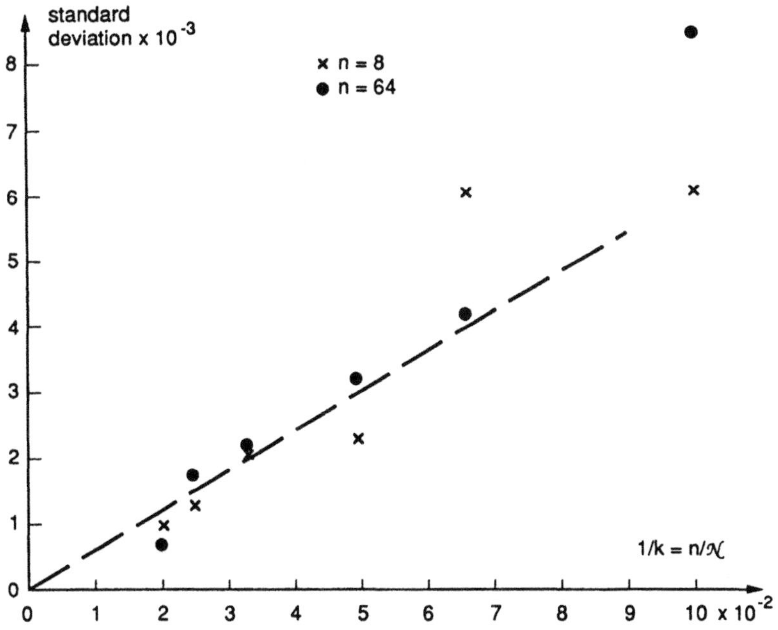

Fig. 5-2 Quadratic classifier degradation for Data *I-I*.

standard deviation [6]. From these results, we may confirm that the standard deviation is very small and roughly proportional to $1/\mathcal{N}$, except the far right-hand side where $\mathcal{N}$ is small and the approximation begins to break down. Thus, the variance is proportional to $1/\mathcal{N}^2$.

An intuitive reason why the standard deviation due to a finite number of design samples is proportional to $1/\mathcal{N}$ may be observed as follows. When the Bayes classifier is implemented, $\Delta\varepsilon$ is always positive and thus generates a positive bias. As (5.70) suggests, the bias is proportional to $1/\mathcal{N}$. Since $\Delta\varepsilon$ varies between 0 and some positive value with an expected value $a/\mathcal{N}$ (where a is a positive number), we can expect that the standard deviation is also proportional to $1/\mathcal{N}$.

In addition, it should be noted that design samples affect the variance of the error in a different way from test samples. When a classifier is fixed, the variations of two test distributions are independent. Thus, $\text{Var}_t\{\hat{\varepsilon}\} =$

$P_1^2 \text{Var}_t\{\hat{\varepsilon}_1\} + P_2^2 \text{Var}_t\{\hat{\varepsilon}_2\}$ as seen in (5.49). On the other hand, when test distributions are fixed and the classifier varies, $\hat{\varepsilon}_1$ and $\hat{\varepsilon}_2$ are strongly correlated with a correlation coefficient close to -1. That is, when $\hat{\varepsilon}_1$ increases, $\hat{\varepsilon}_2$ decreases and vice versa. Thus, when $P_1 = P_2$, $\text{Var}_d\{\hat{\varepsilon}\} = (0.5)^2 \; E_d\{\Delta\varepsilon_1^2\} + (0.5)^2 E_d\{\Delta\varepsilon_2^2\} + 2(0.5)^2 \; E_d\{\Delta\varepsilon_1 \; \Delta\varepsilon_2\} \cong (0.5)^2 \; [E_d\{\Delta\varepsilon_1^2\} + E_d\{(-\Delta\varepsilon_1)^2\} + 2E_d\{\Delta\varepsilon_1(-\Delta\varepsilon_1)\}] = 0$. The covariance of $\hat{\varepsilon}_1$ and $\hat{\varepsilon}_2$ cancels the individual variances of $\hat{\varepsilon}_1$ and $\hat{\varepsilon}_2$.

Effect of Independent Design and Test Samples

When both design and test sample sizes are finite, the error is expressed as

$$\hat{\varepsilon} = \frac{1}{2} + \frac{P_1}{N_1}\sum_{j=1}^{N_1}\hat{\alpha}_j^{(1)} - \frac{P_2}{N_2}\sum_{j=1}^{N_2}\hat{\alpha}_j^{(2)} , \tag{5.98}$$

where

$$\hat{\alpha}_j^{(i)} = \frac{1}{2\pi}\int \frac{e^{j\omega\hat{h}(X_j^{(i)})}}{j\omega} d\omega . \tag{5.99}$$

That is, the randomness comes from $\hat{h}$ due to the finite design samples as well as from the test samples $X_j^{(i)}$.

The expected value and variance of $\hat{\varepsilon}$ can be computed as follows:

$$\bar{\varepsilon} = E\{\hat{\varepsilon}\} = E_t E_d\{\hat{\varepsilon}\} = \frac{1}{2} + P_1\bar{\alpha}_1 - P_2\bar{\alpha}_2 \tag{5.100}$$

where

$$\bar{\alpha}_i = \frac{1}{2\pi}\iint \frac{E_d\{e^{j\omega\hat{h}(X)}\}}{j\omega} p_i(X) d\omega dX$$

$$= \begin{cases} \bar{\varepsilon}_1 - \dfrac{1}{2} & \text{for } i=1 \\[2ex] \dfrac{1}{2} - \bar{\varepsilon}_2 & \text{for } i=2 . \end{cases} \tag{5.101}$$

Substituting (5.101) into (5.100),

$$\bar{\varepsilon} = P_1\bar{\varepsilon}_1 + P_2\bar{\varepsilon}_2 \ . \tag{5.102}$$

This average error is the same as the error of (5.64). That is, the bias of the error due to finite design and test samples is identical to the bias due to finite design samples alone. Finite test samples do not contribute to the bias.

The variance of $\hat{\boldsymbol{\varepsilon}}$ can be obtained from (5.98) as

$$\begin{aligned}\mathrm{Var}\{\hat{\boldsymbol{\varepsilon}}\} &= P_1^2[\frac{1}{N_1}\mathrm{Var}\{\hat{\boldsymbol{\alpha}}_j^{(1)}\} + (1-\frac{1}{N_1})\mathrm{Cov}\{\hat{\boldsymbol{\alpha}}_j^{(1)},\hat{\boldsymbol{\alpha}}_k^{(1)}\}] \\ &+ P_2^2[\frac{1}{N_2}\mathrm{Var}\{\hat{\boldsymbol{\alpha}}_j^{(2)}\} + (1-\frac{1}{N_2})\mathrm{Cov}\{\hat{\boldsymbol{\alpha}}_j^{(2)},\hat{\boldsymbol{\alpha}}_k^{(2)}\}] \\ &- 2P_1P_2\mathrm{Cov}\{\hat{\boldsymbol{\alpha}}_j^{(1)},\hat{\boldsymbol{\alpha}}_k^{(2)}\} \ ,\end{aligned} \tag{5.103}$$

where

$$\begin{aligned}\mathrm{Var}\{\hat{\boldsymbol{\alpha}}_j^{(i)}\} &= E\{[\frac{1}{2\pi}\int\frac{e^{j\omega\hat{\mathbf{h}}(\mathbf{X})}}{j\omega}d\omega]^2\} - (\bar{\varepsilon}_i - \frac{1}{2})^2 \\ &= \frac{1}{4} - (\bar{\varepsilon}_i - \frac{1}{2})^2 = \bar{\varepsilon}_i(1-\bar{\varepsilon}_i) \ ,\end{aligned} \tag{5.104}$$

$$\begin{aligned}\mathrm{Cov}\{\hat{\boldsymbol{\alpha}}_j^{(i)},\hat{\boldsymbol{\alpha}}_\ell^{(k)}\} &= \frac{1}{4\pi^2}\iiiint\frac{E_d\{e^{j\omega_1\hat{\mathbf{h}}(X)}e^{j\omega_2\hat{\mathbf{h}}(Y)}\}}{j\omega_1 j\omega_2}p_i(X)p_k(Y)d\omega_1 d\omega_2 dXdY \\ &-\bar{\alpha}_i\bar{\alpha}_k \ .\end{aligned} \tag{5.105}$$

The second line of (5.104) can be derived from the first line as seen in (5.46). From (5.105), a portion of (5.103) can be expressed as

$$\begin{aligned}&P_1^2\mathrm{Cov}\{\hat{\boldsymbol{\alpha}}_j^{(1)},\hat{\boldsymbol{\alpha}}_k^{(1)}\} + P_2^2\mathrm{Cov}\{\hat{\boldsymbol{\alpha}}_j^{(2)},\hat{\boldsymbol{\alpha}}_k^{(2)}\} - 2P_1P_2\mathrm{Cov}\{\hat{\boldsymbol{\alpha}}_j^{(1)},\hat{\boldsymbol{\alpha}}_k^{(2)}\} \\ &= \frac{1}{4\pi^2}\iiiint\frac{E_d\{e^{j\omega_1\hat{\mathbf{h}}(X)}e^{j\omega_2\hat{\mathbf{h}}(Y)}\}}{j\omega_1 j\omega_2}\tilde{p}(X)\tilde{p}(Y)d\omega_1 d\omega_2 dXdY - (\bar{\varepsilon}-\frac{1}{2})^2 \\ &= \mathrm{Var}_d\{\hat{\boldsymbol{\varepsilon}}\} \ ,\end{aligned} \tag{5.106}$$

where $\mathrm{Var}_d\{\hat{\boldsymbol{\varepsilon}}\}$ is the same one as (5.97). On the other hand, (5.105) can be approximated as

$$\text{Cov}\{\hat{\boldsymbol{\alpha}}_j^{(i)}, \hat{\boldsymbol{\alpha}}_\ell^{(k)}\} \cong \frac{1}{4\pi^2} \iiiint E_d\{\Delta \mathbf{h}(X) \Delta \mathbf{h}(Y)\}$$

$$\times e^{j\omega_1 h(X)} e^{j\omega_1 h(Y)} p_i(X) p_k(Y) d\omega_1 d\omega_2 dX dY$$

$$= \int_{h(X)=0} \int_{h(Y)=0} E_d\{\Delta \mathbf{h}(X) \Delta \mathbf{h}(Y)\} p_i(X) p_k(X) dX dY$$

$$\sim \frac{1}{\mathcal{n}} . \tag{5.107}$$

Equation (5.107) can be derived by replacing $\tilde{p}(X)$ in (5.97) with $p_i(X)$. Equation (5.107) is proportional to $1/\mathcal{n}$ because $E_d\{\Delta \mathbf{h}(X) \Delta \mathbf{h}(Y)\}$ is proportional to $1/\mathcal{n}$.

Substituting (5.104)-(5.107) into (5.103), and ignoring the terms proportional to $1/N_i \mathcal{n}$,

$$\text{Var}\{\hat{\boldsymbol{\varepsilon}}\} \cong P_1^2 \frac{\bar{\varepsilon}_1 (1-\bar{\varepsilon}_1)}{N_1} + P_2^2 \frac{\bar{\varepsilon}_2 (1-\bar{\varepsilon}_2)}{N_2} + \text{Var}_d\{\hat{\boldsymbol{\varepsilon}}\} . \tag{5.108}$$

As we discussed in the previous section, $\text{Var}_d\{\hat{\boldsymbol{\varepsilon}}\}$ is proportional to $1/\mathcal{n}^2$ when the Bayes classifier is used for normal distributions. Therefore, $\text{Var}\{\hat{\boldsymbol{\varepsilon}}\}$ of (5.108) is dominated by the first two terms which are due to the finite test set. A comparison of (5.108) and (5.49) shows that the effect of the finite design set appears in $\bar{\varepsilon}_1$ and $\bar{\varepsilon}_2$ of (5.108) instead of ε_1 and ε_2 of (5.49). That is, the bias due to the finite design set increases the variance proportionally. However, since $(\bar{\varepsilon}_i - \varepsilon_i) \sim 1/\mathcal{n}$, this effect can be ignored. It should be noted that $\text{Var}_d\{\hat{\boldsymbol{\varepsilon}}\}$ could be proportional to $1/\mathcal{n}$ if the classifier is not the Bayes.

Thus, we can draw the following conclusions from (5.102) and (5.108). When both design and test sets are finite,

1. the bias of the classification error comes entirely from the finite design set, and
2. the variance comes predominantly from the finite test set.

5.3 Holdout, Leave-One-Out, and Resubstitution Methods

Bounds of the Bayes Error

When a finite number of samples is given and the performance of a specified classifier is to be estimated, we need to decide which samples are used for designing the classifier and which samples are for testing the classifier.

Upper and lower bounds of the Bayes error: In general, the classification error is a function of two sets of data, the design and test sets, and may be expressed by

$$\varepsilon(\mathcal{P}_D, \mathcal{P}_T) , \tag{5.109}$$

where, $\mathcal{P}$ is a set of two densities as

$$\mathcal{P} = \{p_1(X), p_2(X)\} . \tag{5.110}$$

If the classifier is the Bayes for the given test distributions, the resulting error is minimum. Therefore, we have the following inequality

$$\varepsilon(\mathcal{P}_T,\mathcal{P}_T) \le \varepsilon(\mathcal{P}_D,\mathcal{P}_T) . \tag{5.111}$$

The Bayes error for the true $\mathcal{P}$ is $\varepsilon(\mathcal{P},\mathcal{P})$. However, we never know the true $\mathcal{P}$. One way to overcome this difficulty is to find upper and lower bounds of $\varepsilon(\mathcal{P},\mathcal{P})$ based on its estimate $\hat{\mathcal{P}} = \{\hat{\mathbf{p}}_1(X),\hat{\mathbf{p}}_2(X)\}$. In order to accomplish this, let us introduce from (5.111) two inequalities as

$$\varepsilon(\mathcal{P},\mathcal{P}) \le \varepsilon(\hat{\mathcal{P}},\mathcal{P}) , \tag{5.112}$$

$$\varepsilon(\hat{\mathcal{P}},\hat{\mathcal{P}}) \le \varepsilon(\mathcal{P},\hat{\mathcal{P}}) . \tag{5.113}$$

Equation (5.112) indicates that $\mathcal{P}$ is the better design set than $\hat{\mathcal{P}}$ for testing $\mathcal{P}$. Likewise, $\hat{\mathcal{P}}$ is the better design set than $\mathcal{P}$ for testing $\hat{\mathcal{P}}$. Also, it is known from (5.48) that, if an error counting procedure is adopted, the error estimate is unbiased with respect to test samples. Therefore, the right-hand side of (5.112) can be modified to

$$\varepsilon(\hat{\mathcal{P}},\mathcal{P}) = E_{\hat{\mathcal{P}}_T}\{\varepsilon(\hat{\mathcal{P}},\hat{\mathcal{P}}_T)\} , \tag{5.114}$$

where $\hat{\mathcal{P}}_T$ is another set generated from $\mathcal{P}$ independently of $\hat{\mathcal{P}}$. Also, after taking the expectation of (5.113), the right-hand side may be replaced by

$$E\{\varepsilon(\mathcal{P},\hat{\mathcal{P}})\} = \varepsilon(\mathcal{P},\mathcal{P}) . \tag{5.115}$$

Thus, combining (5.112)-(5.115),

$$E\{\varepsilon(\hat{\mathcal{P}},\hat{\mathcal{P}})\} \le \varepsilon(\mathcal{P},\mathcal{P}) \le E_{\hat{\mathcal{P}}_T}\{\varepsilon(\hat{\mathcal{P}},\hat{\mathcal{P}}_T)\} . \tag{5.116}$$

That is, the Bayes error, $\varepsilon(\mathcal{P},\mathcal{P})$, is bounded by two sample-based estimates [12].

The rightmost term $\varepsilon(\hat{\mathcal{P}},\hat{\mathcal{P}}_T)$ is obtained by generating two independent sample sets, $\hat{\mathcal{P}}$ and $\hat{\mathcal{P}}_T$, from $\mathcal{P}$, and using $\hat{\mathcal{P}}$ for designing the Bayes classifier and $\hat{\mathcal{P}}_T$ for testing. The expectation of this error with respect to $\hat{\mathcal{P}}_T$ gives the upper bound of the Bayes error. Furthermore, taking the expectation of this result with respect to $\hat{\mathcal{P}}$ does not change this inequality. Therefore, $E_{\hat{\mathcal{P}}}E_{\hat{\mathcal{P}}_T}\{\varepsilon(\hat{\mathcal{P}},\hat{\mathcal{P}}_T)\}$ also can be used as the upper bound. This procedure is called the *holdout* (H) method. On the other hand, $\varepsilon(\hat{\mathcal{P}},\hat{\mathcal{P}})$ is obtained by using $\hat{\mathcal{P}}$ for designing the Bayes classifier and the same $\hat{\mathcal{P}}$ for testing. The expectation of this error with respect to $\hat{\mathcal{P}}$ gives the lower bound of the Bayes error. This procedure is called *resubstitution* (R) method.

The holdout method works well if the data sets are generated artificially by a computer. However, in practice, if only one set of data is available, in order to apply the holdout method, we need to divide the available sample set into two independent groups. This reduces the number of samples available for designing and testing. Also, how to divide samples is a serious and non-trivial problem. We must implement a proper dividing algorithm to assure that the distributions of design and test samples are very close. In addition, how to allocate samples to design and test is another problem. Since we know the effects of design and test sample sizes from the discussion of Section 5.2, we may determine how samples should be allocated to design and test by balancing the resulting bias and variance. As seen in Section 5.2, the bias is determined by the size of the design samples, while the variance is primarily determined by the size of the test samples.

A procedure, called the *leave-one-out* (L) method, alleviates the above difficulties of the H method [13]. In the L method, one sample is excluded, the classifier is designed on the remaining $N-1$ samples, and the excluded sample is tested by the classifier. This operation is repeated N times to test all N samples. Then, the number of misclassified samples is counted to obtain the estimate of the error. Since each test sample is excluded from the design sample set, the independence between the design and test sets is maintained. Also, all N samples are tested and $N-1$ samples are used for design. Thus, the available samples are, in this method, more effectively utilized. Furthermore, we do not need to worry about dissimilarity between the design and test distributions. One of the disadvantages of the L method is that N classifiers must be designed, one classifier for testing each sample. However, this problem is easily overcome by a procedure which will be discussed later.

The H and L methods are supposed to give very similar, if not identical, estimates of the classification error, and both provide upper bounds of the Bayes error. In order to confirm this, an experiment was conducted as follows.

Experiment 6: The H and L errors

Data: *I-I* (Normal, $M^TM = 2.56^2$, $\varepsilon = 10\%$)
Dimensionality: $n = 4, 8, 16, 32, 64$
Classifier: Quadratic classifier of (5.54)
Sample size: $\mathcal{N}_1 = \mathcal{N}_2 = kn$ (Design) for H
$N_1 = N_2 = kn$ (Test)
$N_1 = N_2 = kn$ for L
$k = 3, 5, 10, 20, 40$
No. of trials: $\tau = 10$
Results: Table 5-8

The first and second lines of Table 5-8 show the average and standard deviation of the H error estimate, while the third and fourth lines are the average and standard deviation of the L error estimate. Both results are very close.

Operation of the L method: In order to illustrate how the L method works, let us examine the simplest case in which two covariances are equal and known as I. Then, the Bayes classifier is

$$(X-M_1)^T(X-M_1) - (X-M_2)^T(X-M_2) \underset{\omega_2}{\overset{\omega_1}{\gtrless}} t \,. \tag{5.117}$$

Assume that two sample sets, $S_1 = \{X_1^{(1)}, \ldots, X_{N_1}^{(1)}\}$ from ω_1 and $S_2 = \{X_1^{(2)}, \ldots, X_{N_2}^{(2)}\}$ from ω_2, are given. In the R method, all of these samples are used to design the classifier and also to test the classifier. With the given mathemat-

TABLE 5-8

COMPARISON OF THE *H* AND *L* ERRORS FOR DATA *I-I* (%)

		n 4	8	16	32	64
	3	21.25	20.00	20.42	26.35	30.55
		7.97	4.73	5.32	2.25	2.53
		17.92	17.50	23.33	25.36	31.61
		11.63	6.82	3.44	4.01	2.57
	5	13.25	16.50	17.63	21.37	24.58
		5.66	4.56	3.47	2.71	1.89
		12.25	17.75	15.56	20.75	25.91
		3.43	7.40	3.03	2.72	1.70
k	10	10.75	10.63	14.13	16.61	19.55
		2.30	2.55	1.98	1.17	1.28
		9.88	11.50	13.63	15.45	19.05
		3.79	3.13	2.51	2.09	1.52
	20	11.25	10.19	11.75	13.17	14.98
		2.28	1.20	1.41	.98	.67
		11.13	12.47	12.55	12.75	15.25
		1.97	1.69	1.57	1.08	1.07
	40	10.78	10.14	11.44	12.01	12.59
		1.39	1.02	.89	.81	.48
		10.41	10.05	10.22	11.53	12.81
		2.11	1.22	.59	.54	.52

ical form of (5.117) for the classifier, designing means to estimate the necessary parameters - in this case two expected vectors by using the sample means, $\hat{M}_i$, of (5.8). Using the error counting procedure, each sample is tested by

$$(X_k^{(i)}-\hat{M}_1)^T(X_k^{(i)}-\hat{M}_1) - (X_k^{(i)}-\hat{M}_2)^T(X_k^{(i)}-\hat{M}_2) \underset{\omega_2}{\overset{\omega_1}{\gtrless}} t \tag{5.118}$$

$$(i = 1,2 : k = 1,\ldots,N_i) \,.$$

If $X_k^{(1)}$ does not satisfy <, the sample is labeled as an error. Likewise, $X_k^{(2)}$, which does not satisfy >, is labeled as an error. The R error is the number of errors divided by the total number of samples.

On the other hand, in the L method, $X_k^{(i)}$ must be excluded from the design set when $X_k^{(i)}$ is tested. The mean estimate without $X_k^{(i)}$, $\hat{M}_{ik}$, may be computed as

$$\hat{M}_{ik} = \frac{1}{N_i-1}[\sum_{j=1}^{N_i} X_j^{(i)} - X_k^{(i)}] = \hat{M}_i - \frac{1}{N_i-1}(X_k^{(i)}-\hat{M}_i) \,. \tag{5.119}$$

Or,

$$X_k^{(i)}-\hat{M}_{ik} = \frac{N_i}{N_i-1}(X_k^{(i)}-\hat{M}_i) \,. \tag{5.120}$$

Therefore, testing an ω_1-sample, $X_k^{(1)}$, can be carried out as follows.

$$(X_k^{(1)}-\hat{M}_{1k})^T(X_k^{(1)}-\hat{M}_{1k}) - (X_k^{(1)}-\hat{M}_2)^T(X_k^{(1)}-\hat{M}_2)$$

$$= (\frac{N_1}{N_1-1})^2(X_k^{(1)}-\hat{M}_1)^T(X_k^{(1)}-\hat{M}_1) - (X_k^{(1)}-\hat{M}_2)^T(X_k^{(1)}-\hat{M}_2) \underset{\omega_2}{\overset{\omega_1}{\gtrless}} t \,. \tag{5.121}$$

Note that, when $X_k^{(1)}$ is tested, only $\hat{M}_1$ is changed and $\hat{M}_2$ is not changed. Likewise, when an ω_2-sample, $X_k^{(2)}$, is tested,

$$(X_k^{(2)}-\hat{M}_1)^T(X_k^{(2)}-\hat{M}_1) - (X_k^{(2)}-\hat{M}_{2k})^T(X_k^{(2)}-\hat{M}_{2k})$$

$$= (X_k^{(2)}-\hat{M}_1)^T(X_k^{(2)}-\hat{M}_1) - (\frac{N_2}{N_2-1})^2(X_k^{(2)}-\hat{M}_2)^T(X_k^{(2)}-\hat{M}_2) \underset{\omega_2}{\overset{\omega_1}{\gtrless}} t \,. \tag{5.122}$$

Equations (5.121) and (5.122) reveal that the modification from the R method to the L method is simply to multiply a scalar $[N_i/(N_i-1)]^2$ with a distance. Since the distance computation in a high-dimensional space needs much more computation time, the addition of a scalar multiplication is negligibly small. Thus, we can perform both R and L methods simultaneously within the computation time needed to conduct the R method alone. In other words, (5.121) and (5.122) give a simple perturbation equation of the L method from the R method such that we do not need to design the classifier N times.

The perturbation factor of $N_i/(N_i-1)$ is always larger than 1. This increases $(X_k^{(1)}-\hat{M}_1)^T(X_k^{(1)}-\hat{M}_1)$ for an ω_1-sample, $X_k^{(1)}$, and $(X_k^{(2)}-\hat{M}_2)^T(X_k^{(2)}-\hat{M}_2)$ for an ω_2-sample, $X_k^{(2)}$. For ω_1, $X_k^{(1)}$ is misclassified if $>$ is satisfied in (5.121). Therefore, increasing the $(X_k^{(1)}-\hat{M}_1)^T(X_k^{(1)}-\hat{M}_1)$ term by multiplying $[N_1/(N_1-1)]^2$ means that $X_k^{(1)}$ has more chance to be misclassified in the L method than in the R method. The same is true for $X_k^{(2)}$ in (5.122). Thus, the L method gives a larger error than the R method. This is true even if the classifier of (5.117) is no longer the Bayes. That is, when the distance classifier of (5.117) is used, the L error is larger than the R error regardless of the test distributions.

The above discussion may be illustrated in a one-dimensional example of Fig. 5-3, where $\hat{m}_1$ and $\hat{m}_2$ are computed by the sample means of all available

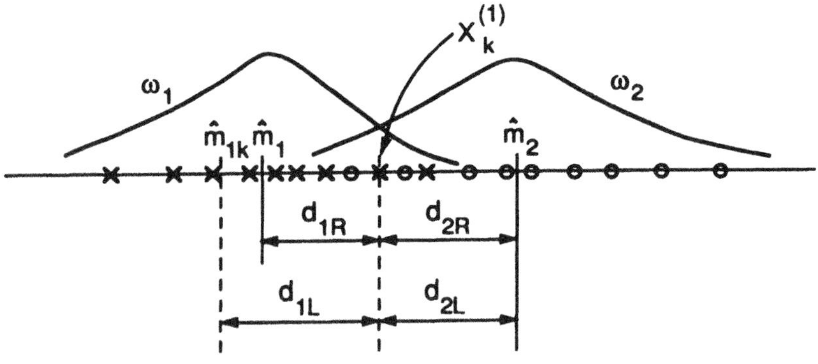

Fig. 5-3 An example of the leave-one-out error estimation.

samples, and each sample is classified according to the nearest mean. For example, $x_k^{(1)}$ is correctly classified by the R method, because $d_{1R}<d_{2R}$ and thus $x_k^{(1)}$ is classified to ω_1. On the other hand, in the L method, $x_k^{(1)}$ must be excluded from estimating the ω_1-mean. The new sample mean, $\hat{m}_{1k}$, is shifted to the left side, thus increasing the distance between $x_k^{(1)}$ and $\hat{m}_{1k}$, d_{1L}. On the other hand, d_{2L} is the same as d_{2R}. Since $d_{1L} > d_{2L}$, $x_k^{(1)}$ is misclassified to ω_2 in the L method.

The *R* and *L* Methods for the Quadratic Classifier

Perturbation equation: The above discussion may be extended to the more complex but more useful quadratic classifier [14]. In the quadratic classifier of (5.54), we need a perturbation equation for the covariance matrix in addition to the mean vector of (5.119) as follows.

$$\hat{\Sigma}_i = \frac{1}{N_i-1}\sum_{j=1}^{N_i}(X_j^{(i)}-\hat{M}_i)(X_j^{(i)}-\hat{M}_i)^T , \tag{5.123}$$

$$\hat{\Sigma}_{ik} = \frac{1}{N_i-2}\left[\sum_{j=1}^{N_i}(X_j^{(i)}-\hat{M}_{ik})(X_j^{(i)}-\hat{M}_{ik})^T - (X_k^{(i)}-\hat{M}_{ik})(X_k^{(i)}-\hat{M}_{ik})^T\right]$$

$$= \frac{N_i-1}{N_i-2}\left[\hat{\Sigma}_i - \frac{N_i}{(N_i-1)^2}(X_k^{(i)}-\hat{M}_i)(X_k^{(i)}-\hat{M}_i)^T\right]$$

$$= \hat{\Sigma}_i + \frac{1}{N_i-2}\hat{\Sigma}_i - \frac{N_i}{(N_i-1)(N_i-2)}(X_k^{(i)}-\hat{M}_i)(X_k^{(i)}-\hat{M}_i)^T . \tag{5.124}$$

The inverse matrix of $\hat{\Sigma}_{ik}$ can be obtained from (2.160)

$$\hat{\Sigma}_{ik}^{-1} = \left(\frac{N_i-2}{N_i-1}\right)\left[\hat{\Sigma}_i^{-1} + \frac{N_i\hat{\Sigma}_i^{-1}(X_k^{(i)}-\hat{M}_i)(X_k^{(i)}-\hat{M}_i)^T\hat{\Sigma}_i^{-1}}{(N_i-1)^2 - N_i\hat{d}_i^2(X_k^{(i)})}\right], \tag{5.125}$$

where $\hat{d}_i^2(X_k^{(i)}) = (X_k^{(i)}-\hat{M}_i)^T\ \hat{\Sigma}_i^{-1}(X_k^{(i)}-\hat{M}_i)$. The L distance, $\hat{d}_{ik}^2(X_k^{(i)})$, is from (5.120) and (5.125)

$$\hat{d}_{ik}^2(X_k^{(i)}) = (X_k^{(i)}-\hat{M}_{ik})^T\hat{\Sigma}_{ik}^{-1}(X_k^{(i)}-\hat{M}_{ik})$$

$$= (\frac{N_i}{N_i-1})^2(X_k^{(i)}-\hat{M}_i)^T\hat{\Sigma}_{ik}^{-1}(X_k^{(i)}-\hat{M}_i)$$

$$= (\frac{N_i}{N_i-1})^2(\frac{N_i-2}{N_i-1})\left[\hat{d}_i^2(X_k^{(i)}) + \frac{N_i\hat{d}_i^4(X_k^{(i)})}{(N_i-1)^2-N_i\hat{d}_i^2(X_k^{(i)})}\right]$$

$$= \hat{d}_i^2(X_k^{(i)}) + \frac{(N_i^2-3N_i+1)\hat{d}_i^2(X_k^{(i)})/(N_i-1)+N_i\hat{d}_i^4(X_k^{(i)})}{(N_i-1)^2-N_i\hat{d}_i^2(X_k^{(i)})} . \tag{5.126}$$

Also, using (2.143), the determinant of $\hat{\Sigma}_{ik}$ can be calculated as follows.

$$|\hat{\Sigma}_{ik}| = \left(\frac{N_i-1}{N_i-2}\right)^n |\hat{\Sigma}_i| \left[1 - \frac{N_i}{(N_i-1)^2}\hat{d}_i^2(X_k^{(i)})\right] . \tag{5.127}$$

Or, taking the logarithm,

$$\ln|\hat{\Sigma}_{ik}| = \ln|\hat{\Sigma}_i| + n \ln\left[1+\frac{1}{N_i-2}\right] + \ln\left[1-\frac{N_i}{(N_i-1)^2}\hat{d}_i^2(X_k^{(i)})\right] . \tag{5.128}$$

Let $\hat{h}_R(X_k^{(i)})$ and $\hat{h}_L(X_k^{(i)})$ be the R and L discriminant functions with $\hat{M}_i$ and $\hat{\Sigma}_i$ replacing M_i and Σ_i for $\hat{h}_R(X_k^{(i)})$, and $\hat{M}_{ik}$ and $\hat{\Sigma}_{ik}$ replacing M_i and Σ_i for $\hat{h}_L(X_k^{(i)})$, respectively. Then, substituting (5.126) and (5.128) into (5.54),

$$\hat{h}_L(X_k^{(i)}) - \hat{h}_R(X_k^{(i)}) = \begin{cases} +g(N_1,\hat{d}_1^2(X_k^{(1)})) & \text{for } \omega_1 \\ -g(N_2,\hat{d}_2^2(X_k^{(2)})) & \text{for } \omega_2 , \end{cases} \tag{5.129}$$

where

$$g(N_i,\hat{d}_i^2(X_k^{(i)})) = \frac{1}{2}\,\frac{(N_i^2-3N_i+1)\hat{d}_i^2(X_k^{(i)})/(N_i-1)+N_i\hat{d}_i^4(X_k^{(i)})}{(N_i-1)^2-N_i\hat{d}_i^2(X_k^{(i)})}$$

$$+\frac{n}{2}\ln\left[1+\frac{1}{N_i-2}\right]+\frac{1}{2}\ln\left[1-\frac{N_i}{(N_i-1)^2}\hat{d}_i^2(X_k^{(i)})\right] . \tag{5.130}$$

When the R method is used to count the number of misclassified samples, $\hat{d}_i^2(X_k^{(i)})$ and $\hat{h}_R(X_k^{(i)})$ must be computed for $k = 1,\ldots,N_i$ and $i = 1,2$. Therefore, the additional computation of the scalar function of (5.130) for each k is a negligible load for a computer in comparison with the computation of $\hat{h}_R(X_k^{(i)})$ for each k, which includes vector-matrix operations in a high-dimensional space. Thus, the computation time of both the R and L methods becomes almost equivalent to the computation time of the R method alone. Remember that, in the R method, we are required to design only one classifier. Since $\hat{h}_L$ can be obtained from $\hat{h}_R$ by a trivial perturbation equation, we do not need to design the classifier N times in the L method.

Proof of $g \geq 0$: The perturbation term, g, of (5.130) is always positive no matter what N_i, $\hat{d}_i^2(X_k^{(i)})$, and n are. The proof is given as follows.

Assuming $N_i > 2$, $|\hat{\Sigma}_{ik}|$ of (5.127) should be positive because $\hat{\Sigma}_{ik}$ is a sample covariance matrix and should be a positive definite matrix. Therefore,

$$1 - \frac{N_i}{(N_i - 1)^2}\hat{d}_i^2(X_k^{(i)}) > 0 \,. \tag{5.131}$$

On the other hand, from (5.130)

$$\frac{\partial g}{\partial \hat{d}_i^2} = \frac{1}{2}\frac{(N_i^2-3N_i+1)/(N_i-1)+2N_i\hat{d}_i^2}{(N_i-1)^2 - N_i\hat{d}_i^2}$$

$$+ \frac{1}{2}\frac{[(N_i^2-3N_i+1)\hat{d}_i^2/(N_i-1)+N_i\hat{d}_i^4]N_i}{[(N_i-1)^2 - N_i\hat{d}_i^2]^2}$$

$$+ \frac{1}{2}\frac{-N_i/(N_i-1)^2}{1-[N_i/(N_i-1)^2]\hat{d}_i^2}$$

$$= \frac{1}{2}\frac{-N_i^2\hat{d}_i^4+N_i(2N_i^2-3N_i+2)\hat{d}_i^2-(N_i-1)(2N_i-1)}{[(N_i-1)^2 - N_i\hat{d}_i^2]^2} \,. \tag{5.132}$$

The term $\partial g/\partial \hat{d}_i^2$ is equal to zero when

$$\hat{d}_i^2 = \frac{1}{N_i} \quad \text{or} \quad \frac{3N_i^3 - 3N_i^2 + N_i}{N_i^2} \,. \tag{5.133}$$

The second solution of (5.133) does not satisfy the condition of (5.131). Since g and $\partial g/\partial \hat{d}_i^2$ for $\hat{d}_i^2 = 0$ are positive and negative, respectively, the first solution of (5.133) gives the minimum g, which is

$$\frac{1}{2}\frac{(N_i^2-3N_i+1)/(N_i-1)+1}{N_i[(N_i-1)^2-1]} + \frac{n}{2}\ln\frac{N_i-1}{N_i-2} + \frac{1}{2}\ln[1 - \frac{1}{(N_i-1)^2}]$$

$$= \frac{1}{2}\frac{1}{N_i(N_i-1)} + \frac{1}{2}\ln\left[\frac{(N_i-1)^2-1}{(N_i-1)^2}\frac{N_i-1}{N_i-2}\right] + \frac{n-1}{2}\ln\frac{N_i-1}{N_i-2}$$

$$= \frac{1}{2}\frac{1}{N_i(N_i-1)} + \frac{1}{2}\ln\frac{N_i}{N_i-1} + \frac{n-1}{2}\ln\frac{N_i-1}{N_i-2} > 0 \qquad (5.134)$$

for $N_i > 2$. The inequality of (5.134) holds since the numerators of the second and third terms are larger than the corresponding denominators.

Comments: Since g of (5.130) is always positive, $\hat{h}_L > \hat{h}_R$ for ω_1-samples and $\hat{h}_L < \hat{h}_R$ for ω_2-samples. Since $h > 0$ is the condition for ω_1-samples to be misclassified and $h < 0$ is the condition for ω_2-samples to be misclassified, the L method always gives a larger error than the R method. This is true for any test distributions, and is not necessarily limited to normal distributions. Note that this conclusion is a stronger statement than the inequality of (5.116), because the inequality of (5.116) holds only for the expectation of errors, while the above statement is for individual samples of individual tests.

Since we have the exact perturbation equation of (5.130), the use of this equation is recommended to conduct the R and L methods. However, for further theoretical analysis, (5.130) is a little too complex. An approximation of (5.130) may be obtained by assuming $N_i >> \hat{d}_i^2$ and $N_i >> 1$. When $\mathbf{X}$ is distributed normally, it is know that $d^2(\mathbf{X})$ has the chi-square distribution with an expected value of n and standard deviation of $\sqrt{2n}$, where $d^2(X) = (X-M)^T\Sigma^{-1}(X-M)$ [see (3.59)-(3.61)]. Therefore, if $N >> n$, the approximation based on $N >> d^2$ is justified. Also, $\ln(1+\delta) \cong \delta$ for a small δ is used to approximate the second and third terms of (5.130). The resulting approximation is

$$g(N_i, \hat{d}_i^2(X_k^{(i)})) \cong \frac{1}{2N_i}[\hat{d}_i^4(X_k^{(i)}) + n] . \qquad (5.135)$$

In order to confirm that the L and R methods give the upper and lower bounds of the Bayes error, the following experiment was conducted.

Experiment 7: Error of the quadratic classifier, L and R

Data: I-Λ (Normal, $n = 8$, $\varepsilon = 1.9\%$)
Classifier: Quadratic classifier of (5.54)
Sample size: $N_1 = N_2 = 12, 50, 100, 200, 400$
No. of trials: $\tau = 40$
Results: Table 5-9 [14]

As expected, the L and R methods bound the Bayes error.

TABLE 5-9

THE BOUNDS OF THE BAYES ERROR BY THE L AND R METHODS

No. of samples per class $N_1 = N_2$	Resubstitution method Mean (%)	Resubstitution method Standard deviation (%)	Leave-one-out method Mean (%)	Leave-one-out method Standard deviation (%)	Bias between two means (%)
12	0.21	1.3	18.54	7.6	18.33
50	1.22	0.9	2.97	1.7	1.75
100	1.44	0.8	2.15	1.0	0.71
200	1.56	0.7	2.00	0.7	0.44
400	1.83	0.5	1.97	0.5	0.14

Effect of removing one sample: Generalizing the above discussion, let us study how the removal of one sample affects the estimate of f which is a function of M and Σ. Let $\hat{M}_R$ and $\hat{\Sigma}_R$ be the sample mean and sample covariance computed from all available samples, and let $\hat{M}_L$ and $\hat{\Sigma}_L$ be the corresponding estimates without a sample Y. From (5.119) and (5.124), we may express $\hat{M}_L$ and $\hat{\Sigma}_L$ in terms of $\hat{M}_R$, $\hat{\Sigma}_R$ and Y as

$$\hat{M}_L = \hat{M}_R - \frac{1}{N-1}(Y-\hat{M}_R) \cong \hat{M}_R - \frac{1}{N}(Y-\hat{M}_R) , \tag{5.136}$$

$$\hat{\Sigma}_L = \hat{\Sigma}_R + \frac{1}{N-2}\hat{\Sigma}_R - \frac{N}{(N-1)(N-2)}(Y-\hat{M}_R)(Y-\hat{M}_R)^T$$

$$\cong \hat{\Sigma}_R + \frac{1}{N}[\hat{\Sigma}_R - (Y-\hat{M}_R)(Y-\hat{M}_R)^T] , \tag{5.137}$$

where $N >> 1$ is assumed. The terms associated with $1/N$ are small deviation terms. Therefore, we may approximate $\hat{M}_R$ and $\hat{\Sigma}_R$ by the true parameters M and Σ whenever they appear in $[\cdot]/N$, resulting in

$$\hat{M}_L \cong \hat{M}_R - \frac{1}{N}(Y-M) , \tag{5.138}$$

$$\hat{\Sigma}_L \cong \hat{\Sigma}_R + \frac{1}{N}[\Sigma - (Y-M)(Y-M)^T] . \tag{5.139}$$

Now, let us consider the problem of estimating $f(M,\Sigma)$ by $f(\hat{M}_Z,\hat{\Sigma}_Z)$, where f is a given function and Z is either R or L, depending on which estimates are used. The estimate $f(\hat{M}_Z,\hat{\Sigma}_Z)$ may be expanded by a Taylor series around $f(M,\Sigma)$ as

$$f(\hat{M}_Z,\hat{\Sigma}_Z) \cong f(M,\Sigma) + \frac{\partial f^T}{\partial M}(\hat{M}_Z - M) + \mathrm{tr}\left\{\frac{\partial f^*}{\partial \Sigma}(\hat{\Sigma}_Z - \Sigma)\right\} \tag{5.140}$$

where

$$\frac{\partial f^*}{\partial \Sigma} = \begin{bmatrix} \frac{\partial f}{\partial c_{11}} & & \frac{1}{2}\frac{\partial f}{\partial c_{ij}} \\ & \ddots & \\ \frac{1}{2}\frac{\partial f}{\partial c_{ij}} & & \frac{\partial f}{\partial c_{nn}} \end{bmatrix} . \tag{5.141}$$

Then, the difference between $f(\hat{M}_L,\hat{\Sigma}_L)$ and $f(\hat{M}_R,\hat{\Sigma}_R)$ is

$$\begin{aligned} \hat{b} &= f(\hat{M}_L,\hat{\Sigma}_L) - f(\hat{M}_R,\hat{\Sigma}_R) \\ &\cong \frac{\partial f^T}{\partial M}(\Delta M_L - \Delta M_R) + \mathrm{tr}\left\{\frac{\partial f^*}{\partial \Sigma}(\Delta\Sigma_L - \Delta\Sigma_R)\right\} \\ &\cong \frac{1}{N}\left[-\frac{\partial f^T}{\partial M}(Y-M) + \mathrm{tr}\left\{\frac{\partial f^*}{\partial \Sigma}[\Sigma - (Y-M)(Y-M)^T]\right\}\right] , \end{aligned} \tag{5.142}$$

where $\Delta M_Z = \hat{M}_Z - M$ and $\Delta\Sigma_Z = \hat{\Sigma}_Z - \Sigma$ ($Z = R$ or L).

Example 1: Let f be

$$f(X,M,\Sigma) = \frac{1}{2}(X-M)^T\Sigma^{-1}(X-M) + \frac{1}{2}\ln|\Sigma| . \tag{5.143}$$

Then,

$$\frac{\partial f}{\partial M} = -\Sigma^{-1}(X-M) , \tag{5.144}$$

$$\frac{\partial f^*}{\partial \Sigma} = \frac{1}{2}[\Sigma^{-1}-\Sigma^{-1}(X-M)(X-M)^T\Sigma^{-1}] \quad \text{[from (A.41)–(A.46)]} . \tag{5.145}$$

If a sample Y is excluded, $\hat{b}$ of (5.142) becomes

$$\hat{b}(X,Y) = \frac{1}{2N}\Big[\{(X-M)^T\Sigma^{-1}(Y-M)\}^2 + n + 2(X-M)^T\Sigma^{-1}(Y-M)$$
$$- (X-M)^T\Sigma^{-1}(X-M) - (Y-M)^T\Sigma^{-1}(Y-M)\Big] . \tag{5.146}$$

Example 2: If f is evaluated at $X = Y$, $\hat{b}$ of (5.146) becomes

$$\hat{b}(Y,Y) = \frac{1}{2N}[d^4(Y) + n] , \tag{5.147}$$

where $d^2(Y) = (Y-M)^T\Sigma^{-1}(Y-M)$. Equation (5.147) is the same as (5.135) except that the true parameters M and Σ are used this time instead of $\hat{M}_i$ and $\hat{\Sigma}_i$ for (5.135).

Resubstitution Error for the Quadratic Classifier

Error expression: When the L method is used, design and test samples are independent. Therefore, when the expectation is taken on the classification error of (5.98), we can isolate two expectations: one with respect to design samples and the other with respect to test samples. In (5.101), the randomness of $\hat{\mathbf{h}}$ comes from design samples, and X is the test sample, independent of the design samples. Therefore, $E_d\{e^{j\omega\hat{\mathbf{h}}(X)}\}$ can be computed for a given X. The expectation with respect to test samples is obtained by computing $\int[\cdot]p_i(X)\,dX$. On the other hand, when the R method is used, design and test simples are no longer independent. Thus, we cannot isolate two expectations. Since X is a design sample as well as a test sample, both contribute to the variation of $\hat{\mathbf{h}}$. Thus, we can no longer use the same argument as in Section 5.2 to compute $E_d\{e^{j\omega\hat{\mathbf{h}}(X)}\}$. However, the relationship between $\hat{\mathbf{h}}_L$ and $\hat{\mathbf{h}}_R$ is given exactly by (5.129) and (5.130) and approximately by (5.147). Therefore, using the approximation of (5.147) for simplicity,

$$\hat{\mathbf{h}}_R(\mathbf{X}_j^{(1)}) \cong \hat{\mathbf{h}}_L(\mathbf{X}_j^{(1)}) - \frac{1}{2N_1}[d_1^4(\mathbf{X}_j^{(1)}) + n] \quad \text{for } \omega_1 , \tag{5.148}$$

$$\hat{\mathbf{h}}_R(\mathbf{X}_j^{(2)}) \cong \hat{\mathbf{h}}_L(\mathbf{X}_j^{(2)}) + \frac{1}{2N_2}[d_2^4(\mathbf{X}_j^{(2)}) + n] \quad \text{for } \omega_2 . \tag{5.149}$$

Applying (5.148), (5.149) and another approximation, $e^{j\omega a/N} \cong 1 + j\omega a/N$ (valid for large N), the classification error by the R method, $\hat{\boldsymbol{\varepsilon}}_R$, may be calculated from (5.98) as

$$\hat{\boldsymbol{\varepsilon}}_R = \frac{1}{2} + \frac{P_1}{N_1}\sum_{j=1}^{N_1}\frac{1}{2\pi}\int\frac{e^{j\omega\hat{\mathbf{h}}_R(\mathbf{X}_j^{(1)})}}{j\omega}d\omega - \frac{P_2}{N_2}\sum_{j=1}^{N_2}\frac{1}{2\pi}\int\frac{e^{j\omega\hat{\mathbf{h}}_R(\mathbf{X}_j^{(2)})}}{j\omega}d\omega$$

$$\cong \frac{1}{2} + \frac{P_1}{N_1}\sum_{j=1}^{N_1}\frac{1}{2\pi}\int\frac{e^{j\omega\hat{\mathbf{h}}_L(\mathbf{X}_j^{(1)})}}{j\omega}[1 - j\omega\frac{d_1^4(\mathbf{X}_j^{(1)})+n}{2N_1}]d\omega$$

$$- \frac{P_2}{N_2}\sum_{j=1}^{N_2}\frac{1}{2\pi}\int\frac{e^{j\omega\hat{\mathbf{h}}_L(\mathbf{X}_j^{(2)})}}{j\omega}[1 + j\omega\frac{d_2^4(\mathbf{X}_j^{(2)})+n}{2N_2}]d\omega$$

$$= \hat{\boldsymbol{\varepsilon}}_L - [\frac{P_1}{N_1^2}\sum_{j=1}^{N_1}\hat{\boldsymbol{\beta}}_j^{(1)} + \frac{P_2}{N_2^2}\sum_{j=1}^{N_2}\hat{\boldsymbol{\beta}}_j^{(2)}] , \tag{5.150}$$

where

$$\hat{\boldsymbol{\beta}}_j^{(i)} = \frac{1}{2\pi}\int\frac{d_i^4(\mathbf{X}_j^{(i)})+n}{2}e^{j\omega\hat{\mathbf{h}}_L(\mathbf{X}_j^{(i)})}d\omega , \tag{5.151}$$

and $\hat{\boldsymbol{\varepsilon}}_L$ is the classification error by the L method.

Moments of the bias: By converting $\hat{\mathbf{h}}_R$ to $\hat{\mathbf{h}}_L$, design and test samples are now independent, and the discussion of Section 5.2 can be directly applied.

Therefore, the statistical properties of the bias, $\hat{\varepsilon}_b = \hat{\varepsilon}_L - \hat{\varepsilon}_R$, can be studied. The expected value of $\hat{\varepsilon}_b$ is

$$E\{\hat{\varepsilon}_b\} \cong \frac{P_1}{N_1}\bar{\beta}_1 + \frac{P_2}{N_2}\bar{\beta}_2 , \tag{5.152}$$

where

$$\bar{\beta}_i = \frac{1}{2\pi}\iint \frac{d_i^4(X)+n}{2} E_d\{e^{j\omega \hat{\mathbf{h}}_L(X)}\} p_i(X)\, d\omega dX . \tag{5.153}$$

And, the variance of $\hat{\varepsilon}_b$ is

$$\begin{aligned} \mathrm{Var}\{\hat{\varepsilon}_b\} &= \frac{P_1^2}{N_1^2}[\frac{1}{N_1}\mathrm{Var}\{\hat{\boldsymbol{\beta}}_j^{(1)}\} + (1-\frac{1}{N_1})\mathrm{Cov}\{\hat{\boldsymbol{\beta}}_j^{(1)},\hat{\boldsymbol{\beta}}_k^{(1)}\}] \\ &+ \frac{P_2^2}{N_2^2}[\frac{1}{N_2}\mathrm{Var}\{\hat{\boldsymbol{\beta}}_j^{(2)}\} + (1-\frac{1}{N_2})\mathrm{Cov}\{\hat{\boldsymbol{\beta}}_j^{(2)},\hat{\boldsymbol{\beta}}_k^{(2)}\}] \\ &+ \frac{2P_1P_2}{N_1N_2}\mathrm{Cov}\{\hat{\boldsymbol{\beta}}_j^{(1)},\hat{\boldsymbol{\beta}}_k^{(2)}\} . \end{aligned} \tag{5.154}$$

Example 3: The explicit expression for $\bar{\beta}_i$ of (5.153) can be obtained by using the same technique used to compute (5.81), if two distributions are normal with $M_1 = 0$, $M_2 = M$, and $\Sigma_1 = \Sigma_2 = I$, and the quadratic classifier of (5.54) is used. For $N_1 = N_2 = N$

$$E_d\{e^{j\omega\hat{\mathbf{h}}_L(X)}\} \cong e^{j\omega h(X)}[1+j\omega E_d\{\Delta\mathbf{h}(X)+\frac{j\omega}{2}\Delta\mathbf{h}^2(X)\}] \cong e^{j\omega h(X)} . \tag{5.155}$$

The last approximation was made because $E_d\{\Delta\mathbf{h} + j\omega\Delta\mathbf{h}^2/2\}$ is proportional to $1/N$. Then, $e^{j\omega h(X)}p_i(X)$ $(i = 1,2)$ are given in (5.78) and (5.79). Thus, the integration of (5.153) merely involves computing the moments of the normal distributions of (5.78) and (5.79), resulting in

$$\bar{\beta}_i \cong \frac{1}{2\sqrt{2\pi M^TM}} e^{\frac{-M^TM}{8}} \left[n^2+(1+\frac{M^TM}{2})n+\{\frac{(M^TM)^2}{16}-\frac{M^TM}{2}-1\} \right] . \tag{5.156}$$

Note that $\bar{\beta}_i$ of (5.156) is exactly twice v_q of (5.81). That is, the bias between the L and R errors is twice the bias between the L and true errors.

In order to confirm (5.156), the following experiment was conducted.

Experiment 8: Bias between the L and R error
Data: *I-I* (Normal, $M^T M = 2.56^2$, $\varepsilon = 10\%$)
Dimensionality: $n = 4, 8, 16, 32, 64$
Classifier: Quadratic classifier of (5.54)
Sample size: $N_1 = N_2 = kn$, $k = 3, 5, 10, 20, 40$
No. of trials: $\tau = 10$
Results: Table 5-10, Fig. 5-3 [6]

The first line of Table 5-10 indicates the theoretical biases from (5.152) and (5.156), and the second and third lines are the average and standard deviation of the 10 trial experiment. Despite a series of approximations, the first and second lines are close except for small k's and large n's, confirming the validity of our discussion.

An important fact is that, from (5.152) and (5.156), $E\{\hat{\varepsilon}_b\}$ is roughly proportional to n^2/N for large n. A simpler explanation for this fact can be obtained by examining (5.153) more closely. Assuming (5.155) and carrying through the integration of (5.153) with respect to ω,

$$\beta_i \cong \int \frac{d_i^4(X) + n}{2} \delta(h(X)) p_i(X) dX$$

$$= \int_{h(X)=0} \frac{d_i^4(X) + n}{2} p_i(X) dX \,. \tag{5.157}$$

It is known that $d_i^2(\mathbf{X})$ is chi-square distributed with an expected value of n and standard deviation of $\sqrt{2n}$, if $\mathbf{X}$ is normally distributed [see (3.59)-(3.61)]. This means that, when n is large, $d_i^2(\mathbf{X})$ is compactly distributed around the expected value n (i.e. $n >> \sqrt{2n}$.) Therefore, $d_i^4(X)$ on the classification boundary should be close to n^2. Thus, β_i should be roughly proportional to n^2.

The analysis of the variance (5.154) is more complex. Though the order of magnitude may not be immediately clear from (5.154), the experimental results, presented in Fig. 5-4 and the third line of Table 5-10, show that the standard deviation is roughly proportional to $1/N$. The intuitive explanation should be the same as that presented in Section 5.2.

TABLE 5-10

BIAS BETWEEN *L* AND *R* ERRORS FOR DATA *I-I* (%)

		n				
		4	8	16	32	64
	3	9.00	13.79	23.03	41.34	77.87
		13.33	15.42	19.69	22.86	30.29
		7.03	5.22	4.12	4.26	3.40
	5	5.40	8.27	13.82	24.80	46.72
		7.50	9.25	10.75	17.75	24.47
		4.56	3.24	2.28	2.69	1.53
k	10	2.70	4.14	6.91	12.40	23.36
		2.25	4.63	6.34	9.58	16.01
		1.84	2.02	1.59	1.61	1.24
	20	1.35	2.07	3.45	6.20	11.68
		1.38	2.09	3.14	5.05	9.56
		1.05	1.00	0.64	0.53	0.45
	40	0.67	1.03	1.73	3.10	5.84
		0.44	1.08	1.55	2.96	5.21
		0.30	0.39	0.30	0.30	0.36

Effect of Outliers

It is widely believed in the pattern recognition field that classifier performance can be improved by removing outliers, points far from a class's inferred mean which seem to distort the distribution. The approach used in this section, namely to analyze the difference between the *R* and *L* parameters, can be

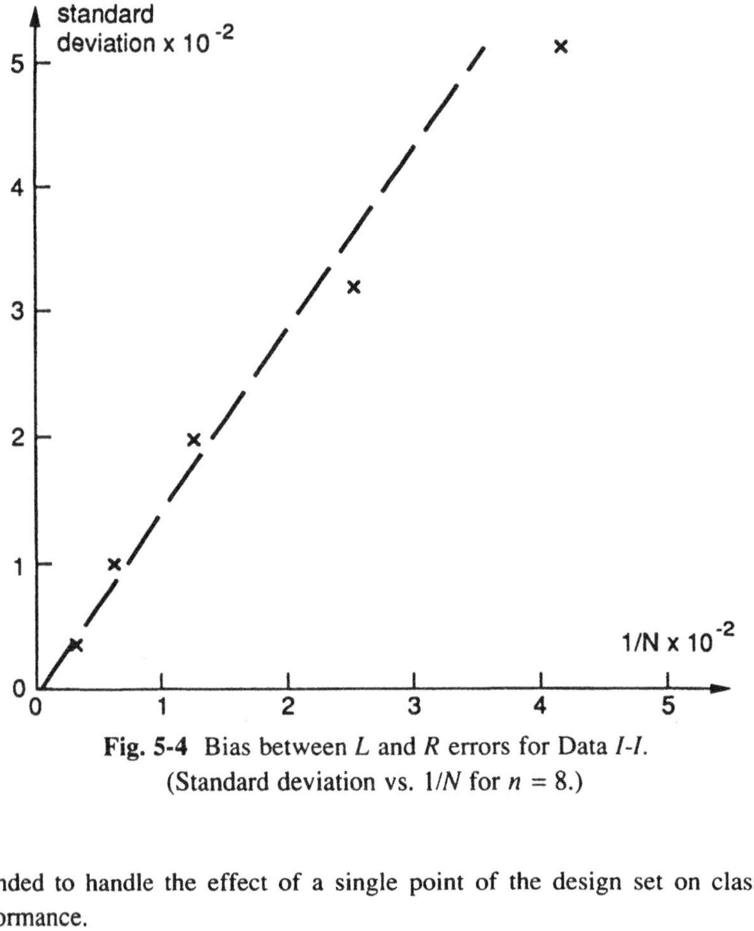

Fig. 5-4 Bias between L and R errors for Data I-I.
(Standard deviation vs. $1/N$ for $n = 8$.)

extended to handle the effect of a single point of the design set on classifier performance.

In order to develop our discussion further, we need to specify the type of the classifier. So, let us study the quadratic classifier of (5.54) here. In the quadratic classifier, we use the discriminant function of $h(X) = f(X,M_1,\Sigma_1) - f(X,M_2,\Sigma_2)$ where f is defined in (5.143). When the estimates $\hat{\mathbf{M}}_1$, $\hat{\mathbf{M}}_2$, $\hat{\mathbf{\Sigma}}_1$, and $\hat{\mathbf{\Sigma}}_2$ are used in the place of M_1, M_2, Σ_1, and Σ_2, the resulting discriminant function becomes $\hat{\mathbf{h}}(X) = f(X,\hat{\mathbf{M}}_1,\hat{\mathbf{\Sigma}}_1) - f(X,\hat{\mathbf{M}}_2,\hat{\mathbf{\Sigma}}_2)$. Furthermore, removing a sample (outlier), Y, from ω_1, $\hat{\mathbf{M}}_1$ and $\hat{\mathbf{\Sigma}}_1$ must be replaced by $\hat{\mathbf{M}}_{1Y}$ and $\hat{\mathbf{\Sigma}}_{1Y}$, and, consequently, $\hat{\mathbf{h}}_Y(X) = f(X,\hat{\mathbf{M}}_{1Y},\hat{\mathbf{\Sigma}}_{1Y}) - f(X,\hat{\mathbf{M}}_2,\hat{\mathbf{\Sigma}}_2)$. The perturbation from $f(X,\hat{\mathbf{M}}_1,\hat{\mathbf{\Sigma}}_1)$ to $f(X,\hat{\mathbf{M}}_{1Y},\hat{\mathbf{\Sigma}}_{1Y})$ is given in (5.146). Therefore,

$$\begin{aligned}\hat{\mathbf{h}}_Y(X) &= f(X,\hat{\mathbf{M}}_{1Y},\hat{\mathbf{\Sigma}}_{1Y}) - f(X,\hat{\mathbf{M}}_2,\hat{\mathbf{\Sigma}}_2) \\ &\cong f(X,\hat{\mathbf{M}}_1,\hat{\mathbf{\Sigma}}_1) + \frac{1}{\mathcal{N}} g_1(X,Y) - f(X,\hat{\mathbf{M}}_2,\hat{\mathbf{\Sigma}}_2) \\ &= \hat{\mathbf{h}}(X) + \frac{1}{\mathcal{N}} g_1(X,Y) \qquad \text{for } Y \varepsilon \omega_1 \,, \end{aligned} \tag{5.158}$$

where

$$g_1(X,Y) = \frac{1}{2}\Big[\{(X-M_1)^T\Sigma_1^{-1}(Y-M_1)\}^2 + n + 2(X-M_1)^T\Sigma_1^{-1}(Y-M_1)$$

$$- (X-M_1)^T\Sigma_1^{-1}(X-M_1) - (Y-M_1)^T\Sigma_1^{-1}(Y-M_1)\Big] \,. \tag{5.159}$$

Likewise, when Y comes from ω_2,

$$\hat{\mathbf{h}}_Y(X) = \hat{\mathbf{h}}(X) - \frac{1}{\mathcal{N}} g_2(X,Y) \qquad \text{for } Y \varepsilon \omega_2 \,, \tag{5.160}$$

where g_2 is the same as (5.159) except that M_2 and Σ_2 are used instead of M_1 and Σ_1.

When this modified classifier is used on an independent set of test samples, the resulting error is, using (5.59),

$$\begin{aligned}\hat{\varepsilon}_Y &= \frac{1}{2} + \frac{1}{2\pi}\iint \frac{e^{j\omega\hat{\mathbf{h}}_Y(X)}}{j\omega}\tilde{p}(X)d\omega dX \\ &\cong \frac{1}{2} + \frac{1}{2\pi}\iint \frac{e^{j\omega\hat{\mathbf{h}}(X)}}{j\omega}[1 \pm \frac{j\omega}{\mathcal{N}} g_i(X,Y)]\tilde{p}(X)d\omega dX \\ &= \hat{\varepsilon} \pm \frac{1}{2\pi}\iint e^{j\omega\hat{\mathbf{h}}(X)}\frac{1}{\mathcal{N}} g_i(X,Y)\tilde{p}(X)d\omega dX \\ &\cong \hat{\varepsilon} \pm \frac{1}{2\pi}\iint e^{j\omega h(X)}\frac{1}{\mathcal{N}} g_i(X,Y)\tilde{p}(X)d\omega dX \,, \end{aligned} \tag{5.161}$$

where $+$ and $i = 1$ are used for $Y \varepsilon \omega_1$ and $-$ and $i = 2$ are for $Y \varepsilon \omega_2$. The approximation in the last line involves replacing $e^{j\omega\hat{\mathbf{h}}(X)}$ by $e^{j\omega h(X)}$. Unlike the case of the R error, (5.161) keeps $\tilde{p}(X)$ in its integrand. This makes the integral in (5.161) particularly easy to handle. If the quadratic classifier is the Bayes classifier, the integration with respect to ω results in

$$\Delta\hat{\varepsilon}_Y = \pm \int \delta(h(X)) \frac{1}{\mathcal{N}} g_i(X,Y)\tilde{p}(X)\, dX$$

$$= \pm \int_{h(X)=0} \frac{1}{\mathcal{N}} g_i(X,Y)\tilde{p}(X)\, dX = 0\,. \tag{5.162}$$

That is, as long as $\tilde{p}(X) = 0$ at $h(X) = 0$, the effect of an individual sample is negligible. Even if the quadratic classifier is not optimal, $\Delta\hat{\varepsilon}_Y$ is dominated by a $1/\mathcal{N}$ term. Thus, as one would expect, as the number of design samples becomes larger, the effect of an individual sample diminishes.

In order to confirm the above results, the following experiment was conducted.

Experiment 9: Effect of removing one sample
Data: *I-I*, *I-4I*, *I-Λ* (Normal, $n = 8$)
Classifier: Quadratic classifier of (5.54)
Design samples: $\mathcal{N}_1 = \mathcal{N}_2 = 24, 40, 80, 160, 320$
Test: Theoretical using (3.119)-(3.128)
No. of trials: $\tau = 10$
Results: Table 5-11 [6]

Table 5-11 shows that, even if the squared distance of Y ($\varepsilon\omega_1$) from M_1, d^2, is much larger than n, the effect is still negligible. The expected value of $\mathbf{d}^2$ is n when $\mathbf{X}$ is distributed normally.

5.4 Bootstrap Methods

Bootstrap Errors

Bootstrap method: So far, we have studied how to bound the Bayes error based on available sample sets. That is, we draw τ sample sets $S_1, \ldots, S_\tau$, from the true distributions, $\mathcal{P}$, as seen in Fig. 5-5, where each sample set contains N_1 ω_1-samples and N_2 ω_2-samples. For each S_i, we can apply the L and R methods to obtain $\hat{\varepsilon}_{Li}$ and $\hat{\varepsilon}_{Ri}$. The averages of these $\hat{\varepsilon}_{Li}$'s and $\hat{\varepsilon}_{Ri}$'s over τ sets approximate the upper and lower bounds of the Bayes error, $E\{\hat{\varepsilon}_L\}$ and $E\{\hat{\varepsilon}_R\}$. The standard deviations of τ $\hat{\varepsilon}_{Li}$'s and $\hat{\varepsilon}_{Ri}$'s indicate how $\hat{\varepsilon}_L$ and $\hat{\varepsilon}_R$ vary. However, in many cases in practice, only one sample set

TABLE 5-11

EFFECT OF REMOVING ONE SAMPLE

Case	n	Error without removing Y (%)	Bias between errors with and without removing Y (%)		
			$d^2 = n$	$d^2 = 2n$	$d^2 = 3n$
	24	20.18	0.689	0.769	0.762
I-I	40	15.61	0.211	0.279	0.274
(ε = 10%)	80	12.04	0.035	0.027	0.018
	160	11.04	0.010	0.014	0.013
	320	10.53	0.006	0.009	0.011
	24	23.53	1.213	1.451	1.356
I-$4I$	40	16.19	0.423	0.619	0.658
(ε = 9%)	80	11.79	0.060	0.091	0.083
	160	10.32	0.005	0.014	0.013
	320	9.52	0.006	0.012	0.015
	24	5.58	0.555	0.664	0.673
I-Λ	40	3.70	0.088	0.110	0.103
(ε = 1.9%)	80	2.54	0.007	0.008	0.003
	160	2.25	0.000	0.001	0.001
	320	2.08	0.000	0.001	0.001

is available, say S_1, from which we wish to learn as much about the statistical properties as possible that these S_i's may have.

One possible way of doing this is to generate ℓ artificial sample sets $S_{11}^*, \ldots, S_{1\ell}^*$ from S_1, and study the statistical properties of these S_{1i}^*'s ($i = 1, \ldots, \ell$), hoping that these statistical properties are close to the ones of the S_i's ($i = 1, \ldots, \tau$). This technique is called the *bootstrap method*, and the artificial samples are called the *bootstrap samples* [15]. The bootstrap method may be applied to many estimation problems. However, in this book, we discuss this technique only for the estimation of classification errors.

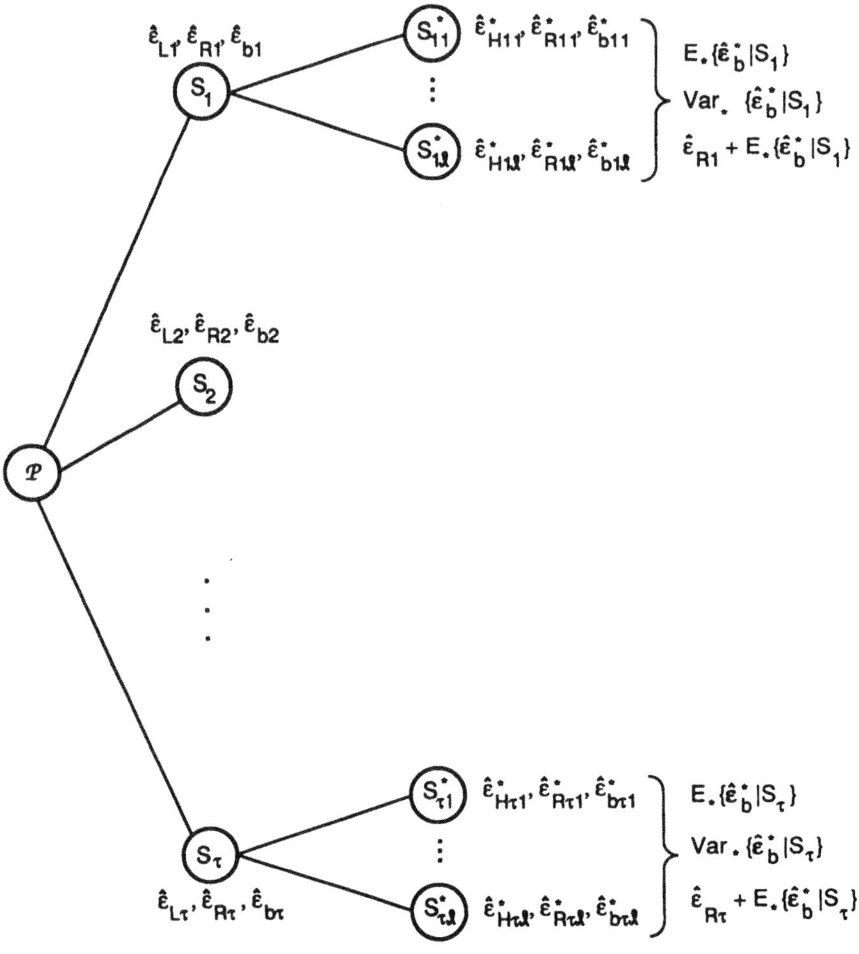

Fig. 5-5 Bootstrap sample generation.

There could be many possible ways to generate artificial samples. One is to generate samples normally around the existing samples. This leads to a nonparametric technique called the *Parzen approach* with the *normal kernel function*, which will be discussed extensively in Chapters 6 and 7. In this section, we discuss the case in which samples are generated randomly at the points where the existing samples in S_1 are located.

Bootstrap errors: Let us assume that S_1 consists of N_1 ω_1-samples, $X_1^{(1)}, \ldots, X_{N_1}^{(1)}$, and N_2 ω_2-samples, $X_1^{(2)}, \ldots, X_{N_2}^{(2)}$. Then, we may express the density function of ω_i by collection of N_i impulses which are located at the existing sample points, $X_1^{(i)}, \ldots, X_{N_i}^{(i)}$. That is,

$$p_i^*(X) = \frac{1}{N_i} \sum_{j=1}^{N_i} \delta(X - X_j^{(i)}) \quad i = 1,2 , \tag{5.163}$$

where * indicates something related to the bootstrap operation. In the bootstrap operation, the density function of (5.163) is treated as the true density from which samples are generated. Therefore, in this section, $X_j^{(i)}$ is considered a given fixed vector and is not random as it was in the previous sections.

When samples are drawn from $p_i^*(X)$ randomly, we select only the existing sample points with random frequencies. Thus, the N_i samples drawn from $p_i^*(X)$ form a random density function

$$\hat{\mathbf{p}}_i^*(X) = \sum_{j=1}^{N_i} \mathbf{w}_j^{(i)} \delta(X - X_j^{(i)}) \quad i = 1,2 . \tag{5.164}$$

Within each class, the $\mathbf{w}_j^{(i)}$'s are identically distributed under the condition $\sum_{j=1}^{N_i} \mathbf{w}_j^{(i)} = 1$. Their statistical properties are known as

$$E\{\mathbf{w}_j^{(i)}\} = \frac{1}{N_i} , \tag{5.165}$$

$$E\{\Delta\mathbf{w}_j^{(i)} \Delta\mathbf{w}_k^{(i)}\} = \frac{1}{N_i^2} \delta_{jk} - \frac{1}{N_i^3} , \tag{5.166}$$

$$E\{\Delta\mathbf{w}_j^{(i)} \Delta\mathbf{w}_\ell^{(k)}\} = 0 \qquad \text{for } i \neq k , \tag{5.167}$$

where $\Delta w_j^{(i)} = w_j^{(i)} - 1/N_i$.

The H error in the bootstrap procedure, $\hat{\boldsymbol{\varepsilon}}_H^*$, is obtained by generating samples, designing a classifier based on $\hat{\mathbf{p}}_i^*(X)$, and testing $p_i^*(X)$ of (5.163). On the other hand, the R error, $\hat{\boldsymbol{\varepsilon}}_R^*$, is computed by testing $\hat{\mathbf{p}}_i^*(X)$. The bias between them can be expressed by

$$\hat{\boldsymbol{\varepsilon}}_b^* = \hat{\boldsymbol{\varepsilon}}_H^* - \hat{\boldsymbol{\varepsilon}}_R^*$$

$$= \frac{1}{2\pi} \iint \frac{e^{j\omega \hat{\mathbf{h}}^*(X)}}{j\omega} \left[P_1 \sum_{j=1}^{N_1} \left[\frac{1}{N_1} - \mathbf{w}_j^{(1)} \right] \delta(X - X_j^{(1)}) \right.$$

$$\left. - P_2 \sum_{j=1}^{N_2} \left[\frac{1}{N_2} - \mathbf{w}_j^{(2)} \right] \delta(X - X_j^{(2)}) \right] d\omega dX$$

$$= P_1 \sum_{j=1}^{N_1} \boldsymbol{\gamma}_j^{(1)} - P_2 \sum_{j=1}^{N_2} \boldsymbol{\gamma}_j^{(2)} , \tag{5.168}$$

where

$$\boldsymbol{\gamma}_j^{(i)} = - \frac{\Delta \mathbf{w}_j^{(i)}}{2\pi} \int \frac{e^{j\omega \hat{\mathbf{h}}^*(X_j^{(i)})}}{j\omega} d\omega . \tag{5.169}$$

Quadratic classifier: When a quadratic classifier is used, $\hat{\mathbf{h}}^*(X)$ in (5.169) becomes

$$\hat{\mathbf{h}}^*(X) = f(X, \hat{\mathbf{M}}_1^*, \hat{\boldsymbol{\Sigma}}_1^*) - f(X, \hat{\mathbf{M}}_2^*, \hat{\boldsymbol{\Sigma}}_2^*) , \tag{5.170}$$

where $f(\cdot,\cdot,\cdot)$ is defined in (5.143). The bootstrap parameters, $\hat{\mathbf{M}}_i^*$, and $\hat{\boldsymbol{\Sigma}}_i^*$, are

$$\hat{\mathbf{M}}_i^* = \sum_{j=1}^{N_i} \mathbf{w}_j^{(i)} X_j^{(i)} , \tag{5.171}$$

$$\hat{\boldsymbol{\Sigma}}_i^* = \sum_{j=1}^{N_i} \mathbf{w}_j^{(i)} (X_j^{(i)} - \hat{M}_i)(X_j^{(i)} - \hat{M}_i)^T . \tag{5.172}$$

Note that $\hat{M}_i = (\Sigma_{j=1}^{N_i} X_j^{(i)})/N_i$ instead of $\hat{\mathbf{M}}_i^*$ is used to compute $\hat{\boldsymbol{\Sigma}}_i^*$. In the conventional sample covariance matrix, the sample mean is used, because the true expected vector is not available. However, the true expected vector, $\hat{M}_i$, is available in the bootstrap operation, and the use of $\hat{M}_i$ instead of $\hat{\mathbf{M}}_i^*$ simplifies the discussion significantly. Their expectations are

$$E_*\{\hat{\mathbf{M}}_i^*\} = \sum_{j=1}^{N_i} E\{\mathbf{w}_j^{(i)}\}X_j^{(i)} = \frac{1}{N_i}\sum_{j=1}^{N_i} X_j^{(i)} = \hat{M}_i \,, \tag{5.173}$$

$$E_*\{\hat{\mathbf{\Sigma}}_i^*\} = \sum_{j=1}^{N_i} E\{\mathbf{w}_j^{(i)}\}(X_j^{(i)}-\hat{M}_i)(X_j^{(i)}-\hat{M}_i)^T$$

$$= \frac{N_i-1}{N_i}\hat{\Sigma}_i \cong \hat{\Sigma}_i \,, \tag{5.174}$$

where E_* indicates the expectation with respect to the $\mathbf{w}$'s.

$f(X,\hat{\mathbf{M}}_i^*,\hat{\mathbf{\Sigma}}_i^*)$ can be expanded around $f(X,\hat{M}_i,\hat{\Sigma}_i)$ by the Taylor series as

$$f(X,\hat{\mathbf{M}}_i^*,\hat{\mathbf{\Sigma}}_i^*) \cong f(X,\hat{M}_i,\hat{\Sigma}_i) + \frac{\partial f^T}{\partial \hat{M}_i}\Delta\hat{\mathbf{M}}_i + \mathrm{tr}\left\{\frac{\partial f^*}{\partial \hat{\Sigma}_i}\Delta\hat{\mathbf{\Sigma}}_i\right\}, \tag{5.175}$$

where $\Delta\hat{\mathbf{M}}_i = \hat{\mathbf{M}}_i^* - \hat{M}_i$, $\Delta\hat{\mathbf{\Sigma}}_i = \hat{\mathbf{\Sigma}}_i^* - \hat{\Sigma}_i$, and $\partial f^*/\partial\hat{\Sigma}_i$ is defined in (5.141). Since $\hat{h}(X) = f(X,\hat{M}_1,\hat{\Sigma}_1) - f(X,\hat{M}_2,\hat{\Sigma}_2)$,

$$\Delta\hat{\mathbf{h}}(X) = \hat{\mathbf{h}}^*(X) - \hat{h}(X)$$

$$\cong \frac{\partial f^T}{\partial \hat{M}_1}\Delta\hat{\mathbf{M}}_1 - \frac{\partial f^T}{\partial \hat{M}_2}\Delta\hat{\mathbf{M}}_2 + \mathrm{tr}\left[\frac{\partial f^*}{\partial \hat{\Sigma}_1}\Delta\hat{\mathbf{\Sigma}}_1 - \frac{\partial f^*}{\partial \hat{\Sigma}_2}\Delta\hat{\mathbf{\Sigma}}_2\right]. \tag{5.176}$$

The partial derivatives of (5.176) can be obtained by (5.144) and (5.145).

Bootstrap Expectation

Using the approximation of (5.60), (5.169) can be approximated as

$$\boldsymbol{\gamma}_j^{(i)} \cong -\frac{\Delta\mathbf{w}_j^{(i)}}{2\pi}\int \frac{e^{j\omega\hat{h}(X_j^{(i)})}}{j\omega}[1+j\omega\Delta\hat{\mathbf{h}}(X_j^{(i)}) + \frac{(j\omega)^2}{2}\Delta\hat{\mathbf{h}}^2(X_j^{(i)})]d\omega \,. \tag{5.177}$$

The third term is a third order variation with the combination of $\Delta\mathbf{w}_j^{(i)}$ and $\Delta\hat{\mathbf{h}}^2$, and can be ignored. Thus, our analysis will focus on the first and second terms only. With this in mind, substituting (5.171), (5.172), and (5.176) into (5.177) produces

$$\boldsymbol{\gamma}_j^{(i)} \cong -\frac{\Delta \mathbf{w}_j^{(i)}}{2\pi} \int \frac{e^{j\omega \hat{h}(X_j^{(i)})}}{j\omega} d\omega$$

$$- \frac{1}{2\pi} \int e^{j\omega \hat{h}(X_j^{(i)})} [\frac{\partial f^T}{\partial \hat{M}_1} \sum_{k=1}^{N_1} \Delta \mathbf{w}_j^{(i)} \Delta \mathbf{w}_k^{(1)} X_k^{(1)}$$

$$- \frac{\partial f^T}{\partial \hat{M}_2} \sum_{k=1}^{N_2} \Delta \mathbf{w}_j^{(i)} \Delta \mathbf{w}_k^{(2)} X_k^{(2)}$$

$$+ \sum_{k=1}^{N_1} \Delta \mathbf{w}_j^{(i)} \Delta \mathbf{w}_k^{(1)} (X_k^{(1)} - \hat{M}_1)^T \frac{\partial f^*}{\partial \hat{\Sigma}_1} (X_k^{(1)} - \hat{M}_1)$$

$$- \sum_{k=1}^{N_2} \Delta \mathbf{w}_j^{(i)} \Delta \mathbf{w}_k^{(2)} (X_k^{(2)} - \hat{M}_2)^T \frac{\partial f^*}{\partial \hat{\Sigma}_2} (X_k^{(2)} - \hat{M}_2)] d\omega \,. \tag{5.178}$$

Using the expectations in (5.165)-(5.167), $E_*\{\boldsymbol{\gamma}_j^{(i)}\}$ becomes

$$E_*\{\boldsymbol{\gamma}_j^{(i)}\} \cong \frac{(-1)^i}{2\pi} \int e^{j\omega \hat{h}(X_j^{(i)})} [\frac{\partial f^T}{\partial \hat{M}_i} \sum_{k=1}^{N_i} (\frac{\delta_{jk}}{N_i^2} - \frac{1}{N_i^3}) X_k^{(i)}$$

$$+ \sum_{k=1}^{N_i} (\frac{\delta_{jk}}{N_i^2} - \frac{1}{N_i^3}) (X_k^{(i)} - \hat{M}_i)^T \frac{\partial f^*}{\partial \hat{\Sigma}_i} (X_k^{(i)} - \hat{M}_i)] d\omega$$

$$\cong \frac{(-1)^i}{2\pi N_i^2} \int e^{j\omega \hat{h}(X_j^{(i)})} [\frac{\partial f^T}{\partial \hat{M}_i} (X_j^{(i)} - \hat{M}_i)$$

$$+ (X_j^{(i)} - \hat{M}_i)^T \frac{\partial f^*}{\partial \hat{\Sigma}_i} (X_j^{(i)} - \hat{M}_i) - \text{tr} \left[\frac{\partial f^*}{\partial \hat{\Sigma}_i} \hat{\Sigma}_i \right]] d\omega \,, \tag{5.179}$$

where an approximation of $N-1 \cong N$ is used to obtain the second line from the first. Now, substituting the partial derivatives of (5.144) and (5.145) into (5.179),

$$E_*\{\boldsymbol{\gamma}_j^{(i)}\} = \frac{(-1)^i}{2\pi N_i^2} \int e^{j\omega \hat{h}(X_j^{(i)})} [-(X_j^{(i)} - \hat{M}_i)^T \hat{\Sigma}_i^{-1} (X_j^{(i)} - \hat{M}_i)$$

$$+ \frac{1}{2} (X_j^{(i)} - \hat{M}_i)^T \hat{\Sigma}_i^{-1} (X_j^{(i)} - \hat{M}_i) - \frac{1}{2} \{(X_j^{(i)} - \hat{M}_i)^T \hat{\Sigma}_i^{-1} (X_j^{(i)} - \hat{M}_i)\}^2$$

$$- \frac{1}{2} n + \frac{1}{2} (X_j^{(i)} - \hat{M}_i)^T \hat{\Sigma}_i^{-1} (X_j^{(i)} - \hat{M}_i)] d\omega$$

$$= \frac{(-1)^{i+1}}{N_i^2} \frac{1}{2\pi} \int \frac{\hat{d}_i^4 (X_j^{(i)}) + n}{2} e^{j\omega \hat{h}(X_j^{(i)})} d\omega \,, \tag{5.180}$$

where $\hat{d}_i^2(X) = (X - \hat{M}_i)^T \hat{\Sigma}_i^{-1} (X - \hat{M}_i)$. Thus, the expectation of the bootstrap bias for a quadratic classifier given a sample set $S_1 = \{X_1^{(1)}, \ldots, X_{N_1}^{(1)}, X_1^{(2)}, \ldots, X_{N_2}^{(2)}\}$ becomes

$$E_* \{ \hat{\boldsymbol{\varepsilon}}_b^* | S_1 \} = \frac{P_1}{N_1^2} \sum_{j=1}^{N_1} \hat{\beta}_j^{*(1)} + \frac{P_2}{N_2^2} \sum_{j=1}^{N_2} \hat{\beta}_j^{*(2)} \,, \tag{5.181}$$

where

$$\hat{\beta}_j^{*(i)} = \frac{1}{2\pi} \int \frac{\hat{d}_i^4 (X_j^{(i)}) + n}{2} e^{j\omega \hat{h}(X_j^{(i)})} d\omega \,. \tag{5.182}$$

Note that (5.151) and (5.182) are very similar. The differences are $\hat{d}_i^2$ vs. d_i^2 and $\hat{h}$ vs. $\hat{\mathbf{h}}_L$. The discriminant function $\hat{h}$ of (5.182) is designed with $\hat{M}_i$ and $\hat{\Sigma}_i$, the sample mean and sample covariance of the sample set S_1. The test samples $X_j^{(i)}$ are the members of the same set, S_1. Therefore, $\hat{h}$ is the same as the R discriminant function $\hat{h}_R$, while $\hat{\mathbf{h}}_L$ of (5.151) is the L discriminant function. For a given S_1, $\hat{h}_R$ is a fixed function. However, if a random set, **S**, replaces the fixed set, S_1, the discriminant function becomes a random variable, $\hat{\mathbf{h}}_R$. As shown in (5.148) and (5.149), the difference between $\hat{\mathbf{h}}_L$ and $\hat{\mathbf{h}}_R$ is proportional to $1/N$. Thus, the difference between $e^{j\omega \hat{\mathbf{h}}_L}$ and $e^{j\omega \hat{\mathbf{h}}_R}$ is proportional to $1/N$. Also, it can be shown that the difference between $\hat{d}_i^2$ and d_i^2 is proportional to $1/N$. Thus, ignoring terms with $1/N$, $\hat{\boldsymbol{\varepsilon}}_b$ of (5.150) and $E_* \{ \hat{\boldsymbol{\varepsilon}}_b^* | \mathbf{S} \}$ of (5.181) (note that **S** is now a random set) become equal and have the same statistical properties. Practically, this means that estimating the expected error rate using the L and bootstrap methods should yield the same results.

These conclusions have been confirmed experimentally.

Experiment 10: Bootstrap errors

Data: I-I, I-$4I$, I-Λ (Normal, $n = 8$)

Classifier: Quadratic classifier of (5.54)

No. of bootstrap sets: $\ell = 100$

Sample size: $N_1 = N_2 = 24, 40, 80, 160, 320$

No. of trials: $\tau = 10$

Results: Table 5-12 [6]

In Table 5-12(a), the means and standard deviations of $\hat{\varepsilon}_L$ and $\hat{\varepsilon}_b$ $(= \hat{\varepsilon}_L - \hat{\varepsilon}_R)$ of the 10 trials are presented for the conventional L and R methods. Table 5-12(b) shows the corresponding terms in the bootstrap method: $\hat{\varepsilon}_R + E_*\{\hat{\varepsilon}_b^* | S\}$ and $E_*\{\hat{\varepsilon}_b^* | S\}$ respectively. $E_*\{\hat{\varepsilon}_b^* | S_i\}$ is obtained by taking the average of $\hat{\varepsilon}_{bi1}^*, \ldots, \hat{\varepsilon}_{bi\ell}^*$ [see Fig. 5-5]. This is the bootstrap estimation of the bias between the H and R errors given S_i, and varies with S_i. The random variable $E_*\{\hat{\varepsilon}_b^* | \mathbf{S}\}$ with a random $\mathbf{S}$ should be compared with $\hat{\varepsilon}_b$ of Table 5-12(a). If this bias estimate is close to the bias between $\hat{\varepsilon}_{Hi}$ and $\hat{\varepsilon}_{Ri}$ of S_i, the bootstrap bias could be added to $\hat{\varepsilon}_{Ri}$ to estimate $\hat{\varepsilon}_{Hi}$. The term $\hat{\varepsilon}_R + E_*\{\hat{\varepsilon}_b^* | S\}$ of Table 5-12(b) shows this estimation of $\hat{\varepsilon}_H$, and should be compared with $\hat{\varepsilon}_L$ of Table 5-12(a). The table shows that $\hat{\varepsilon}_L$ of (a) and $\hat{\varepsilon}_R + E_*\{\hat{\varepsilon}_b^* | S\}$ of (b) are close in both mean and standard deviation for a reasonable size of N. The biases, $\hat{\varepsilon}_b$ of (a) and $E_*\{\hat{\varepsilon}_b^* | \mathbf{S}\}$ of (b), are also close in the mean, but the standard deviations of $E_*\{\hat{\varepsilon}_b^* | \mathbf{S}\}$ are consistently smaller than the ones of $\hat{\varepsilon}_b$.

Bootstrap Variance

The variance with respect to the bootstrap samples can be evaluated in a fashion similar to (5.154)

$$\begin{aligned} \mathrm{Var}_*\{\hat{\varepsilon}_b^* | S\} = {} & P_1^2 [\sum_{j=1}^{N_1} \mathrm{Var}_*\{\gamma_j^{(1)}\} + \sum_{j=1}^{N_1} \sum_{\substack{k=1 \\ j \neq k}}^{N_1} \mathrm{Cov}_*\{\gamma_j^{(1)}, \gamma_k^{(1)}\}] \\ & + P_2^2 [\sum_{j=1}^{N_2} \mathrm{Var}_*\{\gamma_j^{(2)}\} + \sum_{j=1}^{N_1} \sum_{\substack{k=1 \\ j \neq k}}^{N_2} \mathrm{Cov}_*\{\gamma_j^{(2)}, \gamma_k^{(2)}\}] \\ & - 2P_1 P_2 \sum_{j=1}^{N_1} \sum_{k=1}^{N_2} \mathrm{Cov}_*\{\gamma_j^{(1)}, \gamma_k^{(2)}\} . \end{aligned} \tag{5.183}$$

TABLE 5-12

COMPARISON BETWEEN CONVENTIONAL AND BOOTSTRAP METHODS

Data	N	$\hat{\varepsilon}_L$		$\hat{\varepsilon}_b = \hat{\varepsilon}_L - \hat{\varepsilon}_R$		$\mathrm{Var}\{\hat{\varepsilon}_R\}$
		Mean (%)	Standard deviation (%)	Mean (%)	Standard deviation (%)	(%)
	24	17.08	4.89	13.54	3.14	0.11
	40	13.38	6.04	7.63	3.88	0.07
I-I	80	11.19	2.47	4.06	1.29	0.04
	160	11.28	2.35	2.16	1.09	0.03
	320	10.67	0.80	0.89	0.37	0.01
	24	18.33	4.79	14.79	3.86	0.12
	40	13.75	3.23	8.88	2.97	0.06
I-4I	80	11.19	2.72	4.00	1.56	0.08
	160	9.88	1.58	2.28	0.68	0.01
	320	10.09	0.83	0.98	0.40	0.01
	24	5.00	3.43	4.38	3.02	0.01
	40	3.63	1.99	1.75	1.21	0.02
I-Λ	80	2.31	1.10	0.88	0.94	0.01
	160	2.34	0.90	0.41	0.36	0.00
	320	2.17	0.48	0.17	0.14	0.00

(a) Conventional L and R error estimates.

Because the samples from each class are bootstrapped independently, $\mathrm{Cov}_*\{\boldsymbol{\gamma}_j^{(1)}, \boldsymbol{\gamma}_k^{(2)}\} = 0$.

Using a property of the inverse Fourier transform,

$$\boldsymbol{\gamma}_j^{(i)} = -\frac{\Delta \mathbf{w}_j^{(i)}}{2\pi} \int \frac{e^{j\omega \hat{\mathbf{h}}^*(X_j^{(i)})}}{j\omega} d\omega = -\frac{1}{2} sign(\hat{\mathbf{h}}^*(X_j^{(i)})) \Delta \mathbf{w}_j^{(i)} . \tag{5.184}$$

The variance of $\boldsymbol{\gamma}_j^{(i)}$ is

TABLE 5-12

COMPARISON BETWEEN CONVENTIONAL AND BOOTSTRAP METHODS

Data	N	$\hat{\varepsilon}_R + E_*\{\hat{\varepsilon}_b^* \mid \mathbf{S}\}$		$E_*\{\hat{\varepsilon}_b^* \mid \mathbf{S}\}$		$\mathrm{Var}_*\{\hat{\varepsilon}_b^* \mid \mathbf{S}\}$
		Mean (%)	Standard deviation (%)	Mean (%)	Standard deviation (%)	Mean (%)
I-I	24	12.77	4.17	9.23	1.38	0.18
	40	11.68	4.44	5.92	1.90	0.08
	80	10.67	2.50	3.55	0.56	0.04
	160	11.17	1.94	2.05	0.44	0.02
	320	10.78	0.91	1.00	0.11	0.01
I-4I	24	15.08	4.35	11.54	1.26	0.21
	40	12.10	2.27	7.22	0.92	0.12
	80	10.82	3.12	3.63	0.54	0.04
	160	9.56	1.23	1.96	0.33	0.02
	320	10.14	0.77	1.03	0.15	0.01
I-Λ	24	4.14	1.69	3.52	0.84	0.10
	40	3.74	1.95	1.86	0.67	0.03
	80	2.26	1.08	0.82	0.24	0.01
	160	2.35	0.80	0.42	0.17	0.01
	320	2.18	0.53	0.18	0.07	0.00

(b) Bootstrap error estimates.

$$\mathrm{Var}_*\{\boldsymbol{\gamma}_j^{(i)}\} = E_*\{\boldsymbol{\gamma}_j^{(i)2}\} - E_*^2\{\boldsymbol{\gamma}_j^{(i)}\}$$

$$= \frac{1}{4}E\{\Delta\mathbf{w}_j^{(i)2}\} - E_*^2\{\boldsymbol{\gamma}_j^{(i)}\}$$

$$\cong \frac{1}{4}\left(\frac{1}{N_i^2} - \frac{1}{N_i^3}\right), \tag{5.185}$$

where $E_*^2\{\boldsymbol{\gamma}_j^{(i)}\}$ is proportional to $1/N_i^4$ from (5.180) and therefore can be ignored. $\mathrm{Cov}_*\{\gamma_j^{(i)},\gamma_k^{(i)}\}$ may be approximated by using the first term only of (5.178). Again, using (5.184),

$$\mathrm{Cov}_*\{\gamma_j^{(i)},\gamma_k^{(i)}\} = E_*\{\gamma_j^{(i)}\gamma_k^{(i)}\} - E_*\{\gamma_j^{(i)}\}E_*\{\gamma_k^{(i)}\}$$

$$\cong \frac{1}{4} sign(\hat{h}(X_j^{(i)}))sign(\hat{h}(X_k^{(i)}))E\{\Delta \mathbf{w}_j^{(i)}\Delta \mathbf{w}_k^{(i)}\} - E_*\{\gamma_j^{(i)}\}E_*\{\gamma_k^{(i)}\}$$

$$\cong -\frac{1}{4N_i^3} sign(\hat{h}(X_j^{(i)}))sign(\hat{h}(X_k^{(i)})) \qquad \text{for } j \neq k \ , \tag{5.186}$$

where $E\{\Delta \mathbf{w}_j^{(i)}\Delta \mathbf{w}_k^{(i)}\} = -1/N_i^3$ for $j \neq k$ by (5.166), and $E_*\{\gamma_j^{(i)}\}E_*\{\gamma_k^{(i)}\}$ is proportional to $1/N_i^4$ by (5.180) and therefore can be ignored.

Thus, substituting (5.185) and (5.186) into (5.183) and using $\mathrm{Cov}_*\{\gamma_j^{(1)},\gamma_k^{(2)}\} = 0$,

$$\mathrm{Var}_*\{\hat{\varepsilon}_b^*|S\} \cong \frac{1}{4}\sum_{i=1}^{2}\frac{P_i^2}{N_i}\left[1-\sum_{j=1}^{N_i}\frac{sign(\hat{h}(X_j^{(i)}))}{N_i}\sum_{k=1}^{N_i}\frac{sign(\hat{h}(X_k^{(i)}))}{N_i}\right]$$

$$= \frac{1}{4}\sum_{i=1}^{2}\frac{P_i^2}{N_i}[1-(1-2\hat{\varepsilon}_{iR})(1-2\hat{\varepsilon}_{iR})]$$

$$= \sum_{i=1}^{2}P_i^2\frac{\hat{\varepsilon}_{iR}(1-\hat{\varepsilon}_{iR})}{N_i} \ . \tag{5.187}$$

Note that $\Sigma sign(\hat{h}(X_j^{(i)}))/N_i = (-1)^i$ [(# of correctly classified ω_i-samples by $\hat{h} \underset{\omega_2}{\overset{\omega_1}{\gtrless}} 0)/N_i$ − (# of misclassified ω_i-samples by $\hat{h} \underset{\omega_2}{\overset{\omega_1}{\gtrless}} 0)/N_i$] $= (-1)^i[(1-\hat{\varepsilon}_{iR}) - \hat{\varepsilon}_{iR}]$]$= (-1)^i(1-2\hat{\varepsilon}_{iR})$. Since $\hat{h}$ is the R discriminant function for the original sample set, the resulting error is the R error. The last column of Table 5-12(a) shows the variance of $\hat{\varepsilon}_R$, which is computed by the 10 trials of the conventional R method. This should be compared with the last column of Table 5-12(b), $\mathrm{Var}_*\{\hat{\varepsilon}_b^*|S\}$. Both are close as (5.187) predicts. $\mathrm{Var}_*\{\hat{\varepsilon}_b^*|S_i\}$ is the variance of $\hat{\varepsilon}_{bi1}^*,\ldots,\hat{\varepsilon}_{bi\ell}^*$ [see Fig. 5-5]. The last column is the average of $\mathrm{Var}\{\hat{\varepsilon}_b^*|S_i\}$ over i.

Note that (5.187) is the variance expression of the R error estimate.

Computer Projects

1. Repeat Experiment 1.

2. Repeat Experiment 4. Also, estimate the asymptotic error for each n by using the line fitting procedure.

3. Repeat Experiment 5. Also, estimate the asymptotic error for each n by using the line fitting procedure.

4. Repeat Experiment 6.

5. Repeat Experiment 9.

6. Repeat Experiment 10.

Problems

1. The Fisher criterion, $f = (m_2 - m_1)^2/(\sigma_1^2 + \sigma_2^2)$, measures the class separability between two one-dimensional distributions. Compute the bias and variance of $\mathbf{f}$ when these parameters are estimated by using N samples from $N_x(0,1)$ for ω_1 and N samples from $N_x(1,4)$ for ω_2.

2. Let $f(m)$ be a function of m, where m is the expected value of a one-dimensional normal distribution and is estimated by the sample mean $\hat{\mathbf{m}}$ using N samples. Expand $f(\hat{\mathbf{m}})$ around $f(m)$ up to the fourth order term, and confirm that $E\{\mathbf{0}^{(3)}\} = 0$ and $E\{\mathbf{0}^{(4)}\} \sim 1/N^2$.

3. Compute the bias and variance of $\hat{\boldsymbol{\mu}}$ (not $\hat{\boldsymbol{\mu}}_1$ and $\hat{\boldsymbol{\mu}}_2$ separately) for normal distributions.

4. In order for a linear classifier $h(X) = V^T X + v_0 \underset{\omega_2}{\overset{\omega_1}{\gtrless}} 0$ to be optimum by minimizing the error of (5.37), prove that V and v_0 must satisfy

$$P_1 \int_{h(X)=0} p_1(X)\, dX = P_2 \int_{h(X)=0} p_2(X)\, dX ,$$

$$P_1 \int_{h(X)=0} X p_1(X)\, dX = P_2 \int_{h(X)=0} X p_2(X)\, dX .$$

5. Derive v_i of (5.92) for Data *I-I*.

6. A quadratic classifier for zero-mean distributions is given as

$$h(X) = X^T [\Sigma_1^{-1} - \Sigma_2^{-1}] X \underset{\omega_2}{\overset{\omega_1}{\gtrless}} t .$$

In the design phase, Σ_1 and Σ_2 are estimated by

$$\hat{\Sigma}_1 = \frac{1}{N} \sum_{i=1}^{N} X_i X_i^T \quad \text{and} \quad \hat{\Sigma}_2 = \frac{1}{N} \sum_{i=1}^{N} Y_i Y_i^T ,$$

where X_i and Y_i are samples from ω_1 and ω_2 respectively. For testing X_k, X_k is excluded from design to get $\hat{\Sigma}_{1k}$. Prove

$$h(X_k, \hat{\Sigma}_{1k}, \hat{\Sigma}_2) - h(X_k, \hat{\Sigma}_1, \hat{\Sigma}_2) = \frac{d_k^2 (d_k^2 - 1)}{N - d_k^2} ,$$

where

$$d_k^2 = X_k^T \hat{\Sigma}_1^{-1} X_k .$$

7. Modify the Procedure III of Section 3.2 to the leave-one-out method.

8. Assuming $M_1 = 0$, $M_2 = M = [m\ 0 \ldots 0]^T$, and $\Sigma_1 = \Sigma_2 = I$, compute the integral of (5.153) along the Bayes boundary ($x_1 = \sqrt{M^T M}/2$) to obtain β_1. Use $h(X) = \sqrt{M^T M} x_1 - M^T M/2$, $d_1^4(X) = (\Sigma_{i=1}^n x_i^2)^2$, and $p_1(X) = (2\pi)^{-n/2} \exp[-\frac{1}{2} \Sigma_{i=1}^n x_i^2]$.

9. N boxes have equal probability of getting a sample. When N samples are thrown, the ith box receives $\mathbf{k}_i$ samples. Defining $\mathbf{w}_i = \mathbf{k}_i/N$, prove that

(1) $E\{\mathbf{w}_i\} = 1/N$,

(2) $E\{(\mathbf{w}_i - 1/N)(\mathbf{w}_j - 1/N)\} = \delta_{ij}/N^2 - 1/N^3$.

10. Let the bootstrap sample covariance matrix be

$$\hat{\boldsymbol{\Sigma}} = \sum_{j=1}^{N} \mathbf{w}_j (X_j - \hat{\mathbf{M}}^*)(X_j - \hat{\mathbf{M}}^*)^T$$

instead of (5.172). Compute the expected value of $\hat{\boldsymbol{\Sigma}}$.

References

1. G. J. McLachlan, Error rate estimation in discriminant analysis: recent advances, in "Advances in Multivariate Statistical Analysis," ed. A. K. Gupta, D. Reidel Publishing Co., Dordrecht, 1987.
2. D. J. Hand, Recent advances in error rate estimation, *Pattern Recognition Letters*, 4, pp. 335-346, 1986.
3. A. K. Jain and B. Chandrasekaran, Dimensionality and sample size considerations in pattern recognition practice, in "Handbook of Statistics 2," ed. P. R. Krishnaiah and L. N. Kanal, North Holland, Amsterdam, 1982.
4. K. Fukunaga and R. R. Hayes, Effects of sample size in classifier design, *Trans. IEEE Pattern Anal. and Machine Intell.*, PAMI-11, pp. 873-885, 1989.
5. G. F. Hughes, On the mean accuracy of statistical pattern recognizers, *Trans. IEEE Inform. Theory*, IT-14, pp. 55-63, 1968.
6. K. Fukunaga and R. R. Hayes, Estimation of classifier performance, *Trans. IEEE Pattern Anal. and Machine Intell.*, PAMI-11, pp. 1087-1101, 1989.
7. S. Raudys and V. Pikelis, On dimensionality, sample size, classification error, and complexity of classification algorithm in pattern recognition, *Trans. IEEE Pattern Anal. Machine Intell.*, PAMI-2, pp. 242-252, 1980.
8. D. H. Foley, Considerations of sample and feature size, *Trans. IEEE Inform. Theory*, IT-18, pp. 618-626, 1972.
9. S. John, Errors in discrimination, *Ann. Math. Stat.*, 32, pp. 1125-1144, 1961.
10. C. P. Han, Distribution of discriminant function in circular models, *Inst. Stat. Math. Ann.*, 22, pp. 117-125, 1970.

11. G. J. McLachlan, Some expected values for the error rates of the sample quadratic discriminant function, *Australian Journal of Statistics,* 17(3), pp. 161-165, 1975.

12. M. Hills, Allocation rules and their error rate, *J. Royal Stat. Soc. Ser.*, B28, pp. 1-31, 1966.

13. P. A. Lachenbruch and R. M. Mickey, Estimation of error rates in discriminant analysis, *Technometrics,* 10, pp. 1-11, 1968.

14. K. Fukunaga and D. L. Kessell, Estimation of classification errors, *Trans. IEEE Computers,* C-20, pp. 1521-1527, 1971.

15. B. Efron, Bootstrap methods: Another look at the jackknife, *Ann. Stat.*, 7, pp. 1-26, 1979.

Chapter 6

NONPARAMETRIC DENSITY ESTIMATION

So far we have been discussing the estimation of parameters. Thus, if we can assume we have a density function that can be characterized by a set of parameters, we can design a classifier using estimates of the parameters. Unfortunately, we often cannot assume a parametric form for the density function, and in order to apply the likelihood ratio test we somehow have to estimate the density functions using an unstructured approach. This type of approach is called *nonparametric estimation*, while the former is called *parametric estimation*. Since, in nonparametric approaches, the density function is estimated locally by a small number of neighboring samples, the estimate is far less reliable with larger bias and variance than the parametric counterpart.

There are two kinds of nonparametric estimation techniques available: one is called the *Parzen density estimate* and the other is the *k-nearest neighbor density estimate*. They are fundamentally very similar, but exhibit some different statistical properties. Both are discussed in this chapter.

It is extremely difficult to obtain an accurate density estimate nonparametrically, particularly in high-dimensional spaces. However, our goal here is not to get an accurate estimate. Our goal is, by using these estimates, to design a classifier and evaluate its performance. For this reason, the accuracy of the estimate is not necessarily a crucial issue. Classification and performance evaluation will be discussed in Chapter 7. The intention of this chapter is to make the reader familiar with the fundamental mathematical properties related to nonparametric density estimation in preparation for the material presented in Chapter 7.

6.1 Parzen Density Estimate

Parzen Density Estimate

In order to estimate the value of a density function at a point X, we may set up a small *local region* around X, $L(X)$. Then, the *probability coverage* (or *probability mass*) of $L(X)$ may be approximated by $p(X)v$ where v is the volume of $L(X)$. This probability may be estimated by drawing a large number of samples, N, from $p(X)$, counting the number of samples, k, falling in $L(X)$, and computing k/N. Equating these two probabilities, we may obtain an estimate of the density function as

$$\hat{\mathbf{p}}(X)v = \frac{\mathbf{k}(X)}{N} \quad or \quad \hat{\mathbf{p}}(X) = \frac{\mathbf{k}(X)}{Nv} . \tag{6.1}$$

Note that, with a fixed v, $\mathbf{k}$ is a random variable and is dependent on X. A fixed v does not imply the same v throughout the entire space, and v could still vary with X. However, v is a preset value and is not a random variable.

Kernel expression: The estimate of (6.1) has another interpretation. Suppose that 3 samples, X_3, X_4, and X_5, are found in $L(X)$ as shown in Fig. 6-1. With v and N given, $\hat{p}(X)$ becomes $3/Nv$. On the other hand, if we set up a uniform *kernel function*, $\kappa(\cdot)$, with volume v and height $1/v$ around all existing samples, the average of the values of these kernel functions at X is also $3/Nv$. That is, [1-4]

$$\hat{\mathbf{p}}(X) = \frac{1}{N} \sum_{i=1}^{N} \kappa(X - \mathbf{X}_i) . \tag{6.2}$$

As seen in Fig. 6-1, only the kernel functions around the 3 samples, X_3, X_4, and X_5, contribute to the summation of (6.2).

Once (6.2) is adopted, the shape of the kernel function could be selected more freely, under the condition $\int \kappa(X)\, dX = 1$. For one-dimensional cases, we may seek optimality and select a complex shape. However, in a high-dimensional space, because of its complexity, the practical selection of the ker-

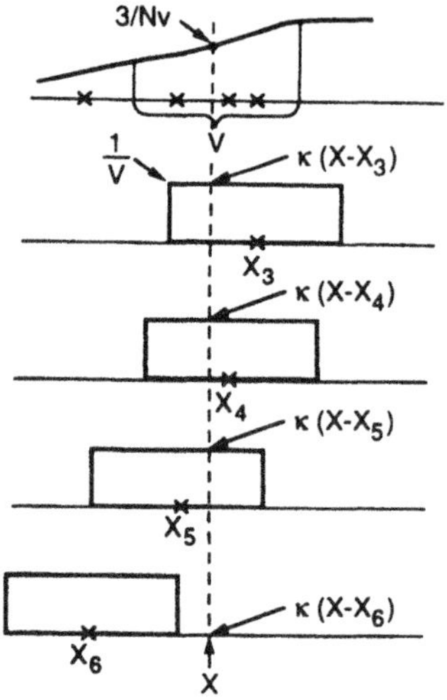

Fig. 6-1 Parzen kernel density estimate.

nel function is very limited to either a normal or uniform kernel. In this book, we will use the following kernel which includes both normal and uniform kernels as special cases:

$$\kappa(X) = \frac{m\Gamma(\frac{n}{2})\Gamma^{n/2}(\frac{n+2}{2m})}{(n\pi)^{n/2}\Gamma^{n/2+1}(\frac{n}{2m})} \times \frac{1}{r^n |A|^{1/2}}$$

$$\times \exp\left[-\left\{\frac{\Gamma(\frac{n+2}{2m})}{n\Gamma(\frac{n}{2m})} X^T(r^2A)^{-1}X\right\}^m\right], \tag{6.3}$$

where $\Gamma(\cdot)$ is the gamma function, and m is a parameter determining the shape of the kernel. It may be verified that, for any value of m, the covariance matrix of the kernel density (6.3) is r^2A. The parameter m determines the rate at which the kernel function drops off. For $m = 1$, (6.3) reduces to a simple normal kernel. As m becomes large, (6.3) approaches a uniform (hyperelliptical) kernel, always with a smooth roll-off. The matrix A determines the shape of the hyperellipsoid, and r controls the size or volume of the kernel. Other coefficients are selected to satisfy the two conditions mentioned previously:

$\int \kappa(X)dX = 1$ and $\Sigma_\kappa = r^2 A$ where Σ_κ is the covariance matrix of $\kappa(X)$.

Convolution expression: Equation (6.2) can be rewritten in convolution form as

$$\hat{\mathbf{p}}(X) = \hat{\mathbf{p}}_s(X) * \kappa(X) \triangleq \int \hat{\mathbf{p}}_s(Y)\kappa(X-Y)dY , \tag{6.4}$$

where $\hat{\mathbf{p}}_s$ is an impulsive density function with impulses at the locations of existing N samples.

$$\hat{\mathbf{p}}_s(Y) = \frac{1}{N}\sum_{i=1}^{N}\delta(Y-\mathbf{X}_i) . \tag{6.5}$$

That is, the estimated density $\hat{\mathbf{p}}(X)$ is obtained by feeding $\hat{\mathbf{p}}_s(X)$ through a linear (noncausal) filter whose impulse response is given by $\kappa(X)$. Therefore, $\hat{\mathbf{p}}(X)$ is a smoothed version of $\hat{\mathbf{p}}_s(X)$.

Moments of $\hat{\mathbf{p}}(X)$: The first and second order moments of (6.4) can be easily computed. First, let us compute the expected value of $\hat{\mathbf{p}}_s(X)$ as

$$E\{\hat{\mathbf{p}}_s(X)\} = \frac{1}{N}\sum_{i=1}^{N}\int \delta(X-Z)p(Z)dZ = \frac{1}{N}\sum_{i=1}^{N}p(X) = p(X) . \tag{6.6}$$

That is, $\hat{\mathbf{p}}_s(X)$ is an unbiased estimate of $p(X)$. Then, the expected value of $\hat{\mathbf{p}}(X)$ of (6.4) may be computed as

$$E\{\hat{\mathbf{p}}(X)\} = \int E\{\hat{\mathbf{p}}_s(Y)\}\kappa(X-Y)dY$$

$$= \int p(Y)\kappa(X-Y)dY = p(X)*\kappa(X) . \tag{6.7}$$

Also,

$$E\{\hat{\mathbf{p}}^2(X)\} = \frac{1}{N^2}\left[\sum_{i=1}^{N}\int \kappa^2(X-Z)p(Z)dZ \right.$$

$$\left. + \sum_{i=1}^{N}\sum_{\substack{j=1 \\ i\neq j}}^{N}\iint \kappa(X-Y)\kappa(X-Z)p(Y)p(Z)dYdZ \right]$$

$$= \frac{1}{N} p(X) * \kappa^2(X) + (1 - \frac{1}{N})[p(X) * \kappa(X)]^2 . \tag{6.8}$$

Therefore, the variance of $\hat{\mathbf{p}}(X)$ is

$$\text{Var}\{\hat{\mathbf{p}}(X)\} = \frac{1}{N}[p(X) * \kappa^2(X) - [p(X) * \kappa(X)]^2] . \tag{6.9}$$

Approximations of moments: In order to approximate the moments of $\hat{\mathbf{p}}(X)$, let us expand $p(Y)$ around X by a Taylor series up to the second order terms as

$$p(Y) \cong p(X) + \nabla p^T(X)(Y-X) + \frac{1}{2}\text{tr}\{\nabla^2 p(X)(Y-X)(Y-X)^T\} . \tag{6.10}$$

Then, $p(X) * \kappa(X)$ may be approximated by

$$\begin{aligned} p(X) * \kappa(X) &= \int p(Y)\kappa(Y-X)dY \\ &\cong p(X)\int \kappa(Y-X)dY \\ &\quad + \frac{1}{2}\text{tr}\{\nabla^2 p(X)\int (Y-X)(Y-X)^T \kappa(Y-X)dY\} , \end{aligned} \tag{6.11}$$

where the first order term disappears because $\kappa(\cdot)$ is a symmetric function. Since $\int \kappa(Y-X)dY = 1$ and $\int (Y-X)(Y-X)^T \kappa(Y-X)dY = r^2 A$ for $\kappa(\cdot)$ of (6.3), (6.11) can be expressed by

$$p(X) * \kappa(X) \cong p(X)[1 + \frac{1}{2}\alpha(X) r^2] , \tag{6.12}$$

where

$$\alpha(X) = \text{tr}\left\{ \frac{\nabla^2 p(X)}{p(X)} A \right\} . \tag{6.13}$$

Similarly,

$$\begin{aligned} p(X) * \kappa^2(X) &\cong p(X)\int \kappa^2(Y-X)dY \\ &\quad + \frac{1}{2}\text{tr}\{\nabla^2 p(X)\int (Y-X)(Y-X)\kappa^2(Y-X)dY\} . \end{aligned} \tag{6.14}$$

Although $\kappa(\cdot)$ is a density function, $\kappa^2(\cdot)$ is not. Therefore, $\int \kappa^2(Y)dY$ has a value not equal to 1. Let

$$w = \int \kappa^2(Y)dY \ . \tag{6.15}$$

Then, $\kappa^2(\cdot)/w$ becomes a density function. Therefore, (6.14) becomes

$$p(X)*\kappa^2(X) \cong wp(X) + \frac{w}{2}\text{tr}\{\nabla^2 p(X)\int (Y-X)(Y-X)^T \frac{\kappa^2(Y-X)}{w} dY\}$$

$$= wp(X)[1 + \frac{1}{2}\beta(X)r^2] \ , \tag{6.16}$$

where

$$\beta(X) = \text{tr}\left\{\frac{\nabla^2 p(X)}{p(X)} B\right\} \tag{6.17}$$

and $r^2 B$ is the covariance matrix of $\kappa^2(X)/w$.

Substituting (6.12) and (6.16) into (6.7) and (6.9), the moments of $\hat{\mathbf{p}}(X)$ are approximated by

$$E\{\hat{\mathbf{p}}(X)\} \cong p(X)[1 + \frac{1}{2}\alpha(X)r^2] \qquad 2nd \text{ order approximation}$$

$$\cong p(X) \qquad 1st \text{ order approximation} \ , \tag{6.18}$$

$$\text{Var}\{\hat{\mathbf{p}}(X)\} \cong \frac{1}{N}[wp(X)\{1 + \frac{1}{2}\beta(X)r^2\} - p^2(X)\{1 + \frac{1}{2}\alpha(X)r^2\}^2]$$

$$2nd \text{ order approximation}$$

$$\cong \frac{1}{N}[wp(X) - p^2(X)] \qquad 1st \text{ order approximation} \ . \tag{6.19}$$

Note that the variance is proportional to $1/N$ and thus can be reduced by increasing the sample size. On the other hand, the bias is independent of N, and is determined by $\nabla^2 p(X)$, A, and r^2.

Normal kernel: When the kernel function is normal with zero expected vector and covariance matrix $r^2 A$, $N_X(0,r^2 A)$, $\kappa^2(X)$ becomes normal as $cN_X(0,r^2 A/2)$ where $c = 2^{-n/2}(2\pi)^{-n/2}|A|^{-1/2}r^{-n}$. Therefore,

$$w = \frac{1}{2^{n/2}(2\pi)^{n/2} |A|^{1/2} r^n} , \tag{6.20}$$

$$\beta(X) = \frac{1}{2}\alpha(X) . \tag{6.21}$$

Uniform kernel: For a uniform kernel with the covariance matrix r^2A,

$$\kappa(Y) = \begin{cases} 1/v & inside\ L(X) \\ 0 & outside\ L(X) . \end{cases} \tag{6.22}$$

where

$$L(X) = \{Y : d(Y,X) \le r\sqrt{n+2}\} , \tag{6.23}$$

$$d^2(Y,X) = (Y-X)^T A^{-1}(Y-X) , \tag{6.24}$$

and

$$v = \int_{L(X)} dY = \frac{\pi^{n/2}}{\Gamma(\frac{n+2}{2})} |A|^{1/2}(r\sqrt{n+2})^n . \tag{6.25}$$

Then, $\kappa^2(X)$ is also uniform in $L(X)$ with the height $1/v^2$. Therefore,

$$w = \int_{L(X)} \kappa^2(Y)dY = \frac{1}{v} . \tag{6.26}$$

Also, since the covariance matrix of $\kappa(X)$ is r^2A, the covariance matrix of $\kappa^2(X)/w$ is also r^2A as

$$\int_{T(X)} (Y-X)(Y-X)^T \frac{1}{v} dY = r^2A . \tag{6.27}$$

Therefore, for the uniform distribution of (6.22),

$$B = A \quad \text{and} \quad \beta(X) = \alpha(X) . \tag{6.28}$$

Note that w's for both normal and uniform kernels are proportional to r^{-n} or v^{-1}. In particular, $w = 1/v$ for the uniform kernel from (6.26). Using this relation, the first order approximation of the variance can be simplified further as follows:

$$\mathrm{Var}\{\hat{\mathbf{p}}(X)\} \cong \frac{1}{N}\left[\frac{p(X)}{v} - p^2(X)\right]$$

$$= p^2(X)\left[\frac{1}{Nvp(X)} - \frac{1}{N}\right] \cong p^2(X)\left[\frac{1}{k} - \frac{1}{N}\right]$$

$$\cong \frac{p^2(X)}{k}, \tag{6.29}$$

where $p \cong k/Nv$ and $N \gg k$ are used. This suggests that the second term of (6.19) is much smaller than the first term, and can be ignored. Also, (6.29) indicates that $k \rightarrow \infty$ is required along with $N \rightarrow \infty$ for the Parzen density estimate to be consistent. These are the known conditions for asymptotic unbiasness and consistency [2].

Convolution of normal distributions: If $p(X)$ is assumed to be normal and a normal kernel is selected for $\kappa(X)$, (6.7) and (6.9) become trivial to evaluate. When two normal densities $N_X(0,A)$ and $N_X(0,B)$ are convolved, the result is also a normal density of $N_X(0,K)$, where

$$K^{-1} = B^{-1} - B^{-1}(B^{-1} + A^{-1})^{-1}B^{-1}$$

$$= A^{-1} - A^{-1}(A^{-1} + B^{-1})^{-1}A^{-1} . \tag{6.30}$$

In particular, if $A = \Sigma$ and $B = r^2\Sigma$

$$K = (1 + r^2)\Sigma . \tag{6.31}$$

Optimal Kernel Size

Mean-square error criterion: In order to apply the density estimate of (6.1) (or (6.2) with the kernel function of (6.3)), we need to select a value for r [5-11]. The optimal value of r may be determined by minimizing the *mean-square error* between $\hat{\mathbf{p}}(X)$ and $p(X)$ with respect to r.

$$MSE\{\hat{\mathbf{p}}(X)\} = E\{[\hat{\mathbf{p}}(X) - p(X)]^2\} . \tag{6.32}$$

This criterion is a function of X, and thus the optimal r also must be a function of X. In order to make the optimal r independent of X, we may use the *integral mean-square error*

$$IMSE = \int MSE\{\hat{\mathbf{p}}(X)\}dX \ . \tag{6.33}$$

Another possible criterion to obtain the globally optimal r is $E_X\{MSE\{\hat{\mathbf{p}}(\mathbf{X})\}\} = \int MSE\{\hat{\mathbf{p}}(X)\}p(X)dX$. The optimization of this criterion can be carried out in a similar way as the *IMSE*, and produces a similar but a slightly smaller r than the *IMSE*. This criterion places more weight on the *MSE* in high density areas, where the locally optimal r's tend to be smaller.

Since we have computed the bias and variance of $\hat{\mathbf{p}}(X)$ in (6.18) and (6.19), $MSE\{\hat{\mathbf{p}}(X)\}$ may be expressed as

$$MSE\{\hat{\mathbf{p}}(X)\} = [E\{\hat{\mathbf{p}}(X)\} - p(X)]^2 + \text{Var}\{\hat{\mathbf{p}}(X)\} \ . \tag{6.34}$$

In this section, only the **uniform kernel function** is considered. This is because the Parzen density estimate with the uniform kernel is more directly related to the k nearest neighbor density estimate, and the comparison of these two is easier. Since both normal and uniform kernels share similar first and second order moments of $\hat{\mathbf{p}}(X)$, the normal kernel function may be treated in the same way as the uniform kernel, and both produce similar results.

When the first order approximation is used, $\hat{\mathbf{p}}(X)$ is unbiased as in (6.18), and therefore $MSE = \text{Var} = p/Nv - p^2/N$ as in (6.29). This criterion value is minimized by selecting $v = \infty$ for a given N and p. That is, as long as the density function is linear in $L(X)$, the variance dominates the *MSE* of the density estimate, and can be reduced by selecting larger v. However, as soon as $L(X)$ is expanded and picks up the second order term of (6.10), the bias starts to appear in the *MSE* and it grows with r^2 (or $v^{2/n}$) as in (6.18). Therefore, in minimizing the *MSE*, we select the best compromise between the bias and the variance. In order to include the effect of the bias in our discussion, we have no choice but to select the second order approximation in (6.18). Otherwise, the *MSE* criterion does not depend on the bias term. On the other hand, the variance term is included in the *MSE* no matter which approximation of (6.19) is used, the first or second order. If the second order approximation is used, the accuracy of the variance may be improved. However, the degree of improvement may not warrant the extra complexity which the second order approximation brings in. Furthermore, it should be remembered that the optimal r will be a function of $p(X)$. Since we never know the true value of

$p(X)$ accurately, it is futile to seek the more accurate but more complex expression for the variance. After all, what we can hope for is to get a rough estimate of r to be used.

Therefore, using the second order approximation of (6.18) and the first order approximation of (6.29) for simplicity,

$$MSE\{\hat{\mathbf{p}}(X)\} \cong \frac{p(X)}{Nv} + \frac{1}{4}\alpha^2(X)p^2(X)r^4 . \tag{6.35}$$

Note that the first and second terms correspond to the variance and squared bias of $\hat{\mathbf{p}}(X)$, respectively.

Minimization of MSE: Solving $\partial MSE/\partial r = 0$ [5], the resulting optimal r, r^*, is

$$r^*(X) = \left[\frac{n}{c\alpha^2 p}\right]^{\frac{1}{n+4}} \times N^{-\frac{1}{n+4}}$$

$$= \left[\frac{n\Gamma(\frac{n+2}{2})}{\pi^{1/2}(n+2)^{n/2}p\,|A|^{1/2}\alpha^2}\right]^{\frac{1}{n+4}} \times N^{-\frac{1}{n+4}} , \tag{6.36}$$

where $v = cr^n$ and

$$c = \frac{\pi^{n/2}(n+2)^{n/2}\,|A|^{1/2}}{\Gamma(\frac{n+2}{2})} . \tag{6.37}$$

The resulting mean-square error is obtained by substituting (6.36) into (6.35).

$$MSE^*\{\hat{\mathbf{p}}(X)\} = \frac{n+4}{4}\left[\frac{\Gamma^{4/n}(\frac{n+2}{2})p^{2+4/n}\alpha^2}{n(n+2)^2\pi^2\,|A|^{2/n}}\right]^{\frac{n}{n+4}} \times N^{-\frac{4}{n+4}} . \tag{6.38}$$

When the integral mean-square error of (6.33) is computed, v and r are supposed to be constant, being independent of X. Therefore, from (6.35)

$$IMSE = \frac{1}{Nv}\int p(X)dX + \frac{1}{4}r^4\int \alpha^2(X)p^2(X)dX$$

$$= \frac{1}{Nv} + \frac{1}{4} r^4 \int \alpha^2(X) p^2(X) dX \ . \tag{6.39}$$

Again, by solving $\partial IMSE / \partial r = 0$ [5],

$$r^* = \left[\frac{n}{c \int \alpha^2(X) p^2(X) dX} \right]^{\frac{1}{n+4}} \times N^{-\frac{1}{n+4}}$$

$$= \left[\frac{n \Gamma(\frac{n+2}{2})}{\pi^{n/2} (n+2)^{n/2} |A|^{1/2} \int \alpha^2(X) p^2(X) dX} \right]^{\frac{1}{n+4}} \times N^{-\frac{1}{n+4}} \ . \tag{6.40}$$

The resulting criterion value is obtained by substituting (6.40) into (6.39),

$$IMSE^* = \frac{n+4}{4} \left[\frac{\Gamma^{4/n}(\frac{n+2}{2}) \int \alpha^2(X) p^2(X) dX}{n(n+2)^2 \pi^2 |A|^{2/n}} \right]^{\frac{n}{n+4}} \times N^{-\frac{4}{n+4}} \ . \tag{6.41}$$

Optimal Metric

Another important question in obtaining a good density estimate is how to select the metric, A of (6.3). The discussion of the optimal A is very complex unless the matrix is diagonalized. Therefore, we first need to study the effect of linear transformations on the various functions used in the previous sections.

Linear transformation: Let Φ be a non-singular matrix used to define a linear transformation. This transformation consists of a rotation and a scale change of the coordinate system. Under the transformation, a vector and metric become

$$Z = \Phi^T X \ , \tag{6.42}$$

$$A_Z = \Phi^T A_X \Phi \ . \tag{6.43}$$

The distance of (6.24) is invariant since

$$(Y-X)^T A_X^{-1} (Y-X) = (W-Z)^T A_Z^{-1} (W-Z) \ , \tag{6.44}$$

where $W = \Phi^T Y$. The following is the list of effects of this transformation on various functions. Proofs are not given but can be easily obtained by the reader.

(1) $p_Z(Z) = |\Phi|^{-1} p_X(X)$ [*Jacobian*] , (6.45)

(2) $\nabla^2 p_Z(Z) = |\Phi|^{-1} \Phi^{-1} \nabla^2 p_X(X) \Phi^{T^{-1}}$

[from (6.10),(6.42), and (6.45)] , (6.46)

(3) $r(Z) = r(X)$ [from (6.44)] , (6.47)

(4) $v(Z) = |\Phi| v(X)$ [from (6.25),(6.43), and (6.47)] , (6.48)

(5) $MSE\{\hat{p}_Z(Z)\} = |\Phi|^{-2} MSE\{\hat{p}_X(X)\}$ [from (6.32) and (6.45)] , (6.49)

(6) $IMSE_Z = |\Phi|^{-1} IMSE_X$ [from (6.33) and (6.42)] . (6.50)

Note that both *MSE* and *IMSE* depend on Φ. The mean-square error is a coordinate dependent criterion.

Minimization of IMSE: We will now use the above results to optimize the integral mean-square error criterion with respect to the matrix A. However, it is impossible to discuss the optimization for a general $p(X)$. We need to limit the functional form of $p(X)$. Here, we choose the following form for $p(X)$:

$$p(X) = |B|^{-1/2} g((X-M)^T B^{-1} (X-M)) , \tag{6.51}$$

where $g(\cdot)$ does not involve B or M. The $p(X)$ of (6.51) covers a large family of density functions including the ones in (6.3). The expected vector, M, can be assumed to be zero, since all results should be independent of a mean shift. Now, we still have the freedom to choose the matrix A in some optimum manner. We will manipulate the two matrices B and A to simultaneously diagonalize each, thus making the analysis easier. That is,

$$\Phi^T B \Phi = I \quad \text{and} \quad \Phi^T A \Phi = \Lambda \tag{6.52}$$

and

$$p(Z) = g(Z^T Z) , \tag{6.53}$$

where Λ is a diagonal matrix with components $\lambda_1, \ldots, \lambda_n$.

In the transformed Z-space, $IMSE_Z^*$ of (6.41) becomes

$$IMSE_Z^* = c_1 \left[c_2 \int \mathrm{tr}^2 \{ \nabla^2 p_Z(Z) \frac{\Lambda}{|\Lambda|^{1/n}} \} dZ \right]^{\frac{n}{n+4}} , \tag{6.54}$$

where c_1 and c_2 are positive constants. $IMSE_Z^*$ can be minimized by minimizing $\mathrm{tr}^2\{\cdot\}$ with respect to Λ. Since Λ is normalized by $|\Lambda|^{1/n}$ such that

$$\left| \frac{\Lambda}{|\Lambda|^{1/n}} \right| = 1 , \tag{6.55}$$

the scale of the matrix has no effect. Thus, we will minimize $\mathrm{tr}^2\{\cdot\}$ with respect to λ_i's with the constraint

$$|\Lambda| = \prod_{i=1}^{n} \lambda_i = 1 . \tag{6.56}$$

Now, $\mathrm{tr}\{\cdot\}$ can be evaluated as

$$\mathrm{tr}\{ \nabla^2 p_Z(Z) \Lambda \} = \sum_{i=1}^{n} \lambda_i \frac{\partial^2 p_Z(Z)}{\partial z_i^2} = \theta \sum_{i=1}^{n} \lambda_i , \tag{6.57}$$

where

$$\theta = \frac{\partial^2 p_Z(Z)}{\partial z_i^2} = \frac{\partial}{\partial z_i} \left[\frac{dg(Z^T Z)}{d(Z^T Z)} \frac{\partial (Z^T Z)}{\partial z_i} \right] = 2 \frac{dg(Z^T Z)}{d(Z^T Z)} . \tag{6.58}$$

Thus, the criterion to be optimized is

$$\begin{aligned} J &= \mathrm{tr}^2 \{ \nabla^2 p_Z(Z) \Lambda \} - \mu (\prod_{i=1}^{n} \lambda_i - 1) \\ &= \theta^2 \sum_{i=1}^{n} \sum_{j=1}^{n} \lambda_i \lambda_j - \mu (\prod_{i=1}^{n} \lambda_i - 1) , \end{aligned} \tag{6.59}$$

where μ is a Lagrange multiplier. Taking the derivative of J with respect to λ_k and setting the result equal to zero,

$$\frac{\partial J}{\partial \lambda_k} = \theta^2(\lambda_k + \sum_{i=1}^{n} \lambda_i) - \frac{\mu}{\lambda_k} = 0 \tag{6.60}$$

or

$$\lambda_k^2 + \lambda_k(\sum_{i=1}^{n} \lambda_i) = \frac{\mu}{\theta^2} \qquad (k = 1, \ldots, n) . \tag{6.61}$$

In order to satisfy (6.61), all λ_i's must be equal. Since $|\Lambda| = 1$, the solution of (6.61) must be

$$\Lambda = I . \tag{6.62}$$

That is, in the transformed Z-space, the optimal matrix A_Z is I for $B_Z = I$. Therefore, the optimal matrix A to use in the original X-space is identical to B of (6.51) [5]. The neighborhoods should take the same ellipsoidal shape as the underlying distribution. For the normal distribution we see that the covariance matrix $B = \Sigma$ is indeed optimal for A.

It is important to notice that (6.62) is the locally optimal metric regardless of the location, because $IMSE^*$ of (6.54) is minimized not after but before taking the integration. The same result can be obtained by minimizing MSE^* of (6.38).

Normal Case

In order to get an idea of what kind of numbers should be used for r, in this section let us compute the optimal r for a normal distribution. The partial derivatives $\nabla p(X)$ and $\nabla^2 p(X)$ for $N_X(M, \Sigma)$ are

$$\nabla p(X) = -p(X)\Sigma^{-1}(X-M) , \tag{6.63}$$

$$\nabla^2 p(X) = p(X)[\Sigma^{-1}(X-M)(X-M)^T\Sigma^{-1} - \Sigma^{-1}] . \tag{6.64}$$

For the simplest case in which $M = 0$ and $\Sigma = I$,

$$\mathrm{tr}\{\nabla^2 p(X)\} = p(X)(X^TX - n) = p(X)(\sum_{i=1}^{n} x_i^2 - n) . \tag{6.65}$$

Note that the optimal A is also I in this case. It is easy to show that, if $p(X) = N_X(0,I)$, then $p^2(X) = 2^{-n/2}(2\pi)^{-n/2}N_X(0,I/2)$. Therefore,

$$\int \mathrm{tr}^2\{\nabla^2 p(X)\}dX = \frac{1}{2^{n/2}(2\pi)^{n/2}} \frac{n(n+2)}{4} . \tag{6.66}$$

Accordingly, from (6.40)

$$r^* = \left[\frac{2^{n+2}\Gamma(\frac{n+2}{2})}{(n+2)^{n/2+1}} \right]^{\frac{1}{n+4}} \times N^{-\frac{1}{n+4}} . \tag{6.67}$$

TABLE 6-1

OPTIMAL ***r*** OF THE UNIFORM KERNEL FUNCTION FOR NORMAL DISTRIBUTIONS

n	4	8	16	32	64	128
r^*	$0.94N^{-1/8}$	$0.89N^{-1/12}$	$0.86N^{-1/20}$	$0.85N^{-1/36}$	$0.85N^{-1/68}$	$0.85N^{-1/132}$
$r^*\sqrt{n+2}$	$2.29N^{-1/8}$	$2.81N^{-1/12}$	$3.66N^{-1/20}$	$4.98N^{-1/36}$	$6.92N^{-1/68}$	$9.72N^{-1/132}$

Table 6-1 shows these r^*'s for various values of n. Remember that the above discussion is for the uniform kernel, and that the radius of the hyperellipsoidal region is $r\sqrt{n+2}$ according to (6.23). Therefore, $r^*\sqrt{n+2}$'s are also presented to demonstrate how large the local regions are.

6.2 *k* Nearest Neighbor Density Estimate

Statistical Properties

***kNN* density estimate:** In the Parzen density estimate of (6.1), we fix v and let $\mathbf{k}$ be a random variable. Another possibility is to fix k and let $\mathbf{v}$ be a random variable [12-16]. That is, we extend the local region around X until the kth nearest neighbor is found. The local region, then, becomes random, $\mathbf{L}(X)$, and the volume becomes random, $\mathbf{v}(X)$. Also, both are now functions of X. This approach is called the *k nearest neighbor* (*kNN*) density estimate. The *kNN* approach can be interpreted as the Parzen approach with a uniform kernel function whose size is adjusted automatically, depending on the location. That is, with k fixed throughout the entire space, v becomes larger in low density areas and smaller in high density areas. The kNN density estimate may be rewritten from (6.1) as [12-14]

$$\hat{\mathbf{p}}(X) = \frac{k-1}{N\mathbf{v}(X)} . \tag{6.68}$$

The reason why $(k-1)$ is used instead of k will be discussed later.

Density of coverage: Although the density function of $\mathbf{v}$ is not available, the density function of the coverage (the probability mass in the local region), $\mathbf{u}$, may be obtained as follows [17].

Let $L(X)$ and $\Delta L(X)$ be defined by

$$L(X) = \{Y : d(Y,X) \le \ell\} \text{ and } \Delta L(X) = \{Y : \ell < d(Y,X) \le \ell + \Delta\ell\} \tag{6.69}$$

and

$$u = \int_{L(X)} p(Y)dY \quad \text{and} \quad \Delta u = \int_{\Delta L(X)} p(Y)dY , \tag{6.70}$$

where $d^2(Y,X) = (Y-X)^T A^{-1}(Y-X)$. Also, let two events G and H be defined as

$$G = \{(k-1) \text{ samples in } L(X)\} , \tag{6.71}$$

$$H = \{1 \text{ sample in } \Delta L(X)\} . \tag{6.72}$$

Then, the probability of the kth NN in $\Delta L(X)$ is

$$Pr\{G \text{ and } H\} = Pr\{G\}Pr\{H \mid G\} , \tag{6.73}$$

where

$$Pr\{G\} = \begin{bmatrix} N \\ k-1 \end{bmatrix} u^{k-1}(1-u)^{N-k+1} , \tag{6.74}$$

$$Pr\{H \mid G\} = \begin{bmatrix} N-k+1 \\ 1 \end{bmatrix} \left[\frac{\Delta u}{1-u} \right] \left[1 - \frac{\Delta u}{1-u} \right]^{N-k} . \tag{6.75}$$

Note that the coverage of $\Delta L(X)$ in the complementary domain of $L(X)$ is $\Delta u/(1-u)$. Substituting (6.74) and (6.75) into (6.73) and using $\{1-\Delta u/(1-u)\} \to 1$ as $\Delta u \to 0$, the probability of (6.73) becomes the product of Δu and a function of u, $p_u(u)$. Therefore, $p_u(u)$ should be the density function of $\mathbf{u}$, where $\mathbf{u}$ is the coverage of $\mathbf{L}(X)$ whose boundary is determined by the kth NN.

$$p_u(u) = \frac{N!}{(k-1)!(N-k)!} u^{k-1}(1-u)^{N-k} \quad 0 \le u \le 1 \ . \tag{6.76}$$

That is, $p_u(u)$ is a *Beta distribution* $Be(k,N-k+1)$. Also, note that the distribution of $\mathbf{u}$ is independent of the underlying distribution, $p(X)$.

More generally, the joint density function of $\mathbf{u}_1, \ldots, \mathbf{u}_k$ may be obtained as [17]

$$p(u_1, \ldots, u_k) = \frac{N!}{(N-k)!}(1 - u_k)^{N-k} \ , \tag{6.77}$$

where $\mathbf{u}_i$ is the coverage of $\mathbf{L}_i(X)$, the region extended until the ith NN is found. Note that the joint density depends on u_k only. The marginal density of $\mathbf{u}_k$ can be obtained by integrating (6.77) with respect to $u_1, \ldots, u_{k-1}$ as

$$\int_0^{u_k} \cdots \int_0^{u_2} p(u_1, \ldots, u_k) du_1 \ldots du_{k-1} = \frac{N!}{(k-1)!(N-k)!} u_k^{k-1}(1-u_k)^{N-k} \ . \tag{6.78}$$

Equation (6.78) is the same as (6.76).

The relationship between u and v may be obtained by integrating (6.10) over $L(X)$ with respect to Y. That is,

$$u(X) \cong p(X)v(X) + \frac{1}{2}\text{tr}\{\nabla^2 p(X) \int_{L(X)} (Y-X)(Y-X)^T dY\}$$

$$= p(X)v(X)[1 + \frac{1}{2}\alpha(X)r^2(X)] \ , \tag{6.79}$$

where α is given in (6.13). Note that $\int (Y-X)(Y-X)^T dY = vr^2 A$ from (6.27). The term $[1+\alpha r^2/2]$ of (6.79) appeared in (6.18) in the Parzen case. Again, $u = pv$ gives the first order approximation, and (6.79) is the second order approximation of u in terms of v.

Moments of $\hat{\mathbf{p}}(X)$: When the first order approximation of $u = pv$ is used, from (6.68) and (6.76)

$$E\{\hat{\mathbf{p}}(X)\} \cong \int_0^1 \frac{(k-1)p}{Nu} p_u(u) du = p(X) \ , \tag{6.80}$$

where the following formula is used

$$\int_0^1 x^b(1-x)^c dx = \frac{\Gamma(b+1)\Gamma(c+1)}{\Gamma(b+c+2)} . \tag{6.81}$$

Equation (6.80) indicates that $\hat{\mathbf{p}} = (k-1)/N\mathbf{v}$ is unbiased as long as $u = pv$ holds. If $k/N\mathbf{v}$ is used instead, the estimate becomes biased. This is the reason why $(k-1)$ is used in (6.68) instead of k. The variance of $\hat{\mathbf{p}}(X)$ also can be computed under the approximation of $u = pv$ as

$$\begin{aligned}\mathrm{Var}\{\hat{\mathbf{p}}(X)\} &\cong \int_0^1 \frac{(k-1)^2p^2}{N^2u^2} p_u(u)du - p^2 \\ &= p^2(X)\left[\frac{1}{k-2}\left(1-\frac{1}{N}\right) - \frac{1}{N}\right] \cong \frac{p^2(X)}{k-2} .\end{aligned} \tag{6.82}$$

Comparison of (6.29) and (6.82) shows that the variance of the *kNN* density estimate is larger than the one for the Parzen density estimate. Also, (6.82) indicates that, in the *kNN* density estimate, k must be selected larger than 2. Otherwise, a large variance may result.

Second order approximation: When the second order approximation is needed, (6.79) must be used to relate u and v. However, since r^2 and v are related by $v = cr^n$, it is difficult to solve (6.79) for v and a series of approximations is necessary. Since $\hat{\mathbf{p}} = (k-1)/N\mathbf{v}$, the computation of the first and second order moments of $\hat{\mathbf{p}}(X)$ requires $E\{\mathbf{v}^{-1}\}$ and $E\{\mathbf{v}^{-2}\}$. We start to derive $\mathbf{v}^{-1}$ from (6.79) as

$$\begin{aligned}\mathbf{v}^{-1} &\cong p\left[\mathbf{u}^{-1} + \frac{1}{2}\alpha c^{-2/n}\mathbf{v}^{2/n}\mathbf{u}^{-1}\right] \\ &\cong p\left[\mathbf{u}^{-1} + \frac{1}{2}\alpha(cp)^{-2/n}\mathbf{u}^{2/n-1}\right] ,\end{aligned} \tag{6.83}$$

where the approximation of $u = pv$ is applied to the second term to obtain the second line from the first. Note that the second term was ignored in the first order approximation and therefore is supposed to be much smaller than the first term. Thus, using $u = pv$ to approximate the second term is justified. From (6.83)

$$\mathbf{v}^{-2} \cong p^2\left[\mathbf{u}^{-2} + \alpha(cp)^{-2/n}\mathbf{u}^{2/n-2} + \frac{1}{4}\alpha^2(cp)^{-4/n}\mathbf{u}^{4/n-2}\right] . \tag{6.84}$$

On the other hand, from (6.76) and (6.81),

$$E\{\mathbf{u}^{-m}\} = \frac{\Gamma(k-m)\Gamma(N+1)}{\Gamma(k)\Gamma(N+1-m)} \quad \text{for} \quad k-m > 0\,. \tag{6.85}$$

Therefore,

$$E\{\mathbf{u}^{-1}\} = \frac{N}{k-1} \quad \text{and} \quad E\{\mathbf{u}^{-2}\} = \frac{N(N-1)}{(k-1)(k-2)} \tag{6.86}$$

and

$$E\{\mathbf{u}^{\delta-1}\} = \frac{\Gamma(k-1+\delta)\Gamma(N+1)}{\Gamma(k)\Gamma(N+\delta)} = \frac{N}{k-1}\,\frac{\Gamma(k-1+\delta)}{\Gamma(k-1)}\,\frac{\Gamma(N)}{\Gamma(N+\delta)}\,, \tag{6.87}$$

$$E\{\mathbf{u}^{\delta-2}\} = \frac{\Gamma(k-2+\delta)\Gamma(N+1)}{\Gamma(k)\Gamma(N-1+\delta)} = \frac{N(N-1)}{(k-1)(k-2)}\,\frac{\Gamma(k-2+\delta)}{\Gamma(k-2)}\,\frac{\Gamma(N-1)}{\Gamma(N-1+\delta)} \tag{6.88}$$

where $\Gamma(x+1) = x\Gamma(x)$ is used. It is known that

$$\frac{\Gamma(x+\delta)}{\Gamma(x)} \cong x^{\delta} \tag{6.89}$$

is a good approximation for large x and small δ. Therefore, applying this approximation,

$$E\{\mathbf{u}^{\delta-1}\} \cong (\frac{k-1}{N})^{\delta-1} \quad \text{and} \quad E\{\mathbf{u}^{\delta-2}\} \cong \frac{N}{k-1}(\frac{k-2}{N-2})^{\delta-1}\,. \tag{6.90}$$

Combining (6.83), (6.84), (6.86), and (6.90),

$$E\{\hat{\mathbf{p}}(X)\} = \frac{k-1}{N}E\{\mathbf{v}^{-1}\} \cong p(X)[1+\frac{1}{2}\alpha(X)(cp(X))^{-2/n}(\frac{k-1}{N})^{2/n}]$$

$$\cong p(X)[1+\frac{1}{2}\alpha(X)(cp(X))^{-2/n}(\frac{k}{N})^{2/n}]\,, \tag{6.91}$$

$$E\{\hat{\mathbf{p}}^2(X)\} = (\frac{k-1}{N})^2E\{\mathbf{v}^{-2}\}$$

$$\cong p^2\left[\left\{1+\frac{1}{k-2}(1-\frac{1}{N})-\frac{1}{N}\right\} + \alpha(cp)^{-2/n}(\frac{k-1}{N})(\frac{k-2}{N-1})^{2/n-1}\right.$$

$$+ \frac{1}{4}\alpha^2(cp)^{-4/n}(\frac{k-1}{N})(\frac{k-2}{N-1})^{4/n-1}\Bigg]$$

$$\cong p^2\left[(1+\frac{1}{k}) + \alpha(cp)^{-2/n}(\frac{k}{N})^{2/n} + \frac{1}{4}\alpha^2(cp)^{-4/n}(\frac{k}{N})^{4/n}\right], \tag{6.92}$$

where $N \gg k \gg 1$ is assumed. Therefore, the variance and mean-square error of $\hat{\mathbf{p}}(X)$ are

$$\mathrm{Var}\{\hat{\mathbf{p}}(X)\} \cong \frac{p^2(X)}{k}, \tag{6.93}$$

$$MSE\{\hat{\mathbf{p}}(X)\} \cong p^2\left[\frac{1}{k} + \frac{1}{4}\alpha^2(cp)^{-4/n}(\frac{k}{N})^{4/n}\right]. \tag{6.94}$$

Again, in (6.94) the first and second terms are the variance and the squared bias respectively. It must be pointed out that the series of approximations used to obtain (6.91)-(6.94) is valid only for large k. For small k, different and more complex approximations for $E\{\hat{\mathbf{p}}(X)\}$ and $\mathrm{Var}\{\hat{\mathbf{p}}(X)\}$ must be derived by using (6.87) and (6.88) rather than (6.90). As in the Parzen case, the second order approximation for the bias and the first order approximation for the variance may be used for simplicity. Also, note that the *MSE* of (6.94) becomes zero as $k \rightarrow \infty$ and $k/N \rightarrow 0$. These are the conditions for the *kNN* density estimate to be asymptotically unbiased and consistent [14].

Optimal Number of Neighbors

Optimal k: In order to apply the *kNN* density estimate of (6.68), we need to know what value to select for k. The optimal k under the approximation of $u = pv$ is ∞, by minimizing (6.82) with respect to k. That is, when $L(X)$ is small and $u = pv$ holds, the variance dominates the *MSE* and can be reduced by selecting larger k or larger $L(X)$. As $L(X)$ becomes larger, the second order term produces the bias and the bias increases with $L(X)$. The optimal k is determined by the rate of the variance decrease and the rate of bias increase.

The optimal k, k^*, may be found by minimizing the mean-square error of (6.94). That is, solving $\partial MSE/\partial k = 0$ for k yields [5]

$$k^*(X) = \left[\frac{n(cp)^{4/n}}{\alpha^2}\right]^{\frac{n}{n+4}} \times N^{\frac{4}{n+4}}$$

$$= \left[\frac{n(n+2)^2\pi^2 p^{4/n} |A|^{2/n}}{\Gamma^{4/n}(\frac{n+2}{2})\alpha^2}\right]^{\frac{n}{n+4}} \times N^{\frac{4}{n+4}} . \quad (6.95)$$

As in the Parzen case, the optimal k is a function of X. Equation (6.95) indicates that k^* is invariant under any non-singular transformation. That is,

$$k^*(Z) = k^*(X) . \quad (6.96)$$

Also, k^* and r^* of (6.36) are related by

$$p(X) = \frac{k^*(X)}{Ncr^{*n}(X)} . \quad (6.97)$$

This indicates that both the Parzen and kNN density estimates become optimal in the same local range of $L(X)$. The resulting mean-square error is obtained by substituting (6.95) into (6.94).

$$MSE^*\{\hat{p}(X)\} = \frac{n+4}{4}\left[\frac{\Gamma^{4/n}(\frac{n+2}{2})p^{2+4/n}\alpha^2}{n(n+2)^2\pi^2 |A|^{2/n}}\right]^{\frac{n}{n+4}} \times N^{-\frac{4}{n+4}} . \quad (6.98)$$

Note that (6.98) and (6.38) are identical. That is, both the Parzen (with the uniform kernel) and kNN density estimates produce the same optimal MSE.

The globally optimal k may be obtained by minimizing the integral mean-square error criterion. From (6.94), with a fixed k,

$$IMSE = \frac{1}{k}\int p^2(X)dX + \frac{1}{4}c^{-4/n}\left(\frac{k}{N}\right)^{4/n}\int \alpha^2(X)p^{2-4/n}(X)dX . \quad (6.99)$$

Solving $\partial IMSE/\partial k = 0$ generates [5]

$$k^* = \left[\frac{nc^{4/n} \int p^2(X)dX}{\int \alpha^2(X) p^{2-4/n}(X)dX} \right]^{\frac{n}{n+4}} \times N^{\frac{4}{n+4}}$$

$$= \left[\frac{n(n+2)^2 \pi^2 \int p^2(X)dX}{\Gamma^{4/n}(\frac{n+2}{2}) \int \alpha^2(X) p^{2-4/n}(X)dX} \right]^{\frac{n}{n+4}} \times N^{\frac{4}{n+4}} . \tag{6.100}$$

The resulting *IMSE* is

$$IMSE^* = \frac{n+4}{4} \left[\frac{\Gamma^{4/n}(\frac{n+2}{2}) [\int p^2(X)dX]^{4/n} \int \alpha^2(X) p^{2-4/n}(X)dX}{n(n+2)^2 \pi^2 |A|^{2/n}} \right]^{\frac{n}{n+4}}$$

$$\times N^{-\frac{4}{n+4}} . \tag{6.101}$$

It should be pointed out that $E_X\{MSE\{\hat{\mathbf{p}}(\mathbf{X})\}\}$ can be minimized by a similar procedure to obtain the globally optimal k. The resulting k^* is similar but slightly smaller than k^* of (6.100).

Optimal metric: The optimal metric also can be computed as in the Parzen case. Again, a family of density functions with the form of (6.51) is studied with the metric of (6.24). In order to diagonalize both B and A to I and Λ respectively, X is linearly transformed to Z. In the transformed Z-space, $IMSE_Z^*$ becomes, from (6.101) and (6.13),

$$IMSE_Z^* = c_1 \left[c_2 \int p_Z^{-4/n}(Z) \mathrm{tr}^2 \left\{ \nabla^2 p_Z(Z) \frac{\Lambda}{|\Lambda|^{1/n}} \right\} dZ \right]^{\frac{n}{n+4}} , \tag{6.102}$$

where c_1 and c_2 are positive constants. $IMSE_Z^*$ can be minimized with respect to Λ by minimizing

$$J = \mathrm{tr}^2\{\nabla^2 p_Z(Z)\Lambda\} - \mu(\prod_{i=1}^{n} \lambda_i - 1) , \tag{6.103}$$

which is identical to (6.59).

Therefore, the optimal metric A for the kNN density estimate is identical to B. Also, note that the same optimal metric is obtained by minimizing MSE^* of (6.98), and thus the metric is optimal locally as well as globally.

Normal example: The optimal k for a normal distribution can be computed easily. For a normal distribution with zero expected vector and identity covariance matrix,

$$\int p^2(X)dX = \frac{1}{(2\pi)^{n/2}2^{n/2}} , \tag{6.104}$$

$$\int p^{-4/n}(X)\mathrm{tr}^2\{\nabla^2 p(X)\}dX = \frac{\pi^{2-n/2}n^{2+n/2}(n^2-6n+16)}{2^n(n-2)^{2+n/2}} . \tag{6.105}$$

Substituting (6.104) and (6.105) into (6.100), and noting that the optimal metric A is I in this case,

$$k^* = \left[\frac{(n+2)^2(n-2)^{2+n/2}}{\Gamma^{4/n}(\frac{n+2}{2})n^{1+n/2}(n^2-6n+16)} \right]^{\frac{n}{n+4}} \times N^{\frac{4}{n+4}} . \tag{6.106}$$

TABLE 6-2

OPTIMAL k FOR NORMAL DISTRIBUTIONS

n	4	8	16	32	64	128
k^*	$0.75N^{1/2}$	$0.94N^{1/3}$	$0.62N^{1/5}$	$0.34N^{1/9}$	$0.17N^{1/17}$	$0.09N^{1/33}$
N for $k^*=5$	4.4×10	1.5×10^2	3.4×10^4	3.2×10^{10}	9.2×10^{24}	3.8×10^{57}

Table 6-2 shows k^* for various values of n [5]. Also, Table 6-2 shows how many samples are needed for k^* to be 5. Note that N becomes very large after $n = 16$. This suggests how difficult it is to estimate a density function in a high-dimensional space, unless an extremely large number of samples is available.

Distance to Neighbors

Distance to *kNN*: From (6.25), the distance to the kth nearest neighbor may be expressed in terms of the corresponding volume as

$$\mathbf{d}_{kNN}(X) = \frac{\Gamma^{1/n}(\frac{n+2}{2})}{\pi^{1/2}|A|^{1/2n}}\mathbf{v}^{1/n}(X) . \tag{6.107}$$

The distance is a random variable due to $\mathbf{v}$. Using the first order approximation of $u = pv$ and knowing the density function of $\mathbf{u}$ as (6.76), the mth order moments of $\mathbf{d}_{kNN}(X)$ can be obtained as [18]

$$E\{\mathbf{d}^m_{kNN}(X)\} = \int_0^1 d^m_{kNN}(X)p_u(u)du \cong \nu p^{-m/n}(X) , \tag{6.108}$$

where

$$\nu = \frac{\Gamma^{m/n}(\frac{n+2}{2})}{\pi^{m/2}|\Sigma|^{m/2n}} \frac{\Gamma(k+m/n)}{\Gamma(k)} \frac{\Gamma(N+1)}{\Gamma(N+1+m/n)} . \tag{6.109}$$

Note that $A = \Sigma$ is used as the optimal matrix. The overall average of this distance in the entire space is

$$E_X E\{\mathbf{d}^m_{kNN}(\mathbf{X})\} \cong \nu E_X\{p^{-m/n}(\mathbf{X})\} . \tag{6.110}$$

$E_X\{p^{-m/n}(\mathbf{X})\}$ for normal and uniform distributions can be expressed as

(a) Normal:

$$E_X\{p^{-m/n}(\mathbf{X})\} = (2\pi)^{m/2}|\Sigma|^{m/2n}(1-\frac{m}{n})^{-n/2} . \tag{6.111}$$

(b) Uniform [see (6.22)]:

$$E_X\{p^{-m/n}(\mathbf{X})\} = (2\pi)^{m/2}|\Sigma|^{m/2n}\Gamma^{-m/n}(\frac{n+2}{2})(\frac{n+2}{2})^{m/2} , \tag{6.112}$$

where both the normal and uniform distributions have zero expected vector and covariance matrix Σ. Substituting (6.109), (6.111), and (6.112) into (6.110),

(a) Normal:

$$E_X E\{\mathbf{d}^m_{kNN}(\mathbf{X})\} \cong \Gamma^{m/n}\left(\frac{n+2}{2}\right) 2^{m/2} \left(1 - \frac{m}{n}\right)^{-n/2}$$

$$\times \frac{\Gamma(k+m/n)}{\Gamma(k)} \frac{\Gamma(N+1)}{\Gamma(N+1+m/n)} . \tag{6.113}$$

(b) Uniform:

$$E_X E\{\mathbf{d}^m_{kNN}(\mathbf{X})\} \cong (n+2)^{m/2} \frac{\Gamma(k+m/n)}{\Gamma(k)} \frac{\Gamma(N+1)}{\Gamma(N+1+m/n)} . \tag{6.114}$$

The reader may check that $\Gamma^{1/n}\ 2^{1/2}\ (1-1/n)^{-n/2}$ for normal and $(n+2)^{1/2}$ for uniform with $m = 1$ are close for a large n (10.3 and 10.1 respectively for $n = 100$).

Effect of parameters: Let us examine (6.108) and (6.109) with $m = 1$. These equations reveal how $E\{\mathbf{d}_{kNN}(X)\}$ is affected by such parameters as n, k, N, and $p(X)$. The effect of k appears only in the second term of (6.109). When $m = 1$ and n is large, $\Gamma(k+1/n)/\Gamma(k) \cong k^{1/n}$ is close to 1 regardless of the value of k. This means that the average distance to the first *NN* is almost the same as the average distance to the second *NN*, and so on. The effect of N, which appears in the third term of (6.109), is also minimal, since $\Gamma(N+1)/\Gamma(N+1+1/n) \cong N^{-1/n} \cong 1$ for large n. The effect of the location is observed as $p^{-1/n}(X)$ in (6.108). When n is large, $p^{-1/n}(X) \cong 1$ regardless of the value of $p(X)$ unless $p(X)$ is either extremely large or small. Thus, $E\{\mathbf{d}_{kNN}(X)\}$ is highly influenced only by n and $|\Sigma|$. On the other hand, in the global *kNN* distance $E_X E\{\mathbf{d}_{kNN}(\mathbf{X})\}$, the $|\Sigma|$ term in v cancels with the $|\Sigma|$ of $E_X\{p^{-1/n}(\mathbf{X})\}$, and only n determines the averaged *kNN* distance. This is true because the distances are normalized by Σ as in (6.24). Table 6-3 shows $E_X E\{\mathbf{d}_{kNN}(\mathbf{X})\}$ for various n, k, and N for normal and uniform distributions with covariance matrix I [18]. The parameter values are $n = 10$, $k = 1$, and $N = 100$, unless otherwise indicated. It can be observed from Table 6-3 that the effects of k and N are not significant for $n = 10$. This behavior is even more apparent for higher-dimensions.

Although the above results are contrary to our intuition, they could be better understood by observing the volume to the kth *NN*, $\mathbf{v}_{kNN}$, instead of the distance. For example, $d_{2NN}/d_{NN} = 2.551/2.319 \cong 1.1$ and is close to 1 for a 10-dimensional normal distribution from Table 6-3. However, the ratio of the corresponding volumes is $v_{2NN}/v_{NN} = (d_{2NN}/d_{NN})^{10} \cong 2.6$, which is not close to 1. That is, the effect of k on $\mathbf{v}_{kNN}$ is significant. The same is true for the

TABLE 6-3

THE AVERAGE DISTANCE TO THE *k*th NEAREST NEIGHBOR

	Normal	Uniform
$n = 5$	1.147	0.966
10	2.319	2.078
20	3.886	3.626
$N = 50$	2.484	2.226
100	2.319	2.078
200	2.164	1.940
400	2.020	1.810
$k = 1$	2.319	2.078
2	2.551	2.286
3	2.679	2.400

effects of N and $p(X)$ on $\mathbf{v}_{kNN}$. Since we estimate a density function by (6.68), if k or N is changed, $\mathbf{v}$ must be changed accordingly. Because of the nth power, a reasonable change of the volume is translated to a very small change of the distance for a large n.

In order to show the effect of the location on $E\{\mathbf{d}_{kNN}(X)\}$, the following experiment was conducted.

Experiment 1: *NN* distance

Data: $N(0,I)$, $n = 10$
kNN: $k = 1$
Sample size: $N = 100$
No. of trials: $\tau = 10$
Results: Fig. 6-2 [18]

Figure 6-2 shows the averaged *NN* distances and the standard deviations of 10 trails vs. the distance from the center, ℓ. Also, theoretical curves computed from (6.108) are plotted by dotted lines. The theoretical and experimental curves match closely until $\ell = 4$, where most samples are located. Also, note that the standard deviation is very small. This is predicted theoretically,

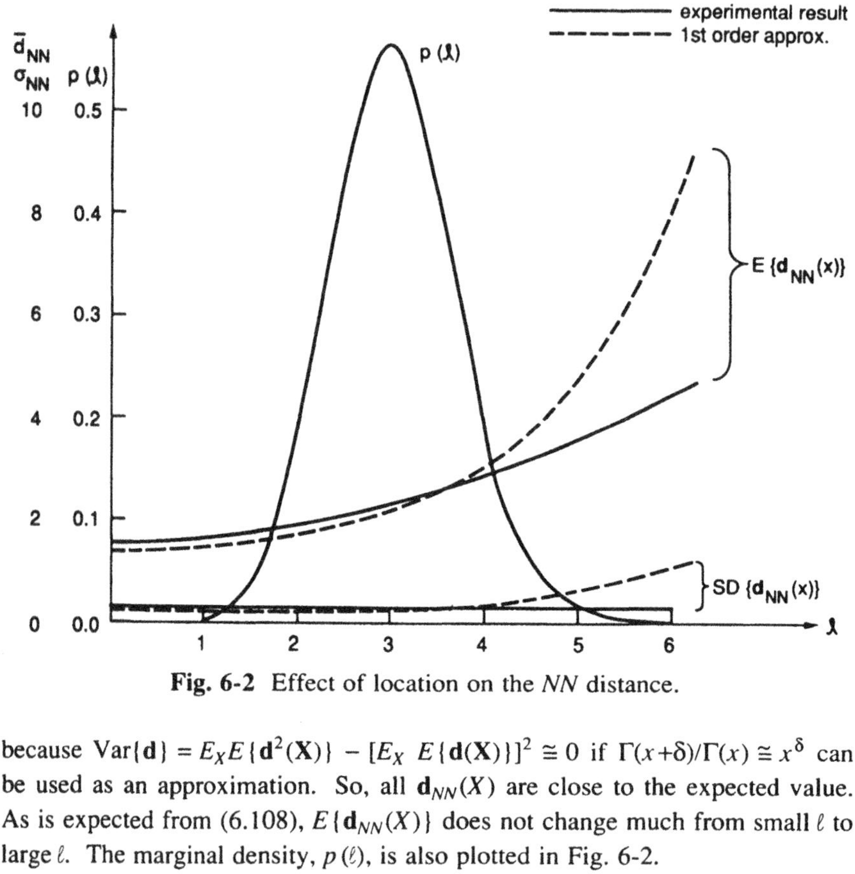

Fig. 6-2 Effect of location on the *NN* distance.

because $\text{Var}\{\mathbf{d}\} = E_X E\{\mathbf{d}^2(\mathbf{X})\} - [E_X\ E\{\mathbf{d}(\mathbf{X})\}]^2 \cong 0$ if $\Gamma(x+\delta)/\Gamma(x) \cong x^\delta$ can be used as an approximation. So, all $\mathbf{d}_{NN}(X)$ are close to the expected value. As is expected from (6.108), $E\{\mathbf{d}_{NN}(X)\}$ does not change much from small ℓ to large ℓ. The marginal density, $p(\ell)$, is also plotted in Fig. 6-2.

Intrinsic Dimensionality

Whenever we are confronted with high-dimensional data sets, it is usually advantageous for us to discover or impose some structure on the data. Therefore, we might assume that the generation of the data is governed by a certain number of underlying parameters. The minimum number of parameters required to account for the observed properties of the data, n_e, is called the *intrinsic* or *effective dimensionality* of the data set, or, equivalently, the data generating process. That is, when n random variables are functions of n_e variables such as $\mathbf{x}_i = g_i(\mathbf{y}_1, \ldots, \mathbf{y}_{n_e})$ $(i = 1, \ldots, n)$, the intrinsic dimensionality of the X-space is n_e. The geometric interpretation is that the entire data set lies on a topological hypersurface of n_e-dimension.

The conventional technique used to measure the dimensionality is to compute the eigenvalues and eigenvectors of the covariance matrix and count the number of dominant eigenvalues. The corresponding eigenvectors form the effective subspace. Although this technique is powerful, it is limited because it is based on a linear transformation. For example, in Fig. 6-3, a one-

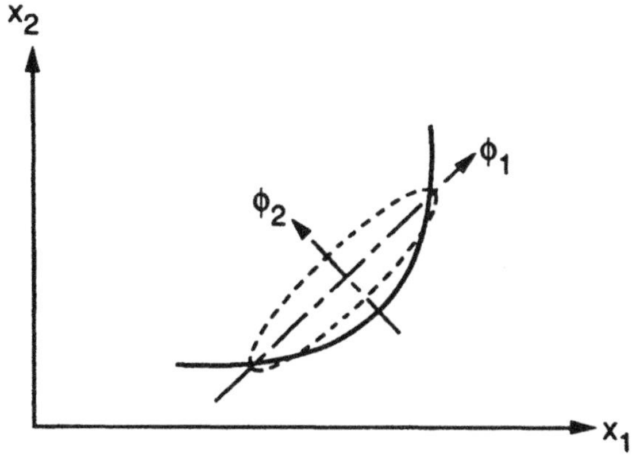

Fig. 6-3 Intrinsic dimensionality and linear mapping.

dimensional distribution is shown by a solid line. The eigenvalues and eigenvectors of this distribution are the same as the ones of the two-dimensional normal distribution of the dotted line. Thus, the conventional technique fails to demonstrate the intrinsic dimensionality, which is one for this example.

The intrinsic dimensionality is, in essence, a local characteristic of the distribution, as shown in Fig. 6-4. If we establish small local regions around X_1, X_2, X_3, etc., the dimensionality within the local region must be close to 1 [19],[20]. Because of this, the intrinsic dimensionality is sometimes called the *local dimensionality*. This approach is similar to the local linearization of a nonlinear function.

When k nearest neighbors are used to estimate dimensionality, the estimate relies on the local properties of the distribution and is not related to the global properties. Thus, the estimated dimensionality must be the intrinsic dimensionality. Keeping this in mind, let us compute the ratio of two NN distances from (6.108)-(6.110)

$$\frac{E\{\mathbf{d}_{(k+1)NN}(X)\}}{E\{\mathbf{d}_{kNN}(X)\}} \cong \frac{E_X E\{\mathbf{d}_{(k+1)NN}(\mathbf{X})\}}{E_X E\{\mathbf{d}_{kNN}(\mathbf{X})\}} \cong 1 + \frac{1}{kn} , \tag{6.115}$$

where use has been made of $\Gamma(x+1) = x\Gamma(x)$. Measuring the left-hand side from the given data set and solving (6.115) for n, we can obtain the local dimensionality [18],[21].

In succeeding chapters, we will discuss the effect of dimensionality in various nonparametric operations. The dimensionality is the most important parameter in determining nonparametric properties as was already seen in $E\{\mathbf{d}_{NN}^m(X)\}$ of (6.108). However, note that the dimensionality in nonparametric operations automatically means the intrinsic or local dimensionality. Without realizing this fact, readers may often find a discrepancy between theoretical and experimental results.

Experiment 2: The Gaussian pulse is a popular waveform which reasonably approximates many signals encountered in practice. The waveform is characterized by three parameters, $\mathbf{a}$, $\mathbf{m}$, and $\boldsymbol{\sigma}$, as

$$\mathbf{x}(t) = \mathbf{a} \exp\left[-\frac{(t-\mathbf{m})^2}{2\boldsymbol{\sigma}^2}\right] . \tag{6.116}$$

When these three parameters are random, the resulting random process $\mathbf{x}(t)$ has an intrinsic dimensionality of 3. In order to verify this, 250 waveforms were generated with uniform distributions for $\mathbf{a}$, $\mathbf{m}$, and $\boldsymbol{\sigma}$ in the following ranges.

$$\begin{aligned} &0.7 \leq \mathbf{a} \leq 1.3 , \\ &0.3 \leq \mathbf{m} \leq 0.7 , \\ &0.2 \leq \boldsymbol{\sigma} \leq 0.4 . \end{aligned} \tag{6.117}$$

The waveforms were time-sampled at 8 points in $0 \leq t \leq 1.05$ with increment 0.15, forming eight-dimensional random vectors. These vectors lie on a three-dimensional warped surface in the eight-dimensional space. The *kNN* distances of each sample for $k = 1, 2, 3$, and 4 were computed, and averaged over 250 samples. These averages were used to compute the intrinsic dimensionality of the data by (6.115). Table 6-4 shows the results. The procedure estimated the intrinsic dimensionality accurately.

TABLE 6-4

ESTIMATION OF INTRINSIC DIMENSIONALITY

		Gaussian pulse	Double exponential
Averaged *kNN* distance	1*NN*	0.74	0.77
	2*NN*	0.99	1.02
	3*NN*	1.14	1.19
	4*NN*	1.26	1.31
Intrinsic dimension estimated by	1*NN* & 2*NN*	3.02	3.13
	2*NN* & 3*NN*	3.19	2.97
	3*NN* & 4*NN*	3.13	3.14
	Average	3.11	3.08

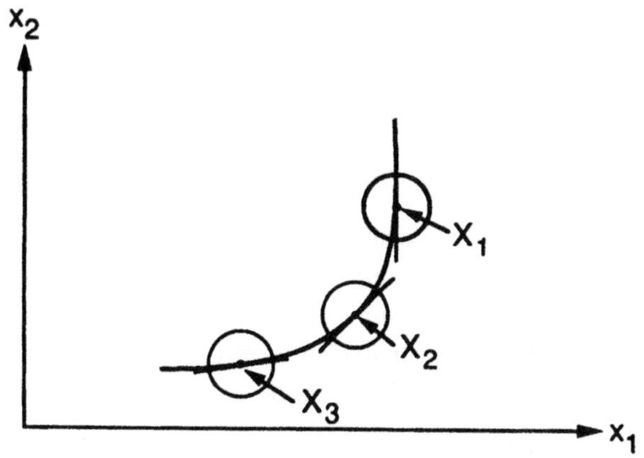

Fig. 6-4 Local subsets of data.

Experiment 3: A similar experiment was conducted for a double exponential waveform as

$$\mathbf{x}(t) = \mathbf{a} \exp \left[-\frac{|t-\mathbf{m}|}{\boldsymbol{\tau}} \right] , \tag{6.118}$$

where three parameters are uniformly distributed in

$$\begin{aligned} 0.7 \leq \mathbf{a} \leq 1.3 \; , \\ 0.3 \leq \mathbf{m} \leq 0.7 \; , \\ 0.3 \leq \boldsymbol{\tau} \leq 0.6 \; . \end{aligned} \tag{6.119}$$

Using eight sampling points and 250 waveforms, the intrinsic dimensionality of the data was estimated, and the results are shown in Table 6-4. Again, fairly accurate estimates of the intrinsic dimensionality (which is 3) were obtained.

Experiment 4: The intrinsic dimensionalities of Data RADAR were estimated by (6.115). They were found to be 19.8 for Chevrolet Camaro and 17.7 for Dodge Van, down from the original dimensionality of 66. This indicates that the number of features could be reduced significantly. Although this technique does not suggest how to reduce the number of features, the above numbers could serve as a guide to know how small the number of features should be.

Very Large Number of Classes

Another application in which the *kNN* distance is useful is a classification scenario where the number of classes is very large, perhaps in the hundreds. For simplicity, let us assume that we have N classes whose expected vectors M_i $(i = 1,\ldots,N)$ are distributed uniformly with a covariance matrix I, and each class is distributed normally with the covariance matrix $\sigma^2 I$.

When only a pair of classes, ω_i and ω_j, is considered, the Bayes classifier becomes a bisector between M_i and M_j, and the resulting error is

$$\varepsilon_p = \int_{d(M_i,M_j)/2\sigma}^{\infty} \frac{1}{\sqrt{2\pi}} e^{-x^2/2} dx \quad \text{(pairwise error)} , \tag{6.120}$$

where $d(M_i,M_j)$ is the Euclidean distance between M_i and M_j. Equation (6.120) indicates that ε_p depends only on the signal-to-noise ratio, $d(M_i,M_j)/\sigma$. When the number of classes is increased, M_i is surrounded by many neighboring classes as seen in Fig. 6-5, where M_{kNN} is the center of the kth nearest

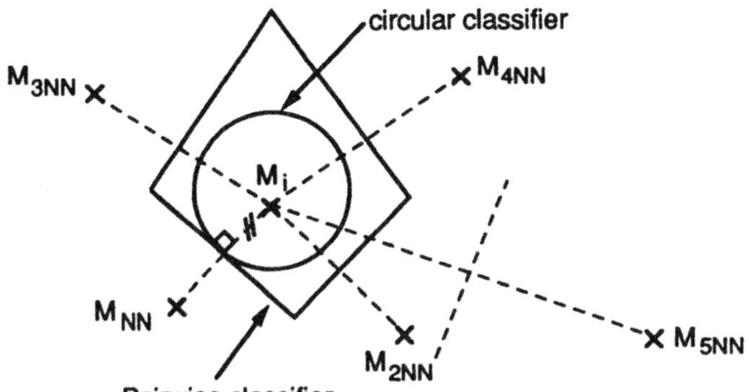

Fig. 6-5 Distribution of class centers and classifiers.

neighbor class. If the distance to the closest neighbor, $d(M_i,M_{NN})$, is much smaller than the distances to the other neighbors, the pairwise error between ω_i and ω_{NN} dominates the total error. However, (6.108) and (6.109) suggest that $d(M,M_{kNN})$ is almost the same, regardless of k. The number of classes, N, and the distribution of the M_i's (uniform, normal and so on) have very little effect. Only the dimensionality, n, has a significant effect on $d(M,M_{kNN})$. Since all neighboring M_j's are equally distanced from M_i, the error from each pair, ε_p, can be added up to produce a large total error, ε_t. Figure 6-6 shows experimental results indicating the relationship between ε_t and $\sigma/E_X E\{\mathbf{d}_{\mathbf{NN}}(\mathbf{X})\}$ for various values of n. Note that n is the intrinsic dimension of the distribution of the M_i's.

Experiment 5: Error for N-class problem

Data: M_i – uniform with mean 0 and covariance I
X – $N(M_i,\sigma^2 I)$ $i = 1,\ldots,N$

Dimensionality: $n = 5, 10, 20$

Sample size: $N = 10n$ ($10n$ classes)
$10n$ samples/class

No. of trials: $\tau = 10$

Classifier: Bisectors between the generated M_i's.

Results: Fig. 6-6 [18]

Although the results are not shown here, the experiment confirmed that these curves are almost invariant for various values of N and distributions of M_i's. The theoretical saturation error for $\sigma \to \infty$ is $(1-1/N) \cong 1$ (100%) for N-class problem.

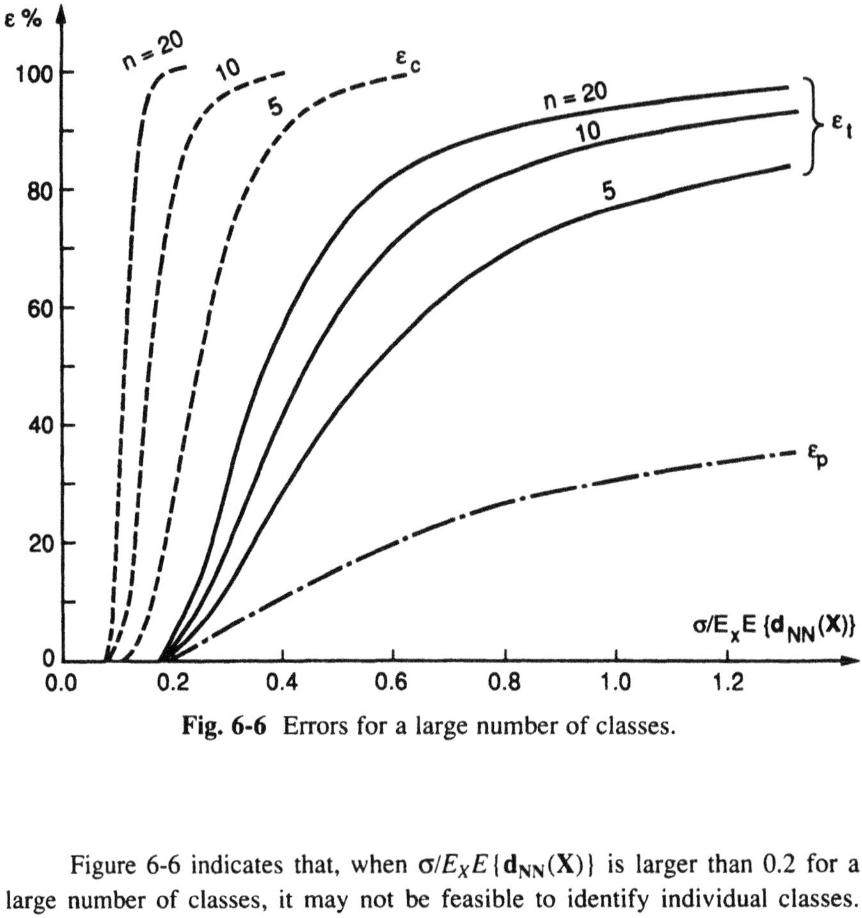

Fig. 6-6 Errors for a large number of classes.

Figure 6-6 indicates that, when $\sigma/E_X E\{\mathbf{d}_{NN}(\mathbf{X})\}$ is larger than 0.2 for a large number of classes, it may not be feasible to identify individual classes. Therefore, before trying to design any classifier, it is advisable to confirm that the classes are well separated pairwise. One way to evade this difficulty is to assemble the classes into a smaller number (L) of groups, and to treat it as an L-class problem. The errors, which occur among classes within the same group, are considered as correct classification. Only the error from a class of one group to a class of another group is treated as the error between groups. Thus, the error between groups is normally much smaller than the error between classes.

It has been found experimentally that ε_p and ε_t are very roughly related by $\varepsilon_t \cong (2 + 0.2n)\varepsilon_p$ for small σ. That is, ε_t is about equivalent to the errors due to 4 and 6 neighbors for n = 10 and 20 respectively, assuming all distances to these neighbors are equal and the pairwise errors are added without mutual interation. For large σ, ε_p tends to saturate at 50% while ε_t does at 100%. Thus, the above empirical equation does not hold.

When one class is surrounded by many other classes, we may design a circular, one-class classifier. That is, X is classified to ω_i if $d(X,M_i)< d(M_i,M_{NN})/2$ [see Fig. 6-5]. Then, the error from ω_i, ε_c, is

$$\varepsilon_c = \int_{d(M_i,M_{NN})/2\sigma}^{\infty} \frac{n}{2^{n/2}\Gamma(\frac{n+2}{2})} \ell^{n-1} e^{-\ell^2/2} d\ell \quad \text{(circular error)} , \tag{6.121}$$

where the integrand is the marginal density function of the distance from the center and is derived from $N_X(O,I)$. Note that the density function of the squared-distance, ζ, is given in (3.59) for $N_X(O,I)$. Therefore, the integrand of (6.121) may be obtained from (3.59) by applying a transformation $\ell = \sqrt{\zeta}$. The ε_c computed from (6.121) is plotted (dotted lines) in Fig. 6-6. As is seen in Figs. 6-5 and 6-6, the circular classifier is worse than the pairwise bisector classifier.

6.3 Expansion by Basis Functions

Expansion of Density Functions

Basis functions: Another approach to approximating a density function is to find an expansion in a set of *basis functions* $\phi_i(X)$ as

$$p(X) = \sum_{i=1}^{\infty} c_i \phi_i(X) . \tag{6.122}$$

If the basis functions satisfy

$$\int \kappa(X)\phi_i(X)\phi_j^*(X)dX = \lambda_i \delta_{ij} , \tag{6.123}$$

we say that the $\phi_i(X)$'s are orthogonal with respect to the *kernel* $\kappa(X)$. The term $\phi_i^*(X)$ is the complex conjugate of $\phi_i(X)$, and equals $\phi_i(X)$ when $\phi_i(X)$ is a real function. If the basis functions are orthogonal with respect to $\kappa(X)$, the coefficients of (6.122) are computed by

$$\lambda_i c_i = \int \kappa(X) p(X) \phi_i^*(X) dX . \tag{6.124}$$

When $\kappa(X)$ is a density function, (6.123) and (6.124) may be expressed by

$$E\{\phi_i(X)\phi_j^*(X)\} = \lambda_i \delta_{ij} , \tag{6.125}$$

$$E\{p(X)\phi_i^*(X)\} = \lambda_i c_i . \tag{6.126}$$

When we terminate the expansion of (6.122) for $i = m$, the squared error is given by

$$\begin{aligned}\bar{\varepsilon}^2 &= \int \kappa(X)\{p(X) - \sum_{i=1}^{m} c_i \phi_i(X)\}\{p(X) - \sum_{i=1}^{m} c_i \phi_i(X)\}^* dX \\ &= \int \kappa(X)\{\sum_{i=m+1}^{\infty} c_i \phi_i(X)\}\{\sum_{i=m+1}^{\infty} c_i \phi_i(X)\}^* dX \\ &= \sum_{i=m+1}^{\infty} \lambda_i |c_i|^2 . \end{aligned} \tag{6.127}$$

Thus, $\lambda_i |c_i|^2$ represents the error due to the elimination of the ith term in the expansion. This means that, if we can find a set of basis functions such that $\lambda_i |c_i|^2$ decreases quickly as i increases, the set of basis functions forms an economical representation of the density function.

There is no known procedure for choosing a set of basis functions in the general multivariate case. Therefore, we will only consider special cases where the basis functions are well defined.

Both the *Fourier series* and the *Fourier transform* are examples of expanding a function in a set of basis functions. The characteristic function of a density function is a Fourier transform and is thus one kind of expansion of a density function. Here we seek a simpler kind of expansion.

One-dimensional case: When a density function is one-dimensional, we may try many well-known basis functions, such as *Fourier series*, *Legendre*, *Gegenbauer*, *Jacobi*, *Hermite*, and *Leguerre* polynomials, etc. [22]. Most of them have been developed for approximating a waveform, but obviously we can look at a one-dimensional density function as a waveform.

As a typical example of the expansion, let us study the Hermite polynomial which is used to approximate a density function distorted from a normal distribution. That is,

$$p(x) = \frac{1}{(2\pi)^{1/2}\sigma}\exp(-\frac{x^2}{2\sigma^2})[\sum_{i=0}^{\infty} c_i \phi_i(x)] \ , \tag{6.128}$$

$$\kappa(x) = \frac{1}{(2\pi)^{1/2}\sigma}\exp(-\frac{x^2}{2\sigma^2}) \ , \tag{6.129}$$

$$\phi_i(x) = (-\sigma)^i \exp\left[\frac{x^2}{2\sigma^2}\right] \frac{d^i \exp(-x^2/(2\sigma^2))}{dx^i}$$

$$= \left[\frac{x}{\sigma}\right]^i - \begin{bmatrix} i \\ 2 \end{bmatrix} \left[\frac{x}{\sigma}\right]^{i-2} + 1 \cdot 3 \begin{bmatrix} i \\ 4 \end{bmatrix} \left[\frac{x}{\sigma}\right]^{i-4} - \ldots . \tag{6.130}$$

The orthogonal condition is given by

$$\int_{-\infty}^{+\infty} \frac{1}{(2\pi)^{1/2}\sigma}\exp(-\frac{x^2}{2\sigma^2})\phi_i(x)\phi_j(x)dx = i!\delta_{ij} \ . \tag{6.131}$$

The coefficients c_i can be obtained by

$$i!c_i = \int_{-\infty}^{+\infty} \kappa(x) \frac{p(x)}{(2\pi)^{-1/2}\sigma^{-1}\exp(-x^2/(2\sigma^2))} \phi_i(x)dx$$

$$= \int_{-\infty}^{+\infty} p(x)\phi_i(x)dx$$

$$= \frac{m_i}{\sigma^i} - \begin{bmatrix} i \\ 2 \end{bmatrix} \frac{m_{i-2}}{\sigma^{i-2}} + 1 \cdot 3 \begin{bmatrix} i \\ 4 \end{bmatrix} \frac{m_{i-4}}{\sigma^{i-4}} - \ldots , \tag{6.132}$$

where m_i is the ith moment of $p(x)$ as

$$m_i = \int_{-\infty}^{+\infty} x^i p(x)dx \ . \tag{6.133}$$

For example, if $p(x)$ has zero-mean and has σ^2 as the variance, then

$$c_0 = \frac{m_0}{\sigma^0} = 1 \ , \tag{6.134}$$

$$c_1 = \frac{m_1}{\sigma} = 0 \ , \tag{6.135}$$

$$2!c_2 = \frac{m_2}{\sigma^2} - \begin{bmatrix} 2 \\ 2 \end{bmatrix} \frac{m_0}{\sigma^0} = 0 \ , \tag{6.136}$$

$$3!c_3 = \frac{m_3}{\sigma^3} - \begin{bmatrix} 3 \\ 2 \end{bmatrix} \frac{m_1}{\sigma} = \frac{m_3}{\sigma^3} , \tag{6.137}$$

$$4!c_4 = \frac{m_4}{\sigma^4} - \begin{bmatrix} 4 \\ 2 \end{bmatrix} \frac{m_2}{\sigma^2} + 1 \cdot 3 \begin{bmatrix} 4 \\ 4 \end{bmatrix} \frac{m_0}{\sigma^0} = \frac{m_4}{\sigma^4} - 3 . \tag{6.138}$$

Therefore, terminating at $i = 4$, we have an approximation of a density function $p(x)$ in terms of $\phi_i(X)$ and the moments of $p(x)$ as

$$p(x) \cong \frac{1}{(2\pi)^{1/2}\sigma} \exp\left(-\frac{x^2}{2\sigma^2}\right) \left[1 + \frac{m_3}{3!\sigma^3}\phi_3(x) + \frac{1}{4!}\left(\frac{m_4}{\sigma^4} - 3\right)\phi_4(x) \right]$$

$$= \frac{1}{(2\pi)^{1/2}\sigma} \exp\left(-\frac{x^2}{2\sigma^2}\right) \left[1 + \frac{m_3}{3!\sigma^3}\left\{ \left(\frac{x}{\sigma}\right)^3 - \begin{bmatrix} 3 \\ 2 \end{bmatrix}\left(\frac{x}{\sigma}\right) \right\} \right.$$

$$\left. + \frac{1}{4!}\left(\frac{m_4}{\sigma^4} - 3\right)\left\{ \left(\frac{x}{\sigma}\right)^4 - \begin{bmatrix} 4 \\ 2 \end{bmatrix}\left(\frac{x}{\sigma}\right)^2 + 1 \cdot 3 \begin{bmatrix} 4 \\ 4 \end{bmatrix} \right\} \right] . \tag{6.139}$$

Because of the complexity involved in the multivariate case, it is not as easy to find general basis functions or to calculate the coefficients.

Density Function of Binary Inputs

Basis functions for binary inputs: When the n inputs are binary numbers +1 or −1, it is known that a linear combination of 2^n independent basis functions can yield any density function without error.

$$p(X) = \sum_{i=0}^{2^n-1} c_i \phi_i(X) . \tag{6.140}$$

Table 6-5 shows the truth table that specifies $p(X)$. Again, it is hard to say how we should select the 2^n basis functions. However, a typical set of basis

TABLE 6-5

SPECIFICATION OF *A* DENSITY FUNCTION OF BINARY VARIABLES

X	x_1	x_2	...	x_n	$p(X)$
X_0	−1	−1	...	−1	$p(X_0)$
X_1	+1	−1	...	−1	$p(X_1)$
⋮	⋮	⋮	⋮	⋮	⋮
X_{2^n-1}	+1	+1	...	+1	$p(X_{2^n-1})$

functions is given as follows [23]:

$$\phi_0(X) = 1 \,,$$

$$\phi_1(X) = \frac{x_1 - a_1}{(1 - a_1^2)^{1/2}} \,,$$

$$\vdots$$

$$\phi_n(X) = \frac{x_n - a_n}{(1 - a_n^2)^{1/2}} \,, \tag{6.141}$$

$$\phi_{n+1}(X) = \frac{x_1 - a_1}{(1 - a_1^2)^{1/2}} \frac{x_2 - a_2}{(1 - a_2^2)^{1/2}} \,,$$

$$\vdots$$

$$\phi_{2^n-1}(X) = \frac{x_1 - a_1}{(1 - a_1^2)^{1/2}} \cdots \frac{x_n - a_n}{(1 - a_n^2)^{1/2}} \,,$$

which is a complete orthonormal set with the kernel

$$\kappa(X) = \frac{1}{2^n} \prod_{i=1}^{n} (1 + a_i)^{(1+x_i)/2} (1 - a_i)^{(1-x_i)/2} \,. \tag{6.142}$$

That is,

$$\sum_{\ell=0}^{2^n-1} \kappa(X_\ell)\phi_i(X_\ell)\phi_j(X_\ell) = \delta_{ij} \ . \tag{6.143}$$

The a_i's are control parameters and must be in the range $0 < a_i < 1$. The c_i's can be calculated by

$$c_i = \sum_{\ell=0}^{2^n-1} \kappa(X_\ell)p(X_\ell)\phi_i(X_\ell) \ . \tag{6.144}$$

Two special cases of the above expansion are well known.

The Walsh function: Selecting $a_i = 0$ $(i = 1, \ldots, n)$, the basis functions become

$$\begin{aligned} &\phi_0(X) = 1, \quad \phi_1(X) = x_1, \quad \ldots \quad , \phi_n(X) = x_n \ , \\ &\phi_{n+1}(X) = x_1 x_2, \quad \ldots \quad , \phi_{2^n-1} = x_1 x_2 \ldots x_n \end{aligned} \tag{6.145}$$

with the kernel

$$\kappa(X) = \frac{1}{2^n} \ . \tag{6.146}$$

This set of basis functions is known as the *Walsh functions* and is used often for the expansions of binary functions.

The Bahadur expansion: Let us introduce the following transformation:

$$\mathbf{y}_i = \frac{(\mathbf{x}_i + 1)}{2} \quad \text{or} \quad \mathbf{x}_i = 2\mathbf{y}_i - 1 \ . \tag{6.147}$$

That is, $\mathbf{x}_i = +1$ and -1 correspond to $\mathbf{y}_i = 1$ and 0. Also, let P_i be the marginal probability of $\mathbf{y}_i = 1$,

$$P_i = Pr\{\mathbf{y}_i = +1\} \ . \tag{6.148}$$

Then the expected value and variance of $\mathbf{y}_i$ are given by

$$E\{\mathbf{y}_i\} = 1 \times P_i + 0 \times (1 - P_i) = P_i \ , \tag{6.149}$$

$$\text{Var}\{\mathbf{y}_i\} = (1 - P_i)^2 P_i + (0 - P_i)^2 (1 - P_i) = P_i(1 - P_i) \ . \tag{6.150}$$

If we select a_i as

$$a_i = 2P_i - 1 \qquad \text{or} \qquad P_i = \frac{a_i + 1}{2} , \tag{6.151}$$

then the basis function of (6.141) becomes

$$\begin{aligned} &\phi_0(Y) = 1, \quad \phi_1(Y) = s_1, \quad \dots \quad ,\phi_n(Y) = s_n , \\ &\phi_{n+1}(Y) = s_1 s_2, \quad \dots \quad ,\phi_{2^n-1}(Y) = s_1 s_2 \dots s_n , \end{aligned} \tag{6.152}$$

where

$$s_i = \frac{y_i - P_i}{\{P_i(1 - P_j)\}^{1/2}} = \frac{y_i - E\{\mathbf{y}_i\}}{(Var\{\mathbf{y}_i\})^{1/2}} \tag{6.153}$$

which is the normalized y_i.

On the other hand, the kernel of (6.142) becomes

$$\kappa(Y) = \prod_{i=1}^{n} P_i^{y_i}(1 - P_i)^{1-y_i} . \tag{6.154}$$

If the $\mathbf{y}_i$'s are mutually independent, $p(Y)$ becomes equal to $\kappa(Y)$.

Thus, we can find the expansion of $p(Y)$ as

$$p(Y) = \kappa(Y) \left[\sum_{i=0}^{2^n-1} c_i \phi_i(Y) \right] , \tag{6.155}$$

where the first term $\kappa(Y)$ equals $p(Y)$ under the independence assumption, and all other terms of $[\cdot]$ are the correction terms. The c_i's are calculated by

$$c_i = \sum_{\ell=0}^{2^n-1} \kappa(Y_\ell) \frac{p(Y_\ell)}{\kappa(Y_\ell)} \phi_i(Y_\ell) = \sum_{\ell=0}^{2^n-1} p(Y_\ell)\phi_i(Y_\ell) = E\{\phi_i(\mathbf{Y})\} . \tag{6.156}$$

Thus, (6.155) becomes

$$p(Y) = \left\{ \prod_{i=1}^{n} P_i^{y_i}(1-P_i)^{1-y_i} \right\} \left[1 + \sum_{i<j}\sum \gamma_{ij} s_i s_j + \sum_{i<j<k}\sum\sum \gamma_{ijk} s_i s_j s_k + \dots \right] . \tag{6.157}$$

where γ's are the correlation coefficients of the associated variables.

$$\gamma_{ij} = E\{\mathbf{s}_i \mathbf{s}_j\} = E\left[\frac{\mathbf{y}_i - E\{\mathbf{y}_i\}}{(Var\{\mathbf{y}_i\})^{1/2}} \frac{\mathbf{y}_j - E\{\mathbf{y}_j\}}{(Var\{\mathbf{y}_j\})^{1/2}} \right] , \tag{6.158}$$

$$\gamma_{ijk} = E\{\mathbf{s}_i \mathbf{s}_j \mathbf{s}_k\} = E\left[\frac{\mathbf{y}_i - E\{\mathbf{y}_i\}}{(Var\{\mathbf{y}_i\})^{1/2}} \frac{\mathbf{y}_j - E\{\mathbf{y}_j\}}{(Var\{\mathbf{y}_j\})^{1/2}} \frac{\mathbf{y}_k - E\{\mathbf{y}_k\}}{(Var\{\mathbf{y}_k\})^{1/2}}\right] . \tag{6.159}$$

This expansion is called the *Bahadur expansion* [24]. In this expansion, we can see the effects of the correlations on the approximation of a density function. In general, since the higher-order correlations are usually smaller than lower-order correlations, we may terminate the expansion with a reasonable number of terms and reasonable accuracy.

Example 1: Let us calculate the Bahadur expansions for two density functions, $p_1(Y)$ and $p_2(Y)$, given in Fig. 6-7. We obtain the same basis functions and the same kernels for both $p_1(Y)$ and $p_2(Y)$ as

$$P_1 = \frac{1}{2} \quad \text{and} \quad P_2 = \frac{1}{2} , \tag{6.160}$$

$$s_i = \frac{y_i - 1/2}{1/2} = 2y_i - 1 \quad (i = 1,2) , \tag{6.161}$$

$$\kappa(Y) = (\frac{1}{2})^{y_1}(\frac{1}{2})^{1-y_1}(\frac{1}{2})^{y_2}(\frac{1}{2})^{1-y_2} = \frac{1}{4} . \tag{6.162}$$

	y_1	y_2	$p_1(Y)$	$p_2(Y)$
Y_0	0	0	1/4	1/6
Y_1	1	0	1/4	1/3
Y_2	0	1	1/4	1/3
Y_3	1	1	1/4	1/6

(a)

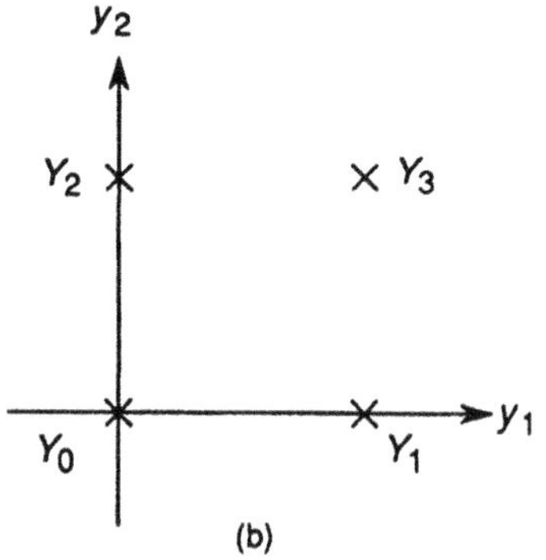

(b)

Fig. 6-7 An example for the Bahadur expansion.

The correlation coefficients of $\mathbf{y}_1$ and $\mathbf{y}_2$ for $p_1(Y)$ and $p_2(Y)$, $\gamma_{12}^{(1)}$ and $\gamma_{12}^{(2)}$, are different and are calculated by

$$\gamma_{12}^{(1)} = \frac{1}{4}\{(2\times 0 - 1)(2\times 0 - 1) + (2\times 1 - 1)(2\times 0 - 1)$$

$$+ (2\times 0 - 1)(2\times 1 - 1) + (2\times 1 - 1)(2\times 1 - 1)\} = 0 \,, \tag{6.163}$$

$$\gamma_{12}^{(2)} = \frac{1}{6}(2\times 0 - 1)(2\times 0 - 1) + \frac{1}{3}(2\times 1 - 1)(2\times 0 - 1)$$

$$+ \frac{1}{3}(2\times 0 - 1)(2\times 1 - 1) + \frac{1}{6}(2\times 1 - 1)(2\times 1 - 1) = -\frac{1}{3} \,. \tag{6.164}$$

Therefore, substituting these results into (6.157), we obtain

$$p_1(Y) = \frac{1}{4} \,, \tag{6.165}$$

$$p_2(Y) = \frac{1}{4}[1 - \frac{1}{3}(2y_1 - 1)(2y_2 - 1)] \,. \tag{6.166}$$

Computer Projects

1. Estimate the mean and variance of the Parzen density estimate, $\hat{\mathbf{p}}(X)$, as follows:

   Data: $N_X(0,I)$, $n = 8$
   Design samples: $N = 100$
   Test points: $[\ell\, 0 \ldots 0]^T, \ldots, [0 \ldots 0\, \ell]^T$
   $\ell = 1, 2, 3, 4, 5$

   Procedure: Parzen
   Kernel: Uniform
   Kernel size: Optimal r
   No. of trials: $\tau = 10$
   Results: Mean and variance vs. ℓ.

2. Repeat Project 1 for a normal kernel.

3. Repeat Project 1 for the *kNN* density estimate with the optimal k.

4. Repeat Projects 1 and 3 for various values of r and k. Plot $IMSE$ vs. r for the Parzen and $IMSE$ vs. k for the kNN. Determine the optimal r and k experimentally.

5. Repeat Experiment 1.

6. Repeat Experiments 2 and 3.

Problems

1. Prove that

   (1) Equation (6.3) is a density function, and

   (2) the covariance matrix of (6.3) is $r^2 A$.

2. Find w of (6.15) for the kernel function of (6.3). Inserting $m = 1$ and ∞ into the w obtained above, confirm that the w's for normal and uniform kernels are obtained.
   [Hint: $\Gamma(\varepsilon) \rightarrow 1/\varepsilon$ as ε goes to zero.]

3. Using a normal kernel, find the optimal r^* and MSE^*. Compare them with the optimal r^* and MSE^* for a uniform kernel.

4. Using $E_X\{MSE\{\hat{\mathbf{p}}(\mathbf{X})\}\}$ instead of $\int MSE\{\hat{\mathbf{p}}(X)\}dX$, find the optimal r and criterion value. Use $p(X) = N_X(0,I)$ and the uniform kernel.

5. Derive the joint density function of coverages, $\mathbf{u}_1, \ldots, \mathbf{u}_k$. Compute the marginal density function of $\mathbf{u}_k$.

6. Using $E_X\{MSE\{\hat{\mathbf{p}}(\mathbf{X})\}\}$ instead of $\int MSE\{\hat{\mathbf{p}}(X)\}dX$, find the optimal k and criterion value. Use $p(X) = N_X(0,I)$.

7. Derive $E_X E\{\mathbf{d}_{kNN}(\mathbf{X})\}$ for the density function of (6.3). Inserting $m = 1$ and ∞ to the above result, confirm that the averaged distances for normal and uniform distributions are obtained.

8. Compute $E_X E\{\mathbf{d}_{kNN}(\mathbf{X})\}$, using the second order approximation $u \cong pv(1 + \alpha r^2/2)$.

9. A density function is given in the figure. Find the Hermite expansion up to the fourth term and show how closely the expansion approximates the density function.

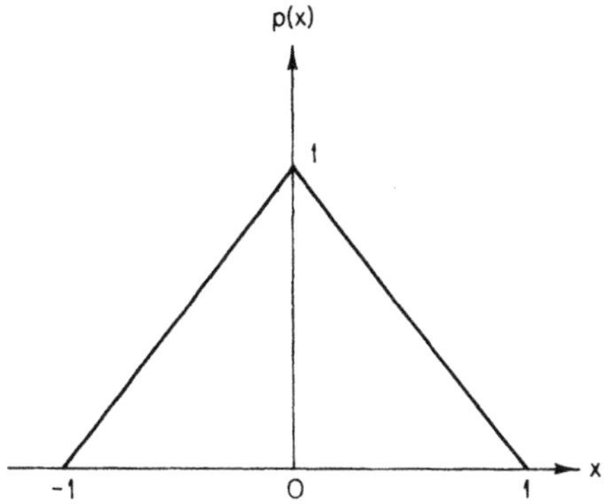

10. A density function of three binary inputs is given in the table. (a) Show the Walsh expansion. (b) Show the Bahadur expansion.

x_1	x_2	x_3	$p(X)$
−1	−1	−1	1/4
+1	−1	−1	1/40
−1	+1	−1	1/40
+1	+1	−1	1/5
−1	−1	+1	1/5
+1	−1	+1	1/40
−1	+1	+1	1/40
+1	+1	+1	1/4

References

1. M. Rosenblatt, Remarks on some nonparametric estimates of a density function, *Ann. Math. Stat.*, 27, pp. 832-837, 1956.

2. E. Parzen, On the estimation of a probability density function and the mode, *Ann. Math. Stat.*, 33, pp. 1065-1076, 1962.

3. T. Cacoullos, Estimation of a multivariate density, *Ann. Inst. Stat. Math.*, 18, pp. 178-189, 1966.

4. L. Devroye and L. Györfi, "Nonparametric Density Estimation: The L_1 View," John Wiley, New York, 1985.

5. K. Fukunaga and L. D. Hostetler, Optimization of *k*-nearest neighbor density estimates, *Trans. IEEE Inform. Theory*, IT-19, pp. 320-326, 1973.

6. J. VanNess, On the dominance of non-parametric Bayes rule discriminant algorithms in high dimensions, *Pattern Recognition*, 12, pp. 355-368, 1980.

7. P. Hall, Large sample optimality of least squares cross-validation in density estimation, *Ann. Stat.*, 11, pp. 1156-1174, 1983.

8. Y. S. Chow, S. German, and L. D. Wu, Consistent cross-validated density estimation, *Ann. Stat.*, 11, pp. 25-38, 1983.

9. T. J. Wagner, Nonparametric estimates of probability densities, *Trans. IEEE Inform. Theory*, IT-21, pp. 438-440, 1975.

10. B. W. Silverman, Choosing the window width when estimating a density, *Biometrika*, 65, pp. 1-11, 1978.

11. D. J. Hand, "Kernel Discriminant Analysis," Research Studies Press, Chichester, UK, 1982.

12. E. Fix and L. J. Hodges, Discriminatory analysis, nonparametric discrimination, consistency properties, Report No. 4, Project 21-49-004, School of Aviation Medicine, Randolph Field, Texas, 1951.

13. E. Fix and L. J. Hodges, Nonparametric discrimination small sample performance, Report No. 11, Project 21-49-004, School of Aviation Medicine, Randolph Field, Texas, 1952.

14. D. O. Loftsgaarden and C. P. Quesenberry, A nonparametric estimate of a multivariate density function. *Ann. Math. Stat.*, 36, pp. 1049-1051, 1965.

15. D. S. Moore and J. W. Yackel, Consistency properties of nearest neighbor density estimates, *Ann. Stat.*, 5, pp. 143-154, 1977.

16. L. Devroye and T. J. Wagner, The strong uniform consistency of nearest neighbor density estimates, *Ann. Stat.*, 5, pp. 536-540, 1977.

17. D. A. S. Fraser, "Nonparametric Methods in Statistics," John Wiley, New York, 1957.

18. K. Fukunaga and T. E. Flick, Classification error for a very large number of classes, *Trans. IEEE Pattern Anal. and Machine Intell.*, PAMI-6, pp. 779-788, 1984.

19. G. V. Trunk, Representation and analysis of signals: statistical estimation of intrinsic dimensionality and parameter identification, *General System*, 13, pp. 49-76, 1968.

20. K. Fukunaga and D. R. Olsen, An algorithm for finding intrinsic dimensionality of data, *Trans. IEEE Computers*, C-20, pp. 176-183, 1971.

21. K. W. Pettis, T. A. Bailey, A. K. Jain, and R. C. Dubes, An intrinsic dimensionality estimator from near-neighbor information. *Trans. IEEE Pattern Anal. and Machine Intell.* PAMI-1, pp. 25-37, 1979.

22. R. Deutsch, "System Analysis Techniques," Prentice-Hall, Englewood Cliffs, NJ, 1969.

23. T. Ito, A note on a general expansion of functions of binary variables, *Inform. and Contr.*, 12, pp. 206-211, 1968.

24. R. R. Bahadur, On classification based on responses to *n* dichotomous items, in "Studies in Item Analysis and Prediction," ed. H. Solomon, Stanford University Press, Stanford, CA, 1967.

Chapter 7

NONPARAMETRIC CLASSIFICATION AND ERROR ESTIMATION

After studying the nonparametric density estimates in Chapter 6, we are now ready to discuss the problem of how to design *nonparametric classifiers* and estimate their *classification errors*.

A nonparametric classifier does not rely on any assumption concerning the structure of the underlying density function. Therefore, the classifier becomes the *Bayes classifier* if the density estimates converge to the true densities when an infinite number of samples are used. The resulting error is the *Bayes error*, the smallest achievable error given the underlying distributions. As was pointed out in Chapter 1, the Bayes error is a very important parameter in pattern recognition, assessing the classifiability of the data and measuring the discrimination capabilities of the features even before considering what type of classifier should be designed. The selection of features always results in a loss of classifiability. The amount of this loss may be measured by comparing the Bayes error in the feature space with the Bayes error in the original data space. The same is true for a classifier. The performance of the classifier may be compared with the Bayes error in the original data space. However, in practice, we never have an infinite number of samples, and, due to the finite sample size, the density estimates and, subsequently, the estimate of the Bayes error have large biases and variances, particularly in a high-dimensional space.

A similar trend was observed in the parametric cases of Chapter 5, but the trend is more severe with a nonparametric approach. These problems are addressed extensively in this chapter.

Both *Parzen* and *kNN* approaches will be discussed. These two approaches offer similar algorithms for classification and error estimation, and give similar results. Also, the *voting kNN procedure* is included in this chapter, because the procedure is very popular, although this approach is slightly different from the *kNN* density estimation approach.

7.1 General Discussion

Parzen Approach

Classifier: As we discussed in Chapter 3, the *likelihood ratio classifier* is given by $-\ln p_1(X)/p_2(X) \gtrless t$, where the threshold t is determined in various ways depending on the type of classifier to be designed (e.g. Bayes, Neyman-Pearson, minimax, etc.). In this chapter, the true density functions are replaced by their estimates discussed in Chapter 6. When the *Parzen density estimate* with a *kernel function* $\kappa_i(\cdot)$ is used, the likelihood ratio classifier becomes

$$-\ln\frac{\hat{p}_1(X)}{\hat{p}_2(X)} = -\ln\frac{\frac{1}{N_1}\sum_{j=1}^{N_1}\kappa_1(X-\mathbf{X}_j^{(1)})}{\frac{1}{N_2}\sum_{j=1}^{N_2}\kappa_2(X-\mathbf{X}_j^{(2)})} \underset{\omega_2}{\overset{\omega_1}{\gtrless}} t\ , \tag{7.1}$$

where $\mathbf{S} = \{\mathbf{X}_1^{(1)},\ldots,\mathbf{X}_{N_1}^{(1)},\mathbf{X}_1^{(2)},\ldots,\mathbf{X}_{N_2}^{(2)}\}$ is the given data set. Equation (7.1) classifies a test sample X into either ω_1 or ω_2, depending on whether the left-hand side is smaller or larger than a threshold t.

Error estimation: In order to estimate the error of this classifier from the given data set, $\mathbf{S}$, we may use the *resubstitution* (R) and *leave-one-out* (L) methods to obtain the lower and upper bounds for the Bayes error. In the R method, all available samples are used to design the classifier, and the same sample set is tested. Therefore, when a sample $\mathbf{X}_k^{(1)}$ from ω_1 is tested, the following equation is used.

$$-\ln \frac{\frac{1}{N_1}\sum_{j=1}^{N_1} \kappa_1(\mathbf{X}_k^{(1)}-\mathbf{X}_j^{(1)})}{\frac{1}{N_2}\sum_{j=1}^{N_2} \kappa_2(\mathbf{X}_k^{(1)}-\mathbf{X}_j^{(2)})} \underset{\omega_2}{\overset{\omega_1}{\gtrless}} t \qquad (R \text{ method}) . \tag{7.2}$$

If < is satisfied, $\mathbf{X}_k^{(1)}$ is correctly classified, and if > is satisfied, $\mathbf{X}_k^{(1)}$ is misclassified. The R estimate of the ω_1-error, ε_{1R}, is obtained by testing $\mathbf{X}_1^{(1)}, \ldots, \mathbf{X}_{N_1}^{(1)}$, counting the number of misclassified samples, and dividing the number by N_1. Similarly, ε_{2R} is estimated by testing $\mathbf{X}_1^{(2)}, \ldots, \mathbf{X}_{N_2}^{(2)}$.

On the other hand, when the L method is applied to test $\mathbf{X}_k^{(1)}$, $\mathbf{X}_k^{(1)}$ must be excluded from the design set. Therefore, the numerator of (7.2) must be replaced by

$$\hat{\mathbf{p}}_{1L}(\mathbf{X}_k^{(1)}) = \frac{1}{N_1-1}\left[\sum_{j=1}^{N_1} \kappa_1(\mathbf{X}_k^{(1)}-\mathbf{X}_j^{(1)}) - \kappa_1(\mathbf{X}_k^{(1)}-\mathbf{X}_k^{(1)})\right] . \tag{7.3}$$

Again, $\mathbf{X}_k^{(1)}$ $(k=1,\ldots,N_1)$ are tested and the misclassified samples are counted. Note that the amount subtracted in (7.3), $\kappa_1(0)$, does not depend on k. When an ω_2-sample is tested, the denominator of (7.2) is modified in the same way.

Typical kernel functions, such as (6.3), generally satisfy $\kappa_i(0) \geq \kappa_i(Y)$ (and subsequently $\kappa_i(0) \geq \hat{\mathbf{p}}_i(Y)$). Then,

$$\hat{\mathbf{p}}_{1L}(\mathbf{X}_k^{(1)}) = \hat{\mathbf{p}}_1(\mathbf{X}_k^{(1)}) + \frac{1}{N_1-1}[\hat{\mathbf{p}}_1(\mathbf{X}_k^{(1)}) - \kappa_1(0)] \leq \hat{\mathbf{p}}_1(\mathbf{X}_k^{(1)}) . \tag{7.4}$$

That is, the L density estimate is always smaller than the R density estimate. Therefore, the left-hand side of (7.2) is larger in the L method than in the R method, and consequently $\mathbf{X}_k^{(1)}$ has more of a chance to be misclassified. Also, note that the L density estimate can be obtained from the R density estimate by simple scalar operations - subtracting $\kappa_1(0)$ and dividing by (N_1-1). Therefore, the computation time needed to obtain both the L and R density estimates is almost the same as that needed for the R density estimate alone.

kNN Approach

Classifier: Using the *kNN* density estimate of Chapter 6, the likelihood ratio classifier becomes

$$-\ln\frac{\hat{\mathbf{p}}_1(X)}{\hat{\mathbf{p}}_2(X)} = -\ln\frac{(k_1-1)N_2\mathbf{v}_2(X)}{(k_2-1)N_1\mathbf{v}_1(X)}$$

$$= -n\ \ln\frac{d_2(\mathbf{X}^{(2)}_{k_2NN},X)}{d_1(\mathbf{X}^{(1)}_{k_1NN},X)} - \ln\frac{(k_1-1)N_2|\Sigma_2|^{1/2}}{(k_2-1)N_1|\Sigma_1|^{1/2}} \underset{\omega_2}{\overset{\omega_1}{\gtrless}} t\ , \tag{7.5}$$

where $v_i = \pi^{n/2}\Gamma^{-1}(n/2+1)|\Sigma_i|^{1/2}d_i^n$ from (B.1), and $d_i^2(Y,X) = (Y-X)^T\Sigma_i^{-1}(Y-X)$. In order to classify a test sample X, the k_1th *NN* from ω_1 and the k_2th *NN* from ω_2 are found, the distances from X to these neighbors are measured, and these distances are inserted into (7.5) to test whether the left-hand side is smaller or larger than t. In order to avoid unnecessary complexity, $k_1 = k_2$ is assumed in this chapter.

Error estimation: The classification error based on a given data set **S** can be estimated by using the L and R methods. When $\mathbf{X}_k^{(1)}$ from ω_1 is tested by the R method, $\mathbf{X}_k^{(1)}$ must be included as a member of the design set. Therefore, when the *kNN*'s of $\mathbf{X}_k^{(1)}$ are found from the ω_1 design set, $\mathbf{X}_k^{(1)}$ itself is included among these *kNN*'s. Figure 7-1 shows how the *kNN*'s are selected and how the distances to the *k*th *NN*'s are measured for $k = 2$. Note in Fig. 7-1 that the locus of points equidistant from $X_k^{(1)}$ becomes ellipsoidal because the distance is normalized by Σ_i. Also, since $\Sigma_1 \neq \Sigma_2$ in general, two different ellipsoids are used for ω_1 and ω_2. In the R method, $\mathbf{X}_k^{(1)}$ and $\mathbf{X}_{NN}^{(1)}$ are the nearest and second nearest neighbors of $\mathbf{X}_k^{(1)}$ from ω_1, while $\mathbf{X}_{NN}^{(2)}$ and $X_{2NN}^{(2)}$ are the nearest and second nearest neighbors of $\mathbf{X}_k^{(1)}$ from ω_2. Thus,

$$-\ln\frac{\hat{\mathbf{p}}_{1R}(\mathbf{X}_k^{(1)})}{\hat{\mathbf{p}}_2(\mathbf{X}_k^{(1)})} = -n\ \ln\frac{d_2(\mathbf{X}_{2NN}^{(2)},\mathbf{X}_k^{(1)})}{d_1(\mathbf{X}_{NN}^{(1)},\mathbf{X}_k^{(1)})} - \ln\frac{N_2|\Sigma_2|^{1/2}}{N_1|\Sigma_1|^{1/2}} \underset{\omega_2}{\overset{\omega_1}{\gtrless}} t \quad (R \text{ method})\ . \tag{7.6}$$

On the other hand, in the L method, $\mathbf{X}_k^{(1)}$ is no longer considered a member of the design set. Therefore, $\mathbf{X}_{NN}^{(1)}$ and $\mathbf{X}_{2NN}^{(1)}$ are selected as the nearest and second nearest neighbors of $\mathbf{X}_k^{(1)}$ from ω_1. The selection of ω_2 neighbors is the same as before. Thus,

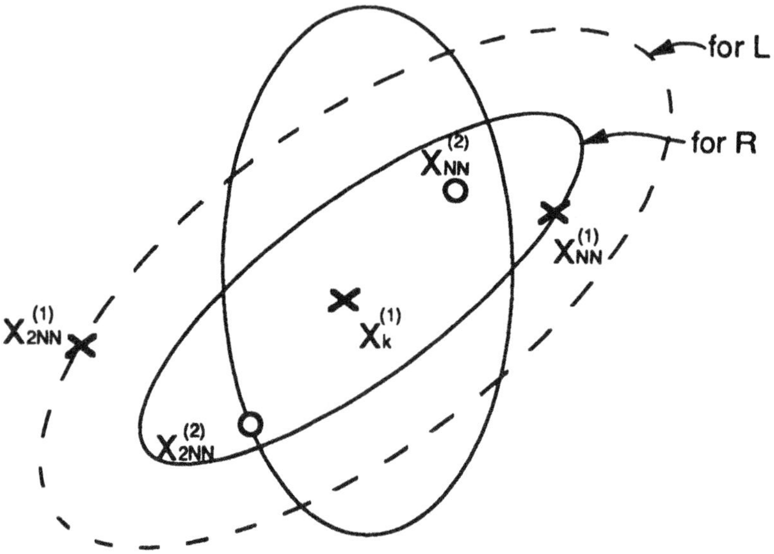

Fig. 7-1 Selection of neighbors.

$$-\ln \frac{\hat{p}_{1L}(\mathbf{X}_k^{(1)})}{\hat{p}_2(\mathbf{X}_k^{(1)})} = -n \ln \frac{d_2(\mathbf{X}_{2NN}^{(2)},\mathbf{X}_k^{(1)})}{d_1(\mathbf{X}_{2NN}^{(1)},\mathbf{X}_k^{(1)})} - \ln \frac{N_2 |\Sigma_2|^{1/2}}{N_1 |\Sigma_1|^{1/2}} \underset{\omega_2}{\overset{\omega_1}{\gtrless}} t \quad (L \text{ method}) . \tag{7.7}$$

Obviously, $d_1(\mathbf{X}_{2NN}^{(1)},\mathbf{X}_k^{(1)}) \geq d_1(\mathbf{X}_{NN}^{(1)},\mathbf{X}_k^{(1)})$, making the left-hand side of (7.7) larger than the left-hand side of (7.6). Thus, $\mathbf{X}_k^{(1)}$ is more likely to be misclassified in the L method than in R method.

Also, note that, in order to find the NN sample, the distances to all samples must be computed and compared. Therefore, when $d_1(\mathbf{X}_{NN}^{(1)},\mathbf{X}_k^{(1)})$ is obtained, $d_1(\mathbf{X}_{2NN}^{(1)},\mathbf{X}_k^{(1)})$ must also be available. This means that the computation time needed to get both the L and R results is practically the same as the time needed for the R method alone.

Voting *kNN* Procedure

The *kNN* approach mentioned above can be modified as follows. Instead of selecting the *k*th *NN* from each class separately and comparing the distances, the *kNN*'s of a test sample are selected from the mixture of classes, and the number of neighbors from each class among the k selected samples is counted. The test sample is then classified to the class represented by a majority of the kNN's. That is,

$$\mathbf{k}_i = \max\{\mathbf{k}_1, \ldots, \mathbf{k}_L\} \quad \rightarrow \quad X \in \omega_i \tag{7.8}$$

$$\mathbf{k}_1 + \ldots + \mathbf{k}_L = k ,$$

where $\mathbf{k}_i$ is the number of neighbors from ω_i ($i = 1, \ldots, L$) among the kNN's. In order to avoid confusion between these two kNN procedures, we will call (7.8) the *voting kNN* procedure and (7.5) the *volumetric kNN* procedure.

For the voting kNN procedure, it is common practice to use the same metric to measure the distances to samples from all classes, although each class could use its own metric. Since the k_i's are integers and a ranking procedure is used, it is hard to find a component of (7.8) analogous with the threshold of (7.5).

It can be shown that the volumetric kNN and voting $(2k-1)NN$ procedures give identical classification results for the two-class problem using the same metric for both classes. For example, let k and $(2k-1)$ be 3 and 5 respectively. In the voting $5NN$ procedure, a test sample is classified to ω_1, if 3, 4, or 5 of the $5NN$'s belong to ω_1. This is equivalent to saying that the 3rd NN from ω_1 is closer to the test sample than the 3rd NN from ω_2.

7.2 Voting *kNN* Procedure—Asymptotic Analysis

In this section, let us study the expected performance of the voting kNN procedure, first for the *asymptotic* case ($N_i = \infty$) and later for the *finite sample* case.

Two-Class *kNN*

NN: We start our discussion with the simplest case, setting $k = 1$ and $L = 2$ in (7.8). That is, in order to classify a test sample, $\mathbf{X}$, the NN sample $\mathbf{X}_{NN}$ is found. Then, $\mathbf{X}$ is classified to either ω_1 or ω_2, depending on the class membership of $\mathbf{X}_{NN}$. An error occurs when $\mathbf{X} \in \omega_1$ but $\mathbf{X}_{NN} \in \omega_2$, or when $\mathbf{X} \in \omega_2$ but $\mathbf{X}_{NN} \in \omega_1$. Therefore, the *conditional risk* given X and X_{NN} is expressed by

$$r_1(X,X_{NN})=Pr\left\{\{\mathbf{X}\varepsilon\omega_1 \text{ and } \mathbf{X}_{NN}\varepsilon\omega_2\} \text{ or } \{\mathbf{X}\varepsilon\omega_2 \text{ and } \mathbf{X}_{NN}\varepsilon\omega_1\} \mid X,X_{NN}\right\}$$
$$=Pr\{\mathbf{X}\varepsilon\omega_1 \text{ and } \mathbf{X}_{NN}\varepsilon\omega_2 \mid X,X_{NN}\}+Pr\{\mathbf{X}\varepsilon\omega_2 \text{ and } \mathbf{X}_{NN}\varepsilon\omega_1 \mid X,X_{NN}\}$$
$$=q_1(X)q_2(X_{NN})+q_2(X)q_1(X_{NN}) \tag{7.9}$$

where

$$q_i(X) = Pr\{X\varepsilon\omega_i \mid X\} : \textit{a posteriori probability} . \tag{7.10}$$

The 2nd line of (7.9) is obtained because the two events in the first line are mutually exclusive. The 3rd line is obtained because $\mathbf{X}$ and $\mathbf{X}_{NN}$ are mutually independent. When an infinite number of samples is available, $\mathbf{X}_{NN}$ is located so close to $\mathbf{X}$ that $q_i(X_{NN})$ can be replaced by $q_i(X)$. Thus, the *asymptotic conditional risk* of the *NN* method is

$$r_1^*(X) = 2q_1(X)q_2(X) = 2\xi(X) \tag{7.11}$$

where

$$\xi(X) = q_1(X)q_2(X) . \tag{7.12}$$

2NN: When k is even, $\mathbf{k}_1 = \mathbf{k}_2$ may occur and a decision cannot be made. In this case, we may set a rule that X be rejected and not counted as an error. In the simplest case of $k = 2$, the rejection occurs when $X_{NN}\varepsilon\omega_1$ and $X_{2NN}\varepsilon\omega_2$, or $X_{NN}\varepsilon\omega_2$ and $X_{2NN}\varepsilon\omega_1$. On the other hand, X is misclassified, when $X\varepsilon\omega_1$ but $X_{NN},X_{2NN}\varepsilon\omega_2$, or $X\varepsilon\omega_2$ but $X_{NN},X_{2NN}\varepsilon\omega_1$. Therefore, the conditional risk is

$$r_2(X,X_{NN},X_{2NN})=q_1(X)q_2(X_{NN})q_2(X_{2NN})+q_2(X)q_1(X_{NN})q_1(X_{2NN}) . \tag{7.13}$$

For the asymptotic case with $q_i(X) = q_i(X_{NN}) = q_i(X_{2NN})$,

$$r_2^*(X) = q_1(X)q_2(X) = \xi(X) \tag{7.14}$$

where $q_1(X) + q_2(X) = 1$ is used.

kNN: Extending the above discussion to larger values of k, the asymptotic conditional risks for odd k and even k are

$$r^*_{2k-1}(X) = \sum_{i=1}^{k} \frac{1}{i} \binom{2i-2}{i-1} \xi^i(X) + \frac{1}{2} \binom{2k}{k} \xi^k(X) , \tag{7.15}$$

$$r^*_{2k}(X) = \sum_{i=1}^{k} \frac{1}{i} \binom{2i-2}{i-1} \xi^i(X) . \tag{7.16}$$

On the other hand, the *conditional Bayes risk* given X is

$$r^*(X) = \min[q_1(X), q_2(X)] = \frac{1}{2} - \frac{1}{2}\sqrt{1-4\xi(X)}$$

$$= \sum_{i=1}^{\infty} \frac{1}{i} \binom{2i-2}{i-1} \xi^i(X) , \tag{7.17}$$

where the 2nd line is the MacLaurin series expansion of the first line. Using (7.15)-(7.17), it is not difficult to prove that these conditional risks satisfy the following inequalities, regardless of ξ [1].

$$\frac{1}{2} r^* \le r^*_2 \le r^*_4 \le \ldots \le r^* \le \ldots \le r^*_3 \le r^*_1 \le 2r^* . \tag{7.18}$$

The proof for $r^* \le r^*_1$ was given in (3.157). Figure 7-2 shows these risks as functions of ξ. The inequalities of (7.18) can also be seen in Fig. 7-2. In addition, $\sqrt{\xi}$ is plotted in Fig. 7-2, because $E\{\sqrt{\xi(\mathbf{X})}\}$ is the Bhattacharyya bound of the Bayes error. Figure 7-2 shows that the *kNN* risks are better bounds than the Bhattacharyya bound. Taking the expectation of these risks with respect to $\mathbf{X}$, the corresponding errors can be obtained. Therefore, these errors also satisfy the inequalities of (7.18). Thus,

$$\frac{1}{2}\varepsilon^* \le \varepsilon^*_{2NN} \le \varepsilon^*_{4NN} \le \ldots \le \varepsilon^* \le \ldots \le \varepsilon^*_{3NN} \le \varepsilon^*_{NN} \le 2\varepsilon^* , \tag{7.19}$$

where

$$\varepsilon^* = E\{r^*(\mathbf{X})\} \quad \text{and} \quad \varepsilon^*_{kNN} = E\{r^*_k(\mathbf{X})\} . \tag{7.20}$$

Equation (7.19) indicates that the error of the voting *NN* procedure is less than twice the Bayes error. This is remarkable, considering that the procedure does not use any information about the underlying distributions and only the class of the single nearest neighbor determines the outcome of the decision.

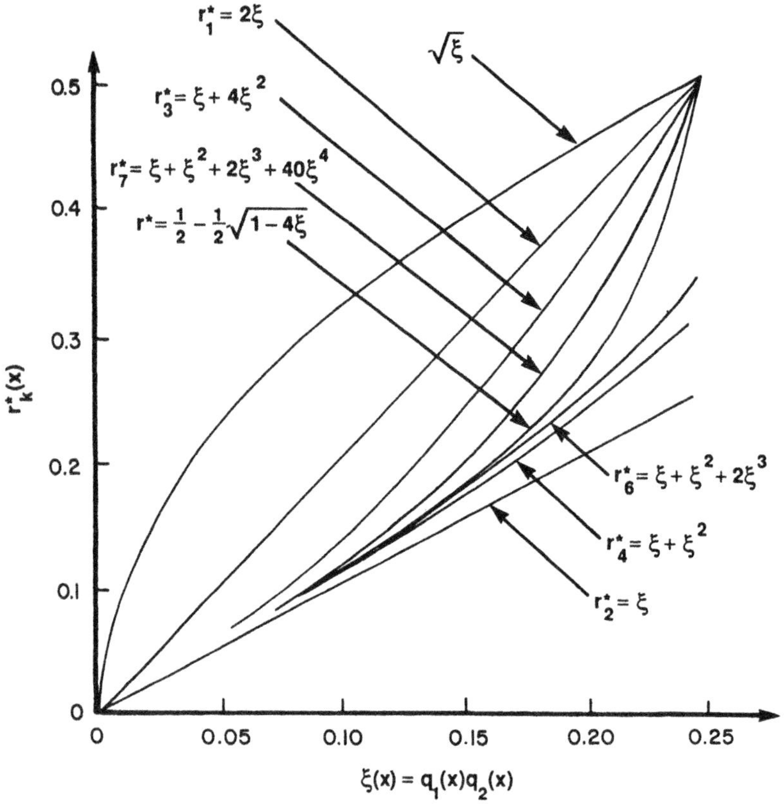

Fig. 7-2 Asymptotic risks vs. ξ.

Example 1: Figure 7-3 gives a simple example to demonstrate how the voting *NN* procedure produces an error between the Bayes error and twice the Bayes error. If the true Bayes classifier is known, samples 5 and 6 from ω_1 and samples 1 and 3 from ω_2 are misclassified. By the voting *NN* procedure, these four samples are indeed misclassified, because their *NN*'s are from the other classes. However, some of these misclassified samples (1 from ω_2 and 5 from ω_1) become the *NN*'s of samples from the other classes (2 from ω_1 and 4 from ω_2), and produce additional errors (2 and 4). This may (for 1 and 5) or may not (for 3 and 6) occur, depending on the distribution of samples. Therefore, roughly speaking, the *NN* error is somewhere between the Bayes error and twice the Bayes error. Also, Fig. 7-3 shows that only 3 samples are misclassified by the voting 2*NN* procedure. For samples 3, 4, and 5, the votes are split and the samples are rejected.

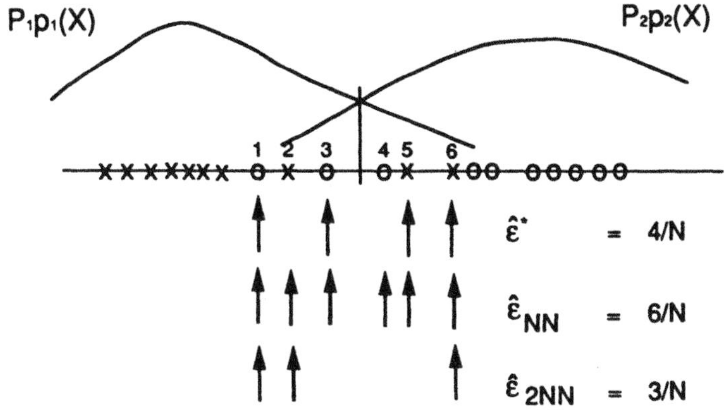

Fig. 7-3 Example of *kNN* classification.

Multiclass *NN*

The voting *NN* procedure can also be applied to general *L*-class problems, in which a test sample is classified to the class of the *NN* sample. The asymptotic conditional risk is

$$r_1^*(X) = q_1(X) \sum_{\substack{j=1 \\ j \neq 1}}^{L} q_j(X) + \ldots + q_L(X) \sum_{\substack{j=1 \\ j \neq L}}^{L} q_j(X)$$

$$= \sum_{i=1}^{L} q_i(X)[1 - q_i(X)] = 1 - \sum_{i=1}^{L} q_i^2(X) \,. \tag{7.21}$$

On the other hand, the Bayes conditional risk is

$$r^*(X) = 1 - \max_j \{q_j(X)\} = 1 - q_\ell(X) \,. \tag{7.22}$$

Using the Schwartz's inequality,

$$(L-1) \sum_{\substack{j=1 \\ j \neq \ell}}^{L} q_j^2(X) \geq [\sum_{\substack{j=1 \\ j \neq \ell}}^{L} q_j(X)]^2 = [1 - q_\ell(X)]^2 = r^{*2}(X) \,. \tag{7.23}$$

Adding $(L-1)q_\ell^2(X)$ to both sides,

$$(L-1) \sum_{j=1}^{L} q_j^2(X) \geq r^{*2}(X) + (L-1)[1 - r^*(X)]^2 \,. \tag{7.24}$$

Substituting (7.24) into (7.21) [1],

$$r_1^*(X) \le 2r^*(X) - \frac{L}{L-1} r^{*2}(X) . \tag{7.25}$$

Equation (7.25) indicates that the *NN* error is still less than twice the Bayes error, but the upper bound becomes larger as L increases.

Estimation of *kNN* Errors

When samples are generated by a computer as in controlled experiments, it is generally desirable to have independent design and test sets. First, design samples are generated and stored. Then, test samples are independently generated, their *kNN*'s are found from the design set, and the number of misclassified test samples is counted. This is the *holdout* (*H*) method for error estimation.

However, with only one set of samples available in practice, we face the problem of deciding whether the sample set should be divided into two groups or used as one group for both design and test. In the parametric case, the latter approach, the *R* method, produces an optimistic bias, as was seen in Chapter 5. However, in the voting *kNN* procedure, we may get different results.

Table 7-1(a) shows how the 3*NN* error can be estimated from a single sample set without dividing it into separate design and test sets. The data column, which lists the samples and their true classes, is given. The 3*NN*'s of each sample are found and listed with their classes in the 1st-*NN*, 2nd-*NN*, and 3rd-*NN* columns. Classification is the result of majority voting among the classes of the 3*NN*'s. Then, the classification column is compared with the true class of the data column. If the classification result matches the true class, the sample is labeled as correct. Otherwise, it is considered an error. The estimate of the 3*NN* error is obtained by counting the number of errors and dividing this by the total number of samples.

Let us examine the first row. When X_1 is tested, X_1 is not included in the design set from which the 3*NN*'s of X_1 are selected. Therefore, this operation utilizes the leave-one-out method. On the other hand, in the resubstitution method, X_1 must be included in the design set. Since X_1 is the closest neighbor of X_1 itself, the 1st-*NN* column of Table 7-1(b) is identical to the data column, and the 1st- and 2nd-*NN* columns of Table 7-1(a) are shifted to the 2nd- and 3rd-*NN* columns in Table 7-1(b). Now, applying the voting 3*NN*

TABLE 7-1

3*NN* ERROR ESTIMATION PROCEDURES

Data		1st *NN*		2nd *NN*		3rd *NN*		Classification	Correct or Error
	ω		ω		ω		ω		
X_1	1	X_3	1	X_{10}	1	X_{23}	2	1	Correct
X_2	2	X_{18}	1	X_{25}	2	X_{36}	1	1	Error
.	.	.	.	.	.	.	.	.	.
.	.	.	.	.	.	.	.	.	.
.	.	.	.	.	.	.	.	.	.
X_N	1	X_{35}	2	X_{536}	2	X_{366}	2	2	Error

$$\hat{\varepsilon}_L = \frac{\#\text{ of errors}}{N}$$

(a) 3*NN* (or 3*NN* leave-one-out)

Data		1st *NN*		2nd *NN*		3rd *NN*		Classification	Correct or Error
	ω		ω		ω		ω		
X_1	1	X_1	1	X_3	1	X_{10}	1	1	Correct
X_2	2	X_2	2	X_{18}	1	X_{25}	2	2	Correct
.	.	.	.	.	.	.	.	.	.
.	.	.	.	.	.	.	.	.	.
.	.	.	.	.	.	.	.	.	.
X_N	1	X_N	1	X_{35}	2	X_{536}	2	2	Error

$$\hat{\varepsilon}_R = \frac{\#\text{ or errors}}{N}$$

(b) 2*NN* (or 3*NN* resubstitution)

procedure to Table 7-1(b), an error occurs only if the classes of the 2nd-*NN* and 3rd-*NN* agree and differ from the class of the 1st-*NN* (see X_N), because the class of the 1st-*NN* is the same as the true class. Therefore, the number of errors counted in Table 7-1(b) is identical to that obtained from the voting 2*NN* procedure using the 2nd-*NN* and 3rd-*NN* columns. In the voting 2*NN* procedure, a sample is rejected if the classes of the 2nd-*NN* and 3rd-*NN* columns disagree (see X_2), and the case is not considered an error. Adding the 1st-*NN* column, this reject case (X_2) becomes correct, but the error case (X_N) still remains an error. Thus, the *L* method version of the voting 2*NN* procedure is the same as the *R* method version of the voting 3*NN* procedure.

An experiment was conducted to compare the performances of two approaches: one is to divide the available sample set into design and test (the *H* method), and the other uses the procedure of Table 7-1(a) (the *L* method).

Experiment 1: *NN* error estimate, *L* and *H*

Data: *I*-Λ (Normal, $n = 8$, $\varepsilon^* = 1.9\%$)

Sample size: $N_1 = N_2 =$ 50–400 (*L*)

50-400 for design, 50-400 for test (*H*)

No. of trials: $\tau = 10$

Metric: $A = I$ (Euclidean)

Results: Fig. 7-4

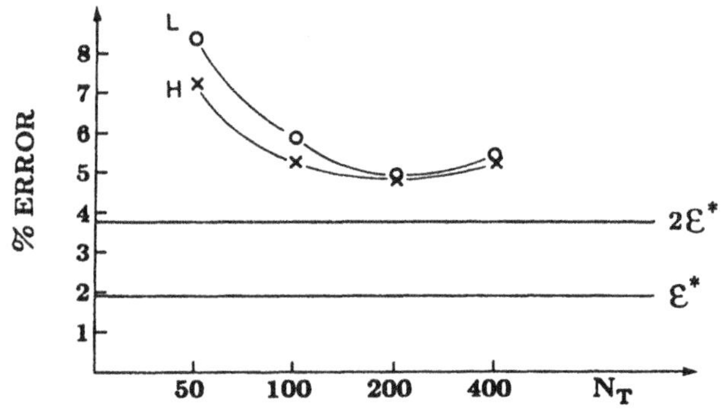

Fig. 7-4 *NN* error estimates by the *H* and *L* methods.

The voting *NN* procedure was applied. N_T indicates the number of test samples per class. In the *H* method, N_T is half of the available sample size, *N*, and $N_T = N$ for the *L* method. Note that the results are fairly close for the same value of N_T. Although the performance of the *L* method is slightly worse, it is better to use the *L* method and double N_T than to divide the data into two groups. Also, note that the experimental curves are above twice the Bayes error, and do not satisfy the inequality of (7.19). This is due to the large bias of this estimation technique, which will be discussed in the next section.

7.3 Voting *kNN* Procedure—Finite Sample Analysis

So far, the asymptotic performance of the voting *kNN* procedure has been studied. That is, the conditional risks and errors were derived based on the assumption that $q_i(\mathbf{X}_{kNN}) = q_i(\mathbf{X})$. However, in the real world, the number of samples available is always finite. So, the question is how many samples are needed so that the observed performance is similar to the asymptotic one [2-7]. In this section, finite sample analysis is presented for the voting *NN* and 2*NN* procedures.

Bias of the *NN* Error

We start our analysis with (7.9). With a finite number of samples, we can no longer assume $q_i(\mathbf{X}_{NN}) = q_i(\mathbf{X})$. Therefore, we define $\boldsymbol{\delta}$ as the difference between $q_i(\mathbf{X})$ and $q_i(\mathbf{X}_{NN})$.

$$q_1(\mathbf{X}_{NN}) = q_1(\mathbf{X}) + \boldsymbol{\delta} \quad \text{and} \quad q_2(\mathbf{X}_{NN}) = q_2(\mathbf{X}) - \boldsymbol{\delta} \,. \tag{7.26}$$

Equation (7.26) holds since $q_1(X) + q_2(X) = 1$ and $q_1(X_{NN})+ q_2(X_{NN}) = 1$. Substituting (7.26) into (7.9),

$$r_1(\mathbf{X},\mathbf{X}_{NN}) = r_1^*(\mathbf{X}) + [q_2(\mathbf{X}) - q_1(\mathbf{X})]\boldsymbol{\delta} \,. \tag{7.27}$$

Thus, the *bias* between the finite sample and asymptotic *NN* errors may be computed by taking the expectation of the second term of (7.27) with respect to both $\mathbf{X}_{NN}$ and $\mathbf{X}$. In order to accomplish this, $q_1(\mathbf{X}_{NN})$ is expanded in a Taylor series around a given X. Terms higher than second order are discarded and $q_1(X)$ is subtracted to obtain

$$\boldsymbol{\delta} \cong \nabla^T q_1(X)(\mathbf{X}_{NN}-X) + \frac{1}{2}\text{tr}\{\nabla^2 q_1(X)(\mathbf{X}_{NN}-X)(\mathbf{X}_{NN}-X)^T\} \,. \tag{7.28}$$

The metric used to measure the *NN* distances is specified by $d^2(Y,X) = (Y-X)^T A^{-1}(Y-X)$. In the case that A is held fixed, this is a *global metric*. However, in the more general case, A may be allowed to vary with X, forming a *local metric*. The same metric is used for both ω_1 and ω_2 in this section. However, a similar analysis could be done, even when two different metrics are adopted for ω_1 and ω_2.

The expectation of (7.28) can be computed in three stages as $E_X E_\rho E_{X_{NN}} \{ \boldsymbol{\delta} | \boldsymbol{\rho}, \mathbf{X} \}$ where $\boldsymbol{\rho}$ is $d(\mathbf{X}, \mathbf{X}_{NN})$.

The first expectation is taken with respect to $\mathbf{X}_{NN}$ given $\mathbf{X} = X$ and $\boldsymbol{\rho} = \rho$. That is, the bias is averaged over all $\mathbf{X}_{NN}$ on the hyperellipsoidal surface, $S(\rho) = \{ Y : \rho = d(Y, X) \}$, specified by a constant ρ. Thus,

$$E_{X_{NN}} \{ \boldsymbol{\delta} | \rho, X \} = \frac{\int_{S(\rho)} \delta p(X_{NN}) dX_{NN}}{\int_{S(\rho)} p(X_{NN}) dX_{NN}}$$

$$\cong \frac{\rho^2}{n} \operatorname{tr} \{ A [\nabla p(X) \nabla^T q_1(X) p^{-1}(X) + \frac{1}{2} \nabla^2 q_1(X)] \} , \tag{7.29}$$

where $p(X)$ is the mixture density function, $P_1 p_1(X) + P_2 p_2(X)$. In order to obtain the second line of (7.29), the following formulas are used, along with δ of (7.28) [see (B.7)-(B.9)]

$$p(X_{NN}) \cong p(X) + \nabla^T p(X)(X_{NN} - X) , \tag{7.30}$$

$$S = \int_{S(\rho)} dY = \frac{n \pi^{n/2} | A |^{1/2}}{\Gamma(\frac{n+2}{2})} \rho^{n-1} , \tag{7.31}$$

$$\int_{S(\rho)} (Y - X)(Y - X)^T dY = \frac{S}{n} r^2 A . \tag{7.32}$$

Note that all odd order terms of $(X_{NN} - X)$ disappear, since $S(\rho)$ is symmetric around X.

In order to take the expectation with respect to $\boldsymbol{\rho}$, we can rewrite (7.29) in terms of $\mathbf{u}$, since the density function of $\mathbf{u}$ is known in (6.76). Using the first order approximation of $u \cong pv$,

$$\mathbf{u} \cong \frac{\pi^{n/2}}{\Gamma(\frac{n+2}{2})} p(X) | A |^{1/2} \boldsymbol{\rho}^n . \tag{7.33}$$

Therefore,

$$E_\rho\{\rho^2\} \cong \frac{\Gamma^{2/n}(\frac{n+2}{2})}{\pi p^{2/n}(X)|A|^{1/n}} E_u\{\mathbf{u}^{2/n}\}$$

$$= \frac{\Gamma^{2/n}(\frac{n+2}{2})}{\pi p^{2/n}(X)|A|^{1/n}} \frac{\Gamma(1+2/n)\Gamma(N+1)}{\Gamma(N+1+2/n)} . \tag{7.34}$$

Finally, combining (7.27), (7.29), and (7.34), and taking the expectation with respect to **X** [8],

$$E\{\hat{\varepsilon}_{NN}\} \cong \varepsilon^*_{NN} + \beta_1 E_X\{|A|^{-1/n}\text{tr}\{AB_1(\mathbf{X})\}\} \tag{7.35}$$

where

$$B_1(X) = p^{-2/n}(X)[q_2(X)-q_1(X)][\nabla p(X)\nabla^T q_1(X)p^{-1}(X)+\frac{1}{2}\nabla^2 q_1(X)] , \tag{7.36}$$

$$\beta_1 = \frac{\Gamma^{2/n}(\frac{n+2}{2})}{n\pi} \frac{\Gamma(1+2/n)\Gamma(N+1)}{\Gamma(N+1+2/n)}$$

$$\cong \frac{\Gamma^{2/n}(\frac{n+2}{2})\Gamma(1+2/n)}{n\pi} N^{-2/n} . \tag{7.37}$$

The second line of (7.37) is obtained by approximating $\Gamma(x+\alpha)/\Gamma(x)$ by x^α for a large integer x and a small α.

Effect of Parameters

Several observations may be made at this point. First, note that the value of β_1 is completely independent of the underlying densities. It depends only on the dimensionality of the data and the sample size, and does not depend on the particular distributions involved. The term inside the expectation in (7.35), on the other hand, does not depend on the sample size. For any given set of distributions this term remains fixed regardless of the number of samples. This term does, however, depend heavily on the selection of the metric, A. These equations, therefore, yield much information about how the bias is effected by each of the parameters of interest (n, N, A, and $p(X)$). Each of these parameters will be discussed separately as follows.

Effect of sample size: Equation (7.37) gives an explicit expression showing how the sample size affects the size of the bias of the *NN* error. Figure 7-5 shows β_1 vs. N for various values of n [8]. The bias tends to drop off

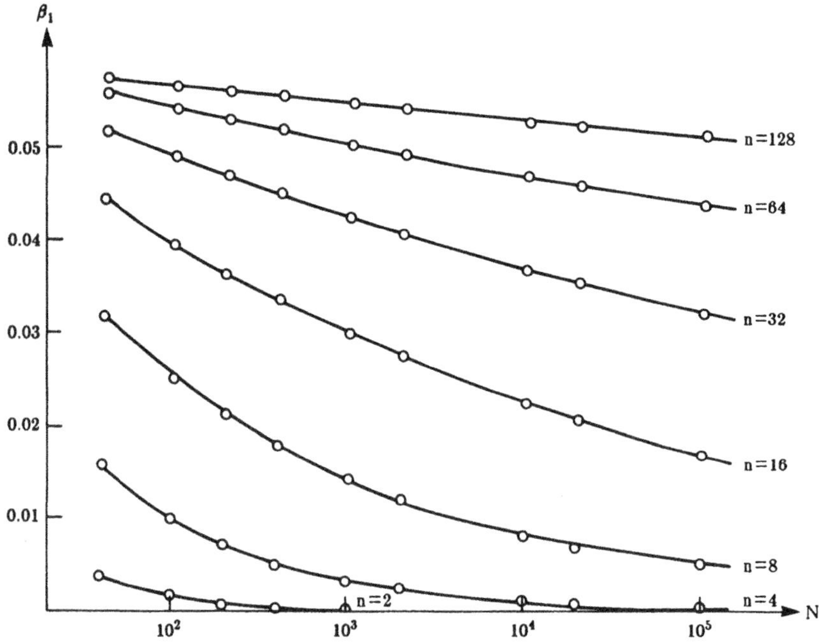

Fig. 7-5 β_1 vs. N.

rather slowly as the sample size increases, particularly when the dimensionality of the data is high. This is not an encouraging result, since it tends to indicate that increasing the sample size N is not an effective means of reducing the bias. For example, with a dimensionality of 64, increasing the number of samples from 1,000 to 10,000 results in only a 6.9% reduction in the bias (β_1 from .0504 to .0469). Further reduction by 6.9% would require increasing the number of samples to over 100,000. Thus it does not appear that the asymptotic *NN* error may be estimated simply by "choosing a large enough N" as generally believed, especially when the dimensionality of the data is high. The required value of N would be prohibitively large.

Effect of dimensionality: The dimensionality of the data appears to play an important role in determining the relationship between the size of the bias and the sample size. As is shown in Fig. 7-5, for small values of n (say, $n \leq 4$), changing the sample size is an effective means of reducing the bias. For larger values of n, however, increasing the number of samples becomes a more and more futile means of improving the estimate. It is in these higher dimensional cases that improved techniques of accurately estimating the Bayes error are needed. It should be pointed out that, in the expression for the bias of the *NN* error, n represents the *local* or *intrinsic* dimensionality of the data as discussed in Chapter 6. In many applications, the intrinsic dimensionality is much smaller than the dimensionality of the observation space. Therefore, in order to calculate β_1, it is necessary that the intrinsic dimensionality be estimated from the data using (6.115).

Effect of densities: The expectation term of (7.35) gives the effect of densities on the size of the bias. In general, it is very hard to determine the effect of this term because of its complexity. In order to investigate the general trends, however, we can compute the term numerically for a normal case.

Experiment 2: Computation of $E_X\{\cdot\}$ of (7.35)
Data: *I-I* (Normal)
M adjusted to give $\varepsilon^* = 2, 5, 10, 20, 30(\%)$
Dimensionality: $n = 2, 4, 8, 16$
Sample size: $N_1 = N_2 = 1600n$
Metric: $A = I$ (Euclidean)
Results: Table 7-2 [8]

In the experiment, B_1 of (7.36) was evaluated at each generated sample point where the mathematical formulas based on the normality assumption were used to compute $p(X)$ and $q_i(X)$. The expectation of (7.35) was replaced by the sample mean taken over 1600n samples per class.

Table 7-2 reveals many properties of the expectation term. But, special attention must be paid to the fact that, once n becomes large (n > 4), its value has little effect on the size of the expectation. This implies that β_1 of (7.37) dominates the effect of n on the bias. That is, the bias is much larger for high-dimensions. This coincides with the observation that, in practice, the *NN* error comes down, contrary to theoretical expectation, by selecting a smaller

TABLE 7-2

ESTIMATES OF THE EXPECTATION TERM
IN (7.35) FOR NORMAL DATA

Bayes Error		$n = 2$	$n = 4$	$n = 8$	$n = 16$
30%	1st order term	3.4	1.2	1.2	1.1
	2nd order term	2.2	1.2	0.4	0.3
	Sum	5.6	2.4	1.6	1.4
20%	1st order term	2.2	1.3	0.9	0.8
	2nd order term	1.8	1.2	1.1	1.0
	Sum	4.0	2.5	2.0	1.8
10%	1st order term	-1.3	-.2	-0.2	-0.2
	2nd order term	4.7	2.1	1.7	1.6
	Sum	3.4	1.9	1.5	1.4
5%	1st order term	-1.9	-1.0	-0.8	-0.6
	2nd order term	3.8	2.3	1.8	1.5
	Sum	1.9	1.3	1.0	0.9
2%	1st order term	-2.0	-1.5	-0.8	-0.7
	2nd order term	3.5	2.3	1.3	1.1
	Sum	1.5	0.8	0.5	0.4

number of features. This happens, because the bias is reduced more than the Bayes error is increased. In order to compare two sets of features in different dimensions, this dependency of the bias on n must be carefully examined. Also, note in Table 7-2 that the second order term due to $\nabla^2 q_1(X)$ is comparable to or even larger than the first order term due to $\nabla q_1(X)$. It is for this reason that the second order term is included in the Taylor series expansion of (7.28).

Effect of metric: The expectation terms of (7.35) also indicates how the matrix, A, affects the bias. Certainly, proper selection of a metric may reduce the bias significantly. Unfortunately, B_1 is a very complex function of X and very hard to estimate for any given set of data. As for optimization of A,

(6.54) shows that an expression of the form $|A|^{-1/n}\text{tr}\{AB_1\}$ is minimized by setting $A = B_1^{-1}$, provided B_1 is a positive definite matrix. However, B_1 might not be positive definite, because of the term $[q_2-q_1]$ in (7.36). Thus, it is not immediately clear how to choose A to minimize the bias. Nevertheless, selection of an appropriate metric remains an important topic in *NN* error estimation [9-10].

Experimental Verification

In order to verify the results mentioned above, the following experiment was run:

Experiment 3: Voting *NN* error estimation,
L method (Table 7-1(a))
Data: *I-I* (Normal, $n = 8$)
M adjusted to give $\varepsilon^* = 2, 5, 10, 20, 30(\%)$
Sample size: $N_1 = N_2 = 20n, 40n, 80n, 160n$
No. of trials: $\tau = 20$
Metric: $A = I$ (Euclidean)
Results: Fig. 7-6 [8]

In Fig. 7-6, the small circle indicates the average of the *NN* errors over 20 trials, and the vertical bar represents ± one standard deviation. According to (7.35), the bias of the *NN* error varies linearly with β_1 for any given set of distributions. Therefore, if we know ε_{NN}^* and $E_X\{\cdot\}$, we can predict the finite sample *NN* errors as linear functions of β_1. The dotted lines of Fig. 7-6 show these predicted *NN* errors for various values of the Bayes error. The $E_X\{\cdot\}$'s of (7.35) are tabulated in Table 7-2. The theoretical asymptotic error, ε_{NN}^*, was estimated by generating a large member (1600n) of samples, calculating the risk at each sample point from (7.11) using the known mathematical expressions for $q_i(X)$ in the normal case, and averaging the result. Note that the averages of these measured $\hat{\varepsilon}_{NN}$'s are reasonably close to the predicted values.

While it may not be practical to obtain the asymptotic *NN* errors simply by increasing the sample size, it may be possible to use information concerning how the bias changes with sample size to our advantage. We could measure $\hat{\varepsilon}_{NN}$ empirically for several sample sizes, and obtain β_1 using either (7.37) or Fig. 7-5. These values could be used in conjunction with (7.35) to obtain an estimate of the asymptotic *NN* error as follows:

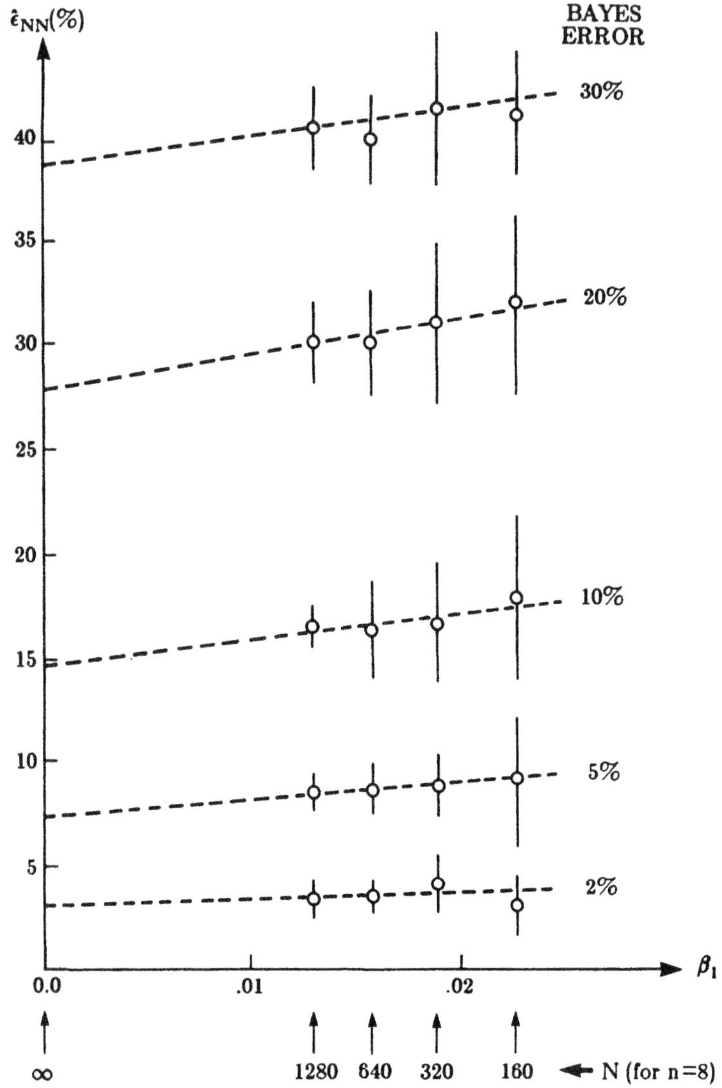

Fig. 7-6 *NN* errors for normal data.

(1) Change the sample size N as $N_1, N_2, \ldots, N_\ell$. For each N_i, calculate β_1 (using the intrinsic dimensionality) and measure $\hat{\varepsilon}_{NN}$ empirically. It is preferable to repeat the experiment several times independently and to average the measured $\hat{\varepsilon}_{NN}$'s.

(2) Plot these ℓ empirical points $\hat{\varepsilon}_{NN}$ vs. β_1. Then, find the line best fitted to these ℓ points. The slope of this line is $E_X\{\cdot\}$ and the y-intercept is ε^*_{NN}, which we would like to estimate.

The reader must be aware that $\hat{\varepsilon}_{NN}$ varies widely (the standard deviation of $\hat{\varepsilon}_{NN}$ for each β_1 is large), and that $\beta_1 = 0$ is far away from the β-region where the actual experiments are conducted. Therefore, a small variation in $\hat{\varepsilon}_{NN}$ tends to be amplified and causes a large shift in the estimate of ε^*_{NN}.

Biases for Other Cases

2NN: The bias of the $2NN$ error can be obtained from (7.13) in a similar fashion, resulting in [8]

$$E\{\hat{\varepsilon}_{2NN}\} \cong \varepsilon^*_{2NN} + \beta_2 E_X\{[|A|^{-1/n}\mathrm{tr}\{AB_2(X)\}]^2\} , \tag{7.38}$$

where

$$B_2(X) = p^{-2/n}(X)[\nabla p(X)\nabla^T q_1(X)p^{-1}(X) + \frac{1}{2}\nabla^2 q_1(X)] , \tag{7.39}$$

$$\beta_2 = \left[\frac{\Gamma^{2/n}(\frac{n+2}{2})}{n\pi}\right]^2 \frac{1+4/n}{1+2/n} \frac{\Gamma(1+4/n)\Gamma(N+1)}{\Gamma(N+1+4/n)}$$

$$\cong \left[\frac{\Gamma^{2/n}(\frac{n+2}{2})}{n\pi}\right]^2 \frac{1+4/n}{1+2/n}\Gamma(1+4/n)N^{-4/n} . \tag{7.40}$$

By comparing (7.40) with (7.37), it can be seen that β_2 is roughly proportional to $N^{-4/n}$ while β_1 is proportional to $N^{-2/n}$. That is, as N increases, the $2NN$ error converges to its asymptotic value more quickly than the NN error - as if the dimensionality, n, were half as large. Also, note that β_2 is significantly smaller than β_1, because $\Gamma^{2/n}/n\pi$ (.088 for $n = 8$ and .068 for $n = 32$) is squared. Many experiments also have revealed that the $2NN$ error is less biased than the NN error [11]. Since their asymptotic errors are related by $\varepsilon^*_{NN} = 2\varepsilon^*_{2NN}$ from (7.11) and (7.14), a better estimate of ε^*_{NN} could be obtained by estimating ε^*_{2NN} first and doubling it.

Multiclass: The *NN* error for multiclass problems can also be obtained in a similar way, starting from (7.21) [8]. The result is

$$E\{\hat{\varepsilon}_{NN}\} \cong \varepsilon^*_{NN} + \beta_1 E_X\{|A|^{-1/n}\mathrm{tr}\{AB_L(\mathbf{X})\}\} , \tag{7.41}$$

where

$$B_L(X) = \sum_{i=1}^{L} p^{-2/n}(X)q_i(X)[-\nabla p(X)\nabla^T q_i(X)p^{-1}(X) + \frac{1}{2}\nabla^2 q_i(X)] . \tag{7.42}$$

Note that β_1 of (7.41) is the same as β_1 of (7.37). This means that the effect of sample size on the bias does not depend on the number of classes.

7.4 Error Estimation

In this section, we return to nonparametric density estimates, and use these estimates to design a classifier and estimate the classification error. Both the Parzen and volumetric *kNN* approaches will be discussed. However, because the analysis of the Parzen approach is simpler than the *kNN* approach, the Parzen approach will be presented first with detailed analysis, and then the *kNN* approach will be discussed through comparison with the Parzen approach.

Classification and error estimation using the Parzen density estimate were discussed in Section 7.1. However, in order to effectively apply this technique to practical problems, we need to know how to determine the necessary parameter values, such as the kernel size, kernel shape, sample size, and threshold.

Effect of the Kernel Size in the Parzen Approach

As we discussed the optimal volume of the Parzen density estimate in Chapter 6, let us consider the problem of selecting the kernel size here. However, density estimation and classification are different tasks, and the optimal solution for one might not be optimal for the other. For example, in density estimation, the mean-square error criterion was used to find the optimal volume. This criterion tends to weight the high density area more heavily than the low density area. On the other hand, in classification, the relationship between the tails of two densities is important. In this case, the mean-square error may not be an appropriate criterion. Despite significant efforts in the past, it is still unclear how to optimize the size of the kernel function for classification. One of the ways to overcome this difficulty is to determine the optimal kernel size experimentally. Assuming that the kernel function of (6.3) is adopted with r as the size control parameter, we may repeat the estimation of the classification error by both L and R methods for various values of r, and plot the results vs. r. The major drawback of this approach is that the estimation procedure must be repeated completely for each value of r.

Experiment 4: Estimation of the Parzen errors, L and R

Data: I-I, I-$4I$, I-Λ (Normal, $n = 8$)
Sample size: $N_1 = N_2 = 100$
No. of trials: $\tau = 10$
Kernel: Normal with $A_1 = \Sigma_1$, $A_2 = \Sigma_2$
Kernel size: $r = 0.6$–3.0
Threshold: $t = 0$
Results: Fig. 7-7 [12]

In Fig. 7-7, the upper and lower bounds of the Bayes error were obtained by the L and R methods, respectively. As seen in Fig. 7-7, the error estimates are very sensitive to r, except for the Data I-I case. Unless a proper r is chosen, the estimates are heavily biased and do not necessarily bound the Bayes error.

In order to understand why the error estimates behave as in Fig. 7-7 and to provide intelligent guidelines for parameter selection, we need a more detailed analysis of the Parzen error estimation procedure.

Effect of the density estimate: In general, the likelihood ratio classifier is expressed by

$$h(X) = -\ln \frac{p_1(X)}{p_2(X)} - t \underset{\omega_2}{\overset{\omega_1}{\gtrless}} 0 , \tag{7.43}$$

where t is the threshold. When the estimates of $p_1(X)$ and $p_2(X)$ are used,

$$\hat{\mathbf{h}}(X) = -\ln \frac{\hat{\mathbf{p}}_1(X)}{\hat{\mathbf{p}}_2(X)} - \hat{t} = h(X) + \Delta\mathbf{h}(X) , \tag{7.44}$$

where $\hat{t}$ is the adjusted threshold. The discriminant function $\hat{\mathbf{h}}(X)$ is a random variable and deviates from $h(X)$ by $\Delta\mathbf{h}(X)$. The effect of $\Delta\mathbf{h}(X)$ on the classification error can be evaluated from (5.65) as

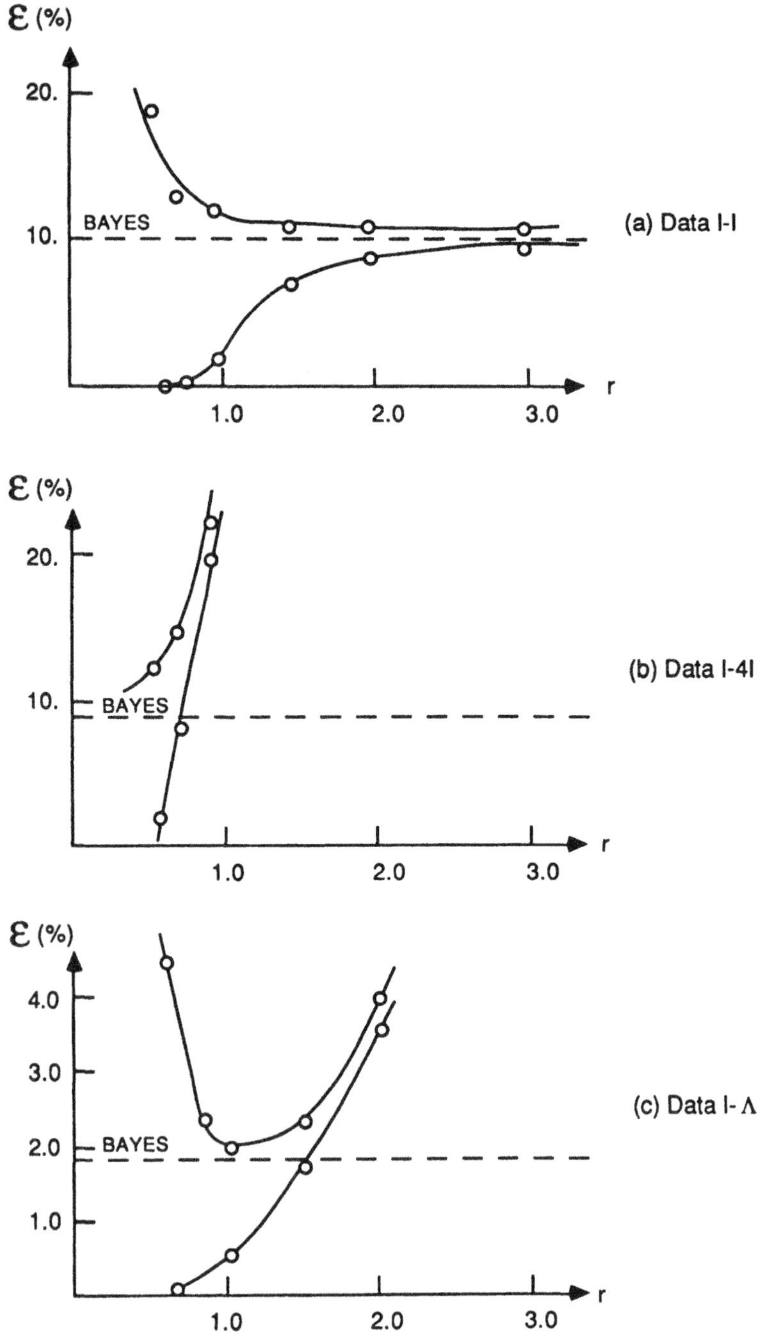

Fig. 7-7 Parzen error for various values of r.

$$E\{\Delta\varepsilon\} \cong \frac{1}{2\pi}\iint E\{\Delta\mathbf{h}(X) + \frac{j\omega}{2}\Delta\mathbf{h}^2(X)\}$$

$$\times e^{j\omega h(X)}[P_1p_1(X) - P_2p_2(X)]d\omega dX \,. \tag{7.45}$$

From (7.44), $\Delta\mathbf{h}(X)$ and $\Delta\mathbf{h}^2(X)$ are derived as follows.

$$\Delta\mathbf{h}(X) = \ln\left[1+\frac{\Delta\mathbf{p}_2(X)}{p_2(X)}\right] - \ln\left[1+\frac{\Delta\mathbf{p}_1(X)}{p_1(X)}\right] - \Delta t$$

$$\cong \frac{\Delta\mathbf{p}_2(X)}{p_2(X)} - \frac{1}{2}\left[\frac{\Delta\mathbf{p}_2(X)}{p_2(X)}\right]^2 - \frac{\Delta\mathbf{p}_1(X)}{p_1(X)} + \frac{1}{2}\left[\frac{\Delta\mathbf{p}_1(X)}{p_1(X)}\right]^2 - \Delta t \,, \tag{7.46}$$

$$\Delta\mathbf{h}^2(X) \cong \left[\frac{\Delta\mathbf{p}_2(X)}{p_2(X)}\right]^2 + \left[\frac{\Delta\mathbf{p}_1(X)}{p_1(X)}\right]^2 - 2\left[\frac{\Delta\mathbf{p}_1(X)}{p_1(X)}\right]\left[\frac{\Delta\mathbf{p}_2(X)}{p_2(X)}\right] + \Delta t^2$$

$$- 2\Delta t\left[\frac{\Delta\mathbf{p}_2(X)}{p_2(X)} - \frac{1}{2}\left[\frac{\Delta\mathbf{p}_2(X)}{p_2(X)}\right]^2 - \frac{\Delta\mathbf{p}_1(X)}{p_1(X)} + \frac{1}{2}\left[\frac{\Delta\mathbf{p}_1(X)}{p_1(X)}\right]^2\right] \tag{7.47}$$

where $\Delta\mathbf{p}_i(X) = \hat{\mathbf{p}}_i(X) - p_i(X)$, $\Delta t = \hat{t} - t$, and the expansions are terminated at the second order terms. The bias of the error estimate may be obtained by taking the expectations of (7.46) and (7.47), inserting them into (7.45), and carrying out the integration.

Parzen kernel: When the Parzen kernel approach is used, $E\{\hat{\mathbf{p}}_i(X)\}$ and $\mathrm{Var}\{\hat{\mathbf{p}}_i(X)\}$ are available in (6.18) and (6.19) respectively. Since $E\{\Delta\mathbf{p}_i(X)\} = E\{\hat{\mathbf{p}}_i(X)\} - p_i(X)$ and $E\{\Delta\mathbf{p}_i^2(X)\} = E\{[\hat{\mathbf{p}}_i(X) - p_i(X)]^2\} = MSE\{\hat{\mathbf{p}}_i(X)\} = \mathrm{Var}\{\hat{\mathbf{p}}_i(X)\} + E^2\{\Delta\mathbf{p}_i(X)\}$,

$$E\left\{\frac{\Delta\mathbf{p}_i(X)}{p_i(X)}\right\} \cong \frac{1}{2}\alpha_i(X)r^2 \,, \tag{7.48}$$

$$E\left\{\left[\frac{\Delta\mathbf{p}_i(X)}{p_i(X)}\right]^2\right\} \cong \frac{s_i}{Np_i(X)r^n} + \frac{1}{4}\alpha_i^2(X)r^4 \,, \tag{7.49}$$

where w_i of (6.15) is expressed by s_ir^{-n} and s_i is given in (6.20) and (6.26) for normal and uniform kernels respectively. The reason why the first and second order approximations are used for the variance and bias respectively was discussed in Chapter 6. If the second order approximation for the variance is adopted, we can obtain a more accurate but complex expression for (7.49). Substituting (7.48) and (7.49) into (7.46) and (7.47),

$$E\{\Delta \mathbf{h}(X)\} \cong \frac{1}{2} r^2(\alpha_2-\alpha_1) + \frac{1}{8} r^4(\alpha_1^2-\alpha_2^2) - \Delta t + \frac{r^{-n}}{2N}\left[\frac{s_1}{p_1} - \frac{s_2}{p_2}\right], \tag{7.50}$$

$$E\{\Delta \mathbf{h}^2(X)\} \cong [\frac{1}{2} r^2(\alpha_2-\alpha_1) - \Delta t]^2 - \frac{\Delta t}{4} r^4(\alpha_1^2-\alpha_2^2) + \frac{r^{-n}}{N}\left[\frac{s_1(1-\Delta t)}{p_1} - \frac{s_2(1+\Delta t)}{p_2}\right]. \tag{7.51}$$

Note that from (6.18) and (6.19) the terms associated with $r^2\alpha_i$ are generated by the bias of the density estimate, and the terms associated with r^{-n}/N come from the variance. The threshold adjustment Δt is a constant selected independently.

Now, substituting (7.50) and (7.51) into (7.45) and carrying out the integration, the bias is expressed in terms of r and N as

$$E\{\Delta \varepsilon\} \cong a_1 r^2 + a_2 r^4 + a_3 r^{-n}/N . \tag{7.52}$$

Here, the constants a_1, a_2, and a_3 are obtained by evaluating the indicated integral expression in (7.45). Here, we assume, for simplicity, that the decision threshold t is set to zero. Because of the complexity of the expressions, explicit evaluation is not possible. However, the constants are only functions of the distributions and the kernel shapes, A_i, and are completely independent of the sample size and the smoothing parameter, r. Hence, (7.52) shows how changes in r and N affect the error performance of the classifier. The $a_1 r^2$ and $a_2 r^4$ terms indicate how biases in the density estimates influence the performance of the classifier, while the $a_3 r^{-n}/N$ term reflects the role of the variance of the density estimates. For small values of r, the variance term dominates (7.52), and the observed error rates are significantly above the Bayes error. As r grows, however, the variance term decreases while the $a_1 r^2$ and $a_2 r^4$ terms play an increasingly significant role. Thus, for a typical plot of the observed error rate versus r, $\hat{\varepsilon}$ decreases for small values of r until a minimum point is reached, and then increases as the bias terms of the density estimates become more significant. This behavior is observed in Fig. 7-7 and is accurately predicted in the expression for $E\{\Delta\varepsilon\}$. It should be noted that although explicit evaluation of a_1 through a_3 is not possible in general, it is reasonable to expect that these constants are positive. It is certainly true that $E\{\Delta\varepsilon\}$ must be positive for any value of r, since the Bayes decision rule is optimal in terms of error performance.

Effect of Other Parameters in the Parzen Approach

With the bias expression of the estimated error, (7.52), we can now discuss the effect of important parameters such as N, t, and the shape of the kernel function.

Effect of sample size: The role of the sample size, N, in (7.52) is seen as a means of reducing the term corresponding to the variance of the density estimates. Hence the primary effect of the sample size is seen at the smaller values of r, where the a_3 term of (7.52) dominates. As r grows, and the a_1 and a_2 terms become dominant, changing the sample size has a decreasing effect on the resulting error rate. These observations were verified experimentally.

Experiment 5: Estimation of the Parzen error, H

Data: I-Λ (Normal, $n = 8$, $\varepsilon^* = 1.9\%$)

Sample size: $N_1 = N_2 = 25, 50, 100, 200$ (Design)

$N_1 = N_2 = 1000$ (Test)

No. of trial: $\tau = 10$

Kernel: Normal with $A_1 = I$, $A_2 = \Lambda$

Kernel size: $r = 0.6$–2.4

Threshold: $t = 0$

Results: Fig. 7-8

Figure 7-8 shows that, for each value of N, the Parzen classifier behaves as predicted by (7.52), decreasing to a minimum point, and then increasing as the biases of the density estimates become significant for larger values of r. Also note that the sample size plays its primary role for small values of r, where the a_3 term is most significant, and has almost no effect at the larger values of r.

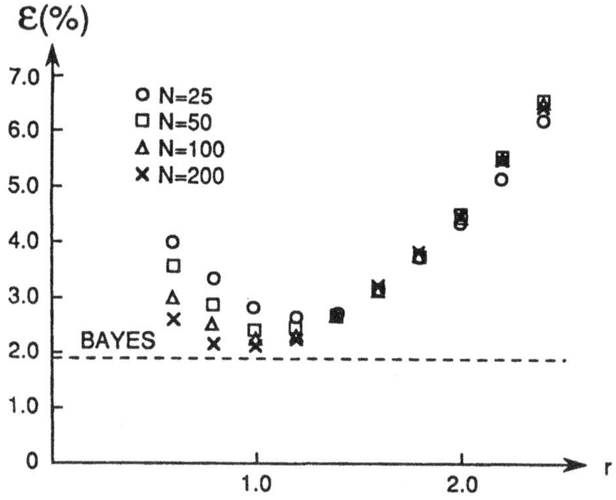

Fig. 7-8 Effect of sample size on Parzen classification.

In order to have $E\{\Delta\varepsilon\} \rightarrow 0$ as $N \rightarrow \infty$, the error expression implies that r must be chosen as a function of N such that $r \rightarrow 0$ and $r^{-n}/N \rightarrow 0$. This is the condition for the consistency of the Parzen density estimate [13], and validates the approximations which we used to obtain (7.52).

The optimal r may now be obtained from (7.52) by solving $\partial E\{\Delta\varepsilon\}/\partial r = 0$. However, $2a_1 r + 4a_2 r^3 - n a_3 r^{-n-1}/N = 0$ is not an easy equation to solve, and the a_i's are hard to obtain. Therefore, it seems better to find the minimum point of the error curve experimentally.

Effect of the decision threshold: Increasing the sample size, N, is seen as a means of improving the performance of the Parzen classifier at small values of r. As n becomes large, however, increasing the sample size becomes more and more futile, and the designer is forced to resort to using larger values of r. This results in a reduction of the variance of the density estimates, at the cost of accepting a larger bias. On the other hand, (7.50) and (7.51) indicate that $E\{\Delta\varepsilon\}$ of (7.45) could be reduced by selecting a proper threshold, Δt, and the kernel covariance matrix, A_i, which determines α_i [see (6.13)]. Here, we will study the effect of Δt, the adjustment of the decision threshold. Theoretically speaking, the optimal Δt can be found by minimizing $E\{\Delta\varepsilon\}$ with respect to Δt. However, in practice, it may not be possible to carry out the integration of (7.45) for such complicated functions of n variables.

The threshold for normal distributions: However, if the $p_i(X)$'s are normal distributions, the effect of the threshold can be analyzed as follows. Recall from (6.7) that the expected value of $\hat{\mathbf{p}}_i(X)$ in the Parzen density estimate is given by $p_i(X) * \kappa_i(X)$. When both $p_i(X)$ and $\kappa_i(X)$ are normal with covariance matrices Σ_i and $r^2\Sigma_i$ respectively, this convolution yields another normal density with mean M_i and covariance $(1+r^2)\Sigma_i$, as shown in (6.31). For larger values of r, the variance of $\hat{\mathbf{p}}_i(X)$ decreases, and the estimate approaches its expected value. Substituting the expected values into the estimated likelihood ratio, one obtains

$$-\ln\frac{\hat{p}_1(X)}{\hat{p}_2(X)} \cong \frac{1}{2}(X-M_1)^T\frac{\Sigma_1^{-1}}{1+r^2}(X-M_1) - \frac{1}{2}(X-M_2)\frac{\Sigma_2^{-1}}{1+r^2}(X-M_2)$$

$$+\frac{1}{2}\ln\frac{|\Sigma_1|}{|\Sigma_2|}\frac{(1+r^2)^n}{(1+r^2)^n} . \tag{7.53}$$

Except for the $1/(1+r^2)$ factors on the inverse covariance matrices, this expression is identical to the true likelihood ratio, $-\ln p_1(X)/p_2(X)$. In fact, the two may be related by

$$-\ln\frac{\hat{p}_1(X)}{\hat{p}_2(X)} \cong \frac{1}{1+r^2}[-\ln\frac{p_1(X)}{p_2(X)}] + \frac{1}{2}(\frac{r^2}{1+r^2})\ln\frac{|\Sigma_1|}{|\Sigma_2|} . \tag{7.54}$$

The true Bayes decision rule is given by $-\ln p_1(X)/p_2(X) \gtrless \ln P_1/P_2$. Using (7.54), an equivalent test may be expressed in terms of the estimated densities:

$$-\ln\frac{\hat{p}_1(X)}{\hat{p}_2(X)} \gtrless t , \tag{7.55}$$

where

$$t = \frac{1}{1+r^2}(\ln\frac{P_1}{P_2}) + \frac{1}{2}(\frac{r^2}{1+r^2})\ln\frac{|\Sigma_1|}{|\Sigma_2|} . \tag{7.56}$$

In all of our experiments, we assume $P_1 = P_2 = 0.5$, so the first term of (7.56) may be neglected. Equation (7.56) gives the appropriate threshold to use when the Parzen classifier with a normal kernel function is used on normal data. This indicates that t can be kept at zero if $\Sigma_1 = \Sigma_2$, but t should be adjusted for each value of r if $\Sigma_1 \neq \Sigma_2$. Otherwise, the classifier based on the Parzen density estimate classifies samples from the original normal distributions with an improper threshold. Figure 7-7 shows exactly that. In Fig. 7-7(a), with $\Sigma_1 = \Sigma_2 = I$, good performance was obtained even for large values of r without adjusting the threshold. When $|\Sigma_1|$ and $|\Sigma_2|$ are different, as with Data *I*-4*I* and *I*-Λ, the performance of the Parzen classifier degrades sharply for larger values of r without adjusting the threshold, as evidenced in Fig. 7-7(b) and (c). Figure 7-9 shows the behavior of the Parzen classifier for these three data sets with t given by (7.56) (Option 1). For low values of r, the classifiers give similar performance to that shown in Fig. 7-7, since the appropriate value of t given in (7.56) is close to zero. As r increases, good performance is obtained for all values of r. Thus, by allowing the decision threshold to vary with r, we are able to make the Parzen classifier much less sensitive to the value of r.

The threshold for non-normal distributions: The decision threshold as used here is simply a means of compensating for the bias inherent in the density estimation procedure. When the data and the kernel functions are normal, we have shown that the bias may be completely compensated for by choosing the value of t given in (7.56). In the non-normal case, we cannot hope to obtain a decision rule equivalent to the Bayes classifier simply by varying t. However, by choosing an appropriate value of t, we can hope to compensate, to some extent, for the bias of the density estimates in a region close to the Bayes decision boundary, providing significant improvement in the performance of the Parzen classifier. Therefore, procedures are needed for determining the best value of t to use when non-normal data is encountered. We present here four possible options. These options, and a brief discussion of their motivation, are given below.

Option 1: Use the threshold as calculated under the normality assumption (7.56). Since for larger values of r the decision rule is dominated by the functional form of the kernels, this procedure may give satisfactory results when the kernels are normal, even if the data is not normal.

Option 2: For each value of r, find the value of t which minimizes the leave-one-out error, and find the optimal t for the resubstitution error separately. This option involves finding and sorting the L and R estimates of the likelihood ratio, and incrementing the values of t through these sorted lists. The error rate used as the estimate is the minimum error rate obtained over all values of t.

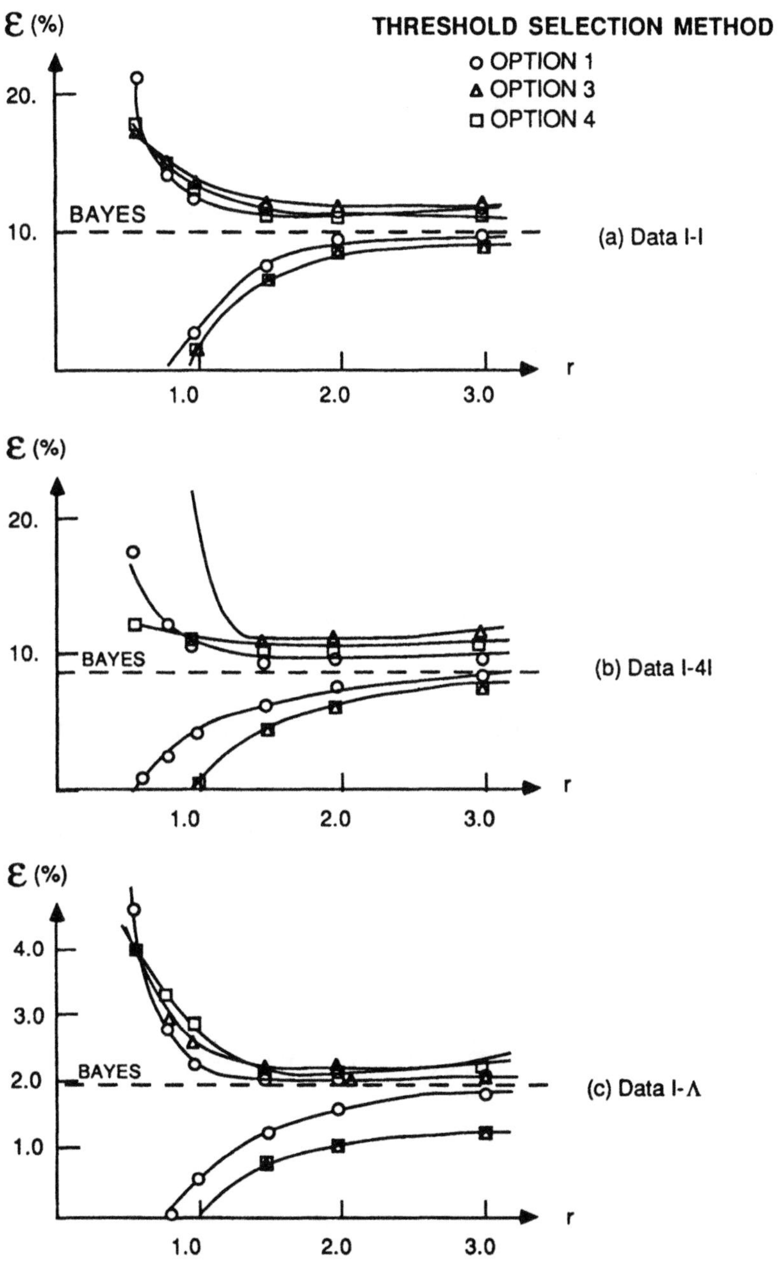

Fig. 7-9 Effect of threshold on Parzen classification.

This option makes no assumptions about the densities of the data or the shape of the kernel function. However, since the value of the threshold is customized to the data being tested, using this option will consistently bias the results low. This is not objectionable in the case of R errors, since the R error is used as a lower bound of the Bayes error. However, using this procedure can give erroneous results for the L error. Options 3 and 4 are designed to alleviate this problem.

Option 3: For each value of r, find the value of t which minimizes the R error, and then use this value of t to find the L error. Since the selection of the threshold has been isolated from the actual values of the L estimates of the likelihood ratio, using this method does in fact help reduce the bias encountered in Option 2. Experimental results will show that this method does give reliable results as long as r is relatively large. When r is small, however, the L estimates of the likelihood ratio are heavily biased as is seen in Fig. 7-9(b), and use of these estimates to determine the threshold may give far from optimal results. An advantage of this option is that it requires no more computation time than Option 2.

Option 4: Under this option, the R error is found exactly as in Option 2, by finding the value of t which minimizes the R error, and using this error rate. In order to find the L error, we use an L procedure to determine the value of t to use for each sample. Hence, under Option 4, we use a different threshold to test each of the N_1+N_2 samples, determining the threshold for each sample from the other N_1+N_2-1 samples in the design set. The exact procedure is as follows.

(1) Find the L density estimates at all samples,

$$\hat{p}_r(X_j^{(r)}) = \frac{1}{N_r-1}[\sum_{k=1}^{N_r} \kappa_r(X_j^{(r)}-X_k^{(r)}) - \kappa_r(X_j^{(r)}-X_j^{(r)})] ,$$

$$\hat{p}_r(X_j^{(i)}) = \frac{1}{N_r}\sum_{k=1}^{N_r} \kappa_r(X_j^{(i)}-X_k^{(r)}) \qquad i \neq r . \tag{7.57}$$

(2) To test sample $X_k^{(\ell)}$:

(a) Modify the density estimates by removing the effect of $X_k^{(\ell)}$ from all estimates

$$\tilde{p}_r(X_j^{(i)}) = \begin{cases} \hat{p}_r(X_j^{(i)}) & r \neq \ell \\ \dfrac{1}{N_r-2}[(N_r-1)\hat{p}_r(X_j^{(i)}) - \kappa_r(X_j^{(i)}-X_k^{(\ell)})] & r = \ell,\ i = \ell \\ \dfrac{1}{N_r-1}[N_r\hat{p}_r(X_j^{(i)}) - \kappa_r(X_j^{(i)}-X_k^{(\ell)})] & r = \ell,\ i \neq \ell\,. \end{cases} \tag{7.58}$$

Let us assume $\ell = 1$ for example. The test sample, $X_k^{(1)}$, was used to compute $\hat{p}_1(\cdot)$ as in (7.57), but never used for $\hat{p}_2(\cdot)$. Therefore, the removal of $X_k^{(1)}$ does not change $\hat{p}_2(\cdot)$ which is the case of the first line of (7.58). The removal of $X_k^{(1)}$, however, affects $\hat{p}_1(\cdot)$ in two different ways, depending on whether $\hat{p}_1(\cdot)$ is evaluated at $X_j^{(1)}$ or $X_j^{(2)}$. $\hat{p}_1(X_j^{(1)})$ is the summation of N_1-1 kernels excluding $\kappa_1(X_j^{(1)}-X_j^{(1)})$ as is seen in the first line of (7.57). Therefore, the further removal of $\kappa_1(X_j^{(1)}-X_k^{(1)})$ can be computed by the second line of (7.58). On the other hand, since $\hat{p}_1(X_j^{(2)})$ is the summation of N_1 kernels as in the second line of (7.57), the removal of $\kappa_1(X_j^{(2)}-X_k^{(1)})$ can be computed by the third line of (7.58). The case with $\ell = 2$ may be discussed similarly.

(b) Calculate the likelihood ratio estimates at all samples $X_j^{(i)} \neq X_k^{(\ell)}$ based on the modified density estimates.

$$\ell(X_j^{(i)}) = -\ln\frac{\tilde{p}_1(X_j^{(i)})}{\tilde{p}_2(X_j^{(i)})} \qquad X_j^{(i)} \neq X_k^{(\ell)}\,. \tag{7.59}$$

(c) Find the value of t which minimizes the error among the N_1+N_2-1 samples (without including $X_k^{(\ell)}$), under the decision rule

$$\ell(X_j^{(i)}) \underset{\omega_2}{\overset{\omega_1}{\gtrless}} t\,. \tag{7.60}$$

This is best accomplished by first sorting the likelihood ratio estimates $\ell(X_j^{(i)})$, and then incrementing the value of t through this list, keeping track of the number of errors for each value of t.

(d) Classify the sample $X_k^{(\ell)}$ using the original density estimates of (7.57) and the value of t found in Step (c):

$$\ell(X_k^{(\ell)}) = -\ln\frac{\hat{p}_1(X_k^{(\ell)})}{\hat{p}_2(X_k^{(\ell)})} \underset{\omega_2}{\overset{\omega_1}{\gtrless}} t \,. \tag{7.61}$$

Count an error if the decided class is not ω_ℓ.

(3) Repeat Step (2) for each sample, counting the resulting number of classification errors.

Although this procedure is by far the most complex computationally, it is the only true L procedure, and gives the most reliable results, particularly for small values of r.

Figure 7-9 shows the results of applying Options 1, 3, and 4 to the three test cases.

Experiment 6: Estimation of the Parzen error, L and R
Same as Experiment 4 except
Threshold: t - Options 1, 3, 4
Results: Fig. 7-9 [12]

In all of the experiments, using the threshold calculated under the normality assumption (Option 1) gave the best performance. This was expected, since both the data and the kernel function are, in fact, normal. It is notable, however, that the use of Option 4 gave performance nearly equal to that of Option 1. Option 3 gave good results also, but performance degraded sharply for small r, particularly for Data *I-4I*, where the covariance determinants are extremely different.

Non-normal example: It is of interest to examine the behavior of the Parzen classifier in a non-normal case where the quadratic classifier is no longer the Bayes classifier. Toward this end, the following experiment was conducted.

Experiment 7: Estimation of the Parzen error, L and R

Data: $p_1(X) = 0.5N_X(M_1,I)+0.5N_X(M_2,I)$

$p_2(X) = 0.5N_X(M_3,I)+0.5N_X(M_4,I)$

$M_1 = [00\dots 0]^T$, $M_2 = [6.58\ 0\dots 0]^T$

$M_3 = [3.29\ 0\dots 0]^T$, $M_4 = [9.87\ 0\dots 0]^T$

$n = 8$, $\varepsilon^* = 7.5\%$

Sample size: $N_1 = N_2 = 100$

No. of trials: $\tau = 10$

Kernel: Normal with $A_1 = A_2 = I$

Kernel size: 0.6-6.0

Threshold: Option 4

Results: Fig. 7-10 [12]

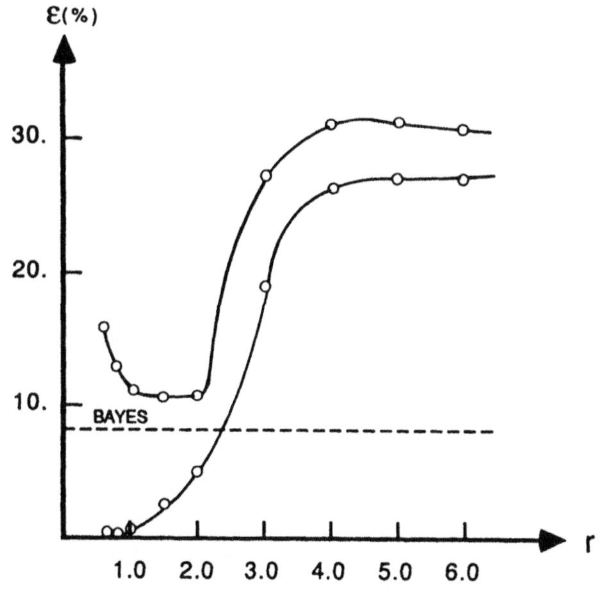

Fig. 7-10 Parzen error for a non-normal test set.

Figure 7-10 shows the results for this experiment. With a moderate value of r, the Bayes error of 7.5% is bounded properly, when the Parzen density estimate for each class represents the given two-modal distribution. On the other hand, as r grows, the density estimate converges to the kernel function itself. Thus, with normal kernels, the likelihood ratio of the estimated densities becomes a quadratic classifier, resulting in the error much higher than the Bayes error. As the result, the curves of Fig. 7-10 is significantly different from the ones of Fig. 7-9, indicating that the selection of a proper r for non-normal cases could be more critical than the one for normal cases. Nevertheless, the Parzen classification does provide usable bounds on the Bayes error.

Selection of the kernel shape: An alternative way of compensating for the biases of the error estimate is the selection of the kernel shape. Equations (7.50) and (7.51) suggest that, if the kernel covariances are selected such that $\alpha_1(X) = \alpha_2(X)$, all terms which are independent of the sample size may be eliminated from the bias expression. Hence, we must find positive definite matrices A_1 and A_2 such that, from (6.13),

$$\mathrm{tr}\left\{ \frac{\nabla^2 p_1(X)}{p_1(X)} A_1 \right\} = \mathrm{tr}\left\{ \frac{\nabla^2 p_2(X)}{p_2(X)} A_2 \right\} . \tag{7.62}$$

In general, $\nabla^2 p_i(X)/p_i(X)$'s are hard to obtain. However, when $p_i(X)$ is normal,

$$\frac{\nabla^2 p_i(X)}{p_i(X)} = \Sigma_i^{-1}(X-M_i)(X-M_i)^T\Sigma_i^{-1} - \Sigma_i^{-1} . \tag{7.63}$$

Therefore, we may obtain a solution of (7.62) in terms of these expected vectors and covariance matrices.

Before going to the general solution of (7.62), let us look at the simplest case, where $\Sigma_1 = \Sigma_2 = \Sigma$ and $A_1 = A_2 = \Sigma$. Using (7.63), (7.62) becomes

$$(X-M_1)^T\Sigma^{-1}(X-M_1) = (X-M_2)^T\Sigma^{-1}(X-M_2) \tag{7.64}$$

which is satisfied by the X's located on the Bayes boundary. On the other hand, since the integration of (7.45) with respect to ω results in $\int [E\{\Delta \mathbf{h}\}\delta(h) + (1/2)E\{\Delta \mathbf{h}^2\}\, d\delta(h)/dh]\, (P_1p_1 - P_2p_2)dX$, the bias is generated only by $E\{\Delta \mathbf{h}(X)\}$ and $E\{\Delta \mathbf{h}^2(X)\}$ on the boundary. Therefore, the selection of $A_1 = A_2 = \Sigma$ seems to be a reasonable choice. Indeed, the error curve of Fig. 7-7(a) shows little bias for large r, without adjusting the threshold.

The general solution of (7.62) is very hard to obtain. However, since (7.62) is a scaler equation, there are many possible solutions. Let us select a solution of the form

$$A_i = \Sigma_i + \gamma_i (X-M_i)(X-M_i)^T , \tag{7.65}$$

where γ_i is a constant to be determined by solving (7.62). Substituting (7.63) and (7.65) into (7.62) and simplifying give

$$[d_1^2(X,M_1)-1][1+\gamma_1 d_1^2(X,M_1)] = [d_2^2(X,M_2)-1][1+\gamma_2 d_2^2(X,M_2)] , \tag{7.66}$$

where $d_i^2(X,M_i) = (X-M_i)^T \Sigma_i^{-1} (X-M_i)$. If we could select $\gamma_i d_i^2(X,M_i) = -1$, (7.66) is satisfied. However, since $(X-M_i)^T A_i^{-1} (X-M_i) = d_i^2(X,M_i)/[1+\gamma_i d_i^2(X,M_i)]$ for A_i of (7.65) from (2.160), $\gamma_i d_i^2(X,M_i) > -1$ must be satisfied for A_i to be positive definite. A simple compromise to overcome this inconsistency is to select a number slightly larger than -1 for $\gamma_i d_i^2(X,M_i)$. This makes $\alpha_1(X) - \alpha_2(X)$ small, although not zero. This selection of the kernel covariance was tested in the following experiment.

Experiment 8: Estimation of the Parzen error, H

Data: *I-I*, *I-4I*, *I-Λ* (Normal, $n = 8$)

Sample size: $N_1 = N_2 = 100$ (Design)

$N_1 = N_2 = 1000$ (Test)

Kernel: Normal, A_i of (7.65), $\gamma_i d_i^2 = -0.8$

Kernel size: $r = 0.6$–2.4

Threshold: $t = 0$

Results: Fig. 7-11

The optimal kernels given in (7.65) were scaled to satisfy $|A_i| = |\Sigma_i|$, allowing direct comparison with the results obtained using the more conventional kernel $A_i = \Sigma_i$ (also shown in Fig. 7-11). The results for Data *I-4I* and *I-Λ* indicate that although the estimates seem less stable at smaller values of r, as r grows the results using (7.65) remain close to the Bayes error while the results using $A_i = \Sigma_i$ degrade rapidly. This implies that the r^2 and r^4 terms of (7.50) and (7.51) have been effectively reduced. Note that for Data *I-I* (Fig. 7-11(a)), the distributions were chosen so that $\alpha_1(X) = \alpha_2(X)$ on the Bayes decision boundary. As a result the r^2 and r^4 terms of (7.50) and (7.51) are already zero, and no improvement is observed by changing the kernel. These experimental results indicate the potential importance of the kernel covariance in designing Parzen classifiers.

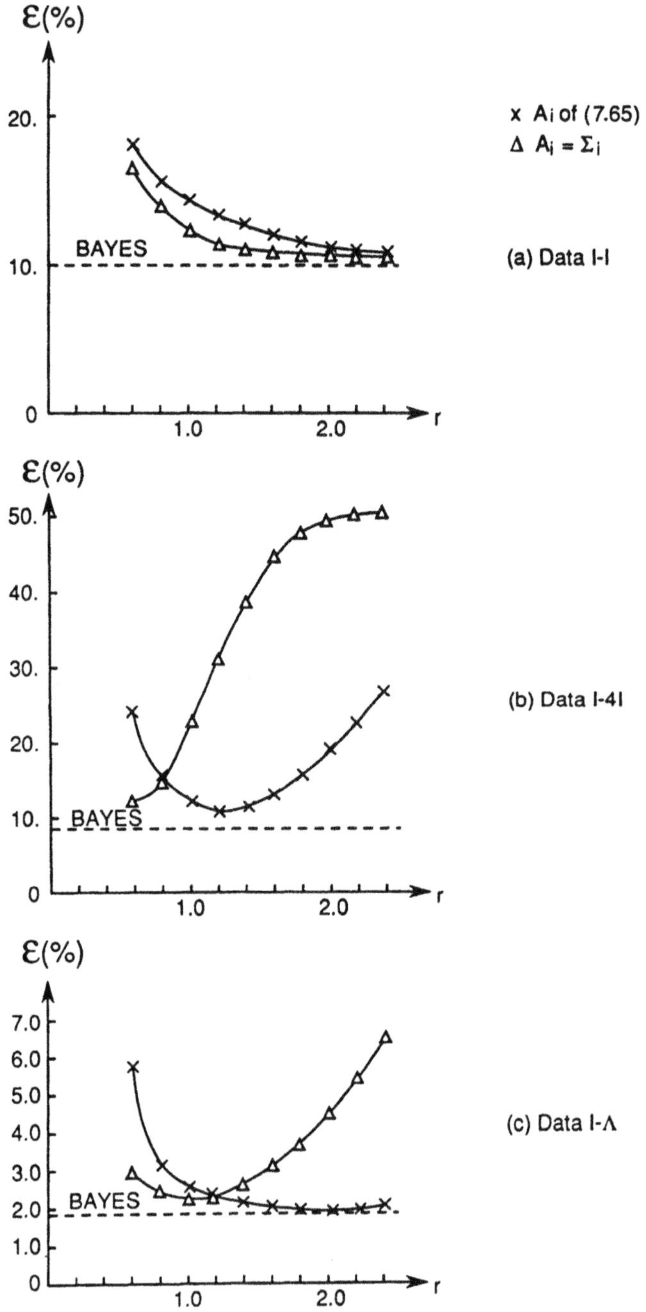

Fig. 7-11 Effect of kernel functions on Parzen classification.

Estimated kernel covariance: So far, we have assumed that the class covariance matrices are known and given. However, is practice, these covariance matrices are unknown and must be estimated from a finite number of samples. This may lead to an optimistically biased error estimate. For example, in Data RADAR, upper and lower bounds of the Bayes error are estimated by the L and R methods. If 720 samples per class are used in this operation with the class covariance matrices estimated from 8800 samples per class, the resulting upper and lower bounds are 17.8% and 16.2% respectively. On the other hand, if the same 720 samples are used to estimate the covariance matrices, bounds of 8.4% and 7.1% result. These bounds are further lowered to 5.2% and 3.8%, when 360 samples per class are used in both the error estimation procedure and the covariance estimation. These results demonstrate that the upper bound of the Bayes error in the L method may be severely biased. Thus, the estimate may no longer give the upper bound of the Bayes error, if the class covariances are estimated from the same data used to form the error estimates. If possible, then, to avoid this bias, one should estimate the class covariances using a large number of independent samples. Once the covariances are estimated accurately, we may use a relatively small sample size for the nonparametric procedures to produce reliable results. However, if additional samples for estimation of the covariance matrices are not available, in order to obtain reliable upper bounds on the Bayes error, one must use leave-one-out type estimates of the kernel covariances when forming the L error estimate. This implies the use of a different covariance matrix for each sample being tested.

In order to show how the kernel covariance can be estimated by the L method, let us study the kernel function of (6.3). In Parzen error estimation, this kernel function is inserted into (7.2) and (7.3) to test a sample $X_k^{(1)}$ from ω_1 in the L method. Using $A_i = \Sigma_i$, which is a good choice in many applications, we need to compute $|\Sigma_i|$ and $d_i^2(X_k^{(1)},X_j^{(i)}) = (X_k^{(1)}-X_j^{(i)})^T \Sigma_i^{-1}(X_k^{(1)}-X_j^{(i)})$. When the covariance matrix Σ_i is not known and needs to be estimated from $X_1^{(i)},\ldots,X_{N_i}^{(i)}$, Σ_i is replaced by its estimate, $\hat{\Sigma}_i$, and subsequently d_i^2 by $\hat{d}_i^2(X_k^{(1)},X_j^{(i)}) = (X_k^{(1)}-X_j^{(i)})^T \hat{\Sigma}_i^{-1}(X_k^{(1)}-X_j^{(i)})$. The L type estimate of the kernel covariance means that, when $X_k^{(1)}$ is tested, $X_k^{(1)}$ must be excluded from the sample set used to estimate Σ_1. Letting $\hat{\Sigma}_{1k}$ be the resulting estimate, $\hat{\Sigma}_1$ and $\hat{d}_1^2$ now must be replaced by $\hat{\Sigma}_{1k}$ and $\hat{d}_{1k}^2$, while $\hat{\Sigma}_2$ and $\hat{d}_2^2$ are kept unchanged. When the sample covariance of (5.9) is used, $|\hat{\Sigma}_{1k}|$ and $\hat{d}_{1k}^2$ can be easily computed from (5.127) and (5.125), resulting in

$$|\hat{\Sigma}_{1k}| = (\frac{N_1-1}{N_1-2})^n |\hat{\Sigma}_1| \left[1 - \frac{N_1}{(N_1-1)^2}\hat{d}_1^2(X_k^{(1)},\hat{M}_1)\right], \tag{7.67}$$

$$\hat{\Sigma}_{1k}^{-1} = (\frac{N_1-2}{N_1-1})\left[\hat{\Sigma}_1^{-1} + \frac{N_1\hat{\Sigma}_1^{-1}(X_k^{(1)}-\hat{M}_1)(X_k^{(1)}-\hat{M}_1)^T\hat{\Sigma}_1^{-1}}{(N_1-1)^2 - N_1\hat{d}_1^2(X_k^{(1)},\hat{M}_1)}\right]. \tag{7.68}$$

Therefore,

$$\hat{d}_{1k}^2(X_k^{(1)},X_j^{(1)}) = (\frac{N_1-2}{N_1-1})\left[\hat{d}_1^2(X_k^{(1)},X_j^{(1)}) + \frac{N_1[(X_k^{(1)}-X_j^{(1)})^T\hat{\Sigma}_1^{-1}(X_k^{(1)}-\hat{M}_1)]^2}{(N_1-1)^2 - N_1\hat{d}_1^2(X_k^{(1)},\hat{M}_1)}\right]$$

$$= (\frac{N_1-2}{N_1-1})\left[\hat{d}_1^2(X_k^{(1)},X_j^{(1)}) + \frac{N_1[\hat{d}_1^2(X_j^{(1)},\hat{M}_1) - \hat{d}_1^2(X_k^{(1)},\hat{M}_1) - \hat{d}_1^2(X_k^{(1)},X_j^{(1)})]^2}{4[(N_1-1)^2 - N_1\hat{d}_1^2(X_k^{(1)},\hat{M}_1)]}\right]. \tag{7.69}$$

Equations (7.67) and (7.69) indicate that, once $\hat{d}_1^2(X_j^{(1)},\hat{M}_1)$ ($j = 1, \ldots, N_1$) are computed and stored, $|\hat{\Sigma}_{1k}|$ and $\hat{d}_{1k}^2(X_k^{(1)},X_j^{(1)})$ can be obtained from $|\hat{\Sigma}_1|$ and $\hat{d}_1^2(X_k^{(1)},X_j^{(1)})$ by scaler computations. This computation time is negligibly small compared with the time needed to compute $\hat{d}_1^2(X_k^{(1)},X_j^{(1)})$, which includes vector and matrix manipulations. The computation of $|\hat{\Sigma}_{2k}|$ and $\hat{d}_{2k}^2(X_k^{(2)},X_j^{(2)})$ when testing $X_k^{(2)}$ from ω_2 is similar.

In order to confirm the validity of the use of the L type covariance for the kernel function, the following experiments were conducted.

Experiment 9: Estimation of the Parzen error, L and R

Data: *I-I*, *I-4I*, *I-Λ* (Normal, $n = 8$)

Sample size: $N_1 = N_2 = 100$

No. of trials: $\tau = 10$

Kernel: $A_i = \Sigma_i$ (True), $A_i = \hat{\Sigma}_{ik}$ (Estimated)

Kernel size: $r = 1.5$

Threshold: Option 4

Results: Table 7-3(a) [14]

Comparison of the performances when the true and estimated covariances are

TABLE 7-3

EFFECT OF ESTIMATED COVARIANCE MATRICES
FOR THE PARZEN APPROACH

Data	Bayes Error (%)	Covariance Used	Leave-one-out Error (%)	σ_L (%)	Resubstitution Error (%)	σ_R (%)
I-I	10	True	11.0	1.8	6.4	1.3
		Estimated	12.6	2.6	5.8	1.3
I-4I	9	True	10.6	2.9	4.8	1.0
		Estimated	11.0	3.2	4.5	1.3
I-Λ	1.9	True	2.0	1.2	1.1	0.9
		Estimated	2.3	0.9	0.8	0.6

(a) Standard data sets

Case	Cov. used	N_{cov}	N	Leave-one-out (%)	Resubstitution (%)
1	$\hat{\Sigma}_i$	8800	720	17.8	16.2
		8800	360	19.5	15.6
2	$\hat{\Sigma}_{ik}(L)$	720	720	23.3	7.1
		360	360	27.4	3.8
3	$\hat{\Sigma}_i$	720	720	8.4	7.1
		360	360	5.2	3.8

(b) Data RADAR

used shows that the estimated covariance always gives a larger upper bound and smaller lower bound than the true covariance, although the differences are small. The standard deviations of 10 trials, σ_L and σ_R, are also presented in Table 7-3.

Experiment 10: Estimation of the Parzen error, L and R

Data: RADAR (Real data, $n = 66$, $\varepsilon^* =$ unknown)

Sample size: $N_1 = N_2 = 720, 360$

No. of trials: $\tau = 1$

Kernel: $A_i = \hat{\Sigma}_i$ for $N_{cov} = 8800$ (Case 1)

$A_i = \hat{\Sigma}_{ik}$ for $N_{cov} = 720, 360$ (Case 2)

$A_i = \hat{\Sigma}_i$ for $N_{cov} = 720, 360$ (Case 3)

N_{cov} - No. of samples to estimate Σ

Kernel size: $r = 9.0$

Threshold: Option 4

Results: Table 7-3(b) [14]

This experiment demonstrates more clearly the importance of the selection of the kernel covariance. Note that even as the sample size used to estimate the covariance matrices becomes small, the L error rates continue to provide reasonable and consistent bounds in Case 2 of Table 7-3(b). This is in contrast to the results given in Case 3 in which the estimated covariances are blindly used without employing the L type covariance. As expected, the bounds become worse as the sample sizes decrease.

Effect of m: Finally, in kernel selection, we need to decide which is better, a normal or uniform kernel. More generally, we may address the selection of m in (6.3). The results using normal kernels ($m = 1$) are shown in Fig. 7-12, in which the upper bounds of the Bayes error are observed to be excellent, but the lower bounds seem much too conservative. This tends to indicate that the normal kernel function places too much weight on the sample being tested in the R error estimate. Hence, one possible approach to improving the lower bound of the Parzen estimate is to use a non-normal kernel function which places less weight on the test sample and more weight on the neighboring samples. The uniform kernel function, with constant value inside a specified region, is one such kernel function. However, if a uniform kernel function is employed, one must decide which decision be made when the density estimates from the two classes are equal, making the Parzen procedure even more complex. A smooth transition from a normal kernel to a uniform kernel may be obtained by using the kernel function of (6.3) and changing m. The parameter m determines the rate at which the kernel function drops off. For $m = 1$, (6.3) reduces to a simple normal kernel. As m becomes large, (6.3)

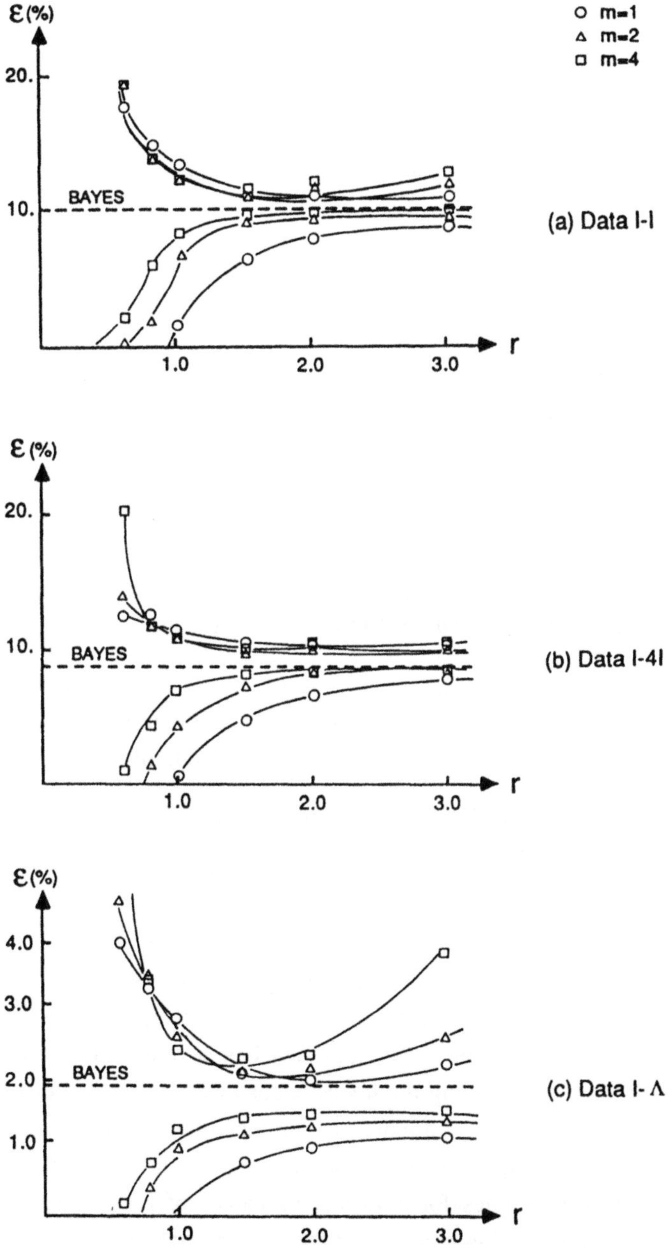

Fig. 7-12 Effect of kernel shape on Parzen classification.

approaches a uniform (hyperelliptical) kernel, always with a smooth roll-off (for finite m), and always with covariance $r^2 A_i$. Using this kernel allows us to use kernel functions close to the uniform kernel, without having to worry about the problem of equal density estimates.

Figure 7-12 shows the performance of the Parzen estimates with $m = 1$ (normal kernel), 2, and 4.

Experiment 11: Estimation of the Parzen error, L and R
Same as Experiment 4 except
Kernel: (6.3), $m = 1, 2, 4$
Threshold: Option 4
Results: Fig. 7-12 [12]

In all cases, using higher values of m (more uniform-like kernel functions) does improve the lower bound while having little effect on the upper bounds of the error.

Estimation of the Bayes Error in the Parzen Approach

So far, we have discussed how to obtain the upper and lower bounds of the Bayes error. In this section, we address the estimation of the Bayes error itself. From (7.52), we can write the expected error rate in terms of r and N as

$$E\{\hat{\varepsilon}\} \cong \varepsilon^* + a_1 r^2 + a_2 r^4 + a_3 r^{-n}/N \, . \tag{7.70}$$

Here, the constants a_1, a_2, a_3, and the desired value of ε^* are unknown and must be determined experimentally. An estimate of ε^* may be obtained by observing the Parzen error rate, $\hat{\varepsilon}$, for a variety of values of r, and finding the set of constants which best fit the experimental results. Any data fitting technique could be used. However, the linear least-square approach is straightforward and easy to implement. This approach has several intuitive advantages over the procedure of accepting the lowest error rate over the various values of r. First, it provides a direct estimate of ε^* rather than an upper bound on the value. Another advantage is that this procedure provides a means of combining the observed error rates for a variety of values of r. Hence, we may be utilizing certain information concerning the higher order properties of the distributions which is ignored by the previous procedures.

As mentioned earlier, it is reasonable to expect that all four of the constants in (7.70) are positive, since the observed error must remain above ε^* for any value of r. In order to ensure stability in the estimate of ε^*, it is advisable to restrict the constants to positive values during the curve fit procedure.

The result of this procedure is illustrated in Fig. 7-13.

Experiment 12: Estimation of the Bayes error, L
Same as Experiment 4 except
Data: I-Λ (Normal, $n = 8$, $\varepsilon^* = 1.9\%$)
Results: Fig. 7-13

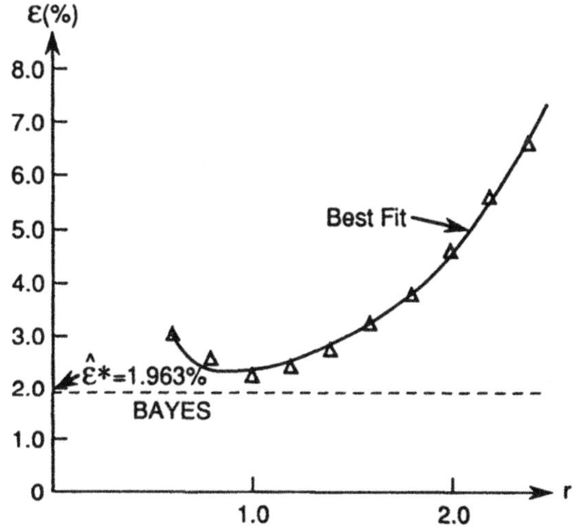

Fig. 7-13 Estimation of the Bayes error.

The best fit of the form given in (7.70) is drawn as a solid line. The resulting estimate of the Bayes error was 1.96% which is extremely close to the true Bayes error of 1.9%. Note the closeness of the fit, indicating that the observed error rates are in fact following the trends predicted.

In order for (7.70) to be valid, the decision threshold t should be selected so that the estimated Bayes decision boundary is relatively close to the actual Bayes decision boundary. As shown in the threshold adjustment section, the optimal value of t may be highly dependent on the value of r, particularly if the covariance determinants for the two classes are very different. Generally, it is advisable to evaluate the Parzen classifier for a variety of values of t, and then apply the curve fit procedure for each value of t. This results in a negligible increase of the computational burden, since the bulk of the time is spent calculating the density estimates, and only a very small percentage comparing the estimates to the thresholds.

Experiment 13: Estimation of the Bayes error, L
Same as Experiment 12 except
Data: I-I, I-$4I$, I-Λ (Normal, $n = 8$)
Threshold: t of (7.56), $r = 0.6$–2.4 in steps of 0.2
Results: Table 7-4

TABLE 7-4

ESTIMATION OF THE BAYES ERROR FOR VARIOUS VALUES OF t

Date I-I ($\varepsilon^* = 10\%$)		Data I-$4I$ ($\varepsilon^* = 9\%$)		Data I-Λ ($\varepsilon^* = 1.9\%$)	
t	$\hat{\varepsilon}^*$ (%)	t	$\hat{\varepsilon}^*$ (%)	t	$\hat{\varepsilon}^*$ (%)
0	11.0	-1.47	3.3	-.252	1.99
		-2.16	7.8	-.373	1.93
		-2.77	8.9	-.477	1.93
		-3.27	9.8	-.563	1.99
		-3.67	9.5	-.632	2.05
		-4.00	9.7	-.686	2.05
		-4.24	9.1	-.729	2.07
		-4.43	11.5	-.764	2.08
		-4.59	10.0	-.791	2.11
		-4.72	9.1	-.813	2.12

For Data I-I, $t = 0$ is the optimal choice for any value of r, and hence only one error estimate ($\hat{\varepsilon}^* = 11.0\%$) is listed. Comparison of the estimated error rates in Table 7-4 with the true error rates indicates that the procedure is providing reasonable estimates of the Bayes error for a wide range of decision thresholds. A particularly bad estimate is obtained for Data I-$4I$ with $t > -2$. Data I-$4I$ is the case in which the covariance determinants of the two classes are very different. Also, it is observed in Fig. 7-7(b) that the error curve increases very quickly. With t ranging from -3 to -5, the error curve becomes more like the one of Fig. 7-7(c), having a down-slope, a minimum at a higher r, and a slower up-slope. This means that smaller biases exist in a wider range of r and that (7.70) fits the actual errors more accurately.

kNN Approach

So far, we have discussed error estimation based on the Parzen density estimate. Similarly, we can develop the argument using the *kNN* density estimation. These two approaches are closely related in all aspects of the error estimation problem, and give similar results. In this section, the *kNN* approach will be presented. However, in order to avoid lengthy duplication, our discussion will be limited.

Bias of the *kNN* error: When the *kNN* density estimate $\hat{\mathbf{p}}_i(X) = (k-1)/N\mathbf{v}_i(X)$ is used, $E\{\hat{\mathbf{p}}_i(X)\}$ and $MSE\{\hat{\mathbf{p}}_i(X)\}$ are available in (6.91) and (6.94) respectively. Therefore, substituting $E\{\Delta\mathbf{p}_i(X)\} = E\{\hat{\mathbf{p}}_i(X)\} - p_i(X)$, and $E\{\Delta\mathbf{p}_i^2(X)\} = E\{[\hat{\mathbf{p}}_i(X) - p_i(X)]^2\} = MSE\{\hat{\mathbf{p}}_i(X)\}$ into (7.46) and (7.47),

$$E\{\Delta\mathbf{h}(X)\} \cong (\gamma_2 - \gamma_1)\left(\frac{k}{N}\right)^{2/n} + \frac{1}{2}(\gamma_1^2 - \gamma_2^2)\left(\frac{k}{N}\right)^{4/n} - \Delta t\ , \tag{7.71}$$

$$E\{\Delta\mathbf{h}^2(X)\} \cong \frac{2}{k} + \Delta t^2 - 2\Delta t\,(\gamma_2 - \gamma_1)\left(\frac{k}{N}\right)^{2/n}$$
$$+ [(\gamma_1 - \gamma_2)^2 - \Delta t\,(\gamma_1^2 - \gamma_2^2)]\left(\frac{k}{N}\right)^{4/n}, \tag{7.72}$$

where

$$\gamma_i(X) = \frac{1}{2}\alpha_i(X)\, r^2\, (v_i p_i)^{-2/n}\ . \tag{7.73}$$

Substituting (7.71) and (7.72) into (7.45) and carring out the integration

$$E\{\Delta\varepsilon\} \cong b_1 \frac{1}{k} + b_2 \left(\frac{k}{N}\right)^{2/n} + b_3 \left(\frac{k}{N}\right)^{4/n} , \tag{7.74}$$

where the b_i's are constant.

Several conclusions can be drawn from (7.74). In order to make $E\{\Delta\varepsilon\} \to 0$, two conditions, $k \to \infty$ and $k/N \to 0$ as $N \to \infty$, must be satisfied. These conditions are identical to the conditions required for asymptotic consistency of the *kNN* density estimate [15]. Since $k/N \cong p_i v_i$, k/N is proportional to r^n, and therefore $(k/N)^{2/n}$ is proportional to r^2. That is, $E\{\Delta\varepsilon\} \cong b_1/k + b_2' r^2 + b_3' r^4$ where b_2' and b_3' are constants different from b_2 and b_3. We may compare this with (7.52), $E\{\Delta\varepsilon\}$ of the Parzen approach. In both cases, we have terms with r^2 and r^4 which are generated by the bias of the density estimate. However, the bias of the *kNN* error does not have an r^{-n}/N term. This is due to the fact that (7.74) describes the behavior of the *kNN* error only for large values of k. A series of approximations based on $N >> k >> 1$ was applied to obtain $E\{\hat{\mathbf{p}}_i(X)\}$ and $MSE\{\hat{\mathbf{p}}_i(X)\}$. If the analysis of the *kNN* error for small values of k is needed, more complicated expressions must be used. In addition to the r^2 and r^4 terms, the *kNN* bias has a constant term b_1/k, which the Parzen bias does not have. This may be related to the fact that the voting *kNN* error with a finite k does not converge to the Bayes error, even under asymptotic conditions. This term can be reduced only by increasing k.

Effect of parameters: In the Parzen approach, the most effective way to reduce the bias of the error estimate is to adjust the threshold properly. Also, in order to assure that the L method gives an upper bound of the Bayes error, the kernel covariance matrix must be estimated either from a large number of independent samples or by an L type estimation technique.

In terms of threshold selection, the method developed for the Parzen approach may be directly applied to the *kNN* approach. The *kNN* density estimates are known to be biased when the size of the design set is limited, and, by choosing an appropriate threshold, one might hope to reduce or eliminate the effect of that bias when classification is performed. There are no usable expressions for t even in the normal case. However, each of the non-normal methods for threshold selection (Options 2, 3, and 4) are directly applicable to the *kNN* problem.

One comment is in order regarding the application of Option 4 to *kNN* estimation. In Step 2 of Option 4 of the Parzen case, it is fairly simple to remove the effect of $X_k^{(\ell)}$ (the test sample) from the density estimates of all the other samples using (7.58). There is no analogous simple modification in the *kNN* case. In order to remove the effect of $X_k^{(\ell)}$ from all other density estimates, one must remove $X_k^{(\ell)}$ from the table of nearest neighbors, rearrange the *NN* table, and recalculate all of the density estimates. This procedure would have to be repeated to test each of the samples in the design set, resulting in a fairly drastic increase in computation time. In practice, modifying each of the density estimates to remove the effect of $X_k^{(\ell)}$ is not nearly as important as finding the threshold by minimizing the error among the remaining $N_1 + N_2 - 1$ samples. That is, modifying the estimates of the likelihood ratios in Step 2 is not necessary to get reliable results - we do it in the Parzen case primarily because it is easy. Thus for *kNN* estimation, Step 2 of Option 4 involves finding and sorting $\ell(X_j^{(i)})$ for all samples $X_j^{(i)} \neq X_k^{(\ell)}$, finding the value of t which minimizes the error among these N_1+N_2-1 samples, and using this value of t to classify $X_k^{(\ell)}$.

Figure 7-14 shows the results of applying Option 4 to the *kNN* estimation problem. For comparison, the results obtained using $t = 0$ are also shown.

Experiment 14: Estimation of the *kNN* error, L and R

Same as Experiment 4, except
Metric: $A_1 = \Sigma_1$ and $A_2 = \Sigma_2$ (Instead of kernel)
No. of neighbors: $k = 1{-}30$ (Instead of kernel size)
Threshold: Option 4 and $t = 0$
Results: Fig. 7-14 [12]

As in the Parzen case, the threshold plays its most significant role when the covariances of the data are different, and particularly when the covariance determinants are different. In Data *I-I*, the bias of the density estimates for ω_1 and ω_2 are nearly equal near the Bayes decision boundary, and hence good results are obtained without adjusting the threshold. However, for Data *I-4I* and *I-*Λ, the *kNN* errors are heavily biased and unusable without adjusting the threshold.

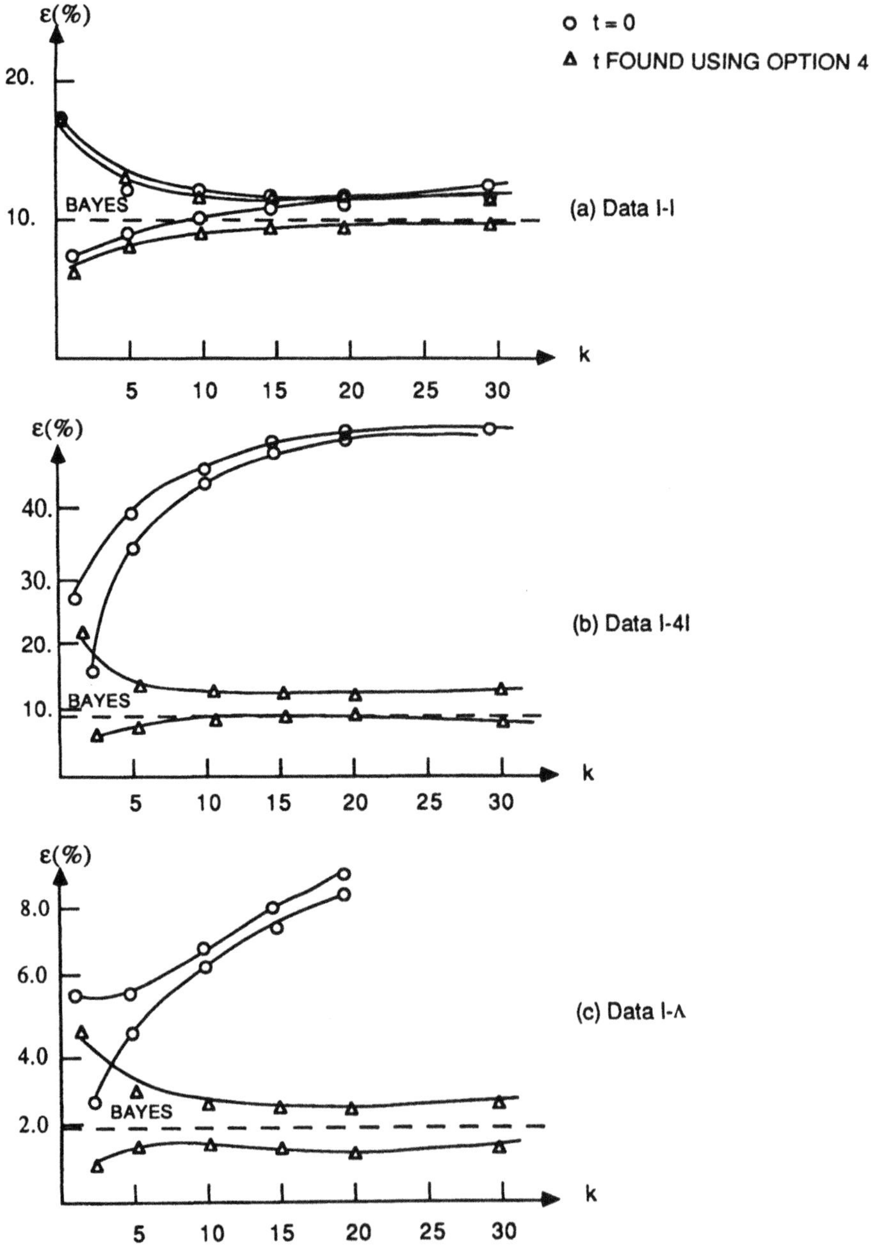

Fig. 7-14 Effect of threshold on *kNN* classification.

As far as the L type estimation of the kernel covariance matrix is concerned, the same procedure used in the Parzen approach can be applied to the *kNN* approach.

Experiment 15: Estimation of the *kNN* error, L and R

Same as Experiment 9, except

No. of neighbors: $k = 10$

Results: Table 7-5(a) [14]

Experiment 16: Estimation of the *kNN* error, L and R

Same as Experiment 10, except

No. of neighbors: $k = 10$

Results: Table 7-5(b) [14]

The conclusions from these experiments are similar to the ones from Experiments 9 and 10.

7.5 Miscellaneous Topics in the *kNN* Approach

In this section, miscellaneous topics related to the *kNN* approach, which were not discussed in the previous sections, will be studied. They are the error control problem (the Neyman-Pearson and minimax tests), data display, procedures to save computational time, and the procedure to reduce the classification error.

Two-Dimensional Data Display

Error control: So far, we have discussed the Bayes classifier for minimum error by using the *kNN* approach. However, the discussion can be easily extended to other hypothesis tests such as the Bayes classifier for minimum cost, the Neyman—Pearson and minimax tests, as long as the volumetric *kNN* is used. As (7.5) indicates, in the likelihood ratio test of the *kNN* approach, two distances, $d_1(X^{(1)}_{k_1NN},X)$ and $d_2(X^{(2)}_{k_2NN},X)$, are measured, and their ratio is compared with a threshold as

$$\frac{d_2(X^{(2)}_{k_2NN},X)}{d_1(X^{(1)}_{k_1NN},X)} \underset{\omega_2}{\overset{\omega_1}{\lessgtr}} e^{-t/n} \left\{ \frac{(k_2-1)N_1 |\Sigma_1|^{1/2}}{(k_1-1)N_2 |\Sigma_2|^{1/2}} \right\}^{1/n} , \tag{7.75}$$

where t must be determined according to which test is performed. For example, t is selected to achieve $\varepsilon_2 = \varepsilon_0$ (ε_0: a preassigned value) for the Neyman-Pearson test, and $\varepsilon_1 = \varepsilon_2$ for the minimax test.

TABLE 7-5

EFFECT OF ESTIMATED COVARIANCE MATRICES FOR THE 10*NN* APPROACH

Data	Bayes Error (%)	Covariance Used	Leave-one-out Error (%)	σ_L (%)	Resubstitution Error (%)	σ_R (%)
I-I	10	True	11.9	2.2	8.7	1.8
		Estimated	13.6	3.2	8.2	1.8
I-4I	9	True	13.6	2.8	9.2	2.6
		Estimated	17.7	5.0	9.0	2.1
I-Λ	1.9	True	2.7	1.0	1.4	0.7
		Estimated	3.2	1.3	1.3	0.6

(a) Standard data sets

Case	Cov used	N_{cov}	N	Leave-one-out (%)	Resubstitution (%)
1	$\hat{\Sigma}_i$	8800	720	22.5	17.8
		8800	360	22.1	18.6
2	$\hat{\Sigma}_{ik}(L)$	720	720	24.3	10.0
		360	360	29.5	6.3
3	$\hat{\Sigma}_i$	720	720	11.5	10.0
		360	360	7.9	6.3

(b) Data RADAR

Equation (7.75) also shows how other parameters, k_i, N_i, and $|\Sigma_i|$, affect the threshold. For example, when two sample sizes, N_1 and N_2, are different, we cannot compare two distances simply as $d_1 \gtrless d_2$ even if $k_1 = k_2$, $|\Sigma_1| = |\Sigma_2|$, and $t = 0$. Instead, we need either to set a threshold as $(d_2/d_1) \lesseqgtr (N_1/N_2)^{1/n}$, or weight two distances differently as $N_2^{1/n} d_2 \lesseqgtr N_1^{1/n} d_1$.

The above argument suggests that thresholding the distance ratio is equivalent to weighting two distances differently. Then, the concept could be applied to the voting kNN approach too. If we adopt $a_i A$ ($a_1 \neq a_2$) as the metric to measure the distance to ω_i-neighbors in the voting kNN procedure, we can control the decision threshold by adjusting the ratio of a_1 and a_2. Furthermore, using $a_i A_i$ ($a_1 \neq a_2$, $A_1 \neq A_2$), we could make the voting kNN virtually equivalent to the volumetric kNN. In this case, A_i could be Σ_i or a more complex matrix like (7.65), and the ratio of a_1 and a_2 still determines the threshold.

Data display: Equation (7.5) also suggests that we may plot data using $y_1 = n\ln d_1(X)$ and $y_2 = n\ln d_2(X)$ as the x- and y-axes, in the same way as we selected $y_i = (X - M_i)^T \Sigma_i^{-1} (X - M_i)$ for the parametric case in Fig. 4-9 [16]. In fact, $n\ln d_i(X)$ is the nonparametric version of the normalized distance $(X-M_i)^T \Sigma_i^{-1} (X-M_i)$, as the following comparison shows:

$$-\ln p_i(X) = \frac{1}{2}(X-M_i)^T \Sigma_i^{-1} (X-M_i) + \{\frac{1}{2}\ln|\Sigma_i| + \frac{n}{2}\ln 2\pi\}$$

for a normal distribution , (7.76)

$$-\ln \hat{p}_i(X) = n\ln d_i(X) + \left\{\ln \frac{N_i c_0 |\Sigma_i|^{1/2}}{k_i - 1}\right\}$$

for the kNN density estimate , (7.77)

where c_0 is the constant relating v_i and d_i as in (B.1). Note that $\hat{p}_i(X) = (k_i-1)/N_i c_0 |\Sigma_i|^{1/2} d_i^n$ is used in (7.77). Using two new variables, $y_1 = n\ln d_1(X)$ and $y_2 = n\ln d_2(X)$, the Bayes classifier becomes a 45° line as

$$n\ln d_2(X) \underset{\omega_2}{\overset{\omega_1}{\lessgtr}} n\ln d_1(X) - \left\{\ln \frac{(k_1-1)N_2 |\Sigma_2|^{1/2}}{(k_2-1)N_1 |\Sigma_1|^{1/2}} + t\right\} , \qquad (7.78)$$

where $\{\cdot\}$ gives the y-cross point.

In order to show what the display of data looks like, the following experiment was conducted.

Experiment 17: Display of data

Data: I-Λ (Normal, n = 8, $\varepsilon^* = 1.9\%$)

Sample size: $N_1 = N_2 = 100$ (L method)

No. of neighbors: $k_1 = k_2 = 5$

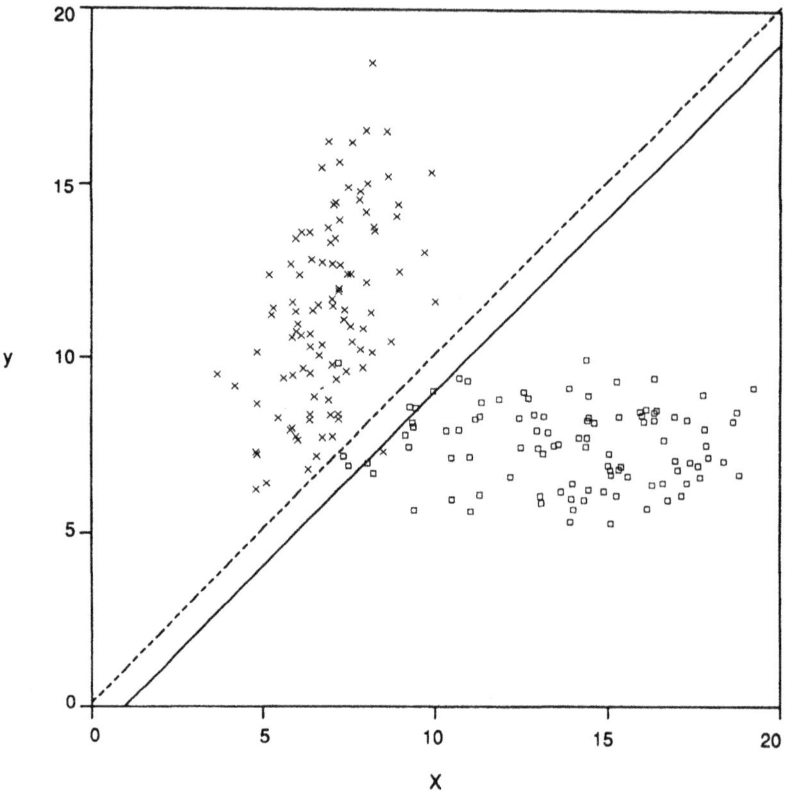

Fig. 7-15 A nonparametric data display with five *NN* distances.

No. of trials: $\tau = 1$
Result: Fig. 7-15

This experiment is the same as the one of Fig. 7-14(c) (Experiment 14), except that the number of trial is one for this experiment while Fig. 7-14(c) shows the average of 10 trials. The solid line shows the 45° line with the y-cross point of $(1/2)\ln|\Sigma_1|/|\Sigma_2|$ where Σ_i is the given ω_i-covariance matrix. From (7.78), this is the threshold value for $t = 0$. The performance of this classifier ($7/200 = 3.5\%$) corresponds to the L-curve without threshold adjustment in Fig. 7-14(c), which is about 5.5% for $k = 5$. The dotted 45° line was selected by using human judgement, minimizing the error among the existing samples. The resulting error is $2/200 = 1\%$. Since the distance to the 5th *NN* for each class is measured according to (7.7), this error is the L error. However, the threshold is fine-tuned to the existing samples (Option 2). Thus, the error is expected to be much smaller than the L-curve of Fig. 7-14(c) (5.5% at $k = 5$), but larger than the R-curve (1.3% at $k = 5$). Note again that the curves of Fig. 7-14(c) were obtained as the 10 trial average by using the threshold of Option 4, while the dotted line of Fig. 7-15 was determined by human judgement for one trial.

In order to apply the Neyman-Pearson test with $\varepsilon_2 = 2\%$ for example, we maintain the 45° slope of the line, and shift it until we find 2 misclassified ω_2-samples out of 100.

Constant risk contours: It is frequently desirable to have risk information about a point in a data display. For the two-class case, the risk at X, $r(X)$, is given by

$$r(X) = \frac{P_1 p_1(X)}{P_1 p_1(X) + P_2 p_2(X)} \quad \text{for } P_1 p_1(X) < P_2 p_2(X) . \tag{7.79}$$

Substituting $p_i(X) = (k_i-1)/N_i c_0 |\Sigma_i|^{1/2} d_i^n(X)$, and taking logarithms,

$$n \ln d_2(X) = n \ln d_1(X) - \left\{ \ln \frac{(k_1-1)N_2 |\Sigma_2|^{1/2}}{(k_2-1)N_1 |\Sigma_1|^{1/2}} + \ln \frac{P_1}{P_2} \right\} + \ln \frac{r(X)}{1-r(X)} . \tag{7.80}$$

Thus, for a given $r(X)$, a contour can be drawn on the display. The resulting contour is a 45° line shifted by $\ln r(X)/[1-r(X)]$ [16]. Similarly, for $P_1 p_1(X) > P_2 p_2(X)$, the numerator of (7.79) is replaced by $P_2 p_2(X)$, and (7.80) is modified to

$$n \ln d_2(X) = n \ln d_1(X) - \left\{ \ln \frac{(k_1-1)N_2 |\Sigma_2|^{1/2}}{(k_2-1)N_1 |\Sigma_1|^{1/2}} + \ln \frac{P_1}{P_2} \right\} - \ln \frac{r(X)}{1-r(X)} . \tag{7.81}$$

Comparison of (7.80) and (7.81) indicates that the constant risk lines are symmetric about the Bayes decision line where $r(X) = 0.5$. As $r(X)$ is decreased, the constant risk lines move farther from the Bayes decision line. This result indicates that points mapped near the Bayes decision line on the display do in fact have a high degree of risk associated with them, while points mapped far from the Bayes decision line have a low degree of risk. This desirable property will be true regardless of the underlying distribution. Table 7-6 shows the amounts of shift for various values of $r(X)$. However, it must be noted that these risk lines should not be drawn around the theoretical Bayes risk line (the solid line of Fig. 7-15). The *kNN* density estimates and subsequently the estimate of $r(X)$ are heavily biased as discussed in the previous sections. In order to compensate these biases, the threshold terms of (7.80) and (7.81) must be adjusted and will differ from the theoretical values indicated in $\{\cdot\}$. Further shift due to $\ln r(X)/(1-r(X))$ must start from the adjusted threshold.

TABLE 7-6

SHIFT OF THRESHOLD DUE TO r

r	0.5	0.4	0.3	0.2	0.1
$\pm\Delta t$	0	0.405	0.847	1.386	2.197

These constant risk lines allow the analyst to identify samples in a reject region easily [17-18]. For a given reject threshold τ, the reject region on the display is the area between two 45° lines specified by $r(X) = \tau$, in which $r(X) > \tau$ is satisfied and accordingly samples are rejected.

Grouped error estimate: An obvious method of error estimation in display is to count the number of ω_1- and ω_2-samples in the ω_2- and ω_1-regions, respectively. Another possible method is to read $\hat{r}(X_i)$ for each X_i, and to compute the sample mean as

$$\hat{\boldsymbol{\varepsilon}} = \frac{1}{N}\sum_{i=1}^{N}\hat{\mathbf{r}}(\mathbf{X}_i) , \tag{7.82}$$

because the Bayes error is expressed by $\varepsilon^* = E\{r(\mathbf{X})\}$. This estimate is called the *grouped estimate* [19-20]. The randomness of $\hat{\boldsymbol{\varepsilon}}$ comes from two sources: one from the estimation of r, $\hat{\mathbf{r}}$, and the other from $\mathbf{X}_i$. When the conventional error-counting process is used, we design a classifier by estimating the density functions using design samples (*design phase*), and count the number of misclassified test samples (*test phase*). As discussed in Chapter 5, with a finite number of samples, the estimated error is biased due to the design samples and has a variance due to the test samples. In the grouped estimate, estimating r corresponds to the design phase and computing the sample mean of $\hat{r}(\mathbf{X}_i)$ corresponds to the test phase. The performance of the grouped estimate has not been fully studied in comparison with the error-counting result. However, if the risk function $r(X)$ is given, the test phase of the grouped estimate has the following advantages.

(1) We can use test samples without knowing their true class assignments. This property could be useful, when a classifier is tested in the field.

(2) The variance due to this test process is less than a half of the variance due to error-counting.

In order to prove that the second property is true, let us compute the variance of (7.82) with the assumption that $r(X)$ is given and $E\{r(\mathbf{X})\} = \varepsilon$. Since the $\mathbf{X}_i$'s are independent and identically distributed,

$$\begin{aligned}
\mathrm{Var}\{\hat{\varepsilon}\} &= \frac{1}{N}\mathrm{Var}\{r(\mathbf{X})\} \\
&= \frac{1}{N}[\varepsilon - \varepsilon^2 - E\{r(\mathbf{X})[1 - r(\mathbf{X})]\}] \\
&\le \frac{1}{N}[\varepsilon - \varepsilon^2 - \frac{1}{2}E\{r(\mathbf{X})\}] \\
&= \frac{1}{2N}(\varepsilon - 2\varepsilon^2)\,,
\end{aligned} \tag{7.83}$$

where $r(1-r) \ge r/2$ for $0 \le r \le 0.5$ is used to obtain the inequality. Note from (5.49) that the variance of error-counting is $\varepsilon(1-\varepsilon)/N$, which is larger than twice (7.83). When the design phase is included, we must add the bias and variance of $\hat{\mathbf{r}}$ to evaluate the total performance of the grouped estimate. Also, note that the bias of $\hat{\mathbf{r}}$ should be removed by the threshold adjustment, as discussed in the previous section. That is, $r(X)$ must be estimated by solving (7.80) or (7.81) for $r(X)$ with the adjusted $\{\cdot\}$ term.

Edited Nearest Neighbor

Edited *kNN*: As seen in Fig. 7-3 for the voting *kNN* approach, the ω_i-samples in the ω_j-region ($i \neq j$) could become close neighbors of some of the ω_j-samples, and this produces extra errors. This is the reason why the *kNN* error is larger than the Bayes error. These extra errors could be reduced by removing ω_i-samples in the ω_j-region (samples 1, 3, 5 and 6 of Fig. 7-3) from the design sample set. In practice, since the exact location of the Bayes boundary is never known, the above operation is replaced by removing the misclassified samples (1, 2, 3, 4, 5 and 6 of Fig. 7-3) by the *kNN* classification [21]. The resulting design set is called the *edited set.* Test samples are classified by the *kNN*'s from the edited set. This algorithm is called the *edited kNN procedure.* It should be noted, however, that some of ω_i-samples in the ω_j-region are correctly classified and not removed, and some of ω_j-samples in the ω_j-region are misclassified and removed. Therefore, the resulting error is not the same as the Bayes error.

Asymptotic analysis: In order to analyze the edited *kNN* procedure, let us study the simplest case of the asymptotic *NN*. In the original sample set, the populations of ω_1 and ω_2 given X are represented by a posteriori probabilities $q_1(X)$ and $q_2(X)$. Applying the voting *NN* classification to the ω_i-samples, $q_i^2(X)$ ($\cong q_i(X)q_i(X_{NN})$) are correctly classified, and $q_i(X)q_j(X)$ ($\cong q_i(X)q_j(X_{NN})$) ($j \neq i$) are misclassified. Therefore, keeping only correctly classified samples, a posteriori probabilities in the edited set, $q_i'(X)$, become

$$q_i'(X) = \frac{q_i^2(X)}{q_1^2(X) + q_2^2(X)} . \tag{7.84}$$

Samples from the original set are classified according to the class of the *NN* from the edited set. The resulting error is

$$r(X) = q_1(X)q_2'(X_{NN}) + q_2(X)q_1'(X_{NN})$$

$$\cong q_1(X)q_2'(X) + q_2(X)q_1'(X)$$

$$= \frac{q_1(X)q_2(X)}{q_1^2(X) + q_2^2(X)}$$

$$= \frac{q_1(X)q_2(X)}{1-2q_1(X)q_2(X)} , \tag{7.85}$$

where $q_i'(X_{NN}) \cong q_i'(X)$ is used for the asymptotic analysis. The last line of (7.85) is the expression of $r(X)$ in terms of $q_1(X)q_2(X)$.

It is easy to show that (7.85) is bounded by the *NN* risk from the upper side and the Bayes risk from the lower side in the range of $0 \le q_1 q_2 \le 0.25$ as

$$\min[q_1(X),q_2(X)] \le \frac{q_1(X)q_2(X)}{1-2q_1(X)q_2(X)} \le 2q_1(X)q_2(X) . \tag{7.86}$$

The proof is left for the reader. Also, (7.85) can be generalized to the case where the k_1NN is used for removing samples and the k_2NN for testing. When both k_1 and k_2 are odd, the resulting error becomes larger than the Bayes error. When k_2 is even, the resulting error becomes smaller than the Bayes error.

Also, the edited *NN* procedure can be applied repeatedly to remove the ω_i-samples in the ω_j-region. The asymptotic analysis also can be carried out by applying (7.85) repeatedly [22]. Figure 7-16 shows the results of the repeated edited *NN* procedure.

Reduction of Computation Time

One of the severe drawbacks of any nonparametric approach is that it requires a large amount of computation time. For the *kNN* approach, this is due to the fact that, in order to find the *kNN*'s, we must compute the distances to all samples. The same is true for the Parzen approach. Because of this computational burden, nonparametric approaches are not popular as a classifier operated on-line. In the off-line operation of the Bayes error estimation, each sample must be tested by computing the distances to other samples. This means that all possible pairwise distances among samples must be computed. This becomes a burden to a computer, slows down the turn-around time, and limits the number of samples we can use even when more samples are available.

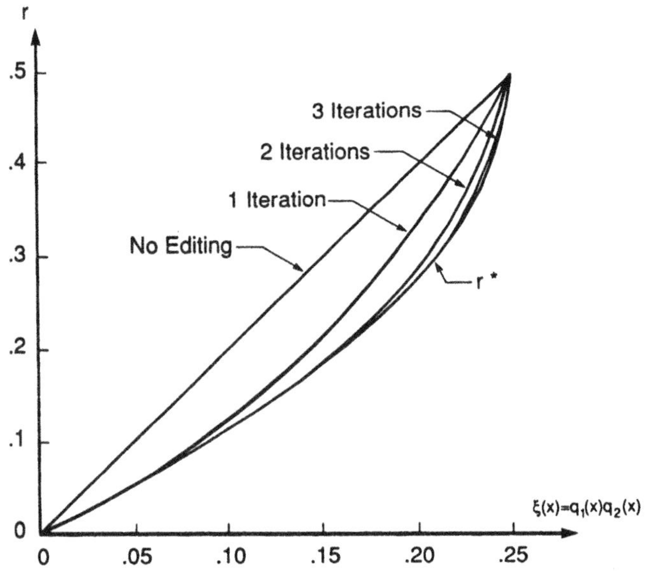

Fig. 7-16 Performance of repeated edited *NN* operations.

In this section, we touch briefly on some past efforts to overcome the above difficulty as follows.

Condensed *NN*: As seen in Fig. 7-3 for the voting *kNN* approach, the samples near the Bayes decision boundary are crucial to the *kNN* decision, but the samples far from the boundary do not affect the decision. Therefore, a systematic removal of these ineffective samples helps to reduce both computation time and storage requirements. This procedure is called the *condensed kNN decision rule* [23].

The risk value, $r(X)$, of each sample can be used as an indicator of how close the sample is located to the boundary. Therefore, we may set a threshold τ, and remove samples with $r(X) < \tau$. In addition, we had better remove all misclassified samples regardless of the value of $r(X)$, in order to avoid extra errors as was discussed in the edited *kNN* procedure. Since the effect of removing samples on the *kNN* error is hard to predict, it is suggested to classify test samples based on the condensed design set and confirm that the resulting error is close to the one based on the original design set.

Branch and bound procedure: The *kNN* computation time could be reduced significantly by applying the *branch and bound technique*, if design samples can be hierarchically decomposed to subsets, sub-subsets and so on [24]. In order to describe the procedure, let us set up a tree structure as in Fig. 7-17 where each node represents a subset, S_k. Each subset is decomposed into

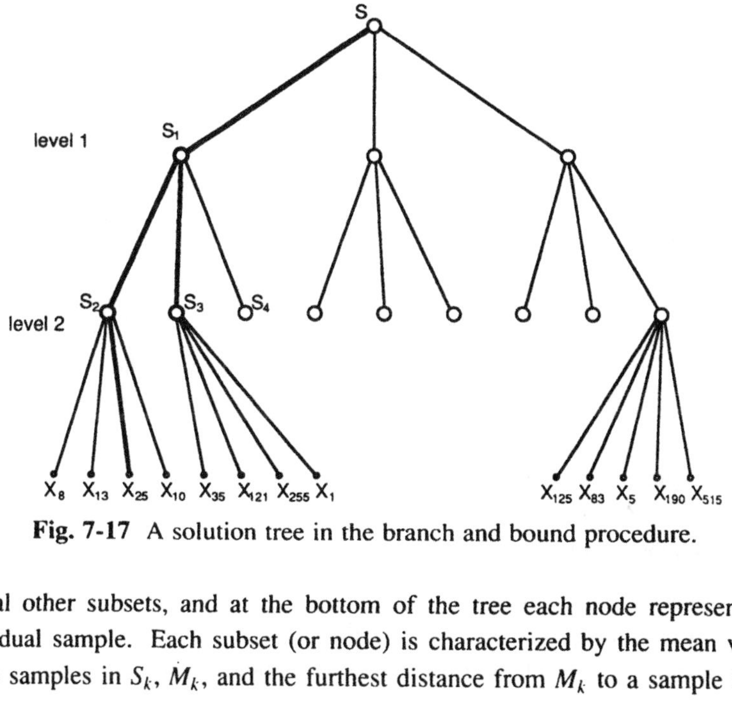

Fig. 7-17 A solution tree in the branch and bound procedure.

several other subsets, and at the bottom of the tree each node represents an individual sample. Each subset (or node) is characterized by the mean vector of the samples in S_k, M_k, and the furthest distance from M_k to a sample in S_k, d_k.

When the *NN* sample of an unknown X is sought, the search begins from the leftmost branch. After comparing the distances from X to X_8, X_{13}, X_{25}, and X_{10}, X_{25} is found as the closest one to X. The computer back-tracks the tree from S_2 to S_1 and then moves to S_3. However, before testing the members of S_3, it is tested whether or not the following inequality is satisfied.

$$d(X,M_3) > d(X,X_{25}) + d_3 . \tag{7.87}$$

If the inequality is satisfied, there is no possibility that the distance between X and any member of S_3 is smaller than $d(X,X_{25})$ [see Fig. 7-18]. Therefore, the search moves to S_4 without testing the members of S_3.

The procedure works well in a low-dimensional space. An experimental result for a uniform distribution in a two-dimensional space shows that only 46 distance computations are needed to find the *NN* among 1000 samples. In this

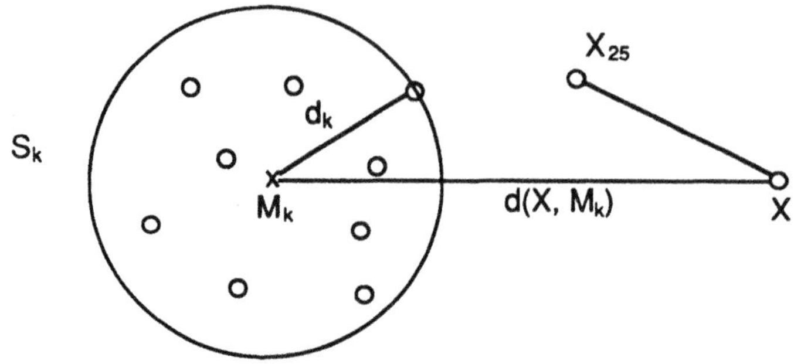

Fig. 7-18 A criterion to eliminate a group of samples.

experiment, the tree consists of 3 levels with each node decomposed to 3 nodes. At the bottom of the tree, there are 27 subsets containing 1000 samples. However, for an 8-dimensional uniform distribution, 451 distance computations are needed to find the *NN* from 3000 samples. The tree is formed with 4 levels and 4 decomposition, which yields 256 subsets at the bottom housing 3000 samples. As discussed in Chapter 6, all pairwise distances among samples become close, as the dimensionality gets high. Therefore, the effectiveness of (7.87) to eliminate subsets diminishes, and only a smaller number of subsets are rejected by satisfying (7.87).

Another problem of this method is how to divide samples into subsets. We will discuss this problem, which is called *clustering*, in Chapter 11. Again, finding clusters becomes more difficult, as the dimensionality goes up.

Computer Projects

1. Repeat Experiment 3 for Data I-Λ. Use (a) I and (b) $(I+\Lambda)/2$ as the metric.

2. Repeat Experiment 5.

3. Repeat Experiment 6.

4. Repeat Experiment 8.

5. Repeat Experiment 9.

6. Repeat Experiment 11.

7. Repeat Experiments 12 and 13.

8. Repeat Experiment 14.

9. Repeat Experiment 17.

Problems

1. Derive the asymptotic 3*NN* and 4*NN* errors for the voting *kNN* procedure, and confirm that the results can also be obtained from (7.15) and (7.16).

2. Two one-dimensional distributions are uniform in [0,2] for ω_1 and [1,4] for ω_2. Assuming $P_1 = P_2 = 0.5$, compute the asymptotic *kNN* errors for k = 1, 2, 3, and 4 in the voting *kNN* procedure, and compare them with the Bayes error.

3. In Problem 2, $\xi(x)$ is either 6/25 or 0 with the probability of 5/12 or 7/12. With this much information, compute the asympotitic *kNN* errors for k = 1, 2, 3, and 4 and the Bayes error. The results must be identical to the ones of Problem 2.

4. Prove that $\min[q_1(X), q_2(X)] = \frac{1}{2} - \frac{1}{2}\sqrt{1-4q_1(X)q_2(X)}$.

5. Assuming $P_1 = P_2$ and $N_1 = N_2 = N$, the Parzen classifier is expressed by

$$\frac{1}{N}\sum_{i=1}^{N}\kappa(X - X_i^{(1)}) \underset{\omega_2}{\overset{\omega_1}{\gtrless}} \frac{1}{N}\sum_{i=1}^{N}\kappa(X - X_i^{(2)}) .$$

Prove that the leave-one-out error is larger than the resubstitution error. Assume $\kappa(0) \geq \kappa(X)$.

6. Express B_1 of (7.36) in terms of M_1, M_2, Σ_1, and Σ_2 for normal **X**.

7. Derive the bias equation for the volumetric 2*NN* error for two-class problems.

8. Derive the bias equation for the volumetric *NN* error for multiclass problems.

9. The risk $r(X)$ is assigned to either 0 or α, depending on whether the classes of X and its NN agree or not. The NN error is computed by $E\{r(\mathbf{X})\}$. Find α which makes this NN error equal to the Bayes error for the uniform distribution of $\xi(X) = q_1(X)q_2(X)$.

10. The edited design samples are selected by using the NN voting procedure, and test samples are classified by the voting $2NN$ procedure. Compute the asymptotic error of this operation. Prove that the resulting error is between the Bayes error and the $2NN$ error without the editing procedure.

References

1. T. M. Cover and P. E. Hart, Nearest neighbor pattern classification, *Trans. IEEE Inform. Theory*, IT-13, pp. 21-27, 1967.
2. T. M. Cover, Rates of convergence for nearest neighbor procedures, *Proc. Hawaii Int. Conf. on System Sciences*, pp. 413-415, 1968.
3. T. J. Wagner, Convergence of the nearest neighbor rule, *Trans. IEEE Inform. Theory*, IT-17, pp. 566-571, 1971.
4. J. Fritz, Distribution-free exponential error bounds for nearest neighbor pattern classification, *Trans. IEEE Inform. Theory*, IT-21, pp. 552-557, 1975.
5. C. J. Stone, Consistent nonparametric regression, *Ann. Stat.*, 5, pp. 595-645, 1977.
6. L. Devroye, On the almost everywhere convergence of nonparametric regression function estimates, *Ann. Stat.*, 9, pp. 1310-1319, 1981.
7. L. Devroye, On the inequality of Cover and Hart in nearest neighbor discrimination, *Trans. IEEE Pattern Anal. and Machine Intell.*, PAMI-3, pp. 75-78, 1981.
8. K. Fukunaga and D. M. Hummels, Bias of nearest neighbor estimates, *Trans. IEEE on Pattern Anal. and Machine Intell.*, PAMI-9, pp. 103-112, 1987.
9. R. D. Short and K. Fukunaga, The optimal distance measure for nearest neighbor classification, *Trans. IEEE Inform. Theory*, IT-27, pp. 622-627, 1981.

10. K. Fukunaga and T. E. Flick, An optimal global nearest neighbor metric, *Trans. IEEE Pattern Anal. and Machine Intell.*, PAMI-6, pp. 314-318, 1984.

11. K. Fukunaga and T. E. Flick, The 2-*NN* rule for more accurate *NN* risk estimation, *Trans. IEEE on Pattern Anal. and Machine Intell.*, PAMI-7, pp. 107-112, 1985.

12. K. Fukunaga and D. H. Hummels, Bayes error estimation using Parzen and *k-NN* procedures, *Trans. IEEE Pattern Anal. and Machine Intell.*, PAMI-9, pp. 634-643, 1987.

13. E. Parzen, On the estimation of a probability density function and the mode, *Ann. Math. Stat.*, 33, pp. 1065-1076, 1962.

14. K. Fukunaga and D. H. Hummels, Leave-one-out procedures for nonparametric error estimates, *Trans. IEEE Pattern Anal. and Machine Intell.*, PAMI-11, pp. 421-423, 1989.

15. D. O. Loftsgaarden and C. P. Quesenberry, A nonparametric estimate of a multivariate density function, *Ann. Math. Stat.*, 36, pp. 1049-1051, 1965.

16. K. Fukunaga and J. M. Mantock, A Nonparametric two-dimensional display for classification, *Trans. IEEE on Pattern Anal. and Machine Intell.*, PAMI-4, pp. 427-436, 1982.

17. M. Hellman, The nearest neighbor classification rule with a reject option, *Trans. IEEE Systems Sci. Cybernet.*, SSC-6, pp. 179-185, 1970.

18. P. A. Devijver, New error bounds with the nearest neighbor rule, *Trans. IEEE Inform. Theory*, IT-25, pp. 749-753, 1979.

19. K. Fukunaga and D. L. Kessell, Nonparametric Bayes error estimation using unclassified samples, *Trans. IEEE on Inform. Theory*, IT-19, pp. 434-440, 1973.

20. K. Fukunaga and L. D. Hostetler, *k*-nearest neighbor Bayes-risk estimation, *Trans. IEEE on Inform. Theory*, IT-21, pp. 258-293, 1975.

21. D. L. Wilson, Asymptotic properties of nearest neighbor rules using edited data, *Trans. IEEE Systems Man Cybernet.*, SMC-2, pp. 408-420, 1972.

22. P. A. Devijver and J. Kittler, On the edited nearest neighbor rule, *Proc. Fifth Internat. Conf. on Pattern Recognition,* Miami Beach, FL, pp. 72-80, 1980.

23. P. E. Hart, The condensed nearest neighbor rule, *Trans. IEEE Inform. Theory,* IT-14, pp. 515-516, 1968.

24. K. Fukunaga and P. M. Narendra, A branch and bound algorithm for computing k-nearest neighbors, *Trans. IEEE Computers,* C-24, pp. 750-753, 1975.

25. J. H. Friedman, F. Baskett and L. J. Shustek, An algorithm for finding nearest neighbors, *Trans. IEEE Computers,* C-24, pp. 1000-1006, 1975.

26. T. P. Yunck, A technique to identify nearest neighbors, *Trans. IEEE Systems Man Cybernet.,* SMC-6, pp. 678-683, 1976.

Chapter 8

SUCCESSIVE PARAMETER ESTIMATION

In the approaches to parameter estimation presented so far, estimates have been determined from all of the observable data in a single calculation. Sometimes, however, it is required to use a procedure which is based on a sequence of observations. In this case, the parameters are first approximated by an initial "guess." Then each observation vector is used in turn to update the estimate. Hopefully, as the number of observations increases, the estimate will converge in some sense toward the true parameters. A major advantage of this successive approach is the fact that an infinite number of observations can be accounted for, using a finite amount of storage.

8.1 Successive Adjustment of a Linear Classifier

When each of the conditional density functions corresponding to the classes to be separated belongs to a known parametric family, the classifier design is fairly straightforward. After the estimates of the unknown parameters have been obtained, the Bayes decision rule is determined. Quite often, however, even the functional form of the conditional densities cannot be assumed. The densities could be approximated by the techniques described in Chapter 6, but, on the other hand, it may be possible to avoid the calculation of the densities completely. Suppose it is decided *a priori* that the decision rule belongs to a parametric family of decision rules. The problem then reduces to that of estimating the parameters of the decision rule. By this approach we sacrifice, perhaps, a certain amount of insight into the nature of the classifier problem. However, this sacrifice is often more than justified by savings in computation.

Suppose, for a two-class problem, we decide to use a linear classifier of the form

$$V^T X + v_0 \underset{\omega_2}{\overset{\omega_1}{\gtrless}} 0 . \tag{8.1}$$

Then, our problem is that of estimating the parameters V and v_0. The linear classifier is chosen because of its simplicity, but it should be recalled from Chapter 4 that (8.1) can include a broad range of nonlinear functions. This is the case if X is considered a vector in a functional space instead of being thought of as the original variable space.

In Chapter 4, we discussed the design of V and v_0 from a given set of observations, provided these are all simultaneously available. In the present case, however, we would rather not store all of the observation vectors simultaneously. Instead, we store only the current parameter estimate and update this estimate each time a single observation vector is presented to the estimation system. This type of system was first developed as a simplified model of *learning* and *decision-making* in early pattern recognition research, and has since been called a *perceptron* [1],[2]. In this model, we have to have an algorithm which modifies the parameters on the basis of the present observation vector and the present values of these parameters.

Linear Classifier for Two-Class Problems

Let us rewrite (8.1) using new notations Z and W as in (4.73).

$$h(Z) = W^T Z = \sum_{i=0}^{n} w_i z_i > 0 , \tag{8.2}$$

where $z_0 = -1$ or $+1$ and $z_i = -x_i$ or $+x_i$ ($i = 1,2, \ldots ,n$) depending on $X \in \omega_1$ or $X \in \omega_2$. Then, the current value of W is updated to the new value of W', as follows [3].

$$(1) \quad W' = W \qquad \text{if} \quad W^T Z > 0 \,, \tag{8.3}$$

$$(2) \quad W' = W + cZ \quad \text{if} \quad W^T Z \le 0 \quad (c > 0) \,. \tag{8.4}$$

Since W of (8.3) correctly classifies the sample, we have no reason to change W. In (8.4), W should be modified to increase $W^T Z$. The updated W' of (8.4) satisfies this condition because

$$W'^T Z = W^T Z + cZ^T Z > W^T Z \,. \tag{8.5}$$

The reader may try to find a function, $W' = f(W,Z)$, which satisfies $f^T(W,Z)Z \ge W^T Z$ for all Z's. Then, it will be realized that there are no other simple, practical solutions than the procedure of (8.3) and (8.4). In (8.4), we still have one control parameter, c, to determine.

There are three common ways to choose c. These are as follows:

(1) *Fixed increment rule:* c = constant

(2) *Absolute correction rule:* Select c large enough to obtain $W'^T Z > 0$. That is,

$$W'^T Z = (W + cZ)^T Z > 0 \quad \text{for} \quad W^T Z \le 0 \,. \tag{8.6}$$

In order to satisfy (8.6), c should satisfy

$$c > \frac{|W^T Z|}{Z^T Z} \,. \tag{8.7}$$

(3) *Gradient correction rule:* When we maximize or minimize a criterion such as the mean-square error between the desired and actual outputs, $\gamma(Z)$ and $W^T Z$, we can determined c by the gradient of the criterion. For example, by analogy with (4.84) we may select c as

$$c = \rho[\gamma(Z) - W^T Z] \,. \tag{8.8}$$

Obviously, c depends on the criterion we select, and ρ should be a positive constant properly chosen.

Example 1: Let us design a classifier which separates the four samples of Fig. 8-1. The samples are presented to the machine in the order $Z_0, Z_1, Z_2, Z_3, Z_0, \ldots$. The fixed increment rule is used with $c = 1$. The sequence of W in the training period is shown in Table 8-1. The term W converges to

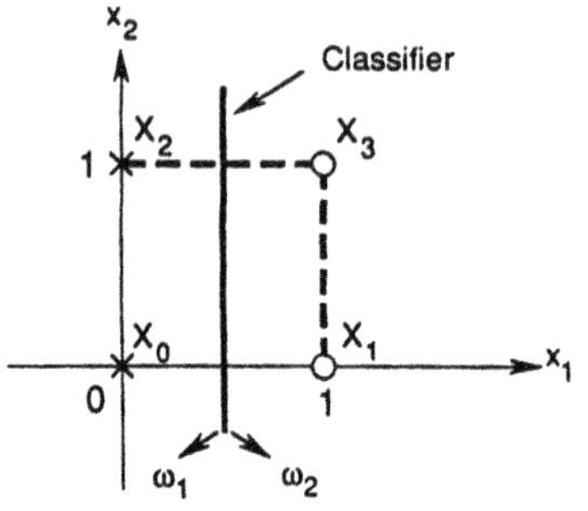

Fig. 8-1 Linearly separable example.

TABLE 8-1

SEQUENCE OF W FOR A LINEARLY SEPARABLE CASE

Iteration	Input	z_0 z_1 z_2	w_0 w_1 w_2	W^TZ	Adjustment
1	Z_0	−1 0 0	0 0 0	0	$W + Z_0$
	Z_1	1 1 0	−1 0 0	−1	$W + Z_1$
	Z_2	−1 0 −1	0 1 0	0	$W + Z_2$
	Z_3	1 1 1	−1 1 −1	−1	$W + Z_3$
2	Z_0	−1 0 0	0 2 0	0	$W + Z_0$
	Z_1	1 1 0	−1 2 0	1	No
	Z_2	−1 0 −1	−1 2 0	1	No
	Z_3	1 1 1	−1 2 0	1	No
3	Z_0	−1 0 0	−1 2 0	1	No

$$2z_1 - 1 > 0 . \tag{8.9}$$

Or, in the original X-space

$$2x_1 - 1 \underset{\omega_2}{\overset{\omega_1}{\gtrless}} 0 . \tag{8.10}$$

As seen in Fig. 8-1, this classifier separates the given four samples correctly.

Example 2: This is an example of a linearly nonseparable case, in which there exists no linear classifier that separates samples without error. Six samples are given in Fig. 8-2, and they are fed into the machine in the order

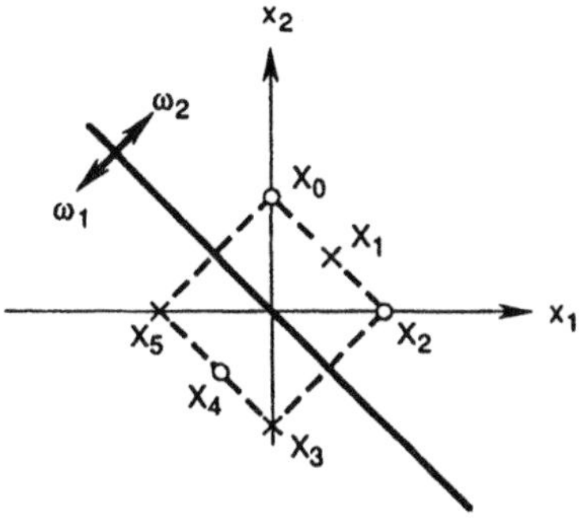

Fig. 8-2 Linearly nonseparable example.

$Z_0, Z_1, \ldots, Z_5, Z_0, \ldots, Z_5, Z_0, \ldots$. The fixed increment rule is used again, with $c = 1$. The sequence of W in the training period is shown in Table 8-2. We have a cyclic sequence of W without convergence, although the best linear classifier $[w_0 \; w_1 \; w_2] = [0 \; 2 \; 2]$ is included in the sequence of W.

Whenever we have an iterative process like this, there is a question of whether the convergence of the process is guaranteed. When two distributions are *linearly separable*, the convergence of the above process for the fixed increment rule with a proper range of ρ can be proved.

Convergence Proof for the Linearly Separable Case

The convergence proof of the fixed increment rule is as follows [3].

Let us eliminate, from a training sequence $Z_1, Z_2, \ldots$, the Z's which do not change W, and call it the *reduced training sequence* $Z_1^*, Z_2^*, \ldots$. Since the eliminated Z's do not affect W, they have no influence on the proof of convergence.

Also, let us assume $c = 1$. This assumption does not reduce the generality of the proof, because a change of c merely corresponds to a change of the coordinate scale. The scale of the coordinate does not affect the structure of the data and the linear classifier.

TABLE 8-2

SEQUENCE OF W FOR A LINEARLY NONSEPARABLE CASE

Iteration	Input	z_0	z_1	z_2	w_0	w_1	w_2	W^TZ	Adjustment
1	Z_0	1	0	2	0	0	0	0	$W+Z_0$
	Z_1	−1	−1	−1	1	0	2	−3	$W+Z_1$
	Z_2	1	2	0	0	−1	1	−2	$W+Z_2$
	Z_3	−1	0	2	1	1	1	1	No
	Z_4	1	−1	−1	1	1	1	−1	$W+Z_4$
	Z_5	−1	2	0	2	0	0	−2	$W+Z_5$
2	Z_0	1	0	2	1	2	0	1	No
	Z_1	−1	−1	−1	1	2	0	−3	$W+Z_1$
	Z_2	1	2	0	0	1	−1	2	No
	Z_3	−1	0	2	0	1	−1	−2	$W+Z_3$
	Z_4	1	−1	−1	−1	1	1	−3	$W+Z_4$
	Z_5	−1	2	0	0	0	0	0	$W+Z_5$
3	Z_0	1	0	2	−1	2	0	−1	$W+Z_0$
	Z_1	−1	−1	−1	0	2	2	−4	$W+Z_1$
	Z_2	1	2	0	−1	1	1	1	No
	Z_3	−1	0	2	−1	1	1	3	No
	Z_4	1	−1	−1	−1	1	1	−3	$W+Z_4$
	Z_5	−1	2	0	0	0	0	0	$W+Z_5$

A reduced sequence of samples generates the corresponding sequence of W^* given by

$$W^*_{k+1} = W^*_k + Z^*_k \,, \tag{8.11}$$

where

$$W^{*T}_k Z^*_k \le 0 \,. \tag{8.12}$$

Since we assume that the two distributions are linearly separable, we should be able to find W_s such that

$$W_s^T Z_k > 0 \quad \text{for all } k\text{'s} \,. \tag{8.13}$$

Selecting

$$a = \max_k Z_k^T Z_k \quad \text{and} \quad b > 0 \,, \tag{8.14}$$

we can select the scale of W so that

$$W_s^T Z_k > \frac{a+b}{2} > 0 \,. \tag{8.15}$$

The change of scale of W does not change the decision rule (8.2).

Now we calculate the distance between W_s and W_k^* as

$$\|W_s - W_k^*\|^2 = \|W_s\|^2 + \|W_k^*\|^2 - 2W_s^T W_k^* \,. \tag{8.16}$$

Hence, using (8.11),

$$\|W_s - W_k^*\|^2 - \|W_s - W_{k+1}^*\|^2 = \|W_k^*\|^2 - \|W_{k+1}^*\|^2$$

$$-2W_s^T(W_k^* - W_{k+1}^*) = -2W_k^{*T} Z_k^* - Z_k^{*T} Z_k^* + 2W_s^T Z_k^* \,. \tag{8.17}$$

Recalling $W_k^{*T} Z_k^* \le 0$ from (8.12) and the inequalities of (8.14) and (8.15), (8.17) becomes

$$\|W_s - W_k^*\|^2 - \|W_s - W_{k+1}^*\|^2 > -a + 2\frac{a+b}{2} > 0 \,. \tag{8.18}$$

Equation (8.18) shows that, whenever a new Z_k^* is applied, $\|W_s - W_k^*\|^2$ decreases by a finite amount (larger than b). Therefore, after a finite number of samples, W_k^* should converge to W_s.

The above convergence proof may be extended to the absolute correction rule by converting it to an equivalent fixed increment rule. This is done by generating artificially a sequence of samples $Z_k = Z_{k+1} = \ldots = Z_{k+u}$ whenever $W_k^T Z_k \le 0$ occurs, and applying the fixed increment rule until $W_{k+u+1}^T Z_k$ becomes positive. That is, $u+1$ corresponds to the value of c which realizes (8.6).

Linear Classifier for Multiclass Problems

The algorithm of designing a linear classifier for the two-class problem can be extended to linear classifiers for the multiclass problem.

For L classes, we set up L linear discriminant functions W_i. The decision rule then becomes

$$W_i^T Y > W_j^T Y \quad (j = 1, \ldots, L:\ j \neq i) \quad \rightarrow \quad Y \in \omega_i \ , \tag{8.19}$$

where Y and W are defined, in terms of X, V, and v_0 of (8.1), by

$$y_0 = 1 \quad \text{and} \quad y_i = x_i \quad (i = 1, \ldots, n) \ ,$$

$$w_i = v_i \quad (i = 0, 1, \ldots, n) \ . \tag{8.20}$$

When all $Y \in \omega_i$ $(i = 1, \ldots, L)$ satisfy (8.19), we call *these L classes linearly separable.* An algorithm to adjust these W's is given as follows:

(1) *If* $W_i^T Y > W_j^T Y$ $(j = 1, \ldots, L: j \neq i)$ for $Y \in \omega_i$, then

$$W_k' = W_k \quad (k = 1, \ldots, L) \ . \tag{8.21}$$

(2) *If* $W_\ell^T Y > W_i^T Y$ and $W_i^T Y > W_j^T Y$ for $Y \in \omega_i$, then

$$W_\ell' = W_\ell - cY, \quad W_i' = W_i + cY, \quad W_j' = W_j \quad (j \neq i, \ell) \ . \tag{8.22}$$

This multiclass problem can be reformulated as a two-class problem, if we extend our dimension to $n \times L$ as

$$W = [W_1^T \ldots W_{i-1}^T W_i^T W_{i+1}^T \ldots W_{\ell-1}^T W_\ell^T W_{\ell+1}^T \ldots W_L^T]^T \ , \tag{8.23}$$

$$Z = [0^T \ldots 0^T \quad Y^T \ 0^T \ldots 0^T \ -Y^T 0^T \ldots 0^T]^T \ , \tag{8.24}$$

for the Y of (8.22). Then, for a reduced sequence of samples, $Z_1^*, Z_2^*, \ldots$, we can obtain a corresponding sequence of W, $W_1^*, W_2^*, \ldots$. These W_k^*'s are related by

$$W_{k+1}^* = W_k^* + cZ_k^* \ . \tag{8.25}$$

Equation (8.25) is equivalent to (8.22). Since (8.25) is the same as (8.11), the convergence of (8.25) and, consequently, the convergence of (8.22) is guaranteed by the proof presented in the previous subsection.

As discussed in Chapter 4, a piecewise linear classifier is often used for separating many classes. Unfortunately, the convergence proof for a piecewise linear classifier is not known. However, similar algorithms to adjust the W's can be found in some references [3],[4].

8.2 Stochastic Approximation

The successive estimation algorithm of the last section does not always converge when the observation vectors are not linearly separable, as seen in Example 2. This fact leads us to look for an estimation algorithm for which convergence is guaranteed. *Stochastic approximation* is a technique that has been developed to find the root or the optimum point of a regression function in random environments [5],[6]. Stochastic approximation can be used for parameter estimation in pattern recognition, and convergence is guaranteed under very general circumstances. It is usually difficult, however, to discuss the rate of convergence.

Before we begin a detailed discussion, let us examine a simple example. Suppose we want to estimate the expected vector from a finite number of observation vectors. Suppose, further, that we want to use a successive estimate. Now the nonsuccessive estimate $\hat{\mathbf{M}}_N$ of the expected vector, based on N observation vectors, $\mathbf{X}_1, \ldots, \mathbf{X}_N$, is given by

$$\hat{\mathbf{M}}_N = \frac{1}{N}\sum_{i=1}^{N}\mathbf{X}_i \, . \tag{8.26}$$

The equation can be modified to

$$\hat{\mathbf{M}}_N = \frac{N-1}{N}\left\{\frac{1}{N-1}\sum_{i=1}^{N-1}\mathbf{X}_i\right\} + \frac{1}{N}\mathbf{X}_N$$

$$= \frac{N-1}{N}\hat{\mathbf{M}}_{N-1} + \frac{1}{N}\mathbf{X}_N \, . \tag{8.27}$$

That is, $\hat{\mathbf{M}}_N$ can be calculated with a new sample $\mathbf{X}_N$ if we store only $\hat{\mathbf{M}}_{N-1}$ and N. Also, the effect of the new sample on the sample mean vector should decrease, with an increase in N, as follows:

$$\mathbf{X}_1, \ \frac{1}{2}\mathbf{X}_2, \ \frac{1}{3}\mathbf{X}_3, \ldots, \ \frac{1}{N}\mathbf{X}_N \, . \tag{8.28}$$

The sequence of coefficients $1, 1/2, 1/3, \ldots, 1/N, \ldots$ is known as a *harmonic sequence.*

The above simple example suggests the following basic approach to successive estimation.

(1) When the mathematical expression for an estimate is available, we may obtain the successive expression of the estimate by separating the estimate calculated from $(N-1)$ samples and the contribution of the Nth sample.

(2) Even when we have to use a search process, in order to minimize or maximize a certain criterion, we may diminish the effect of the Nth sample by using a coefficient which is a decreasing function of N.

Root-Finding Problem

The simplest form of stochastic approximation is seen in finding a root of a *regression function*. This process is also called the *Robbins-Monro*

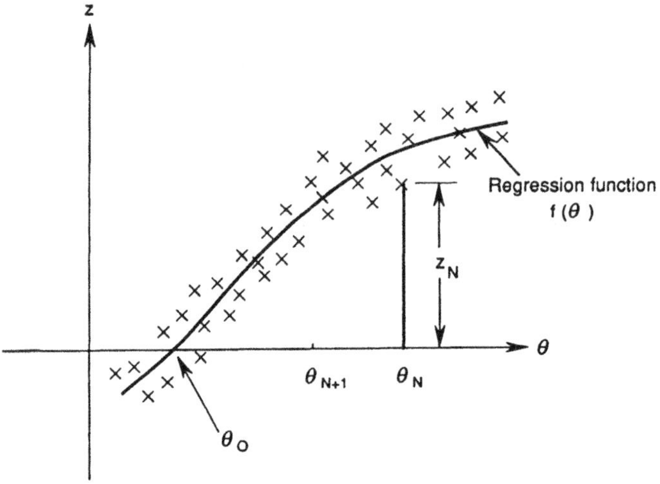

Fig. 8-3 Root-finding problem.

method [7]. Let $\boldsymbol{\theta}$ and $\mathbf{z}$ be two random variables with some correlation, as shown in Fig. 8-3. Our problem is to find the root of the regression function $f(\theta)$, which is defined by

$$f(\theta) = E\{\mathbf{z} \mid \theta\} . \tag{8.29}$$

If we can collect all samples for a fixed θ and estimate $E\{\mathbf{z} \mid \theta\}$, then finding the root of $f(\theta)$ can be carried out by a root-finding technique for a deterministic function such as the Newton method. However, when it is predetermined that only one sample is observed for a given θ and we try to change θ accordingly, the observation of $f(\theta)$ is very noisy and may introduce an erroneous adjustment of θ, particularly around the root.

In the Robbins-Monro method, the new successive estimate $\boldsymbol{\theta}_{N+1}$ based on the present estimate $\boldsymbol{\theta}_N$ and a new observation $\mathbf{z}_N$ is given by

$$\boldsymbol{\theta}_{N+1} = \boldsymbol{\theta}_N - a_N \mathbf{z}_N \,, \tag{8.30}$$

where we assume, without losing any generality, that θ approaches θ_0, the root of (8.29), from the high side; that is, $f(\theta) > 0$ for $\theta > \theta_0$ and $f(\theta) < 0$ for $\theta < \theta_0$, as shown in Fig. 8-3. Also, a_N is assumed to be a sequence of positive numbers which satisfy the following conditions:

$$(1) \quad \lim_{N \to \infty} a_N = 0 \,, \tag{8.31}$$

$$(2) \quad \sum_{N=1}^{\infty} a_N = \infty \,, \tag{8.32}$$

$$(3) \quad \sum_{N=1}^{\infty} a_N^2 < \infty \,. \tag{8.33}$$

Although we will see later how these conditions for a_N are used for the convergence proof, the physical meaning of these equations can be described as follows. Equation (8.31) is similar to the $1/N$ term discussed earlier and allows the process to settle down in the limit. On the other hand, (8.32) insures that there is enough corrective action to avoid stopping short of the root. Equation (8.33) guarantees the variance of the accumulated noise to be finite so that we can correct for the effect of noise.

With a sequence of a_N satisfying (8.31) through (8.33), $\boldsymbol{\theta}_N$ of (8.30) converges toward θ_0 in the mean-square sense and with probability 1, that is,

$$\lim_{N \to \infty} E\{(\boldsymbol{\theta}_N - \theta_0)^2\} = 0 \,, \tag{8.34}$$

$$\lim_{N \to \infty} Pr\{\boldsymbol{\theta}_N = \theta_0\} = 1 \,. \tag{8.35}$$

The harmonic sequence of (8.28) is a suitable candidate for $\{a_N\}$. More generally, a sequence of the form

$$a_N = \frac{1}{N^k} \qquad 1 \ge k > \frac{1}{2} \tag{8.36}$$

satisfies (8.31) through (8.33), although it is not the only possible sequence.

Before discussing the convergence of the Robbins-Monro method, let us consider a feedback system analogous to this process.

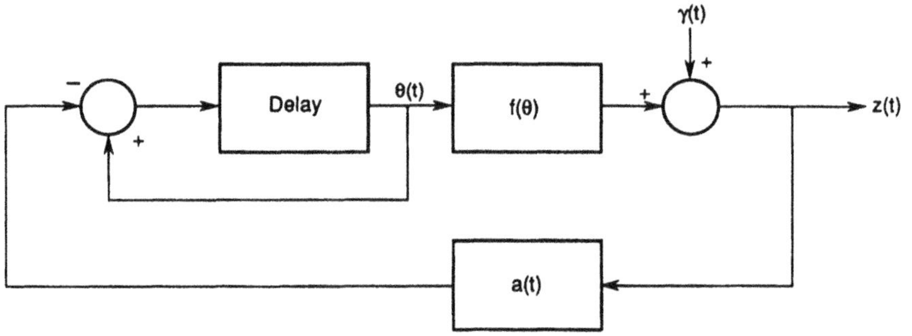

Fig. 8-4 Equivalent feedback circuit.

Figure 8-4 shows an equivalent feedback circuit, where $\gamma(t)$ is a noise process. Instead of a fixed feedback gain, we have a time-decreasing feedback gain $a(t)$. From the conventional design concept of a feedback circuit, one can notice that the decreasing $a(t)$ could guarantee the stability of the circuit without hunting but could also result in a slower response.

Convergence Proof of the Robbins-Monro Method

The convergence of the Robbins-Monro method is proved as follows. First let us divide $\mathbf{z}_N$ into two parts: the regression function $f(\boldsymbol{\theta}_N)$ and noise $\boldsymbol{\gamma}_N$. Then, (8.30) is rewritten as

$$\boldsymbol{\theta}_{N+1} = \boldsymbol{\theta}_N - a_N f(\boldsymbol{\theta}_N) - a_N \boldsymbol{\gamma}_N , \tag{8.37}$$

where

$$\boldsymbol{\gamma}_N = \mathbf{z}_N - f(\boldsymbol{\theta}_N) . \tag{8.38}$$

Then, from the definition of the regression function $f(\theta)$ in (8.29), $\boldsymbol{\gamma}_N$ is a random variable with zero mean as

$$E\{\boldsymbol{\gamma}_N \mid \boldsymbol{\theta}_N\} = E\{\mathbf{z}_N \mid \boldsymbol{\theta}_N\} - f(\boldsymbol{\theta}_N) = 0 . \tag{8.39}$$

Also, it is reasonable to assume that the variance of $\boldsymbol{\gamma}_N$ is bounded, that is,

$$E\{\boldsymbol{\gamma}_N^2\} \le \sigma^2 \tag{8.40}$$

and that $\boldsymbol{\gamma}_N$ and $\boldsymbol{\theta}_N$ are statistically independent.

Next, let us study the difference between θ_0 and $\boldsymbol{\theta}_N$. From (8.37), we have

$$(\boldsymbol{\theta}_{N+1} - \theta_0) = (\boldsymbol{\theta}_N - \theta_0) - a_N f(\boldsymbol{\theta}_N) - a_N \boldsymbol{\gamma}_N . \tag{8.41}$$

Taking the expectation of the square of (8.41)

$$E\{(\boldsymbol{\theta}_{N+1} - \theta_0)^2\} - E\{(\boldsymbol{\theta}_N - \theta_0)^2\}$$

$$= a_N^2 E\{f^2(\boldsymbol{\theta}_N)\} + a_N^2 E\{\boldsymbol{\gamma}_N^2\} - 2a_N E\{(\boldsymbol{\theta}_N - \theta_0) f(\boldsymbol{\theta}_N)\} . \tag{8.42}$$

Therefore, repeating (8.42), we obtain

$$E\{(\boldsymbol{\theta}_N - \theta_0)^2\} - E\{(\boldsymbol{\theta}_1 - \theta_0)^2\}$$

$$= \sum_{i=1}^{N-1} a_i^2 [E\{f^2(\boldsymbol{\theta}_i)\} + E\{\boldsymbol{\gamma}_i^2\}] - 2\sum_{i=1}^{N-1} a_i E\{(\boldsymbol{\theta}_i - \theta_0) f(\boldsymbol{\theta}_i)\} . \tag{8.43}$$

We assume that the regression function is also bounded in the region of interest as

$$E\{f^2(\boldsymbol{\theta}_N)\} \le b . \tag{8.44}$$

Then, (8.43) is bounded by

$$E\{(\boldsymbol{\theta}_N - \theta_0)^2\} - E\{(\boldsymbol{\theta}_1 - \theta_0)^2\}$$

$$\le (b + \sigma^2) \sum_{i=1}^{N-1} a_i^2 - 2\sum_{i=1}^{N-1} a_i E\{(\boldsymbol{\theta}_i - \theta_0) f(\boldsymbol{\theta}_i)\} . \tag{8.45}$$

Let us examine (8.45) term by term. First, since $E\{(\boldsymbol{\theta}_N - \theta_0)^2\}$ is positive and assuming $\boldsymbol{\theta}_1$ is selected so that $E\{(\boldsymbol{\theta}_1 - \theta_0)^2\}$ is finite, the left-hand side of (8.45) is bounded from below. The first term on the right-hand side of (8.45) is finite because of (8.33).

Recall from Fig. 8-3 that the regression function satisfies:

$$\begin{aligned} f(\theta) &> 0 \text{ if } (\theta - \theta_0) > 0 , \\ f(\theta) &= 0 \text{ if } (\theta - \theta_0) = 0 , \\ f(\theta) &< 0 \text{ if } (\theta - \theta_0) < 0 . \end{aligned} \tag{8.46}$$

Therefore,

$$(\theta - \theta_0) f(\theta) \geq 0 , \tag{8.47}$$

and

$$E\{(\boldsymbol{\theta} - \theta_0) f(\boldsymbol{\theta})\} \geq 0 . \tag{8.48}$$

Now consider the following proposition:

$$\lim_{i \to \infty} E\{(\boldsymbol{\theta}_i - \theta_0) f(\boldsymbol{\theta}_i)\} = 0 . \tag{8.49}$$

If (8.49) does not hold, then, because of (8.32), the last term of (8.45) tends toward $-\infty$. But this contradicts the fact that the left-hand side of (8.45) is bounded from below. Hence, (8.49) must hold. Since (8.47) holds for all θ's, (8.49) is equivalent to

$$\lim_{i \to \infty} Pr\{\boldsymbol{\theta}_i = \theta_0)\} = 1 . \tag{8.50}$$

Thus, the convergence with probability 1 is proved. The convergence in mean-square sense has also been proved but this proof is omitted here.

Minimum-Point-Finding Problem

The Robbins-Monro method can be easily modified to seek the minimum point of a regression function instead of the root. As is well known, the minimum point or the optimum point of a function $f(\theta)$ is a root of $df(\theta)/d\theta$. Therefore, if we can measure $df(\theta)/d\theta$, we can apply the Robbins-Monro method directly. Unfortunately, in most applications, the measurement of $df(\theta)/d\theta$ is not available. Therefore, we measure the derivative experimentally and modify $\boldsymbol{\theta}_N$ as

$$\boldsymbol{\theta}_{N+1} = \boldsymbol{\theta}_N - a_N \frac{\mathbf{z}(\boldsymbol{\theta}_N + c_N) - \mathbf{z}(\boldsymbol{\theta}_N - c_N)}{2c_N} . \tag{8.51}$$

This successive equation is called the *Kiefer-Wolfowitz method* [8]. Figure 8-5 illustrates the Kiefer-Wolfowitz method.

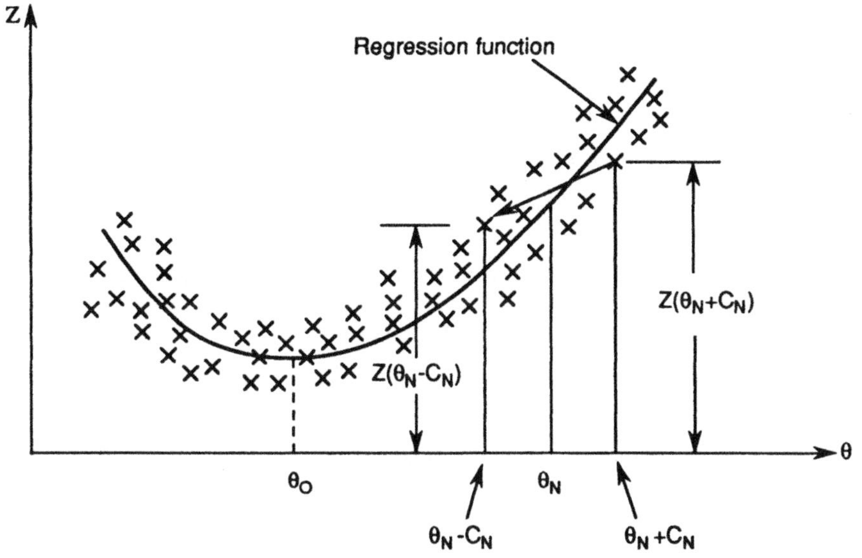

Fig. 8-5 Minimum-point-finding problem.

Both a_N and c_N are sequences of positive numbers. They must vanish in the limit, that is,

$$\lim_{N \to \infty} a_N = 0 , \tag{8.52}$$

$$\lim_{N \to \infty} c_N = 0 , \tag{8.53}$$

so that the process eventually converges. In order to make sure that we have enough corrective action to avoid stopping short of the minimum point, a_N should satisfy

$$\sum_{N=1}^{\infty} a_N = \infty . \tag{8.54}$$

Also, to cancel the accumulated noise effect we must have

$$\sum_{N=1}^{\infty} \left[\frac{a_N}{c_N} \right]^2 < \infty . \tag{8.55}$$

With a_N and c_N satisfying these conditions, it has been proven that $\boldsymbol{\theta}_N$ of (8.51) converges to θ_0 both in the mean-square sense and with probability 1, provided that we have a bounded variance for the noise and a bounded slope for the regression function. The proof is similar to the one for root-finding but is omitted here.

Multidimensional Extension

So far, we have discussed stochastic approximation for a single variable. This has been done mainly for simplicity's sake. The conclusions and the criterion for the selection of a_N are all valid for the multivariate case. The previous discussion, including the convergence proof, can be repeated simply by replacing x^2 by $\|X\|^2$ [9].

Thus, for the Robbins-Monro method, (8.30) can be rewritten as

$$\mathbf{\Theta}_{N+1} = \mathbf{\Theta}_N - a_N \mathbf{Z}_N , \tag{8.56}$$

where both $\mathbf{\Theta}$ and $\mathbf{Z}$ are random vectors with n components. With a_N satisfying (8.31) through (8.33), the convergence in the mean-square sense and with probability 1 is guaranteed, provided that both the noise variances and the regression function are bounded.

For the Kiefer-Wolfowitz method, the partial derivatives should be approximated by

$$\frac{\partial z(\Theta_N)}{\partial \theta_i} \cong \frac{z(\Theta_N + c_N E_i) - z(\Theta_N)}{c_N} \tag{8.57}$$

or

$$\frac{\partial z(\Theta_N)}{\partial \theta_i} \cong \frac{z(\Theta_N + c_N E_i) - z(\Theta_N - c_N E_i)}{2c_N} , \tag{8.58}$$

where E_i is the ith unit coordinate vector $[0 \ldots 0\ 1\ 0 \ldots 0]^T$. Then (8.51) can be extended to

$$\mathbf{\Theta}_{N+1} = \mathbf{\Theta}_N - a_N \begin{bmatrix} \partial z(\mathbf{\Theta}_N)/\partial \theta_1 \\ \vdots \\ \partial z(\mathbf{\Theta}_N)/\partial \theta_n \end{bmatrix} . \tag{8.59}$$

Figure 8-6 shows how the partial derivatives are measured; $n + 1$ observations for (8.57) and $2n$ observations for (8.58) are needed. Again, the convergence in the mean-square sense and with probability 1 is guaranteed, provided that both the noise variances and the slope of the regression function are bounded.

Now we can relate stochastic approximation to the design of a classifier. Let us design a classifier which minimizes the mean-square error between the desired output $\gamma(Z_j)$ and the actual output $W^T Z_j$ as in (4.78). Although we dis-

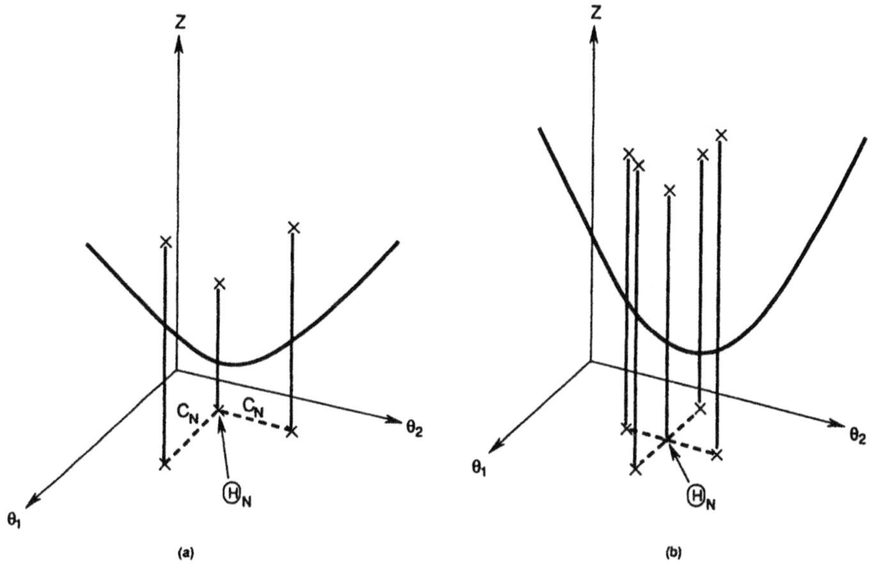

Fig. 8-6 Minimum-point-finding problem for a multivariate case.

cuss only one criterion, the same discussion can be applied to other criteria. The successive adjustment of W of (4.84) can be rewritten as

$$W(\ell+1) = W(\ell) - \rho \frac{\partial \overline{\varepsilon^2}}{\partial W} = W(\ell) - \frac{2\rho}{N} \sum_{i=1}^{N} \{ W^T(\ell) Z_i - \gamma(Z_i) \} Z_i \; . \tag{8.60}$$

That is, $W(\ell)$ is modified by the sample mean vector of $\{W^T(\ell)\mathbf{Z} - \gamma(\mathbf{Z})\}\mathbf{Z}$. Therefore, when we can use all N samples to calculate the sample mean vector for a given W, the successive adjustment becomes a simple optimization process for the regression function. When we can use only one sample at a time to modify $W(\ell)$, (8.60) is converted to

$$W(\ell + 1) = W(\ell) - 2\rho \{ W^T(\ell) Z_i - \gamma(Z_i) \} Z_i \; . \tag{8.61}$$

This is identical to (8.56), the Robbins-Monro method for the multivariate case, where $2\{W^T(\ell)Z_i - r(Z_i)\}Z_i$ corresponds to Z_N of (8.56). Thus, although this is a minimum-point-finding problem, we can calculate the partial derivatives from $W(\ell)$ and Z_i. Therefore, we can apply the simpler Robbins-Monro method rather than the Kiefer-Wolfowitz method.

Example 3: Let us apply the Robbins-Monro method to the six samples, given in Example 2, which are not linearly separable and for which the method of the previous section could not make the sequence of W converge. The result is shown in Table 8-3, where the starting W is $[0\,0\,0]^T$, $\gamma(Z_j) = 3$ for

TABLE 8-3

AN EXAMPLE OF CLASSIFIER DESIGN
BY USING INDIVIDUAL SAMPLES

Iteration	Input	z_0 z_1 z_2	w_0 w_1 w_2	$\gamma-W^TZ$	ρ	$2\rho(\gamma-W^TZ)Z$
1	Z_0	1 0 2	0 0 0	3.0	1/10	0.6 0 1.2
	Z_1	−1 −1 −1	0.6 0 1.2	4.8	1/11	−0.9 −0.9 −0.9
	Z_2	1 2 0	−0.3 −0.9 0.3	5.0	1/12	0.8 1.7 0
	Z_3	−1 0 2	0.6 0.8 0.3	2.9	1/13	−0.4 0 0.9
	Z_4	1 −1 −1	0.1 0.8 1.2	4.9	1/14	0.7 −0.7 −0.7
	Z_5	−1 2 0	0.8 0.1 0.5	3.6	1/15	−0.5 1.0 0
2	Z_0	1 0 2	0.3 1.1 0.5	1.6	1/16	0.2 0 0.4
	⋮				⋮	
	Z_5	−1 2 0	0.4 0.4 0.3	2.5	1/21	−0.2 0.5 0
3	Z_0	1 0 2	0.1 0.9 0.3	2.2	1/22	0.2 0 0.4
	⋮				⋮	
	Z_5	−1 2 0	0.2 0.5 0.3	2.3	1/27	−0.2 0.3 0
4	Z_0	1 0 2	0.1 0.8 0.3	2.3	1/28	0.2 0 0.3
	⋮				⋮	
	Z_5	−1 2 0	0.2 0.5 0.4	2.2	1/33	−0.1 0.3 0
5	Z_5	−1 2 0	0.1 0.5 0.4	2.1	1/39	−0.1 0.2 0
10	Z_5	−1 2 0	0.1 0.5 0.4	2.1	1/69	−0.1 0.1 0
15	Z_5	−1 2 0	0 0.5 0.5	2.0	1/99	0 0.1 0

$j = 0, 1, \ldots, 5$, and ρ is sequenced from 1/10 as 1/10, 1/11, ... This sequence is selected mainly because we felt that all six samples should contribute to the design of the classifier equally, at least at the initial stage, and that the sequence 1, 1/2, 1/3, . . . places too much weight on Z_0. The sequence 1/10, 1/11, . . . does not violate the conditions (8.31) through (8.33). Table 8-3 shows that, after 15 iterations, the sequence of W converges to the optimum classifier, which is $W = [0\;0.5\;0.5]^T$ in this example.

Example 4: For comparison, let us find the sequence of W by using (8.60) instead of (8.61) for the same six samples. This time, W is changed after six samples are received. Table 8-4 shows the result. Starting with

TABLE 8-4

AN EXAMPLE OF CLASSIFIER DESIGN
BY USING THE REGRESSION FUNCTION

Iteration	Input	z_0	z_1	z_2	w_0	w_1	w_2	$\gamma - W^T Z$	ρ	$2\rho(\gamma - W^T Z)Z$			$\frac{1}{6}\Sigma_{i=0}^{5} 2\rho(\gamma - W^T Z_i)Z_i$		
1	Z_0	1	0	2	0	0	0	3	1	6	0	12			
	Z_1	−1	−1	−1	0	0	0	3	1	−6	−6	−6			
	Z_2	1	2	0	0	0	0	3	1	6	12	0			
	Z_3	−1	0	2	0	0	0	3	1	−6	0	12			
	Z_4	1	−1	−1	0	0	0	3	1	6	−6	−6			
	Z_5	−1	2	0	0	0	0	3	1	−6	12	0	0	2	2
2	Z_0	1	0	2	0	2	2	−1	1/2	−0.5	0	−1			
	Z_1	−1	−1	−1	0	2	2	7	1/2	−3.5	−3.5	−3.5			
	Z_2	1	2	0	0	2	2	−1	1/2	−0.5	−1	0			
	Z_3	−1	0	2	0	2	2	−1	1/2	0.5	0	−1			
	Z_4	1	−1	−1	0	2	2	7	1/2	3.5	−3.5	−3.5			
	Z_5	−1	2	0	0	2	2	−1	1/2	0.5	−1	0	0	−1.5	−1.5
3	Z_0	1	0	2	0	0.5	0.5	2	1/3	1.3	0	2.7			
	Z_1	−1	−1	−1	0	0.5	0.5	4	1/3	−2.7	−2.7	−2.7			
	Z_2	1	2	0	0	0.5	0.5	2	1/3	1.3	2.7	0			
	Z_3	−1	0	2	0	0.5	0.5	2	1/3	−1.3	0	2.7			
	Z_4	1	−1	−1	0	0.5	0.5	4	1/3	2.7	−2.7	−2.7			
	Z_5	−1	2	0	0	0.5	0.5	2	1/3	−1.3	2.7	0	0	0	0
4	Z_0				0	0.5	0.5		1/4						

$W = [0\,0\,0]^T$, $\gamma(Z_j) = 3$ ($j = 0, 1, \ldots, 5$), and the sequence of $\rho = 1, 1/2, \ldots,$ the optimum classifier is obtained in two iterations. This is a much faster process than the one of Example 3, in which 15 iterations were needed.

The Method of Potential Functions

In stochastic approximation, successive approximation is applied to estimate a set of parameters which gives either the root or the extremal point of a regression function. The results can be extended to the estimation of the regression function itself [10].

Let us express a regression function $f(X)$ by an expansion of a given set of basis functions as

$$f(X) = \sum_{i=1}^{\infty} \theta_i \xi_i(X) , \tag{8.62}$$

where $\{\theta_i\}$ should satisfy

$$\sum_{i=1}^{\infty} \theta_i^2 < \infty . \tag{8.63}$$

Assuming that the ξ_i's are know and given, the regression function $f(X)$ is characterized by a set of parameters $\Theta = \{\theta_1, \ldots, \theta_\infty\}$. This is somewhat the same as designing a linear classifier in which x_i is used instead of $\xi_i(X)$. The selection of the basis functions is very much problem-oriented and depends on the functional form of $f(X)$. In general, we have to look for ξ_i so that θ_i decreases quickly as i increases. Also, it is common practice to select an orthonormal set of ξ_i for theoretical convenience.

$$E\{\xi_i(\mathbf{X})\xi_j(\mathbf{X})\} = \int \xi_i(X)\xi_j(X)p(X)dX = \delta_{ij} . \tag{8.64}$$

In a noisy environment, for a given X, our observation is a random variable $\mathbf{z}(X)$ whose expected value is $f(X)$. Therefore, if we want to determine the θ_i's to minimize the mean-square error between $\mathbf{z}(\mathbf{X})$ and $\Sigma\theta_i\xi_i(\mathbf{X})$, then we solve

$$\frac{\partial}{\partial \theta_i} E\left[\left\{\mathbf{z}(\mathbf{X}) - \sum_{j=1}^{\infty}\theta_j\xi_j(\mathbf{X})\right\}^2\right] = -2E\left[\left\{\mathbf{z}(\mathbf{X}) - \sum_{j=1}^{\infty}\theta_j\xi_j(\mathbf{X})\right\}\xi_i(\mathbf{X})\right]$$

$$= -2[E\{\mathbf{z}(\mathbf{X})\xi_i(\mathbf{X})\} - \theta_i] = 0 , \tag{8.65}$$

where the ξ_i's are assumed to be orthonormal. Therefore, θ_i is determined by

$$\theta_i = E\{\mathbf{z}(\mathbf{X})\xi_i(\mathbf{X})\} = \iint_{-\infty}^{+\infty} z(X)\xi_i(X)p(z \mid X)p(X)dzdX$$

$$= \int f(X)\xi_i(X)p(X)dX = E\{f(\mathbf{X})\xi_i(\mathbf{X})\} . \tag{8.66}$$

When a successive approximation is required, θ_i can be estimated by the sequence

$$\theta_i(\ell+1)=\theta_i(\ell)-a_\ell \frac{\partial \overline{\varepsilon^2}}{\partial \theta_i}$$

$$=\theta_i(\ell)-2a_\ell\left\{\sum_{j=1}^{\infty}\theta_j(\ell)\xi_j(X_\ell)-z(X_\ell)\right\}\xi_i(X_\ell) \quad (i=1,2,\ldots). \tag{8.67}$$

Or, in vector form,

$$\Theta(\ell+1)=\Theta(\ell)-2a_\ell\{\Theta^T(\ell)\Xi(X_\ell)-z(X_\ell)\}\Xi(X_\ell), \tag{8.68}$$

where $\Theta=[\theta_1\ldots\theta_\infty]^T$ and $\Xi=[\xi_1\ldots\xi_\infty]^T$. This equation suggests the use of the Robbins-Monro method with the sequence a_ℓ satisfying (8.31) through (8.33).

A successive approximation of a functional form $f(X)$, rather than Θ, is also obtained by multiplying (8.68) by $\Xi(X)$. That is,

$$f_{\ell+1}(X)=\Theta^T(\ell+1)\Xi(X)$$

$$=\Theta^T(\ell)\Xi(X)-2a_\ell\{\Theta^T(\ell)\Xi(X_\ell)-z(X_\ell)\}\Xi^T(X_\ell)\Xi(X)$$

$$=f_\ell(X)-\gamma_\ell\kappa(X_\ell,X), \tag{8.69}$$

where

$$\gamma_\ell=2a_\ell\{f_\ell(X_\ell)-z(X_\ell)\}, \tag{8.70}$$

$$\kappa(X_\ell,X)=\Xi^T(X_\ell)\Xi(X). \tag{8.71}$$

This $\kappa(Y,X)$ is called the *potential function*, and the successive approximation of (8.69) is called the *method of potential functions*.

Although we have derived the method of the potential functions from a stochastic approximation point of view, the method can be stated in a more general form as follows.

A function $f(X)$ which is either deterministic or stochastic can be successively approximated by

$$f_{\ell+1}(X)=f_\ell(X)-\gamma_\ell\kappa(X_\ell,X), \tag{8.72}$$

where $f(X)$, its observation $z(X)$, and $\kappa(Y,X)$ are all bounded. The potential function satisfies

$$\kappa(Y,X) = \kappa(X,Y) \tag{8.73}$$

and

$$\kappa(Y,X) = \sum_{i=1}^{\infty} \lambda_i^2 \xi_i(Y) \xi_i(X) . \tag{8.74}$$

The basis functions are orthogonal as

$$\int \xi_i(X) \xi_j(X) k(X) dX = \frac{\delta_{ij}}{\lambda_i^2} , \tag{8.75}$$

where $k(X)$ is a general kernel function, and $k(X) = p(X)$ for stochastic cases as in (8.64). Selecting γ_ℓ as

$$\gamma_\ell = a_\ell \{ f_\ell(X_\ell) - z(X_\ell) \} , \tag{8.76}$$

where a_ℓ satisfies (8.31) through (8.33), the successive approximation of (8.72) converges in probability. The proof is omitted [10].

Although we may select a broad range of potential functions which satisfy the above conditions, we can be a little more specific by using the fact that the potential functions are symmetric with respect to two vectors X and Y. It has been suggested that the distance between X and Y be used as a symmetric function, that is,

$$\kappa(Y,X) = g(\|Y - X\|) . \tag{8.77}$$

Two typical examples of $g(\cdot)$ are

$$\kappa(Y,X) = \exp\{-c\|Y - X\|^2\} \tag{8.78}$$

and

$$\kappa(Y,X) = (1 + \|Y - X\|^2)^{-1} . \tag{8.79}$$

Acceleration of Convergence

As we stated previously, a stochastic approximation converges very slowly. This is the price for guaranteed convergence. There have been many proposals to improve this disadvantage. In this subsection, we discuss two of them.

(1) *Flatter Sequence of a_N:* Since the primary cause of slow convergence is the choice of the decreasing sequence a_N, we can make the sequence decrease more slowly and still guarantees convergence. One way to do this is to change a_N to the next value only when a sign change of z_N is observed in root-finding. As long as the sign of z_N remains the same, we are not close to the root and convergence speed is more important than guaranteed convergence. When a sign change of z_N is observed, we have to start worrying about convergence. The same argument holds for the minimum-point-finding problem, where the sign of slope should be observed instead of the sign of z_N. Table 8-5 shows this altered sequence a_N. Note that the altered sequence satisfies (8.31) through (8.33).

TABLE 8-5

ACCELERATED SEQUENCE OF a_N

Trial:	1	2	3	4	5	6	7	8
Sign of z_N:	+	+	+	−	−	+	+	−
Conventional a_N:	1	1/2	1/3	1/4	1/5	1/6	1/7	1/8
Accelerated a_N:	1	1	1	1/2	1/2	1/3	1/3	1/4

(2) *More Observations for a Given θ:* If we can take many observations for a given θ and calculate the mean, we can obtain the regression function. Therefore, the problem becomes that of the convergence of a deterministic function. As a compromise between this deterministic approach and stochastic approximation, we may select a few observations for a given θ rather than one, take the average of these observations, and use it as z_N. An analogy can be found in a conventional feedback circuit where a filter is used to eliminate noise from the observation signal. Determining how many observations should be averaged to eliminate noise corresponds to the selection of the time constant in filter design.

8.3 Successive Bayes Estimation

Since the estimates of parameters are random vectors, complete knowledge of the statistical properties of the estimates is obtained from their joint density, distribution, or characteristic functions. In this section, we show

how the density function of the estimate can be calculated by a successive process.

Supervised Estimation

Let $\mathbf{X}_1, \ldots, \mathbf{X}_N$ be N samples which are used to estimate the density function of a parameter vector $\boldsymbol{\Theta}$. The samples $\mathbf{X}_i$ are given successively one by one. Thus, using the Bayes theorem, we can obtain a recursive expression for the *a posteriori* density function of $\boldsymbol{\Theta}$, given $X_1, \ldots, X_N$, as

$$p(\Theta | X_1, \ldots, X_N) = \frac{p(X_N | X_1, \ldots, X_{N-1}, \Theta) p(\Theta | X_1, \ldots, X_{N-1})}{p(X_N | X_1, \ldots, X_{N-1})} \quad (8.80)$$

where the *a priori* density function of $\mathbf{X}_N$, $p(X_N | X_1, \ldots, X_{N-1}, \Theta)$, is assumed to be known. If the numerator of (8.80) is available, the denominator can be calculated by integrating the numerator as follows:

$$p(X_N | X_1, \ldots, X_{N-1}) = \int p(X_N | X_1, \ldots, X_{N-1}, \Theta) p(\Theta | X_1, \ldots, X_{N-1}) d\Theta \,. \quad (8.81)$$

Thus (8.80) shows that $p(\Theta | X_1, \ldots, X_N)$ may be calculated from $p(\Theta | X_1, \ldots, X_{N-1})$. Repeating the same operation N times, we may start this sequence of calculations from $p(\Theta)$. The term $p(\Theta)$ is called the *initial* density function of $\boldsymbol{\Theta}$, and reflects our initial knowledge about $\boldsymbol{\Theta}$.

Estimation of an expected vector with a known covariance matrix: Let us estimate the expected vector M of a normal distribution with a known covariance matrix Σ. The initial density function $p(M)$ is assumed to be normal with the expected vector M_0 and covariance matrix Σ_0. Then, after observing the first sample X_1,

$$p(M | X_1) = \frac{p(X_1 | M) p(M)}{\int p(X_1 | M) p(M) dM}$$

$$= c_1 \exp[-\frac{1}{2}(X_1 - M)^T \Sigma^{-1}(X_1 - M) - \frac{1}{2}(M - M_0)^T \Sigma_0^{-1}(M - M_0)]$$

$$= c_2 \exp[-\frac{1}{2}(M - M_1)^T \Sigma_1^{-1}(M - M_1)] \,, \quad (8.82)$$

where

$$M_1 = \Sigma_0(\Sigma_0 + \Sigma)^{-1}X_1 + \Sigma(\Sigma_0 + \Sigma)^{-1}M_0 , \tag{8.83}$$

$$\Sigma_1 = \Sigma_0(\Sigma_0 + \Sigma)^{-1}\Sigma . \tag{8.84}$$

That is, $p(M|X_1)$ is also a normal distribution and its expected vector and covariance matrix are given by (8.83) and (8.84). Since $\int p(X_1|M)p(M)dM$ of (8.82) is independent of M, c_1, and c_2 are independent of M and are constants such that $\int p(M|X_1)dM = 1$.

We repeat the same process, replacing M_0 and Σ_0 of $p(M)$ by M_1 and Σ_1 of $p(M|X_1)$. The resulting density $p(M|X_1,X_2)$ is also normal, and M_2 and Σ_2 are calculated by (8.83) and (8.84) with M_1 and Σ_1 instead of M_0 and Σ_0. Thus, after N iterations,

$$p(M|X_1,\ldots,X_N) = N_M(M_N,\Sigma_N) , \tag{8.85}$$

where $N_M(M_N,\Sigma_N)$ denotes a normal distribution of $\mathbf{M}$ with expected vector M_N and covariance matrix Σ_N. They are given by

$$M_N = \frac{\Sigma}{N}[\Sigma_0 + \frac{\Sigma}{N}]^{-1}M_0 + \Sigma_0[\Sigma_0 + \frac{\Sigma}{N}]^{-1}\left[\frac{1}{N}\sum_{i=1}^{N}X_i\right] , \tag{8.86}$$

$$\Sigma_N = \Sigma_0[\Sigma_0 + \frac{\Sigma}{N}]^{-1}\frac{\Sigma}{N} . \tag{8.87}$$

As N increases, the effect of the initial knowledge of M, M_0, and Σ_0, decreases and finally

$$\lim_{N\to\infty} M_N = \frac{1}{N}\sum_{i=1}^{N}X_i , \tag{8.88}$$

$$\lim_{N\to\infty} \Sigma_N = 0 . \tag{8.89}$$

Thus, M_N for large N is estimated by the sample mean vector, and Σ_N is Σ/N.

Throughout this process, we notice that both *a priori* and *a posteriori* density functions are always normal. Because of this fact, we calculated only M_N and Σ_N recursively instead of calculating the density function. In general, when the *a posteriori* density function after each iteration is a member of the same family as the *a priori* density function and only the parameters of the density function change, we call the density functions a *conjugate* or *reproducing pair*.

In addition to its simplicity of computation, it has been shown that the reproducing density function of $\boldsymbol{\Theta}$ becomes more concentrated and converges toward the true parameter vector Θ in some appropriate sense as $N \rightarrow \infty$ [11].

Many well-known density functions which are reproducing pairs are listed in a reference [11].

Estimation of a covariance matrix with a given expected vector: The successive estimation of a covariance matrix for a normally distributed random vector **X** can be discussed in the same manner as that of the expected vector. Here we assume that the expected vector is known and, without further loss of generality, that it is equal to zero. As we assumed, the *a priori* density function of $p(X|\Sigma)$ is normal. On the other hand, it is known that the sample covariance matrix has a *Wishart distribution*. Therefore, we start from the distribution of a sample covariance matrix $p(\Sigma|\Sigma_0,N_0)$ with N_0 as the number of samples used to compute Σ_0. The term N_0 may be considered as a confidence constant about the initial estimate of Σ_0. Furthermore, instead of calculating $p(\Sigma|\Sigma_0,N_0)$, let us compute $p(K|\Sigma_0,N_0)$ where $K = \Sigma^{-1}$. The reason for doing this is that the covariance matrix is always used in the inverse form for a normal distribution. Then, $p(K|\Sigma_0,N_0)$ is given by

$$p(K|\Sigma_0,N_0) = c(n,N_0)\left|\frac{1}{2}N_0\Sigma_0\right|^{(N_0-1)/2}|K|^{(N_0-n-2)/2}$$

$$\times \exp[-\frac{1}{2}\text{tr}(N_0\Sigma_0K)] , \tag{8.90}$$

where

$$c(n,N_0) = \left\{\pi^{n(n-1)/4}\prod_{i=1}^{n}\Gamma\left[\frac{N_0-i}{2}\right]\right\}^{-1} . \tag{8.91}$$

Using (8.90) as $p(\Theta)$ and applying (8.80) repeatedly, $p(K|X_1,\ldots,X_N)$ also becomes the Wishart distribution and the parameters of the Wishart distribution, Σ_0 and N_0, are updated as follows [12]:

$$\Sigma_N = \frac{\left[\frac{1}{N}\sum_{i=1}^{N} X_i X_i^T\right] + \frac{N_0}{N}\Sigma_0}{1 + \frac{N_0}{N}} , \tag{8.92}$$

$$N_N = N_0 + N . \tag{8.93}$$

Thus, as N increases, Σ_N approaches the sample covariance matrix $(1/N)\Sigma X_i X_i^T$ with zero-mean.

Estimation of an expected vector and a covariance matrix: When both the expected vector and covariance matrix are to be estimated successively, we have to calculate the joint *a posteriori* density function $p(M,\Sigma | X_1, \ldots, X_N)$. When M and Σ are estimated by the sample mean vector and sample covariance matrix and $\mathbf{X}$ is normally distributed, $p(M,K | M_0,\Sigma_0,\mu_0,N_0)$ $(K = \Sigma^{-1})$ is known to be the *Gauss-Wishart distribution* as

$$p(M,K | M_0,\Sigma_0,\mu_0,N_0)$$

$$= (2\pi)^{-n/2} |\mu_0 K|^{1/2} \exp[-\frac{1}{2}\mu_0 (M - M_0)^T K (M - M_0)]$$

$$\times c(n,N_0) | \frac{1}{2} N_0 \Sigma_0 |^{(N_0-1)/2} | K |^{(N_0-n-2)/2} \exp[-\frac{1}{2}\mathrm{tr}(N_0 \Sigma_0 K)] . \tag{8.94}$$

where $c(n,N_0)$ is given in (8.91). The term μ_0 is the confidence constant about the initial estimate of M_0 as N_0 for Σ_0. Again, using (8.94) as $p(\Theta)$ and applying (8.80) repeatedly, $p(M,K | X_1, \ldots, X_N)$ becomes the Gauss-Wishart distribution and the parameters of the distribution, M_0, Σ_0, μ_0, and N_0, are updated as follows [12]:

$$M_N = \frac{\left[\frac{1}{N}\sum_{i=1}^{N} X_i\right] + \frac{\mu_0}{N} M_0}{1 + \frac{\mu_0}{N}} , \tag{8.95}$$

$$\Sigma_N = \frac{1}{1 + \dfrac{N_0}{N}} \left\{ \left[\frac{1}{N} \sum_{i=1}^{N} X_i X_i^T \right] - (1 + \frac{\mu_0}{N}) M_N M_N^T \right.$$

$$\left. + (\frac{N_0}{N} \Sigma_0 + \frac{\mu_0}{N} M_0 M_0^T) \right\} , \tag{8.96}$$

$$\mu_N = \mu_0 + N , \tag{8.97}$$

$$N_N = N_0 + N . \tag{8.98}$$

Unsupervised Estimation

Suppose that we have two distributions characterized by Θ_1 and Θ_2. In successive *unsupervised estimation*, our task is to estimate Θ_1 and Θ_2 successively, assuming that we do not know the true distributions from which the incoming samples are taken. This is also termed *learning without a teacher*. Because of the additional ambiguity we impose, the computation of unsupervised estimation becomes more complex. However, the development of this kind of technique is motivated by the hope that the machine may improve the performance without any outside supervision after initial learning in a supervised mode.

Since we do not know the class of $\mathbf{X}_N$, our guess is that $\mathbf{X}_N$ may belong to ω_i with probability P_i ($i = 1,2$), provided that we know P_i. Therefore, the *a priori* density function of (8.80) becomes

$$p(X_N | X_1, \ldots, X_{N-1}, \Theta_1, \Theta_2) = \sum_{i=1}^{2} p(X_N | X_1, \ldots, X_{N-1}, \Theta_i, \omega_i) P_i \,. \tag{8.99}$$

Hence, if we know the *a priori* density function of each class $p(X_N | X_1, \ldots, X_{N-1}, \Theta_i, \omega_i)$ and the *a priori* class probability P_i, $p(X_N | X_1, \ldots, X_{N-1}, \Theta_1, \Theta_2)$ can be computed by (8.99) and subsequently $p(X_N | X_1, \ldots, X_{N-1})$ by (8.81).

Thus we obtain a recursive expression for the *a posteriori* density function as

$$p(\Theta_1,\Theta_2 \mid X_1,\ldots,X_N)$$

$$= \frac{\sum_{i=1}^{2} p(X_N \mid X_1,\ldots,X_{N-1},\Theta_i,\omega_i)P_i}{p(X_N \mid X_1,\ldots,X_{N-1})} p(\Theta_1,\Theta_2 \mid X_1,\ldots,X_{N-1}) . \quad (8.100)$$

Therefore, as a concept, successive unsupervised estimation of (8.100) is the same as successive supervised estimation of (8.80). However, because of the summation involved in the calculation of *a priori* density function, the reproducing property is lost for all density functions listed previously, including the normal distribution. This means that updating parameters is no longer adequate and we must deal with the recursive estimation of multivariate functions.

Using all available samples at a time, there are more practical techniques available for unsupervised estimation and classification. The problem is stated as the method of finding the *clusters* of given samples and finding the natural boundaries of these clusters without knowing the classes of the samples. This problem will be discussed in Chapter 11.

Computer Projects

1. Generate samples one by one, according to Data I-Λ with $P_1 = P_2 = 0.5$. Find the linear classifier by using three successive adjustments: fixed increment, absolute correction, and gradient correction rules. Find a way to detect the oscillation of the classifier around the steady state and show which samples cause this oscillation.
2. Repeat 1 by using the stochastic approximation of (8.61).
3. Repeat 2 by using the average of k samples in the second term of (8.61). Choose $k = 2$, 4, 8, and 16.
4. Attach the acceleration program of Table 8-5 to Project 2.
5. Attach the acceleration program of Table 8-5 to Project 3.

Problems

1. Repeat Examples 2 and 3 by using

   (a) the absolute correction rule of (8.7), and

   (b) the gradient correction rule of (8.8).

2. Suppose that we have six samples from three classes as (+1,0) and (0,+1) for ω_1, (−1,+1) and (−1,0) for ω_2, and (0,−1) and (+1,−1) for ω_3. Find a linear classifier to separate these three classes by a successive method.

3. In Chapter 4, we discussed a piecewise linear classifier. Propose an algorithm of successive adjustment for a piecewise linear classifier in a multiclass problem.

4. A regression function is given by $f = \theta^3$. Find the root of the regression function by the Robbins-Monro method starting from $\theta = 2$. Assume that the ℓth observation is $z_\ell = \theta_\ell^3 + (-0.3)^\ell$, where $(-0.3)^\ell$ is an additive noise.

5. A regression function is given by $f = -\theta^2$. Find the maximum point of the regression function by the Kiefer-Wolfowitz method. Assume that the observation is $\mathbf{z} = -\theta^2 + 0.3\mathbf{a}$, where $\mathbf{a}$ is either +1 or −1 depending on the face of a tossed coin.

6. Repeat the convergence proof of the Robbins-Monro method for the multivariate case.

7. Repeat Example 4 by using (4.82) so as to minimize (4.74). If the linear classifier does not converge to $a(x_1 + x_2) = 0$ (a is a positive constant), point out the problem of this procedure.

8. The term $\mathbf{x}$ is a random variable +1 or 0 with probability P or $(1 - P)$, respectively. Let $\mathbf{y}$ be the number of 1's out of N observations of $\mathbf{x}$. The *a priori* density function of $\mathbf{y}$, given P and N, is given by

$$Pr\{\mathbf{y} = y \mid P, N\} = \binom{N}{y} P^y (1 - P)^{N-y} ,$$

   which is a binomial distribution. Find the successive Bayes estimate of P. Also show that the binomial distribution is a reproducing pair. (Hint: Start from

$$p(P \mid y_0, N_0) = \begin{bmatrix} N_0 \\ y_0 \end{bmatrix} P^{y_0}(1 - P)^{N_0 - y_0} .$$

9. Let $\mathbf{x}$ be normally distributed with zero-mean and variance σ^2. Find the successive Bayes estimate of σ^2, assuming σ_0^2 as the initial estimate of σ^2 with the confidence constant N_0. (Hint: The sample variance with zero mean has the chi-square distribution.)

10. Let $\mathbf{x}_i$ be the ith sample from the mixture of two normal distributions whose means and variances are 0 and σ^2 for ω_1 and m and σ^2 for ω_2. Assuming $P_1 = P_2 = 0.5$, find the successive unsupervised estimate of m when the first sample $\mathbf{x}_1$ is received. Is $p(m \mid x_1)$ normal? The mean of ω_1, 0, and both variances σ^2 are assumed to be known. The initial density function $p(m)$ is normal with the expected value m_0 and variance σ_0^2.

References

1. F. Rosenblatt, "Principles of Neurodynamics," Spartan Books, Washington, DC, 1962.
2. M. Minsky and S. Papert, "Perceptrons," MIT Press, Cambridge, 1969.
3. N. J. Nilsson, "Learning Machines," McGraw-Hill, New York, 1966.
4. R. O. Duda and H. Fossum, Pattern classification by iteratively determined linear and piecewise linear discriminant functions, *Trans. IEEE Electronic Computers*, EC-15, pp. 220-232, 1966.
5. D. J. Walde, "Optimum Seeking Methods," Prentice-Hall, Englewood Cliffs, New Jersey, 1964.
6. K. S. Fu, "Sequential Methods in Pattern Recognition and Machine Learning," Academic Press, New York, 1968.
7. H. Robbins and S. Monro, A stochastic approximation method, *Ann. Math. Stat.*, 22, pp. 400-407, 1951.
8. J. Kiefer and J. Wolfowitz, Stochastic estimation of the maximum of a regression function, *Ann. Math. Stat.*, 23, pp. 462-466, 1952.
9. J. A. Blum, Multidimensional stochastic approximation procedures, *Ann. Math. Stat.*, 25, pp. 737-744, 1965.

10. E. M. Braverman, The method of potential functions in the problem of training machines to recognize patterns without a teacher, *Autom. and Remote Contr.* [USSR], 27, pp. 1748-1771, 1966.

11. J. Spragins, A note on the iterative application of Bayes' rule, *Trans. IEEE Inform. Theory*, IT-11, pp. 544-549, 1965.

12. D. G. Keehn, A note on learning for Gaussian properties, *Trans. IEEE Inform. Theory*, IT-11, pp. 126-132, 1965.

Chapter 9

FEATURE EXTRACTION AND LINEAR MAPPING FOR SIGNAL REPRESENTATION

Up to now we have discussed how to design a classifier to separate samples into two or more classes, assuming that the variables of these samples are already selected and given. Obviously, the selection of these variables is important and strongly affects classifier design. That is, if the variables show significant differences from one class to another, the classifier can be designed more easily with better performance. Therefore, the selection of variables is a key problem in pattern recognition and is termed *feature selection* or *feature extraction*.

Feature selection is generally considered a process of mapping the original measurements into more effective features. If the mapping is linear, the mapping function is well defined and our task is simply to find the coefficients of the linear function so as to maximize or minimize a criterion. Therefore, if we have a proper criterion for evaluating the effectiveness of features, we can use the well-developed techniques of linear algebra for simple criteria, or, in the case of a complex criterion, we can apply iterative techniques to determine these mapping coefficients. Unfortunately, in many applications of pattern recognition, there are important features which are not linear functions of the original measurements, but are highly nonlinear functions. Then, the basic problem is to find a proper nonlinear mapping function for the given data.

Since we do not have any general algorithm to generate nonlinear mapping functions systematically, the selection of features becomes very much problem-oriented.

In this and the next chapter, we will discuss criteria for measuring feature effectiveness. Since linear mappings are based on these criteria, we discuss linear mappings as well as the criteria. In this chapter, we deal with features for signal representation. Since the evaluation of eigenvalues and eigenvectors is a central problem for signal representation, we will discuss their estimation in this chapter. In the next chapter we will extend the discussion to classification, and features will be evaluated by their effectiveness on class separability.

9.1 The Discrete Karhunen-Loéve Expansion

First, let us discuss feature selection for signal representation. That is, we discuss how closely we can represent samples of a distribution with a set of features. If a small set of features is found to represent the samples accurately, we may say that these features are effective. Although this problem is not directly related to pattern classification, knowledge of the characteristics of individual distributions should help to separate one distribution from others. Also, feature selection for signal representation has wide applications in other areas such as data compression in communication systems.

Another limitation stems from the fact that we seek only features which can be obtained by a linear transformation of the original variables. Figure 9-1 shows that a new feature $\mathbf{y}$ is very effective in representing the given samples, but that $\mathbf{y}$ is a nonlinear function of $\mathbf{x}_1$ and $\mathbf{x}_2$.

Minimum Mean-Square Error

Discrete Karhunen-Loéve expansion: Let $\mathbf{X}$ be an n-dimensional random vector. Then, $\mathbf{X}$ can be represented without error by the summation of n linearly independent vectors as

$$\mathbf{X} = \sum_{i=1}^{n} \mathbf{y}_i \phi_i = \Phi \mathbf{Y} , \tag{9.1}$$

where

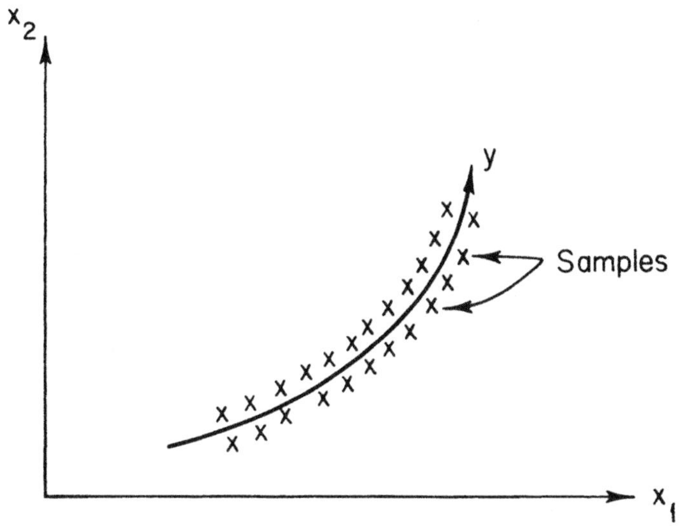

Fig. 9-1 Nonlinear mapping.

$$\Phi = [\phi_1 \ldots \phi_n] \tag{9.2}$$

and

$$\mathbf{Y} = [y_1 \ldots y_n]^T . \tag{9.3}$$

The matrix Φ is deterministic and is made up of n linearly independent column vectors. Thus,

$$|\Phi| \neq 0 . \tag{9.4}$$

The columns of Φ span the n-dimensional space containing $\mathbf{X}$ and are called *basis vectors*. Furthermore, we may assume that the columns of Φ form an orthonormal set, that is,

$$\phi_i^T \phi_j = \begin{cases} 1 & \text{for } i = j \\ 0 & \text{for } i \neq j . \end{cases} \tag{9.5}$$

If the orthonormality condition is satisfied, the components of $\mathbf{Y}$ can be calculated by

$$y_i = \phi_i^T \mathbf{X} \qquad (i = 1, \ldots, n) . \tag{9.6}$$

Therefore, $\mathbf{Y}$ is simply an orthonormal transformation of the random vector $\mathbf{X}$, and is itself a random vector. We may call ϕ_i the ith feature or feature vector, and $\mathbf{y}_i$ the ith component of the sample in the feature (or mapped) space.

Suppose that we choose only m ($<n$) of ϕ_i's and that we still want, at least, to approximate $\mathbf{X}$ well. We can do this by replacing those components of $\mathbf{Y}$, which we do not calculate, with preselected constants and form the following approximation:

$$\hat{\mathbf{X}}(m) = \sum_{i=1}^{m} \mathbf{y}_i \phi_i + \sum_{i=m+1}^{n} b_i \phi_i \; . \tag{9.7}$$

We lose no generality in assuming that only the first m $\mathbf{y}$'s are calculated. The resulting representation error is

$$\Delta\mathbf{X}(m) = \mathbf{X} - \hat{\mathbf{X}}(m) = \mathbf{X} - \sum_{i=1}^{m} \mathbf{y}_i \phi_i - \sum_{i=m+1}^{n} b_i \phi_i = \sum_{i=m+1}^{n} (\mathbf{y}_i - b_i)\phi_i \; . \tag{9.8}$$

Note that both $\hat{\mathbf{X}}$ and $\Delta\mathbf{X}$ are random vectors. We will use the mean-square magnitude of $\Delta\mathbf{X}$ as a criterion to measure the effectiveness of the subset of m features. We have

$$\begin{aligned} \bar{\varepsilon}^2(m) &= E\{\|\Delta\mathbf{X}(m)\|^2\} \\ &= E\left\{ \sum_{i=m+1}^{n} \sum_{j=m+1}^{n} (\mathbf{y}_i - b_i)(\mathbf{y}_j - b_j)\phi_i^T \phi_j \right\} \\ &= \sum_{i=m+1}^{n} E\{(\mathbf{y}_i - b_i)^2\} \; . \end{aligned} \tag{9.9}$$

For every choice of basis vectors and constant terms, we obtain a value for $\bar{\varepsilon}^2(m)$. We would like to make the choice which minimizes $\bar{\varepsilon}^2(m)$.

The optimum choice for b_i is obtained by minimizing $\bar{\varepsilon}^2(m)$ with respect to b_i as follows:

$$\frac{\partial}{\partial b_i} E\{(\mathbf{y}_i - b_i)^2\} = -2[E\{\mathbf{y}_i\} - b_i] = 0 \; . \tag{9.10}$$

Solving (9.10) for b_i

$$b_i = E\{\mathbf{y}_i\} = \phi_i^T E\{\mathbf{X}\} \; . \tag{9.11}$$

That is, we should replace those $\mathbf{y}_i$'s, which we do not measure, by their expected values.

Now, the mean-square error can be written as

$$\bar{\varepsilon}^2(m) = \sum_{i=m+1}^{n} E[(\mathbf{y}_i - E\{\mathbf{y}_i\})^2]$$

$$= \sum_{i=m+1}^{n} \phi_i^T E[(\mathbf{X} - E\{\mathbf{X}\})(\mathbf{X} - E\{\mathbf{X}\})^T]\phi_i$$

$$= \sum_{i=m+1}^{n} \phi_i^T \Sigma_X \phi_i \ , \tag{9.12}$$

where Σ_X is, by definition, the covariance matrix of $\mathbf{X}$. We shall show that the optimum choice for the ϕ_i's is those which satisfy

$$\Sigma_X \phi_i = \lambda_i \phi_i \ , \tag{9.13}$$

that is, the eigenvectors of Σ_X. Thus, inserting (9.13) into (9.12), the minimum mean-square error becomes

$$\bar{\varepsilon}^2(m)_{opt} = \sum_{i=m+1}^{n} \lambda_i \ . \tag{9.14}$$

The expansion of a random vector in the eigenvectors of the covariance matrix is called the discrete version of *the Karhunen-Loéve (K-L) expansion.*

Proof of (9.13): Since we minimize (9.12) under the constraint of orthonormality among the ϕ_i's, let us rewrite the criterion as

$$J = \sum_{i=m+1}^{n} \phi_i^T \Sigma_X \phi_i - \sum_{i=m+1}^{n} \sum_{j=m+1}^{i} \mu_{ij}(\phi_i^T \phi_j - \delta_{ij})$$

$$= \text{tr}[\Phi_{n-m}^T \Sigma_X \Phi_{n-m} - \boldsymbol{\mu}_{n-m}(\Phi_{n-m}^T \Phi_{n-m} - I)] \ , \tag{9.15}$$

where the μ_{ij}'s are Langrange multipliers and Φ_{n-m} and $\boldsymbol{\mu}_{n-m}$ are $n\times(n-m)$ and $(n-m)\times(n-m)$ matrices defined by

$$\Phi_{n-m} = [\phi_{m+1} \ldots \phi_n]_{n\times(n-m)} \ , \tag{9.16}$$

$$\boldsymbol{\mu}_{n-m} = \begin{bmatrix} \mu_{m+1,m+1} & & \frac{1}{2}\mu_{ij} \\ & \ddots & \\ \frac{1}{2}\mu_{ij} & & \mu_{nn} \end{bmatrix} . \tag{9.17}$$

The derivative of J with respect to Φ_{n-m} can be calculated by using (A.13) and (A.14), resulting in

$$\frac{\partial J}{\partial \Phi_{n-m}} = 2[\Sigma_X \Phi_{n-m} - \Phi_{n-m} \boldsymbol{\mu}_{n-m}] . \tag{9.18}$$

Equating $\partial J / \partial \Phi_{n-m}$ to zero,

$$\Sigma_X \Phi_{n-m} = \Phi_{n-m} \boldsymbol{\mu}_{n-m} . \tag{9.19}$$

Certainly, (9.19) is satisfied, if $\boldsymbol{\mu}_{n-m}$ is the diagonal matrix with the $(n-m)$ eigenvalues of Σ_X, $\lambda_{m+1}, \ldots, \lambda_n$, and Φ_{n-m} is the matrix of the corresponding eigenvectors. Thus, the eigenvalues and eigenvectors give a particular solution of (9.19). The minimization of $\bar{\varepsilon}^2(m)$ can be achieved by selecting the smallest $(n-m)$ eigenvalues and the corresponding eigenvectors.

However, there exist many other Φ_{n-m}'s and $\boldsymbol{\mu}_{n-m}$'s which satisfy (9.19). Therefore, we need to show why we choose the eigenvalue and eigenvector matrices as the solution of (9.19).

Multiplying Φ_{n-m}^T to (9.19) from the left side and using the orthonormality of the ϕ_i's,

$$\boldsymbol{\mu}_{n-m} = \Phi_{n-m}^T \Sigma_X \Phi_{n-m} . \tag{9.20}$$

Therefore, $\boldsymbol{\mu}_{n-m}$ is the covariance matrix of the $(n-m)$-dimensional vector $\mathbf{Y}$ after the transformation of $\mathbf{Y} = \Phi_{n-m}^T \mathbf{X}$, and is not necessarily diagonal in general. In the mapped space, $\boldsymbol{\mu}_{n-m}$ has its eigenvalue and eigenvector matrices Λ_{n-m} and Ψ_{n-m}. Therefore, an additional transformation $\mathbf{Z} = \Psi_{n-m}^T \mathbf{Y}$ diagonalizes the covariance matrix $\boldsymbol{\mu}_{n-m}$ as

$$\Sigma_Z = \Lambda_{n-m} = \Psi_{n-m}^T \mu_{n-m} \Psi_{n-m} . \tag{9.21}$$

Note that both Ψ_{n-m} and Λ_{n-m} are $(n-m)\times(n-m)$ matrices, and Ψ_{n-m}^{-1} exists and is equal to Ψ_{n-m}^T. Furthermore, substituting (9.20) into (9.21),

$$\Lambda_{n-m} = (\Phi_{n-m}\Psi_{n-m})^T \Sigma_X (\Phi_{n-m}\Psi_{n-m}) . \tag{9.22}$$

That is, Λ_{n-m} contains the $(n-m)$ eigenvalues of Σ_X, and $(\Phi_{n-m}\ \Psi_{n-m})_{n\times(n-m)}$ consists of the corresponding $(n-m)$ eigenvectors. Let us denote this eigenvector matrix by Φ_{n-m}^*. Then, from (9.22)

$$\Phi_{n-m}^* = \Phi_{n-m}\Psi_{n-m} \quad \rightarrow \quad \Phi_{n-m} = \Phi_{n-m}^* \Psi_{n-m}^T . \tag{9.23}$$

That is, any Φ_{n-m}, which is the solution of (9.19), is obtained from Φ_{n-m}^* by an $(n-m)\times(n-m)$ orthonormal transformation. We call this Φ_{n-m} the member of the Φ_{n-m}^* family.

The mean-square error is invariant among all members of the family as follows:

$$\begin{aligned}
\bar{\varepsilon}^2 &= \mathrm{tr}(\Phi_{n-m}^T \Sigma_X \Phi_{n-m}) \\
&= \mathrm{tr}(\Psi_{n-m} \Phi_{n-m}^{*T} \Sigma_X \Phi_{n-m}^* \Psi_{n-m}^T) \\
&= \mathrm{tr}(\Phi_{n-m}^{*T} \Sigma_X \Phi_{n-m}^* \Psi_{n-m}^T \Psi_{n-m}) \\
&= \mathrm{tr}(\Phi_{n-m}^{*T} \Sigma_X \Phi_{n-m}^*) .
\end{aligned} \tag{9.24}$$

That is, once $\mathbf{X}$ is mapped down to the $(n-m)$-dimensional subspace spanned by $(n-m)$ eigenvectors of Σ_X, further application of an $(n-m)\times(n-m)$ orthonormal transformation would not change the mean-square error. Thus, although any member of the Φ_{n-m}^* family is a legitimate solution of (9.19), we select Φ_{n-m}^* as the representative of the family.

Properties of the *K-L* expansion: Figure 9-2 shows how the *K-L* expansion works for a simple two-dimensional example. A distribution is shown by a contour line of one standard deviation. The eigenvectors ϕ_1 and ϕ_2 of the covariance matrix are the principal axes of the distribution, and the eigenvalues λ_1 and λ_2 are the variances of the distribution along the ϕ_1- and ϕ_2-axes. Since $y_i = \phi_i^T \mathbf{X}$, y_1 and y_2 are the projected values of $\mathbf{X}$ on the ϕ_1- and ϕ_2-

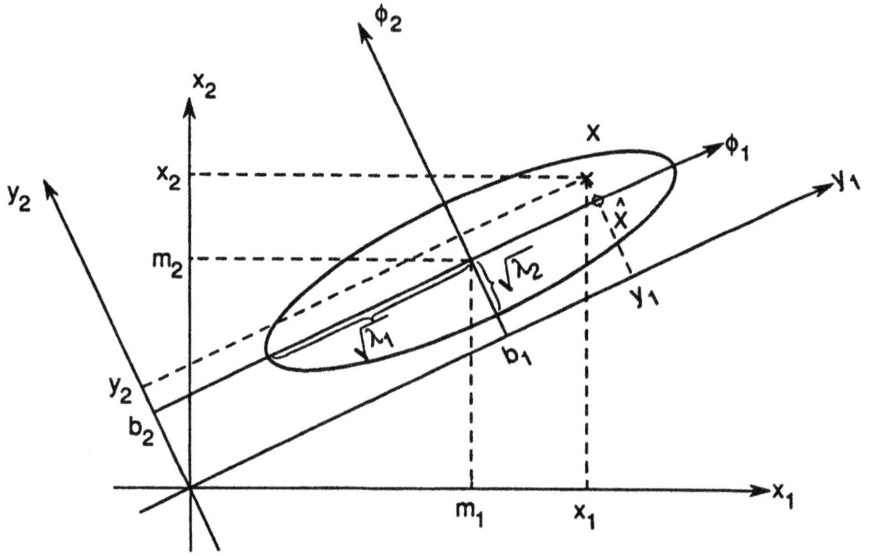

Fig. 9-2 A two-dimensional example of the Karhunen-Loéve expansion.

axes. If $\lambda_2 = E\{(y_2-b_2)^2\}$ is small, y_2 stays close to b_2. Thus, **X** can be approximated by $y_1\phi_1 + b_2\phi_2$, which is $\hat{\mathbf{X}}$ in Fig. 9-2.

Conventionally, the expected vector M is subtracted from **X** before the K-L expansion is applied. This simplifies the discussion. Therefore, from now on in this chapter, we will assume that the expected vector of **X** is zero. Then, the second term of (9.7) disappears, and the expansion is terminated at the mth term. When **X** has a nonzero mean, the deviation of **X** from the mean is approximated by a summation of m eigenvectors, and the mean is added to the approximation to represent **X**.

In the context of pattern recognition, the coefficients $y_1, \ldots, y_n$ in the expansion are viewed as feature values representing the observed vector **X** in the feature space. The feature space has several attractive properties which we can list.

(1) The effectiveness of each feature, in terms of representing **X**, is determined by its corresponding eigenvalue. If a feature, say ϕ_i, is deleted, the mean-square error increases by λ_i. Therefore, the feature with the smallest eigenvalue should be deleted first, and so on. If the eigenvalues are indexed as $\lambda_1 \geq \lambda_2 \geq \ldots \geq \lambda_n \geq 0$, the features should be ordered in the same manner.

(2) The feature values are mutually uncorrelated, that is, the covariance matrix of **Y** is diagonal. This follows since

$$\Sigma_Y = \Phi^T \Sigma_X \Phi = \begin{bmatrix} \lambda_1 & & & & 0 \\ & \lambda_2 & & & \\ & & \cdot & & \\ & & & \cdot & \\ 0 & & & & \lambda_n \end{bmatrix} = \Lambda \,. \tag{9.25}$$

In the special case where **X** is normally distributed, the $\mathbf{y}_i$'s are mutually independent.

(3) The set of m eigenvectors of Σ_X, which correspond to the m largest eigenvalues, minimizes $\overline{\varepsilon}^2(m)$ over all choices of m orthonormal basis vectors. Linear transformations which are not orthonormal are not considered in this chapter. In the case of representing a signal distribution, we are concerned only with transformations which preserve the structure of the distribution.

In order to show how the *K-L* expansion is applied, two simple examples are given here.

Example 1: Let us examine two impulsive distributions as shown in Fig. 9-3(a) and (b), where each impulse carries the probability of 1/4. The expected

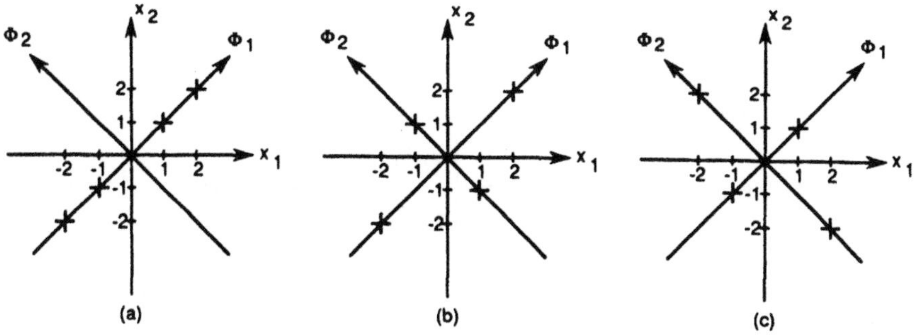

Fig. 9-3 Examples of the Karhunen-Loéve expansion.

vectors are zero in both cases. First, we calculate the covariance matrix Σ_X.

$$\Sigma_{Xa} = \frac{1}{4}\sum_{i=1}^{4} X_i X_i^T = \frac{1}{4}\left\{ \begin{bmatrix} 1 \\ 1 \end{bmatrix} [1 \quad 1] + \begin{bmatrix} 2 \\ 2 \end{bmatrix} [2 \quad 2] + \begin{bmatrix} -1 \\ -1 \end{bmatrix} [-1 \quad -1] \right.$$

$$\left. + \begin{bmatrix} -2 \\ -2 \end{bmatrix} [-2 \quad -2] \right\}$$

$$= \begin{bmatrix} 10/4 & 10/4 \\ 10/4 & 10/4 \end{bmatrix} \quad \text{for Data (a)} , \tag{9.26}$$

$$\Sigma_{Xb} = \frac{1}{4}\sum_{i=1}^{4} X_i X_i^T = \frac{1}{4}\left\{ \begin{bmatrix} -1 \\ +1 \end{bmatrix} [-1 \quad +1] + \begin{bmatrix} 2 \\ 2 \end{bmatrix} [2 \quad 2] \right.$$

$$\left. + \begin{bmatrix} +1 \\ -1 \end{bmatrix} [+1 \quad -1] + \begin{bmatrix} -2 \\ -2 \end{bmatrix} [-2 \quad -2] \right\}$$

$$= \begin{bmatrix} 10/4 & 6/4 \\ 6/4 & 10/4 \end{bmatrix} \quad \text{for Data (b)} . \tag{9.27}$$

Secondly, we calculate the eigenvalues and eigenvectors of Σ_X.

$$\lambda_{1a} = 5, \qquad \lambda_{2a} = 0 ,$$

$$\phi_{1a} = \begin{bmatrix} 1/\sqrt{2} \\ 1/\sqrt{2} \end{bmatrix}, \qquad \phi_{2a} = \begin{bmatrix} 1/\sqrt{2} \\ -1/\sqrt{2} \end{bmatrix} \quad \text{for Data (a)} , \tag{9.28}$$

$$\lambda_{1b} = 4, \qquad \lambda_{2b} = 1 ,$$

$$\phi_{1b} = \begin{bmatrix} 1/\sqrt{2} \\ 1/\sqrt{2} \end{bmatrix}, \qquad \phi_{2b} = \begin{bmatrix} 1/\sqrt{2} \\ -1/\sqrt{2} \end{bmatrix} \quad \text{for Data (b)} . \tag{9.29}$$

Thus, for both cases, the basis vectors become 45° and −45° lines, as shown by ϕ_1 and ϕ_2 of Fig. 9-3.

Finally, let us consider the effect of eliminating one of these basis vectors. For Data (a), $\lambda_{2a} = 0$. Therefore, even if we eliminate ϕ_2 in the *K-L* expansion, the mean-square error is zero. Figure 9-3(a) shows that all four points can be expressed by the first basis vector ϕ_1 without error. On the other hand, for Data (b), $\lambda_{2b} = 1$. Therefore, we expect a mean-square error of 1 by eliminating ϕ_2 in the expansion. From Fig. 9-3(b), we see that only $X_2 = [2\ 2]^T$ and $X_4 = [-2\ -2]^T$ can be expressed by ϕ_1 without error, but $X_1 = [-1\ 1]^T$ and $X_3 = [1\ -1]^T$ have errors of $\sqrt{2}$. Therefore, the mean-square error is $(0^2 + 0^2 + (\sqrt{2})^2 + (\sqrt{2})^2)/4 = 1$, which equals λ_{2b}.

Example 2: In this example, we show why non-orthonormal transformations should not be allowed for signal representation. Suppose that we apply to the distribution of Fig. 9-3(b) the transformation of

$$\mathbf{Y} = \begin{bmatrix} 1/2 & 0 \\ 0 & 2 \end{bmatrix} \begin{bmatrix} 1/\sqrt{2} & 1/\sqrt{2} \\ 1/\sqrt{2} & -1/\sqrt{2} \end{bmatrix} \mathbf{X} = \begin{bmatrix} 1/(2\sqrt{2}) & 1/(2\sqrt{2}) \\ \sqrt{2} & -\sqrt{2} \end{bmatrix} \mathbf{X} . \tag{9.30}$$

That is, after applying the orthonormal transformation of (9.29), the scales of the new axes are changed by factors of 1/2 and 2 to get the distribution of Fig. 9-3(c). Since the distributions of Fig. 9-3(b) and (c) are different, any conclusion about the properties of (c) cannot be applied to (b) directly. For example, if we conclude that the y_2-axis (or ϕ_2) is important from (c), it contradicts the conclusion from (b) that the y_1-axis (or ϕ_1) is important. Since feature extraction for signal representation finds a small number of effective features to approximate a given distribution, any transformation which alters the structure of the distribution should not be allowed.

Data compression: One of the popular applications of the *K-L* expansion is data compression in communication. Suppose we want to send a random process $\mathbf{x}(t)$. If we time-sample this waveform with n sampling points at the transmitter, we need to send n numbers, $\mathbf{x}(t_1), \ldots, \mathbf{x}(t_n)$. However, if we study the properties of the distribution of $\mathbf{X} = [\mathbf{x}(t_1) \ldots \mathbf{x}(t_n)]^T$ and find out that $\mathbf{X}$ can be approximated by a smaller number (m) of $\mathbf{y}_i$'s and ϕ_i's, we can compute these m $\mathbf{y}_i$'s at the transmitter and send them through the communication channel. At the receiving end, we can reconstruct $\mathbf{X}$ by $\Sigma_{i=1}^{m} \mathbf{y}_i \phi_i$ as in Fig. 9-4. Thus, we need to send only m numbers instead of n. As seen in Fig. 9-4, both the transmitter and receiver must have the information of $\phi_1, \ldots, \phi_m$.

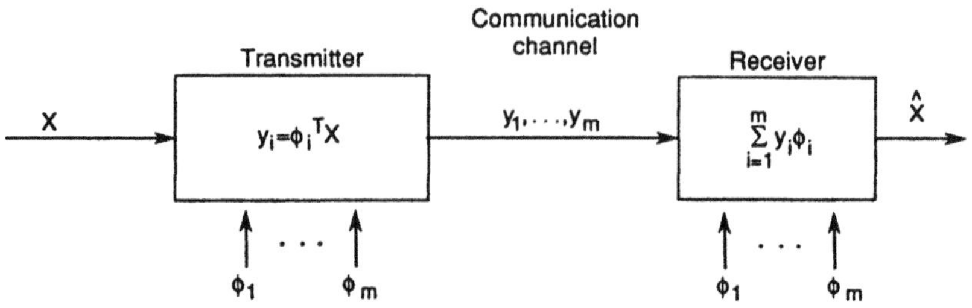

Fig. 9-4 Data compression in communication.

Normalization problems: In the *K-L* expansion, we decide whether or not we select an eigenvector by observing the corresponding eigenvalue. However, the absolute value of the eigenvalue does not give adequate information for selection. The ratio of the eigenvalue to the summation of all eigenvalues expresses the percentage of the mean-square error introduced by eliminating the corresponding eigenvector. Thus, we may use

$$\mu_i = \frac{\lambda_i}{\sum_{j=1}^{n}\lambda_j} = \frac{\lambda_i}{\mathrm{tr}\Sigma_X} \tag{9.31}$$

as a criterion for retaining or deleting the ith eigenvector. Note that

$$\sum_{i=1}^{n}\mu_i = 1 \; . \tag{9.32}$$

Sometimes samples are normalized prior to application of the *K-L* expansion. The magnitude-normalized vector $\mathbf{Z}$ is given by

$$\mathbf{Z} = \frac{\mathbf{X}}{\|\mathbf{X}\|} \tag{9.33}$$

so that

$$\|\mathbf{Z}\| = 1 \; . \tag{9.34}$$

Let Σ_Z and λ_i''s be the covariance matrix of $\mathbf{Z}$ and its eigenvalues. Then the summation of λ_i''s is

$$\sum_{i=1}^{n}\lambda_i' = \mathrm{tr}\Sigma_Z = E\{\mathbf{Z}^T\mathbf{Z}\} = 1 \; , \tag{9.35}$$

where $E\{\mathbf{Z}\} = 0$ is assumed. That is, the λ_i''s are the normalized eigenvalues.

However, it must be noted that the statistical properties of **Z**, including the covariance matrix, are entirely different from those of **X**. Thus, application of the *K-L* expansion to **Z** produces completely different eigenvectors and, therefore, completely different features, than for **X**.

A word of caution is in order for another normalization of

$$\mathbf{z}_i = \frac{\mathbf{x}_i}{\sum_{j=1}^{n} \mathbf{x}_i} . \tag{9.36}$$

In this normalization, the $\mathbf{z}_i$'s are no longer linearly independent, because $\Sigma_{i=1}^{n} \mathbf{z}_i = 1$. Therefore, the covariance matrix of $\mathbf{Z} = [\mathbf{z}_1 \dots \mathbf{z}_n]^T$ becomes singular.

Other Criteria for Signal Representation

In addition to the mean-square error of approximation, there are some other criteria for evaluating features for signal representation. In this section, we will discuss two typical criteria: *scatter measure* and *entropy*.

Scatter measure: One measure of scatter is the expected value of the squared between-sample distance, which is given by

$$\bar{d}_X^2 = E\{\|\mathbf{X}_i - \mathbf{X}_j\|^2\} = E\{\mathbf{X}_i^T\mathbf{X}_i + \mathbf{X}_j^T\mathbf{X}_j\} - E\{\mathbf{X}_i^T X_j + \mathbf{X}_j^T\mathbf{X}_i\} \tag{9.37}$$

where $\mathbf{X}_i$ and $\mathbf{X}_j$ are mutually independent sample vectors taken from a single distribution. By virtue of the independence property, (9.37) becomes

$$\begin{aligned} \bar{d}_X^2 &= 2E\{\mathbf{X}^T\mathbf{X}\} - 2E\{\mathbf{X}^T\}E\{\mathbf{X}\} = 2\,\mathrm{tr}[E\{\mathbf{X}\mathbf{X}^T\} - MM^T] \\ &= 2\,\mathrm{tr}(S - MM^T) = 2\,\mathrm{tr}\,\Sigma_X , \end{aligned} \tag{9.38}$$

where S and Σ_X are the autocorrelation and covariance matrices and M is the expected vector of the distribution.

Let **Y** be an m-dimensional vector mapped from **X** by an orthonormal transformation as

$$\mathbf{Y} = \Phi_m^T \mathbf{X} , \tag{9.39}$$

where $\Phi_m = [\phi_1 \dots \phi_m]_{n \times m}$ consists of m column vectors ϕ_i's, and satisfies

$$\Phi_m^T \Phi_m = I \quad \text{or} \quad \phi_i^T \phi_j = \delta_{ij} . \tag{9.40}$$

Then, the scatter measure in the mapped Y-space, $\overline{d}_Y^2$, is

$$\overline{d}_Y^2 = 2 \operatorname{tr} \Sigma_Y = 2 \operatorname{tr} (\Phi_m^T \Sigma_X \Phi_m)$$

$$= 2 \sum_{i=1}^{m} \phi_i^T \Sigma_X \phi_i . \tag{9.41}$$

Now the feature selection problem may be stated in terms of choosing orthonormal vectors $\phi_1, \ldots, \phi_m$ so as to maximize $\overline{d}_Y^2$. Equation (9.41) is the same as (9.12) except that in (9.41) the summation of chosen terms is maximized while in (9.12) the summation of discarded terms is minimized. Therefore, the optimalization discussion of the K-L expansion can be directly applied to this case, and $\phi_1, \ldots, \phi_m$ should be the eigenvectors of Σ_X, whose eigenvalues are m largest. Thus we can conclude:

(1) The eigenvectors of Σ_X, which correspond to the dominant eigenvalues, are the optimum features among all orthonormal transformations with respect to the scatter criterion $\overline{d}^2$.

(2) From (9.41), the contribution of each feature to the total scatter is twice the value of the corresponding eigenvalue.

Population entropy: The population entropy can be used as a measure of diversity of a distribution, and is defined by

$$h_X = -E\{\ln p(\mathbf{X})\} . \tag{9.42}$$

The entropy is a far more complex criterion than the previous two criteria because the density function of $\mathbf{X}$ is involved.

Again, feature selection consists of finding features so as to maximize h for a given m ($m<n$). As with the scatter measure, we should limit ourselves to structure-preserving, orthonormal transformations.

When the distribution of $\mathbf{X}$ is normal, h of (9.42) becomes

$$h_X = E\{\frac{1}{2}(X - M)^T \Sigma_X^{-1}(X - M) + \frac{1}{2}\ln|\Sigma_X| + \frac{n}{2}\ln(2\pi)\}$$

$$= \frac{n}{2} + \frac{1}{2}\ln|\Sigma_X| + \frac{n}{2}\ln(2\pi) \tag{9.43}$$

which is simply a function of $|\Sigma_X|$.

When an orthonormal transformation $\mathbf{Y} = \Phi_m^T \mathbf{X}$ of (9.39) is applied, the entropy of (9.43) in the mapped Y-space becomes $h_Y(m) = m/2 + (1/2)\ln|\Phi_m^T \Sigma_X \Phi_m| + (m/2)\ln(2\pi)$. Since the first and third terms of the entropy are not a function of Φ_m, we can maximize the entropy under the constraint of orthonormality for Φ_m by maximizing

$$J = \ln|\Phi_m^T \Sigma_X \Phi_m| - \mathrm{tr}[\mu_m(\Phi_m^T \Phi_m - I)] , \tag{9.44}$$

where μ_m is a Lagrange multiplier matrix ($m \times m$) as in (9.15). Using (A.27) and (A.14), the derivative of J with respect to Φ_m is

$$\frac{dJ}{d\Phi_m} = 2[\Sigma_X \Phi_m (\Phi_m^T \Sigma_X \Phi_m)^{-1} - \Phi_m \mu_m] , \tag{9.45}$$

where $\Phi_m^T \Sigma_X \Phi_m$ is the covariance matrix of $\mathbf{Y}$, and generally can be assumed to be nonsingular. Equating (9.45) to zero,

$$\Sigma_X \Phi_m = \Phi_m \mu_m \Sigma_Y . \tag{9.46}$$

Multiplying Φ_m^T from the left side

$$\Phi_m^T \Sigma_X \Phi_m = \mu_m \Sigma_Y . \tag{9.47}$$

Thus, μ_m must be equal to I. Furthermore, we can express Σ_Y by $\Psi_m \Lambda_m \Psi_m^T$ where Ψ_m and Λ_m are the eigenvector and eigenvalue matrices of Σ_Y. Then, (9.46) can be rewritten as

$$\Phi_m^T \Sigma_X \Phi_m = \Psi_m \Lambda_m \Psi_m^T \tag{9.48}$$

or

$$(\Phi_m \Psi_m)^T \Sigma_X (\Phi_m \Psi_m) = \Lambda_m . \tag{9.49}$$

That is, Λ_m contains the m eigenvalues of Σ_X, and $(\Phi_m \Psi_m)$ consists of the m corresponding eigenvectors. Note that

$$\begin{aligned}\ln|(\Phi_m\Psi_m)^T\Sigma_X(\Phi_m\Psi_m)| &= \ln|\Psi_m^T(\Phi_m^T\Sigma_X\Phi_m)\Psi_m| \\ &= \ln\{|\Psi_m^T||\Phi_m^T\Sigma_X\Phi_m||\Psi_m|\} \\ &= \ln|\Phi_m^T\Sigma_X\Phi_m| \ , \end{aligned} \tag{9.50}$$

where $|\Psi_m^T||\Psi_m| = |\Psi_m^T\Psi_m| = |I| = 1$ is used. Therefore, as in the trace criterion of (9.24), each m-dimensional subspace carries a different value of the entropy. But, within a subspace, the entropy of (9.43) is invariant under any orthonormal transformation. It is appropriate to select a subset of eigenvectors of Σ_X as the basis vectors to specify the subspace.

When Φ_m consists of m eigenvectors of Σ_X,

$$\ln|\Phi_m^T\Sigma_X\Phi_m| = \ln|\Lambda_m| = \sum_{i=1}^{m}\ln\lambda_i \ . \tag{9.51}$$

In order to maximize (9.51), we must select m largest eigenvalues.

So far, we have found the best linear mapping by maximizing the entropy for a normal distribution, (9.43). However, the optimization of (9.43) may offer a wider implication [1]. Note that the second line of (9.43) can be obtained by taking the expectation of the first line with respect to any distribution (not limited to a normal distribution) as long as the distribution has the mean M and covariance matrix Σ. We call this family of density functions G_X. That is,

$$G_X = \{p(X): E\{\mathbf{X}\} = M,\ \mathrm{Cov}\{\mathbf{X}\} = \Sigma\} \ . \tag{9.52}$$

On the other hand, the following inequality holds for any two density functions $p_1(X)$ and $p_2(X)$.

$$\begin{aligned}\int\left[\ln\frac{p_1(X)}{p_2(X)}\right]p_2(X)dX &\leq \int\left[\frac{p_1(X)}{p_2(X)} - 1\right]p_2(X)dX \\ &= \int p_1(X)dX - \int p_2(X)dX = 1 - 1 = 0 \ , \end{aligned} \tag{9.53}$$

where $\ln x \leq x - 1$ is used. The equality holds only when $p_1(X) = p_2(X)$. Replacing $p_1(X)$ and $p_2(X)$ by $N_X(M,\Sigma)$ and $p(X) \in G_X$ respectively, (9.53) can be rewritten as

$$\int[-\ln N_X(M,\Sigma)]p(X)dX \geq \int[-\ln p(X)]p(X)dX \ . \tag{9.54}$$

Since (9.43) is equal to the left side of (9.54), we may conclude that (9.43) is the maximum entropy among all density functions in G_X. In other words, the entropy for a normal distribution is the largest for given M and Σ.

When $\mathbf{X}$ is mapped onto $\mathbf{Y}$ by $\mathbf{y}_i = \phi_i^T\mathbf{X}$ $(i = 1, \ldots, m)$, the remaining $\mathbf{y}_i = \phi_i^T\mathbf{X}$ $(i = m+1, \ldots, n)$ form the complementary $(n-m)$-dimensional space of $\mathbf{Y}$, which we will call the $\bar{Y}$-space. Let the feature extraction problem be to minimize the entropy in the $\bar{Y}$-space, instead of maximizing the one in the Y-space as previously discussed. Furthermore, let us assume that the true distribution is not known. Then, often in practice, it is risky to assume a density function and to find the best mapping based on that assumption. If the true distribution is different from the assumed one, the mapping functions might not give a good set of features. Therefore, as a safety precaution, we may find the maximum entropy among all density functions in $G_{\bar{Y}}$, and select the best linear mapping which minimizes the maximum entropy in the $\bar{Y}$-space. This is the *minimax procedure* applied to feature extraction. Thus, we may claim that the selected features are *most reliable*, although they might not be the best.

Restating the above in a mathematical form,

$$\min_{\phi_{m+1},\ldots,\phi_n} \ \max_{p(\bar{Y})\in G_{\bar{Y}}} h_{\bar{Y}}(n-m) \ . \tag{9.55}$$

Using (9.43), max $h_{\bar{Y}}(n-m)$ can be obtained. Thus, (9.55) becomes

$$\min_{\Phi_{n-m}} \left[\frac{n-m}{2} + \frac{1}{2}\ln|\Phi_{n-m}^T\Sigma_X\Phi_{n-m}| + \frac{n-m}{2}\ln(2\pi) \right] , \tag{9.56}$$

where $\Phi_{n-m} = [\phi_{m+1} \cdots \phi_n]$. Applying the same argument as before, the optimum ϕ_i $(i = m+1, \ldots, n)$ are the eigenvectors of Σ_X corresponding to the smallest $(n-m)$ eigenvalues of Σ_X.

Thus, the discussion of (9.43) through (9.51) is not only for the optimization of the entropy for a normal distribution, but also for the selection of most reliable linear features regardless of the true distribution.

In addition, the inequality of (9.53) can be used to measure the closeness of two distributions. That is, the closer (9.53) is to zero, the more similar two distributions are. One of the applications of this similarity measurement is to approximate a given density function $p(X)$ ($=p_2(X)$ in (9.53)) by $\hat{p}(X)$ ($=p_1(X)$ in (9.53)). In this problem, we characterize $\hat{p}(X)$ by a number of parameters. In order to make $\hat{p}(X)$ as close as possible to $p(X)$, we may minimize $-\int[\ln\hat{p}(X)]p(X)dX$ by adjusting the control parameters of $\hat{p}(X)$. This procedure is called the *entropy minimization.* Often in practice, $p(X)$ is not known, but samples, $X_1,\ldots,X_N$, from $p(X)$ are available. Then, we may approximate the expectation part of $-\int[\ln\hat{p}(X)]p(X)dX$ by the sample mean as $(1/N)\Sigma_{i=1}^{N}[-\ln\hat{p}(X_i)]$. Note that the approximate criterion does no longer include $p(X)$.

Example 3: When the components of $\mathbf{X}$ are binary, +1 or −1, and independent, h_X of (9.42) becomes

$$h_X = -\sum_{i=1}^{n}\{P_i \ln P_i + (1-P_i)\ln(1-P_i)\} , \tag{9.57}$$

where P_i and $(1-P_i)$ are the probabilities of $\mathbf{x}_i = +1$ and -1 respectively. Thus, individual variables $\mathbf{x}_i$'s are evaluated by $-\{P_i \ln P_i + (1-P_i)\ln(1-P_i)\}$. When the inputs are not independent, we may use the Bahadur expansion of Chapter 6 as the approximation of $p(X)$ of (9.42). Obviously, h_X becomes much more complex.

General remarks: In the foregoing discussion, we have dealt exclusively with orthonormal linear transformations. This is necessary in order to maintain the structure of the distribution. As seen in Example 2, for a given distribution, we can cause one eigenvalue to dominate the others by an arbitrary amount simply by changing the scales. However, unless we are given some physical reason to introduce such distortion, we would only be selecting the features that are created by the transformation and not related to the original distribution.

Let us also consider the type of criteria we have used. Both the mean-square error and scatter measure are the expected values of some quadratic functions of variables. For this reason, our features are all given in terms of the second-order statistics of the distribution, the covariance or autocorrelation matrix. The eigenvalues of these matrices are invariant under linear orthonormal transformations.

In the statistical literature, the above is generally called *factor analysis* or *principle components analysis.*

On the other hand, when we discuss feature selection for classifying two or more distributions, we will allow a more general class of transformations. This is because the class separability, for example the probability of error due to the Bayes classifier, is invariant under any nonsingular transformations. These transformations preserve the structure of these distributions as far as classification is concerned.

In this section, we concluded that the optimum basis vectors of the *K-L* expansion are the eigenvectors of the covariance matrix of a given distribution. However, it should be pointed out that even if we select the eigenvectors of the autocorrelation matrix as the basis vectors of the expansion for some reason, the discussion is exactly the same as for the covariance matrix. The eigenvalue of the autocorrelation matrix represents the mean-square error due to the elimination of the corresponding eigenvector from the expansion.

9.2 The Karhunen-Loéve Expansion for Random Processes

Continuous *K-L* expansion: Since the *K-L* expansion was originally developed and discussed to represent a random process [2], in this section we relate our previous discussion to the case of random processes, and also add some specific properties of the expansion for random processes.

A random process $\mathbf{x}(t)$, defined in a time domain [0,T], can be expressed as a linear combination of basis functions.

$$\mathbf{x}(t) = \sum_{i=0}^{\infty} \mathbf{y}_i \xi_i(t) \qquad (0 \le t \le T) , \tag{9.58}$$

where the *basis functions* $\xi_i(t)$ are deterministic time functions and the coefficients $\mathbf{y}_i$ are random variables. An infinite number of $\xi_i(t)$ is required in order to form *a complete set.* Therefore, the summation is taken to ∞. The orthonormal condition of $\xi_i(t)$ is given by

$$\int_0^T \xi_i(t)\xi_j^*(t)\,dt = \delta_{ij} , \tag{9.59}$$

where $\xi_j^*(t)$ is the complex conjugate of $\xi_j(t)$. If $\xi_j(t)$ is a real function, $\xi_j^*(t)$ becomes $\xi_j(t)$. The inverse operation to calculate $\mathbf{y}_i$ from $\mathbf{x}(t)$ is

$$\int_0^T \mathbf{x}(t)\xi_i^*(t)\,dt = \mathbf{y}_i . \tag{9.60}$$

The expected value, autocorrelation and covariance functions of $\mathbf{x}(t)$ are defined by

$$m(t) = E\{\mathbf{x}(t)\} , \tag{9.61}$$

$$R(t,\tau) = E\{\mathbf{x}(t)\mathbf{x}^*(\tau)\} , \tag{9.62}$$

$$C(t,\tau) = E[\{\mathbf{x}(t) - m(t)\}\{\mathbf{x}(\tau) - m(\tau)\}^*] . \tag{9.63}$$

For simplicity's sake, let us assume $m(t) = 0$ for $0 \le t \le T$. If the $\xi_i(t)$'s are the *eigenfunctions* of $R(t,\tau)$, they must satisfy the following integral equation:

$$\int_0^T R(t,\tau)\xi_i(\tau)\,d\tau = \lambda_i\xi_i(t) \qquad (i = 1,2,\ldots) , \tag{9.64}$$

where the λ_i's are the *eigenvalues* of $R(t,\tau)$.

These equations are exactly the same as the ones for random vectors. Suppose we take n time-sampled values of these time functions and convert them to vectors as

$$\mathbf{X} = [\mathbf{x}(t_1)\ldots\mathbf{x}(t_n)]^T , \tag{9.65}$$

$$\phi_i = [\xi_i(t_1)\ldots\xi_i(t_n)]^T , \tag{9.66}$$

where each time-sampled value of $\mathbf{x}(t)$, $\mathbf{x}(t_i)$, is a random variable. Then, for example, (9.59) and (9.64) can be rewritten as follows:

$$\sum_{k=1}^{n} \xi_i(t_k)\xi_j^*(t_k) = \phi_i^T\phi_j^* = \delta_{ij} \tag{9.67}$$

and

$$\sum_{k=1}^{n} R(t_\ell, t_k)\xi_i(t_k) = \lambda_i \xi_i(t_\ell) \qquad (i, \ell = 1, 2, \ldots, n) . \tag{9.68}$$

Equation (9.68) can be rewritten in a matrix form to define the eigenvalues and eigenvectors as

$$S\phi_i = \lambda_i \phi_i \qquad (i = 1, 2, \ldots, n) , \tag{9.69}$$

where S is

$$S = \begin{bmatrix} R(t_1,t_1) & \ldots & R(t_1,t_n) \\ \vdots & & \vdots \\ R(t_n,t_1) & \ldots & R(t_n,t_n) \end{bmatrix}$$

$$= \begin{bmatrix} E\{\mathbf{x}(t_1)\mathbf{x}^*(t_1)\} & \ldots & E\{\mathbf{x}(t_1)\mathbf{x}^*(t_n)\} \\ \vdots & & \vdots \\ E\{\mathbf{x}(t_n)\mathbf{x}^*(t_1)\} & \ldots & E\{\mathbf{x}(t_n)\mathbf{x}^*(t_n)\} \end{bmatrix} . \tag{9.70}$$

Since S is an $n \times n$ matrix, we can obtain only n eigenvalues and eigenvectors instead of an infinite number.

Minimum mean-square error: In order to minimize the mean-square error in the continuous version, we can follow a procedure similar to the one for the discrete case. For orthonormal $\xi_i(t)$'s,

$$\bar{\varepsilon}^2 = E\left[\int_0^T \left\{\mathbf{x}(t) - \sum_{i=0}^{m} \mathbf{y}_i \xi_i(t)\right\}\left\{\mathbf{x}(t) - \sum_{i=0}^{m} \mathbf{y}_i \xi_i(t)\right\}^* dt\right]$$

$$= E\left[\int_0^T \left\{\sum_{i=m+1}^{\infty} \mathbf{y}_i \xi_i(t)\right\}\left\{\sum_{i=m+1}^{\infty} \mathbf{y}_i \xi_i(t)\right\}^* dt\right]$$

$$= \sum_{i=m+1}^{\infty} E\{\mathbf{y}_i \mathbf{y}_i^*\} . \tag{9.71}$$

From (9.60), $E\{\mathbf{y}_i \mathbf{y}_i^*\}$ can be calculated by

$$E\{\mathbf{y}_i\mathbf{y}_i^*\} = \int_0^T\int_0^T E\{\mathbf{x}(t)\mathbf{x}^*(\tau)\}\xi_i^*(t)\xi_i(\tau)dtd\tau$$
$$= \int_0^T\int_0^T R(t,\tau)\xi_i(\tau)\xi_i^*(t)d\tau dt \,. \tag{9.72}$$

Therefore, if the $\xi_i(t)$'s are the eigenfunctions of $R(t,\tau)$,

$$E\{\mathbf{y}_i\mathbf{y}_i^*\} = \int_0^T \lambda_i\xi_i(t)\xi_i^*(t)\,dt = \lambda_i \,. \tag{9.73}$$

Hence

$$\bar{\varepsilon}^2 = \sum_{i=m+1}^{\infty} \lambda_i \,. \tag{9.74}$$

Recalling our assumption that $E\{\mathbf{x}(t)\} = 0$ and therefore $E\{\mathbf{y}_i\} = 0$, the result is the same as the one for the discrete version of the K-L expansion.

The difficulty in the continuous K-L expansion is that we have to solve the integral equation of (9.64) in order to obtain eigenvalues and eigenfunctions. Except in very special cases, explicit solutions are hard to obtain. Therefore, in order to get the solution numerically, we have to go to the discrete version; that is, take time-sampled values, calculate the autocorrelation matrix, and find the eigenvalues and eigenvectors.

Stationary Process

***K-L* expansion for an infinite time duration:** For simplicity, the stationary condition is often imposed in many cases when discussing random processes. A random process is called *stationary in the wide sense* if the following two conditions are satisfied:

$$m(t) = m \quad \text{(constant)}\,, \tag{9.75}$$

$$R(t,\tau) = R(t-\tau)\,. \tag{9.76}$$

Equation (9.76) means that the autocorrelation function depends only on $t-\tau$. The functional form of R in the left side with two arguments is not the same as that of R in the right side with one argument. Also, we will continue to assume that $m = 0$. Since our discussion is quite specific, the reader should consult more general texts on random processes for background [3].

For stationary processes, the integral equation of (9.64) becomes

$$\int_{-T/2}^{T/2} R(t-\tau)\xi_i(\tau)\,d\tau = \lambda_i \xi_i(t) \quad (-T/2 \le t \le T/2)\,, \tag{9.77}$$

where the time region is shifted from [0,T] to $[-T/2, T/2]$. Let us extend T to ∞. Then (9.77) becomes

$$\int_{-\infty}^{+\infty} R(t-\tau)\xi_i(\tau)\,d\tau = \lambda_i \xi_i(t) \quad (-\infty \le t \le +\infty)\,. \tag{9.78}$$

Since (9.78) is the convolution integral of $R(t)$ and $\xi_i(t)$, the Fourier transform of this equation becomes

$$\mathcal{S}(j\omega)\Xi_i(j\omega) = \lambda_i \Xi_i(j\omega)\,, \tag{9.79}$$

where $\mathcal{S}(j\omega)$ and $\Xi_i(j\omega)$ are the Fourier transforms of $R(t)$ and $\xi_i(t)$. Particularly, $\mathcal{S}(j\omega)$, the Fourier transform of the autocorrelation function of a random process, is known as the *power spectrum* of the random process $\mathbf{x}(t)$.

In order to solve (9.79) for $\Xi_i(j\omega)$ and λ_i given $\mathcal{S}(j\omega)$, we must find a function of $j\omega$ which becomes the same function, except its size, after it is multiplied by $\mathcal{S}(j\omega)$. Assuming that $\mathcal{S}(j\omega)$ is nowhere flat, such a function must be an impulsive function as

$$\Xi_i(j\omega) = \delta(\omega - \omega_i) \tag{9.80}$$

which corresponds to, in the time domain,

$$\xi_i(t) = e^{j\omega_i t}\,. \tag{9.81}$$

Then, (9.79) becomes

$$\mathcal{S}(j\omega_i) = \lambda_i\,. \tag{9.82}$$

Since (9.80) with any value of ω_i is the solution of (9.79), we may vary ω_i from $-\infty$ to ∞ continuously (or with an extremely small increment). As a result, we have an infinite number of eigenvalues and eigenfunctions. Also, because ω_i takes negative values as well as positive values, the *K-L* expansion of (9.58) must be modified to

$$\mathbf{x}(t) = \sum_{i=-\infty}^{+\infty} \mathbf{y}_i e^{j\omega_i t}\,, \tag{9.83}$$

where $\omega_{-i} = -\omega_i$. With ω_i changing continuously form $-\infty$ to $+\infty$, the summation of (9.83) is replaced with an integration as

$$\mathbf{x}(t) = \frac{1}{2\pi}\int_{-\infty}^{+\infty} \mathbf{y}(\omega)e^{j\omega t}d\omega \,, \tag{9.84}$$

where $\mathbf{y}_i = \mathbf{y}(\omega_i)\Delta\omega/2\pi$. Note that (9.84) is the inverse Fourier transform. Thus, when a random process is stationary, the basis functions of the K-L expansion become the complex exponential, $e^{j\omega t}$, and the coefficient, $\mathbf{y}(\omega)$ (or $\mathbf{y}_i$), is the Fourier transform of $\mathbf{x}(t)$.

Equation (9.83) may be modified to an expansion with real basis functions and real coefficients as follows. Since the ith and $-i$th basis functions, $e^{j\omega_i t}$ and $e^{-j\omega_i t}$, are mutually conjugate, their coefficients, $\mathbf{y}_{-i}$ and $\mathbf{y}_i$, are also conjugate for a real $\mathbf{x}(t)$ from (9.60). Therefore, combining these two terms, (9.83) becomes

$$\mathbf{x}(t) = \mathbf{y}_0 + \sum_{i=1}^{\infty} 2\,|\mathbf{y}_i|\cos(\omega_i t + \angle \mathbf{y}_i) \,, \tag{9.85}$$

where $|\mathbf{y}_i|$ and $\angle \mathbf{y}_i$ are the magnitude and angle of a complex variable $\mathbf{y}_i$.

As far as the eigenvalue is concerned, two eigenfunctions, $e^{j\omega_i t}$ and $e^{-j\omega_i t}$, carry the same eigenvalue, because the power spectrum of a real random process is an even and real function with $\mathcal{S}(j\omega_i) = \mathcal{S}(-j\omega_i)$. Therefore, after combining these two eigenfunctions, $\cos(\omega_i t + \angle \mathbf{y}_i)$ of (9.85) carries the eigenvalues of $\mathcal{S}(j\omega_i)$.

***K-L* expansion for a finite time duration:** When the time domain is limited to a finite duration, the above conclusion is no longer true but still approximately true. When $\mathbf{x}(t)$ is time-sampled at n points, $0, \Delta t, \ldots, (n-1)\Delta t$ for the duration of $T = n\Delta t$, the autocorrelation function is obtained from (9.62) and (9.76) at $(2n-1)$ points in the time domain $[-T,T]$ with the same sampling rate, as shown in Fig. 9-5. Even if $\mathbf{x}(t)$ is shifted along the time axis, there is no effect on $R(t)$. As known in the discrete Fourier transform, these $(2n-1)$ sampling points in the time domain induce $(2n-1)$ sampling points in the frequency domain. Since the duration of $R(t)$ is $(2n-1)\Delta t$, the sampling rate in the frequency domain is

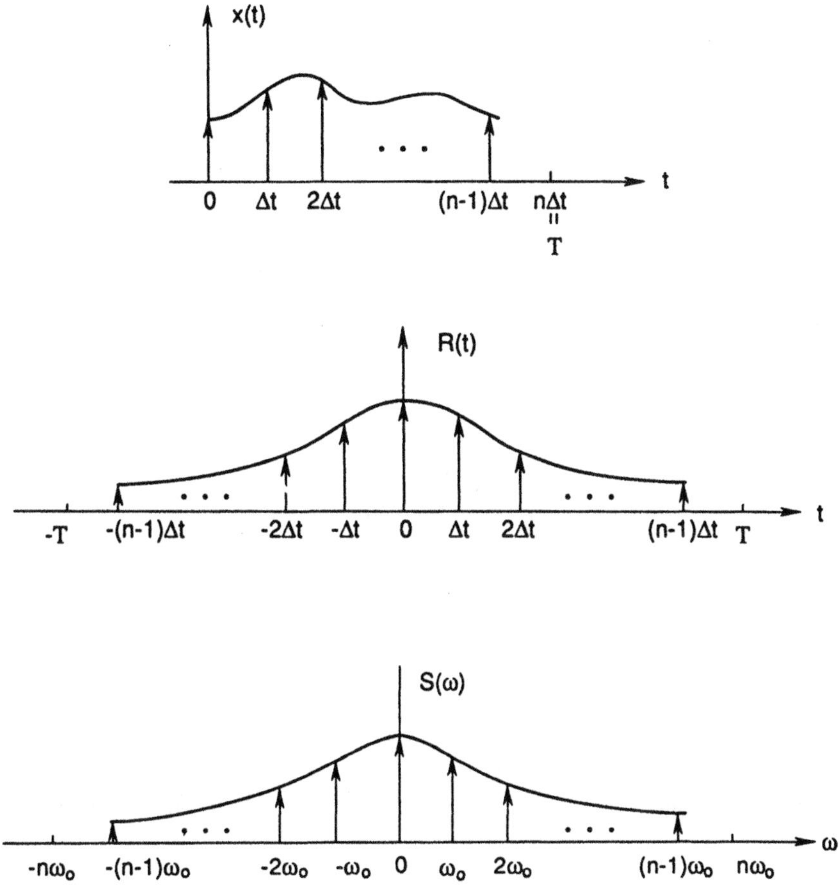

Fig. 9-5 Relationship between the sampling points of $\mathbf{x}(t)$, $R(t)$ and $\mathcal{S}(j\omega)$.

$$\omega_0 = \frac{2\pi}{(2n-1)\Delta t} = \frac{2n\pi}{(2n-1)T} \cong \frac{\pi}{T} . \tag{9.86}$$

Since two eigenfunctions $e^{j\omega_i t}$ and $e^{-j\omega_i t}$ for $i \neq 0$ are combined to form a real eigenfunction as in (9.85), only n real eigenfunctions and eigenvalues are obtained as

$$\xi_i(t) \cong \cos(i\omega_0 t + \theta_i) \,, \tag{9.87}$$

$$\lambda_i \cong \mathcal{S}(ji\omega_0) \tag{9.88}$$

$$(i = 0, 1, \ldots, n-1) \,.$$

Example 4: The autocorrelation matrix of a stationary process has a toeplitz form. A special toeplitz form has known eigenvalues and eigenvectors expressible in closed form as follows [4].

$$\begin{bmatrix} \alpha & 1 & & & \\ 1 & \alpha & 1 & & 0 \\ & & \cdot & & \\ & 1 & & \cdot & \\ & & & \cdot & \\ & & & & 1 \\ 0 & & & 1 & \alpha \end{bmatrix} \begin{bmatrix} \sin\frac{i\pi}{n+1} \\ \vdots \\ \sin\frac{in\pi}{n+1} \end{bmatrix} = [\alpha + 2\cos\frac{i\pi}{n+1}] \begin{bmatrix} \sin\frac{i\pi}{n+1} \\ \vdots \\ \sin\frac{in\pi}{n+1} \end{bmatrix}$$

$$i = 1, 2, \ldots, n \,. \tag{9.89}$$

In order to see how closely (9.87) and (9.88) approximate (9.89), let us compute the eigenvalues and eigenvectors of the given toeplitz matrix by (9.88) and (9.87). Since $R(k)$ of (9.89) is α for $k = 0$, 1 for $k = -1$ and $+1$, and 0 for other k's, the discrete Fourier transform of $R(k)$ with $\Delta t = 1$ or $T = n$ becomes, from (9.86) and (9.88)

$$\mathcal{S}(i) = e^{-j\frac{i\pi}{n-1/2}} + \alpha + e^{j\frac{i\pi}{n-1/2}}$$

$$= \alpha + 2\cos\frac{i\pi}{n-1/2} \tag{9.90}$$

which is close to the eigenvalues of (9.89) particularly for a large n. Since we see a difference between (9.89) and (9.90) in the denominators of the cosine function, let us set up the eigenvalues and eigenfunctions from (9.90) and

(9.87) as $\lambda_i = \alpha + 2\cos i\pi/n^*$ and $\xi_i(k) = \cos(ik\pi/n^* + \theta_i)$, where n^* is an unspecified number closed to n. Then, it is easy to confirm that the left and right sides of (9.89) for $k = 2, \ldots, n-1$ are equal regardless of n^* and θ_i as

$$\cos\left[\frac{i(k-1)\pi}{n^*} + \theta_i\right] + \alpha\cos\left[\frac{ik\pi}{n^*} + \theta_i\right] + \cos\left[\frac{i(k+1)\pi}{n^*} + \theta_i\right]$$

$$= [\alpha + 2\cos\frac{i\pi}{n^*}]\cos\left[\frac{ik\pi}{n^*} + \theta_i\right] \quad (k = 2, \ldots, n-1) . \tag{9.91}$$

However, at the edges of the matrix of (9.89), the first and nth rows, different equations must be satisfied as

$$\alpha\cos\left[\frac{i\pi}{n^*} + \theta_i\right] + \cos\left[\frac{2i\pi}{n^*} + \theta_i\right] = [\alpha + 2\cos\frac{i\pi}{n^*}]\cos\left[\frac{i\pi}{n^*} + \theta_i\right]$$

$$\text{for } k = 1 , \tag{9.92}$$

$$\cos\left[\frac{i(n-1)\pi}{n^*} + \theta_i\right] + \alpha\cos\left[\frac{in\pi}{n^*} + \theta_i\right] = [\alpha + 2\cos\frac{i\pi}{n^*}]\cos\left[\frac{in\pi}{n^*} + \theta_i\right]$$

$$\text{for } k = n . \tag{9.93}$$

Both (9.92) and (9.93) are satisfied by selecting $n^* = n+1$ and $\theta_i = -90^\circ$. Thus, the eigenvalues and eigenvectors become $\lambda_i = \alpha + 2\cos i\pi/(n+1)$ and $\xi_i(k) = \sin ik\pi/(n+1)$ as in (9.89).

9.3 Estimation of Eigenvalues and Eigenvectors

From the previous discussion, we realize that selecting features for signal representation by linear transformations requires a considerable amount of eigenvalue and eigenvector calculation. Theoretically, this is the end of this subject. However, there are many problems to be solved in order to apply the technique to real-life data. Some of the problems, which will be discussed in this section, are the following.

(1) *The number of sampling points for a random process:* In some applications of pattern recognition, the number of variables n is very much

predetermined and cannot be controlled. However, in some other areas, particularly in waveform analysis, we have to determine the number of sampling points n. Furthermore, in waveform analysis, n becomes fairly large, say in the hundreds, and computer time grows rapidly with n. Therefore, proper procedures are needed to select the minimum possible number of sampling points while maintaining sufficient accuracy for representing the random process.

(2) *The number of samples:* We always have to know how many samples (or waveforms) are needed to ensure the accuracy of estimation of eigenvalues and eigenvectors.

Determining the Dimensionality

In this subsection, we will develop a procedure for determining n, the number of time samples taken from a random process $\mathbf{x}(t)$. Before going into the subject, we need to discuss the *perturbation theory* of eigenvalues and eigenvectors.

Perturbation theory: Let us derive first-order approximations for the eigenvectors and eigenvalues of a perturbed matrix in terms of those of the unperturbed matrix.

Let Q_0 be a real, symmetric $n \times n$ matrix and let ΔQ be a real, symmetric perturbation matrix. Let ϕ_i and λ_i, $i = 1, \ldots, n$, be the eigenvectors and eigenvalues, respectively, of Q_0. Assume that the λ_i's are distinct. We wish to obtain a first-order approximation of the eigenvectors and eigenvalues of Q in terms of the ϕ_i's and λ_i's, where

$$Q = Q_0 + \Delta Q . \tag{9.94}$$

These may be obtained by retaining the terms of first order or lower of the equation

$$(Q_0 + \Delta Q)(\phi_i + \Delta\phi_i) = (\lambda_i + \Delta\lambda_i)(\phi_i + \Delta\phi_i) , \tag{9.95}$$

where

$$Q_0\phi_i = \lambda_i\phi_i . \tag{9.96}$$

The resulting equation is

$$Q_0\Delta\phi_i + \Delta Q\phi_i \cong \lambda_i \Delta\phi_i + \Delta\lambda_i\phi_i . \tag{9.97}$$

To calculate $\Delta\lambda_i$, we premultiply (9.97) by ϕ_i^T and, since $\phi_i^T Q_0 = \lambda_i \phi_i^T$ and $\phi_i^T \phi_j = \delta_{ij}$, we have

$$\Delta\lambda_i \cong \phi_i^T \Delta Q \phi_i \ . \tag{9.98}$$

Since n ϕ_j's form a complete set of basis vectors, we can write $\Delta\phi_i$ as a linear combination of the ϕ_j's as follows:

$$\Delta\phi_i = \sum_{j=1}^{n} b_{ij}\phi_j \ , \tag{9.99}$$

where

$$b_{ij} = \phi_j^T \Delta\phi_i \ . \tag{9.100}$$

If we premultiply (9.97) by ϕ_j^T and rearrange, we have for $i \neq j$

$$b_{ij} \cong \frac{\phi_j^T \Delta Q \phi_i}{\lambda_i - \lambda_j} \qquad (i \neq j) \ . \tag{9.101}$$

To determine b_{ii} we impose a first-order normalization condition on $\phi_i + \Delta\phi_i$, that is, we require

$$\|\phi_i + \Delta\phi_i\|^2 = 1 \cong \|\phi_i\|^2 + 2\phi_i^T \Delta\phi_i = 1 + 2\phi_i^T \Delta\phi_i \tag{9.102}$$

and it follows that

$$\phi_i^T \Delta\phi_i = b_{ii} \cong 0 \ . \tag{9.103}$$

Noting that $\phi_i^T Q_0 \phi_i = \lambda_i$ and $\phi_i^T Q_0 \phi_j = 0$ for $i \neq j$, we summarize this section as follows:

$$\lambda_i + \Delta\lambda_i \cong \phi_i^T Q \phi_i \tag{9.104}$$

and

$$b_{ij} \cong \begin{cases} \dfrac{\phi_i^T Q \phi_j}{\lambda_i - \lambda_j} & \text{for } i \neq j \\ 0 & \text{for } i = j \ . \end{cases} \tag{9.105}$$

Effect of doubling sampling rate: Let us begin our discussion with a simple example. Let $\mathbf{x}(t)$ be sampled at four instants, t_2, t_4, t_6, and t_8, as shown by the solid vertical lines in Fig. 9-6(a). Then, the autocorrelation matrix S has four eigenvalues whose magnitudes are indicated by the solid lines in Fig. 9-6(b). Let the number of sampling points be doubled to include t_1, t_3, t_5, and t_7. Now S has eight eigenvalues, as shown by the dashed lines in Fig. 9-6(b). The first four eigenvalues are close to the eigenvalues derived in the four-sampling case. The remaining four eigenvalues are those which result from doubling the sampling rate. If these four eigenvalues are small, the

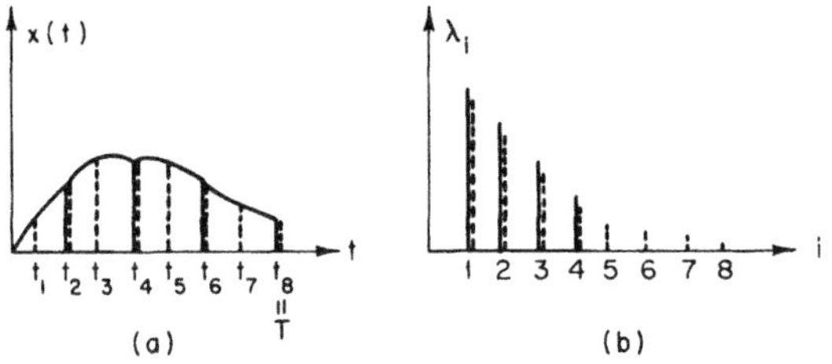

Fig. 9-6 A typical (a) waveform and (b) its eigenvalues.

error committed by deleting the corresponding features is also small. If the new features are unimportant, the features derived in the four-sampling case adequately represent $\mathbf{x}(t)$.

In general, suppose the dimension is $2n$. Then, we would have a $2n \times 2n$ autocorrelation matrix, S^{2n}. If the summation of some n of the $2n$ eigenvalues of S^{2n} is small compared to the summation of all $2n$ eigenvalues, n is sufficiently large. However, the computation of eigenvalues is time-consuming. Therefore, we introduce a simpler test for n by using the perturbation result.

Let the elements of the $2n$-dimensional vector X^{2n} be ordered so that

$$\mathbf{X}^{2n} = [\mathbf{x}(t_2)\,\mathbf{x}(t_4)\ldots\mathbf{x}(t_{2n})\,\mathbf{x}(t_1)\,\mathbf{x}(t_3)\ldots\mathbf{x}(t_{2n-1})]^T = [\mathbf{X}_e^{nT}\;\mathbf{X}_d^{nT}]^T , \tag{9.106}$$

where e stands for even and d for odd. Then, S^{2n} is given by

$$S^{2n} = E\{\mathbf{X}^{2n}\mathbf{X}^{2nT}\} = \begin{bmatrix} E\{\mathbf{X}_e^n\mathbf{X}_e^{nT}\} & E\{\mathbf{X}_e^n\mathbf{X}_d^{nT}\} \\ E\{\mathbf{X}_d^n\mathbf{X}_e^{nT}\} & E\{\mathbf{X}_d^n\mathbf{X}_d^{nT}\} \end{bmatrix} = \begin{bmatrix} S_{11}^n & S_{12}^n \\ S_{12}^{nT} & S_{22}^n \end{bmatrix} . \tag{9.107}$$

For large n, S_{11}^n, S_{12}^n, and S_{22}^n are nearly equal. We write S^{2n} as

$$S^{2n} = \begin{bmatrix} S_{11}^n & S_{11}^n \\ S_{11}^n & S_{11}^n \end{bmatrix} + \begin{bmatrix} 0 & S_{12}^n - S_{11}^n \\ S_{12}^{nT} - S_{11}^n & S_{22}^n - S_{11}^n \end{bmatrix} = S_0^{2n} + \Delta S^{2n} . \tag{9.108}$$

Now if

$$\Phi^n = [\phi_1^n \ldots \phi_n^n] \tag{9.109}$$

is the eigenvector matrix of S_{11}^n, then

$$\Phi_0^{2n} = \frac{1}{\sqrt{2}} \begin{bmatrix} \Phi^n & \Phi^n \\ \Phi^n & -\Phi^n \end{bmatrix} \tag{9.110}$$

is the eigenvector matrix of S_0^{2n}. Since ΔS^{2n} is small for large n, the eigenvalues of S^{2n} are given approximately from (9.104) by the diagonal elements of

$$G^{2n} = \Phi_0^{2nT} S^{2n} \Phi_0^{2n} = \begin{bmatrix} G_{11}^n & G_{12}^n \\ G_{12}^{nT} & G_{22}^n \end{bmatrix}, \tag{9.111}$$

where

$$G_{11}^n = \frac{1}{2} \Phi^{nT} (S_{11}^n + S_{12}^n + S_{12}^{nT} + S_{22}^n) \Phi^n , \tag{9.112}$$

$$G_{12}^n = \frac{1}{2} \Phi^{nT} (S_{11}^n - S_{12}^n + S_{12}^{nT} - S_{22}^n) \Phi^n , \tag{9.113}$$

and

$$G_{22}^n = \frac{1}{2} \Phi^{nT} (S_{11}^n - S_{12}^n - S_{12}^{nT} + S_{22}^n) \Phi^n . \tag{9.114}$$

We define a criterion J_n as [5]

$$J_n = \frac{\mathrm{tr} G_{22}^n}{\mathrm{tr}(G_{11}^n + G_{22}^n)} . \tag{9.115}$$

That is, J_n is approximately the ratio of the sum of the n smaller eigenvalues of S^{2n} to the sum of all $2n$ eigenvalues. If $J_n << 1$, n samples are sufficient, and the assumption concerning the smallness of ΔS^{2n} is reinforced. Using (9.112), (9.114), and the orthonormality of Φ^n, we can rewrite J_n as

$$J_n = \frac{\mathrm{tr}(S_{11}^n - S_{12}^n - S_{12}^{nT} + S_{22}^n)}{2\,\mathrm{tr}(S_{11}^n + S_{22}^n)} . \tag{9.116}$$

Or, recalling (9.106) and (9.107), we can write J_n in terms of the autocorrelation function, $R(t, \tau)$, of $\mathbf{x}(t)$ as

$$J_n = \frac{1}{2} \frac{\sum_{i=1}^{n} \{R(t_{2i},t_{2i}) - R(t_{2i},t_{2i-1}) - R(t_{2i-1},t_{2i}) + R(t_{2i-1},t_{2i-1})\}}{\sum_{i=1}^{n} \{R(t_{2i},t_{2i}) + R(t_{2i-1},t_{2i-1})\}} . \tag{9.117}$$

The advantage of this procedure is that J_n can be obtained from the autocorrelation matrix directly without computing the eigenvalues.

In stationary processes, $R(t_{2i},t_{2i}) = R(t_{2i-1},t_{2i-1}) = R(0)$, and $R(t_{2i-1},t_{2i}) = R(t_{2i}-t_{2i-1}) = R(T/(2n))$. Therefore,

$$J_n = \frac{R(0) - R(\frac{T}{2n})}{2R(0)} . \tag{9.118}$$

Example 5: Let us calculate J_n of (9.118) for $R(\tau) = \exp(-|\tau|)$ and $T = 1$. In this example

$$J_n = \frac{1}{2} \left[1 - \exp\left(-\frac{1}{2n} \right) \right] . \tag{9.119}$$

If $2n = 8$, we have $J_n \cong 0.06$ which indicates that four eigenvalues of S are very small compared to the other four. Thus, we would expect to gain little additional characterization of $\mathbf{x}(t)$ by increasing n further.

Example 6: Let $R(\tau)$ be a triangular function as

$$R(\tau) = \begin{cases} R(0)(1 - \frac{|\tau|}{T_0}) & (|\tau| \le T_0) \\ 0 & (|\tau| > T_0) . \end{cases} \tag{9.120}$$

If $T \le T_0$, J_n is given by

$$J_n = \frac{T}{4nT_0} . \tag{9.121}$$

The result of this example is useful in problems where stationarity may be assumed, but $R(\tau)$ is unknown. We assume the triangular form and determine the necessary n for a given T.

Estimation of Eigenvalues and Eigenvectors

Moments of eigenvalues and eigenvectors: Having chosen n, our next task is to estimate the eigenvalues and eigenvectors λ_i and ϕ_j $(j = 1, \ldots, n)$ of the autocorrelation matrix S. To do this, we calculate the sample autocorrelation matrix $\hat{\mathbf{S}}$ by

$$\hat{\mathbf{S}} = \frac{1}{N}\sum_{i=1}^{N}\mathbf{X}_i\mathbf{X}_i^T \tag{9.122}$$

and calculate the eigenvalues and eigenvectors $\boldsymbol{\lambda}_{\hat{j}}$ and $\hat{\boldsymbol{\phi}}_j$ $(j = 1, \ldots, n)$ of $\hat{\mathbf{S}}$.

It is important to note that $\boldsymbol{\lambda}_{\hat{j}}$ and $\hat{\boldsymbol{\phi}}_j$ are estimates of λ_j and ϕ_j and that they are random variables and vectors. They are functions of $\mathbf{X}_1, \ldots, \mathbf{X}_N$. In this section, we shall show approximate formulas for the expected values and variances of these estimates. Using these formulas, we can determine a value of N such that the estimates are sufficiently accurate.

The statistics of the eigenvectors and eigenvalues of a matrix of random variables have been studied previously [6-7]. The general approach is to calculate the distribution of $\hat{\mathbf{S}}$, and from this find the distribution of the eigenvectors and eigenvalues.

However, since $\hat{\mathbf{S}} \cong S$ for N sufficiently large, we may use the approximations (9.104) and (9.105) to express $\hat{\boldsymbol{\phi}}_i$ and $\boldsymbol{\lambda}_{\hat{i}}$, that is,

$$\hat{\boldsymbol{\phi}}_i \cong \phi_i + \sum_{\substack{j=1\\ j\neq i}}^{n}\frac{\phi_i^T\hat{\mathbf{S}}\phi_j}{\lambda_i - \lambda_j}\phi_j \tag{9.123}$$

and

$$\boldsymbol{\lambda}_{\hat{i}} \cong \phi_i^T\hat{\mathbf{S}}\phi_i \qquad (i = 1, \ldots, n) . \tag{9.124}$$

First, we consider the expected value of the estimate. Since $S = E\{\mathbf{X}\mathbf{X}^T\}$, the expected value of $\hat{\mathbf{S}}$ of (9.122) becomes

$$E\{\hat{\mathbf{S}}\} = \frac{1}{N}\sum_{i=1}^{N}E\{\mathbf{X}\mathbf{X}^T\} = S . \tag{9.125}$$

Therefore,

$$E\{\phi_i^T \hat{\mathbf{S}} \phi_j\} = \phi_i^T E\{\hat{\mathbf{S}}\} \phi_j = \phi_i^T S \phi_j = \lambda_i \delta_{ij} . \tag{9.126}$$

It follows from (9.123) and (9.124) that

$$E\{\hat{\boldsymbol{\phi}}_i\} \cong \phi_i \quad \text{and} \quad E\{\boldsymbol{\lambda}_i\} \cong \lambda_i . \tag{9.127}$$

Thus, the estimates are unbiased when only the first order approximations are used. This is due to the fact that the estimate of S is unbiased. However, as seen in (5.3) and (5.4), the bias comes from the second order term of the approximation, while the variance comes from the first order. Furthermore, since the eigenvalues and eigenvectors are functions of S, (5.18) suggests that the biases must be proportional to $1/N$. Thus,

$$E\{\hat{\boldsymbol{\phi}}_i\} \cong \phi_i + \frac{1}{N}\psi_i \quad \text{and} \quad E\{\boldsymbol{\lambda}_i\} \cong \lambda_i + \frac{1}{N}\mu_i , \tag{9.128}$$

where ψ_i are μ_i are the functions of S, although the functional forms are too complex to determine. The asymptotic values can be obtained experimentally by the procedure of (5.6).

From (5.19), the variances are also proportional to $1/N$. Since the variances can be obtained from the first order approximation as in (5.4), their approximated values may be computed as follows. The variance of $\boldsymbol{\lambda}_i$ and the covariance matrix of $\hat{\boldsymbol{\phi}}_i$ are given by

$$\text{Var}\{\boldsymbol{\lambda}_i\} = E\{(\boldsymbol{\lambda}_i - \lambda_i)^2\} = E\{\boldsymbol{\lambda}_i^2\} - \lambda_i^2 \cong E\{(\phi_i^T \hat{\mathbf{S}} \phi_i)^2\} - \lambda_i^2 , \tag{9.129}$$

$$\text{Cov}\{\hat{\boldsymbol{\phi}}_i\} = E\{(\hat{\boldsymbol{\phi}}_i - \phi_i)(\hat{\boldsymbol{\phi}}_i - \phi_i)^T\}$$

$$\cong \sum_{\substack{j=1 \\ j\neq i}}^{n} \sum_{\substack{k=1 \\ k\neq i}}^{n} \frac{E\{\phi_i^T \hat{\mathbf{S}} \phi_j \phi_i^T \hat{\mathbf{S}} \phi_k\}}{(\lambda_i - \lambda_j)(\lambda_i - \lambda_k)} \phi_j \phi_k^T . \tag{9.130}$$

Or, as a simpler alternative of (9.130), we may look at the mean-square error between $\hat{\boldsymbol{\phi}}_i$ and ϕ_i as

$$E\{\|\hat{\phi}_i - \phi_i\|^2\} = \text{tr}\,[\text{Cov}\{\hat{\phi}_i\}]$$

$$\cong \sum_{\substack{j=1 \\ j \neq i}}^{n} \frac{E\{(\phi_i^T \hat{\mathbf{S}} \phi_j)^2\}}{(\lambda_i - \lambda_j)^2} . \tag{9.131}$$

Note that both (9.129) and (9.131) are expressed in terms of $E\{(\phi_i^T \hat{\mathbf{S}} \phi_j)^2\}$.

Normal cases: When $\mathbf{X}$ is normally distributed, $E\{(\phi_i^T \hat{\mathbf{S}} \phi_j)^2\}$ can be computed as follows.

Since $\hat{\mathbf{S}}$ is given by (9.122),

$$\phi_i^T \hat{\mathbf{S}} \phi_j = \frac{1}{N} \sum_{k=1}^{N} \mathbf{y}_{ik} \mathbf{y}_{jk} , \tag{9.132}$$

where

$$\mathbf{y}_{ik} = \phi_i^T \mathbf{X}_k . \tag{9.133}$$

If both sides of (9.132) are squared and the expectation is taken, the result is

$$E\{(\phi_i^T \hat{\mathbf{S}} \phi_j)^2\} = \frac{1}{N^2} \sum_{k=1}^{N} \sum_{\ell=1}^{N} E\{\mathbf{y}_{ik} \mathbf{y}_{jk} \mathbf{y}_{i\ell} \mathbf{y}_{j\ell}\}$$

$$= \frac{1}{N^2} \sum_{\substack{k=1 \\ k \neq \ell}}^{N} \sum_{\ell=1}^{N} E\{\mathbf{y}_{ik} \mathbf{y}_{jk}\} E\{\mathbf{y}_{i\ell} \mathbf{y}_{j\ell}\} + \frac{1}{N^2} \sum_{k=1}^{N} E\{\mathbf{y}_{ik}^2 \mathbf{y}_{jk}^2\} , \tag{9.134}$$

since the $\mathbf{X}_k$'s are independent. Now

$$E\{\mathbf{y}_{ik} \mathbf{y}_{jk}\} = \phi_i^T E\{\mathbf{X}_k \mathbf{X}_k^T\} \phi_j = \lambda_i \delta_{ij} \qquad (k = 1, \ldots, N) \tag{9.135}$$

and (9.134) may be rewritten as

$$E\{(\phi_i^T \hat{\mathbf{S}} \phi_j)^2\} = \frac{N-1}{N} \lambda_i^2 \delta_{ij} + \frac{1}{N} E\{\mathbf{y}_i^2 \mathbf{y}_j^2\} . \tag{9.136}$$

The second subscript on $\mathbf{y}$ is dropped since the $\mathbf{X}_k$'s are identically distributed.

When $\mathbf{X}$ is normally distributed with zero mean, the $\mathbf{y}_i$'s are also normal with $E\{\mathbf{y}_i\} = 0$ from (9.133) and $E\{\mathbf{y}_i \mathbf{y}_j\} = \lambda_i \delta_{ij}$ from (9.135). This means that the $\mathbf{y}_i$'s are mutually independent. Therefore,

$$E\{\mathbf{y}_i^2\mathbf{y}_j^2\} = \begin{cases} 3\lambda_i^2 & \text{for } i = j \\ \lambda_i\lambda_j & \text{for } i \neq j . \end{cases} \tag{9.137}$$

Inserting (9.137) into (9.136),

$$E\{(\phi_i^T\hat{\mathbf{S}}\phi_j)^2\} = \lambda_i^2\delta_{ij} + \frac{1}{N}(\lambda_i^2\delta_{ij} + \lambda_i\lambda_j) . \tag{9.138}$$

Substituting (9.138) into (9.129) and (9.131),

$$\mathrm{Var}\{\boldsymbol{\lambda}_i\} \cong \frac{2}{N}\lambda_i^2 , \tag{9.139}$$

$$E\{\|\hat{\boldsymbol{\phi}}_i - \phi_i\|^2\} \cong \frac{1}{N}\sum_{\substack{j=1 \\ j\neq i}}^{n} \frac{\lambda_i\lambda_j}{(\lambda_i-\lambda_j)^2} = \frac{\gamma_i}{N} . \tag{9.140}$$

The variance of the eigenvalue, normalized by λ_i^2, is approximately $2/N$ regardless of the value of λ_i. On the other hand, the variation of $\hat{\boldsymbol{\phi}}_i$ depends on how close some of other eigenvalues are to λ_i. When $\lambda_j/\lambda_i \cong 1$, γ_i of (9.140) can become very large. This seems to be a serious problem. However, this problem is not as critical as it appears to be. Let us consider a simple 3-dimensional example in which $\lambda_1 = \lambda_2 = 1$ and $\lambda_3 = 0.1$. Applying the *K-L* expansion, we discard ϕ_3 and map down $\mathbf{X}$ onto the two-dimensional subspace spanned by ϕ_1 and ϕ_2. The covariance matrix of $\mathbf{y}_1 = \phi_1^T\mathbf{X}$ and $\mathbf{y}_2 = \phi_2^T\mathbf{X}$ is I, and we cannot identify the principal axes of the distribution in the Y-space. In fact, ϕ_1 and ϕ_2 are indefinite, and (9.140) indicates that the variations of $\hat{\boldsymbol{\phi}}_1$ and $\hat{\boldsymbol{\phi}}_2$ are infinite. However, in this case, we do not need to obtain the accurate estimates of ϕ_1 and ϕ_2 individually, as long as the subspace spanned by ϕ_1 and ϕ_2 is accurately estimated.

Example 7: We now present a numerical example that illustrates some interesting points.

Let $\mathbf{x}(t)$ be a stationary, normal random process with

$$R(\tau) = \exp(-a\,|\tau|) . \tag{9.141}$$

If $\mathbf{x}(t)$ is time-sampled at $t = \ell T/n$ ($\ell = 0, \ldots, n-1$), the autocorrelation matrix S becomes a matrix whose element $s_{\ell m}$ is

$$s_{\ell m} = \exp(-a\,|\ell - m|\,\frac{T}{n}) = \rho^{|\ell - m|/n} \qquad (\ell, m = 0, \ldots, n-1)\,, \tag{9.142}$$

where

$$\rho = \exp(-aT)\,. \tag{9.143}$$

The error coefficients of (9.140) are determined by the eigenvalues of S. By varying ρ and n of (9.142), we have a family of S matrices. Let us then examine the error coefficients of various matrices in the family.

(1) *Fixed* ρ*:* For each value of n, we have n error coefficients, $\gamma_1, \ldots, \gamma_n$. We order γ_i according to decreasing magnitude of λ_i.

Figure 9-7 is a plot of γ_i for $\rho = 0.1$ [5]. The variation of the eigenvector estimate tends to increase as the value of the corresponding eigenvalue decreases. Therefore, a larger number of samples is needed to estimate these eigenvectors with smaller eigenvalues. Fortunately, the eigenvectors with smaller eigenvalues are less important for signal representation, and thus the accuracy of the estimates is not as critical as the one for the eigenvectors with larger eigenvalues. The range of the error coefficients is on the order of 100.

(2) *Variation of the largest coefficient:* Suppose we must measure all of the eigenvectors with a certain accuracy. Then, when the dimension is n, $\gamma_{\max} = \max\{\gamma_1, \ldots, \gamma_n\}$ is the constraining factor. Thus, the variation of $\gamma_{\max}$ with n indicates how the sample size must grow with n to maintain a fixed accuracy.

Figure 9-8 shows the variation of $\gamma_{\max}$ with n for various values of ρ. We see that $\gamma_{\max}$ grows roughly as n^2 [5].

Computer Projects

1. Generate 50, 100, and 200 samples from a normal distribution with zero mean and the covariance matrix Λ of Data *I*-Λ. For each sample size, calculate the sample covariance matrix and their eigenvalues. Repeat this experiment 10 times and average the estimated eigenvalues. Using the estimation technique of (5.6), find the asymptotic values for these eigenvalues.

2. (a) Compute the eigenvalues and eigenvectors of (4.126) where $n = 10$ and $\rho = \exp(-0.1)$.

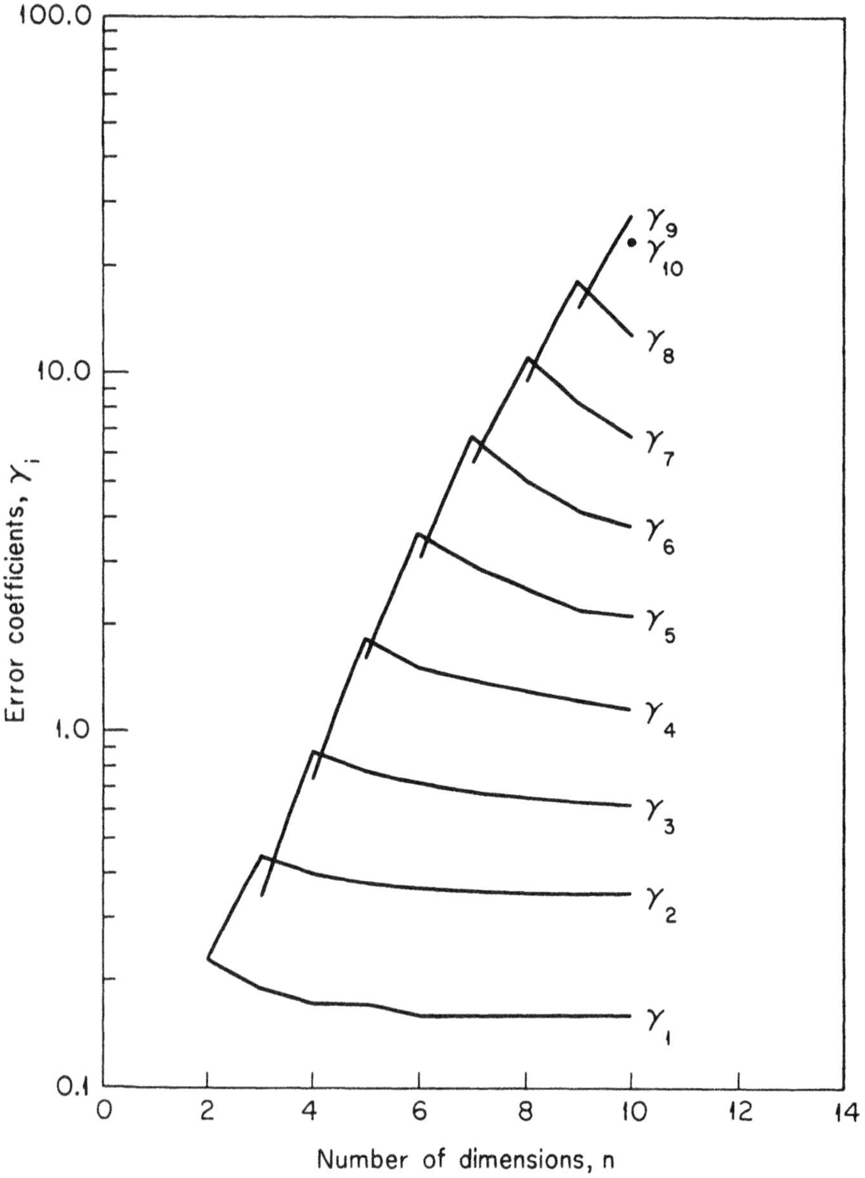

Fig. 9-7 Error coefficients for $\rho = 0.1$.

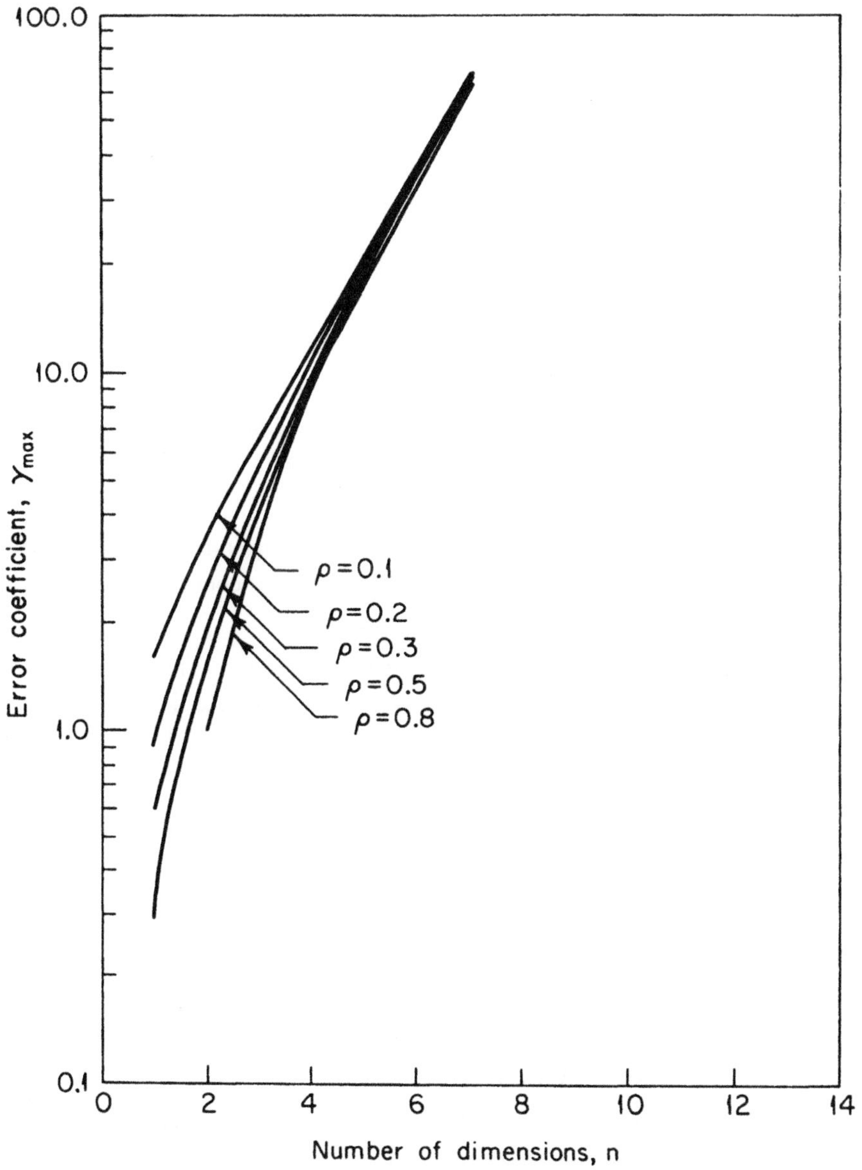

Fig. 9-8 Value of the maximum error coefficient.

(b) Compute the power spectrum of an autocorrelation function $R(t) = \exp(-|t|)$. Assuming that the random process is time-sampled in $0 \le t < 1$ with increment of 0.1, determine the sampling points in the power spectrum. Compare the eigenvalues and eigenvectors obtained in (b) with the ones obtained in (a).

3. Repeat Project 2 for $R(t) = 2/(20t^2 + 1)$.

4. Repeat Example 7 to obtain Figs. 9-7 and 9-8.

Problems

1. The density function of a two-dimensional random vector $\mathbf{X}$ consists of four impulses at (0,3), (0,1), (1,0), and (3,0) with probability of 1/4 for each.

(a) Find the *K-L* expansion. Compute the mean-square error when one feature is eliminated. Compute the contribution of each impulse point to the mean-square error.

(b) Repeat (a) without subtracting the mean vector. That is, express $\mathbf{X}$ by the summation of two basis vectors, optimize the basis vectors without subtracting the mean vector, and compute the mean-square error when one vector is eliminated.

2. Let $\mathbf{X}^{(1)}$ and $\mathbf{X}^{(2)}$ be samples from ω_1 and ω_2 respectively. The between-class scatter matrix is defined by

$$S_b = E\{(\mathbf{X}^{(1)} - \mathbf{X}^{(2)})(\mathbf{X}^{(1)} - \mathbf{X}^{(2)})^T\} .$$

Find S_b in terms of the expected vectors and covariance matrices of two classes.

Find the linear orthonormal transformation from an n-dimensional $\mathbf{X}$ to an m-dimensional $\mathbf{Y}$ by maximizing trS_b.

3. Calculate $E\{-\ln p_1(X)|\omega_2\}$ where $p_i(X)$ $(i = 1,2)$ is a normal distribution with the expected vector M_i and covariance matrix Σ_i.

Assuming $M_1 = M_2$ and $\Sigma_1 = I$, find the linear orthonormal transformation from an n-dimensional $\mathbf{X}$ to an m-dimensional $\mathbf{Y}$ which maximizes $E\{-\ln p_1(X)|\omega_2\}$.

4. A stationary process $\mathbf{x}(t)$ is observed in $0 \le t < 1$. The mean and autocorrelation function of $\mathbf{x}(t)$ are given by 0 and $\exp(-4|t|)$. Find the necessary sampling points which assure approximately that the eigenvalues larger than 10% of the largest eigenvalue are retained.

5. The figure shows a block diagram of a linear filter problem, where $s(t)$ is the original signal, $\mathbf{x}(t)$ is the observed signal with $s(t)$ and noise $\mathbf{n}(t)$ added, and $\hat{\mathbf{s}}(t)$ is the estimate of $s(t)$. The impulse response $h(t,\tau)$ of the optimum linear filter is found by minimizing

$$E\left[\frac{1}{T}\int_0^T \{s(t) - \hat{\mathbf{s}}(t)\}^2 dt\right] = E\left[\frac{1}{T}\int_0^T \left\{s(t) - \int_0^T h(t,\tau)\mathbf{x}(\tau)d\tau\right\}^2 dt\right]$$

with respect to $h(t,\tau)$. Find the optimum $h(t,\tau)$ by using the vector-matrix approach.

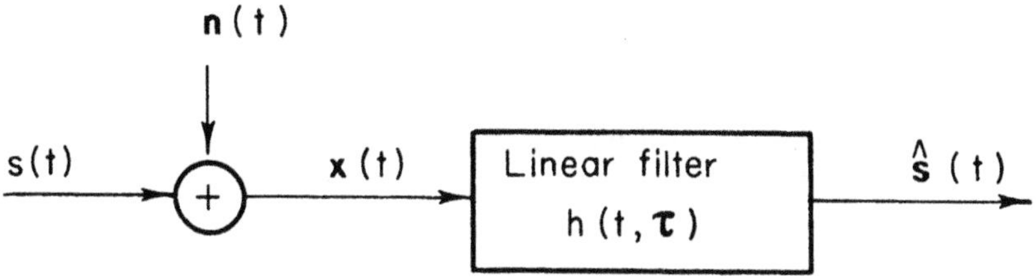

6. The autocorrelation function of a Poisson process is given by $\lambda t + \lambda^2 t\tau$ for $\tau \ge t$ and $\lambda\tau + \lambda^2 t\tau$ for $t \ge \tau$.

Assuming $0 \le t,\ \tau \le T$, find the sampling interval or the number of sampling points to assure that, even if we double the sampling rate, the summation of the newly generated eigenvalues is less than ε% of the summation of total eigenvalues. Find the necessary number of sampling points to assure $\varepsilon = 0.1\%$ for $\lambda = 1$ and $T = 1$.

7. A stationary process is normally distributed in [0, 1] with the covariance function of $\exp(-|t|)$. Assuming that the process is time-sampled at 10 points, find the necessary number of samples (waveforms) to assure $E\{\|\hat{\boldsymbol{\phi}}_{10} - \boldsymbol{\phi}_{10}\|^2\} \le 0.1$.

References

1. T. Y. Young, The reliability of linear feature extractor, *Trans. IEEE Computers*, C-20, pp. 967-971, 1971.
2. H. L. VanTrees, "Detection, Estimation, and Modulation Theory: Part I," Wiley, New York, 1968.
3. A. Papoulis, "Probability, Random Variables, and Stochastic Processes," McGraw-Hill, New York, 1965.
4. B. Noble and J. W. Daniel, "Applied Linear Algebra (Second Edition)," Prentice-Hall, Englewood Cliffs, New Jersey, 1977.
5. K. Fukunaga and W. L. G. Koontz, Representation of random processes using the finite Karhunen-Loéve expansion, *Inform. and Contr.*, 16, pp. 85-101, 1970.
6. J. H. Wilkinson, "Algebraic Eigenvalue Problem," Oxford Univ. Press, London and New York, 1965.
7. T. W. Anderson, "An Introduction to Multivariate Statistical Analysis," Wiley, New York, 1962.

Chapter 10

FEATURE EXTRACTION AND LINEAR MAPPING FOR CLASSIFICATION

When we have two or more classes, feature extraction consists of choosing those features which are most effective for preserving class separability. Class separability criteria are essentially independent of coordinate systems, and are completely different from the criteria for signal representation. Furthermore, class separability depends not only on the class distributions but also on the classifier to be used. For example, the optimum feature set for a linear classifier may not be the optimum set for other classifiers for the same distributions. In order to avoid this additional complexity, let us assume that we seek the optimum feature set with reference to the Bayes classifier; this will result in the minimum error for the given distributions. Then, class separability becomes equivalent to the probability of error due to the Bayes classifier, which is the best we can expect.

Therefore, theoretically speaking, the Bayes error is the optimum measure of feature effectiveness. Also, in practice, the Bayes error calculated experimentally is one of the most popular criteria. That is, having selected a set of features intuitively from given data, estimate the Bayes error in the feature space by the procedures discussed in Chapter 7.

A major disadvantage of the Bayes error as a criterion is the fact that an explicit mathematical expression is not available except for a very few special cases and, therefore, we cannot expect a great deal of theoretical development. In Chapter 3, we showed that, even for normal distributions, the calculation of the Bayes error requires a numerical integration, except for the equal covariance case.

In this chapter, several criteria which have explicit mathematical expressions will be discussed. These expressions are derived from some physical notions. However, the reader should be reminded that, whenever a criterion is proposed, the performance of the criterion has to be discussed in relation to the Bayes error.

10.1 General Problem Formulation

Difference Between Signal Representation and Classification

Feature extraction for classification which will be discussed in this chapter is different in many respects from feature extraction for signal representation in Chapter 9, particularly in the criteria to be used and in the transformations to be allowed.

Criteria: As an example, let us look at the distribution of height and weight for males as in Fig. 10-1. Since these two variables are highly correlated (a taller person tends to be heavier and vice versa), the distribution shows a football shape. As discussed in Chapter 9, the principal axis ϕ_1 with a larger eigenvalue is a better vector than ϕ_2 to represent the vectors of this distribution. That is, the selection of ϕ_1 produces a smaller mean-square error of representation than the selection of ϕ_2. The same is true for the female distribution, and even for the mixture of two distributions. However, as seen in Fig. 10-1, if the two distributions are mapped onto ϕ_1, the marginal density functions are heavily overlapped. On the other hand, if they are mapped onto ϕ_2, the marginal densities are well separated with little overlap. Therefore, for classification purposes, ϕ_2 is a better feature than ϕ_1, preserving more of the classification information.

The same argument can be applied to the problem of classifying two different human races. In order to describe a human being, we may use such characteristics as two eyes, one mouth, two hands, two legs and so on. However, none of these features are useful for classifying caucasians and orientals.

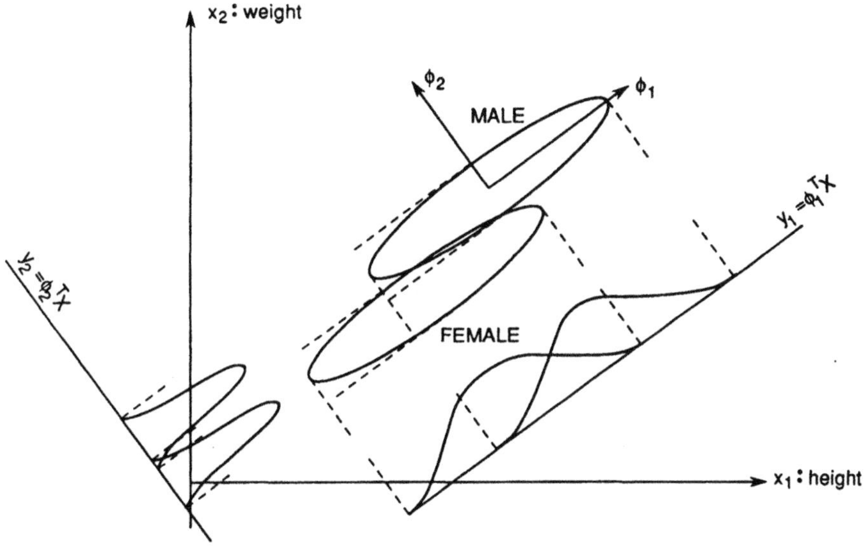

Fig. 10-1 An example of feature extraction for classification.

Thus, feature extraction for classification cannot be discussed as a simple extension of Chapter 9. In particular, the criteria to evaluate the effectiveness of features must be a measure of the overlap or class separability among distributions, and not a measure of fit such as the mean-square error.

Transformations: When feature extraction for signal representation was discussed, we limited our discussion only to orthonormal transformations, because the shape of the distribution had to be preserved. The mean-square error is a coordinate-dependent criterion except for orthonormal transformations. On the other hand, the overlap or class separability among distributions is invariant under any nonsingular transformation, including both linear and nonlinear mappings. However, any singular transformation maps $\mathbf{X}$ onto a lower-dimensional $\mathbf{Y}$, losing some of the classification information. Therefore, we can present feature extraction for classification as a search, among all possible singular transformations, for the best subspace which preserves class separability as much as possible in the lowest possible dimensional space.

Ideal Features for Classification

It is always advantageous to know what are the best features for classification, even though those features might be too complex to obtain in practice. Since the Bayes classifier for the L-class problem compares a posteriori probabilities, $q_1(X), \ldots, q_L(X)$, and classifies X to the class whose a posteriori probability is the largest, these L functions carry sufficient information to set up the Bayes classifier. Furthermore, since $\sum_{i=1}^{L} q_i(X) = 1$, only $(L-1)$ of these L functions are linearly independent. Thus, these $(L-1)$ features are the smallest set needed to classify L classes. Also, the Bayes error in this $(L-1)$-dimensional feature space is identical to the Bayes error in the original X-space. That is, by the transformation of $y_i = q_i(X)$, $i = 1, \ldots, (L-1)$, from an n-dimensional space to an $(L-1)$-dimensional space, no classification information is lost. Thus, we call $\{q_1(X), \ldots, q_{L-1}(X)\}$ the *ideal feature set for classification*. Figure 10-2 shows the distributions of three classes in the original X-space as well as in the ideal feature space. No matter

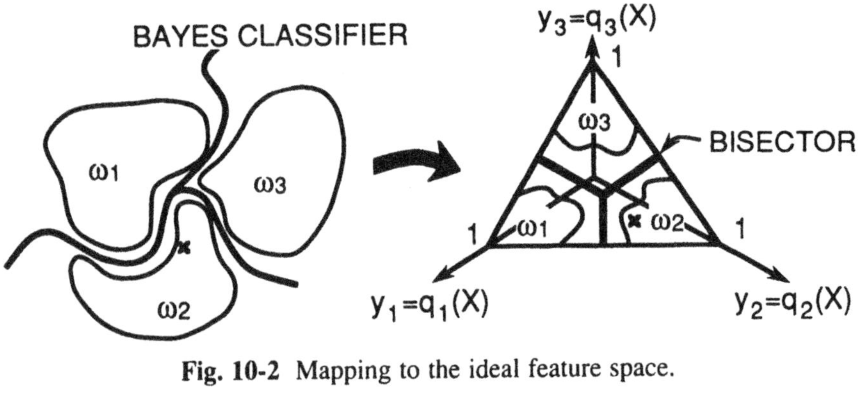

Fig. 10-2 Mapping to the ideal feature space.

how the distributions are in the X-space, the three classes of the ideal features are distributed in the two-dimensional plane to satisfy $\mathbf{y}_1 + \mathbf{y}_2 + \mathbf{y}_3 = 1$. Since the Bayes classifier classifies X according to the largest $q_i(X)$, the Bayes classifier in the feature space becomes a *piecewise bisector classifier* which is the simplest form of a classifier for the three-class problem.

Figure 10-3 shows how the ideal features are translated to other forms, depending on the conditions. The features of the second line, $\ln p_i(X)$, are obtained by taking the logarithm of the first line. Note that the term $\ln p(X)$ is common for all classes and is irrelevant to classification. Also, in feature

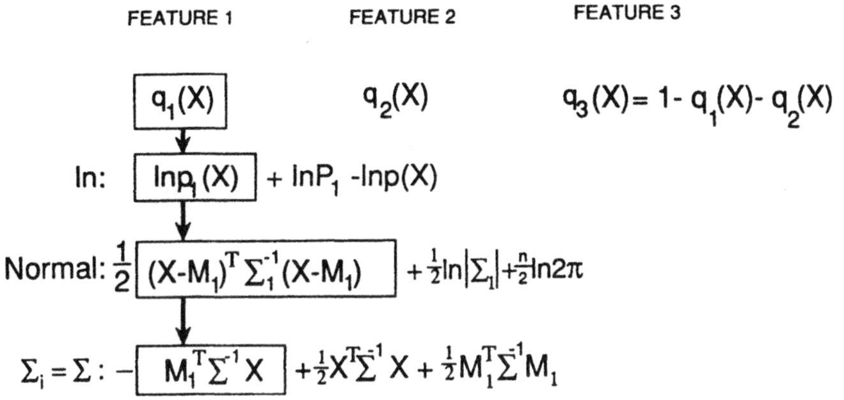

Fig. 10-3 The ideal features.

extraction, additive and multiplicative constants do not alter the subspace onto which distributions are mapped. Therefore, the term $\ln P_i$ is not included in the feature function. If the distributions are normal, the quadratic equations of X in the third line are the ideal features. Furthermore, if the covariance matrices of all classes are the same, the linear functions of X in the fourth line become the ideal features.

10.2 Discriminant Analysis

The Bayes error is the best criterion to evaluate feature sets, and a posteriori probability functions are the ideal features. However, in practice, a posteriori probability functions are hard to obtain, and their estimates, obtained through nonparametric density estimation techniques of Chapter 6, normally have severe biases and variances. As for the Bayes error, we can estimate it and use it to evaluate given feature sets, as discussed in Chapter 7; however this is time-consuming. Unfortunately, the Bayes error is just too complex and useless as an analytical tool to extract features systematically. Therefore, we need simpler criteria associated with systematic feature extraction algorithms.

There are two types of criteria which are frequently used in practice. One is based on a family of functions of scatter matrices, which are conceptually simple and give systematic feature extraction algorithms. The criteria used measure the class separability of L classes, but do not relate to the Bayes error directly. The other is a family of criteria which give upper bounds of the Bayes error. The Bhattacharyya distance of (3.152) is one of these criteria.

However, the criteria are only for two-class problems, and are based on normality assumption.

Scatter Matrices and Separability Criteria

In *discriminant analysis* of statistics, within-class, between-class, and mixture scatter matrices are used to formulate criteria of class separability.

A *within-class scatter matrix* shows the scatter of samples around their respective class expected vectors, and is expressed by

$$S_w = \sum_{i=1}^{L} P_i E\{(\mathbf{X}-M_i)(\mathbf{X}-M_i)^T \mid \omega_i\} = \sum_{i=1}^{L} P_i \Sigma_i \ . \tag{10.1}$$

On the other hand, a *between-class scatter matrix* is the scatter of the expected vectors around the mixture mean as

$$S_b = \sum_{i=1}^{L} P_i (M_i - M_0)(M_i - M_0)^T \ , \tag{10.2}$$

where M_0 represents the expected vector of the mixture distribution and is given by

$$M_0 = E\{\mathbf{X}\} = \sum_{i=1}^{L} P_i M_i \ . \tag{10.3}$$

The *mixture scatter matrix* is the covariance matrix of all samples regardless of their class assignments, and is defined by

$$S_m = E\{(\mathbf{X}-M_0)(\mathbf{X}-M_0)^T\} = S_w + S_b \ . \tag{10.4}$$

All these scatter matrices are designed to be invariant under coordinate shifts.

In order to formulate criteria for class separability, we need to convert these matrices to a number. This number should be larger when the between-class scatter is larger or the within-class scatter is smaller. There are several ways to do this, and typical criteria are the following:

(1) $J_1 = \mathrm{tr}(S_2^{-1} S_1)$, (10.5)

(2) $J_2 = \ln |S_2^{-1} S_1| = \ln |S_1| - \ln |S_2|$, (10.6)

$$(3) \quad J_3 = \text{tr}\, S_1 - \mu(tr\, S_2 - c)\,, \tag{10.7}$$

$$(4) \quad J_4 = \frac{\text{tr}\, S_1}{\text{tr}\, S_2}\,, \tag{10.8}$$

where S_1 and S_2 are one of S_b, S_w, or S_m. The following remarks pertain to these criteria:

(1) Many combinations of S_b, S_w, and S_m for S_1 and S_2 are possible. Typical examples are $\{S_b,S_w\}$, $\{S_b,S_m\}$, and $\{S_w,S_m\}$ for $\{S_1,S_2\}$.

(2) The optimization of J_1 is equivalent to the optimization of $\text{tr}(A^T S_1 A)$ with respect to A under the constraint $A^T S_2 A = I$ where A is an $n \times m$ transformation matrix [see Problem 2]. The same is true for J_2.

(3) For J_2, S_b cannot be used, because the rank of S_b is $(L-1)$ from (10.2) and (10.3) and $|S_b| = 0$ for $(L-1) < n$.

(4) As we will discuss later, the optimization of J_1 and J_2 results in the same linear features. Recall that the trace and determinant criteria produced the same linear features for signal representation in Chapter 9. Furthermore, these optimal features are the same no matter which combination of S_b, S_w, and S_m is used for S_1 and S_2. Therefore, we may choose any combination for our discussion without worrying about which combination is better.

(5) The logarithm of the determinant is used for J_2 in this book, although many references cite $|S_1|/|S_2|$. By using the logarithm, J_2 in an n-dimensional space can be computed by adding the J_2 values of individual features, if the features are independent. This property is called the *additive property of independent features*.

(6) When J_3 is used, $\text{tr}\, S_1$ is optimized, subject to the constraint $\text{tr}\, S_2 = c$ [see Problem 3]. That is, μ is a Lagrange multiplier and c is a constant.

(7) As we will discuss later, J_1 and J_2 are invariant under any nonsingular linear transformation, while J_3 and J_4 are dependent on the coordinate system.

In this book, we will discuss only the optimization of J_1 and J_2 in detail. Similar discussions are found in [1] for J_3 and [2] for J_4.

Optimum Linear Transformation

Since it is very difficult, if not impossible, to discuss general nonlinear transformations, our discussion will be limited to linear transformations. A linear transformation from an n-dimensional $\mathbf{X}$ to an m-dimensional $\mathbf{Y}$ (m < n) is expressed by

$$\mathbf{Y} = A^T \mathbf{X} , \tag{10.9}$$

where A is an $n \times m$ rectangular matrix and the column vectors are linearly independent. However, contrary to the case for signal representation, these column vectors do not need to be orthonormal. Since all three scatter matrices, S_b, S_w, and S_m, have the form of a covariance matrix, S_1 and S_2 in the Y-space can be calculated from S_1 and S_2 in the X-space by

$$S_{iY} = A^T S_{iX} A \qquad (i = 1,2) . \tag{10.10}$$

Thus, the problem of feature extraction for classification is to find the A which optimizes one of the J's in the Y-space.

Optimization of J_1: Let $J_1(m)$ be the value of J_1 in an m-dimensional Y-space. Then,

$$J_1(m) = \text{tr}(S_{2Y}^{-1} S_{1Y}) = \text{tr}\{(A^T S_{2X} A)^{-1} (A^T S_{1X} A)\} . \tag{10.11}$$

Taking the derivative of (10.11) with respect to A, by using (A.16),

$$\frac{\partial J_1(m)}{\partial A} = -2 S_{2X} A\, S_{2Y}^{-1} S_{1Y} S_{2Y}^{-1} + 2 S_{1X} A\, S_{2Y}^{-1} . \tag{10.12}$$

Equating (10.12) to zero, the optimum A must satisfy

$$(S_{2X}^{-1} S_{1X}) A = A (S_{2Y}^{-1} S_{1Y}) . \tag{10.13}$$

Two matrices S_{1Y} and S_{2Y} can be simultaneously diagonalized to μ_m and I_m by a linear transformation $\mathbf{Z} = B^T \mathbf{Y}$ such that

$$B^T S_{1Y} B = \mu_m \qquad \text{and} \qquad B^T S_{2Y} B = I_m , \tag{10.14}$$

where B is an $m \times m$ nonsingular square matrix and B^{-1} exists.

It is easy to show that the criterion value is invariant under this nonsingular transformation from **Y** to **Z**.

$$
\begin{aligned}
\mathrm{tr}(S_{2Z}^{-1}S_{1Z}) &= \mathrm{tr}\{(B^TS_{2Y}B)^{-1}(B^TS_{1Y}B)\} \\
&= \mathrm{tr}(B^{-1}S_{2Y}^{-1}B^{T^{-1}}B^TS_{1Y}B) \\
&= \mathrm{tr}(S_{2Y}^{-1}S_{1Y}B\,B^{-1}) \\
&= \mathrm{tr}(S_{2Y}^{-1}S_{1Y}) \,. \qquad (10.15)
\end{aligned}
$$

Using (10.14), (10.13) is rewritten as

$$(S_{2X}^{-1}S_{1X})A = A(B\,\mu_mB^{-1}) \qquad (10.16)$$

or

$$(S_{2X}^{-1}S_{1X})(AB) = (AB)\mu_m \,. \qquad (10.17)$$

Equation (10.17) shows that the components of μ_m and the column vectors of (AB) are the m eigenvalues and eigenvectors of $S_{2X}^{-1}S_{1X}$. Although both S_{1X} and S_{2X} are symmetric, $S_{2X}^{-1}S_{1X}$ is not necessarily symmetric. However, the eigenvalues and eigenvectors of $S_{2X}^{-1}S_{1X}$ are obtained as the result of simultaneous diagonalization of S_{1X} and S_{2X}, as discussed in Chapter 2. As the result, the eigenvalues are real and positive, and the eigenvectors are real and orthonormal with respect to S_{2X}.

Since the trace of a matrix is the summation of the eigenvalues,

$$J_1(n) = \mathrm{tr}(S_{2X}^{-1}S_{1X}) = \lambda_1 + \ldots + \lambda_n \,, \qquad (10.18)$$

$$J_1(m) = \mathrm{tr}(S_{2Y}^{-1}S_{1Y}) = \mu_1 + \ldots + \mu_m \,, \qquad (10.19)$$

where the λ_i's and μ_i's are the eigenvalues of $S_{2X}^{-1}S_{1X}$ and $S_{2Y}^{-1}S_{1Y}$ respectively. Since the μ_i's are also the eigenvalues of $S_{2X}^{-1}S_{1X}$ from (10.17), we can maximize (or minimize) $J_1(m)$ by selecting the largest (or smallest) m eigenvalues. The corresponding m eigenvectors form the transformation matrix.

The above argument indicates that, by projecting **X** onto the m eigenvectors of $S_{2X}^{-1}S_{1X}$, we can form an m-dimensional subspace which is spanned by these m eigenvectors. Then, $J_1(m)$ is the summation of the corresponding m eigenvalues. Further application of any $m \times m$ nonsingular linear transformation would not change the value of $J_1(m)$. Therefore, we may conclude that the value of $J_1(m)$ is attached to the subspace and is invariant regardless of the selection of the coordinate system in the subspace. Thus, it is appropriate to represent the subspace by the set of m eigenvectors of $S_{2X}^{-1}S_{1X}$.

Comparing feature extraction for classification in this chapter with the one for signal representation in Chapter 9, it should be noted that both algorithms are identical, selecting the eigenvectors of a matrix as the optimum linear features. However, different matrices are used for different purposes: $S_2^{-1}S_1$ for classification and the covariance matrix for signal representation.

Two-class problems: Let $J_1 = \text{tr}(S_w^{-1}S_b)$ be the criterion for two-class problems. For two-class problems, S_b becomes

$$S_b = P_1(M_1-M_0)(M_1-M_0)^T + P_2(M_2-M_0)(M_2-M_0)^T$$
$$= P_1P_2(M_2-M_1)(M_2-M_1)^T , \tag{10.20}$$

where $P_1M_1 + P_2M_2 = M_0$ is used to obtain the second line from the first. Since S_b of (10.20) is composed of one vector (M_2-M_1), the rank of S_b is one. Since S_w is the averaged covariance matrix, it generally has full rank and S_w^{-1} exists. Therefore, the rank of $S_w^{-1}S_b$ is also one. That is,

$$\lambda_1 \neq 0 \quad \text{and} \quad \lambda_2 = \ldots = \lambda_n = 0 . \tag{10.21}$$

On the other hand, $\text{tr}(S_w^{-1}S_b)$ is the summation of these eigenvalues,

$$\lambda_1 = \text{tr}(S_w^{-1}S_b) = P_1P_2(M_2-M_1)^TS_w^{-1}(M_2-M_1) . \tag{10.22}$$

The corresponding eigenvector is

$$\phi_1 = \frac{S_w^{-1}(M_2-M_1)}{\|S_w^{-1}(M_2-M_1)\|} , \tag{10.23}$$

where the denominator is a constant selected to satisfy $\|\phi_1\| = 1$. The reader can confirm that $S_w^{-1}S_b\phi_1 = \lambda_1\phi_1$ is satisfied by using ϕ_1 of (10.23), λ_1 of (10.22), and S_b of (10.20).

Equation (10.21) indicates that, for two-class problems, only one feature is needed, and the others do not contribute to the value of J_1. The mapping function is

$$y_1 = \phi_1^T\mathbf{X} = c(M_2-M_1)^TS_w^{-1}\mathbf{X} , \tag{10.24}$$

where c is a constant. Note from (4.27) that (10.24) is the optimum linear classifier without including the threshold term, when $f(\eta_1, \eta_2, P_1\sigma_1^2 + P_2\sigma_2^2)$ is optimized with respect to V. If we were to select one vector to project two distributions, the vector perpendicular to the optimum hyperplane should be the one. The above argument suggests that, by projecting two distributions onto $V = S_w^{-1}(M_2 - M_1)$, we can preserve all classification information, as long as the class separability is measured by $\text{tr}(S_w^{-1} S_b)$.

***L*-class problems:** Two-class problems can be extended to L-class problems, still using $J_1 = \text{tr}(S_w^{-1} S_b)$. Since the M_i's are related by (10.3), only $(L-1)$ of them are linearly independent. Therefore, S_b of (10.2) has the rank $(L-1)$, and subsequently the rank of $S_w^{-1} S_b$ is $(L-1)$. This means that $(L-1)$ eigenvalues of $S_w^{-1} S_b$ are nonzero and the others are zero. Thus, without losing the criterion value, we can map **X** onto the $(L-1)$-dimensional subspace spanned by the $(L-1)$ eigenvectors corresponding to these nonzero eigenvalues.

Recall that the number of ideal features was $(L-1)$. In order to classify L distributions, we need at least $(L-1)$ features. The optimization of $\text{tr}(S_w^{-1} S_b)$ also produces $(L-1)$ features without losing classifiability, as long as the classifiability is measured by $\text{tr}(S_w^{-1} S_b)$.

It is commonly considered that a pattern recognition system consists of two parts; a feature extractor and a classifier, as shown in Fig. 10-4. However,

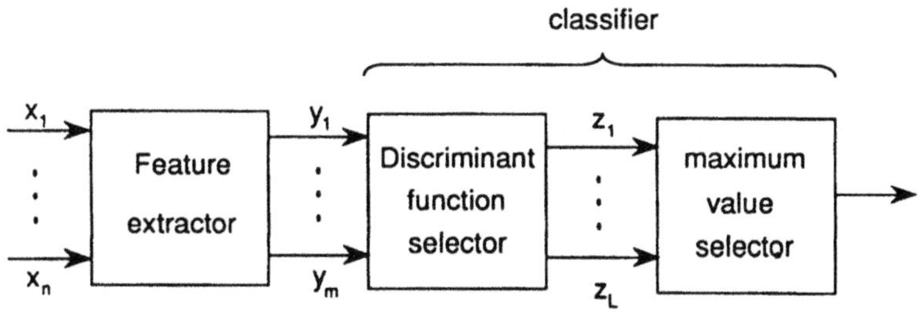

Fig. 10-4 Structure of a classifier.

when the classifier part is examined more closely, it is found to consist of a discriminant function selector, which chooses a posteriori probability functions for the Bayes classifier, and a maximum value selector, which decides the class assignment of the test sample. When we apply an optimization technique to find the smallest possible number of features with the largest possible value for a criterion, the mathematical procedure automatically combines the feature extractor and the discriminant function selector, and selects $(L-1)$ features as the optimal solution. After all, the functions of these two blocks are the same, namely to reduce the number of variables. There is no theoretical reason to divide this operation into two stages. Particularly, when both blocks do linear transformations, the combination of two linear transformations is just another linear transformation. Generally, engineers like to see intermediate results showing how variables are transformed down step by step, and gain some physical insights. However, we cannot expect an optimization procedure to divide the process into several steps and produce intermediate results.

When an optimization procedure selects the $(L-1)$ optimum features without reducing the criterion value, one would intuitively wonder why the number of classes alone should determine the number of features regardless of the distributions. However, once the mathematical process of optimization is understood, it may be recognized that the above conclusion is reasonable and sound after all. Indeed, we can select $(L-1)$ features for the combination of the trace criterion, $\text{tr}(S_w^{-1}S_b)$, and linear transformation. Also, $(L-1)$ a posteriori probability functions (the ideal features for classification) may be obtained by the nonlinear transformation, which minimizes the Bayes error.

Since neither compromise nor approximation were used in the optimization process, the quality of the selected features depends solely on how accurately the criterion, $\text{tr}(S_w^{-1}S_b)$, measures the class separability. Generally speaking, $\text{tr}(S_w^{-1}S_b)$ is a good measure when the distributions are unimodal and separated by the scatter of means. However, if the distributions are multimodal and share the same mean as in Fig. 10-5(a), there is no scatter of M_1 and M_2 around M_0. Subsequently, $\text{tr}(S_w^{-1}S_b)$ is not a good measure of class separability. For this case, we can find *clusters*, and treat this as a four-class problem rather than a two-class one. Then $\text{tr}(S_w^{-1}S_b)$ gives 3 good features. How to find clusters will be discussed in Chapter 11. The same is true for the case of Fig. 10-5(b). This case is better handled as a six-class problem by finding three clusters from each class. However, the clustering technique is not so effective for the case of Fig. 10-5(c) in which unimodal distributions share the same mean. This case will be studied later in relation to the optimization of the

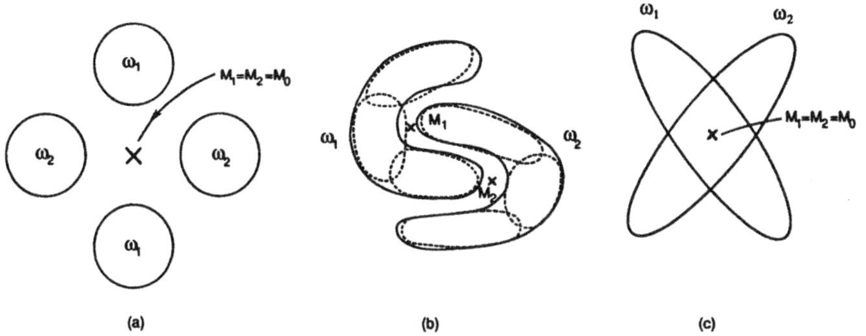

Fig. 10-5 Examples for which $\text{tr}(S_w^{-1} S_b)$ does not work.

Bhattacharyya distance. These examples suggest that, in order to utilize the feature extraction algorithm of $\text{tr}(S_w^{-1} S_b)$ effectively, we need to study the data structure carefully and adapt our procedure accordingly.

Same features for different matrices: So far, we have studied feature extraction by using the criterion of $\text{tr}(S_2^{-1} S_1)$ with $S_1 = S_b$ and $S_2 = S_w$. In this section we will show that other combinations of S_b, S_w, and S_m for S_1 and S_2 give the same optimum features as the ones for $S_1 = S_b$ and $S_2 = S_w$.

Let us consider, as an example,

$$J_1 = \text{tr}(S_m^{-1} S_w) . \tag{10.25}$$

Since this criterion measures the averaged covariance matrix normalized by the mixture scatter matrix, the criterion must be minimized, contrary to the maximization of $\text{tr}(S_w^{-1} S_b)$. According to (10.17), the minimization is achieved by selecting the eigenvectors of $S_m^{-1} S_w$ corresponding to the m smallest eigenvalues. Let Φ and Λ be the eigenvector and eigenvalue matrices of $S_m^{-1} S_w$. Then

$$S_m^{-1} S_w \Phi = \Phi \Lambda . \tag{10.26}$$

Or

$$S_w \Phi = S_m \Phi \Lambda \,. \tag{10.27}$$

Using $S_m = S_w + S_b$ from (10.4), (10.27) can be converted to

$$S_w \Phi = (S_w + S_b) \Phi \Lambda \,, \tag{10.28}$$

$$S_b \Phi \Lambda = S_w \Phi (I - \Lambda) \,, \tag{10.29}$$

$$S_w^{-1} S_b \Phi = \Phi (\Lambda^{-1} - I) \,. \tag{10.30}$$

Equation (10.30) shows that Φ is also the eigenvector matrix of $S_w^{-1} S_b$, and its eigenvalue matrix is $(\Lambda^{-1} - I)$. When the components of Λ, λ_i, are ordered from the largest to the smallest as

$$\lambda_1 \geq \ldots \geq \lambda_n \,, \tag{10.31}$$

the corresponding components of $(\Lambda^{-1} - I)$ are reversely ordered as

$$\frac{1}{\lambda_1} - 1 \leq \ldots \leq \frac{1}{\lambda_n} - 1 \,. \tag{10.32}$$

That is, ϕ_i corresponds to the ith largest eigenvalue of $S_m^{-1} S_w$ as well as the ith smallest eigenvalue of $S_w^{-1} S_b$. Therefore, the m eigenvectors of $S_m^{-1} S_w$ corresponding to the m smallest eigenvalues are the same as the m eigenvectors of $S_w^{-1} S_b$ corresponding to the m largest eigenvalues.

Similar derivations are obtained for other combinations of S_b, S_w, and S_m for S_1 and S_2.

Optimization of J_2: The optimization of J_2 can be carried out in a similar way as that for J_1. The criterion value in the m-dimensional Y-space is

$$J_2(m) = \ln |S_{1Y}| - \ln |S_{2Y}|$$
$$= \ln |A^T S_{1X} A| - \ln |A^T S_{2X} A| \,. \tag{10.33}$$

Taking the derivative of (10.33) with respect A by using (A.28),

$$\frac{\partial J_2(m)}{\partial A} = 2 S_{1X} A\, S_{1Y}^{-1} - 2 S_{2X} A\, S_{2Y}^{-1} \,. \tag{10.34}$$

Equating (10.34) to zero, the optimal A must satisfy

$$(S_{2X}^{-1}S_{1X})A = A(S_{2Y}^{-1}S_{1Y}) \,. \tag{10.35}$$

Since (10.35) and (10.13) are identical, the feature extraction to optimize (10.35) gives the same result as the one to optimize (10.13).

The value of $J_2(n)$ can be expressed in terms of the eigenvalues of $S_{2X}^{-1}S_{1X}$ as

$$J_2(n) = \ln \lambda_1 + \ldots + \ln \lambda_n \,. \tag{10.36}$$

Therefore, in order to maximize (or minimize) $J_2(m)$, the m largest (or smallest) eigenvalues of $S_{2X}^{-1}S_{1X}$ and the m corresponding eigenvectors are selected.

Optimization of the Bhattacharyya Distance

As discussed in Chapter 3, the Bhattacharyya distance of (3.152) is a convenient measure of class separability, if the number of classes is two. Furthermore, (3.152) gives an upper bound of the Bayes error, if the distributions are normal. However, the optimization of this criterion is not so easy, because two different types of functions, trace and determinant, are combined in the criterion. Therefore, in this book, we present the optimum solutions only for special cases, and the suboptimum solutions for the general case.

Optimization of μ_1: When $\Sigma_1 = \Sigma_2$, the second term of the Bhattacharyya distance disappears, and we need to maximize the first term only. From (3.152), μ_1 is

$$\mu_1 = \frac{1}{8}(M_2-M_1)^T\overline{\Sigma}^{-1}(M_2-M_1) = \frac{1}{8}\,\mathrm{tr}\,\{\overline{\Sigma}^{-1}(M_2-M_1)(M_2-M_1)^T\} \,, \tag{10.37}$$

where $\overline{\Sigma} = (\Sigma_1 + \Sigma_2)/2$ and $\overline{\Sigma}$ is the same as S_w if $P_1 = P_2 = 0.5$. Equation (10.37) is the same as $\mathrm{tr}(S_w^{-1}S_b)$ with S_b of (10.20), replacing S_w with $\overline{\Sigma}$ and ignoring the multiplicative constant. Therefore, from the previous discussion, only one linear feature is needed to maximize this criterion, and the mapping function is, from (10.24)

$$y = (M_2 - M_1)^T \overline{\Sigma}^{-1} \mathbf{X} . \tag{10.38}$$

Optimization of μ_2: When $M_1 = M_2$, the first term of the Bhattacharyya distance disappears, and we need to maximize the second term only. From (3.152), μ_2 is

$$\begin{aligned}\mu_2 &= \frac{1}{2} \ln \frac{\left| \frac{\Sigma_1 + \Sigma_2}{2} \right|}{\sqrt{|\Sigma_1|}\sqrt{|\Sigma_2|}} \\ &= \frac{1}{4} \{ \ln |\Sigma_1^{-1}(\Sigma_1 + \Sigma_2)\Sigma_2^{-1}(\Sigma_1 + \Sigma_2)| - n \ln 4 \} \\ &= \frac{1}{4} \{ \ln |\Sigma_2^{-1}\Sigma_1 + \Sigma_1^{-1}\Sigma_2 + 2I| - n \ln 4 \} .\end{aligned} \tag{10.39}$$

Therefore, the optimum linear transformation is found by maximizing

$$J(m) = \ln |(A^T\Sigma_2 A)^{-1}(A^T\Sigma_1 A) + (A^T\Sigma_1 A)^{-1}(A^T\Sigma_2 A) + 2I_m| \tag{10.40}$$

where I_m is the m-dimensional identity matrix while I of (10.39) is n-dimensional. As seen in the derivation of the third line of (10.39) from the second, I represents $\Sigma_i^{-1}\Sigma_i$. Therefore, by the transformation, I is converted to $(A^T\Sigma_i A)^{-1}(A^T\Sigma_i A) = I_m$, which is independent of A.

Taking the derivative of (10.40) with respect A,

$$\begin{aligned}\frac{\partial J(m)}{\partial A} = -2[\cdot]^{-1}[&\{\Sigma_{2X} A\, \Sigma_{2Y}^{-1}\Sigma_{1Y}\Sigma_{2Y}^{-1} - \Sigma_{1X} A\, \Sigma_{2Y}^{-1}\} \\ &+ \{\Sigma_{1X} A\, \Sigma_{1Y}^{-1}\Sigma_{2Y}\Sigma_{1Y}^{-1} - \Sigma_{2X} A\, \Sigma_{1Y}^{-1}\}] ,\end{aligned} \tag{10.41}$$

where $\Sigma_{iX} = \Sigma_i$, $\Sigma_{iY} = A^T\Sigma_{iX}A$, and $[\cdot]$ is the summation of three matrices in (10.40). Although it seems very complex to solve $\partial J(m)/\partial A = 0$ for A, the first $\{\cdot\}$ and second $\{\cdot\}$ of (10.41) can be made zero separately as follows.

$$(\Sigma_{2X}^{-1}\Sigma_{1X})A = A(\Sigma_{2Y}^{-1}\Sigma_{1Y}) \quad \text{for the first } \{\cdot\} , \tag{10.42}$$

$$(\Sigma_{1X}^{-1}\Sigma_{2X})A = A(\Sigma_{1Y}^{-1}\Sigma_{2Y}) \quad \text{for the second } \{\cdot\} . \tag{10.43}$$

In order to satisfy both (10.42) and (10.43) simultaneously, A must be the eigenvectors of both $\Sigma_{2X}^{-1}\Sigma_{1X}$ and $\Sigma_{1X}^{-1}\Sigma_{2X}$. Since these two matrices are related by $\Sigma_{2X}^{-1}\Sigma_{1X} = (\Sigma_{1X}^{-1}\Sigma_{2X})^{-1}$, they share the same eigenvector matrix and their eigenvalue matrices are Λ for $\Sigma_{2X}^{-1}\Sigma_{1X}$ and Λ^{-1} for $\Sigma_{1X}^{-1}\Sigma_{2X}$. Thus, by selecting m eigenvectors of $\Sigma_{2X}^{-1}\Sigma_{1X}$, we satisfy both (10.42) and (10.43) simultaneously, and can make $\partial J(m)/\partial A$ of (10.41) zero. The value of $J(n)$ in the original n-dimensional space is

$$J(n) = \sum_{i=1}^{n} \ln(\lambda_i + \frac{1}{\lambda_i} + 2) , \tag{10.44}$$

where the λ_i's are the eigenvalues of $\Sigma_{2X}^{-1}\Sigma_{1X}$. Therefore, in order to maximize $J(m)$, we must select the m eigenvectors of $\Sigma_{2X}^{-1}\Sigma_{1X}$ corresponding to the m largest $(\lambda_i + 1/\lambda_i + 2)$ terms.

Each eigenvalue of $\Sigma_{2X}^{-1}\Sigma_{1X}$ is the ratio of the ω_1- and ω_2-variances along the corresponding eigenvector. If the ω_1-variance is larger or smaller than the ω_2-variance along ϕ_i, λ_i becomes larger or smaller than one. In either case, $\lambda_i + 1/\lambda_i + 2$ becomes larger than 4, because $x + 1/x \geq 2$ for $x \geq 0$. On the other hand, when two variances are the same, λ_i becomes one and $\lambda_i + 1/\lambda_i + 2$ becomes 4 which is the smallest value for this term. Therefore, this algorithm is very effective in picking the features along which the variances of two classes are different, as in Fig. 10-5(c).

For dominant μ_1: When $M_1 \neq M_2$ and $\Sigma_1 \neq \Sigma_2$, there is no known procedure available to optimize μ of (3.152). Therefore, we must seek either an iterative process or a suboptimum solution to find A. When the first term μ_1 is dominant, we may use the following procedure to find the suboptimal solution.

(1) Compute the eigenvalues and eigenvectors of $\bar{\Sigma}^{-1}(M_2-M_1)(M_2-M_1)^T$, λ_i and ϕ_i, where $\bar{\Sigma} = (\Sigma_1 + \Sigma_2)/2$. Since the rank of the matrix is one, only λ_1 is nonzero and the other λ_i's are zero. Use ϕ_1 as the first feature and transform $\mathbf{X}$ to $\mathbf{y}_1 = \phi_1^T\mathbf{X}$. All information of class separability due to mean-difference is preserved in this feature.

(2) By $\mathbf{y}_i = \phi_i^T \mathbf{X}$ ($i = 2, \ldots, n$), map $\mathbf{X}$ onto the $(n-1)$-dimensional subspace which is orthogonal to ϕ_1 with respect to $\bar{\Sigma}$. In this subspace, there is no information of class separability due to mean-difference.

(3) In the $(n-1)$-dimensional Y-space, compute $\Sigma_{2Y}^{-1}\Sigma_{1Y}$ and its eigenvalues and eigenvectors, μ_i's and ψ_i's. Note that the ψ_i's are orthonormal with respect to Σ_{2Y} in the Y-space.

(4) Select the ψ_i's which correspond to the $(m-1)$ largest $(\mu_i + 1/\mu_i + 2)$ terms, and transform $\mathbf{Y}$ to $\mathbf{z}_i = \psi_i^T \mathbf{Y}$ ($i = 1, \ldots m-1$).

(5) Form an m-dimensional vector as $[\mathbf{y}_1 \mathbf{z}_1 \ldots \mathbf{z}_{m-1}]^T$. If desired, find the orthonormal basis vectors which are the eigenvectors of the covariance matrix of $[\mathbf{y}_1 \mathbf{z}_1 \ldots \mathbf{z}_{m-1}]^T$.

For dominant μ_2: When the second term μ_2 is dominant, we may select the eigenvectors of $\Sigma_{2X}^{-1}\Sigma_{1X}$ as seen in the optimization of μ_2, while checking how much information of class separability due to the first term μ_1 is distributed in these eigenvectors. The eigenvalue and eigenvector matrices of $\Sigma_{2X}^{-1}\Sigma_{1X}$, Λ and Φ, satisfy

$$\Phi^T \Sigma_{1X} \Phi = \Lambda \quad \text{and} \quad \Phi^T \Sigma_{2X} \Phi = I \,. \tag{10.45}$$

Applying an $n \times n$ transformation $\mathbf{Y} = \Phi^T \mathbf{X}$, the Bhattacharyya distance can be rewritten as

$$\mu = \sum_{i=1}^{n} \left[\frac{1}{4} \frac{\{\phi_i^T (M_2 - M_1)\}^2}{1 + \lambda_i} + \frac{1}{4} \{ \ln(\lambda_i + \frac{1}{\lambda_i} + 2) - \ln 4 \} \right] . \tag{10.46}$$

The second term of (10.46) is the same as (10.44) except for a constant ln4, and shows how the variance-difference of $\mathbf{y}_i$ contributes to the Bhattacharyya distance. In addition, (10.46) includes the first term, the effect of the mean-difference in $\mathbf{y}_i$. Thus, we can select the m eigenvectors of $\Sigma_{2X}^{-1}\Sigma_{1X}$ which correspond to the m largest $[\cdot]$ terms in (10.46).

Divergence: The *divergence* is another criterion of class separability similar to the Bhattacharyya distance. Most properties of the divergence can be discussed in terms similar to those used for the Bhattacharyya distance.

In pattern recognition, the key variable is the likelihood ratio or minus-log-likelihood ratio of two density functions. Therefore, if we have some way to evaluate the density functions of the likelihood ratio for ω_1 and ω_2, it is almost equivalent to evaluating the Bayes error. Unfortunately, this is not an easy task. The simplest version of this type of approach might be to use the expected values of the minus-log-likelihood ratio for ω_1 and ω_2 and to evaluate the class separability by the difference of the expected values of two classes. Thus, the divergence is defined as [3]

$$D = E\left\{ - \ln \frac{p_1(\mathbf{X})}{p_2(\mathbf{X})} \mid \omega_2 \right\} - E\left\{ - \ln \frac{p_1(\mathbf{X})}{p_2(\mathbf{X})} \mid \omega_1 \right\} . \qquad (10.47)$$

Since we consider only expected values in the divergence, we cannot expect a close relationship between the divergence and the Bayes error. A closer relationship can be obtained by normalizing the means by the standard deviations, but the expression might become very complicated.

When two density functions are normal, the divergence becomes

$$D = \int \left[\frac{1}{2}(X-M_1)^T \Sigma_1^{-1} (X-M_1) - \frac{1}{2}(X-M_2)^T \Sigma_2^{-1}(X-M_2) + \frac{1}{2} \ln \frac{|\Sigma_1|}{|\Sigma_2|} \right]$$

$$\times \left\{ \frac{1}{(2\pi)^{n/2} |\Sigma_2|^{1/2}} \exp[-\frac{1}{2}(X-M_2)^T \Sigma_2^{-1}(X-M_2)] \right.$$

$$\left. - \frac{1}{(2\pi)^{n/2} |\Sigma_1|^{1/2}} \exp[-\frac{1}{2}(X-M_1)^T \Sigma_1^{-1}(X-M_1)] \right\} dX$$

$$= \frac{1}{2} \operatorname{tr}\{(\Sigma_1^{-1} + \Sigma_2^{-1})(M_2-M_1)(M_2-M_1)^T\} + \frac{1}{2} \operatorname{tr}(\Sigma_1^{-1}\Sigma_2 + \Sigma_2^{-1}\Sigma_1 - 2I)$$

$$(10.48)$$

The form of (10.48) is close to that of the Bhattacharyya distance with first and second terms indicating class separabilities due to mean- and covariance-differences. The advantage of the divergence is that both the first and second terms are expressed by the trace of a matrix, while the Bhattacharyya distance is the combination of trace and determinant. Thus, it is sometimes easier to use the divergence for theoretical discussions. However, the weaker link to the Bayes error prevents the divergence from wider applications.

10.3 Generalized Criteria

The discussion of the previous section suggests that extracting features for classification is the same as finding the discriminant functions in classifier design. As seen in Fig. 10-4, the discriminant functions are the final analog outputs in a classifier before the decision-making logic is applied, and the number of discriminant functions, $(L-1)$, is the smallest number needed for L-class classification problems. Furthermore, finding the optimum linear transformation is the same as designing the optimum linear classifier. Thus, the entire discussion of Chapter 4 can be directly applied to feature extraction.

Two-Class Problems

For two-class problems, we can map $\mathbf{X}$ onto a one-dimensional subspace of $\mathbf{y}_1 = \phi_1^T\mathbf{X}$, in which the criterion $\mathrm{tr}(S_w^{-1}S_b)$ becomes

$$J_1(1) = \mathrm{tr}(S_{wy_1}^{-1} S_{by_1}) = \frac{P_1(\eta_1-\eta_0)^2 + P_2(\eta_2-\eta_0)^2}{P_1\sigma_1^2 + P_2\sigma_2^2} , \tag{10.49}$$

where $\eta_i = E\{\mathbf{y}_1 | \omega_i\} = \phi_1^T M_i$, $\eta_0 = E\{\mathbf{y}_1\} = \phi_1^T M_0$, and $\sigma_i^2 = \mathrm{Var}\{\mathbf{y}_1 | \omega_i\} = \phi_1^T \Sigma_i \phi_1$. The other criteria of scatter matrices also can be expressed as the functions of η_1, η_2, σ_1^2, and σ_2^2. Therefore, as was already seen in Chapter 4, we may introduce the generalized criteria, $f(\eta_1,\eta_2,\sigma_1^2,\sigma_2^2)$, and treat the criteria of scatter matrices as special cases. The optimization of $f(\eta_1,\eta_2,\sigma_1^2,\sigma_2^2)$ with respect to the mapping function was discussed extensively in Chapter 4, resulting in

$$\mathbf{y}_1 = q_1(\mathbf{X}) \quad \text{for nonlinear mapping,} \tag{10.50}$$

$$\mathbf{y}_1 = (M_2-M_1)^T[s\Sigma_1 + (1-s)\Sigma_2]^{-1}\mathbf{X} \quad \text{for linear mapping,} \tag{10.51}$$

where

$$s = \frac{\partial f/\partial\sigma_1^2}{\partial f/\partial\sigma_1^2 + \partial f/\partial\sigma_2^2} . \tag{10.52}$$

When f is a function of S_b, S_w, and S_m, Σ_1 and Σ_2 never appear separately, but always appear in a combined form of $S_w = P_1\Sigma_1 + P_2\Sigma_2$. Subsequently, after mapping to one-dimension, σ_1^2 and σ_2^2 always appear in the same form of $P_1\sigma_1^2 + P_2\sigma^2$ $(= \phi_1^T S_w \phi_1)$. Therefore, this particular family of criteria is expressed by $f(\eta_1,\eta_2,P_1\sigma_1^2 + P_2\sigma_2^2)$, and s of (10.52) becomes P_1.

Thus, $\mathbf{y}_1$ of (10.51) becomes $(M_2-M_1)^T S_w^{-1}\mathbf{X}$ which is the same as (10.24).

L-Class Problems [4]

The above argument can be extended to more general L-class problems [4-7].

Class separability criteria: let $f(M_1, \ldots, M_L, S_m)$ be a family of criteria for class separability. For simplicity, we assume in this section that the covariance matrices are always used in the combined form of $\Sigma_{i=1}^{L} P_i \Sigma_i = S_w$. This criterion includes functions of S_b, S_w, and S_m as special cases. The discussion of this section can be extended to a more general criterion of $f(M_1, \ldots, M_L, \Sigma_1, \ldots, \Sigma_L)$, but with more complexity.

Feature extraction selects an $(L-1)$-dimensional $Y(\mathbf{X})$ from an n-dimensional $\mathbf{X}$ by maximizing (or minimizing) the criterion. Without losing generality, we also assume for simplicity that the mixture means are zero vectors in both the X- and Y-spaces.

Since our criterion of class separability is invariant under a coordinate shift and nonsingular linear transformation, we whiten S_m such that

$$f(M_1, \ldots, M_L, S_m) = f(D_1, \ldots, D_L, I) , \tag{10.53}$$

where

$$D_i = \Lambda^{-1/2}\Phi^T M_i = S_m^{-1/2} M_i \tag{10.54}$$

and Λ and Φ are the eigenvalue and eigenvector matrices of S_m. Further application of any orthonormal transformation keeps the value of f the same as well as keeps the mixture scatter matrix I. This means that the value of f does not depend on the absolute position of each D_i, but depends only on the relative positions of the D_i's. Since the relative positions of the D_i's may be specified by a set of $D_i^T D_j$'s for all possible combinations of i and j, the criterion can be rewritten as a function of the $D_i^T D_j$'s as

$$f(D_1, \ldots, D_L, I) = g(r_{11}, r_{21}, \ldots, r_{LL}) , \tag{10.55}$$

where

$$r_{ij} = D_i^T D_j = M_i^T S_m^{-1} M_j \qquad i \geq j . \tag{10.56}$$

Note that $D_i^T D_j = D_j^T D_i$ and only the $D_i^T D_j$'s for $i \geq j$ are used. The criterion of (10.55) can be optimized by solving

$$\delta g = \sum_{i=1}^{L}\sum_{j=1}^{i} \frac{\partial g}{\partial r_{ij}} \Bigg|_{r_{ij}=r_{ij}^*} \delta r_{ij} = 0 \,, \tag{10.57}$$

where r_{ij}^* is the optimum value of r_{ij}. The same result can be obtained by optimizing another criterion J as

$$J = \sum_{i=1}^{L}\sum_{j=1}^{i} \beta_{ij} r_{ij} \,, \tag{10.58}$$

where

$$\beta_{ij} = \frac{\partial g}{\partial r_{ij}} \Bigg|_{r_{ij}=r_{ij}^*} . \tag{10.59}$$

Rewriting this criterion in matrix form

$$\begin{aligned} J &= \operatorname{tr}(B\,R) = \operatorname{tr}(B\,\mathcal{D}^T\mathcal{D}) \\ &= \operatorname{tr}(B\,\mathcal{M}^T S_m^{-1}\mathcal{M}) \\ &= \operatorname{tr}\{S_m^{-1}(\mathcal{M}B\,\mathcal{M}^T)\} \\ &= \operatorname{tr}(S_m^{-1}\,\mathcal{S}_b) \,, \end{aligned} \tag{10.60}$$

where

$$B = \begin{bmatrix} \beta_{11} & & \frac{1}{2}\beta_{ij} \\ & \ddots & \\ \frac{1}{2}\beta_{ij} & & \beta_{LL} \end{bmatrix} , \tag{10.61}$$

$$R = \begin{bmatrix} r_{11} & \dots & r_{L1} \\ \vdots & & \vdots \\ r_{L1} & \dots & r_{LL} \end{bmatrix} , \tag{10.62}$$

$$\mathcal{D} = [D_1 \ldots D_L] \,, \tag{10.63}$$

$$\mathcal{M} = [M_1 \ldots M_L] \,, \tag{10.64}$$

$$\mathcal{S}_b = \mathcal{M} B \mathcal{M}^T \,. \tag{10.65}$$

Note from (10.60) that $\mathcal{S}_b$ is a *generalized between-class scatter matrix*, with B determined by the functional form of the criterion.

Example 1: When $f = \mathrm{tr}(S_m^{-1} S_b)$ is used,

$$f = \mathrm{tr}(S_m^{-1} S_b) = \sum_{i=1}^{L} P_i M_i^T S_m^{-1} M_i \,. \tag{10.66}$$

Therefore,

$$\frac{\partial J}{\partial r_{ij}} = P_i \delta_{ij} \tag{10.67}$$

and

$$\mathcal{S}_b = S_b \,. \tag{10.68}$$

Example 2: When $f = \mathrm{tr}(S_w^{-1} S_b)$ is used, we could find $\partial g / \partial r_{ij}$ after replacing S_w by $S_m - S_b$. However, it is simpler to replace the criterion $f(M_1, \ldots, M_L, S_m)$ by another one $f(M_1, \ldots, M_L, S_w)$ and repeat the same discussion. The result becomes $J = \mathrm{tr}(S_w^{-1} \mathcal{S}_b)$ with the same $\mathcal{S}_b$ as (10.65).

Optimum nonlinear features: When **X** is mapped onto an $(L-1)$-dimensional **Y**, the class separability in the Y-space is measured by $J_Y = \mathrm{tr}(S_{mY}^{-1} \mathcal{S}_{bY})$, where S_{mY} and $\mathcal{S}_{bY}$ are the $(L-1)\times(L-1)$ mixture and generalized between-class scatter matrices in the Y-space. The optimization of the criterion with respect to the mapping function $Y(X)$ can be carried out by solving, for $Y(X)$,

$$\delta J_Y = \sum_{i=1}^{L} \frac{\partial J_Y^T}{\partial M_{iY}} \delta M_{iY} + \mathrm{tr} \left[\frac{\partial J_Y^*}{\partial S_{mY}} \delta S_{mY} \right] = 0 \tag{10.69}$$

where $\partial J_Y^* / \partial S_{mY}$ is defined as in (A.40) for a symmetric matrix S_{mY}, and

$$M_{iY} = \int Y(X) p_i(X) dX \,, \quad \delta M_{iY} = \int \delta Y(X) p_i(X) dX \,, \tag{10.70}$$

$$S_{mY} = \int Y(X)Y^T(X)p(X)dX \ ,$$

$$\delta S_{mY} = \int [Y(X)\delta Y^T(X) + \delta Y(X)Y^T(X)]p(X)dX \ . \tag{10.71}$$

Substituting (10.70) and (10.71) into (10.69),

$$\delta J_Y = \int \delta Y^T(X) \left[\sum_{i=1}^{L} \frac{\partial J_Y}{\partial M_{iY}} p_i(X) + 2 \frac{\partial J_Y^*}{\partial S_{mY}} Y(X)p(X) \right] dX = 0 \ . \tag{10.72}$$

In order to satisfy (10.72) regardless of $\delta Y(X)$, the $[\cdot]$ term in the integrand must be equal to zero. Therefore,

$$\frac{\partial J_Y^*}{\partial S_{mY}} Y(X) = -\frac{1}{2} \sum_{i=1}^{L} \frac{\partial J_Y}{\partial M_{iY}} \frac{p_i(X)}{p(X)}$$

$$= -\frac{1}{2} \sum_{i=1}^{L} \frac{1}{P_i} \frac{\partial J_Y}{\partial M_{iY}} q_i(X)$$

$$= -\frac{1}{2} \frac{\partial J_Y}{\partial \mathcal{M}_Y} P^{-1} Q(X) \ , \tag{10.73}$$

where

$$\frac{\partial J_Y}{\partial \mathcal{M}_Y} = \left[\frac{\partial J_Y}{\partial M_{1Y}} \ \cdots \ \frac{\partial J_Y}{\partial M_{LY}} \right] , \tag{10.74}$$

$$P = \begin{bmatrix} P_1 & & 0 \\ & \ddots & \\ 0 & & P_L \end{bmatrix} , \tag{10.75}$$

$$Q(X) = [q_1(X) \ \dots \ q_L(X)]^T \ . \tag{10.76}$$

Note that $q_i(X) = P_i p_i(X)/p(X)$ is the a posteriori probability function. The two derivatives $\partial J_Y^*/\partial S_{mY}$ and $\partial J_Y/\partial \mathcal{M}_Y$ can be computed from (10.60) as

$$\frac{\partial J_Y^*}{\partial S_{mY}} = -S_{mY}^{-1}\mathcal{S}_{bY}S_{mY}^{-1} \quad [\textit{from } (A.45)] \,, \tag{10.77}$$

$$\frac{\partial J_Y}{\partial \mathcal{M}_Y} = 2\, S_{mY}^{-1}\mathcal{M}_Y B \,. \tag{10.78}$$

Substituting (10.77) and (10.78) into (10.73),

$$\mathcal{S}_{bY}S_{mY}^{-1}Y(X) = \mathcal{M}_Y B\, P^{-1}Q(X) \,. \tag{10.79}$$

Since the dimensionality of $Y(X)$ is $(L-1)$, the $(L-1)\times(L-1)$ matrix of $\mathcal{S}_{bY}$ is nonsingular in general and $\mathcal{S}_{bY}^{-1}$ exists. Therefore, the $y_i(X)$'s can be expressed as linear functions of the $q_i(X)$'s. That is, the ideal features are the solutions to optimizing $f(M_1, \ldots, M_L, S_m)$, regardless of the functional form, f. This conclusion enhances the use of $f(M_1, \ldots, M_L, S_m)$ as the class separability criterion. Even when $\mathcal{S}_{bY}$ is singular, we can solve (10.79) for linearly independent $y_i(X)$'s such that the $y_i(X)$'s become linear functions of the $q_i(X)$'s.

Optimum linear features: When $(L-1)$ linear features are sought, $Y(X) = A^TX$ where A is an $n\times(L-1)$ transformation matrix, and $\delta Y(X) = \delta A^TX$ since the variation of Y comes from the variation of the mapping function A. Substituting this $\delta Y(X)$ into (10.72),

$$\delta J_Y = \int X^T\delta A\left[\sum_{i=1}^{L}\frac{\partial J_Y}{\partial M_{iY}}p_i(X) + 2\frac{\partial J_Y^*}{\partial S_{mY}}A^TX\,p(X)\right]dX$$

$$= \mathrm{tr}\left\{\delta A\left[\sum_{i=1}^{L}\frac{\partial J_Y}{\partial M_{iY}}M_{iX}^T + 2\frac{\partial J_Y^*}{\partial S_{mY}}A^TS_{mX}\right]\right\} = 0\,, \tag{10.80}$$

where $M_{iX} = E\{\mathbf{X}\,|\,\omega_i\}$ and $S_{mX} = E\{\mathbf{X}\mathbf{X}^T\}$. In order to satisfy (10.80) regardless of δA, the $[\cdot]$ term must be zero. Thus,

$$2\frac{\partial J_Y^*}{\partial S_{mY}}A^TS_{mX} = -\sum_{i=1}^{L}\frac{\partial J_Y}{\partial M_{iY}}M_{iX}^T \,. \tag{10.81}$$

Substituting (10.77) and (10.78) into (10.81),

$$\mathcal{S}_{bY} S_{mY}^{-1} A^T S_{mX} = \mathcal{M}_Y B \mathcal{M}_X^T . \tag{10.82}$$

Furthermore, since $\mathcal{M}_Y = A^T \mathcal{M}_X$ and $\mathcal{S}_{bX} = \mathcal{M}_X B \mathcal{M}_X^T$, (10.82) is modified to

$$\mathcal{S}_{bY} S_{mY}^{-1} A^T = A^T \mathcal{S}_{bX} S_{mX}^{-1} . \tag{10.83}$$

Or, taking the transpose,

$$(S_{mX}^{-1} \mathcal{S}_{bX}) A = A (S_{mY}^{-1} \mathcal{S}_{bY}) . \tag{10.84}$$

Note that (10.84) is the same as (10.13) except that the generalized between-class scatter matrix, $\mathcal{S}_b$, is used in (10.84). Therefore, using the same argument to solve (10.13), we can conclude that the optimum linear features are the eigenvectors of $S_{mX}^{-1} \mathcal{S}_{bX}$ which correspond to the largest $(L-1)$ eigenvalues.

10.4 Nonparametric Discriminant Analysis [8]

So far we have stated repeatedly that only $(L-1)$ features are needed for the classification of L classes. However, unless a posteriori probability functions are selected, $(L-1)$ features are suboptimal in the Bayes sense, although they are optimal with regard to a criterion used. Therefore, if the estimate of the Bayes error in the feature space is much larger than the one in the original variable space, some method must be devised to augment the feature extraction process.

One possibility is to artificially increase the number of classes. In this way we can increase the rank of S_b, and subsequently the number of features. This could be accomplished by dividing each class into a number of clusters as seen in Fig. 10-5(a) and (b). For those cases where multimodal behavior is present and a clustering algorithm can be found that "properly" identifies the clusters, this may work well. As a second possibility [9], after determining the $(L-1)$ features, we could remove them leaving a subspace orthogonal to the extracted features. If $\text{tr}(S_w^{-1} S_b)$ is used as a criterion, the first $(L-1)$-dimensional subspace contains all classification information due to the scatter of mean vectors, while the second $(n-L+1)$-dimensional space contains the information due to covariance-differences. Therefore, in order to select additional features from the $(n-L+1)$-dimensional subspace, $\text{tr}(S_w^{-1} S_b)$ is no longer an appropriate criterion to use. A different criterion such as the second term of the Bhattacharyya distance must be adopted. Unfortunately, such a criterion is available only for two-class cases, and we do not know how to handle general L-class problems, in which all means are the same [10].

A more fundamental problem is the parametric nature of the scatter matrices. If the distributions are significantly non-normal, the use of such parametric forms cannot be expected to accurately indicate which features should be extracted to preserve complex structures needed for classification.

In this section, a nonparametric form of discriminant analysis is presented which overcomes both of the previously mentioned problems. The basis of the extension is a nonparametric between-class scatter matrix which measures between-class scatter on a local basis, using k-nearest neighbor (kNN) techniques, and is generally of full rank. As the result, neither artificial class generation nor sequential methods are necessary. In addition, the nonparametric nature of the scatter matrix inherently leads to extracted features that preserve structure important for classification.

Nonparametric Scatter Matrix and Linear Mapping

In this section only the two-class problem will be discussed for simplicity, although an extension to the general L-class problem is possible.

Nonparametric between-class scatter matrix: We begin by defining a *nonparametric between-class scatter matrix*, denoted $\mathcal{S}_b$, as

$$\mathcal{S}_b = P_1 E\{(\mathbf{X}^{(1)}-\mathbf{X}_{NN}^{(2)})(\mathbf{X}^{(1)}-\mathbf{X}_{NN}^{(2)})^T \mid \omega_1\}$$
$$+ P_2 E\{(\mathbf{X}^{(2)}-\mathbf{X}_{NN}^{(1)})(\mathbf{X}^{(2)}-\mathbf{X}_{NN}^{(1)})^T \mid \omega_2\} , \qquad (10.85)$$

where $\mathbf{X}^{(i)}$ refers to samples from ω_i, and $\mathbf{X}_{NN}^{(j)}$ is the NN of $\mathbf{X}^{(i)}$ from the ω_j-samples ($i \neq j$). Note that the NN is selected from the other class, and that the vector, $X_{NN}^{(j)} - X^{(i)}$ ($i \neq j$), points to the other class locally at $X^{(i)}$. Equation (10.85) is the scatter matrix of these vectors. Recall that the between-class scatter matrix, S_b, for two-class was given in (10.20) as the scatter matrix of one vector, M_2-M_1, which points from M_1 to M_2 (and also from M_2 to M_1 if the sign is ignored). Therefore, $\mathcal{S}_b$ of (10.85) may be considered as a nonparametric version of S_b.

Instead of using only the NN, we might prefer to include information about kNN's. A natural approach to accomplish this would be the replacement of $\mathbf{X}_{NN}^{(\cdot)}$ by $(1/k)\Sigma_{j=1}^{k}\mathbf{X}_{jNN}^{(\cdot)}$. We call the sample mean of the kNN's the *local mean*. For a given sample $\mathbf{X}_\ell$, the ω_i-local mean is computed as

$$\mathcal{M}_i(\mathbf{X}_\ell) = \frac{1}{k}\sum_{j=1}^{k}\mathbf{X}_{jNN}^{(i)} , \tag{10.86}$$

where $\mathbf{X}_{jNN}^{(i)}$ is the jth NN from ω_i to the sample $\mathbf{X}_\ell$. Observe that, as k approaches N_i, the total number of samples in ω_i, $\mathcal{M}_i(\cdot)$ approaches the ω_i-mean vector, M_i. Using (10.86), a more general form of (10.85) can be defined as

$$\begin{aligned}\mathcal{S}_b = {} & P_1 E\{(\mathbf{X}^{(1)}-\mathcal{M}_2(\mathbf{X}^{(1)}))(\mathbf{X}^{(1)}-\mathcal{M}_2(\mathbf{X}^{(1)}))^T \mid \omega_1\} \\ & + P_2 E\{(\mathbf{X}^{(2)}-\mathcal{M}_1(\mathbf{X}^{(2)}))(\mathbf{X}^{(2)}-\mathcal{M}_1(\mathbf{X}^{(2)}))^T \mid \omega_2\} .\end{aligned} \tag{10.87}$$

It is of interest to study the behavior of $\mathcal{S}_b$ when $k = N_i$. This corresponds to replacing $\mathcal{M}_i(\cdot)$ with M_i. We denote the resulting between-class scatter matrix as S_b'.

$$\begin{aligned}S_b' &= P_1 E\{(\mathbf{X}-M_2)(\mathbf{X}-M_2)^T \mid \omega_1\} + P_2 E\{(\mathbf{X}-M_1)(\mathbf{X}-M_1)^T \mid \omega_2\} \\ &= P_1\{\Sigma_1 + (M_1-M_2)(M_1-M_2)^T\} + P_2\{\Sigma_2 + (M_2-M_1)(M_2-M_1)^T\} \\ &= (P_1\Sigma_1 + P_2\Sigma_2) + (M_2-M_1)(M_2-M_1)^T .\end{aligned} \tag{10.88}$$

On the other hand, from (10.20),

$$S_b = \sum_{i=1}^{2} P_i(M_i-M_0)(M_i-M_0)^T = P_1P_2(M_2-M_1)(M_2-M_1)^T . \tag{10.89}$$

Therefore, S_b' and S_b are related by

$$S_b' = S_w + \frac{1}{P_1P_2}S_b . \tag{10.90}$$

Or, multiplying S_w^{-1} from the left side

$$S_w^{-1}S_b' = I + \frac{1}{P_1P_2}S_w^{-1}S_b . \tag{10.91}$$

That is, the features selected by maximizing $\mathrm{tr}(S_w^{-1}S_b')$ must be the same as the ones from $\mathrm{tr}(S_w^{-1}S_b)$. Thus, the parametric feature extraction obtained by maximizing $\mathrm{tr}(S_w^{-1}S_b)$ is a special case of feature extraction with the more general nonparametric criterion $\mathrm{tr}(S_w^{-1}\mathcal{S}_b)$.

Further understanding of $\mathcal{S}_b$ is obtained by examining the vector $(X_\ell - \mathcal{M}_\ell(X_\ell))$. Figure 10-6 shows an example of these vectors for $k = 1$.

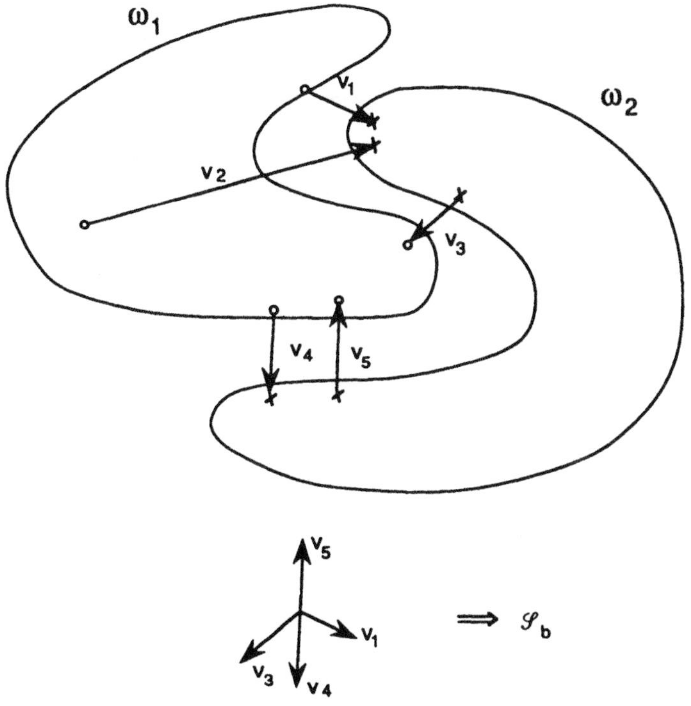

Fig. 10-6 Nonparametric between-class scatter.

Pointing to the *NN* from the other class, each vector indicates the direction to the other class locally. If we select these vectors only from the samples located in the classification boundary (V_1, V_3, V_4, V_5, etc.), the scatter matrix of these vectors should specify the subspace in which the boundary region is embedded. Samples which are far away from the boundary (V_2, etc.) tend to have larger magnitudes. These large magnitudes can exert a considerable influence on the scatter matrix and distort the information of the boundary structure. Therefore, some method of deemphasizing samples far from the boundary seems appropriate. To accomplish this we can use a weighting function for each $(X_\ell - \mathcal{M}_\ell(X_\ell))$. The value of the *weighting function*, denoted as w_ℓ, for X_ℓ is defined as

$$w_i = \frac{\min\{d^\alpha(X_i, X_{kNN}^{(1)}), d^\alpha(X_i, X_{kNN}^{(2)})\}}{d^\alpha(X_i, X_{kNN}^{(1)}) + d^\alpha(X_i, X_{kNN}^{(2)})} , \tag{10.92}$$

where α is a control parameter between zero and infinity, and $d(X_i, X_{kNN}^{(i)})$ is the distance from X_i to its kNN from ω_i. Observe that if α is selected as n, w_i corresponds to the kNN risk estimate of Chapter 7.

This weighting function has the property that near the classification boundary it takes on values close to 0.5 and drops off to zero as we move away from the classification boundary. The control parameter, α, adjusts how rapidly w_i falls to zero as we move away.

The final discrete form for $\mathcal{S}_b$ is expressed by

$$\mathcal{S}_b = \frac{1}{N}\sum_{i=1}^{N_1} w_i (X_i^{(1)} - \mathcal{M}_2(X_i^{(1)}))(X_i^{(1)} - \mathcal{M}_2(X_i^{(1)}))^T$$

$$+ \frac{1}{N}\sum_{i=1}^{N_2} w_i (X_i^{(2)} - \mathcal{M}_1(X_i^{(2)}))(X_i^{(2)} - \mathcal{M}_1(X_i^{(2)}))^T , \tag{10.93}$$

where $N = N_1 + N_2$, and the expectations of (10.87) are replaced by the sample means and P_i by N_i/N.

Optimum linear mapping: We now turn to the problem of the choice for S_2. We could choose S_2 as either the parametric S_w in (10.1), the parametric S_m in (10.4), or we could define a nonparametric extension of S_2 based on one of the parametric forms. In this section, S_w is selected as S_2. This choice is based on the observation that some form of global normalization is appropriate. This is readily recognized when the Euclidean distance is used to determine the kNN's. Intuitively, it is appropriate to apply the Euclidean metric to data whose covariance matrix is the identity matrix. However, transforming two data sets simultaneously so that both have $\Sigma_i = I$ is generally not possible. As a compromise, we transform the data so that the averaged covariance matrix, S_w, becomes the identity matrix. Then, $\mathcal{S}_b$ is computed in the transformed space. In addition, using S_w as S_2, the parametric scatter criterion $\text{tr}(S_w^{-1} S_b)$ becomes a special case of the nonparametric scatter criterion $\text{tr}(S_w^{-1} \mathcal{S}_b)$ as in (10.91), when the local means approach the class means.

We now present the algorithm in its entirety.

(1) Whiten the data with respect to S_w. That is, transform $\mathbf{X}$ to $\mathbf{Y}$ by $\mathbf{Y} = \Lambda^{-1/2}\Phi^T\mathbf{X}$ where Λ and Φ are the eigenvalue and eigenvector matrices of S_w.

(2) Select k and α.

(3) In the Y-space, compute $\mathcal{S}_b$ of (10.93) using w_i of (10.92) for weighting.

(4) Select the m eigenvectors of $\mathcal{S}_b$, $\psi_1, \ldots, \psi_m$, which correspond to the m largest eigenvalues.

(5) Then, $\mathbf{Z} = \Psi_m^T\Lambda^{-1/2}\Phi^T\mathbf{X}$ is the optimum linear mapping where $\Psi_m = [\psi_1 \ldots \psi_m]$. Note that this transformation matrix is orthonormal with respect to S_w as

$$\Psi_m^T\Lambda^{-1/2}\Phi^T S_w \Phi\Lambda^{-1/2}\Psi_m = I \, . \tag{10.94}$$

Experiment 1: In order to verify the algorithm, two groups of three-dimensional data were generated. The first two variables were generated uniformly as shown in Fig. 10-7. The third variable, independent of other two,

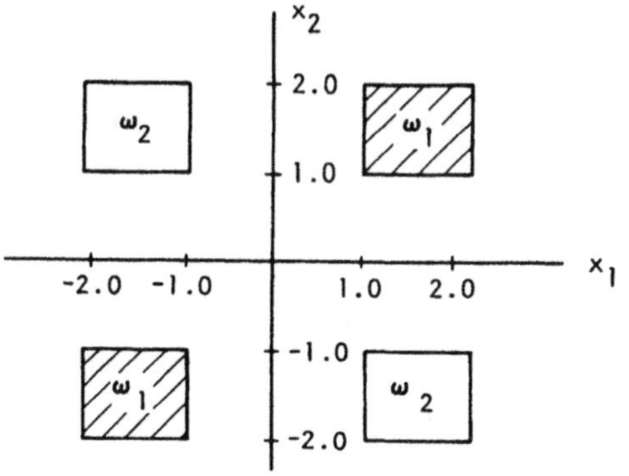

Fig. 10-7 An example of distributions.

was normally distributed with zero mean and unit variance for both classes. Each class was comprised of 100 samples. After applying the nonparametric feature extraction procedure with $k = 3$ and $\alpha = 2$, the following eigenvalues and eigenvectors were obtained.

$$\lambda_1 = 0.56 \ , \qquad \lambda_2 = 0.40 \ , \qquad \lambda_3 = 0.04 \ ,$$
$$\phi_1 = \begin{bmatrix} -0.59 \\ -0.29 \\ -0.03 \end{bmatrix} , \ \phi_2 = \begin{bmatrix} 0.28 \\ -0.58 \\ -0.05 \end{bmatrix} , \ \phi_3 = \begin{bmatrix} 0.03 \\ -0.07 \\ 1.00 \end{bmatrix} , \tag{10.95}$$

where the eigenvalues are normalized so that $\lambda_1 + \lambda_2 + \lambda_3 = 1$. The eigenvalues clearly indicate that only two features are needed. Furthermore, it is observed that both ϕ_1 and ϕ_2 effectively exclude the third variable, which possesses no structure that would assist in classification.

Experiment 2: As warped distributions, Gaussian pulses of (6.116) and double exponential waveforms of (6.118) were used. These two random processes were time-sampled at eight points, forming eight-dimensional random vectors. Since both processes are controlled by three random variables, as shown in Experiments 6-2 and 6-3, their intrinsic dimensionality is three, and samples from each class lie on a three-dimensional warped surface in the eight-dimensional space. The number of samples generated was 250 per class.

The nonparametric feature extraction procedure with $k = 3$ and $\alpha = 2$ was applied for the classification of these two classes. The resulting normalized eigenvalues were 0.45, 0.18, 0.11, 0.08, 0.06, 0.05, 0.04, and 0.03, indicating that most of the classification information is concentrated on the first feature. Figure 10-8 shows the plot of samples in the subspace spanned by $\mathbf{y}_1 = \phi_1^T\mathbf{X}$ and $\mathbf{y}_2 = \phi_2^T\mathbf{X}$, where ϕ_1 and ϕ_2 are the eigenvectors corresponding to the eigenvalues $\lambda_1 = 0.45$ and $\lambda_2 = 0.18$ respectively [8]. Figure 10-8 clearly shows that the first extracted feature embodies the majority of the classification structure, as its 0.45 eigenvalue predicts. The second extracted feature, while not effective if used alone (as its eigenvalue of 0.18 suggests), assists to show how two distributions are separated.

For comparison, Fig. 10-9 shows the plot from the Karhunen-Loéve expansion [8]. That is, the covariance matrix of the mixture of two classes was computed, from which the eigenvalues and eigenvectors are obtained. The plot is the distribution of samples in the subspace spanned by $\mathbf{y}_1 = \phi_1^T\mathbf{X}$ and $\mathbf{y}_2 = \phi_2^T\mathbf{X}$ where ϕ_1 and ϕ_2 correspond to two largest eigenvalues. Figure 10-9 shows that the *K-L* expansion gives a poor selection of two features for classification.

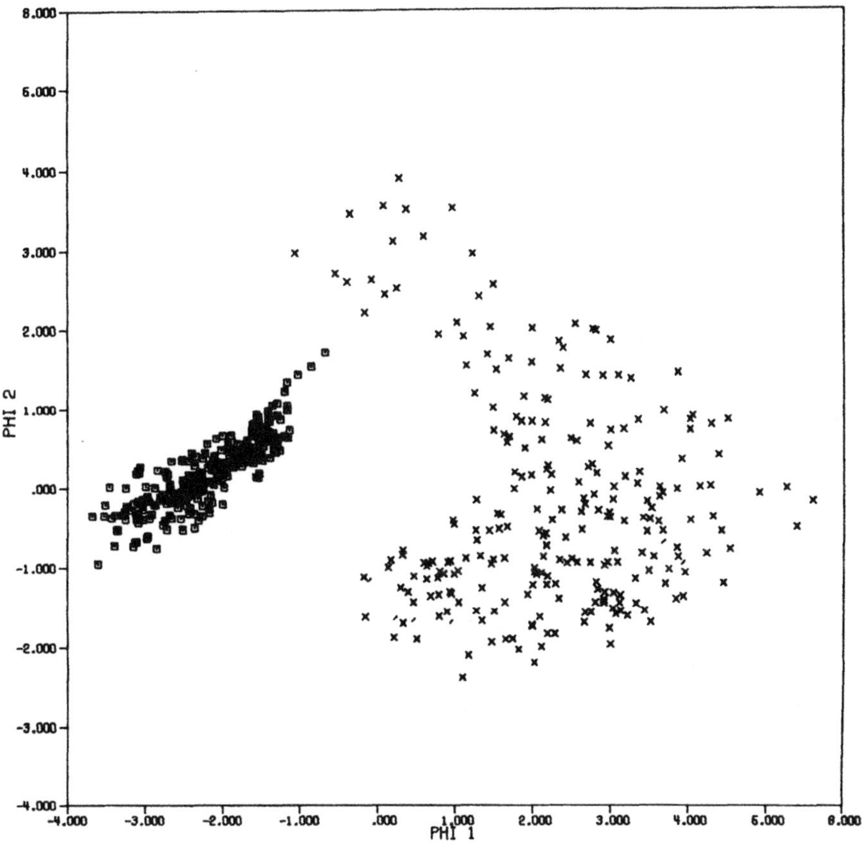

Fig. 10-8 Plot by the nonparametric discriminant analysis.

Linear Classifier Design

Linear classifier design is a special case of feature extraction, involving the selection of a linear mapping to reduce the dimensionality to one. Classification is then performed by specifying a single threshold.

When $L = 2$, parametric discriminant analysis always results in the extraction of a single feature. Thus, parametric discriminant analysis for the two-class case is essentially linear classifier design.

For linear classifier design using the nonparametric procedure, we select the eigenvector corresponding to the largest eigenvalue as our linear transformation.

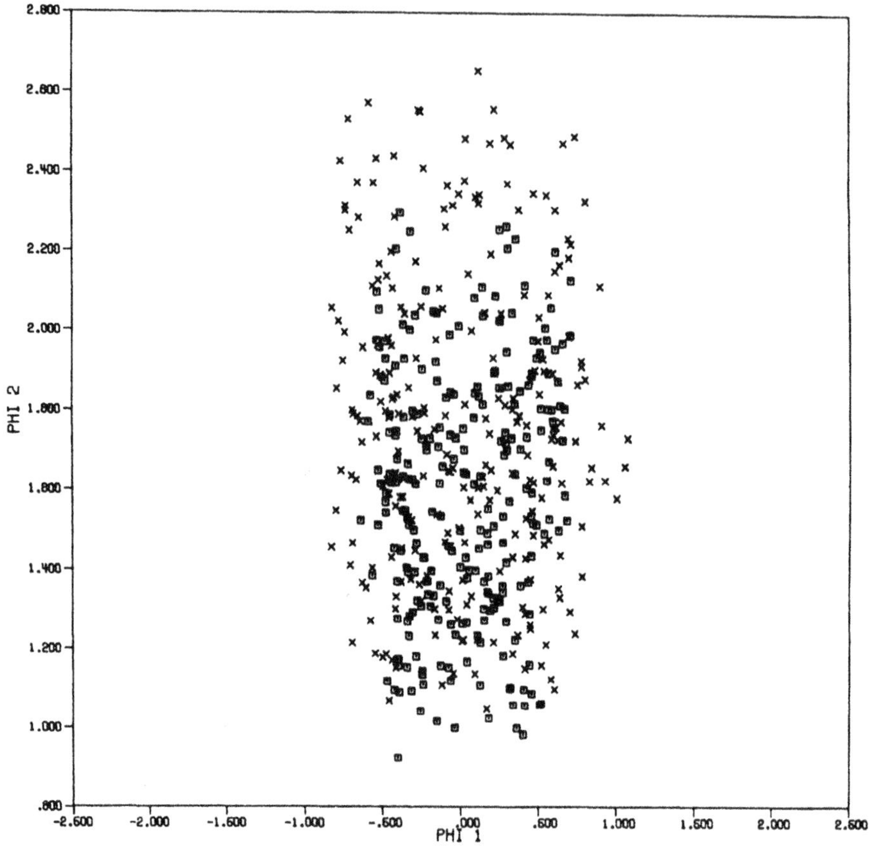

Fig. 10-9 Plot by the Karhunen-Loéve expansion.

Experiment 3: Linear classifiers were designed to classify two normal distributions with expected vectors and covariance matrices as

$$M_1 = \begin{bmatrix} 0 \\ 0 \end{bmatrix} , \quad \Sigma_1 = I , \quad \text{and} \quad M_2 = \begin{bmatrix} 2 \\ 3 \end{bmatrix} , \quad \Sigma_2 = \begin{bmatrix} 2 & 0 \\ 0 & 4 \end{bmatrix} . \tag{10.96}$$

The theoretically optimal linear classifier was designed by Procedure I in Section 4.2 (just after (4.46)). The error was 9.3%.

Then, both parametric and nonparametric discriminant analyses were applied by maximizing $\text{tr}(S_w^{-1} S_b)$ and $\text{tr}(S_w^{-1} \mathcal{S}_b)$. For these procedures, 100 samples per class were generated for design. After a linear transformation $\mathbf{y} = \phi_1^T \mathbf{X}$ was found, the means and variances of $\mathbf{y}$ for ω_1 and ω_2 were computed by $\phi_1^T M_i$ and $\phi_1^T \Sigma_i \phi_1$ $(i = 1,2)$. Since $\mathbf{y}$ is normal for normal $\mathbf{X}$, the minimum error in the y-space can be obtained by using a normal error table. This test process eliminates the variation of the estimated error due to a finite number of test samples. Also, $k = 3$ and $\alpha = 2$ were used to determine the weighting coefficients in the nonparametric procedure. The resulting errors were 9.7% for parametric approach and 9.4% for nonparametric one. Thus, not only was the performance of the nonparametric procedure close to the optimal linear classifier, but it was in fact superior to the parametric procedure.

Experiment 4: In this experiment, samples were uniformly distributed in the areas shown in Fig. 10-10. The true error of zero is achieved by selecting

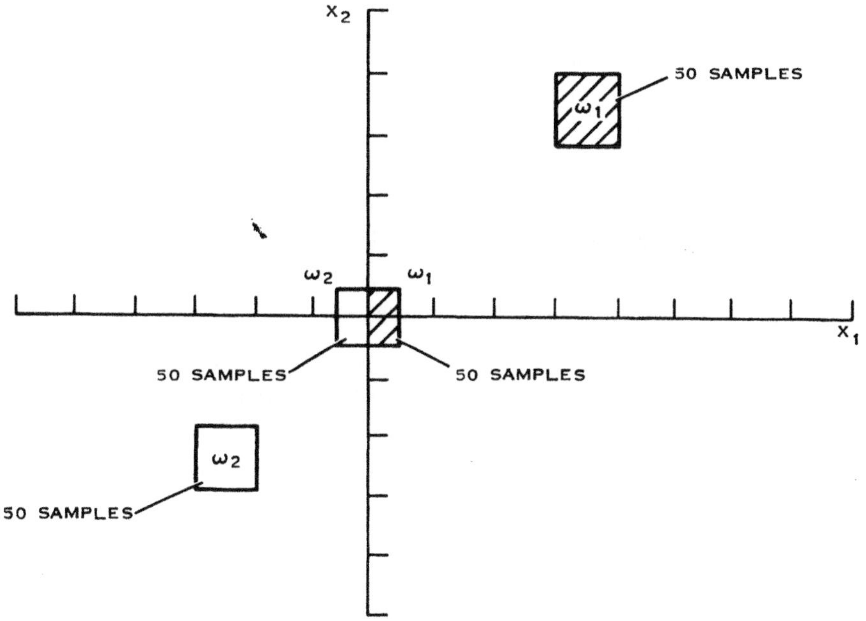

Fig. 10-10 An example of distributions.

the x_1-axis as the only feature. For comparison, all three mappings were computed as before. Since the data sets were not normally distributed, there is no reason to assume that the procedure of Section 4.2 would necessarily be optimal even if Procedures II and III are used. The average error of Procedures II and III was 5.4%. On the other hand, parametric and nonparametric discriminant analyses resulted in the errors of 5.6% and 3.4%, respectively.

The above two experiments provide additional justification for the nonparametric feature extraction algorithm.

Distributional Testing

Another application of the nonparametric scatter matrices is in the testing of structural similarity of two distributions. The ability to compare two distributions has numerous applications. One can gather data sets at different times or under different conditions and distributional testing can then be used to determine whether they are similar or not. When only a single measurement is taken, the problem can be solved in a fairly straightforward manner. However, multiple measurements present a problem.

One method of testing the similarity of two distributions in a high-dimensional space is to compare the mean vectors and covariance matrices of the distributions. Two covariance matrices can be more easily compared by simultaneously diagonalizing them and checking whether or not the diagonal terms of the second matrix are close to one. Also, the Bhattacharyya distance is used to measure the closeness of two distributions. Although these tests are simple and adequate for most applications, more sophisticated tests are needed for distributions severly distorted from normal.

A second alternative is to estimate the degree of overlap of the two distributions. The Bayes error could be estimated by nonparametric techniques such as the Parzen and *kNN* approaches as discussed in Chapter 7. However, this method fails to indicate the subspace in which the differences are most prominent, or what type of differences exists.

The test of this section requires no distributional assumptions, and produces an eigenvalue and eigenvector decomposition that is ranked by distributional similarity.

To develop the test we first separate $\mathcal{S}_b$ into two parts

$$\mathcal{S}_{b1} = \frac{1}{N_1}\sum_{\ell=1}^{N_1} w_\ell (X_\ell^{(1)} - \mathcal{M}_2(X_\ell^{(1)}))(X_\ell^{(1)} - \mathcal{M}_2(X_\ell^{(1)}))^T , \qquad (10.97)$$

$$\mathcal{S}_{b2} = \frac{1}{N_2}\sum_{\ell=1}^{N_2} w_\ell (X_\ell^{(2)} - \mathcal{M}_1(X_\ell^{(2)}))(X_\ell^{(2)} - \mathcal{M}_1(X_\ell^{(2)}))^T . \qquad (10.98)$$

We can interpret $\mathcal{S}_{bi}$ as a *nonparametric between-class scatter matrix computed with respect to* ω_i. In addition we will define two *nonparametric within-class scatter matrices*, denoted by $\mathcal{S}_{w\cdot 1}$ and $\mathcal{S}_{w\cdot 2}$, as

$$\mathcal{S}_{w\cdot 1} = \frac{1}{N_1}\sum_{\ell=1}^{N_1} w_\ell (X_\ell^{(1)} - \mathcal{M}_1(X_\ell^{(1)}))(X_\ell^{(1)} - \mathcal{M}_1(X_\ell^{(1)}))^T , \tag{10.99}$$

$$\mathcal{S}_{w\cdot 2} = \frac{1}{N_2}\sum_{\ell=1}^{N_2} w_\ell (X_\ell^{(2)} - \mathcal{M}_2(X_\ell^{(2)}))(X_\ell^{(2)} - \mathcal{M}_2(X_\ell^{(2)}))^T . \tag{10.100}$$

The only difference between $\mathcal{S}_{w\cdot i}$ and $\mathcal{S}_{bi}$ is the class of the local mean used in the computation. If the two distributions are identical, it is expected that $\mathcal{S}_{w\cdot 1} \cong \mathcal{S}_{b1}$ and $\mathcal{S}_{w\cdot 2} \cong \mathcal{S}_{b2}$. This suggests that the matrix products $\mathcal{S}_{w\cdot 1}^{-1}\mathcal{S}_{b1}$ and $\mathcal{S}_{w\cdot 2}^{-1}\mathcal{S}_{b2}$ should be close to I. To reduce the number of comparisons from n^2 for each matrix product we can diagonalize $\mathcal{S}_{w\cdot 1}^{-1}\mathcal{S}_{b1}$ and $\mathcal{S}_{w\cdot 2}^{-1}\mathcal{S}_{b2}$. The diagonalization of $\mathcal{S}_{w\cdot i}^{-1}\mathcal{S}_{bi}$ may be achieved by simultaneously diagonalizing $\mathcal{S}_{wi}$ and $\mathcal{S}_{bi}$. The n diagonal elements of each matrix can then be compared.

Before presenting the experimental results we make a final note about $\mathcal{S}_{w\cdot i}$. For the sample $X_\ell^{(i)}$, when the local mean $\mathcal{M}_i(X_\ell^{(i)})$ is computed, we do not consider $X_\ell^{(i)}$ as its own *NN*.

Experiment 5: The first experiment consists of two parts. First, two normal distributions with mean vectors equal to the zero vector and covariance matrices equal to the identity matrix were compared. The distributions were two-dimensional. One hundred samples per class were generated, k was chosen as three, and α was chosen as zero, i.e. $w_\ell = 1$ or no weighting. Two matrices $\mathcal{S}_{w\cdot 1}^{-1}\mathcal{S}_{b1}$ and $\mathcal{S}_{w\cdot 2}^{-1}\mathcal{S}_{b2}$ were computed. The mean values and standard deviations of the eigenvalues for four trials are summarized in Table 10-1 [8]. The fact that the eigenvalues are less than one is not particularly surprising. Recall that when we computed $\mathcal{S}_{w\cdot i}$ it was necessary to exclude the sample X_ℓ from our *kNN* determination. As such, this tends to make the within-class distances larger than the between-class distances, resulting in eigenvalues smaller than one.

To complete the experiment a second comparison was performed. A normal distribution was compared with a uniform distribution, both two-dimensional with mean vector equal to the zero vector and covariance matrix equal to the identity matrix. As before, 100 samples per class were used, k was chosen as three, and α was chosen as zero. The mean value and standard

TABLE 10-1

EIGENVALUE RESULTS FOR FOUR TRIALS

	ω_1 - Normal ω_2 - Normal				ω_1 - Normal ω_2 - Uniform			
	$\mathcal{S}_{w\cdot 1}^{-1}\mathcal{S}_{b1}$		$\mathcal{S}_{w\cdot 2}^{-1}\mathcal{S}_{b2}$		$\mathcal{S}_{w\cdot 1}^{-1}\mathcal{S}_{b1}$		$\mathcal{S}_{w\cdot 2}^{-1}\mathcal{S}_{b2}$	
λ's	λ_1	λ_2	λ_1	λ_2	λ_1	λ_2	λ_1	λ_2
Mean	0.79	0.61	0.96	0.66	1.63	0.95	1.52	0.89
Standard Deviation	0.06	0.13	0.17	0.06	0.22	0.21	0.20	0.16

deviation results of the eigenvalue calculations for four trials are presented in Table 10-1 [8]. When compared to the normal vs. normal results, a distributional difference is evident.

Experiment 6: In the second experiment the time sampled-gaussian pulse was compared with the time-sampled double exponential pulse. Refer to Experiments 6-2 and 6-3 for additional information about these data sets.

To provide a reference, two eight-dimensional normal distributions (not time-sampled gaussian pulses) were generated, both with mean vector equal to the zero vector and covariance matrix equal to the identity matrix. The resulting eigenvalues were 1.36, 1.21, 1.11, 1.06, 0.89, 0.88, 0.79, and 0.57 for $\mathcal{S}_{w\cdot 1}^{-1}\mathcal{S}_{b1}$ and 1.29, 1.19, 1.11, 1.08, 0.93, 0.81, 0.70, and 0.57 for $\mathcal{S}_{w\cdot 2}^{-1}\mathcal{S}_{b2}$ for a single trial.

To assure that we would be testing for structural differences, both time-sampled data sets were independently whitened, i.e., mean vector transformed to the zero vector and covariance matrix transformed to the identity matrix. When the whitened time-sampled data sets were compared, the eigenvalues were 34.4, 17.3, 14.3, 10.6, 6.6, 3.9, 2.7, and 1.4 for $\mathcal{S}_{w\cdot 1}^{-1}\mathcal{S}_{b1}$ and 0.87, 0.75, 0.67, 0.52, 0.41, 0.32, 0.23, and 0.14 for $\mathcal{S}_{w\cdot 2}^{-1}\mathcal{S}_{b2}$. These results clearly indicate that significant distributional differences exist. In addition they indicate why the $\mathcal{S}_{w\cdot i}^{-1}\mathcal{S}_{bi}$ should not be combined. It is possible that if they are combined, the eigenvectors of the result may not exhibit the same level of discrimination. This is due to the fact that the eigenvalues are averaged in some fashion.

As well as having the ability to test distributional differences, if the eigenvectors are computed, the axes of major difference can be plotted. This is shown in Fig. 10-11 where we project the data down onto the two eigenvectors

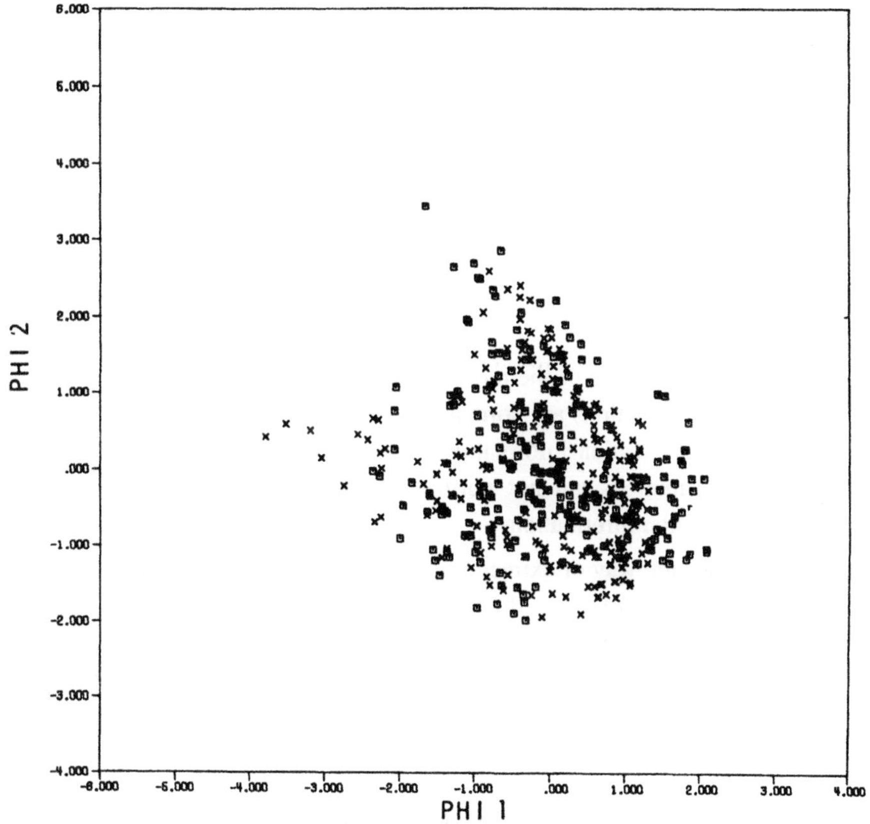

Fig. 10-11 Plot of structure difference.

of $\mathcal{S}_{w1}^{-1}\mathcal{S}_{b1}$ with corresponding eigenvalues, 34.4 and 17.3 [8]. The two distributions of Fig. 10-11 seem to be very similar at a glance. This is due to the fact that they share the same mean vector as well as the same covariance matrix. Therefore, we must look for, in Fig. 10-11, the more detailed structural difference beyond the first and second order statistics.

10.5 Sequential Selection of Quadratic Features [11]

So far, we have limited our discussion to linear transformations, because general nonlinear transformations are hard to define and analyze. However, in practical classification problems, we need to focus our attention on a particular nonlinear function, which is the quadratic discriminant function. The quadratic discriminant functions are the ideal features for normal distributions, and are expected to be reasonably good features even for non-normal (but unimodal) distributions. Thus, the quadratic equation of

$$h(X)=\frac{1}{2}(X-M_1)^T\Sigma_1^{-1}(X-M_1)-\frac{1}{2}(X-M_2)^T\Sigma_2^{-1}(X-M_2)+\frac{1}{2}\ln\frac{|\Sigma_1|}{|\Sigma_2|} \tag{10.101}$$

must be the first candidate of the most effective feature for the classification of two classes. If distributions are normal, $h(X)$ is the sufficient statistic, and carries all of the classification information. No extra features are needed. However, if the distributions are not normal, there exist other features carrying some of classification information.

One systematic way of extracting quadratic features for non-normal cases is to select $h(X)$ of (10.101) as the first feature, and then find the subspace, Y, orthogonal to $h(X)$. In the next stage, the quadratic discriminant function $h(Y)$ in the Y-subspace is selected as the second feature, and the sub-subspace orthogonal to $h(Y)$ is found. This process is repeated until classification information is exhausted in the subspace.

Orthogonal space to $h(X)$: The *orthogonal space to $h(X)$* may be defined as an $(n-1)$-dimensional hypersurface on which a certain (possibly nonlinear) projection of two normal distributions are identical. It should be noted that this definition of orthogonality is not conventional. Without losing generality, let us assume that two covariance matrices are diagonal, I and Λ. Given two means M_1 and M_2, we can move the coordinate origin by C such that two mean vectors in the new coordinate system satisfy

$$(M_2 - C) = \Lambda^{1/2}(M_1 - C) . \tag{10.102}$$

Such a C can be uniquely obtained by solving (10.102) for C as

$$C = (I - \Lambda^{1/2})^{-1}(M_2 - \Lambda^{1/2}M_1) , \tag{10.103}$$

where none of the components of Λ, the λ_i's, are assumed to be one. When $\lambda_i = 1$, C of (10.103) cannot be determined. This case will be discussed later. Also, note that two covariance matrices I and Λ are related by

$$\Lambda = \Lambda^{1/2} I \Lambda^{1/2} . \tag{10.104}$$

Equations (10.102) and (10.104) imply that, if two distributions are normal,

$$\mathbf{X}^{(2)} = \Lambda^{1/2}\mathbf{X}^{(1)} , \tag{10.105}$$

where $\mathbf{X}^{(i)}$ is $\mathbf{X}$ from ω_i. For non-normal distributions, (10.102) and (10.104) do not necessarily imply (10.105).

The significance of (10.105) is the fact that it allows us to relate two normal distributions with $\Sigma_1 = I$ and $\Sigma_2 = \Lambda$ to one another after performing a simple mean shift using (10.103).

To proceed with the development we replace $\Lambda^{1/2}$ in (10.105) with e^{-B} where B is a matrix chosen to satisfy $\Lambda^{1/2} = e^{-B}$. Rewriting (10.105) we get

$$\mathbf{X}^{(2)} = e^{-B}\mathbf{X}^{(1)} . \tag{10.106}$$

Using (10.106) it is possible to express the two random vectors in the following form with t and $\mathbf{X}_0$ as parameters:

$$\mathbf{X}^{(1)} = e^{-Bt}\mathbf{X}_0 , \tag{10.107}$$

$$\mathbf{X}^{(2)} = e^{-B(t+1)}\mathbf{X}_0 . \tag{10.108}$$

These equations suggest that corresponding samples of $\mathbf{X}^{(1)}$ and $\mathbf{X}^{(2)}$ are located on a trajectory of the following differential equation

$$\frac{d}{dt}\mathbf{X}(t) = B\mathbf{X}(t) \quad \text{with} \quad \mathbf{X}(0) = \mathbf{X}_0 . \tag{10.109}$$

Given an $\mathbf{X}_0$ on a trajectory of (10.109), for any $\mathbf{X}$ on that trajectory there is a t such that

$$\mathbf{X} = \mathbf{X}(t) = e^{-Bt}\mathbf{X}(0) = \Lambda^{t/2}\mathbf{X}(0) . \tag{10.110}$$

Figure 10-12 shows an example.

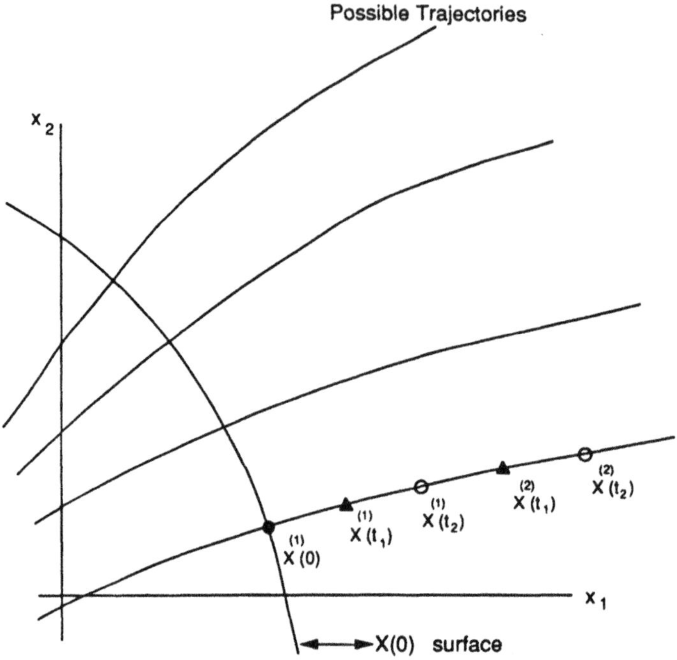

Fig. 10-12 Possible trajectories in two-dimensional space.

The ith component of $\mathbf{X}(t)$, denoted by $\mathbf{x}_i(t)$, satisfies

$$\frac{\mathbf{x}_i(t)}{\mathbf{x}_i(0)} = \lambda_i^{t/2} . \tag{10.111}$$

Raising to the $(\alpha/\ln\lambda_i)$th power, (10.111) can be converted to make the right-hand side independent of i, as

$$\frac{sign(\mathbf{x}_i(t))}{sign(\mathbf{x}_i(0))} \left| \frac{\mathbf{x}_i(t)}{\mathbf{x}_i(0)} \right|^{\frac{\alpha}{\ln\lambda_i}} = e^{\alpha t/2} \quad (i = 1, \ldots, n) , \tag{10.112}$$

where $sign(\cdot)$ is the sign function and α is introduced to scale the exponential term. Note that (10.112) holds for any value of α, and thus we can choose the value of α freely. Generally, it is suggested to select an α so that $\alpha/\ln\lambda_i$ is as close as possible to one for all i. This will minimize data distortion.

Example 3: Let two normal distributions be characterized by

$$M_1 = \begin{bmatrix} 8 \\ 2 \end{bmatrix} , \quad \Sigma_1 = I \quad , \quad \text{and} \quad M_2 = \begin{bmatrix} 4 \\ 4 \end{bmatrix} , \quad \Sigma_2 = \begin{bmatrix} 0.25 & 0 \\ 0 & 4 \end{bmatrix} . \tag{10.113}$$

Substituting (10.113) into (10.103), $C = [0 \ \ 0]^T$. Also, from (10.112)

$$\left[\frac{x_1(t)}{x_1(0)} \right]^{\frac{\alpha}{\ln 0.25}} = \left[\frac{x_2(t)}{x_2(0)} \right]^{\frac{\alpha}{\ln 4}} . \tag{10.114}$$

Or,

$$x_1(t)x_2(t) = x_1(0)x_2(0) . \tag{10.115}$$

Figure 10-13 shows the three trajectories of (10.115) for $x_1(0) = 8$ and

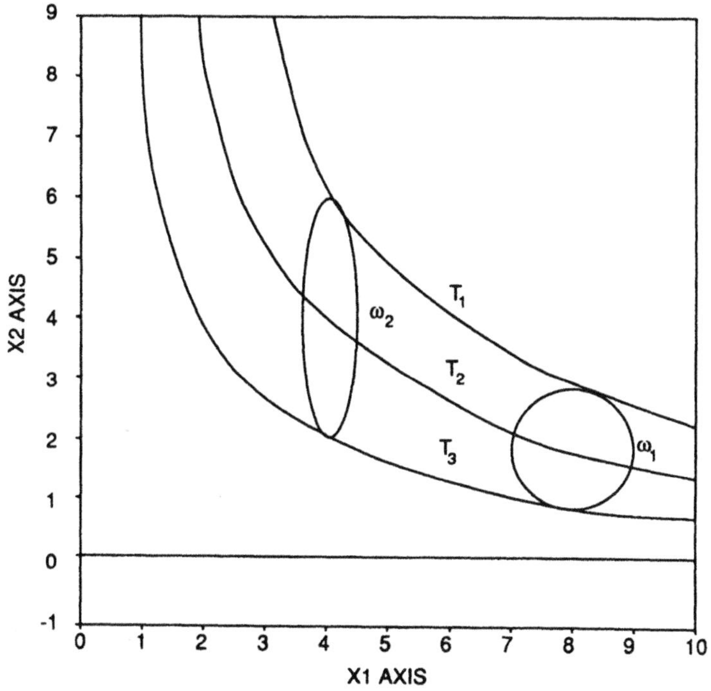

Fig. 10-13 Three trajectories for a normal example.

$x_2(0) = 3, 2, 1$, denoted as T_1, T_2, and T_3, respectively.

Note that if $\mathbf{X}(0)$ is always selected on an $(n-1)$-dimensional surface across which each trajectory passes through exactly once, then the n-dimensional space of X could be transformed to another n-dimensional space consisting of one variable t, or a function of t, and the $(n-1)$-dimensional $\mathbf{X}(0)$

surface. Since all corresponding samples of the two normal distributions are located on the same trajectories, the projection of the two normal distributions onto the $\mathbf{X}(0)$ surface would be identical. Thus, the $\mathbf{X}(0)$ surface is the subspace orthogonal to $h(X)$ of (10.101).

Selection of the orthogonal subspace: It is desirable to select, regardless of the distributions, the same $(n-1)$-dimensional surface to facilitate the transformation to the new n-dimensional space. This can achieved by introducing the new variables $\mathbf{y}_i$ as

$$\mathbf{y}_i(t) = sign(\mathbf{x}_i(t))\,|\mathbf{x}_i(t)|^{\frac{\alpha}{\ln\lambda_i}} . \tag{10.116}$$

Then, (10.112) becomes

$$\frac{\mathbf{y}_i(t)}{\mathbf{y}_i(0)} = e^{\alpha t/2} \qquad (i = 1,\ldots,n) . \tag{10.117}$$

In the Y-coordinate system all of the trajectories are lines beginning at the origin. Since all the lines start at the origin, a natural selection of the $\mathbf{Y}(0)$ (formerly $\mathbf{X}(0)$) surface is a *unit sphere around the origin.*

Example 4: Two normal distributions of Example 3 are transformed to y_1 and y_2. Selecting $\alpha = \ln 4$, two means in the y-space, M_{1Y} and M_{2Y}, are calculated from (10.116) as

$$M_{1Y} = \begin{bmatrix} 8^{\frac{\ln 4}{\ln 0.25}} \\ 2^{\frac{\ln 4}{\ln 4}} \end{bmatrix} = \begin{bmatrix} 0.125 \\ 2 \end{bmatrix} , \tag{10.118}$$

$$M_{2Y} = \begin{bmatrix} 4^{\frac{\ln 4}{\ln 0.25}} \\ 4^{\frac{\ln 4}{\ln 4}} \end{bmatrix} = \begin{bmatrix} 0.25 \\ 4 \end{bmatrix} . \tag{10.119}$$

Note that we can control the scales of the y_i's by α. Figure 10-14 shows two distributions as well as three trajectories in the Y-space. The T_i's in Fig. 10-14 correspond to the respective T_i's in Fig. 10-13.

This formulation standardizes the transformation to an $(n-1)$-dimensional $\mathbf{Y}(0)$ surface and the variable that is a function of t, regardless of distributions. By converting to multidimensional spherical coordinates r, $\theta_1,\ldots,\theta_{n-1}$ as

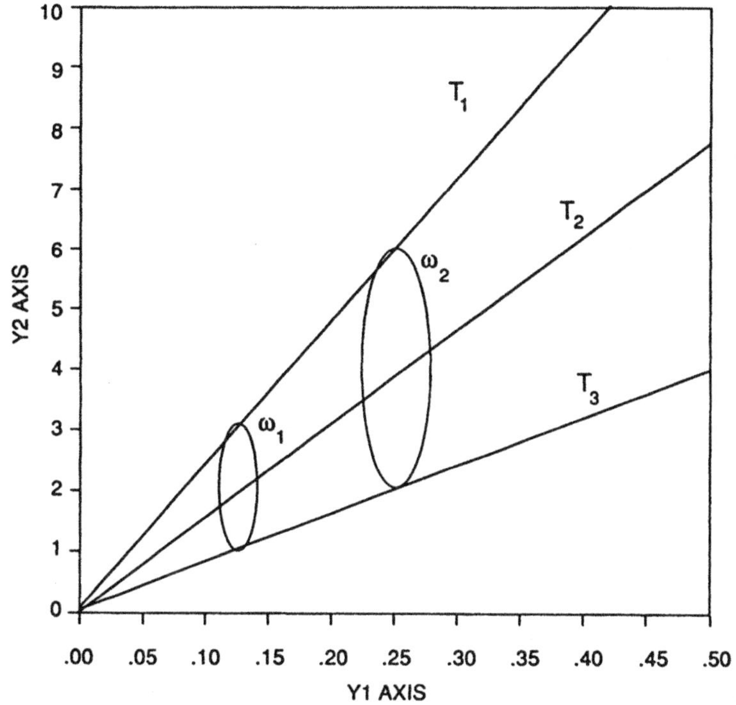

Fig. 10-14 *Y* coordinate representation.

$$r = (\sum_{i=1}^{n} y_i^2)^{1/2} ,$$

$$\theta_1 = arctan(\frac{y_2}{y_1}) ,$$

$$\theta_2 = arctan[\frac{(y_1^2 + y_2^2)^{1/2}}{y_3}] ,$$

.

.

.

$$\theta_{n-1} = arctan \left[\frac{(\sum_{i=1}^{n-1} y_i^2)^{1/2}}{y_n} \right] . \qquad (10.120)$$

Note that the range of r is $(0,\infty)$, the range of θ_1 is $(0,2\pi)$, and the ranges of $\theta_2, \ldots, \theta_{n-1}$ are $(0,\pi)$.

Feature extraction algorithm: We now detail the systematic feature extraction procedure.

(1) Compute the sample mean vector and covariance matrix for each class.

(2) Compute $h(X)$ in (10.101), and select this as a feature.

(3) If $h(X)$ is an effective feature, retain it and continue. Otherwise, stop.

(4) Simultaneously diagonalize the data.

(5) Compute C in (10.103), and use it to translate the data sets. Select an α.

(6) For each sample X in the data set compute Y using (10.116).

(7) Convert Y to multidimensional spherical coordinates using (10.120). Do not compute the radial component, r. The $(n-1)$ components $\theta_1, \ldots, \theta_{n-1}$ are orthogonal to $h(X)$.

(8) Go to Step (2).

For two normal distributions, the algorithm will stop after testing the second extracted feature. This will occur because in the mapped θ-coordinate system, if we disregard r, the two distributions will have identical mean vectors and covariance matrices. Hence, the second extracted feature, h in the $(n-1)$-dimensional mapped space, will not have any capability of discrimination.

We now address the case when C does not exist. From (10.103), C does not exist when any $\lambda_i = 1$. As an aid to the discussion, let us assume that there are ℓ instances of $\lambda_i = 1$ and that the features are ordered so that $\lambda_j \neq 1$ $(j = 1, \ldots, n-\ell)$, and $\lambda_i = 1$ $(i = n-\ell+1, \ldots, n)$. We can now deal with the two cases separately. The first $(n-\ell)$ features are readily handled by the nonlinear mapping algorithm. For the remaining ℓ features we need to reexamine our process of finding the orthogonal space to $h(X)$. Since the covariance matrices are both I for these ℓ features $(\lambda_i = 1)$, the hypersurface and the projection technique are simple to determine. The hypersurface is chosen as the hyperplane that bisects the mean-difference vector, and linear projection is used. Refer to Fig. 10-15, which illustrates this. It is seen that the mapping

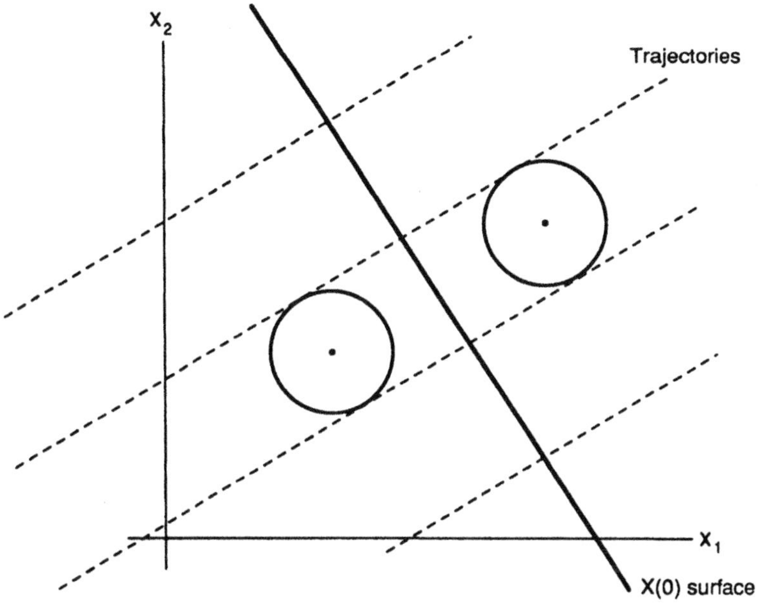

Fig. 10-15 Hypersurface and trajectories for features with $\lambda_i = 1$.

algorithm for the ℓ features with $\lambda_i = 1$ is a linear transformation. Because of this linearity, there is no possibility that there will be any mean vector or covariance matrix differences in the (ℓ−1)-dimensional subspace. This implies that the h computed in the (ℓ−1)-dimensional subspace will not exhibit any discriminatory ability. Specifically, the mean vectors will be identical and the covariance matrices will both be I. As a result, there is no need to map the ℓ features down to an (ℓ−1)-dimensional space. All of our discriminatory ability is contained in the mean-difference, and this information is included in the $h(X)$ computed for all n features, i.e., prior to the mapping procedure. This observation allows us to easily modify the nonlinear mapping algorithm. Add Step (4′) after Step (4) and before Step (5) as follows: (4′) Discard all features with $\lambda_i = 1$.

One final topic deserves mention. In Step (7) we convert to a multidimensional spherical coordinate system. The retained axes are the angular coordinates. Since these angles have finite ranges, we should carefully consider where these angles are measured from. For example, if the positive T_2 line of Fig. 10-14 is chosen as the reference line, the distribution of the angle, θ_1, is centered at $0°$ as seen in Fig. 10-16(a). On the other hand, if the negative T_2 line of Fig. 10-14 is used, the distribution of θ_1 is centered at π as in Fig. 10-

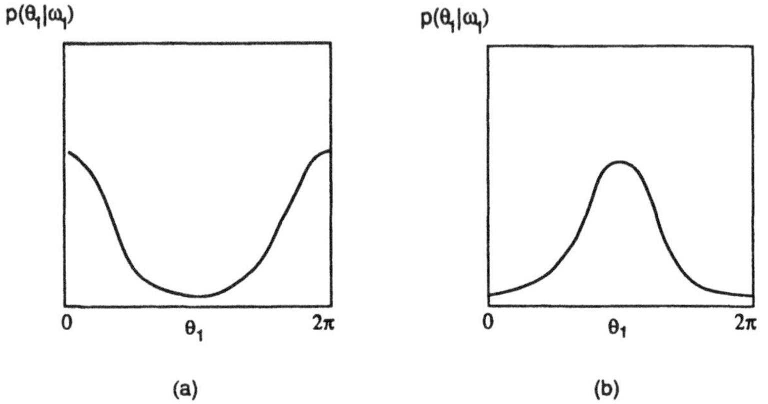

Fig. 10-16 Distributions of an angle.

16(b). Since we will be using $h(X)$ in the θ coordinate system, and $h(X)$ is essentially a normal classifier, it seems reasonable to try to avoid the situation in Fig. 10-16(a). This can be accomplished by rotating the θ coordinate system so that the global mean vector is approximately in the midrange of θ_1.

To demonstrate the performance of the nonlinear mapping algorithm, the results from two experiments follow. Note that for the experiments in these examples α was computed using the following formula:

$$\alpha = \frac{1}{n} \sum_{i=1}^{n} |\ln \lambda_i| . \tag{10.121}$$

Experiment 7: In the first experiment both data sets were drawn from normal distributions. Each class consisted of 100 three-dimensional samples. The mean vectors and covariances matrices were

$$M_1 = \begin{bmatrix} -1.00 \\ -3.75 \\ -1.00 \end{bmatrix}, \quad \Sigma_1 = I \quad \text{and} \quad M_2 = \begin{bmatrix} 0 \\ 0 \\ 0 \end{bmatrix}, \quad \Sigma_2 = 1.7I . \tag{10.122}$$

These values were chosen to provide a Bayes error of approximately 9%. A nonparametric error estimate of the data indicated an error rate of 9%. The first feature was computed using $h(X)$. A nonparametric error estimate of the single feature indicated an error rate of 9%. This result is consistent with the fact that the original classes were actually jointly normal. The data set was reduced to two-dimension using the nonlinear mapping algorithm. A nonparametric error estimate in the two-dimensional subspace indicated an error rate of 49%, which implies the two distributions were essentially identical. When a second feature was extracted from this subspace and combined with the first feature, there was no change in the nonparametric error estimate.

Experiment 8: In the second experiment the first distribution was 100 normal samples with $M_1 = [-1 \ \ -4 \ \ -1]^T$ and $\Sigma_1 = I$. The second distribution was formed using two normal distributions with parameters

$$M_{21} = \begin{bmatrix} 2 \\ 0 \\ 0 \end{bmatrix}, \qquad \Sigma_{21} = \begin{bmatrix} 0.1 & 0 & 0 \\ 0 & 4.1 & 0 \\ 0 & 0 & 4.1 \end{bmatrix},$$

$$M_{22} = \begin{bmatrix} -2 \\ 0 \\ 0 \end{bmatrix}, \qquad \Sigma_{22} = \begin{bmatrix} 0.1 & 0 & 0 \\ 0 & 4.1 & 0 \\ 0 & 0 & 4.1 \end{bmatrix}, \tag{10.123}$$

where the second subscript serves as an identifier for the two clusters. Fifty samples from each cluster were combined to provide 100 samples. A nonparametric error estimate of the data set indicated an error rate of 8%. The first feature was extracted, and a nonparametric error estimate indicated an 11% error rate. The data set was reduced to two-dimension using the nonlinear mapping algorithm. A nonparametric error estimate in the two-dimensional subspace produced an error rate of 40%, indicating improvement was possible. A second feature was extracted in the two-dimensional subspace. The resulting nonparametric error estimate of the two features was 8%. Since this was equal to the error rate of the original data, the feature extraction process was terminated.

10.5 Feature Subset Selection

Up to now, we have assumed that the features are functions of all the original variables, thus preserving as much classification information as possible contained in the original variables. This assumption is reasonable in many applications of pattern recognition, particularly for the classification of random processes. A feature extractor for random processes may be interpreted as a filter, with the output time-sampled values to be functions of all input time-sampled values. However, in some other applications such as medical diagnosis, we need to evaluate the effectiveness of individual tests (variables) or their combinations for classification, and select only the effective ones. This problem is called *feature subset selection.* The best subset of m variables out of n may be found by evaluating a criterion of class separability for all possible combinations of m variables. However, the number of all possible combinations, $\binom{n}{m}$, becomes prohibitive even for modest values of m and n. For example, with $n = 24$ and $m = 12$, the number becomes 2,704,156. Therefore, we need some procedures to avoid the exhaustive search.

Backward and Forward Selections

In this section, we will discuss two *stepwise search techniques* which avoid exhaustive enumeration [12-14]. Although the procedures are simple, they do not guarantee the selection of the best subset.

Backward selection: Let us study a simple example in which two features are chosen out of four as in Fig. 10-17(a). The subset of features a, b,

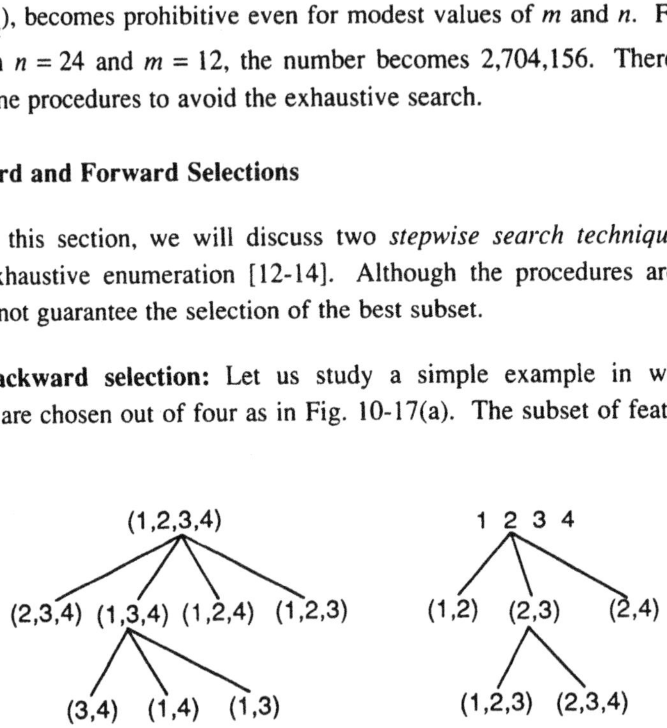

(a) Backward selection (b) Forward selection

Fig. 10-17 Stepwise feature subset selection.

and c is denoted by (a,b,c). A criterion of class separability is selected, and its value for (a,b,c) is expressed by $J_3(a,b,c)$ where the subscript indicates the number of features in the subset. The *backward selection* procedure starts from the full set (1,2,3,4). Then, eliminating one feature from four, all possible subsets of three features are obtained and their criterion values are evaluated. If $J_3(1,3,4)$ is the largest among the four J_3's, (1,3,4) is selected as the best subset of three variables. Then, eliminating one more feature only from (1,3,4), we can obtain the subsets of two features, among which the subset with the largest J_2 is chosen as the best solution of the problem.

Forward selection: The *forward selection* procedure starts from the evaluation of individual features as shown in Fig. 10-17(b). Let the problem be to select three features out of four. If $J_1(2)$ is the largest among all $J_1(\cdot)$'s, one feature is added to feature 2 to form the subset of two features. If $J_2(2,3)$ is the largest among all $J_2(2,\cdot)$'s, one more feature is added to (2,3) to form the subset of three features. Among all possible $(2,3,\cdot)$'s, the best subset is the one which gives the largest $J_3(2,3,\cdot)$.

The reason why these stepwise searchs cannot necessarily select the optimum subset may be better understood by observing the forward selection procedure. Suppose that $\mathbf{x}_1$ and $\mathbf{x}_2$ of Fig. 10-1 are two features among n, from which m features are to be selected. Since the ω_1- and ω_2-marginal density functions of $\mathbf{x}_1$ are heavily overlapped, $\mathbf{x}_1$ drops out when individual features are evaluated. The same is true for $\mathbf{x}_2$. Thus, one of the other features, say $\mathbf{x}_5$, is selected as the best single feature. At the next stage, only combinations of $\mathbf{x}_5$ and others are examined, and so on. As the result, the combination of features including both $\mathbf{x}_1$ and $\mathbf{x}_2$ might not come up for evaluation at the later stages. As seen in Fig. 10-1, although $\mathbf{x}_1$ and $\mathbf{x}_2$ are poor features individually, their combination gives a good feature space in which the ω_1- and ω_2-distributions are well separated. The forward selection procedure could fail to pick that information. This phenomenon is observed frequently when two features are highly correlated. In general, it is true for signal representation that we can eliminate one feature when two features are highly correlated. This is due to the fact that the second feature gives little extra information for representing signals. For an example of Fig. 10-1, knowing one's height (x_1) we can well guess the weight (x_2). On the other hand, highly correlated features could enhance class separability significantly, as seen in Fig. 10-1. Eliminating one, we might lose vital information for classification.

Thus, both backward and forward selection procedures give simple search techniques which avoid exhaustive enumeration. However, the selection of the optimal subset is not guaranteed.

Branch and Bound Procedure [15]

Branch and bound methods have been developed to obtain optimal solutions to combinatorial problems without involving exhaustive enumeration [16-19]. In this section, we formulate the feature subset selection as a combinatorial optimization problem, and develop an efficient algorithm for selecting feature subsets. The subset selected by this procedure is guaranteed to be the best among all possible combinations of features.

Basic branch and bound procedure: Rather than enumerating the subsets of m features, we will find it more convenient to enumerate the subsets of $\bar{m} = n - m$ features *discarded* from the n feature set. Let $(z_1, \ldots, z_{\bar{m}})$ denote the set of those $\bar{m}$ discarded features. Each variable z_i can take on integer values in $\{1, \ldots, n\}$. However, since the order of the z_i's is immaterial, every permutation of the sequence $\{z_1, \ldots, z_{\bar{m}}\}$ will yield the same value of the criterion. Moreover, all the z_i's should be different. Hence, it is sufficient to consider the sequences which satisfy

$$z_1 < z_2 < \ldots < z_{\bar{m}} . \tag{10.124}$$

We will discuss more general enumeration of the subsets later.

The feature selection criterion is a function of the m features obtained by deleting the $\bar{m}$ features from the n feature set. However, for notational convenience, we write the criterion as $J_{\bar{m}}(z_1, \ldots, z_{\bar{m}})$. Then the subset selection problem is to find the optimum sequence $(z_1^*, \ldots, z_{\bar{m}}^*)$ such that

$$J_{\bar{m}}(z_1^*, \ldots, z_{\bar{m}}^*) = \max_{z_1, \ldots, z_{\bar{m}}} J_{\bar{m}}(z_1, \ldots, z_{\bar{m}}) . \tag{10.125}$$

If the criterion were to be minimized instead, all the inequalities in the following discussion would be reversed.

Enumeration of the sequences $(z_1, \ldots, z_{\bar{m}})$ satisfying (10.124) can be illustrated by a solution tree. Figure 10-18 is a solution tree corresponding to $n = 6$ and $m = 2$ ($\bar{m} = 4$). A node at level i is labeled by the value of z_i. Also, each node can be identified by the sequence of discarded features; for example, (1,4) for node A in Fig. 10-18. At level 1 of Fig. 10-18, z_1 can only assume values 1, 2, or 3, because, with z_1 greater than 3, it would not be possible to have sequences $(z_1, \ldots, z_4)$ satisfying (10.124). Similar considerations govern the enumeration at other levels of the tree, and the largest value for z_i must be $(m+i)$ in general.

Let us assume that the criterion J satisfies *monotonicity*, which is defined by

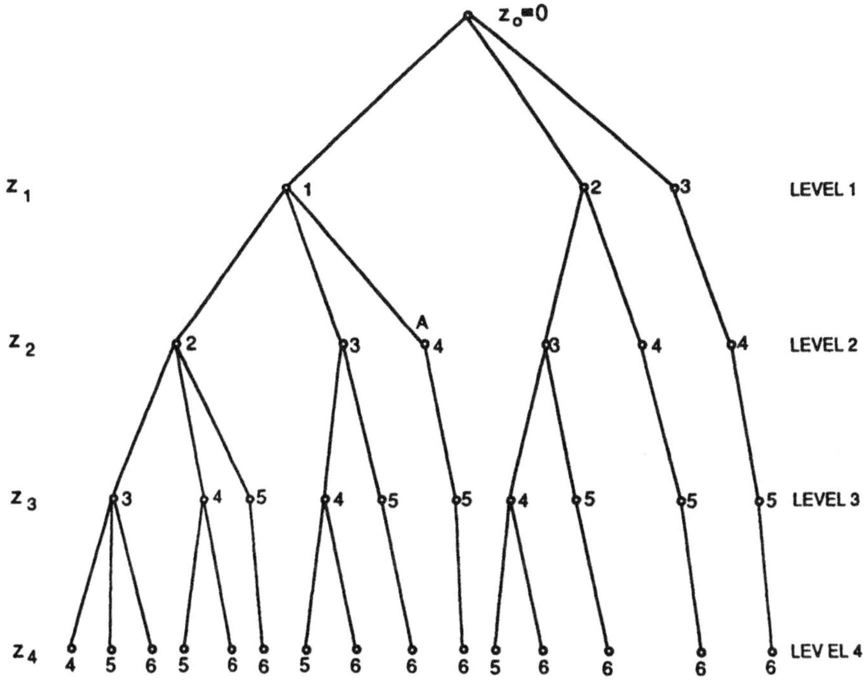

n = 6, m = 2 ($\overline{m}$ = 4)

Fig. 10-18 The solution tree for the basic algorithm.

$$J_1(z_1) \geq J_2(z_1, z_2) \geq \ldots \geq J_{\overline{m}}(z_1, \ldots, z_{\overline{m}}) . \tag{10.126}$$

The monotonicity is not particularly restrictive, as it merely implies that a subset of features should be no better than any larger set that contains the subset. Indeed, a large variety of feature selection criteria do satisfy the monotonicity relation. They are the Bayes error, asymptotic *kNN* error, distance measures such as the Bhattacharyya distance, and the functions of the scatter matrices.

Let α be the best (maximum) value of $J_{\overline{m}}(z_1, \ldots, z_{\overline{m}})$ found so far in the search. If

$$J_k(z_1, \ldots, z_k) \leq \alpha \quad \text{for} \quad k < \overline{m} , \tag{10.127}$$

then by (10.126)

$$J_{\bar{m}}(z_1, \ldots, z_k, z_{k+1}, \ldots, z_{\bar{m}}) \le J_k(z_1, \ldots, z_k) \le \alpha \tag{10.128}$$

for all possible $\{z_{k+1}, \ldots, z_{\bar{m}}\}$.

This means that, whenever the criterion evaluated for any node is less than α, all nodes that are successors of that node also have criterion values less than α, and therefore cannot be optimal. This forms the basis for the branch and bound algorithm.

The branch and bound algorithm successively generates portions of the solution tree and computes the criterion for the nodes explored. Whenever a suboptimal partial sequence of nodes is found to satisfy (10.128), the subtree under the node is implicitly rejected, and enumeration begins on partial sequences which have not yet been explored.

We shall give a simple procedure for enumerating the partial sequences with $z_1 < \ldots < z_k$ as follows.

Basic algorithm:

(1) *Initialization:* Set $\alpha = -\infty$, the level $i = 1$, and $z_0 = 0$.

(2) *Generate successors:* Initialize $LIST(i)$ which is the list of the feature values that z_i can assume given the values of $(z_1, \ldots, z_{i-1})$. That is,

$$LIST(i) = \{z_{i-1}+1,\ z_{i-1}+2, \ldots, m+i\} \quad (i = 1, \ldots, \bar{m}) . \tag{10.129}$$

(3) *Select new node:*

If $LIST(i)$ is empty, go to (5). Otherwise, set $z_i = k$, where

$$J_i(z_1, \ldots, z_{i-1}, k) = \max_{j \in LIST(i)} J_i(z_1, \ldots, z_{i-1}, j) . \tag{10.130}$$

Delete k from $LIST(i)$.

(4) *Check bound:*

If $J_i(z_1, \ldots, z_i) < \alpha$, go to (5). If level $i = \bar{m}$, go to (6). Otherwise, set $i = i + 1$ (advance to a new level) and go to (2).

(5) *Backtrack to lower level:*

Set $i = i - 1$. If $i = 0$, terminate the algorithm. Otherwise go to (3).

(6) *Last level:*

Set $\alpha = J_{\bar{m}}(z_1, \ldots, z_{\bar{m}})$ and set $(z_1^*, \ldots, z_{\bar{m}}^*) = (z_1, \ldots, z_{\bar{m}})$. Go to (5).

The functioning of the algorithm is as follows. Starting from the root of the tree, the successors of the current node are enumerated in *LIST*(i). The successor, for which the partial criterion $J_i(z_1, \ldots, z_i)$ is maximum (the most promising node), is picked as the new current node, and the algorithm moves on to the next higher level. The lists *LIST*(i) at each level i keep track of the nodes that have not been explored. Whenever the partial criterion is found to be less than α, the algorithm backtracks to the previous level and selects a hitherto unexplored node for expansion. Whenever the algorithm reaches the last level $\bar{m}$, α is updated to be the current value of $J_{\bar{m}}(z_1, \ldots, z_{\bar{m}})$ and the current sequence $(z_1, \ldots, z_{\bar{m}})$ is saved as $(z_1^*, \ldots, z_{\bar{m}}^*)$. When all the nodes in *LIST*(i) for a given i are exhausted, the algorithm backtracks to the previous level. When the algorithm backtracks to level 0, it terminates. Upon termination, the current value of $(z_1^*, \ldots, z_{\bar{m}}^*)$ gives the complement of the optimum set of m features, and the current value of α gives the optimum value of the criterion. The procedure guarantees that all sequences are either explicitly evaluated or implicitly rejected, and thus the sequence $(z_1^*, \ldots, z_{\bar{m}}^*)$ gives the best subset of features among all possible subsets.

Alternate enumeration: The enumeration scheme of the basic algorithm is direct and simple. The partial sequences enumerated (see for example, Fig. 10-18) satisfy (10.124). Relation (10.124) ensures that no two equivalent sequences are enumerated. That is, a permutation of a previously enumerated sequence will not be enumerated again.

On the other hand, we note that, with reference to Fig. 10-18, the nodes at a given level do not all have the same number of terminal nodes. Node (1,2) has 6 terminal successors, while node (1,4) has only one. As a result, if the suboptimality test (10.128) is satisfied for node (1,2) (i.e., if $J_2(1,2) < \alpha$), six sequences are rejected as being suboptimal, while for node (1,4) only the single sequence (1,4,5,6) would be rejected. Therefore, we would like nodes with more successors to have a greater probability of the suboptimality test (10.128) being satisfied: i.e., those nodes should have smaller values of the criterion J_k than the ones with fewer successors.

One way to accomplish the above is to initially rank the features from good to bad, and reorder them with 1 as the single feature whose removal from the full set of n features yields the smallest value of the criterion, and n as the worst single feature. The basic algorithm is then applied to the ordered features. Thus, at level 1, $J_1(1) < J_1(2) < J_1(3)$.

This reordering will obviously be effective at the first level, but there is no guarantee that, at successive levels, nodes with more successors will always have smaller values of the criterion.

If we remove the restriction (10.124), we can order the features at each level to realize maximum advantage of the suboptimality test (10.128). This results in a slightly more involved enumeration procedure because we have to ensure that the sequences enumerated would still be unique to a permutation.

The alternate enumeration scheme is based on the same tree structure as before. But, the successors of each node are ordered at each level so that successors with the smaller values of the partial criterion will be nodes which will have larger number of successors in turn.

Following is the improved algorithm, the branch and bound algorithm employing the new enumeration scheme.

Improved algorithm: The following notation will be used in the improved algorithm.

LIST (i): an *ordered* list of the features enumerated at level i.

POINTER (i): The pointer to the element of *LIST* (i) being currently considered. For example, if the current element in *LIST* (i) is the kth, then *POINTER* $(i) = k$.

SUCCESSOR (i,k): number of successors that the kth element in *LIST* (i) can have.

AVAIL: a list of available feature values that *LIST* (i) can assume.

(1) *Initialization:*

Set $\alpha = -\infty$, $AVAIL = \{1,2, \dots ,n\}$, $i = 1$, $LIST(0) = \{0\}$, $SUCCESSOR(0,1) = m + 1$, $POINTER(0) = 1$.

(2) *Initialize LIST(i):*

Set $NODE = POINTER(i-1)$. Compute $J_i(z_1, \dots ,z_{i-1},k)$ for all k in *AVAIL*. Rank the features in *AVAIL* in the increasing order of $J_i(z_1, \dots ,z_{i-1},k)$ and store the smallest r of these in *LIST* (i) in the increasing order (with the first element in *LIST* (i) being the feature in *AVAIL* yielding the smallest J_i), where $r = SUCCESSOR(i-1, NODE)$. Set $SUCCESSOR(i,j) = r - j + 1$ for $j = 1,2,\ldots,r$. Remove $LIST(i)$ from $AVAIL$.

(3) *Select new mode:*

If $LIST(i)$ is empty, go to (5). Otherwise, set $z_i = k$, where k is the last element in $LIST(i)$. Set $POINTER(i) = j$, where j is the current number of elements in $LIST(i)$. Delete k from $LIST(i)$.

(4) *Check Bound:*

If $J_i(z_1,\ldots,z_i) < \alpha$, return z_i to $AVAIL$ and go to (5).

If level $i = \overline{m}$, go to (6). Otherwise set $i = i + 1$, and go to (2).

(5) *Backtrack:*

Set $i = i - 1$. If $i = 0$, terminate the algorithm. Otherwise, return z_i to $AVAIL$ and go to (3).

(6) *Final level, Update bound:*

Set $\alpha = J_{\overline{m}}(z_1,\ldots,z_{\overline{m}})$ and save $(z_1,\ldots,z_{\overline{m}})$ as $(z_1^*,\ldots,z_{\overline{m}}^*)$. Return $z_{\overline{m}}$ to $AVAIL$. Go to (5).

At the conclusion of the algorithm, $(z_1^*,\ldots,z_{\overline{m}}^*)$ will give the complement of the best feature set as before. Figure 10-19 illustrates, for a random example, the tree enumerated including the nodes which were rejected by the suboptimality test (10.128). At level 1, features 4, 3, and 6 were enumerated because $J_1(4) < J_1(3) < J_1(6) < J_1(1), J_1(2), J_1(5)$. The $SUCCESSOR$ variables determine the number of successor nodes the current node will have at the next level. $AVAIL$ keeps track of the feature values that can be enumerated at any level. The algorithm is thus totally independent of the ordering of the features. No sequence is enumerated more than once (even as a permutation) and all possible sequences are considered either explicitly or implicitly, guaranteeing optimality of the subset sought. Moreover, the suboptimality test (10.128) is always used to the best advantage, rendering the algorithm very efficient. Also, the ordering of the nodes does not mean extra computation, because the partial criteria would be evaluated for the successors of each node anyway.

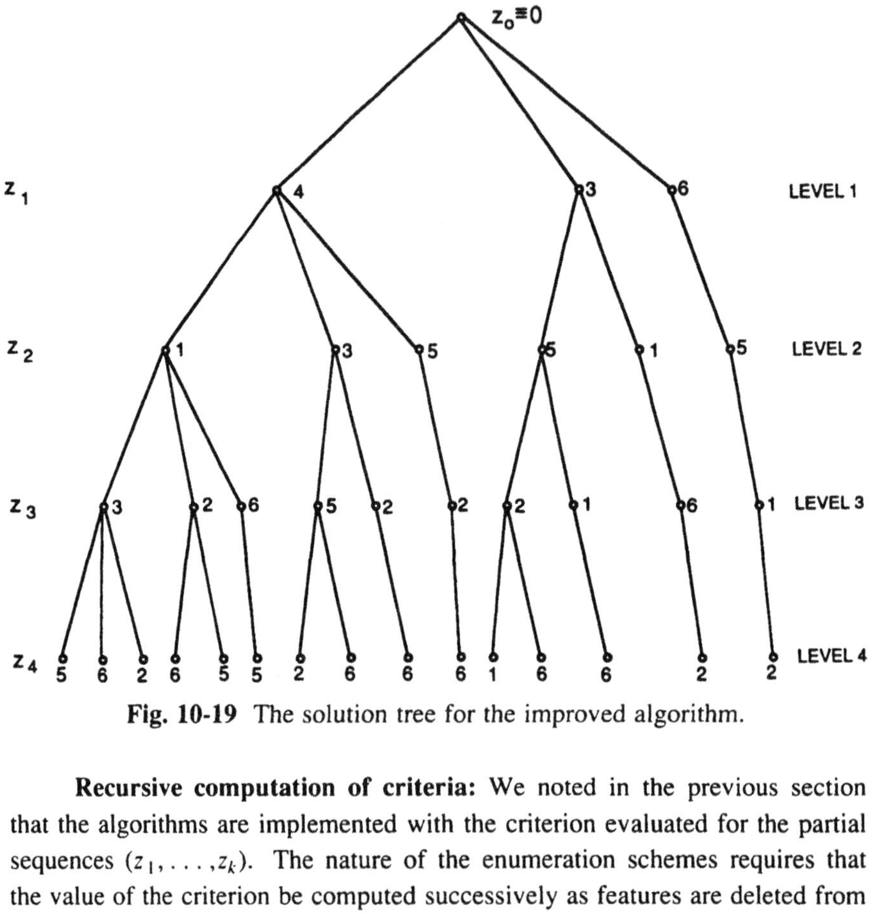

Fig. 10-19 The solution tree for the improved algorithm.

Recursive computation of criteria: We noted in the previous section that the algorithms are implemented with the criterion evaluated for the partial sequences $(z_1, \ldots, z_k)$. The nature of the enumeration schemes requires that the value of the criterion be computed successively as features are deleted from the full set. For a class of criteria, it is possible to evaluate the criterion recursively, as a new feature is deleted from the present partial set. Recursive computation results in substantial computational savings. We will derive recursive equations for the class of quadratic criteria. The function of the scatter matrices is a example of quadratic criteria. The criterion always takes the form of

$$J_k = X_k^T S_k^{-1} X_k \, , \tag{10.131}$$

where X_k is a k-dimensional vector and S_k is a $k \times k$ scatter matrix, when k features are present. Also, the Bhattacharyya distance for the normal case has the first term in the quadratic form (10.131). The determinant term of the

Bhattacharyya distance can also be computed recursively as we will see later.

The inversion of S_k is the major computational effort in evaluating (10.131) as features are successively deleted from the full set of features. When the ith feature is deleted, it is necessary to compute the inverse of S_k with the ith row and column deleted. Without loss of generality, let the feature being deleted correspond to the kth row and column of S_k.

$$S_k = \begin{bmatrix} S_{k-1} & D \\ D^T & s_{kk} \end{bmatrix} . \tag{10.132}$$

A fundamental identity in matrix algebra gives S_k^{-1} in terms of S_{k-1}^{-1} as

$$S_k^{-1} = \begin{bmatrix} S_{k-1}^{-1} + \frac{1}{a} S_{k-1}^{-1} D D^T S_{k-1}^{-1} & -\frac{1}{a} S_{k-1}^{-1} D \\ -\frac{1}{a} D^T S_{k-1}^{-1} & \frac{1}{a} \end{bmatrix} , \tag{10.133}$$

where

$$a = s_{kk} - D^T S_{k-1}^{-1} D . \tag{10.134}$$

The reader can verify that the multiplication of (10.132) and (10.133) gives I. If we write

$$S_k^{-1} = \begin{bmatrix} A & C \\ C^T & b \end{bmatrix} , \tag{10.135}$$

then, by (10.133) and (10.135), it can be verified that

$$S_{k-1}^{-1} = A - \frac{1}{b} C C^T . \tag{10.136}$$

Hence, S_{k-1}^{-1} can be computed from S_k^{-1} with little computational effort. With reference to branch and bound algorithms, the inverse matrices S_k^{-1} are stored for each level. The inverse at any level is computed from that at the previous level using the recursive equation (10.136). Whenever the algorithm back-tracks and proceeds down another branch, the inverse for the new S_k can be recomputed from the inverse at the level at which the branching occurred. For example, in Fig. 10-18, after (2,4,5,6) is explored, the algorithm backtracks to the node (2,3). The value of S_k^{-1} for the node (2,3) can be computed from the current value of S_k^{-1} at level 1. The S_k^{-1} for level 2 is updated to be this value as feature 3 is now chosen to be z_2.

It is also possible to recursively compute the quadratic $X_k^T S_k^{-1} X_k$ for $k-1$ features given its value with k features and the S_k^{-1} matrix from the previous level. This is useful in Step (3) of branch and bound algorithms, where it is necessary to compute the criterion after deleting one feature at a time from a partial set. This avoids computation of S_{k-1}^{-1} during this step. Once a node is selected however (Step (4)), the S_k^{-1} for the new level has to be updated using (10.136).

Let the criterion with k features be denoted by $J_k = X_k^T S_k^{-1} X_k$, and let us assume that the kth feature is being deleted as before.

The criterion with $k-1$ features is now $J_{k-1} = X_{k-1}^T S_{k-1}^{-1} X_{k-1}$, where

$$X_k = [\underset{k-1}{X_{k-1}^T}\ \underset{1}{x_k}]^T \,, \tag{10.137}$$

and S_{k-1} is defined as in (10.132).

From (10.136),

$$\begin{aligned} X_{k-1}^T S_{k-1}^{-1} X_{k-1} &= X_{k-1}^T [A - \frac{1}{b} C C^T] X_{k-1} \\ &= X_{k-1}^T A \, X_{k-1} - \frac{1}{b} (C^T \, X_{k-1})^2 \,. \end{aligned} \tag{10.138}$$

Consider

$$\begin{aligned} X_k^T S_k^{-1} X_k &= [X_{k-1}^T x_k] \begin{bmatrix} A & C \\ C^T & b \end{bmatrix} \begin{bmatrix} X_{k-1} \\ x_k \end{bmatrix} \\ &= X_{k-1}^T A \, X_{k-1} + 2 \, x_k C^T X_{k-1} + b \, x_k^2 \,. \end{aligned} \tag{10.139}$$

Equations (10.138) and (10.139) together give

$$\begin{aligned} X_{k-1}^T S_{k-1}^{-1} X_{k-1} &= X_k^T S_k^{-1} X_k - [b \, x_k^2 + 2 x_k \, C^T X_{k-1} + \frac{1}{b} (C^T X_{k-1})^2] \\ &= X_k^T S_k^{-1} X_k - \frac{1}{b} \{ [C^T \;\; b] X_k \}^2 \,. \end{aligned} \tag{10.140}$$

Note that $[C^T \;\; b]$ is a row of S_k^{-1} corresponding to the feature being deleted. Hence $[C^T \;\; b]X_k$ is merely the inner product of that row with X_k. Thus, the $J_i(z_1, \ldots, z_{i-1}, j)$ in the algorithms can be directly evaluated from $J_{i-1}(z_1, \ldots, z_{i-1})$ by (10.140) without actually having to compute S_{k-1}^{-1} for all the variables j. Incidentally, (10.140) also furnishes proof that J is monotonic.

The determinant term in the Bhattacharyya distance for the normal case can be computed recursively.

Let S_k denote a matrix with k features. It is necessary to evaluate $|S_{k-1}|$, when the kth feature is deleted from S_k. Recalling that at every level of the algorithm we have S_k^{-1} available (used in the quadratic term). Thus, $|S_{k-1}|$ can be directly computed from $|S_k|$ of (10.132) as follows:

$$
\begin{aligned}
|S_k| &= \begin{vmatrix} S_{k-1} - \dfrac{1}{s_{kk}} DD^T & 0 \\ D^T & s_{kk} \end{vmatrix} \\
&= s_{kk} \left| S_{k-1} - \frac{1}{s_{kk}} DD^T \right| \\
&= s_{kk} |S_{k-1}| \left(1 - \frac{1}{s_{kk}} D^T S_{k-1}^{-1} D\right) \\
&= (s_{kk} - D^T S_{k-1}^{-1} D) |S_{k-1}| \,,
\end{aligned}
\tag{10.141}
$$

where the third line is obtained from the second by (2.143). The ratio of two determinants, $s_{kk} - D^T S_{k-1}^{-1} D$, is readily available from the (k,k) element of S_k^{-1} as seen in (10.133) and (10.134).

Experiment 9: The algorithms were tested on multispectral data acquired from airborne remote sensing scanners at the Laboratory for Applications of Remote Sensing (LARS) at Purdue University.

The data comprised of 423 sample vectors each from two classes; Soybean and Corn. There were 12 data channels, corresponding to 12 bands of the spectrum in which the sensing was performed. Each channel is a feature, and the problem was to select a subset of the channels which was best according to a given criterion. The criterion used was $J = \text{tr}(S_w^{-1} S_b)$ with the estimated means and covariance matrices.

Table 10-2 shows the number of subsets evaluated for three algorithms: two from the basic algorithm and one from the improved one.

TABLE 10-2

THE RESULTS OF THE BRANCH AND BOUND PROCEDURE

	NUMBER OF SUBSETS ENUMERATED			
Case	Exhaustive search	Basic algorithm without initial ordering	Basic algorithm with initial ordering	Improved algorithm
$\binom{12}{4}$	495	100	42	32
$\binom{24}{12}$	2,704,156	Did not terminate after 600 sec. CPU time (CDC 6500)	13,369 (249 sec. CPU time)	6,256 (140 sec. CPU time)

In the first algorithm, features are ordered according to the wave-lengths of the spectrum bands from the shortest to the longest, while in the second algorithm, features are ordered according to the class separability of individual feature. The basic algorithm was used for both cases. The third is the improved algorithm. Table 10-2 shows significant saving achieved by the basic algorithm with initial ordering and the improved algorithm [15].

Experiment 10: To evaluate the performance of the algorithms for a larger problem, an additional set of 12 features was generated by taking the square of 12 features of Experiment 9. The covariance matrices and the means were computed for the 24 feature set. It is to be expected that the resulting 24 feature set is very correlated, and there may be several subsets that yield very close values of the criterion.

Again, significant saving was achieved by the basic algorithm with initial ordering and the improved algorithm. The superiority of the improved algorithm is to be expected, because in the large variable problem the initial ordering scheme for the basis algorithm will not be very effective at higher levels. In fact, the basic algorithm without initial ordering did not even terminate after 600 seconds of computation (by CDC6500). Table 10-2 summarizes the results [15]. Table 10-3 gives the number of nodes expanded (subsets

TABLE 10-3

SUMMARY OF BEHAVIOR OF ALGORITHMS

Algorithm		LEVEL 1	2	3	4	5	6	7	8	9	10	11	12
Basic with ordering	No. of nodes enumerated	13	91	370	776	1376	2083	2961	3656	4185	2953	2248	771
	No. of nodes rejected	0	9	89	152	293	290	669	691	2325	1107	1718	746
Improved	No. of nodes enumerated	13	91	323	631	1091	1674	2024	1742	1242	910	347	188
	No. of nodes rejected	0	13	90	127	199	452	756	800	466	633	180	168

enumerated) at each level and the number of nodes for which the inequality (10.128) was satisfied (subsets rejected) at each level [15]. Because of the reordering of the features, every node that was rejected at each level of the improved algorithm results in a large number of suboptimal sequences being discovered. Hence, fewer nodes are enumerated overall in the improved algorithm than in the basic algorithm. The additional complexity of the improved algorithm appears justified in the light of its efficiency. Also, the improved algorithm is independent of the initial ordering of the features.

Computer Projects

1. Find the suboptimal linear features from Data I-Λ by maximizing the Bhattacharyya distance.

   (a) Use the algorithm for μ_1 dominant.

(b) Use the algorithm for μ_2 dominant.

2. Repeat Experiment 2. Change the parameters N, n, α, and k to see the effects.

3. Repeat Experiment 3 for Data I-Λ.

4. Repeat Experiment 6.

5. Repeat Experiment 8.

6. Repeat Experiment 10 for Data I-Λ.

Problems

1. The density functions of three classes consist of three impulses for each class as in the figure, each impulse carrying the probability of 1/3.

   (a) Select one linear feature which maximizes $\mathrm{tr}(S_w^{-1} S_b)$.

   (b) Select one linear feature which maximizes $\mathrm{tr}(S_w^{-1} S_b)$ between ω_1 and ω_2.

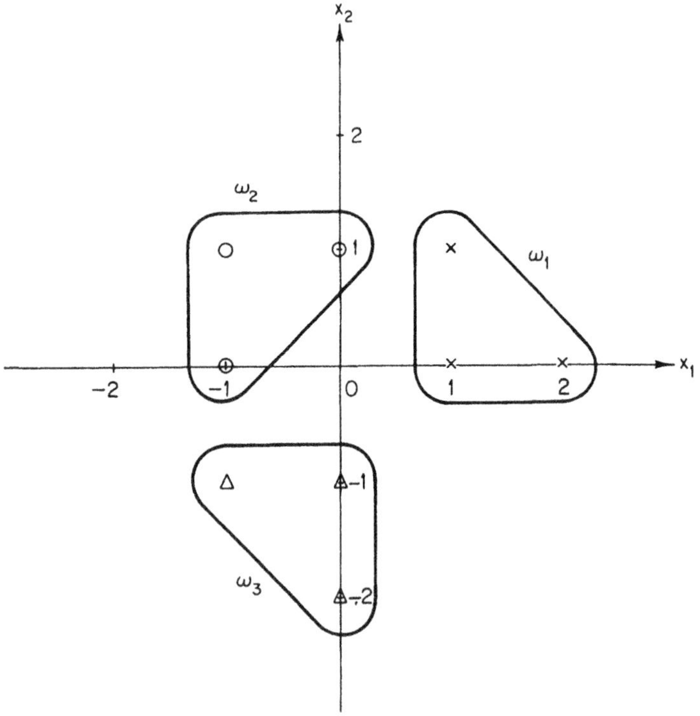

2. Find the optimum linear features to maximize $\mathrm{tr}(A^T S_1 A)$ under a constraint $A^T S_2 A = I$, where A is an $n \times m$ $(m<n)$ transformation matrix.

3. Find the optimum linear features to maximize $\mathrm{tr}(A^T S_1 A)$ under a constraint $\mathrm{tr}(A^T S_2 A) = c$, where A is an $n \times m$ $(m<n)$ matrix, and c is a constant. Point out the difference between Problems 2 and 3.

4. Let $\lambda_1, \ldots, \lambda_n$ be the eigenvalues of $S_2^{-1} S_1$, and $\mu_1, \ldots, \mu_m$ be the eigenvalues of $(A^T S_2 A)^{-1}(A^T S_1 A)$ where A is an $n \times m$ $(m<n)$ transformation matrix. Prove $\lambda_i \geq \mu_i$.

5. Show how to find the suboptimum linear features to maximize the divergence, when the second term is dominant. Is it possible to obtain the explicit solutions to find linear features by optimizing the first term of the divergence?

6. Let $f(M_1, \ldots, M_L, S_m)$ be a class separability criterion.

   (a) Prove that $\Sigma_{i=1}^{L} (\partial f / \partial M_{iY}) = 0$ must be satisfied in order for f to be invariant under a coordinate shift $Y(X) = Y^*(X) + V$ where $Y^*(X)$ is the optimal solution. The mixture mean of $Y(\mathbf{X})$ is assumed to be zero.

   (b) Prove that $\Sigma_{i=1}^{L} (\partial f / \partial M_{iY}) M_{iY}^T = -2(\partial f^* / \partial S_{mY})\, S_{mY}$ must be satisfied in order for f to be invariant under nonsingular linear transformations $Y(X) = B^T Y^*(X)$.

7. Let $J = \mathrm{tr}\{S_w^{-1}(M_1 M_1^T + M_2 M_2^T - M_1 M_2^T - M_2 M_1^T)\}$ be the class separability criterion where

$$M_1 = \begin{bmatrix} 1 \\ 1 \end{bmatrix}, \quad M_2 = \begin{bmatrix} -1 \\ -1 \end{bmatrix}, \quad \Sigma_1 = \Sigma_2 = I, \quad P_1 = P_2 = 0.5 .$$

   Compute $\mathcal{S}_b$, and find one linear feature which maximizes $\mathrm{tr}(S_w^{-1} \mathcal{S}_b)$.

8. Let $f(M_1, \ldots, M_L, S_m)$ be the class separability criterion. Find the value of f for the ideal features in terms of asymptotic NN errors.

9. Define the nonparametric within-class and mixture scatter matrices, and prove that they are the same as the parametric ones, S_w and S_m, when the local means approach the class means.

10. Two normal distributions are characterized by

$$M_1 = \begin{bmatrix} 8 \\ 1 \end{bmatrix}, \quad \Sigma_1 = I, \quad \text{and} \quad M_2 = \begin{bmatrix} 15 \\ 2 \end{bmatrix}, \quad \Sigma_2 = \begin{bmatrix} 4 & 0 \\ 0 & 9 \end{bmatrix}.$$

(a) Plot the trajectories passing through (15, 1), (15, 2), and (15, 3) in the original X-space.

(b) Plot the trajectories in the Y-space, corresponding to the three trajectories in the X-space. Use $\alpha = \ln 2$.

References

1. G. S. Sebestyen, "Decision-Making Process in Pattern Recognition," Macmillan, New York, 1962.
2. S. S. Wilks, "Mathematical Statistics," Wiley, New York, 1963.
3. S. Kullback, "Information Theory and Statistics," Wiley, New York, 1959.
4. K. Fukunaga and R. D. Short, A Class of feature extraction criteria and its relation to the Bayes risk estimate, *Trans. IEEE on Inform. Theory,* IT-26, pp. 59-65, 1980.
5. K. Fukunaga and R. D. Short, Nonlinear feature extraction with a general criterion function, *Trans. IEEE on Inform. Theory,* IT-24, pp. 600-607, 1978.
6. K. Fukunaga and S. Ando, The optimum nonlinear features for a scatter criterion in discriminant analysis, *Trans. IEEE on Inform. Theory,* IT-23, pp. 453-459, 1977.
7. P. A. Devijver, Relationships between statistical risks and least-mean-square-error design criterion in pattern recognition, *Proc. 1st Intern. Joint Conf. Pattern Recog.,* Washington, DC, 1973.
8. K. Fukunaga and J. M. Mantock, Nonparametric discriminant analysis, *Trans. IEEE on Pattern Anal. and Machine Intell.,* PAMI-5, pp. 671-678, 1983.
9. D. H. Foley and J. W. Sammon, An optimal set of discriminant vectors, *Trans. IEEE Computers,* C-24, pp. 281-289, 1975.
10. S. Watanabe and N. Takvasa, Subspace methods in pattern recognition, *Proc. 1st Intern. Joint Conf. Pattern Recog.,* Washington, DC, 1973.

11. K. A. Brakke, J. M. Mantock, and K. Fukunaga, Systematic feature extraction, *Trans. IEEE on Pattern Anal. and Machine Intell.*, PAMI-4, pp. 291-297, 1982.

12. A. N. Mucciardi and E. E. Gose, A comparison of seven techniques for choosing subsets of pattern recognition properties, *Trans. IEEE Computers*, C-20, pp. 1023-1031, 1971.

13. A. W. Whitney, A Direct method of nonparametric measurement selection, *Trans. IEEE Computers*, C-20, pp. 1100-1103, 1971.

14. T. Marill and D. M. Green, On the effectiveness of receptors in recognition systems, *Trans. IEEE Inform. Theory*, IT-9, pp. 11-27, 1963.

15. P. M. Narendra and K. Fukunaga, A branch and bound algorithm for feature subset selection, *Trans. IEEE Computers*, C-26, pp. 917-922, 1977.

16. S. W. Golomb and L. D. Baumert, Backtrack programming, *J. ACM*, 12, pp. 516-524, 1965.

17. A. L. Chernyavskii, Algorithms for the solution of combinatorial problems based on a method of implicit enumeration, *Automat. and Remote Contr.* 33, pp. 252-260, 1972.

18. E. L. Lawler and D. E. Wood, Branch and bound methods: a survey, *Oper. Res.*, 149, No. 4, 1966.

19. N. J. Nilsson, "Problem Solving Methods in Artificial Intelligence," McGraw-Hill, New York, 1971.

Chapter 11

CLUSTERING

In the preceding chapters, we have presented a considerable body of design theory for pattern recognition. Procedures for classifier design, parameter estimation, and density estimation have been discussed in detail. We have consistently assumed the existence of a training set of classified samples. In this chapter, we will focus our attention on the classification of samples without the aid of a training set. We will refer to this kind of classification as *clustering* or *unsupervised classification*.

There are many instances where classification must and can be performed without *a priori* knowledge. Consider, for example, the biological taxonomy problem. Over the years, all known living things have been classified according to certain observable characteristics. Of course, plants and animals have never borne labels indicating their kingdoms, phylae, and so on. Rather, they have been categorized according to their observable characteristics without outside supervision.

The clustering problem is not well defined unless the resulting classes of samples are required to exhibit certain properties. The choice of properties or, equivalently, the definition of a cluster, is the fundamental issue in the clustering problem. Given a suitable definition of a cluster, it is possible to distinguish between good and bad classifications of samples.

In this chapter, two approaches to clustering will be addressed. One is called the *parametric approach* and the other is the *nonparametric approach.*

In most parametric approaches, *clustering criteria* are defined, and given samples are classified to a number of clusters so as to optimize the criteria. The most commonly used criteria are the class separability measures which were introduced in Chapter 10. That is, the class assignment which maximizes the class separability measure is considered to be the best clustering result. In this approach, the structure (parametric form) of the classification boundary is determined by the criterion. The *clustering algorithm*, which determines efficiently the best classification with respect to the criterion, is normally an iterative algorithm. In another parametric approach, a mathematical form is assumed to express the distribution of the given data. A typical example is the summation of normal distributions. In this case, the clustering problem consists of finding the parameter values for this distribution which best fit the data.

On the other hand, neither clustering criteria nor assumed mathematical forms for the distribution are used in the nonparametric approach. Instead, samples are separated according to the *valley* of the density function. The valley may be considered as the natural boundary which separates the modes of the distributions. This boundary could be complex and not expressible by any parametric form.

In addition, clustering may be viewed as the selection of representatives. In general, a density function may be approximated by the Parzen density estimate around the representatives. Then, we may try to reduce the number of representatives while maintaining the degree of approximation. An iterative procedure to choose the representatives is discussed in this chapter.

11.1 Parametric Clustering

In this section, we will present, first, a general-purpose clustering algorithm based on a generalized criterion. Then, the discussion for a specific criterion follows.

General Clustering Algorithm

The clustering algorithm developed in this section applies to a wide range of criteria. However, it is necessary to specify the form of the criterion as well as some other details of the clustering problem at the outset.

Clustering criterion: Assume that we want to classify N samples, $X_1, \ldots, X_N$. These vectors are not denoted as random vectors because, in the clustering problem, they are assumed to be fixed and known. Each sample is to be placed into one of L classes, $\omega_1, \ldots, \omega_L$, where L is assumed to be given. The class to which the ith sample is assigned is denoted ω_{k_i} $(i = 1, \ldots, N)$. For convenience, let the value of k_i be an integer between 1 and L. A *classification* Ω is a vector made up of the ω_{k_i}'s, and a *configuration* X^* is a vector made up of the X_i's, that is,

$$\Omega = [\omega_{k_1} \ldots \omega_{k_N}]^T \tag{11.1}$$

and

$$X^* = [X_1^T \ldots X_N^T]^T \ . \tag{11.2}$$

The clustering criterion J is a function of Ω and X^* and can be written

$$J = J(\omega_{k_1}, \ldots, \omega_{k_N}; X_1, \ldots, X_N) = J(\Omega; X^*) \ . \tag{11.3}$$

By definition, the best classification Ω_0 satisfies either

$$J(\Omega_0; X^*) = \max_{\Omega} \text{ or } \min_{\Omega} J(\Omega; X^*) \tag{11.4}$$

depending on the criterion. For the remainder of this section, we will discuss only the minimization problem, since the maximization is similar.

Example 1: Six vectors, $X_1, \ldots, X_6$, of Fig. 11-1 are given. The problem is to find class assignments of these vectors to one of two classes so as to minimize a criterion. Let $J = \mathrm{tr}(S_m^{-1} S_w)$ be the criterion where S_w and S_m are the within-class and mixture scatter matrices defined in (10.1) and (10.4).

For each classification, for example $\{X_1, X_2, X_5\} \in \omega_1$ and $\{X_3, X_4, X_6\} \in \omega_2$ as shown by dotted lines, or $\{X_1, X_2, X_3\} \in \omega_1$ and $\{X_4, X_5, X_6\} \in \omega_2$ as shown by solid lines, the mean vectors and covariance matrices for ω_1 and ω_2 are estimated, and S_w, S_m, and J can be computed.

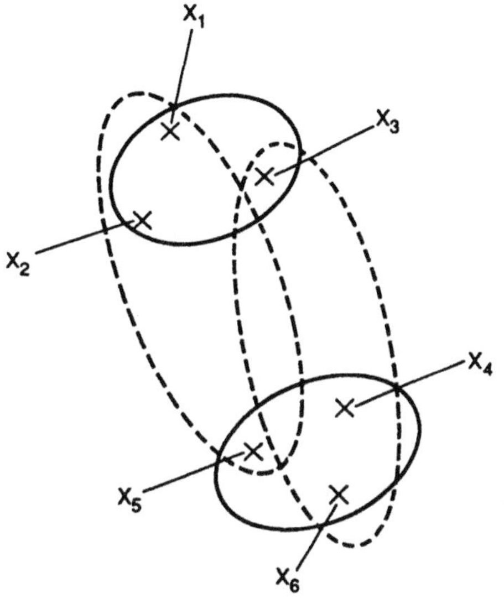

Fig. 11-1 An example of clustering.

Note that S_w varies depending on the class assignment but S_m does not. The class assignment by the solid lines would give the minimum J (the smallest within-class scatter) among all possible combinations of class assignments.

Clustering algorithm: For a given clustering problem, the configuration X^* is fixed. The clustering algorithm varies only the classification Ω. Ordinary steepest descent search techniques cannot be applied because of the discrete and unordered nature of Ω. Still, it is possible to define an iterative search algorithm based on variations in J with respect to variations in Ω.

Suppose, at the ℓth iteration, the classification is $\Omega(\ell)$, where

$$\Omega(\ell) = [\omega_{k_1(\ell)} \dots \omega_{k_N(\ell)}]^T . \tag{11.5}$$

If the ith sample is reclassified from its present class $k_i(\ell)$ to class j, the clustering criterion varies by an amount $\Delta J(i,j,\ell)$, which is given by

$$\Delta J(i,j,\ell) = J(\omega_{k_1(\ell)}, \dots, \omega_{k_{i-1}(\ell)}, \omega_j, \omega_{k_{i+1}(\ell)}, \dots, \omega_{k_N(\ell)}; X^*) - J(\Omega(\ell); X^*) . \tag{11.6}$$

If $\Delta J(i,j,\ell)$ is negative, reclassification of the ith sample to class j yields a classification that is improved in terms of J. This fact is the basis of the following algorithm:

(1) Choose an initial classification $\Omega(0)$.

(2) Given the ℓth classification $\Omega(\ell)$, calculate $\Delta J(i,j,\ell)$ for $j = 1,2,\ldots,L$ and $i = 1,2,\ldots,N$.

(3) For $i = 1,2,\ldots,N$, reclassify the ith sample to class t, where

$$\Delta J(i,t,\ell) = \min_j \Delta J(i,j,\ell) . \tag{11.7}$$

Decide ties involving $j = k_i(\ell)$ in favor of the present classification. Decide other ties arbitrarily. This step forms $\Omega(\ell + 1)$.

(4) If $\Omega(\ell + 1) \neq \Omega(\ell)$, return to Step (2). Otherwise the algorithm is complete.

The algorithm is simply the iterative application of a classification rule based on the clustering criterion. Here, we adopted a procedure in which all of the samples are reclassified simultaneously at each iteration. An alternative approach is to reclassify each sample one at a time, resulting in similar but slightly different clusters. In these iterative procedures, there is no guarantee that the algorithm converges. Even if it does converge, we cannot be certain that the absolute minimum of J has been obtained. Therefore, we must depend on empirical evidence to justify the algorithm.

In contrast to these potential weaknesses, the algorithm described above is very efficient. Like any good search algorithm, it surveys a small subset of classifications in a systematic and adaptive manner. It is easily programmable for any criterion of the form of (11.3).

Determining the number of clusters: So far, we have ignored the problem of determining the number of classes L, and have assumed that L is given. However, in practice, L is rarely known. We not only need to determine L but also the proper class assignment. For that purpose, we may run the clustering procedure for the various values of L, and find the best classification for each value of L. Let J_L^* be the optimal criterion value for a given L after the clustering procedure has converged. If J_L^* decreases as L increases, and either reaches the minimum point at L_0 or becomes flat after L_0, then we may use L_0 as the proper number of classes. Unfortunately, many of the popular criteria do not have this favorable property. For example, consider $J = \mathrm{tr}(S_m^{-1} S_w)$ of Example 1. As L increases, samples are divided into smaller groups, and consequently the within-class scatter becomes smaller. This means that J might decrease monotonically with L. Finally, when L becomes N, the total number of samples, each class consists of one sample only, and there is no within-class scatter ($J = 0$). Although $L = N$ minimizes this criterion, this is obviously not the solution we want.

It appears, therefore, that some external method of controlling L is necessary. Unfortunately, no unified theory for determining L has been fully developed and accepted.

Merging and splitting: After a number of classes is obtained, we may consider the merging of two classes into a single class or the splitting of a class into a number of classes.

Basically, merging is desirable in two instances. The first is when two classes are very similar. The similarity may be measured in a number of ways. The Euclidean distance between two mean vectors is the simplest measure but is not an accurate one. The Bhattacharyya distance of (3.152), based on the normal assumption, could be a reasonable compromise between simplicity and accuracy. The second instance in which merging may be appropriate is when the population of a class is very small. In this case, the class may be merged with the most similar class, even when the similarity is not very close.

Deciding whether or not a class is to be split is a more complex problem. Too large a population suggests that the class is a candidate for a split. Multimodal and nonsymmetric distributions as well as distributions with large variances along one direction are also candidates for splitting. In order to identify these characteristics, various tests are necessary. Splitting a class may be carried out by applying the clustering procedure to the samples in the class.

It goes without saying that this kind of merging and splitting is very heuristic. Its merit lies in the fact that it is efficient and requires a minimum of human interaction.

Multiple dichotomy: It is somewhat more satisfying to adopt an approach which depends entirely on the clustering criterion J. One such approach has been suggested [1] and is outlined as follows.

Suppose that for $L = 2$ there are several distinct classifications which yield a nearly minimal value of J. If these classifications differ only in the classification of a few samples, there is no reason to suppose the existence of more than two classes. If the classifications are grossly different, however, then it is evident that several classes are actually present.

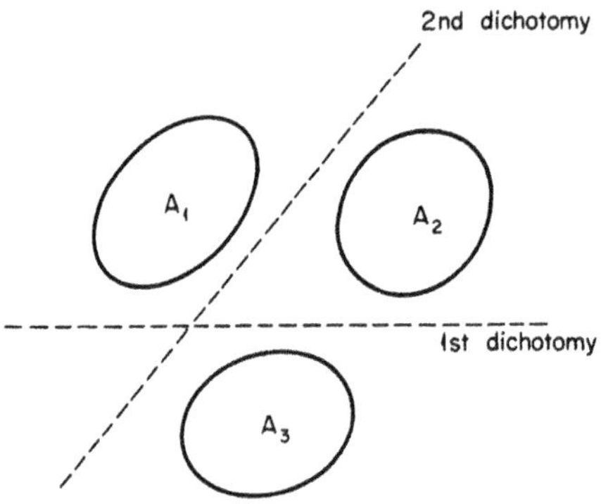

Fig. 11-2 Multiple dichotomy of three classes of samples.

Figure 11-2 illustrates two possible dichotomies of a collection of samples apparently containing three classes A_1, A_2, and A_3. One dichotomy separates the samples into $A_1 \cup A_2$ and A_3, while the other results in the two classes A_1 and $A_2 \cup A_3$. Thus, A_3, A_1, and $\overline{A_1 \cup A_3} = A_2$ are seen to be distinct classes ($\bar{A}$ is the complement of the set A.)

Now let us consider the more general case where there are k dichotomies of a collection of samples containing L classes. Each dichotomy separates these samples into two groups. Let S_{ij} be the set of all samples assigned to group j by the ith dichotomy for $j = 1,2$ and $i = 1, \ldots, k$. Assume that the following two conditions hold.

(a) A dichotomy places each class into only one group, that is, classes are not split by dichotomies.

(b) For each pair of classes, there is at least one dichotomy which does not assign the two classes to the same group.

Select one group from each of the k dichotomies and form a subset C as the intersection of these k groups. By condition (a), if C contains one sample, then it must contain all of the samples of that class. By condition (b), for any other class, there is at least one of the k selected groups to which that class does not belong. Therefore, if C is nonempty, then C contains one and only one class. Hence, in order to construct all the L classes, we consider the 2^k subsets of the form.

$$C(j_1, \ldots, j_k) = \bigcap_{i=1}^{k} S_{ij_i} , \tag{11.8}$$

where each j equals 1 or 2. Each nonempty C is a class. In our example, we have

$$S_{11} = A_1 \cup A_2, \quad S_{12} = A_3, \quad S_{21} = A_1, \quad S_{22} = A_2 \cup A_3 , \tag{11.9}$$

so that

$$\begin{aligned} C(1, 1) &= S_{11} \cap S_{21} = A_1 , \\ C(1, 2) &= S_{11} \cap S_{22} = A_2 , \\ C(2, 1) &= S_{12} \cap S_{21} = 0 , \\ C(2, 2) &= S_{12} \cap S_{22} = A_3 , \end{aligned} \tag{11.10}$$

which is in agreement with our earlier argument.

The multiple dichotomy approach has a stronger theoretical basis than the merging and splitting procedure. Further, it relies on no numerical criterion other than J. However, implementation of the multiple dichotomy approach can be difficult, especially when the true number of classes is large. In addition, the conditions (a) and (b) mentioned above are rarely satisfied in practice. These difficulties may be overcome somewhat by imposing a hierarchical structure on the classes. The samples are divided into a small number of classes, each class is divided further, and so on. Under this strategy, we need not find every possible dichotomy of the entire collection of samples.

At this point, we depart from general discussion of the clustering algorithm. Obviously, the discussion is incomplete. We have a basis, however, to develop and implement clustering procedures. Therefore, let us turn our attention to the detailed derivations of clustering procedures.

Nearest Mean Reclassification Algorithm [2-5]

In this section, we will discuss clustering procedures based on parameters such as mean vectors and covariance matrices. We will show that the criteria of class separability discussed in Chapter 10 play an important role, and that the iterative algorithms of the previous section take on simple forms.

Criteria: Clustering can be considered as a technique to group samples so as to maximize class separability. Then, all of the criteria which were discussed in Chapter 10 may be used as clustering criteria. In this section only functions of scatter matrices are discussed due to the following reasons:

(1) The extension to multiclass problems is straightforward. In this respect, the Bhattacharyya distance has a severe disadvantage, since it can be applied only to two-class problems.

(2) Most clustering techniques are based on the scatter of mean vectors. Finding clusters based on covariance-differences is extremely difficult, unless some mathematical structure is imposed on the distribution. Therefore, the functions of scatter matrices fit well to clustering problems.

(3) The simplicity of the criteria is a significant advantage, because in clustering we have the additional complexity of unknown class assignment.

For feature extraction, we could choose any combination of S_b, S_w, and S_m as S_1 and S_2 to form a criterion $J = \text{tr}(S_2^{-1} S_1)$. However, for clustering it is preferable to use S_m as S_2, because S_m is independent of class assignment. It would be too complicated if we had to recompute the inverse of S_2 each time the class assignment was altered in iteration. Therefore, our choice is limited to either $\text{tr}(S_m^{-1} S_b)$ or $\text{tr}(S_m^{-1} S_w)$. These two criteria are the same, because $\text{tr}(S_m^{-1} S_b) = \text{tr}\{S_m^{-1}(S_m - S_w)\} = n - \text{tr}(S_m^{-1} S_w)$. In this chapter, we will use $J = \text{tr}(S_m^{-1} S_w)$.

Another important consideration in selecting criteria for clustering is to ensure that the clustering procedures give the same classification for a given set of samples regardless of the coordinate system of these samples. The chosen criterion, $J = \text{tr}(S_m^{-1} S_w)$, satisfies this condition, since the criterion is invariant under any nonsingular linear transformation.

Clustering algorithm: Let us assume that $M_0 = 0$ and $S_m = I$ without losing generality. If the given samples do not satisfy these conditions, we can shift the coordinate origin and whiten the data with respect to S_m. Then, using (10.1) the criterion is rewritten as

$$J = \mathrm{tr}\, S_w = \sum_{r=1}^{L} \frac{N_r}{N} \frac{1}{N_r} \sum_{j=1}^{N_r} (X_j^{(r)} - M_r)^T (X_j^{(r)} - M_r)$$

$$= \frac{1}{N} \sum_{r=1}^{L} \sum_{j=1}^{N_r} \| X_j^{(r)} - M_r \|^2 . \tag{11.11}$$

Changing the class assignment of X_i from the current class k_i to class j at the ℓth iteration, we delete from (11.11) the term $\|X_i - M_{k_i}(\ell)\|^2$ and insert a new term $\|X_i - M_j(\ell)\|^2$. Thus,

$$\Delta J(i,j,\ell) = \frac{1}{N} \{ \|X_i - M_j(\ell)\|^2 - \|X_i - M_{k_i}(\ell)\|^2 \} . \tag{11.12}$$

Since the second term of (11.12) is independent of j, the reclassification of X_i at the ℓth iteration can be carried out by

$$\|X_i - M_t(\ell)\| = \min_j \|X_i - M_j(\ell)\| \quad \rightarrow \quad X \in \omega_t . \tag{11.13}$$

In words, the algorithm becomes:

(1) Choose an initial classification, $\Omega(0)$, and calculate $M_1(0), \ldots, M_L(0)$.

(2) Having calculated sample mean vectors $M_1(\ell), \ldots, M_L(\ell)$ at the ℓth iteration, reclassify each X_i according to the nearest $M_j(\ell)$.

(3) If the classification of any X_i is changed, calculate the new sample mean vectors $M_1(\ell+1), \ldots, M_L(\ell+1)$ for the new class assignment, and repeat from Step (2). Otherwise, stop.

This algorithm is called the *nearest mean reclassification rule.*

Figure 11-3 shows how the iterative process works. At the ℓth step, samples are divided to three clusters, and their sample means, $M_i(\ell)$'s, are computed. All samples are now reclassified according to the nearest means. That is, the new boundary is piecewise linear, bisecting each pair of $M_i(\ell)$'s. In Fig. 11-3, there are three clearly separated clusters. We can see that the boundary is indeed improved by this operation.

From the above discussion, some properties of the nearest mean reclassification algorithm become evident. They are:

(1) Clusters are divided by piecewise linear bisectors. Only the means contribute to determine the boundary and covariance matrices do not affect the boundary.

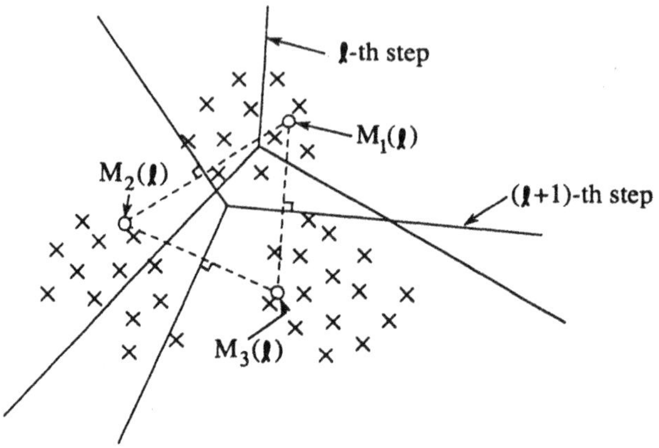

Fig. 11-3 An example of the nearest mean reclassification algorithm.

(2) The number of clusters must be preassigned.

(3) The initial classification, $\Omega(0)$, may be given randomly. No matter how $\Omega(0)$ is given, the $M_i(0)$'s are computed and the reclassification of samples according to the nearest $M_i(0)$'s results in a piecewise linear boundary. This is equivalent to selecting the number of vectors, $M_i(0)$'s, initially according to the number of clusters. Random class assignment does not impose any extra instability on the algorithm.

In order to verify the algorithm, the following experiment was conducted.

Experiment 1: One hundred samples were generated from each of Data *I*-Λ, and mixed together to form 200 samples. Then, these samples were classified to two clusters. Table 11-1 shows the *confusion matrix* of this experiment [5]. All 100 samples from ω_1 with 19 samples from ω_2 were assigned to one cluster, and 81 samples from ω_2 are assigned to the other cluster. The error rate is 19/200 = 0.095. Recall that we got 5% error for this data by designing the optimum linear classifier in Chapter 4. Considering the fact that any covariance information was not used in this clustering algorithm, the error rate of 9.5% is reasonable. Furthermore, since all error samples came from one class, we could improve the error rate simply by adjusting the decision threshold.

Convergence [5]: The nearest mean reclassification algorithm is not guaranteed to converge. In this section, we will discuss the conditions under

TABLE 11-1

CONFUSION MATRIX FOR THE NEAREST MEAN RECLASSIFICATION ALGORITHM

		Assigned class	
		1	2
Actual class	1	100	0
	2	19	81

which the separating hyperplane converges for two normal distributions with equal covariance matrices.

Let us assume that two normal distributions are $N_X(M_1,\Sigma_1)$ and $N_X(M_2,\Sigma_2)$ after normalization and that $\Sigma_1 = \Sigma_2 = \Sigma$. The normalization makes $S_m = I$ and $M_0 = 0$. The Bayes classifier in this case becomes linear as

$$(M_2 - M_1)^T \Sigma^{-1} X + c = 0 , \tag{11.14}$$

where c is a constant. Since $S_m = I = \Sigma + P_1 M_1 M_1^T + P_2 M_2 M_2^T$ and $M_0 = 0 = P_1 M_1 + P_2 M_2$,

$$\Sigma = I - P_1 M_1 M_1^T - P_2 M_2 M_2^T = I - \frac{P_2}{P_1} M_2 M_2^T , \tag{11.15}$$

$$M_2 - M_1 = \frac{1}{P_1} M_2 . \tag{11.16}$$

Using (2.160),

$$\Sigma^{-1} = I + \frac{\dfrac{P_2}{P_1} M_2 M_2^T}{1 - \dfrac{P_2}{P_1} M_2^T M_2} . \tag{11.17}$$

Substituting (11.16) and (11.17) into (11.14), the Bayes classifier is

$$\frac{1}{P_1 - P_2 M_2^T M_2} M_2^T X + c = 0 . \tag{11.18}$$

Thus, the optimum hyperplane for the equal covariance case is always in the direction of M_2 which is the same as the mean-difference vector M_2-M_1. This property, which the original coordinate system does not have, is a significant advantage of the normalized coordinate system.

For the equal covariance case, we can show that the algorithm converges to M_2-M_1 from a wide range of initial classifications. After a given iteration, samples are separated by a hyperplane whose direction is, say V ($\|V\| = 1$), as shown in Fig. 11-4. Also, the position of the hyperplane is specified by ℓ_1 and

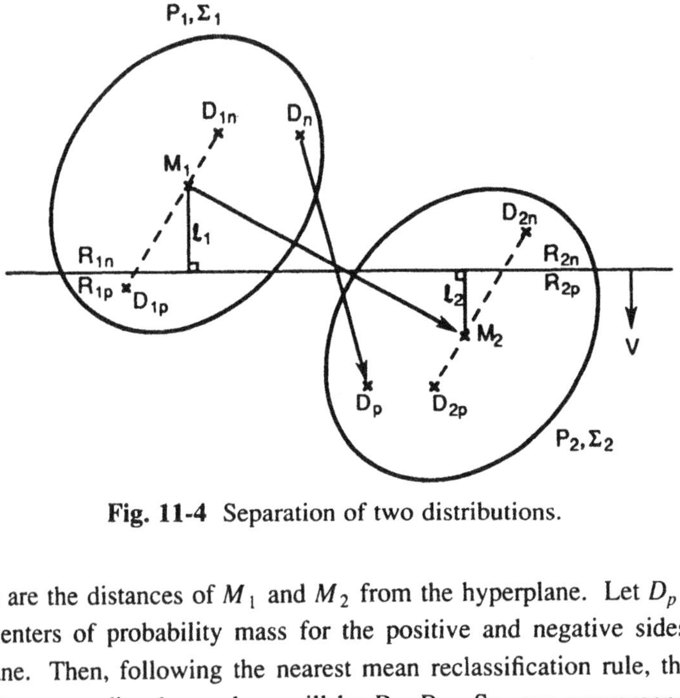

Fig. 11-4 Separation of two distributions.

ℓ_2 which are the distances of M_1 and M_2 from the hyperplane. Let D_p and D_n be the centers of probability mass for the positive and negative sides of the hyperplane. Then, following the nearest mean reclassification rule, the direction of the succeeding hyperplane will be D_p-D_n. So, our convergence proof is to show that the angle between D_p-D_n and M_2-M_1 is smaller than the angle between V and M_2-M_1.

Since the hyperplane separates each distribution into two parts, the positive and negative sides, we have four probability masses R_{ij} ($i = 1,2;\ j = p,n$), as shown in Fig. 11-4. Let D_{ij} and q_{ij} be the mean vectors and populations of these probability masses. Then,

$$D_{ip} = M_i + \frac{a_i}{\sigma_i b_i} \Sigma_i V \ , \tag{11.19}$$

$$D_{in} = M_i - \frac{a_i}{\sigma_i (1-b_i)} \Sigma_i V \ , \tag{11.20}$$

$$q_{ip} = P_i b_i \ , \tag{11.21}$$

$$q_{in} = P_i (1-b_i) \ , \tag{11.22}$$

where

$$a_i = \frac{1}{\sqrt{2\pi}} \int_{\pm \ell_i/\sigma_i}^{\infty} \zeta \exp[-\frac{1}{2}\zeta^2] d\zeta = \frac{1}{\sqrt{2\pi}} \exp[-\frac{1}{2} \left(\frac{\ell_i}{\sigma_i} \right)^2] \ , \tag{11.23}$$

$$b_i = \frac{1}{\sqrt{2\pi}} \int_{\pm \ell_i/\sigma_i}^{\infty} \exp[-\frac{1}{2}\zeta^2] d\zeta = 1 - \Phi \left(\pm \frac{\ell_i}{\sigma_i} \right) \ , \tag{11.24}$$

$$\sigma_i^2 = V^T \Sigma_i V \ , \tag{11.25}$$

and Φ is the normal error function. The sign + or − is selected, depending on whether M_i is located in R_{in} or R_{ip}. The details of the derivation of (11.19) through (11.25) are left to the reader. However, the following information could be helpful in deriving (11.19) through (11.25). Since $\mathbf{X}$ is normal, $\mathbf{y} = V^T \mathbf{X}$ is also normal with the variance of (11.25). In the y-space, the probability of mass for the positive side, b_i, can be computed by (11.24). The vector $D_{ij} - M_i$ has the direction of $\Sigma_i V$, and the projections of $D_{ij} - M_i$ on V $(j = p,n)$ are $V^T(D_{ip} - M_i) = a_i \sigma_i / b_i$ and $V^T(D_{in} - M_i) = -a_i \sigma_i / (1-b_i)$. These are obtained by computing the expected values of $\mathbf{y}$ for the positive and negative sides. From D_{ij} and q_{ij}, D_p and D_n are obtained as

$$D_p = \frac{q_{1p} D_{1p} + q_{2p} D_{2p}}{q_{1p} + q_{2p}} \ , \tag{11.26}$$

$$D_n = \frac{q_{1n} D_{1n} + q_{2n} D_{2n}}{q_{1n} + q_{2n}} \ . \tag{11.27}$$

Substituting (11.19) through (11.22) into (11.26) and (11.27),

$$D_p - D_n = \frac{P_1 P_2 (b_1 - b_2)(M_1 - M_2) + \{P_1 (a_1/\sigma_1)\Sigma_1 + P_2 (a_2/\sigma_2)\Sigma_2\} V}{(P_1 b_1 + P_2 b_2)\{1 - (P_1 b_1 + P_2 b_2)\}} . \tag{11.28}$$

For the equal covariance case,

$$\Sigma_1 = \Sigma_2 = \Sigma \quad \text{and} \quad \sigma_1 = \sigma_2 = \sigma . \tag{11.29}$$

Furthermore, under the normalization of $S_m = I$ and $M_0 = 0$, Σ and $M_2 - M_1$ are expressed as functions of M_2 as in (11.15) and (11.16). Therefore, (11.28) becomes

$$D_p - D_n = c_1 M_2 + c_2 V , \tag{11.30}$$

where

$$c_1 = \frac{P_2 (b_2 - b_1) - (1/\sigma)(P_2/P_1)(P_1 a_1 + P_2 a_2) M_2^T V}{(P_1 b_1 + P_2 b_2)\{1 - (P_1 b_1 + P_2 b_2)\}} , \tag{11.31}$$

$$c_2 = \frac{(1/\sigma)(P_1 a_1 + P_2 a_2)}{(P_1 b_1 + P_2 b_2)\{1 - (P_1 b_1 + P_2 b_2)\}} . \tag{11.32}$$

The normal of the new hyperplane has a component in the direction of V and another in the direction of M_2. If the coefficient of M_2, c_1, has the same sign as $M_2^T V$, the successive hyperplane becomes more nearly parallel to M_2. Since c_2 and the denominator of c_1 are positive, we need to show that the numerator of c_1 and $M_2^T V$ have the same sign. We examine only the case where $M_2^T V > 0$. The discussion for $M_2^T V < 0$ is similar to the one for $M_2^T V > 0$. For $M_2^T V > 0$, we see from Fig. 11-4 that

$$\ell_1 + \ell_2 = (M_2 - M_1)^T V = \frac{1}{P_1} M_2^T V . \tag{11.33}$$

Using (11.33), the condition for convergence becomes

$$b_2 - b_1 > \frac{\ell_1 + \ell_2}{\sigma} (P_1 a_1 + P_2 a_2) . \tag{11.34}$$

It is easily seen that the inequality of (11.34) is not satisfied for certain combinations of parameters. However, the region of parameters where (11.34) is satisfied can be calculated numerically. The result is shown in Fig. 11-5.

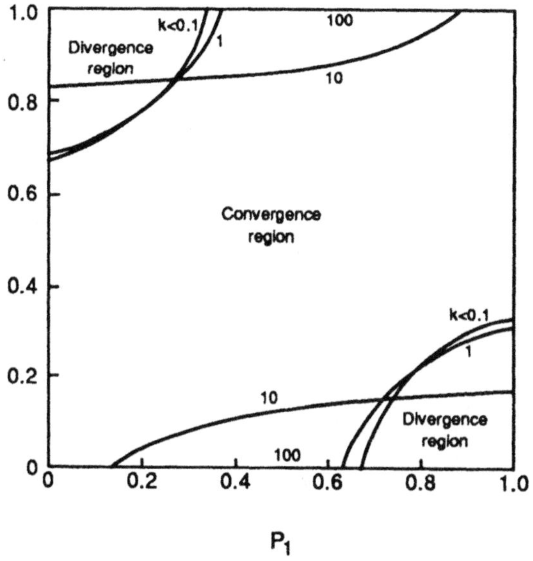

Fig. 11-5 Region of convergence.

Equations (11.23) and (11.24) with (11.34) show that we have three parameters in (11.34), ℓ_1/σ, ℓ_2/σ, and P_1 ($P_2 = 1 - P_1$), or

$$k = \frac{\ell_1 + \ell_2}{\sigma}, \quad \gamma = \frac{\ell_1}{\ell_1 + \ell_2}, \quad \text{and} \quad P_1 . \tag{11.35}$$

In Fig. 11-5, the convergence regions of γ and P_1 are plotted for various values of k [5]. The figure shows that convergence is quite likely in practice, except for either extreme P_1's or γ's.

Branch and bound procedure [6]: The nearest mean reclassification algorithm works fine for many applications. However, there is no guarantee of the convergence of the iterative process. Also, the process might stop at a locally minimum point and fail to find the globally minimum point.

Since assigning a class to each sample is a combinatorial problem, the *branch and bound procedure* discussed in Chapter 10 may be applied to find the optimum class assignment.

Figure 11-6 shows a solution tree for the clustering problem with four samples and three clusters. In general, there are L^N different Ω's for classify-

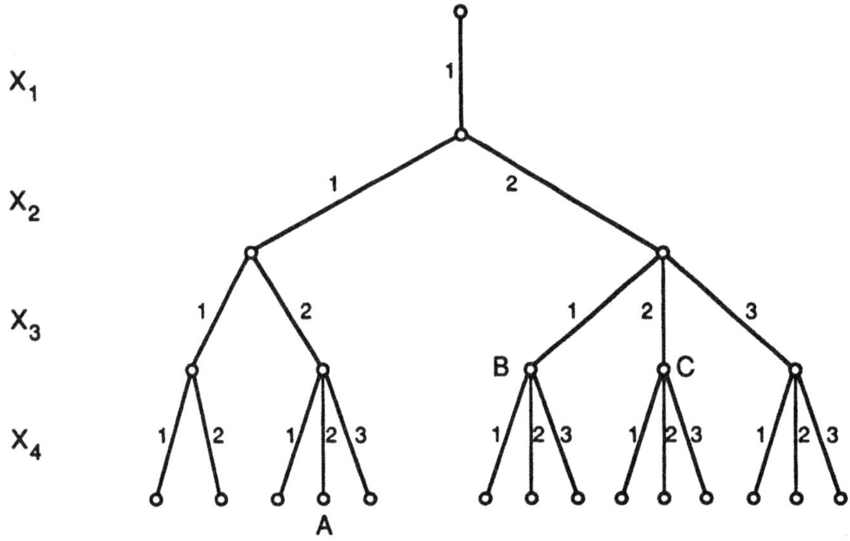

Fig. 11-6 A solution tree for clustering.

ing N sample vectors into L clusters. However, since the label of each cluster may be chosen arbitrarily, each classification could have several different expressions for Ω. For example, $\Omega = [1\ 1\ 2\ 2]$ and $\Omega = [2\ 2\ 3\ 3]$ are the same classification, both indicating that X_1 and X_2 are in one cluster and X_3 and X_4 are in one of the other clusters. In order to eliminate this duplication, we assign the first sample X_1 to cluster 1, the second sample X_2 to either cluster 1 or 2, and so on, as shown in Fig. 11-6.

In order for the branch and bound procedure to work effectively, we need to have a criterion which satisfies the *monotonicity condition*. Let $J_m(\Omega_m)$ be the criterion to be minimized for $\Omega_m = [\omega_{k_1} \ldots \omega_{k_m}]$, where the subscript m indicates the number of sample vectors involved. Then, the monotonicity condition is stated as

$$J_{m+1}(\Omega_m, \omega_{k_{m+1}}) \geq J_m(\Omega_m) . \tag{11.36}$$

That is, the J of a node is smaller than the J's for all nodes which are successors of the node.

Let α be the value of J_N which is the current smallest among all cases tested so far for the classification of N samples (for example, $\alpha = J(A)$). Then, the branch and bound procedure checks at each node (for example, at B) whether or not the following inequality is satisfied

$$J_m(\Omega_m) \geq \alpha \ . \tag{11.37}$$

If yes, then from (11.36), all successors of this node have J's larger than α. It means that the optimum classification does not exist in the subtree under the node. Thus, the subtree is rejected without further tests, and the search back-tracks to the next node (for example, C). This elimination of subtrees makes the branch and bound procedure a very efficient tree search technique. When (11.37) is not satisfied, the search moves down to a node in the next level. The node selected for the next evaluation is determined by

$$J_{m+1}(\Omega_m, t) = \min_{\ell} J_{m+1}(\Omega_m, \ell) \ . \tag{11.38}$$

That is, X_{m+1} is assigned to cluster t, and the search goes on.

The criterion $J = \text{tr}(S_m^{-1} S_w)$ satisfies the monotonicity condition with a minor modification. Again, assuming $S_m = I$, (11.11) is the criterion to be minimized. Since the number of samples is determined by the level of the solution tree and is independent of Ω, let us delete it from the criterion and rewrite the criterion for m samples, $X_1, \ldots, X_m$, as

$$J_m(\Omega_m) = \sum_{r=1}^{L} \sum_{j=1}^{m_r} \| X_j^{(r)} - M_r \|^2 \ , \tag{11.39}$$

where m_r is the number of ω_r-samples among $X_1, \ldots, X_m$. When X_{m+1} is added into cluster ℓ, M_ℓ must be modified to M'_ℓ, including the effect of X_{m+1}, and $\| X_{m+1} - M'_\ell \|^2$ must be added to the summation. Thus,

$$J_{m+1}(\Omega_m, \ell) = J_m(\Omega_m) + \Delta J(\ell) \ , \tag{11.40}$$

where

$$\Delta J(\ell) = \| X_{m+1} - M'_\ell \|^2 + \sum_{j=1}^{m_\ell} \{ \| X_j^{(\ell)} - M'_\ell \|^2 - \| X_j^{(\ell)} - M_\ell \|^2 \} \ . \tag{11.41}$$

The new ℓ-class mean, M'_ℓ, can be obtained as

$$\begin{aligned} M'_\ell &= \frac{1}{m_\ell + 1} \left(\sum_{j=1}^{m_\ell} X_j^{(\ell)} + X_{m+1} \right) \\ &= M_\ell + \frac{1}{m_\ell + 1} (X_{m+1} - M_\ell) \ , \end{aligned} \tag{11.42}$$

or

$$X_j^{(\ell)} - M_\ell' = (X_j^{(\ell)} - M_\ell) - \frac{1}{m_\ell + 1}(X_{m+1} - M_\ell) . \tag{11.43}$$

Substituting (11.43) into (11.41) and using $M_\ell = (1/m_\ell)\Sigma_{j=1}^{m_\ell} X_j^{(\ell)}$,

$$\Delta J(\ell) = \frac{m_\ell}{m_\ell + 1}\|X_{m+1} - M_\ell\|^2 \geq 0 . \tag{11.44}$$

Since $\Delta J(\ell) \geq 0$, from (11.40) the criterion has the monotonicity property.

Note that (11.40), (11.44), and (11.42) provide recursive equations for computing $J_{m+1}(\Omega_m,\ell)$ and M_ℓ' from $J_m(\Omega_m)$, M_ℓ, and X_{m+1}. Also, (11.38), (11.40), and (11.44) indicate that the selection of the next node can be made by minimizing $\Delta J(\ell)$ with respect to ℓ.

For a large N, the number of nodes is huge. Thus, the initial selection of α becomes critical. One way of selecting a reasonably low initial α is to apply the iterative nearest mean reclassification algorithm to get a suboptimal solution and use the resulting criterion value as the initial α. The branch and bound procedure gives the final solution which is guaranteed to be optimum globally.

Also, it is possible to make the procedure more efficient by reordering the samples [6].

Normal Decomposition

Piecewise quadratic boundary: The nearest mean reclassification rule can be extended to include more complex boundaries such as quadratic ones. Following the same iterative process, the algorithm would be stated as follows:

(1) Choose an initial classification, $\Omega(0)$, and calculate $P_i(0)$, $M_i(0)$ and $\Sigma_i(0)$ $(i = 1, \ldots, L)$.

(2) Having calculated class probabilities, $P_i(\ell)$, and sample means and covariance matrices, $M_i(\ell)$ and $\Sigma_i(\ell)$, at the ℓth iteration, reclassify each X_j according to the smallest $(1/2)(X_j-M_i)^T \Sigma_i^{-1}(X_j-M_i)+(1/2)\ln|\Sigma_i|-\ln P_i$. The class probability for ω_i is estimated by the number of ω_i-samples divided by the total number of samples.

(3) If the classification of any X_j is changed, calculate the $P_i(\ell+1)$, $M_i(\ell+1)$ and $\Sigma_i(\ell+1)$ for the new class assignment, and repeat from Step (2).

Otherwise stop.

This process is identical to the nearest mean reclassification algorithm, but results in a piecewise quadratic boundary. Also, since the estimation of the covariance matrices is involved, the process is more computer-time consuming and more sensitive to parameters such as sample size, dimensionality, distributions, and so on.

More fundamentally, the clustering techniques mentioned above may have a serious shortcoming, particularly when a mixture distribution consists of several overlapping distributions. An important goal of finding clusters is to decompose a complex distribution into several normal-like distributions. If we could approximate a complex distribution by the summation of several normal distributions, it would be much easier to discuss all aspects of pattern recognition, including feature extraction, classifier design, and so on. However, the clustering procedures discussed above decompose a mixture as in Fig. 11-7(b) rather than as in Fig. 11-7(a). The hatched distribution of cluster 1 in Fig. 11-7(b) includes the tail of the ω_2-distribution and does not include the tail of the ω_1-distribution. As a result, the mean and covariance matrix of the hatched distribution in Fig. 11-7(b) could be significantly different from the ones for the hatched distribution of Fig. 11-7(a). Thus, the representation of a complex distribution by the parameters obtained from the clustering procedures described above could be very poor.

Decomposition of a distribution into a number of normal distributions has been studied extensively [7]. The two most common approaches are the *method of moments* and *maximum likelihood estimation*. In the former method, the parameters of normal distributions are estimated from the higher order moments of the mixture distribution (for example, the third and fourth order moments [8]). This approach is complex and not very reliable for high-dimensional cases. Therefore, in this chapter, only the latter approach is presented in detail.

Maximum likelihood estimate [9-10]: In order to obtain the hatched distribution of Fig. 11-7(a) from $p(X)$, it is necessary to impose a mathematical structure. Let us assume that $p(X)$ consists of L normal distributions as

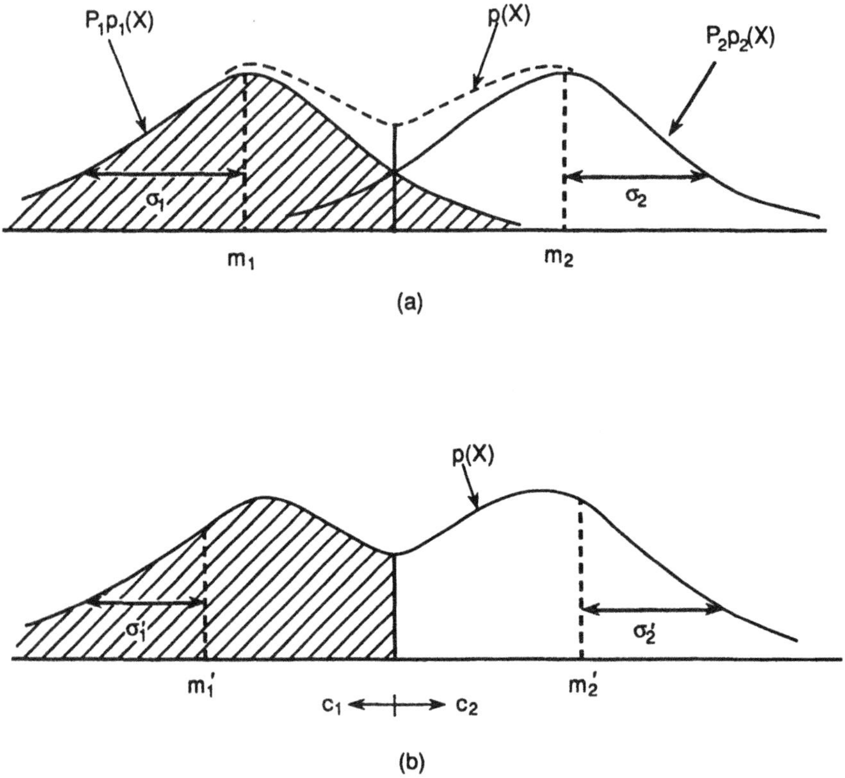

Fig. 11-7 An example of the shortcoming of the clustering technique.

$$p(X) = \sum_{i=1}^{L} P_i p_i(X) \, , \tag{11.45}$$

where $p_i(X)$ is normal with the expected vector M_i and covariance matrix Σ_i. Under this assumption, our problem is to estimate P_i, M_i, and Σ_i from N available samples, $X_1, \ldots, X_N$, drawn from $p(X)$. One way of solving this problem is to apply the *maximum likelihood estimation* technique. The maximum likelihood estimates may be obtained by maximizing $\Pi_{j=1}^{N} p(X_j)$ with respect to P_i, M_i, and Σ_i under a constraint $\Sigma_{i=1}^{L} P_i = 1$. Taking the logarithm of $\Pi_{j=1}^{N} p(X_j)$, the criterion to be maximized is

$$J = \sum_{j=1}^{N} \ln p(X_j) - \mu(\sum_{i=1}^{L} P_i - 1) \, , \tag{11.46}$$

where μ is a Lagrange multiplier.

First, computing the derivative of J with respect to P_i,

$$\frac{\partial J}{\partial P_i} = \sum_{j=1}^{N} \frac{p_i(X_j)}{p(X_j)} - \mu = \frac{1}{P_i} \sum_{j=1}^{N} q_i(X_j) - \mu = 0 \,, \tag{11.47}$$

where $q_i(X) = P_i p_i(X)/p(X)$ is the a posteriori probability of ω_i, and satisfies $\Sigma_{i=1}^{L} q_i(X) = 1$. Since $\Sigma_{i=1}^{L} P_i(\partial J/\partial P_i) = \Sigma_{j=1}^{N}(\Sigma_{i=1}^{L} q_i(X_j)) - (\Sigma_{i=1}^{L} P_i)\mu = N - \mu = 0$,

$$\mu = N \,, \tag{11.48}$$

and from (11.47)

$$P_i = \frac{1}{N} \sum_{j=1}^{N} q_i(X_j) \,. \tag{11.49}$$

Next, the derivative of J with respect to M_i can be computed as

$$\frac{\partial J}{\partial M_i} = \sum_{j=1}^{N} \frac{P_i}{p(X_j)} \frac{\partial p_i(X_j)}{\partial M_i} = \sum_{j=1}^{N} q_i(X_j) \Sigma_i^{-1} (X_j - M_i) = 0 \,. \tag{11.50}$$

Using $\Sigma_{j=1}^{N} q_i(X_j) = N P_i = N_i$ where N_i is the number of ω_i-samples, (11.50) can be solved for M_i, resulting in

$$M_i = \frac{1}{N_i} \sum_{j=1}^{N} q_i(X_j) X_j \,. \tag{11.51}$$

At last, the derivative of J with respect to Σ_i is, from (A.9) and (A.23),

$$\begin{aligned} \frac{\partial J}{\partial \Sigma_i} &= \sum_{j=1}^{N} \frac{P_i}{p(X_j)} \frac{\partial p_i(X_j)}{\partial \Sigma_i} \\ &= \sum_{j=1}^{N} q_i(X_j) [\Sigma_i^{-1} (X_j - M_i)(X_j - M_i)^T \Sigma_i^{-1} - \Sigma_i^{-1} \\ &\quad - \frac{1}{2} \text{diag}[\Sigma_i^{-1} (X_j - M_i)(X_j - M_i)^T \Sigma_i^{-1} - \Sigma_i^{-1}]] = 0, \end{aligned} \tag{11.52}$$

where diag$[A]$ is a diagonal matrix, keeping only the diagonal terms of A. Equation (11.52) can be solved for Σ_i yielding

$$\Sigma_i = \frac{1}{N_i} \sum_{j=1}^{N} q_i(X_j)(X_j - M_i)(X_j - M_i)^T \,. \tag{11.53}$$

By solving (11.49), (11.51), and (11.53), we can obtain the optimum solution. However, since $q_i(X)$ is a function of P_k, M_k, and Σ_k ($k = 1, \ldots, L$), it is very difficult to obtain the solution explicitly. Therefore, we must solve these equations iteratively. The process can be described as follows.

(1) Choose an initial classification, $\Omega(0)$, and calculate P_i, M_i, and Σ_i ($i = 1, \ldots, L$).

(2) Having calculated $P_i^{(\ell)}$, $M_i^{(\ell)}$, and $q_i^{(\ell)}(X_j)$, compute $P_i^{(\ell+1)}$, $M_i^{(\ell+1)}$, and $\Sigma_i^{(\ell+1)}$ by (11.49), (11.51), and (11.53), respectively. The new $q_i^{(\ell+1)}(X_j)$ can be calculated as

$$q_i^{(\ell+1)}(X_j) = \frac{P_i^{(\ell+1)} p_i^{(\ell+1)}(X_j)}{\sum_{k=1}^{L} P_k^{(\ell+1)} p_k^{(\ell+1)}(X_j)} , \tag{11.54}$$

where the superscript indicates the (ℓ+1)st iteration, and $p_i^{(\ell+1)}(X)$ is a normal density function with mean $M_i^{(\ell+1)}$ and covariance matrix $\Sigma_i^{(\ell+1)}$. Note that each sample X_j carries L probability values $q_1(X_j), \ldots, q_L(X_j)$ instead of being assigned to one of the L classes.

(3) When $q_i^{(\ell+1)}(X_j) = q_i^{(\ell)}(X_j)$ for all $i = 1, \ldots, L$ and $j = 1, \ldots, N$, then stop. Otherwise, increase ℓ by 1 and go to Step (2).

In the maximum likelihood estimation technique, the criterion (the first term of (11.46)) may be used to determine the number of clusters. The maximized criterion value, J_L, is obtained for a given L, and the procedure is repeated for various values of L. The criterion J_L tends to increase with increasing L, and reach a flat plateau at L_0. This means that, even if we use more normal distributions than L_0, the mixture distribution cannot be better approximated. Therefore, L_0 is the proper number of clusters to use in approximating the mixture distribution.

In order to verify the procedure, the following two experiments were run.

Experiment 2: One hundred samples per class were generated from two-dimensional normal distributions specified by

$$M_1 = M_2 = \begin{bmatrix} 0 \\ 0 \end{bmatrix} , \quad \Sigma_1 = \begin{bmatrix} 1 & -0.7 \\ -0.7 & 1 \end{bmatrix} , \quad \text{and} \quad \Sigma_2 = \begin{bmatrix} 1 & 0.7 \\ 0.7 & 1 \end{bmatrix} . \tag{11.55}$$

The sample means and covariance matrices of the generated samples were

$$\hat{M}_1 = \begin{bmatrix} -0.06 \\ 0.21 \end{bmatrix}, \quad \hat{\Sigma}_1 = \begin{bmatrix} 0.91 & -0.65 \\ -0.65 & 1.17 \end{bmatrix},$$

$$\hat{M}_2 = \begin{bmatrix} 0.11 \\ 0.19 \end{bmatrix}, \quad \hat{\Sigma}_2 = \begin{bmatrix} 1.03 & 0.62 \\ 0.62 & 0.81 \end{bmatrix}. \tag{11.56}$$

These two hundred samples were mixed, and initially assigned to either ω_1 or ω_2 depending on $x_2 \geq 0$ or $x_2 < 0$ (x_2 is the second variable). After 10 iterations, the parameters became

$$\hat{P}_1 = 0.61 \ , \quad \hat{P}_2 = 0.39 \ ,$$

$$\hat{M}_1 = \begin{bmatrix} 0.07 \\ 0.36 \end{bmatrix}, \quad \hat{\Sigma}_1 = \begin{bmatrix} 0.87 & -0.47 \\ -0.47 & 1.04 \end{bmatrix},$$

$$\hat{M}_2 = \begin{bmatrix} -0.04 \\ -0.06 \end{bmatrix}, \quad \hat{\Sigma}_2 = \begin{bmatrix} 1.12 & 0.66 \\ 0.66 & 0.78 \end{bmatrix}. \tag{11.57}$$

Note that the two distributions share the same mean and are heavily overlapped. This means that finding clusters must be very difficult. Despite the expected difficulty, the procedure found two reasonable clusters successfully. Without imposing the mathematical structure of (11.45), no other clustering technique works properly for this example.

Experiment 3: One hundred samples per class were generated from 8-dimensional normal distributions of Data I-Λ, and initially assigned to either ω_1 or ω_2 depending on $x_8 \leq 0$ or $x_8 > 0$ (x_8 is the eighth variable). After 20 iterations, samples were classified to either ω_1 or ω_2, depending on whether $q_1(X) > q_2(X)$ or $q_1(X) < q_2(X)$. Table 11-2 shows the resulting confusion matrix. This error of 2.5% is very close to the Bayes error of 1.9%, and is much better than the 9.5% error of the nearest mean reclassification algorithm [see Table 11-1].

In order to confirm that the mixture distribution was properly decomposed into two normal distributions, a quadratic classifier was designed based on P_i, M_i, and Σ_i obtained from the two clusters. Independently, 100 samples per class were generated according to Data I-Λ, and classified by the quadratic classifier. The resulting error was 2.5%. Considering the fact that the holdout method (design and test samples are selected independently) always produces an error larger than the Bayes error, the designed classifier was very closed to the Bayes.

TABLE 11-2

CONFUSION MATRIX FOR THE MAXIMUM LIKELIHOOD ESTIMATION ALGORITHM

		Assigned class	
		1	2
Actual class	1	98	2
	2	3	97

In order to determine the proper number of clusters, the experiment was repeated for various values of L. For a given L, P_i and $p_i(X)$ $(i = 1, \ldots L)$ of (11.45) were estimated, and subsequently the first term of (11.46), $J = \Sigma_{j=1}^{N} \ln p(X_j)$, was computed. Figure 11-8 shows J/N vs. L. The curves are flat for $L \geq 2$ and $N = 400, 800$, indicating that two normal distributions are adequate to represent this data. The number of samples assigned to each cluster is N/L on the average. Therefore, when N/L becomes smaller (for example $N/L = 50$ for $N = 200$ and $L = 4$), each cluster may not have an adequate sample size to estimate the covariance matrix properly. This is the reason that the curve decreases as L increases for $N = 200$ in Fig. 11-8.

So far, we have presented the recursive equations to estimate a priori probabilities, mean vectors, and covariance matrices. However, in some applications, we can assume some of the parameter values or the relationship among the parameters as follows:

(1) all covariance matrices are equal [see Problem 2],

(2) all mean vectors are equal, or

(3) a priori probabilities are known [see Problem 3].

With the above conditions, the maximum likelihood estimation technique can be applied to estimate the remaining parameters. Because of the additional information, we can obtain a better estimate with faster convergence.

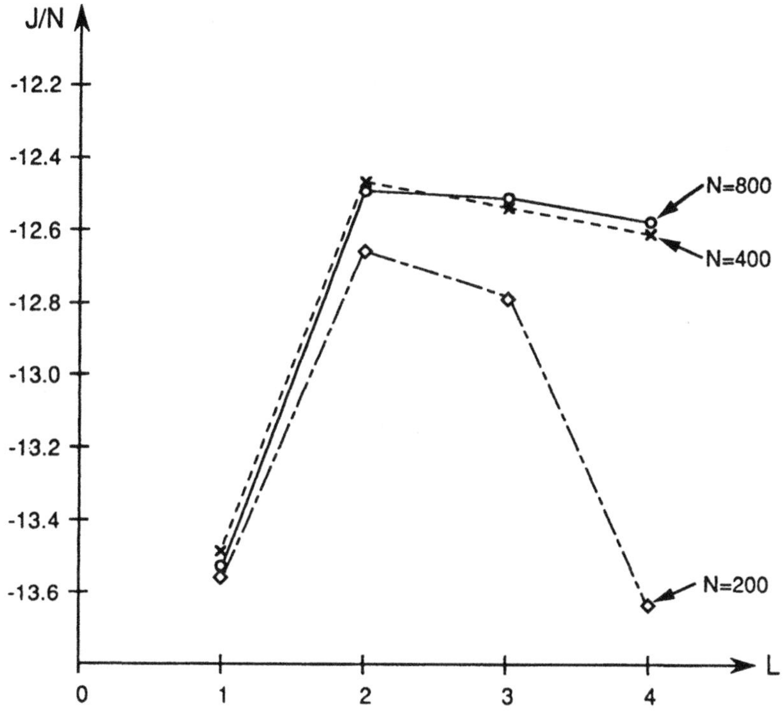

Fig. 11-8 Criterion value vs. L for Data I-Λ.

11.2 Nonparametric Clustering

When a mixture density function has peaks and valleys as shown in Fig. 11-9, it is most natural to divide the samples into clusters according to the valley. However, the valley may not have a parametric structure such as hyperplanes, quadratic surfaces, and so on. As discussed in the previous section, the parametric structure of the boundary comes from either the use of a parametric criterion or from the underlying assumption that the distribution consists of several normal distributions. For the distribution of Fig. 11-9, we cannot expect to get reasonable clusters by a parametric boundary.

In order to find the valley of a density function in a high-dimensional space, we need a nonparametric technique to characterize the local structure of the valley. There are many nonparametric clustering procedures available. However, most of them are implicitly or explicitly based on the estimate of the density gradient. In Fig. 11-9, if we estimate the gradient of the density func-

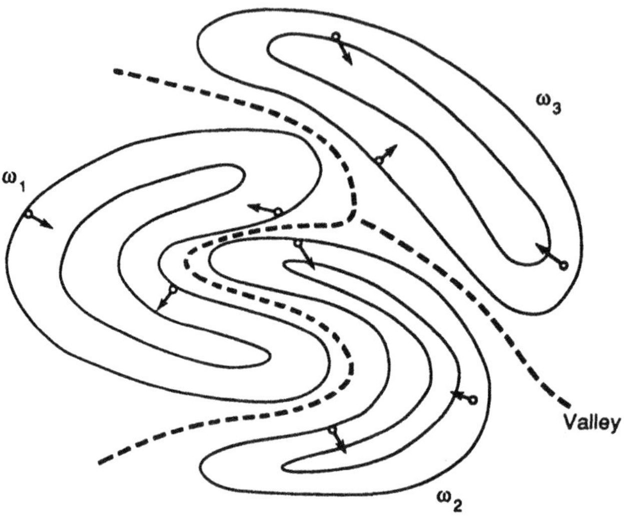

Fig. 11-9 Clusters separated by the valley.

tion at each existing sample point (as indicated by arrows) and move the sample toward the direction of the gradient, samples move away from the valley area. Repeating this process, the valley becomes wider at each iteration, and samples form compact clusters. This procedure is called the *valley-seeking* procedure.

Thus, the valley-seeking procedure consists of two problems: one is how to estimate the gradient of a density function, and the other is how to utilize the estimate to form clusters.

Estimation of Density Gradient

In this section, we develop the estimation technique of the density gradient, and discuss how to apply this technique to pattern recognition problems.

Estimation of density gradient [11]: In order to estimate the gradient of a density function at X, let us select an ellipsoidal local region $\Gamma(X)$ with radius r, specified by

$$\Gamma(X) = \{Y: d(Y,X) \le r\} \;, \tag{11.58}$$

where

$$d^2(Y,X) = (Y-X)^T A^{-1}(Y-X) \tag{11.59}$$

and A is the metric to measure the distance. The expected vector of $\mathbf{Y}$ in $\Gamma(X)$, which is called the *local mean*, can be computed as

$$M(X) = E\{(\mathbf{Y}-X)\mid\Gamma(X)\} = \int_{\Gamma(X)} (Y-X)\frac{p(Y)}{u_0}dY \,, \tag{11.60}$$

where

$$u_0 = \int_{\Gamma(X)} p(Y)dY \cong p(X)v \tag{11.61}$$

and v is the volume of $\Gamma(X)$. The term u_0 is the coverage of $\Gamma(X)$, and $p(Y)/u_0$ of (11.60) gives the conditional density function of $\mathbf{Y}$ given $\Gamma(X)$. Expanding $p(Y)$ around X by a Taylor series

$$p(Y) \cong p(X) + (Y-X)^T \nabla p(X) \,. \tag{11.62}$$

Substituting (11.61) and (11.62) into (11.60),

$$M(X) \cong \int_{\Gamma(X)} (Y-X)(Y-X)^T \frac{1}{v} dY \frac{\nabla p(X)}{p(X)} = \frac{r^2}{n+2} A \frac{\nabla p(X)}{p(X)} \tag{11.63}$$

or

$$\frac{\nabla p(X)}{p(X)} \cong \frac{n+2}{r^2} A^{-1} M(X) \,, \tag{11.64}$$

where the integration of (11.63) is obtained from (B.6). Equation (11.64) indicates that, by measuring the local mean $M(X)$ in $\Gamma(X)$, $\nabla p(X)/p(X)$ can be estimated. Particularly, the formula becomes simpler if the Euclidean metric $A = I$ is used.

The normalization of $\nabla p(X)$ by $p(X)$ has an advantage, particularly in clustering. In clustering, it is desirable that samples around the valley area have stronger signal as to which direction the gradients point. Since $p(X)$ is low at the valley, $\nabla p(X)$ is amplified by being divided by $p(X)$. On the other hand, at the peak area, $p(X)$ is high and $\nabla p(X)$ is depressed by being divided by $p(X)$.

Figure 11-10 illustrates how the local mean is related to the gradient of a density function. In $\Gamma(X)$, we tend to have more samples from the higher density side than from the lower density side. As a result, the sample mean of local samples generally points in the direction of the higher density side.

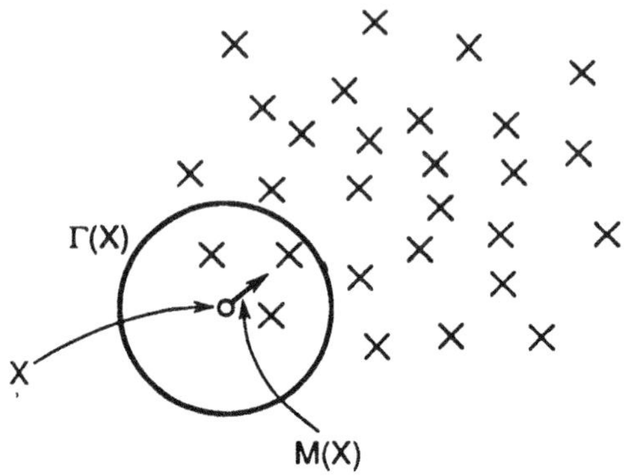

Fig. 11-10 Local mean as the gradient estimate.

The estimate of the density gradient can be applied to many pattern recognition problems besides clustering. They are briefly discussed as follows.

Gradient of $q_i(X)$: The Bayes classifier is the hypersurface on which X satisfies $q_1(X) = q_2(X) = 0.5$ for two-class problems. The vector perpendicular to this hypersurface at X is the gradient of $q_1(X)$, $\nabla q_1(X)$, which indicates the local linear classifier, classifying local samples Y around X as

$$\nabla q_1^T(X)(Y-X) \underset{\omega_2}{\overset{\omega_1}{\lessgtr}} 0 . \tag{11.65}$$

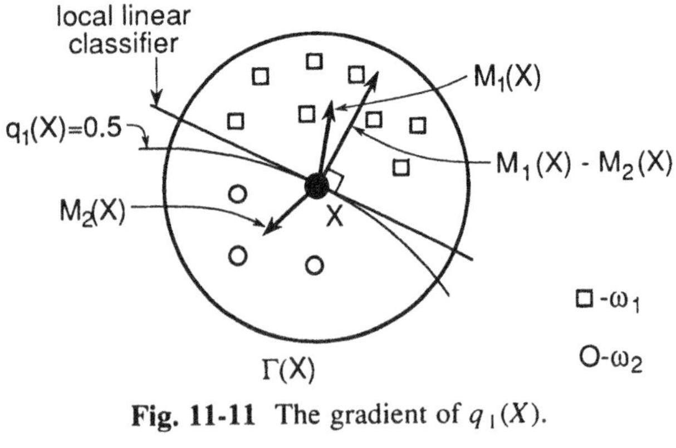

Fig. 11-11 The gradient of $q_1(X)$.

Figure 11-11 shows an example. Note that $\nabla q_2(X) = -\nabla q_1(X)$, since $q_1(X) + q_2(X) = 1$.

The gradient $\nabla q_1(X)$ can be estimated from the local means as

$$\nabla q_1(X) = \nabla\left[\frac{P_1 p_1(X)}{p(X)}\right]$$

$$= q_1(X) q_2(X)\left[\frac{\nabla p_1(X)}{p_1(X)} - \frac{\nabla p_2(X)}{p_2(X)}\right]$$

$$= \frac{n+2}{r^2} q_1(X) q_2(X)[M_1(X) - M_2(X)] , \tag{11.66}$$

where the Euclidean metric $A = I$ is used. Since $q_1(X)q_2(X)$ is a scalar, the direction of the vector $\nabla q_1(X)$ is determined by $M_1(X)-M_2(X)$, as shown in Fig. 11-11.

Normality test [12]: When $p(X)$ is normal with zero mean and covariance matrix I, $\nabla p(X)/p(X)$ can be obtained by differentiating $\ln p(X)$ with respect to X [see (B.11)], resulting in

$$\frac{\nabla p(X)}{p(X)} = -X . \tag{11.67}$$

Equation (11.67) suggests that, by adding the estimate of $\nabla p(X)/p(X)$ to X, the resulting vector should point toward the coordinate origin if **X** is normally distributed. This property can be used to test the normality of a given set of samples. The procedure is described as follows.

(1) Whiten the samples. After the whitening process, the samples have zero mean and covariance matrix I.

(2) Estimate $\nabla p(X)/p(X)$ by the local mean $M(X)$ of (11.60), and add it to X. Use $A = I$.

(3) The data passes the normality test by satisfying

$$\frac{1}{N}\sum_{i=1}^{N}\|X_i + \frac{n+2}{r^2}M(X_i)\|^2 < t , \tag{11.68}$$

where t is a threshold. Various properties of this test as well as the selection procedures of related parameters, including t, can be found in [12].

Data filter [11]: A data filter eliminates noise from a given set of samples and produces the *skeleton hypersurface*. The filter could be an effective tool for determining the intrinsic dimensionality of samples. Figure 11-12

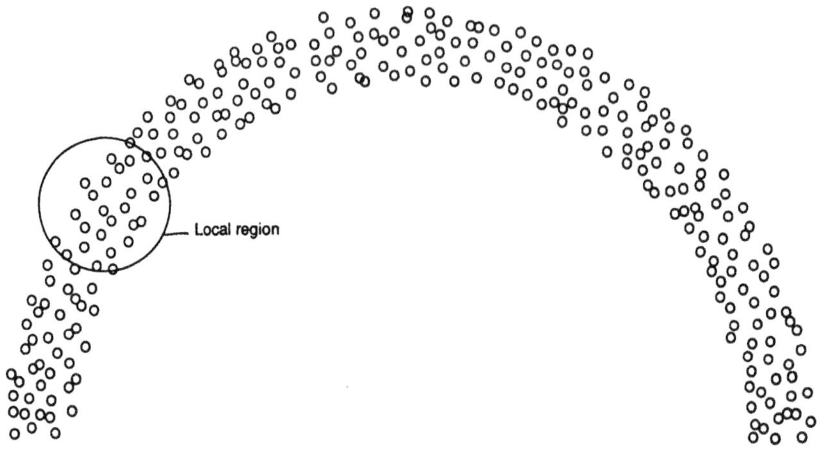

Fig. 11-12 Noisy data set.

shows a distribution of samples which, judged subjectively, is intrinsically one- or two-dimensional. Let us assume that the distribution is one-dimensional, and that unwanted noise is responsible for the two-dimensional scatter. As discussed in Chapter 6, the intrinsic dimensionality is determined by observing the local dimensionalities. Selecting a local region, as shown in Fig. 11-12, the dimensionality in the local region is two, because the two-dimensional scatter of noise has the same order of magnitude as the size of the local region. In order to eliminate the noise, we can measure the density gradient at each sample point X_j, and move X_j toward the direction of the gradient. The amount of the move could be controlled by another parameter, which is multiplied to the local mean vector $M(X_j)$. Repeating this process, samples are merged to a curve having little two-dimensional scatter. This curve is the skeleton of the distribution. After obtaining the skeleton, the local dimensionality is measured, which is one in the example of Fig. 11-12.

Clustering Algorithms

After estimating the gradient of a density function, we now need an algorithm to find clusters. As discussed in data filter, one way of finding clusters is to move samples toward the direction of the gradient by $\rho M(X)$ where ρ is a control parameter. The procedure must be repeated until all samples in each cluster converge to one vector. This is conceptually simple, but computationally cumbersome. So, if possible, we would like to change only class assignment without altering sample vectors. Also, it is preferable to avoid iterative operations. There are many ways to accomplish this. However, in this section we present only two: one is a non-iterative process, and the other is an iterative one.

Graph theoretic approach [13]: One way to avoid an iterative operation is to form trees as shown in Fig. 11-13. In this figure a node representing

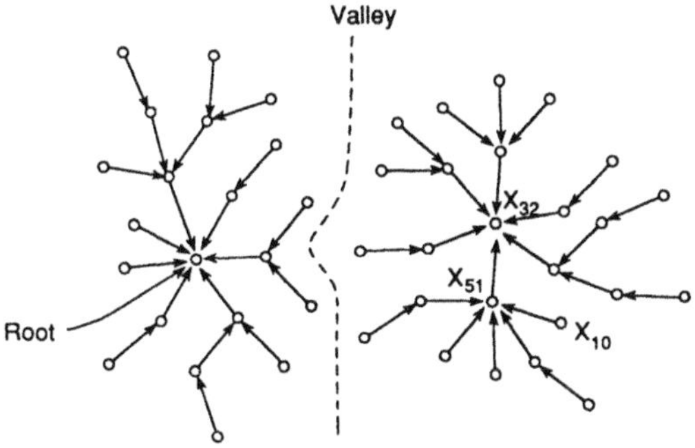

Fig. 11-13 Graph theoretic clustering.

X_{10} initiates a branch (or an arrow) pointing another node X_{51}, which is called the *predecessor* of X_{10}. Then, X_{51} initiates another branch to point to X_{32}, and so on. Thus, each sample becomes an initial node and leads into a final node through a series of branches, each branch pointing from one node to its predecessor. A series of branches is called a *directed path*. We will implement an algorithm such that there is no directed path from a node to itself (i.e. no cycle). At the top of a tree, the *final node* (such as X_{32}) does not have a predecessor and is called the *root* of a tree. Note that each node except the final node has one and only one predecessor, but each could be the predecessor of a number of nodes, including zero. This type of tree is called a *directed tree*. Since the concept of this tree-formation comes from graph theory, we call this the *graph theoretic approach*.

In order to form directed trees for the clustering problem, we need an algorithm to select the predecessor of each sample. If we could select, as the predecessor of X, a sample along the steepest ascent path starting from X, samples will be divided by the valley of the density function, and a tree is formed for each cluster as shown in Fig. 11-13. The quality of the result depends wholly on the quality of the estimation technique for the density gradient, particularly in the low density area of the valley.

The density gradient at X can be estimated by the local mean $M(X)$ as in (11.64). Asymptotically, the sample at the local mean can be the predecessor of X. However, in practice, with a finite number of samples, none of the existing local samples in $\Gamma(X)$ is located exactly at the local mean. Therefore, we need a procedure to pick up an existing local sample which is closest to the local mean.

When two samples are located close together, the steepness of the slope from X_j to X_ℓ can be measured by

$$s_{\ell j} = \frac{p(X_\ell) - p(X_j)}{\|X_\ell - X_j\|} . \tag{11.69}$$

Then, the predecessor X_k is the one which has the steepest slope from X_j among samples in $\Gamma(X_j)$, satisfying

$$s_{kj} = \max_{X_\ell \in \Gamma(X_j)} s_{\ell j} . \tag{11.70}$$

Equation (11.69) has another interpretation. Expanding $p(X_\ell)$ around X_j by a Taylor series

$$\begin{aligned} p(X_\ell) &\cong p(X_j) + \nabla p^T(X_j)(X_\ell - X_j) \\ &= p(X_j) + \|X_\ell - X_j\| \nabla^T p(X_j) \frac{X_\ell - X_j}{\|X_\ell - X_j\|} . \end{aligned} \tag{11.71}$$

Thus

$$s_{\ell j} \cong \nabla^T p(X_j) \frac{X_\ell - X_j}{\|X_\ell - X_j\|} = \|\nabla p(X_j)\| \cos\theta_{\ell j} , \tag{11.72}$$

where $\theta_{\ell j}$ is the angle between the two vectors, $\nabla p(X_j)$ and $(X_\ell - X_j)$. Since $\|\nabla p(X_j)\|$ is independent of ℓ, (11.70) and (11.72) suggest that X_k is the sample which gives the smallest angle between $\nabla p(X_j)$ and $(X_k - X_j)$ among all local samples in $\Gamma(X_j)$. That is, X_k is the closest sample to the steepest ascent line from X_j. Thus, the predecessor of X_j can be determined by measuring the angle between the local mean and $(X_\ell - X_j)$.

In addition, when nodes approach the root of the tree and s_{kj} of (11.70) becomes either zero or negative, we need rules to identify the root as follows.

(1) $s_{kj} < 0$: X_j is a root.

(2) $s_{kj} = 0$: Consider the set $\pi(X_j) = \{X_k | X_k \in \Gamma(X_j), s_{kj} = 0\}$. Eliminate from $\pi(X_j)$ any X_k, from which there exists a directed path to X_j. If the resulting $\pi(X_j)$ is empty, X_j is a root. Otherwise, the predecessor of X_j is X_t which satisfies

$$\|X_t - X_j\| = \min_{X_k \in \pi(X_j)} \|X_k - X_j\| . \tag{11.73}$$

The similar result may be obtained without computing local means. The density values of (11.69) can be estimated by using any nonparametric technique such as the Parzen or *kNN* approach as discussed in Chapter 6. For example, if the Parzen approach with a uniform kernel function is used, $\hat{p}(X_j) = \hat{\tau}(X_j)/Nv$, where $\hat{\tau}(X_j)$ is the number of samples in $\Gamma(X_j)$, N is the total number of samples, and v is the volume of $\Gamma(X_j)$. Since N and v are independent of j, we may ignore them and replace $\hat{p}(X_j)$ by $\hat{\tau}(X_j)$. For the *kNN* approach, $\hat{p}(X_j) = (k-1)/N\hat{v}(X_j)$, where k is a preset number and $\hat{v}(X_j)$ must be measured. Since k and N are independent of j in this case, $\hat{p}(X_j)$ is replaced by $1/\hat{v}(X_j)$ in (11.69). Thus, using $\hat{p}(\cdot)$ in the place of $p(\cdot)$ in (11.69), (11.70) determines the predecessor of each sample.

The graph theoretic approach has a number of advantages. It is a non-iterative process, and does not require an initial class assignment. Also, the number of clusters needs not be preassigned. After the predecessor of each sample is found, a computer keeps track of the connections of samples to identify the number of isolated trees automatically.

In the graph theoretic approach, a crucial parameter is the size of the local region $\Gamma(X)$. A density function is not a smooth function with a few peaks, but a noisy function with many local peaks and valleys. With a small $\Gamma(X)$, the algorithm tends to pick up many clusters separated by the local valleys due to noise. On the other hand, if $\Gamma(X)$ is too large, all peaks and valleys are smoothed out and the algorithm produces only one cluster. In order to find a proper size for $\Gamma(X)$, it is suggested to run the algorithm for various sizes of $\Gamma(X)$, and observe the resulting number of clusters. Normally, as the size of $\Gamma(X)$ is changed from a small value to a large one, the number of clusters starts from a large value, drops down and stays at a certain level for a while, and then starts to drop again. The plateau at the middle is a reasonable and stable operating range, from which we can determine the size of $\Gamma(X)$ and the number of clusters.

Iterative valley-seeking: A nonparametric version of the nearest mean reclassification algorithm can be developed by defining a *nonparametric within-class scatter matrix* as

$$\mathcal{S}_{w'} = \sum_{i=1}^{L} P_i \frac{1}{N_i} \sum_{j=1}^{N_i} (X_j^{(i)} - \mathcal{M}_i(X_j^{(i)}))(X_j^{(i)} - \mathcal{M}_i(X_j^{(i)}))^T , \tag{11.74}$$

where $\mathcal{M}_i(X_j^{(i)})$ is the sample mean of kNN's to $X_j^{(i)}$ from ω_i as

$$\mathcal{M}_i(X_j^{(i)}) = \frac{1}{k} \sum_{\ell=1}^{k} X_{\ell NN}^{(i)} . \tag{11.75}$$

We will call $\mathcal{M}_i(X_j^{(i)})$ the *local* ω_i*-mean* of $X_j^{(i)}$. This is the kNN version of the local mean. On the other hand, the local ω_i-mean for the Parzen approach is the sample mean of ω_i-samples in the local region $\Gamma(X_j)$ with a fixed radius. Comparing (11.74) with (10.99) and (10.100), we note that the weighting coefficients of (10.99) and (10.100) are not included in (11.74). Since w_ℓ requires knowledge of the true class assignment of the samples, their use is deemed inappropriate for clustering.

The criterion for class separability is set as $J = \text{tr}(S_m^{-1} \mathcal{S}_{w'})$ just as $J = \text{tr}(S_m^{-1} S_{w'})$ is used for the parametric counterpart. When k approaches N_i, the local ω_i-mean becomes the global ω_i-mean M_i, and consequently (11.74) becomes the parametric within-class scatter matrix $S_{w'}$. Thus, the nearest mean reclassification algorithm is a special case of the optimization of $J = \text{tr}(S_m^{-1} \mathcal{S}_{w'})$. On the other hand, when $k << N_i$, we can develop the nonparametric reclassification algorithm by repeating the derivation of (11.13) with $\mathcal{M}_i(X_j)$ this time instead of M_i then, resulting in

$$\|X_j - \mathcal{M}_t(X_j)\| = \min_{\ell} \|X_j - \mathcal{M}_\ell(X_j)\| \quad \rightarrow \quad X_j \in \omega_t . \tag{11.76}$$

Note that (11.76) is applied only after the data is whitened with respect to S_m. This procedure may be called the *nearest local-mean reclassification* algorithm. In this algorithm, the local ω_i-means must be updated each time the class assignment is changed.

Another possible definition of the nonparametric within-class scatter matrix is

$$\mathcal{S}_{w'} = \sum_{i=1}^{L} P_i \frac{1}{N_i} \sum_{j=1}^{N_i} (X_j^{(i)} - X_{kNN}^{(i)})(X_j - X_{kNN}^{(i)})^T , \tag{11.77}$$

where $X_{kNN}^{(i)}$ is the kth NN of $X_j^{(i)}$ from ω_i. This time, we use the kth NN itself instead of the sample mean of the kNN's. Then, by a derivation similar to before, $X_j^{(i)}$ is reclassified to ω_t by

$$\|X_j - X_{kNN}^{(t)}\| = \min_{\ell} \|X_j - X_{kNN}^{(\ell)}\| \quad \to \quad X_j \in \omega_t \tag{11.78}$$

after whitening the data with respect to S_m.

Under the current class assignment, the density function of ω_ℓ at X_j can be estimated by using the kNN approach as

$$\hat{P}_\ell \hat{p}_\ell(X_j) = \frac{N_\ell}{N} \frac{k-1}{N_\ell \hat{v}_\ell(X_j)} = \frac{k-1}{Nc\|X_j - X_{kNN}^{(\ell)}\|^n} , \tag{11.79}$$

where c is a constant relating the radius to the volume. Selecting the smallest $\|X_j - X_{kNN}^{(\ell)}\|$ means selecting the largest $\hat{P}_\ell \hat{p}_\ell(X_j)$. Therefore, the reclassification algorithm of (11.78) suggests that we evaluate $\hat{P}_\ell \hat{p}_\ell(X_j)$ by (11.79) at each X_j, and classify X_j to the class which has the largest $\hat{P}_\ell \hat{p}_\ell(X_j)$.

When the Parzen approach with a uniform kernel function is used, $\hat{P}_\ell \hat{p}_\ell(X_j)$ is estimated by

$$\hat{P}_\ell \hat{p}_\ell(X_j) = \frac{N_\ell}{N} \frac{k_\ell(X_j)}{N_\ell v} = \frac{k_\ell(X_j)}{Nv} , \tag{11.80}$$

where v is a fixed volume of the local region around X_j, and $k_\ell(X_j)$ is the number of ω_ℓ-samples in the local region. Then, (11.78) is converted to

$$k_t(X_j) = \max_{\ell} k_\ell(X_j) \quad \to \quad X_j \in \omega_t \, . \tag{11.81}$$

The formulas of (11.78) and (11.81) have a computational advantage over the formula of (11.76). When (11.76) is used, we need to recompute the local means at each iteration. This is not required for (11.78) and (11.81).

When (11.81) is used, we set the local region around each sample with a fixed volume v, and tabulate samples in the local regions with their current class assignments, as shown in Fig. 11-14. Then, finding the class with the highest population, each sample is reclassified to that class. For example, in Fig. 11-14, X_1 is reclassified to ω_2 because the local region of X_1 contains one ω_1-sample and two ω_2-samples. After all samples are reclassified, the class labels of samples in the table are revised, and the same operation is repeated. In this iteration, only class labels are processed and no mean vector computation is involved. The same is true for (11.78). In the operation of (11.78),

		1st NN		2nd NN		3rd NN		4th NN		
	ω		ω		ω		ω		ω	
X_1	1	X_5	2	X_8	2	X_{13}	1			$X_1 \to \omega_2$
X_2	3	X_6	1	X_{21}	1					$X_2 \to \omega_1$
$\vdots$	$\vdots$	$\vdots$	$\vdots$	$\vdots$	$\vdots$					$\vdots$
X_{1000}	5	X_{35}	5	X_{15}	5	X_{210}	6	X_{361}	5	$X_{1000} \to \omega_5$

Fig. 11-14 Iterative class assignment.

after tabulating neighbors of each sample, the sample is classified to ω_t when the kth NN from ω_t appears first in the sequence of $1NN$, $2NN$, $\ldots$. For example, in Fig. 11-14 with $k = 2$, X_1 has a sequence of neighbors as $\omega_2, \omega_2, \omega_1, \ldots$, and the second NN from ω_2 appears first in the sequence. Accordingly, X_1 is reclassified to ω_2. Again, no mean computation is involved in each iteration.

Because of the above computational advantage, let us use (11.81) as the updating scheme of class assignment, and study the properties of the valley-seeking algorithm. The algorithm can be stated as follows [14-15].

(1) Whiten the data with respect to S_m.

(2) Assign the number of clusters, L. Choose an initial classification, $\Omega(0)$.

(3) Set a local spherical region around each sample, $\Gamma(X_j)$, with a fixed radius, and list samples in $\Gamma(X_j)$ with the current class assignment, as in Fig. 11-14.

(4) Reclassify X_j according to the majority of classes among all neighboring samples in $\Gamma(X_j)$.

(5) If any change in class assignment occurs, revise the class labels of all neighbors in the table and go to Step (4). Otherwise stop.

In order to understand how this procedure works, let us study the one-dimensional example of Fig. 11-15. Suppose that, at the ℓth iteration, samples are divided into 7 clusters as shown. A sample X_1 is not reclassified from ω_2 because all neighboring samples of X_1 in $\Gamma(X_1)$ belong to ω_2 currently. On the other hand, X_2 on the boundary between ω_5 and ω_6 is most likely reclassified to ω_6, because the number of neighbors from ω_6 tends to be larger than the number of ω_5-neighbors. This is due to the fact that the density function on the ω_6-side is higher than the one on the ω_5-side. Reclassifying X_2

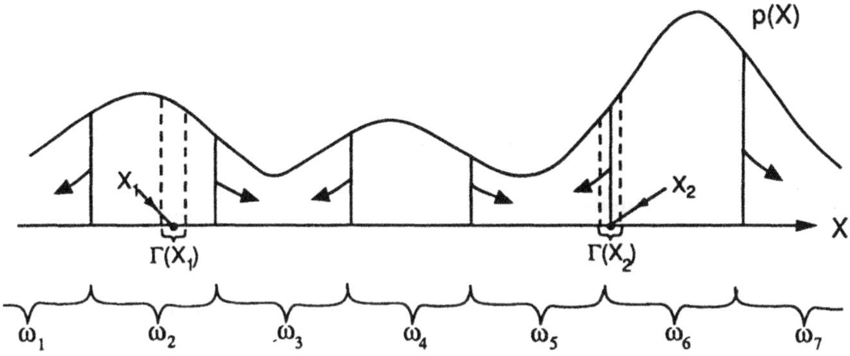

Fig. 11-15 An example of the valley-seeking clustering.

into ω_6 results in a shift of the boundary toward the ω_5-side, as the arrow indicates. This is equivalent to saying that the direction of the density gradient is estimated by using the numbers of samples on both sides of the boundary, and the boundary is moved toward the lower density side. Applying this process to all boundaries repeatedly, the leftmost boundary of Fig. 11-15 moves out to $-\infty$, leaving the ω_1-cluster empty, the second and third leftmost boundaries merge to one, making the ω_3-cluster empty, and so on. As a result, at the end of iteration, only ω_2, ω_4, and ω_6 keep many samples and the others become empty. The procedure works in the same way even in a high-dimensional space.

A number of comments can be made about this iterative valley-seeking procedure. The procedure is nonparametric, and divides samples according to the valley of a density function. The density gradient is estimated, but in a crude way. The number of clusters must be preassigned, but we can always assign a larger number of clusters than we actually expect to have. Many of initial clusters could become empty, and only true clusters separated by the valleys will keep samples. As far as computation time is concerned, it takes a lot of computer time to find neighbors for each sample and form the table of Fig. 11-14. However, this operation is common for all nonparametric clustering procedures, including the graph theoretic approach. The iterative process of this algorithm revises only the class assignment according to the majority of classes in $\Gamma(X)$. This operation does not take much computation time.

The volume of $\Gamma(X)$ affects the performance of this algorithm, just as it did in the graph theoretic approach. The optimum volume should be determined experimentally, as was done for the graph theoretic approach.

Experiment 4: Seventy five samples per class were generated according to

$$\begin{bmatrix} \mathbf{x}_1 \\ \mathbf{x}_2 \end{bmatrix} = 20 \begin{bmatrix} \cos \boldsymbol{\theta} \\ \sin \boldsymbol{\theta} \end{bmatrix} + \begin{bmatrix} m_1 \\ m_2 \end{bmatrix} + \begin{bmatrix} \mathbf{n}_1 \\ \mathbf{n}_2 \end{bmatrix}, \tag{11.82}$$

where $\mathbf{n}_1$ and $\mathbf{n}_2$ are independent and normally distributed with zero mean and unit variance for both ω_1 and ω_2, $[m_1\ m_2]$ is [0 0] for ω_1 and [0 −20] for ω_2, and $\boldsymbol{\theta}$ is normally distributed with $E\{\boldsymbol{\theta}|\omega_1\} = \pi$, $E\{\boldsymbol{\theta}|\omega_2\} = 0$, and $\text{Var}\{\boldsymbol{\theta}|\omega_1\} = \text{Var}\{\boldsymbol{\theta}|\omega_2\} = (\pi/4)^2$. After the data was whitened with respect to the mixture covariance matrix, both graph theoretic and iterative valley-seeking algorithms were applied, resulting in the same clustering result, as shown in Fig. 11-16 [13-14].

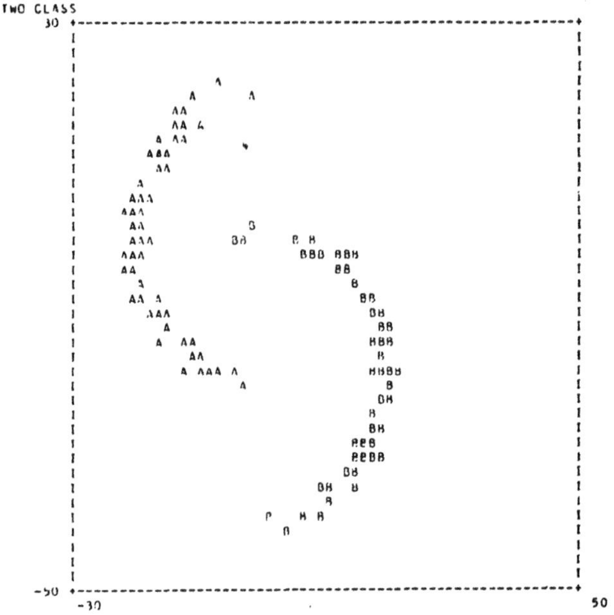

Fig. 11-16 Classification of a two-class example.

Table 11-3 shows the selected radius for $\Gamma(X)$, and the number of iterations required to reach the final clusters in the iterative valley-seeking algorithm [14].

Experiment 5: Fifty samples per class were generated from three classes. Two of them were the same ones as Experiment 4 except

TABLE 11-3

PERFORMANCE OF THE VALLEY-SEEKING ALGORITHM

Experiment	Number of samples	Number of clusters	Radius of $\Gamma(X)$	Number of iterations
4	150	2	1.0	8
5	150	3	0.75	10

$[m_1\ m_2] = [20\ 0]$ for ω_2 instead of $[0\ -20]$. The third distribution was normal with the mean and covariance matrix

$$M_3 = \begin{bmatrix} 10 \\ 0 \end{bmatrix} \quad \text{and} \quad \Sigma_3 = \begin{bmatrix} 16 & 0 \\ 0 & 1 \end{bmatrix} . \tag{11.83}$$

Again, after the data was whitened with respect to the mixture covariance matrix, both the graph theoretic and iterative valley-seeking algorithms produced the same clustering result, as shown in Fig. 11-17 [13-14]. The

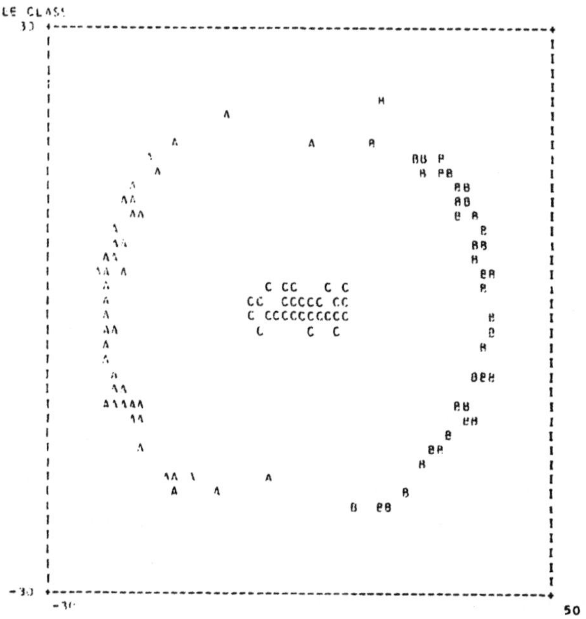

Fig. 11-17 Classification of a three-class example.

radius of $\Gamma(X)$ and the number of iterations in the latter algorithm are listed in Table 11-3 [14].

General comments: We have discussed both parametric and nonparametric clustering techniques. The question here is which technique is better under what conditions. Generally speaking, nonparametric techniques do not require the knowledge of the number of clusters beforehand. This is certainly true for the graph theoretic approach. Even for the iterative valley-seeking procedure, we can preassign a larger number of clusters than what is actually needed, and let the procedure select automatically the necessary number of clusters. Therefore, if we do not have any a priori knowledge about the data structure, it is most natural to adopt a nonparametric clustering technique and find out how the data is naturally divided into clusters.

However, nonparametric procedures are in general very sensitive to the control parameters, especially the size of the local region. Therefore, it is necessary to run experiments for a wide range of sizes, and the results must be carefully examined. Also, nonparametric procedures are normally very computationally intensive.

Furthermore, nonparametric clustering techniques have two fundamental flaws described as follows.

(1) We cannot divide a distribution into a number of clusters unless the valley actually exists. For example, the ω_1-distribution of Fig. 11-9 could be obtained as the result of the valley-seeking procedure, but the distribution cannot be divided into 2 or 3 clusters by any nonparametric method even if it is desirable to do so. When a distribution is wrapped as the ω_1-distribution of Fig. 11-9, it is sometimes prefered to decompose the distribution into several normal distributions for further analysis of data structure or designing a classifier.

On the other hand, the parametric procedures do not depend on the natural boundary of clusters, but depend only on the criterion. With a preassigned number of clusters, the procedures seek the boundary to optimize the criterion value. Therefore, we can divide the ω_1-distribution of Fig. 11-9 into 2, 3, or 4 clusters as we like. After examining the clustering results for various numbers of clusters, we may decide which number of clusters is most appropriate for a particular application. Previously, we stated that it is a disadvantage of parametric clustering techniques to have to know the number of clusters beforehand. But, that property may work sometimes as an advantage as discussed above.

(2) As seen in Fig. 11-7(b), the resulting clusters of nonparametric clustering procedures contain the tails of other distributions and do not contain their own tails. Thus, the mean and covariance matrix of each cluster do not represent the true ones of the underlying distribution. In order to obtain proper parameters of the underlying distributions, we need to impose a parametric structure such as the summation of normal distributions.

11.3 Selection of Representatives

In the previous sections, we have discussed algorithms to find clusters from a distribution. A similar but slightly different problem is to reduce the number of samples while maintaining the structure of the distribution. This may be viewed as selecting a small number of representatives from a distribution. Besides clustering, the reduction of sample size has a number of applications. A typical example is to divide a set of available samples into design and test sets. In this case, we must assure that design and test distributions are similar.

Nonparametric Data Reduction

Generally, it is not appropriate to assume a mathematical structure when the sample size is reduced. Therefore, a nonparametric procedure must be adopted to guide through the operation.

Data reduction algorithm [16-17]: Let us study the Parzen approach to the problem of sample size reduction. Given N samples drawn from $p(X)$, we wish to select Q samples ($Q < N$) so that the Parzen density estimates for the N sample set and the Q sample set are close.

Let $\hat{p}_N(X)$ be the density estimate based on N samples. Then

$$\hat{p}_N(X) = \frac{1}{N}\sum_{i=1}^{N}\kappa(X - X_i) , \tag{11.84}$$

where $\kappa(\cdot)$ is the kernel function. Similarly, when Q representatives, $Y_1, \ldots, Y_Q$, are selected, the density function is estimated by

$$\hat{p}_Q(X) = \frac{1}{Q}\sum_{i=1}^{Q}\kappa(X - Y_i)\ . \tag{11.85}$$

In order to measure the similarity between $\hat{p}_N(X)$ and $\hat{p}_Q(X)$, the entropy criterion of Chapter 9 is used. Replacing $p_1(X)$ and $p_2(X)$ of (9.53) by $\hat{p}_Q(X)$ and $\hat{p}_N(X)$ respectively, we obtain the entropy inequality as

$$\int[-\ln\hat{p}_Q(X)]\hat{p}_N(X)dX \geq \int[-\ln\hat{p}_N(X)]\hat{p}_N(X)dX\ , \tag{11.86}$$

where the equality holds only for $\hat{p}_Q(X) = \hat{p}_N(X)$. Thus, the best $\hat{p}_Q(X)$ may be found by minimizing the lefthand side of (11.86). The criterion may be simplified by approximating the expectation with respect to $\hat{p}_N(X)$ in (11.86) by the sample mean over the existing samples $X_1, \ldots, X_N$, as

$$J = \frac{1}{N}\sum_{i=1}^{N}[-\ln\hat{p}_Q(X_i)] = \frac{1}{N}\sum_{i=1}^{N}[-\ln\{\frac{1}{Q}\sum_{j=1}^{Q}\kappa(X_i-Y_j)\}]\ . \tag{11.87}$$

In order to find the best Q representatives from the existing samples $X_1, \ldots, X_N$, we would like to minimize J over all possible Q element subsets of the original N element set. Unfortunately, an exhaustive search of all $\binom{N}{Q}$ subsets is not computationally feasible. Instead, we will settle for the minimum J for subsets formed by replacing one element of the representative set by the best candidate not yet selected.

An iterative procedure is as follows:

(1) Select an initial assignment of Q samples from the N sample data set. Call the Q sample set *STORE* and the remaining $N-Q$ samples *TEST*.

(2) For each element, X_t, in *TEST*, compute the change in J that results if the sample is transferred to *STORE*.

$$\Delta J_1(X_t) = \frac{1}{N}\sum_{i=1}^{N}\left[\ln\left\{\frac{1}{Q}\sum_{j=1}^{Q}\kappa(X_i-Y_j)\right\}\right.$$

$$\left. - \ln\left\{\frac{1}{Q+1}\left[\sum_{j=1}^{Q}\kappa(X_i-Y_j) + \kappa(X_i-X_t)\right]\right\}\right]\ . \tag{11.88}$$

(3) Pick the element, X_t, corresponding to the smallest ΔJ_1 (and call it X_t^*).

(4) For each element, X_s, in *STORE*, compute the change in J that results if the sample is transferred to *TEST*.

$$\Delta J_2(X_s) = \frac{1}{N}\sum_{i=1}^{N}\left[\ln\left\{\frac{1}{Q+1}\left[\sum_{j=1}^{Q}\kappa(X_i-Y_j) + \kappa(X_i-X_t^*)\right]\right\}\right.$$

$$\left. - \ln\left\{\frac{1}{Q}\left[\sum_{j=1}^{Q}\kappa(X_i-Y_j) + \kappa(X_i-X_t^*) - \kappa(X_i-X_s)\right]\right\}\right] . \qquad (11.89)$$

(5) Find the element, X_s, corresponding to the smallest ΔJ_2 (and call it X_s^*).

(6) The change of J due to these two operations is $\Delta J = \Delta J_1(X_t^*) + \Delta J_2(X_s^*)$. In order to minimize J, we would like to have $\Delta J < 0$. If X_s^* exists to satisfy $\Delta J < 0$, transfer X_s^* to *TEST*, transfer X_t^* to *STORE*, and go to Step (2).

(7) Otherwise, find the element, X_t, corresponding to the next smallest ΔJ_1 (and call it X_t^*).

(8) If X_t^* exists, go to Step (4).

(9) Otherwise, stop.

Generally, this kind of iterative process produces a result which depends on the initial selection of Q representatives in *STORE*. However, Steps (7) and (8) allow us to search more possible combinations of X_t and X_s and thus insure that the final representative set is less dependent on the initial assignment.

The *kNN* approach also can be applied in a similar way as the Parzen approach. The *kNN* density estimate is

$$\hat{p}_N(X) = \frac{k-1}{Ncd_N^n(X)} , \qquad (11.90)$$

where $d_N(X)$ is the distance from X to its kth *NN* among N samples. The same formula is used when Q samples are used to estimate the density function. Thus, the entropy criterion of (11.87) becomes

$$J = \frac{1}{N}\sum_{i=1}^{N}[-\ln \hat{p}_Q(X_i)] = \frac{1}{N}\sum_{i=1}^{N}[n \ln d_Q(X_i) + \ln \frac{cQ}{k-1}] . \tag{11.91}$$

The same iterative procedure can be used to find the best Q samples by minimizing J of (11.91).

As in most iterative techniques, a good initial guess usually is of considerable importance. The following is a method to perform the initial assignment when $Q = N/2$.

An initial assignment procedure: We discuss a procedure to generate an initial assignment for the case with $Q = N/2$. The basis of the procedure lies in an intuitive observation. If a subset with size $N/2$, called *STORE*, is optimally chosen, then we suspect that, on average, the *NN* of a sample, X, in *STORE* might be the second *NN* of X using all N samples.

The procedure is best explained with the aid of Fig. 11-18. In Fig. 11-18(a) the *NN* of X_1 is X_{23}, the *NN* of X_{23} is X_{17}, and X_{17} and X_{40} are mutual *NN*. Figures 11-18(b) and (c) represent two other possible *NN* progressions.

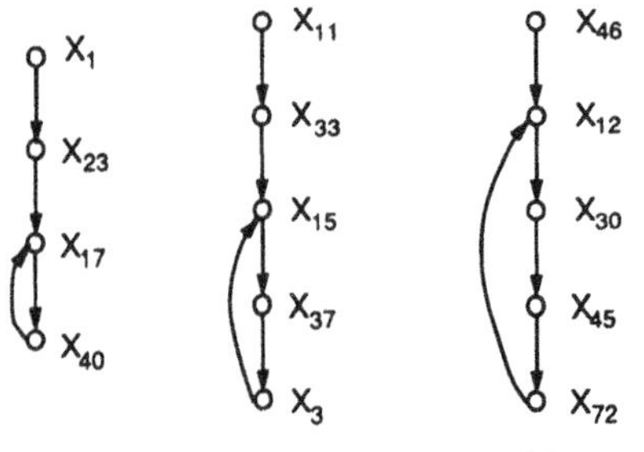

Fig. 11-18 Three examples of *NN* progressions.

We may form the initial assignment by simply assigning every other sample in a *NN* progression to the initial assignment of *STORE*. Thus for Fig. 11-18(a) the initial assignment for *STORE* would consist of either X_1 and X_{17}, or X_{23} and X_{40}.

We now state the procedure.

(1) Get the first sample, and follow the complete progression of its

NN's, assigning alternate samples to *STORE*. Flag every sample in the progression.

(2) Find the next unflagged sample. Follow its *NN* progression, assigning alternate samples to *STORE*. This is done until the progression ends or leads to a previously flagged sample. Flag every sample in the progression.

(3) Repeat Step (2) until all samples are flagged.

If sufficient storage is available to store a table of *kNN*'s for each sample ($k = 4$ or 5), the entire process of initial assignment and criterion minimization can be done very efficiently.

Reduced Parzen classifier [17]: In pattern recognition, the quadratic classifier is very popular. However, in practice with non-normal distributions, it is frequently observed that the error of a quadratic classifier is much larger than the Bayes error estimated by a nonparametric technique. On the other hand, nonparametric classifiers are too complex and time-consuming for on-line operation. Thus, there is a need to fill the gap between these two kinds of classifiers.

One possible solution is to divide each class into several clusters, and design a piecewise quadratic classifier as in (4.149). This approach contains both quadratic and nonparametric classifiers as special cases. If each class has only one cluster, it becomes a quadratic classifier, while, if each sample is viewed as a cluster, it becomes a Parzen classifier.

The most elaborate procedure to design a piecewise quadratic classifier would be to decompose the distribution of each class into several normal distributions as shown in (11.45). Note that only this method gives reasonable estimates of a priori probabilities, means, and covariance matrices. The other clustering procedures fail to do so, because they divide samples as in Fig. 11-7(b) instead of Fig. 11-7(a). The entire clustering operation must be repeated by preassigning various numbers of clusters. The resulting classification error for each preassigned number of clusters is estimated and compared with the Bayes error estimated by a nonparametric technique. The final number of clusters must be as small as possible while maintaining an error close to the Bayes error.

A somewhat simpler approach is to select Q representatives from each class as discussed in this section, and to set a kernel function at each representative to form the Parzen density estimate as in (11.85). The classification can be carried out by comparing the density estimates for ω_1 and ω_2 as

$$-\ln\frac{\hat{p}_1(X)}{\hat{p}_2(X)} \underset{\omega_2}{\overset{\omega_1}{\gtrless}} t \,. \tag{11.92}$$

This classifier is called the *reduced Parzen classifier*. It is generally too complex to select a different kernel function for each representative. So, we may use a normal kernel function with the covariance matrix $r^2\Sigma_i$, where Σ_i is the global covariance matrix of ω_i and r is a parameter controlling the size of the kernel. This approach is simpler because a common kernel function is used within the same class and is prespecified, instead of being estimated and varying locally, as in the approach of (11.45). As discussed in Chapter 7, the sensitive parameters are the size of the kernel, r, the decision threshold, t of (11.92), and the estimate of Σ_i.

In order to verify the above argument, two experimental results are presented.

Experiment 6: The reduced Parzen classifier for Data *I*-Λ was designed and tested as follows:

(1) One hundred samples per class were generated from Data *I*-Λ, and Experiment 7-6 was repeated. From Fig. 7-9, $r = 2$ was chosen as the kernel size.

(2) The sample reduction algorithm in this section was applied to select Q representatives from 100.

(3) Using the Parzen density estimates of (11.85) for ω_1 and ω_2 with $r = 2$, the original 100 samples per class were classified as in (11.92). The threshold t was selected so as to minimize the classification error. The optimum t is different for each different value of Q.

(4) Independently, 100 samples per class were generated and tested by the classifier designed above.

Figure 11-19 shows the plot of the error vs. Q [17]. The error curve is the average of 10 trials, and the standard deviations are shown by vertical bars. Note that the above error estimation is based on the holdout method, in which design and test samples are independent so that the error becomes larger than the Bayes error (1.9%). The error curve is almost flat up to one representative. For normal distributions, selecting the expected vector as the one representative from each class and the covariance matrix as the kernel covariance, the reduced

Parzen classifier becomes quadratic, which is the Bayes classifier. So, the error curve of Fig. 11-19 should be flat down to $Q = 1$. However, since we select representatives from the existing design samples, they may or may not be close to the expected vector. If not, we see that the error curve is flat up to $Q = 2$ or 3 and starts to increase for smaller Q's.

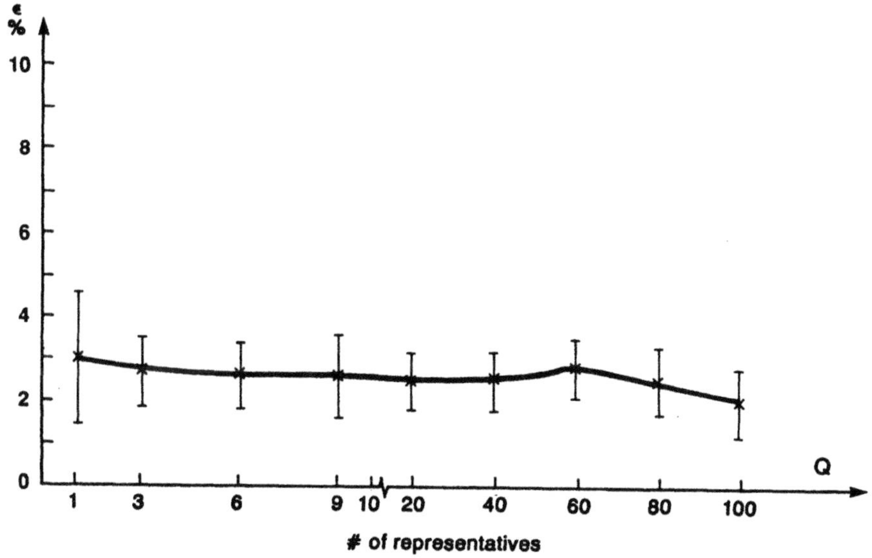

Fig. 11-19 The error of the reduced Parzen classifier for a normal case.

Experiment 7: In order to test a non-normal case, the data of Experiment 7-7 was studied. The data is 8-dimensional, and each class consists of two normal distributions. From Fig. 7-10, $r = 1.5$ was chosen. The procedure of Experiment 6 was repeated for this data, and the result is shown in Fig. 11-20 [17]. Figure 11-20 shows that the error curve is flat for $Q \geq 6$. We found that, when $Q = 6$, three representatives are selected from each cluster.

These experiments suggest an interesting fact. It has been believed that a nonparametric procedure needs a large number of samples for high-dimensional data, in order to reliably estimate the Bayes error. Any nonparametric operation with a large number of samples requires a large amount of computer time. The results of the experiments in this section contradict these common beliefs, and suggest that we may need only a relatively small number of samples (or representatives) after all. However, as Experiment 7-10 and Table 7-3(b) suggest, we may still need a large number of samples to estimate the covariance matrices, which are used to form the kernel functions.

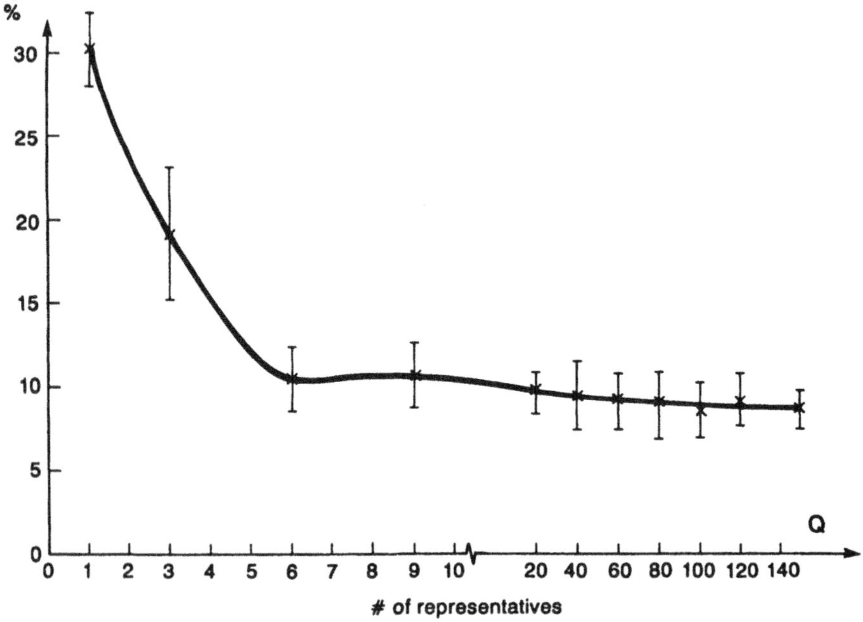

Fig. 11-20 The error of the reduced Parzen classifier for a non-normal case.

Parametric Data Reduction

In parametric approaches, our main concern is to maintain the expected vector and autocorrelation (or covariance) matrix while reducing the number of samples.

Representation of a sample matrix: Let us express N samples in a matrix form as

$$U = [X_1 \dots X_N] \tag{11.93}$$

which is an $n \times N$ rectangular matrix, called the *sample matrix*. Then, the sample autocorrelation matrix can be expressed by

$$\hat{S} = \frac{1}{N}\sum_{i=1}^{N} X_i X_i^T = \frac{1}{N} U U^T . \tag{11.94}$$

Since $\hat{S}$ is an $n \times n$ matrix, $\hat{S}$ has the $n \times n$ eigenvalue and eigenvector matrices, Λ and Φ, such that

$$\hat{S}\Phi = \Phi\Lambda . \tag{11.95}$$

Or

$$(UU^T)\Phi = \Phi(N\Lambda) = \Phi\mu \; , \tag{11.96}$$

where μ is the eigenvalue matrix of UU^T and $\mu = N\Lambda$. Multiplying U^T from the left side, we can convert (11.96) to

$$(U^TU)_{N\times N}(U^T\Phi)_{N\times n} = (U^T\Phi)_{N\times n}\mu_{n\times n} \; , \tag{11.97}$$

where U^TU is an $N\times N$ matrix, $U^T\Phi$ consists of n eigenvectors of U^TU, and the components of μ are the n eigenvalues of U^TU. Since $(U^T\Phi)^T(U^T\Phi) = \Phi^TUU^T\Phi = \mu \neq I$, we change the scales of the eigenvectors by multiplying $\mu^{-1/2}$ from the right side so that (11.97) can be rewritten as

$$(U^TU)\Psi = \Psi\mu \; , \tag{11.98}$$

where

$$\Psi = U^T\Phi\mu^{-1/2} \; . \tag{11.99}$$

That is, Ψ consists of the n eigenvectors of U^TU, and satisfies the orthonormal condition as

$$\Psi^T\Psi = \mu^{-1/2}\Phi^TUU^T\Phi\mu^{-1/2} = I \; . \tag{11.100}$$

From (11.99), U can be expressed in terms of Φ, Ψ, and Λ as

$$U = \Phi\mu^{1/2}\Psi^T = \sqrt{N}\Phi\Lambda^{1/2}\Psi^T \; . \tag{11.101}$$

This expression of a sample matrix is called *singular value decomposition* [18]. Singular value decomposition is an effective technique to represent a rectangular (non-square) matrix by eigenvalues and eigenvectors.

Data reduction: Now our problem is to reduce the number of samples while maintaining the expected vector and autocorrelation matrix. Let us introduce another sample matrix V which consists of Q sample vectors. In order that both U and V share the same autocorrelation matrix

$$\hat{S} = \frac{1}{N}UU^T = \frac{1}{Q}VV^T \; . \tag{11.102}$$

Using (11.101), both U and V can be expressed by

$$U = \sqrt{N}\,\Phi\Lambda^{1/2}\Psi^T , \tag{11.103}$$

$$V = \sqrt{Q}\,\Phi\Lambda^{1/2}\Xi^T , \tag{11.104}$$

where Ψ ($N \times n$) and Ξ ($Q \times n$) are the eigenvector matrices of U^TU and V^TV respectively, and Φ and Λ are the eigenvector and eigenvalue matrices of $\hat{S}$. Note that, although $(UU^T)_{n\times n}$ and $(VV^T)_{n\times n}$ share the same eigenvector matrix, Φ, $(U^TU)_{N\times N}$ and $(V^TV)_{Q\times Q}$ have different eigenvector matrices, Ψ and Ξ. Furthermore, since $\sqrt{N}\,\Psi^T = \Lambda^{-1/2}\Phi^TU$ from (11.103), $\sqrt{N}\,\Psi^T$ is the sample matrix in the whitened space, where the sample autocorrelation matrix becomes I. Similarly, $\sqrt{Q}\,\Xi^T$ is the reduced sample matrix in that space. Then, (11.104) shows the transformation which converts $\sqrt{Q}\,\Xi^T$ back to the original space.

As in (11.100), the n column vectors of Ξ are orthonormal to satisfy

$$\Xi^T\Xi = I . \tag{11.105}$$

The second condition is that U and V must have the same mean vector. Without losing generality, let us assume that the mean is zero. Then,

$$\frac{1}{N}U\,1_N = \frac{1}{Q}V\,1_Q = 0 , \tag{11.106}$$

where 1_k is a vector with all k components being equal to 1 as $1_k = [1 \dots 1]^T$. Or, substituting (11.103) and (11.104) into (11.106),

$$\frac{1}{\sqrt{N}}\Psi^T 1_N = \frac{1}{\sqrt{Q}}\Xi^T 1_Q = 0 . \tag{11.107}$$

When the sample matrix U is given, we can compute Φ, Ψ, and Λ. Therefore, our problem is to find Ξ by solving (11.105) and (11.107). Then, V can be computed by (11.104). Now Ξ consists of $n\times Q$ elements. To determine those $n\times Q$ unknowns we have $n\times n$ equations from (11.105) and n equations from (11.107). Therefore, in general when Q is smaller than $n+1$, there are many possible solutions. But when $Q = n+1$, we have a unique solution as follows:

$$\Xi^T_{n\times(n+1)} = [F_{n\times n}G_{n\times 1}] , \tag{11.108}$$

$$F = I - \alpha\,1_n 1_n^T , \tag{11.109}$$

$$G = -\,\theta_n 1_n , \tag{11.110}$$

where

$$\alpha = \frac{\sqrt{n+1} - 1}{n\sqrt{n+1}} , \tag{11.111}$$

$$\theta = \frac{1}{\sqrt{n+1}} . \tag{11.112}$$

The derivation of (11.108) through (11.112) has been omitted for brevity, but the reader may easily verify that Ξ of (11.108) satisfies both (11.105) and (11.107).

Substituting (11.109) and (11.110) into (11.108),

$$\Xi^T = \begin{bmatrix} 1-\alpha & -\alpha & \dots & -\alpha & -\theta \\ -\alpha & 1-\alpha & & & -\theta \\ \vdots & & \ddots & -\alpha & \vdots \\ -\alpha & & -\alpha & 1-\alpha & -\theta \end{bmatrix} . \tag{11.113}$$

Note that Ξ^T of (11.113) is data independent, because $\sqrt{n+1}\,\Xi^T$ is the reduced sample matrix of $(n+1)$ samples for the mean 0 and the covariance matrix I. This sample matrix is transformed by (11.104) into the space where the original data and its sample covariance matrix are given.

Example 2: For $n = 2$, $\sqrt{n+1}\,\Xi^T$ becomes

$$\sqrt{3}\,\Xi^T = \begin{bmatrix} 1.366 & -0.366 & -1 \\ -0.366 & 1.366 & -1 \end{bmatrix} . \tag{11.114}$$

Computer Projects

1. Repeat Experiment 1.
2. Repeat Experiments 2 and 3.
3. Apply the graph theoretic valley-seeking technique to Data I-Λ.
4. Apply the iterative valley-seeking technique to Data I-Λ.
5. Repeat Experiments 6 and 7.

Problems

1. A random variable $\mathbf{x}$ is uniformly distributed in [a, b]. From N samples $\mathbf{x}_1, \ldots, \mathbf{x}_N$ drawn from the distribution, find the maximum likelihood estimates of a and b.

2. Assume that a distribution can be decomposed to L normal clusters and all clusters share the same covariance matrix. Find the recursive equations to compute the a priori probabilities, the mean vectors, and the common covariance matrix of L clusters by using the maximum likelihood estimation technique. Point out the difference between this procedure and the nearest mean reclassification algorithm.

3. Assume that a distribution consists of L normal clusters and $P_1 = \ldots = P_L$. Find the recursive equations to compute the means and covariance matrices of L clusters by using the maximum likelihood estimation technique.

4. A kurtosis matrix is defined by

$$K = E\{(X^T X)XX^T\} - (n+2)I \ .$$

When a density function consists of L normal clusters with the mean vectors M_i and the common covariance matrix Σ, K can be rewritten as

$$K = \sum_{i=1}^{L} P_i M_i M_i^T [\mathrm{tr}(\Sigma + M_i M_i^T) - (n+2)] \ .$$

Since the rank of the above equation is $(L-1)$, only $(L-1)$ eigenvalues of K are non-zero. Using this property, we can estimate the number of modes when clusters are normal and share the same covariance matrix. Prove that the second equation is equal to the first one for $\Sigma = I$.

5. A density function of a random variable $\mathbf{x}$ can be estimated by the Parzen method with the kernel function

$$\kappa(y) = \begin{cases} 0 & \text{for } y^2 \geq 1 \\ \frac{3}{4}(1-y^2) & \text{for } y^2 < 1 \ . \end{cases}$$

The derivative of the Parzen density estimate, $d\hat{p}(x)/dx$, can be used as an estimate of the density gradient. Confirm that this method of gradient estimation coincides with (11.64).

6. The product of two normal distributions, $N(M_1,\Sigma_1)$ and $N(M_2,\Sigma_2)$, gives another normal distribution, $N(M_0,\Sigma_0)$, multiplied by a constant, c.

(a) Derive the relations between the three means and covariance matrices.

(b) Samples are drawn from $N(M_1,\Sigma_1)$, and a normal window function $N(X,\Sigma_2)$ is set at X. Using these samples and the given window function, estimate the mean and covariance matrix of $N(M_0,\Sigma_0)$.

(c) Using $\hat{M}_0$ and $\hat{\Sigma}_0$ and the given window function, estimate M_1 and Σ_1. This procedure could be used to estimate a local covariance matrix even when the samples are drawn from a non-normal distribution.

7. Two density functions are estimated by the Parzen method. Find the expression for the class separability criterion $\int p_1(X)p_2(X)dX$.

(a) Use a normal kernel function with kernel covariance $r^2\Sigma_i$ for ω_i.

(b) Use a hyperspherical uniform kernel with radius r for both ω_1 and ω_2.

8. Let class separability be measured by

$$J = \frac{1}{N}\sum_{i=1}^{N}\sum_{j=1}^{i} f(X_i,X_j)g(c_i,c_j) \ ,$$

where

$$f(X_i,X_j) = \begin{cases} 1 & \text{for } \|X_i-X_j\| \le r \\ 0 & \text{for } \|X_i-X_j\| > r \ , \end{cases}$$

$$g(c_i,c_j) = \begin{cases} 1 & \text{when } X_i \text{ and } X_j \text{ belong to different classes,} \\ 0 & \text{when } X_i \text{ and } X_j \text{ belong to the same class.} \end{cases}$$

That is, J counts the number of pairs whose members are close and yet come from different classes. Prove that the minimization of J by an iterative process leads to the iterative valley-seeking procedure of (11.81).

9. Formulate the selection of representatives by a branch and bound procedure.

10. By using the singular value decomposition technique, show how to decompose an $n \times m$ $(m < n)$ two-dimensional image to m basis images, and how to evaluate the effectiveness of these basis images.

References

1. S. Watanabe, "Knowing and Guessing," Wiley, New York, 1969.
2. D. J. Hall and G. B. Ball, ISODATA: A novel method of data analysis and pattern classification, Technical report, Stanford Research Institute, Menlo Park, CA, 1965.
3. G. B. Ball, Data analysis in the social sciences: What about the details?, *Proc. Fall Joint Computer Conference*, pp. 533-559, Washington, DC, 1965.
4. J. MacQueen, Some methods for classification and analysis of multivariate observations, *Proc. Fifth Berkeley Symposium on Math. Statist. and Prob.*, pp. 281-297, Berkeley, CA, 1967.
5. K. Fukunaga and W. L. G. Koontz, A criterion and an algorithm for grouping data, *Trans. IEEE Computers*, C-19, pp. 917-923, 1970.
6. W. L. G. Koontz, P. M. Narendra, and K. Fukunaga, A branch and bound clustering algorithm, *Trans. IEEE Computers*, C-24, pp. 908-915, 1975.
7. D. M. Titterington, A. F. M. Smith, and U. E. Makov, "Statistical Analysis of Finite Mixture Distributions," Wiley, New York, 1985.
8. K. Fukunaga and T. E. Flick, Estimation of the parameters of a Gaussian mixture using the method of moments, *Trans. IEEE Pattern Anal. and Machine Intell.*, PAMI-5, pp. 410-416, 1983.
9. N. E. Day, Estimating the components of a mixture of normal distributions, *Biometrika*, 56, pp. 463-474, 1969.
10. J. H. Wolfe, Pattern clustering by multivariate mixture analysis, *Multivar. Behav. Res.*, 5, pp. 329-350, 1970.
11. K. Fukunaga and L. D. Hostetler, The estimation of the gradient of a density function, with applications in pattern recognition, *Trans. IEEE Inform. Theory*, IT-21, pp. 32-40, 1975.

12. K. Fukunaga and T. E. Flick, A test of Gaussian-ness of a data set using clustering, *IEEE Trans. Pattern Anal. and Machine Intell.*, PAMI-8, pp. 240-247, 1986.

13. W. L. G. Koontz, P. M. Narendra, and K. Fukunaga, A graph-theoretic approach to nonparametric cluster analysis, *Trans. IEEE Computers*, C-25, pp. 936-944, 1975.

14. W. L. G. Koontz and K. Fukunaga, A nonparametric valley-seeking technique for cluster analysis, *Trans. IEEE Computers*, C-21, pp. 171-178, 1972.

15. W. L. G. Koontz and K. Fukunaga, Asymptotic analysis of a nonparametric clustering technique, *Trans. IEEE Computers*, C-21, pp. 967-974, 1972.

16. K. Fukunaga and J. M. Mantock, Nonparametric data reduction, *Trans. IEEE Pattern Anal. and Machine Intell.*, PAMI-6, pp. 115-118, 1984.

17. K. Fukunaga and R. R. Hayes, The reduced Parzen classifier, *Trans. IEEE Pattern Anal. and Machine Intell.*, PAMI-11, pp. 423-425, 1989.

18. P. A. Wintz, Transform picture coding, *Proc. IEEE*, pp. 58-68, 1969.

Appendix A

DERIVATIVES OF MATRICES

In this appendix, the derivatives of matrices will be discussed for various cases. The following notations are used throughout this appendix.

$R = [r_{ij}]$: nonsymmetric matrix of $n \times n$

$S = [s_{ij}]$: symmetric matrix of $n \times n$

$A = [a_{ij}]$: rectangular matrix of $n \times m$

$B = [b_{ij}]$: specified differently for each formula.

Matrix Inversion

When r_{ij} is a function of a scalar x, the derivative of R with respect to x is defined as the matrix of each element r_{ij} differentiated with respect to x.

$$\frac{\partial R}{\partial x} = \left[\frac{\partial r_{ij}}{\partial x} \right] . \tag{A.1}$$

Applying this to the product $RR^{-1} = I$ for a nonsingular R gives

$$\frac{\partial R^{-1}}{\partial x} = -R^{-1} \frac{\partial R}{\partial x} R^{-1} . \tag{A.2}$$

For $x = r_{ij}$,

$$\frac{\partial R^{-1}}{\partial r_{ij}} = -R^{-1} I_{ij} R^{-1} , \tag{A.3}$$

where I_{ij} is a matrix with an i,j component of 1 and all other components equal to 0.

For a symmetric matrix S, $s_{ij} = s_{ji}$. Therefore,

$$\frac{\partial S}{\partial s_{ij}} = I_{ij} + I_{ji} - \delta_{ij} I_{ij} = I_{ij}^* , \tag{A.4}$$

where I_{ij}^* for $i \neq j$ is a matrix with 1's as the i,j and j,i components and 0's as the others. When $i=j$, $I_{ii}^* = I_{ii}$. Thus, from (A.2) and (A.4),

$$\frac{\partial S^{-1}}{\partial s_{ij}} = -S^{-1} I_{ij}^* S^{-1} . \tag{A.5}$$

Furthermore,

$$\frac{\partial^2 S^{-1}}{\partial s_{ij} \partial s_{k\ell}} = S^{-1} I_{ij}^* S^{-1} I_{k\ell}^* S^{-1} + S^{-1} I_{k\ell}^* S^{-1} I_{ij}^* S^{-1} . \tag{A.6}$$

Trace

Let f be a trace function as

$$f = \mathrm{tr}(S^{-1} B) . \tag{A.7}$$

From (A.5),

$$\frac{\partial f}{\partial s_{ij}} = -\mathrm{tr}(S^{-1} I_{ij}^* S^{-1} B) = -\mathrm{tr}(I_{ij}^* S^{-1} B S^{-1}) = -[\theta_{ij} + \theta_{ji} - \delta_{ij} \theta_{ij}] , \tag{A.8}$$

where θ_{ij} is the i,j component of $\Theta = S^{-1} B S^{-1}$. Therefore,

$$\begin{aligned} \frac{\partial f}{\partial S} &= -[\Theta + \Theta^T - \mathrm{diag}[\Theta]] \\ &= -[S^{-1}(B + B^T) S^{-1} - \mathrm{diag}[S^{-1} B S^{-1}]] , \end{aligned} \tag{A.9}$$

where diag[R] is a diagonal matrix, keeping only the diagonal terms of R.

Similar formula can be obtained for a nonsymmetric R, by using I_{ij} instead of I_{ij}^* in (A.8),

$$\frac{\partial}{\partial R}\text{tr}(R^{-1}B) = -R^{-1}B^TR^{-1} , \tag{A.10}$$

where $\text{tr}(I_{ij}\Theta) = \theta_{ji}$ is used.

The derivatives of other trace functions are listed as follows:

(1) $$\frac{d}{dA}\text{tr}(AB) = \frac{d}{dA}\text{tr}(BA) = B^T \quad (B: m\times n) , \tag{A.11}$$

(2) $$\frac{d}{dA}\text{tr}(A^TB) = \frac{d}{dA}\text{tr}(BA^T) = B \quad (B: n\times m) , \tag{A.12}$$

(3) $$\frac{d}{dA}\text{tr}(A^TRA) = (R + R^T)A , \tag{A.13}$$

(4) $$\frac{d}{dA^T}\text{tr}(A^TRA) = A^T(R + R^T) , \tag{A.14}$$

(5) $$\frac{d}{dA}\text{tr}\{(A^TSA)^{-1}R\} = \frac{d}{dA}\text{tr}\{R(A^TSA)^{-1}\}$$

$$= -SA(A^TSA)^{-1}(R + R^T)(A^TSA)^{-1} , \tag{A.15}$$

(6) $$\frac{d}{dA}\text{tr}\{(A^TS_2A)^{-1}(A^TS_1A)\} = \frac{d}{dA}\text{tr}\{(A^TS_1A)(A^TS_2A)^{-1}\}$$

$$= \frac{d}{dA_1}\text{tr}\{(A_1^TS_2A_1)^{-1}(A^TS_1A)\}\,|_{A_1=A}$$

$$+ \frac{d}{dA_2}\text{tr}\{(A^TS_2A)^{-1}(A_2^TS_1A_2)\}\,|_{A_2=A}$$

$$= -2S_2A(A^TS_2A)^{-1}(A^TS_1A)(A^TS_2A)^{-1}$$

$$+ 2S_1A(A^TS_2A)^{-1} . \tag{A.16}$$

When (A.16) is set to be equal to zero,

$$S_2^{-1}S_1A = A(A^TS_2A)^{-1}(A^TS_1A) . \tag{A.17}$$

Determinant

The derivative of $|R|$ with respect to r_{ij} can be obtained as

$$\frac{\partial |R|}{\partial r_{ij}} = |R_{ij}| \,, \tag{A.18}$$

where $|R_{ij}|$ is the cofactor of r_{ij}. Therefore,

$$\frac{\partial |R|}{\partial R} = (\text{adj } R)^T = |R| R^{-1^T} \,, \tag{A.19}$$

where (adj R) is the adjoint matrix of R, and $R^{-1} = (\text{adj } R)/|R|$. Furthermore,

$$\frac{\partial \ln |R|}{\partial R} = \frac{1}{|R|} \frac{\partial |R|}{\partial R} = R^{-1^T} \,. \tag{A.20}$$

When a matrix, S, is symmetric, the above equations are modified to

$$\frac{\partial |S|}{\partial s_{ij}} = |S_{ij}| + |S_{ji}| - \delta_{ij} |S_{ij}| = (2 - \delta_{ij}) |S_{ij}| \,, \tag{A.21}$$

$$\frac{\partial |S|}{\partial S} = |S| [2S^{-1} - \text{diag}[S^{-1}]] \,, \tag{A.22}$$

$$\frac{\partial \ln |S|}{\partial S} = 2S^{-1} - \text{diag}[S^{-1}] \,. \tag{A.23}$$

Furthermore, using (A.5),

$$\frac{\partial^2 \ln |S|}{\partial S \partial s_{k\ell}} = -[2S^{-1} I_{k\ell}^* S^{-1} - \text{diag}[S^{-1} I_{k\ell}^* S^{-1}]] \tag{A.24}$$

or

$$\frac{\partial^2 \ln |S|}{\partial s_{ij} \partial s_{k\ell}} = -(2 - \delta_{ij})(\gamma_{ik}\gamma_{j\ell} + \gamma_{i\ell}\gamma_{jk} - \delta_{k\ell}\gamma_{ik}\gamma_{j\ell}) \,, \tag{A.25}$$

where γ_{ij} is the i,j component of S^{-1}.

The derivatives of other determinant functions are listed as follows:

(1) $$\frac{d}{dA} |A^T S A| = 2 |A^T S A| S A (A^T S A)^{-1} \,, \tag{A.26}$$

(2) $$\frac{d}{dA} \ln |A^T S A| = 2SA(A^T S A)^{-1} , \qquad (A.27)$$

(3) $$\frac{d}{dA} \{\ln |A^T S_1 A| - \ln |A^T S_2 A|\}$$

$$= 2\{S_1 A(A^T S_1 A)^{-1} - S_2 A(A^T S_2 A)^{-1}\} . \qquad (A.28)$$

When (A.28) is set to be equal to zero, (A.17) is satisfied.

Special Cases

Let us consider a special case in which $S = \Lambda$ (a diagonal matrix with components λ_i), and $s_{ij} = c_{ij}$. The derivatives of three functions, $f_1 = \text{tr}(\Lambda^{-1} M M^T)$, $f_2 = \text{tr}(\Lambda^{-1} M X^T)$, and $f_3 = \ln |\Sigma|$, with respect to M and c_{ij} are of particular interest, where both M and X are column vectors. These derivatives are listed here for the reader's convenience, because they are frequently used in Chapter 5.

The first function to be considered is a trace function of (A.7) with a symmetric B or a squared distance as

$$f_1 = \text{tr}(\Lambda^{-1} M M^T) = M^T \Lambda^{-1} M . \qquad (A.29)$$

The derivatives of f_1 are computed as follows:

$$\frac{\partial f_1}{\partial M} = 2\Lambda^{-1} M \quad \text{and} \quad \frac{\partial^2 f_1}{\partial M^2} = 2\Lambda^{-1} , \qquad (A.30)$$

$$\frac{\partial f_1}{\partial c_{ij}} = -(2 - \delta_{ij})[\Lambda^{-1} M M^T \Lambda^{-1}]_{ij} = -(2 - \delta_{ij}) \frac{m_i m_j}{\lambda_i \lambda_j} \quad \text{from (A.8)} ,$$

(A.31)

$$\frac{\partial^2 f}{\partial c_{ij}^2} = 2M^T [\Lambda^{-1} I_{ij}^* \Lambda^{-1} I_{ij}^* \Lambda^{-1}] M = \frac{2 - \delta_{ij}}{\lambda_i \lambda_j} \left[\frac{m_i^2}{\lambda_i} + \frac{m_j^2}{\lambda_j} \right] \quad \text{from (A.6)} ,$$

(A.32)

where m_i is the ith component of M, and $[K]_{ij}$ is the i,j component of K.

The second function is a trace function of (A.7) with a nonsymmetric B as

$$f_2 = \mathrm{tr}(\Lambda^{-1} M X^T) = X^T \Lambda^{-1} M = M^T \Lambda^{-1} X \ . \tag{A.33}$$

The derivatives of f_2 are

$$\frac{\partial f_2}{\partial c_{ij}} = -\frac{1}{\lambda_i \lambda_j}(m_i x_j + m_j x_i - \delta_{ij} m_i x_i) \quad \text{from (A.8)}\ , \tag{A.34}$$

$$\frac{\partial^2 f_2}{\partial c_{ij}^2} = 2M^T [\Lambda^{-1} I_{ij}^* \Lambda^{-1} I_{ij}^* \Lambda^{-1}] X$$

$$= \frac{2}{\lambda_i \lambda_j}\left[\frac{m_i x_i}{\lambda_i} + \frac{m_j x_j}{\lambda_j} - \delta_{ij}\frac{m_i x_i}{\lambda_i}\right] \quad \text{from (A.6)}\ . \tag{A.35}$$

The third function is a determinant function as

$$f_3 = \ln|\Lambda|\ . \tag{A.36}$$

The derivatives of f_3 are

$$\frac{\partial f_3}{\partial c_{ij}} = \frac{\delta_{ij}}{\lambda_i} \quad \text{from (A.23)}\ , \tag{A.37}$$

$$\frac{\partial^2 f_3}{\partial c_{ij}^2} = -(2 - \delta_{ij})\frac{1}{\lambda_i \lambda_j} \quad \text{from (A.25)}\ . \tag{A.38}$$

Special Derivatives

Let f be a function of a mean vector M and covariance matrix Σ. When their estimates $\hat{M}$ and $\hat{\Sigma}$ are used, $f(\hat{M},\hat{\Sigma})$ can be expanded around $f(M,\Sigma)$ by a Taylor series as

$$f(\hat{M},\hat{\Sigma}) \cong f(M,\Sigma) + \sum_{i=1}^{n} \frac{\partial f}{\partial m_i}(\hat{m}_i - m_i) + \sum_{i=1}^{n}\sum_{j=1}^{i} \frac{\partial f}{\partial c_{ij}}(\hat{c}_{ij} - c_{ij})$$

$$= f(M,\Sigma) + \frac{\partial f^T}{\partial M}(\hat{M} - M) + \mathrm{tr}\left\{\frac{\partial f^*}{\partial \Sigma}(\hat{\Sigma} - \Sigma)\right\}, \tag{A.39}$$

where

$$\frac{\partial f^*}{\partial \Sigma} = \begin{bmatrix} \frac{\partial f}{\partial c_{11}} & & \frac{1}{2}\frac{\partial f}{\partial c_{ij}} \\ & \ddots & \\ \frac{1}{2}\frac{\partial f}{\partial c_{ij}} & & \frac{\partial f}{\partial c_{nn}} \end{bmatrix} = \frac{1}{2}\left[\frac{\partial f}{\partial \Sigma} + \text{diag}\left[\frac{\partial f}{\partial \Sigma}\right]\right] . \tag{A.40}$$

That is, because of the symmetry of Σ, $\partial f^* / \partial \Sigma$ is not the same as $\partial f / \partial \Sigma$ whose i,j component is $\partial f / \partial c_{ij}$.

Let us examine $\partial f^* / \partial \Sigma$ for two different types of f as

$$f_1 = \text{tr}(\Sigma^{-1} M M^T) = M^T \Sigma^{-1} M , \tag{A.41}$$

$$f_2 = \ln |\Sigma| . \tag{A.42}$$

Then, from (A.9) and (A.23)

$$\frac{\partial f_1}{\partial \Sigma} = -[2\Sigma^{-1} M M^T \Sigma^{-1} - \text{diag}[\Sigma^{-1} M M^T \Sigma^{-1}]] , \tag{A.43}$$

$$\frac{\partial f_2}{\partial \Sigma} = 2\Sigma^{-1} - \text{diag}[\Sigma^{-1}] . \tag{A.44}$$

Substituting (A.43) and (A.44) into (A.40),

$$\frac{\partial f_1^*}{\partial \Sigma} = -\Sigma^{-1} M M^T \Sigma^{-1} , \tag{A.45}$$

$$\frac{\partial f_2^*}{\partial \Sigma} = \Sigma^{-1} . \tag{A.46}$$

Comparing (A.45) and (A.46) with (A.10) and (A.20), we can conclude that, in both cases, $\partial f_i^* / \partial \Sigma$ is obtained by differentiating f_i with respect to Σ as though Σ is a nonsymmetric matrix.

Reference

S. R. Searle, "Matrix Algebra Useful for Statistics," John Wiley, New York, 1982.

Appendix B

MATHEMATICAL FORMULAS

For quick reference, a list of formulas frequently used in this book is presented here as follows.

Volume and Surface Area

$$v = c_0 |A|^{1/2} r^n : \quad \text{volume with radius } r \tag{B.1}$$

$$c_0 = \pi^{n/2} \Gamma^{-1} \left(\frac{n+2}{2} \right) \tag{B.2}$$

$$L(X) = \{Y: \ d(Y,X) \le r\} \tag{B.3}$$

$$d^2(Y,X) = (Y-X)^T A^{-1} (Y-X) \tag{B.4}$$

$$v_0 = c_0 |A|^{1/2} (r\sqrt{n+2})^n : \quad \text{the volume of a region } L(X) \text{ which satisfies} \tag{B.5}$$

$$\int_{L(X)} (Y-X)(Y-X)^T \frac{1}{v_0} dY = r^2 A \tag{B.6}$$

$$S = c_0 n |A|^{1/2} r^{n-1} : \quad \text{surface area with radius } r \tag{B.7}$$

$S_0 = c_0 |A|^{1/2} r^{n-1}$: the area of a surface $S(X)$ which satisfies (B.8)

$$\int_{S(X)} (Y-X)(Y-X)^T \frac{1}{S_0} dY = r^2 A \quad \text{(B.9)}$$

Properties Related to Normal Distributions

$$p(X) = N_X(M, \Sigma) = \frac{1}{(2\pi)^{n/2} |\Sigma|^{1/2}} \exp[-\frac{1}{2}(X-M)^T \Sigma^{-1} (X-M)] \quad \text{(B.10)}$$

$$\nabla p(X) = \frac{\partial p(X)}{\partial X} = -p(X) \Sigma^{-1} (X-M) \quad \text{(B.11)}$$

$$\nabla^2 p(X) = \frac{\partial^2 p(X)}{\partial X^2} = p(X)[\Sigma^{-1}(X-M)(X-M)^T \Sigma^{-1} - \Sigma^{-1}] \quad \text{(B.12)}$$

$$p^m(X) = m^{-n/2} (2\pi)^{-n(m-1)/2} |\Sigma|^{-(m-1)/2} N_X(M, \frac{\Sigma}{m}) \quad \text{(B.13)}$$

Properties Related to Gamma and Beta Densities

Gamma density:

$$p(x) = \frac{\alpha^{\beta+1}}{\Gamma(\beta+1)} x^\beta e^{-\alpha x} \qquad 0 \le x \quad \text{(B.14)}$$

$$E\{\mathbf{x}\} = \frac{\beta+1}{\alpha} \quad \text{(B.15)}$$

$$\text{Var}\{\mathbf{x}\} = \frac{\beta+1}{\alpha^2} \quad \text{(B.16)}$$

Beta density:

$$p(x) = \frac{\Gamma(\alpha+\beta+2)}{\Gamma(\alpha+1)\Gamma(\beta+1)} x^\alpha (1-x)^\beta \qquad 0 \le x \le 1 \quad \text{(B.17)}$$

$$E\{\mathbf{x}\} = \frac{\alpha+1}{\alpha+\beta+2} \quad \text{(B.18)}$$

$$E\{\mathbf{x}^2\} = \frac{(\alpha+1)(\alpha+2)}{(\alpha+\beta+2)(\alpha+\beta+3)} \tag{B.19}$$

Gamma function:

$$\Gamma(\beta+1) = \alpha^{\beta+1}\int_0^\infty x^\beta e^{-\alpha x} dx \tag{B.20}$$

$$\frac{\Gamma(\alpha+1)\Gamma(\beta+1)}{\Gamma(\alpha+\beta+2)} = \int_0^1 x^\alpha (1-x)^\beta dx \tag{B.21}$$

$$\Gamma(x+1) = x\Gamma(x) \tag{B.22}$$

$$\Gamma(x+1) = x! \quad \text{for } x = 0,1,2,\ldots \tag{B.23}$$

$$\Gamma\left(\frac{1}{2}\right) = \sqrt{\pi} \tag{B.24}$$

$$\Gamma(x+\frac{1}{2}) = \frac{1\cdot 3\cdot 5\cdot \ldots \cdot(2x-1)}{2^x}\sqrt{\pi} \quad \text{for } x = 1,2,3,\ldots \tag{B.25}$$

$$\frac{\Gamma(x+\delta)}{\Gamma(x)} \cong x^\delta \quad \text{for a large x and a small } \delta \tag{B.26}$$

Moments of the Parzen and *kNN* Density Estimates

Parzen:

$$\hat{\mathbf{p}}(X) = \frac{\mathbf{k}(X)}{Nv} \tag{B.27}$$

$$E\{\hat{\mathbf{p}}(X)\} \cong p(X)[1 + \frac{1}{2}\alpha(X)r^2] \quad \text{(2nd order approx.)} \tag{B.28}$$

$$\alpha(X) = \operatorname{tr}\left\{\frac{\nabla^2 p(X)}{p(X)}A\right\} \tag{B.29}$$

$$\operatorname{Var}\{\hat{\mathbf{p}}(X)\} \cong \frac{1}{N}wp(X) \quad \text{(1st order approx.)} \tag{B.30}$$

$$w = \int \kappa^2(Y)dY \tag{B.31}$$

$$= 2^{-n/2}(2\pi)^{-n/2}|A|^{-1/2}r^{-n} \quad \text{for normal} \tag{B.32}$$

$$= \pi^{-n/2}(n+2)^{-n/2}\Gamma\left(\frac{n+2}{2}\right)|A|^{-1/2}r^{-n} \quad \text{for uniform} \tag{B.33}$$

***kNN*:** $$\hat{\mathbf{p}}(X) = \frac{k-1}{N\mathbf{v}(X)} \tag{B.34}$$

$$E\{\hat{\mathbf{p}}(X)\} \cong p(X)[1+\frac{1}{2}\alpha(X)(cp(X))^{-2/n}\left(\frac{k}{N}\right)^{2n}] \quad \text{(2nd order approx.)} \tag{B.35}$$

$$c = c_0|A|^{1/2} \quad [c_0 \text{ from (B.2)}] \tag{B.36}$$

$$\text{Var}\{\hat{\mathbf{p}}(X)\} \cong \frac{p^2(X)}{k} \quad \text{(1st order approx.)} \tag{B.37}$$

Appendix C

NORMAL ERROR TABLE

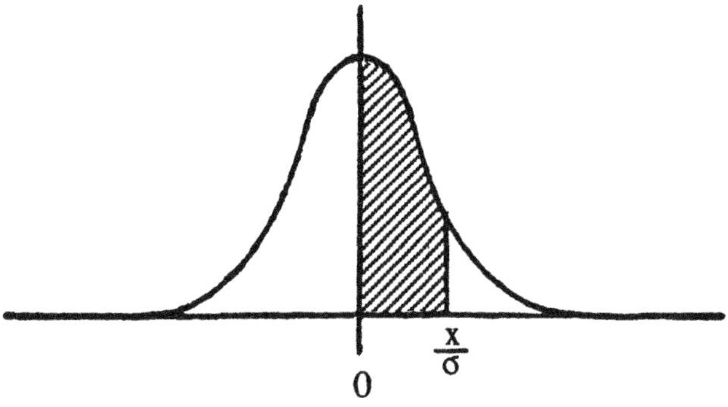

Each figure in the body of the table is preceded by a decimal point.

x/σ	0.00	0.01	0.02	0.03	0.04	0.05	0.06	0.07	0.08	0.09
0.0	00000	00399	00798	01197	01595	01994	02392	02790	03188	03586
0.1	03983	04380	04776	05172	05567	05962	06356	06749	07142	07535
0.2	07926	08317	08706	09095	09483	09871	10257	10642	11026	11409
0.3	11791	12172	12552	12930	13307	13683	14058	14431	14803	15173
0.4	15554	15910	16276	16640	17003	17364	17724	18082	18439	18793
0.5	19146	19497	19847	20194	20450	20884	21226	21566	21904	22240
0.6	22575	22907	23237	23565	23891	23215	24537	24857	25175	25490
0.7	25804	26115	26424	26730	27035	27337	27637	27935	28230	28524
0.8	28814	29103	29389	29673	29955	30234	30511	30785	31057	31327
0.9	31594	31859	32121	32381	32639	32894	33147	33398	33646	33891
1.0	34134	34375	34614	34850	35083	35313	35543	35769	35993	36214
1.1	36433	36650	36864	37076	37286	37493	37698	37900	38100	38298
1.2	38493	38686	38877	39065	39251	39435	39617	39796	39973	40147
1.3	40320	40490	40658	40824	40988	41149	41308	41466	41621	41774
1.4	41924	42073	42220	42364	42507	42647	42786	42922	43056	43189
1.5	43319	43448	43574	43699	43822	43943	44062	41179	44295	44408
1.6	44520	44630	44738	44845	44950	45053	45154	45254	45352	45449
1.7	45543	45637	45728	45818	45907	45994	46080	46164	46246	46327
1.8	46407	46485	46562	46638	46712	46784	46856	46926	46995	47062
1.9	47128	47193	47257	47320	47381	47441	47500	47558	47615	47670
2.0	47725	47778	47831	47882	47932	47982	48030	48077	48124	48169
2.1	48214	48257	48300	48341	48382	48422	48461	48500	48537	48574
2.2	48610	48645	48679	48713	48745	48778	48809	48840	48870	48899
2.3	48928	48956	48983	49010	49036	49061	49086	49111	49134	49158
2.4	49180	49202	49224	49245	49266	49286	49305	49324	49343	49361
2.5	49379	49396	49413	49430	49446	49461	49477	49492	49506	49520
2.6	49534	49547	49560	49573	49585	49598	49609	49621	49632	49643
2.7	49653	49664	49674	49683	49693	49702	49711	49720	49728	49736
2.8	49744	49752	49760	49767	49774	49781	49788	49795	49801	49807
2.9	49813	49819	49825	49831	49836	49841	49846	49851	49856	49861
3.0	49865									
3.5	4997674									
4.0	4999683									
4.5	4999966									
5.0	4999997133									

Appendix D

GAMMA FUNCTION TABLE

n	0	1	2	3	4	5	6	7	8	9
1.0	1.0000	.9943	.9888	.9835	.9784	.9735	.9687	.9642	.9597	.9555
1.1	.9514	.9474	.9436	.9399	.9364	.9330	.9298	.9267	.9237	.9209
1.2	.9182	.9156	.9131	.9108	.9085	.9064	.9044	.9025	.9007	.8990
1.3	.8975	.8960	.8946	.8934	.8922	.8912	.8902	.8893	.8885	.8879
1.4	.8873	.8868	.8864	.8860	.8858	.8857	.8856	.8856	.8857	.8859
1.5	.8862	.8866	.8870	.8876	.8882	.8889	.8896	.8905	.8914	.8924
1.6	.8935	.8947	.8959	.8972	.8986	.9001	.9017	.9033	.9050	.9068
1.7	.9086	.9106	.9126	.9147	.9168	.9191	.9214	.9238	.9262	.9288
1.8	.9314	.9341	.9368	.9397	.9426	.9456	.9487	.9518	.9551	.9584
1.9	.9618	.9652	.9688	.9724	.9761	.9799	.9837	.9877	.9917	.9958

In order to compute the gamma function outside the above range, apply $\Gamma(x+1) = x\Gamma(x)$ for $x > 0$ recursively. For examples

$$\Gamma(3.38) = 2.38\Gamma(2.38) = 2.38\{1.38\Gamma(1.38)\} = 2.918$$

$$\Gamma(0.38) = \Gamma(1.38)/0.38 = 2.338$$

INDEX

E

F

G

H

M

Printed and bound by CPI Group (UK) Ltd, Croydon, CR0 4YY
03/10/2024
01040414-0012